The
Mac OS® X
Tiger™ Book

D1443779

The Mac OS® X Tiger™ Book

Andy Ihnatko

WILEY

Wiley Publishing, Inc.

The Mac OS® X Tiger™ Book

Published by
Wiley Publishing, Inc.
111 River Street
Hoboken, N.J. 07030
www.wiley.com

Copyright © 2005 by Wiley Publishing, Inc.

Published by Wiley Publishing, Inc., Indianapolis, Indiana
Published simultaneously in Canada

ISBN-13: 978-0-7645-7957-8

ISBN-10: 0-7645-7957-6

Manufactured in the United States of America

10 9 8 7 6 5 4 3 2

1K/RY/QV/QV/IN

To My Mother, out of love and respect as well as in anticipation of her maybe finally cutting me a little slack about the ponytail already.

Credits

Acquisitions Editor
Michael Roney

Project Editor
Tim Borek

Technical Editor
Dennis Cohen

Copy Editors
Nancy Rapoport
Scott Tullis

Editorial Manager
Robyn Siesky

Vice President and Executive Group Publisher
Richard Swadley

Vice President and Publisher
Barry Pruett

Project Coordinator
Maridee Ennis

Layout and Graphics
Carrie A. Foster
Denny Hager
Jennifer Heleine
Amanda Spagnuolo

Quality Control Technician
Amanda Briggs
Brian H. Walls

Book Designer
Marie Kristine Parial-Leonardo

Proofreading and Indexing
Joan Griffitts
Christine Pingleton

Cover Image
Anthony Bunyan

Special Help
Robyn Siesky
Maureen Spears

Preface

And now, we come to Tiger, aka Mac OS X 10.4. If you're a student of film or a fan of film or maybe an assistant-managership at Blockbuster was the best you could do for a summer gig, you're gripping this book with tense fingers. If you had any fingernails left, they'd be puncturing the lovely metallic cover, straight through to the dedication page.

Plenty of flicks have broken past the "sequels always suck" maxim. *The Godfather, Part II* featured Pacino at the top of his game, and possibly the best (and certainly the most violent) male-male kiss in film history. The first *Star Trek* movie was a rejected TV pilot script in which the crew of the Enterprise dressed like intergalactic dental hygienists. But the second! All we need to say is *Khannnnnnnnn!!!* at a histrionic, eyeball-shaking outburst, and the DVD is as good as bought. As for *The Empire Strikes Back,* never has an ending that was so completely depressing been so completely satisfying.

Still, there's *Godfather: Part III.* Which will provoke a deep sigh that dislodges barely-suppressed memories of the Ewoks in *Return Of The Jedi.* And then you start thinking *Jaguar . . . Panther . . .* (ulp) . . . *Tiger!*

So if your mouth has suddenly gone very, very dry right now, well, your endocrine system can be forgiven.

But there's no need to worry. Steve Jobs isn't the head of a movie studio (apart from Pixar). He's the head of Apple, and with Tiger, Mac OS X truly becomes spectacular. Apple had a stiff challenge ahead of them: to throw out everything that was old, stable, functional, and familiar about the Macintosh operating system and start again from scratch. 10.0 and 10.1 were basic, just something that Apple could release as a starting point. The fact that they didn't bother to come up with a catchy name for it suggests that it probably wasn't meant to be a staple of your daily workflow. There were Marx brothers named Ted and Larry; you've never heard of them and you were never meant to.

With 10.2, it was time to start calling the new OS "Jaguar." It was the first version of X that was up to the challenge of being your one-and-only operating system. With Panther, Apple refined everything that had come before. They polished the Finder, made the networking features easier to manage, and installed dozens of little tweaks that enhanced fit and function.

The Compulsory portion of this particular competition has been completed: Mac OS X has been the best, most powerful, the easiest OS on the planet for a while now. But with Tiger, X enters a thrilling new phase: Apple starts working to collect Freestyle points. X always had great search features, but its new Spotlight technology infests every nook and cranny of the Mac experience with the ability to find anything, on any basis, at your slightest whim. X has always given you the opportunity to automate tasks with AppleScript, but now Automator lets you streamline processes by just clicking and dragging boxes together, without having to write a single line of instructions.

Even the new iChat wants in on the action. Multiple panes of live, lifelike video of friends, family, and even mortal enemies are arranged around a virtual meetspace, each one rotated, lit, and reflected like they're the Phantom Zone panels that imprisoned General Zod in *Superman II*.

 Note

Please don't allow the preceding paragraph to remind you of *Superman III*, in which Richard Pryor — after a three-week instructional course in computing — builds a supercomputer that takes over the world, causing plenty of wacky hijinx to ensue. Remember: Tiger breaks the mold of Third Sequels. There's really nothing to worry about. I promise. I'm a little sorry that I even brought it up.

So it's exciting. We're no longer satisfied with the concept of actually managing to get our computers to print something. We're all a-twitter: surely a company that fills our screen with a layer of vaguely-gelatinous tools for looking up our next appointment and a webcam image from Beijing is only *this far away* from giving us one of those flying cars that folds up into a suitcase, like in "The Jetsons."

WHY THIS BOOK DEMANDED TO BE WRITTEN

Ah, well. Let's get on with the business of this book, namely, to make sure that you actually buy it instead of continuing to browse it here in the bookstore.

And hey, I'm not going to make you feel guilty for having stood here in the aisle for so long. Here in the Tiger edition of the book, we've added pages while dropping the price, provoking a startlingly good value for the money (particularly when you factor in the fact that Chapters 9 through 13, when torn from the book and tiled on the floor, form a centimeter-resolution map that pinpoints the exact location of an immense pirate hoard which has remained undisturbed near the Massachusetts coastline for nearly four centuries. Swear to God. As your friend and author, I only hope and pray that someone else hasn't gotten to it before you, in which case it'd really be impossible for you or your attorneys to prove that the above claim is a fraud).

Still, you have to be careful with your money. Why don't you buy yourself a coffee and a sticky bun and move to one of those overstuffed club chairs down by the Biography section? You're the backbone of the American publishing industry: you *deserve* to be pampered!

Comfy? Good. You probably want to know what I had in mind when I put this book together. This book is geared towards five different groups of people:

1. **Folks who are old hands at the Macintosh, but new to Tiger.** Some of you might be coming in from even *earlier* incarnations of the Mac OS. Hey, man: I been there. Actually, I *are* there, because while at this writing I've been using Tiger for nearly three months now, Tiger's official release is still a long ways away, and thus I can't simply rush to the bookstore and start scamming information off the shelves like *some* users I could mention.

   That was uncalled for. My apologies. Lack of sleep, you see. Won't happen again.

2. **Folks who are Macintosh *users,* but who don't feel as though they're really getting the most out of their Macs.** I have friends who've been Mac users for ten years, and yet when I told them that they could open their PowerBooks and download their email from my hotel suite without any difficulty because I was "sharing" my Internet connection through my own Mac's wireless networking card, it was as though I'd told them that all Macs manufactured after 2002 could produce moist, delicious, fresh Toll House Cookies by installing a piece of software and keeping an oven mitt next to the DVD slot. And I'm still amazed that there are folks who've never automated their Mac with AppleScript!

   Not to worry. Buy this book and I'll help spackle some of the gaps in your Macintosh education.

3. **Family members and personal friends, who have seen the sort of car I drive and who are therefore eager to pep up my royalty checks.** Good for you; I'm way too proud to accept charity, but still, I'm eager to get another step closer to that Mini Cooper I've had my eye on.

4. **New Mac users.** Folks who have heard of and seen Macs, and who've occasionally been blinded by the purple aura of peace, happiness, and productivity that each and every Macintosh user gives off, and who have finally declared that they're ready to be happy. Welcome, welcome, welcome. As Brother Cadfael often says in his series of murder mysteries, he might have come late to the order of monks, but he came when called. And I'm glad you're here.

5. **New Mac users who are used to the Windows way of doing things.** I been *there,* too. The Mac has been my primary OS for (good Lord) nearly twenty years, now, and I didn't even *start* using Windows on a daily basis until Windows XP came along. So much of my struggle to Deal With It was a simple case of dealing with things that weren't necessarily inferior to the Mac way of doing things. . . but instead, were simply Different. I mean, honestly: I turn the computer *off* by pushing a button marked "Start"? Can that *really* be right?

So for you, dear Microsoft expatriate, I have included an entire chapter that details the bare fundamentals of the Macintosh user interface.

Okay. That's nearly all of you. If you're not a Windows user or a neophyte Mac user or a Mac user with years of experience, or one of my relatives, you're probably qualified to write one of these books instead of buying one, so I'd be foolish to try to go after your consumer dollars. As for the rest of you: gimme gimme gimme.

Thus, I'm pretty confident that you'll like what you see. But if you decide to postpone your purchase for another day, throw me a bone and smudge up the pages with frosting and sticky glaze from that cinnamon roll you're eating. It'll convince future browsers that this book is worth thumbing through from start to finish, perhaps even suggesting that you had read some stuff that caused you to howl with laughter. It'll also make the bookseller feel funny about returning the book unsold, which can only help to boost the book's numbers.

Some of you have already purchased this title, and what can I say to *you* except

GOD BLESS YOU, BOOK PURCHASER!

I mean, honestly. Other authors forget what a miserable experience it is to have to wake up every morning at 6 A.M. and put on a name badge and a paper hat. But not me; I'm grateful for every book I sell and for every day that ends without me reeking of frying medium and pity.

Actually, I feel as though I ought to give you a little something to show my appreciation. How about this: when you're making scrambled eggs, keep testing the skillet by flicking water onto it from your fingertips. The temperature is perfect when the water immediately boils away. Then pour in the eggs and let them sit. Resist the urge to keep stirring them around; letting them sit is the difference between moist, fluffy clouds of eggs and dried, rubbery squibs of hate. Don't start moving the mixture around until it starts getting a little dry at the very edges. Then slowly scrape the bottom of the pan — you're turning the eggs over more than stirring them up — and prevent overcooking by occasionally removing the pan from the heat from time to time. When the surface goes from glossy to moist, the eggs are ready to plate and serve.

This will be one of the ten best pieces of advice you'll ever get in your life. Love often dies with the first forkful of hard, bland scrambled eggs, and if you can master the above procedure you'll be well on your way to attracting and keeping your perfect mate. Why have you never seen this advice on the Oprah show? Because Oprah doesn't love you as much as I love you.

Oh, and it occurs to me that many of you might have paid full price for the book. Extra thanks to you. Don't get the tops of your ears pierced because that's cartilage and it'll hurt like bloody hell. On the whole that information is probably even more valuable than the egg thing.

THE USER INTERFACE OF THIS BOOK

So, how get you started? First, let's introduce you to the unique structure of the book that you hold in your hands. There are a couple of book elements that you need to know about.

Sidebars

You'll notice these sidebars scattered here and there throughout the pages of the book. Sidebars are where I take the opportunity to digress. I share information that might enhance your understanding of the topic at hand, that adds new perspective, or that I Just Plain Find Interesting.

> ### A BOOK YOU SHOULD BUY AFTER BUYING THIS ONE
>
> Actually, I got the idea from Martin Gardner's *The Annotated Alice,* in which the complete text of Lewis Carroll's classic is accompanied by sidebars that explain just exactly what the guy was talking about. You know, on the off-chance that you're not aware that mercurous nitrate was a key chemical used in the manufacture of felt, and that as a result, hatmakers often suffered from mercury poisoning and exhibited psychotic behavior.
>
> The book's still in print and led to a whole line of "annotated" classics. Definitely worth a look.

Ideally, the effect of these footnotes will be like the "commentary track" you'd find on a good DVD of a great movie. Possibly it's like having some idiot in the audience yelling at the screen while you're trying to enjoy *Vertigo*. Hard to tell. My hopes are high, and frankly you might as well just grin and bear it because there really isn't much you can do about it at this point.

Though I suppose you could just put this book back on the shelf and spend the dough on Roger Ebert's Movie Yearbook instead. Hmm. That honestly never occurred to me. Well, okay, the man has a Pulitzer and everything, but did he ever teach you how to network two computers via Firewire? Just don't do anything rash; that's all I ask.

Notes

And then there are those comments that I inserted because I'm undisciplined and uncontrollable — and I need to comment on the discussion at hand. Right now. With sidebars, there's sort of an implied warranty. If you read the sidebar, you'll probably learn something useful but not essential. But notes are mostly here because I have a hard time controlling my impulses. All I can promise is that each note certainly seemed like a good idea at the time, and my heart was in the right place, absolutely.

Note

See, as a writer, the most difficult part of the job is figuring out just how much Coke you need to drink before sitting down at the keyboard, and how often to redose over the course of the day. Some people need the assistance of university medical facilities and complex nuclear imaging devices to monitor the seratonin levels of their brains. All I have to do is read back the stuff I've written over the past hour or so. I'm on an HMO so it's a real time and money saver.

BOOK ORGANIZATION

The book's chopped up into three major sections:

Part I: Using Tiger

The bulk of it's dedicated to the nuts-and-bolts details of installing and using Tiger. This book is ecumenical, embracing geeks of all skill levels. If you already know what the yellow button in a window's title bar does, feel free to skip around until you find something that provokes that not unpleasant sensation of mild confusion.

Part II: The Technical Bits

There are areas that few users of Mac OS X seem to bother with, such as Unix and AppleScript. That's because you really don't have to. Unix is the OS that lurks underneath Tiger's slick façade, and AppleScript is a resource for automating your Mac's functions and writing your own software.

"Unix?" "Writing your own software?" From way over here (in Boston, several months in the past) I can hear some of you getting up, misshelving this book somewhere convenient, and then stalking off to the Cartoons and Humor section to see if there's a new Garfield anthology. Well, that's why these chapters were quarantined. But you really ought to read about this stuff. There's a difference between a User and a Power User, and it's the difference between knowing Unix and AppleScript . . . and only having heard of those things. It's also often the difference between leaving the office at 4:30 and still being stuck working when Letterman's starting his monologue.

Part III: Bonus Material

"The Professor and Mary-Ann" of the book. Here are items that are interesting and informative but don't necessarily fit in with the other two sections. Think of these as the bonus materials that come on a decent DVD.

Acknowledgments

Body and soul were held together shakily, but successfully, during the production of this book, thanks in no small part to the indulgence and efforts of a whole bunch of people.

First on your ballots, first in our hearts: to them that raised me.

My pals John Welch and Rich Siegel are the sort of geeks whom geeks get in touch with for answers and advice, and this geek is grateful that they never thought to block me from their iChat buddy lists.

When you're writing about a secret pre-release operating system, you can't just Google for technical information and practical background. Lots of people at Apple filled that breach bravely and generously. My particular thanks go to Mike Shebanek; if I'd asked him just a few more questions, I'd probably have had to install a big red Bat-Phone in his office.

My agent, Carole McClendon, diligently and skillfully handled all the business stuff, which left me free to focus on the role of Sensitive Artiste.

And let's not leave out my editors, Mike Roney and Tim Borek. Good editors make you want to write better; bad ones make you want to move to a line of work that centers around figuring out if a basket of french fries is done or not. Suffice to say that I'm at the end of this project and I'm not wearing a hair net and a name badge.

About the Author

Andy Ihnatko describes himself as "The world's 42nd most-beloved industry personality," because "it's vaguely-credible but utterly impossible to prove or disprove, and thus precisely the sort of tagline I was looking for."

An unabashed geek ("The bashings ended when I left high school for Rensselaer Polytechnic, thank God"), Andy's been writing about tech since 1989. In the past, he's written for every single magazine or website with the word "Mac" in it, highlighted by ten years as *MacUser* and then *Macworld*'s back-page opinion columnist. He's currently the *Chicago Sun-Times*' technology columnist.

In his pursuit of "heroically-stupid applications of technology," Andy has built an animatronic Darth Vader doll that could be controlled over the Internet via telepresence to hassle his roomate's cats and has written and published a complete set of plans and instructions for converting any Classic-style Macintosh into a fully-functional 2.5-gallon aquarium. "The Original MacQuarium" was one of the Internet's first e-books and can be downloaded from several sites after a quick Google search.

This is Andy's fifth book. Andy lives in Boston with his two goldfish, Click and Drag. He invites you to visit his aptly named "Colossal Waste of Bandwidth" at www.andyi.com.

Contents

PART I

Using Tiger

Why Having Chosen Mac OS X Was by No Means a Dopey Idea

In This Chapter

If Your Computer Was Really Your Friend, It Wouldn't Crash On You So Often • Tiger Is Non-Crashy and Faster
Tiger Is Non-Crashy and Faster and Easier To Use • In Most States, Your Spouse Owns Half of That $2,000 Mac
U2's Next Album Isn't Coming Out On 8-track • You Can Run Nearly Any App
Tiger's Got a Creamy Nougat Center of Thick, Rich Unix

I suppose I should start off by stressing that I am totally on your side. I'm your pal; I'm your friend. I don't think I'm willing to cosign a car loan for you or anything like that, but on the whole, when you picture Andy Ihnatko in your mind, just take a stock mental image of St. Francis of Assissi and add a hat and a downright stupid quantity of personal electronics, and you'll have me down to a T. Two reasons for this visualization: First, because I really do want you to be a happy, capable, and proud user of Mac OS X Tiger; and secondly, I'm spending all this time writing a chapter telling you why Tiger is a great OS.

Honestly, I'm to be commended. Those people who seek out and eradicate disease, hunger, poverty, et al.? Punks, all of 'em. When the Nobel Prize committee comes to their senses and starts recognizing the intense personal sacrifices committed in the name of computer books, I expect to be eating lutefisk front-and-center with the best of 'em.

Look at it this way: I already have your money. And yet, here I am, sitting in a hotel room in Kauai, reassuring you about the wisdom of Mac OS X, when I'm supposed to be at the beach competing in the Xbox Pipeline Masters Tournament — a surf contest that I was *heavily* favored to win. Plus, there were going to be girls there, probably. So why am I doing this? Exactly. Selfless dedication to the needs of you, the reader. No, don't thank me; honestly, I just don't know any other way.

So I wanna start off by reaffirming the reasons why Mac OS X is the best thing since sliced cat's pajamas. Some of you (guessing by the adoption numbers available in 2004) are still migrating to X from earlier versions of the Mac OS. Others are coming here from Windows.

And even if you're upgrading from a previous version of X, all the basic concepts of Why Mac OS X Continues To Be A Good Idea bear repeating. As Mac users, our most adorable communal attribute is our eagerness to evangelize. Let's say that you're flying to New York and the guy in the middle seat is using a Windows notebook. Naturally, you're going to harangue him about your Mac, but are you *sure* you have enough material to maintain a one-sided conversation for the *entire* four-hour flight? Forewarned is forearmed. By mastering the bromides in this chapter, you'll have the information you need to convert another poor unfortunate to the True Path.

REDUCE BULK, REDUCE STRESS

It's probably a good idea to just tear this whole chapter out of the book and keep it in a coat pocket or purse, for discreet reference when these opportunities arise, or to hand off to someone who's on the fence. You won't miss a single trick, plus there's an excellent chance that you'll be forced to go out and buy another copy of the book. It's called "Smart Marketing," people.

IF YOUR COMPUTER WAS *REALLY* YOUR FRIEND, IT WOULDN'T CRASH ON YOU SO OFTEN

We all like to have a little variety thrown into our workday. But when your computer freezes up on you 20 minutes before the deadline of a critical project and you know that you had plenty of unsaved changes, well, you yearn for the stable, reliable, hour-to-hour routine of a life in the federal prison system.

Every edition of the Macintosh operating system before Mac OS X was a steady evolution of the same OS that shipped with the original Macintosh 128K in 1984, which means it uses the same methods of managing programs and memory that were in vogue during the Reagan Administration. Sure, it made sense back then; with the ever-present threat of an intercontinental thermonuclear holocaust hanging over our heads, all of a computer's programs crashing at once really didn't seem like such a big problem, all things considered.

Thankfully, times have changed. New ideas about OS architecture and memory management were developed and perfected and started to appear in Windows and other operating systems, while the Macintosh OS was stuck in the early 1980s. Before too long, the Mac got a bad reputation: It was known as that one operating system that always crashes, taking all of your work down with it; and it was also known for being about as agile as a pig ice-skating on three legs, one of which was actually wearing a skate.

Such slings and arrows are a thing of the past, thanks to protected memory and preemptive multitasking. *Protected memory* is a memory-management scheme in which the operating system isolates every piece of running software, assigning it a private, walled-off little box of memory.

A SPECIAL WORD FOR FORMER WINDOWS USERS

If you **are** coming to the Mac OS X fresh from Windows, let me say straight off: This is going to be great. Our Kool-Aid is just **so** much better than theirs. The only downside is that nearly all private insurers categorize the removal of the Microsoft Quality Control and Rights Management chips from your brainstem as elective surgery. Well, let me assure you that it's a simple outpatient procedure and in time, you'll think of it as the best $1,100 you ever spent.

Just keep some ice on the sutures, and the pain, swelling, and scarring will be kept to a cozy minimum.

interests, the "cooperation" was marginal at best. When a running app needed to perform a function, it would seize complete control of the CPU and only relinquished it to other running apps when its immediate task was complete. It all usually happened so fast the user barely noticed, but still, cooperative multitasking is *fake* multitasking.

▼ **Note**

For a flawless demo of the limits of cooperative multitasking, just pull down a menu in Mac OS 9. Every other function comes to a dead stop; the snippet of code that handles the menu bar now completely owns the Mac, and nothing else can happen until you let go of the mouse button. If you don't have Mac OS 9 handy, go and brush your teeth while your significant other is exfoliating. You can try as best you can, but you can't get around the fact that there's just one sink and one mirror.

Under the old scheme, the OS used one big memory space for all software. When one app trashed its space, it also trashed the space that every other app used. Result: *Boom.* One app might accidentally write data to a bit of memory that another app is using. Again: Boom. The difference between protected memory and the way the Mac OS used to do things is like the difference between roommates living in a two-bedroom apartment and sharing an open loft space. Oscar Madison can decorate his bedroom with day-old newspapers and week-old pizzas, and it won't affect Felix Unger in the slightest.

Preemptive multitasking is a bit more complicated. Essentially, it's the way that the OS juggles multiple tasks. The old OS could run multiple apps, sure, but it used an unsophisticated scheme called *cooperative multitasking.* Those of you who've ever worked with Humans before see the flaw in this scheme right away: It only works if all of the running apps cooperate with each other; and because software is an ego-driven tangle of selfish personal

The old Mac OS fakes real multitasking well, but X is better. The OS prioritizes all of the apps' ongoing tasks so that no one app can tie up the CPU.

As a result, Mac OS X is way more stable and feels way more responsive. Applications can indeed freeze up, but each piece of software, including the OS itself, runs in its own little bunker of protected memory. One malcontented piece of code can't bring down the entire Mac.

Under Mac OS 9, you're probably forced to restart your Mac once a day. As a longtime Mac OS X user, I can tell you that the only times I ever restart my Mac are when I've installed new software that requires me to do so. This way is better.

▼ **Note**

Still, let's not completely pooh-pooh the advantages of using a computer that can crash at any given moment with the slightest provocation and take all of your open documents down with it. When I upgraded to Mac OS X, my only big disappointment with it was that I suddenly couldn't use "My Mac crashed and ate all my work" as an excuse any more. It was almost as bad as when I replaced my 12-year-old Pontiac with my first brand-new car. All of a sudden, people started expecting me to show up at work **on time** and stuff. It was a very stressful turn of events.

TIGER IS NON-CRASHY *AND* FASTER

Mac OS X was written from the ground up, recycling little. Along the way, all of its basic code was enhanced and covered with Teflon to make it slicker and more aerodynamic.

If that weren't enough, Mac OS X is optimized to take full advantage of modern Mac hardware, such as the G4's Velocity Engine coprocessor, the absurdly advanced architecture of the G5, machines with multiple microprocessors, and even new technologies for sharing the processing power of several Macs across a network. One of the five most powerful supercomputers on the planet is a roomful of Macs that act like a single brain. It's Mac OS X that makes this possible, and it's unique throughout the entire industry.

Thanks to X's support of multiprocessing, any time Apple wants to make a faster Mac, all it needs to do is add more processors. Figure 1-1 is a graph of how hard a two-processor Mac works while playing music, building a DVD, *and* emulating a Windows PC all at once!

Bottom line: The first time you boot your old computer with Mac OS X, you'll feel as though you've taken the stock engine out of your Volkswagen and replaced it with something you tore out of a Porsche while its owner was off in Vail.

Figure 1-1
The Activity Monitor is the Mac's "dashboard" for examining performance.

TIGER IS NON-CRASHY *AND* FASTER *AND* EASIER TO USE

I've been focusing on *technical* advances that have been made in the field of OS architecture since 1984. But Apple spent a colossal amount of time reconsidering how Humans interact with computers, and (by extension) how computers can be encouraged not to be such truculent free-willed nincompoops.

From the Dock to the new Aqua user interface and beyond, Mac OS X's elegance and ease is as big an improvement over Mac OS 9 as Mac OS 9 is over any version of Windows. Check out Chapter 8, which is all about the universal and holistic Dock (Figure 1-2), Mac OS X's biggest and best basic improvement to the Mac interface.

Figure 1-2
The Dock. The glorious, wonderful, funderful Dock is just one of the Mac's many X-only user-interface innovations.

▼ **Note**

Gosh, you're *still* reading this chapter? I'm terribly flattered. I think that Mac OS X has already made a smashing case for itself at this point in the proceedings, and if you're reading the rest of this, it can only mean that you're enjoying the writing. It's an overwhelming vote of confidence and I shall endeavor to be worthy of it.

IN MOST STATES, YOUR SPOUSE LEGALLY OWNS HALF OF THAT $2,000 MAC

Funny, isn't it, that when you come home after blowing thousands of dollars of the household budget on a new toy, *other* members of the house actually insist on getting a turn at the keyboard, too! I mean, really. Does the simple but effective phrase "Mine mine mine mine *mine!!!*" mean nothing to these people?

The petty demands of your spouse and your kids will still sting, but at least they can't mess around with your personal files and customized settings. Mac OS X is a true multiuser operating system. If you set up the Mac with separate accounts for Mom, Dad, and little D'Artagnian, it's like owning three different Macs. Mom and Dad don't have to look at their kid's Sailor Moon desktop picture, and the kid will never pore through Mom and Dad's copy of Quicken and learn that the folks blew his entire college fund on that

new Cadillac Escalade parked outside. Chapter 18 is all about sharing your Mac and its resources with other people.

U2'S NEXT ALBUM ISN'T COMING OUT ON 8-TRACK

Mac OS X is the present, and it's the future. There is no serious ongoing development of Mac OS 9 software. Every important app, every utility that shaves an hour of work out of your day, every incredible new piece of hardware, every revolutionary Internet resource, every component of iLife that awakens talents in you that you've hitherto envied only in others (as well as every efficient mechanism for locating and viewing pictures of scantily clad people on the Internet) will be available solely and exclusively for Macs running OS X. Not Mac OS 9.

YOU CAN RUN NEARLY ANY APP

God knows why you'd want to run apps not specifically written for Mac OS X, but you can. Mac OS X can bamboozle all of your old OS 9 software into thinking it isn't running on the most advanced OS on the planet. It's sort of like when aliens abduct Amish people and make their spaceship look like it's made out of pine lumber and hay, just to keep them from freaking out. Read Chapter 10 to see me heap additional derisive abuse upon the idea of running old apps, which I also parenthetically talk about how to actually do. But the main thrust is on pouring you a nice hot cup of General Foods International® Coffee and browbeating you into forsaking all that is non-Mac OS X in this world.

On top of *that,* you can also run most Windows apps, by buying a special piece of Windows-emulation software sold by Microsoft. And because Mac OS X has a creamy nougat center of thick, rich Unix, you can also run hundreds of free, commercial-grade apps written and supported by the open-source software community. Oh, wait. . . did I mention that Tiger's got a creamy nougat center of thick, rich Unix?

TIGER'S GOT A CREAMY NOUGAT CENTER OF THICK, RICH UNIX

And this is the point in the pitch when the car salesman talks about how this model has a Hanley-style fuel-injection system instead of an old-fashioned venturi carburetor: you haven't the foggiest idea what either term means, but so long as it makes the car go faster, that's all you're interested in.

Unix makes the Mac go better. No question. It means that your Mac is more stable; it's more secure from attacks by viruses and Trojan horses and evil, egg-sucking weasel system crackers trying to sneak in through its connections to the rest of the world. It also works with almost any network up to and including the one that controls the group consciousness of the hyperintelligent race of cyborgs that shall surely enslave us all some day.

With Unix at the heart of X, the Macintosh community gets a lot of things for "free." That's literally true; open-source software (in which the apps are copyrighted, but they're authored by the entire developer community and can be freely distributed) is a big deal in Unix, and everything from games to audio-recording apps to a complete suite of Microsoft Office–compatible apps are available for little more than the cost of duplication, if anything (see Figure 1-3).

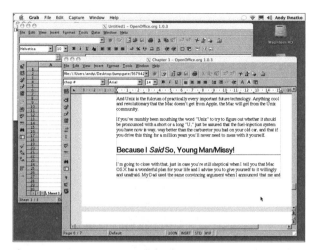

Figure 1-3
Open Office, a Microsoft Office–compatible suite of apps, is free for the downloading.

▼ Note

Plus, there are a lot of bars and clubs near the Massachusetts Institute of Technology where you won't get anywhere with anybody unless you're wearing a wristwatch with more than 2MB of flash storage and can honestly claim to be running some sort of Unix at home. Word to the wise.

But getting things for free is also metaphorically true. Apple tried — twice — to create its own next-generation operating system from the ground up. Both times, they quickly got bogged down in the infinite and stubborn details of forging revolution. Ten seconds after they decided to base Mac OS X around Unix, the new OS inherited all of Unix's advantages. It's aggressively a network-friendly OS; it's secure; it's extensible; it's based on international standards; and it's supported and maintained by uncountable developers, which means that when something very basic breaks, chances are excellent that the problem is already well understood and easy for Apple to fix.

And Unix is the fulcrum of practically every important future technology. Anything cool and revolutionary that the Mac doesn't get from Apple, the Mac will inherit from the Unix community.

So I've sold you on the Unix and given you the technical reasons why it's a very good thing for the Mac. But if you've numbly been mouthing the word Unix to try to figure out whether it should be pronounced with a short or a long *U*, just be assured that the fuel-injection system you have now is way, way better than the carburetor you had on your old car; and that if you drive this thing for a million years, you'll never need to mess with it yourself. If you do care to learn a little about Unix, however, and you want to take that giant leap forward towards enlightenment and productivity, be sure to check out Chapter 20, taking a deep breath first if necessary.

TIGER'S WHERE ALL THE *ACTION* IS, BABY!

If you're thrown off by all of the rah-rah-rah Macintosh boosterism in this chapter, I warn you that (a) it's well merited, and (b) you've probably already got ten coffee stains on this book, so don't even think of trying to return it.

I don't know if you read my credentials before buying this humble tome, but I write about *all* forms of technology. My newspaper column isn't just about Macs: it's about Windows and Linux and PDAs and wristwatches that go *pinggg!* in clever ways. Mac OS X is my primary operating system of choice, but I use Windows each and every day, and of the. . . um. . . dash it. . . (Andy does a quick 360 of his office) *nine* functioning computers in this room, four of them are running operating systems other than

Mac OS X. I'm a Mac user and an Apple fan, but it's not for lack of choice or lack of options. Windows is harder to use, it's inconsistent, it's nearly impossible to master, it's baffling and unpredictable at times, and, quite simply, it's not a cutting-edge OS. Historically, Windows has lagged at least two years behind Mac OS in terms of speed, stability, and features.

Just look at Spotlight, Tiger's built-in system-level resource for retrieving information on your Mac. "What is an operating system?" Well, theoreticists have been revising the answer ever since the term "Operating System" was invented. One of the newest and most promising of the Big Ideas is to give the OS the responsibility of organizing and tracking all the info on your hard drive. Sure, you'll still have to put stuff in files, and you're going to continue to create and name documents, but in the Push-Button World of Tomorrow, getting a hold of that Word document that someone emailed you last week — the report explaining why, precisely, there was any need whatsoever for your studio to continue to make terrible movies starring former *Saturday Night Live* cast members — will be your computer's job, not yours. Instead of navigating through files and folders, you'll just ask for a list of Word documents received last week that talk about SNL, and bango! It's there.

If you own a Mac, the Push-Button World of Tomorrow is here today. If you have Windows, you'll be delighted to hear that it'll be part of the OS in a year. Or more.

It's hard to ignore Apple and Microsoft's track records. Windows XP came out in 2001, and apart from two large maintenance updates, has remained unchanged ever since. The differences between Mac OS X 10.0 and Tiger, on the other hand, are nearly as profound as the difference between X and Windows itself.

WHY MICROSOFT IS THE WAY IT IS

It's not that Microsoft is full of dopes, slackers, and layabouts. No more than any company with a staff greater than, say, four, anyway. It's just that Apple and Microsoft have achieved their success through two nearly opposite algorithms. Apple continues to be a highly profitable and successful company through innovation. If they *stop* being the first to bring power and sophistication to consumers, well, they become Just Another Computer Company. It's actually more complicated than that (give me 40 minutes and I'll explain why Steve Jobs is the Walt Disney of technology, maintaining a clear vision of what his company's role is in the world), but that'll do for now.

Microsoft is by nature far more conservative. They don't work with technology: they work with *markets*. They couldn't be the first to sell a mouse-driven graphical operating system because the market didn't exist. Not until Apple created it, at least. They sell to people who are buying, which a fantastically successful model for business — and remember, a business' first obligation to its customers is to *stay* in business — but it's also one that keeps Microsoft permanently at the back of the pack.

After all, your customers can't tell you to make something that they've never heard of, you know?

And what about Linux? It easily matches Tiger for power and in many ways exceeds it in raw speed. But it's not an invisible OS that simply does what you need it to do. It requires regular hands-on maintenance, like a muscle car. Because it's been built by thousands of hands, it doesn't work consistently from task to task. If anything, the only thing that you can count on is that its developers think you're a lot more experienced than you actually are. Yes, Linux works with digital cameras; yes, there's iPhoto-like software for cataloguing and organizing your photos. However, whereas plugging your camera into a Mac is the first step of a one-click process to import its contents, on Linux it's the first step of a 71-step process for getting your computer to recognize and work with the camera. You can do better. And congratulations: you *are.* You've got Tiger. I can't tell you how impressed I am with your choice.

I'm going to close with that, just in case you're still skeptical when I tell you that Mac OS X has a wonderful plan for your life, and I advise you to give yourself to it willingly and unafraid. My dad used the same argument when I announced that a couple of friends and I were going to drive to Rhode Island and get the album art from R.E.M.'s *Automatic for the People* tattooed across our backs. It was *very* effective, and I avoided making the worst mistake of my life.

Instead, I got Weird Al Yankovic's *Dare To Be Stupid* cover, and have gotten nothing but compliments on it ever since.

Installarama

In This Chapter

Before You Install: Sit, Drink, and Think • Part I: Installing Basic Files
Part II: Configuring a New Installation • Installing Applications
Getting Software Updates

Ah! A fresh, new copy of the operating system. Such a feeling of . . . what am I looking for? The crisp feeling of smelling the first cool dew of spring. Hearing an announcement that pitchers and catchers are reporting to training camps. Spotting the unexpected and delightful appearance of shorts on your UPS guy for the first time this year (seasonal climes only).

Oh, and the dread: the crushingly cold feeling that you are atoning for the bad karma accumulated from every past life in one fell swoop as you gamely try to upgrade to Tiger from a previous edition of the Mac OS and, because your toddler chose a rather spectacularly bad moment to yank out your Mac's power cord, your hitherto friendly and complacent computer is about to turn into Linda Blair.

 Note
Clarification: the young, Satan-possessed Linda Blair from *The Exorcist,* not the grown-up version who did all those "women in prison" movies many years later.

Well, chin up. Unless you bought a new Mac with Tiger preinstalled, installing a Tiger upgrade is just Something You'll Have To Do. Plus, remember that back during one of your previous incarnations through the Wheel of Life you just blithely went ahead and pulled the lever to guillotine Marie Antoinette, just because an angry mob told you to? Well, *I* sure do. She was my favorite auntie! Never forgot a single birthday, she did. And she wouldn't just fob me off with a gift certificate, either. Quality stuff from Fabergé, every single time.

So there will come a time when you must atone for past sins of your past lives. Never lose your fear that one day, the Universe will finally turn its attention to you and cause a system crash of such profound and divine thoroughness that your only recourse is to reinstall from scratch.

BEFORE YOU INSTALL: SIT, DRINK, AND THINK.

Actually, Step One of any install process is to go to the fridge, pour yourself a glass of something cold and entertaining, and sit in the comfy chair in your living room. It's time for bold, Alexander the Great–style thinking, preparation, and strategizing.

I don't want to create the impression that installing Tiger is like lofting elephants over the Alps. The Installer program you'll find on your Tiger setup disc takes care of everything for you and holds your hand the whole way, stopping every once in a while to ask you a critical question or to see if Sir or Madam could use another pillow. But things go so much more smoothly if you prepare beforehand. Questions you should be asking yourself:

Do I feel lucky today, punk? Well, *do* I?

And yes, that's a serious question. You should always be a bit timid about installing newly released software. Apple voraciously tests all of its code before it's shipped, but even if 10,000 people have tested the new OS, it may still ship with bugs that won't be discovered until 1 million people start using it 7 days a week in real-world situations. It's also unlikely that one of those testers had a Soviet-made label printer and a Finlandian DVD burner installed. So you

might be trying to make the new OS do something that's never been tried before.

Apple OS software has a good track record for reliability. Still, it's something you should always keep in mind. If a piece of software is absolutely critical to your life — and gosh, your operating system sure is — you might consider waiting a couple of weeks before updating it. By then, Apple will have discovered and fixed any obscure bugs that cause, say, all of your files to become unrecoverable mincemeat.

Should I upgrade my existing copy of Mac OS X, or have the Installer build a brand-new copy of the OS from the ground up?

That's probably the most important question to ask yourself. The Installer gives you three install options: Upgrade, Archive and Install, and Erase and Install. The latter takes an absolutely scorched-earth approach. Your whole hard drive will be erased and you'll lose all of your apps and documents. It's a true Colonel Kurtz solution, if you're hip to *Apocalypse Now.* You're calling in an air strike on your Mac; it'll be like no one's ever used this machine.

THE TRUE COLONEL KURTZ SOLUTION

There's also Erase and Install, which erases everything before installing Tiger. It's a good choice if you're receiving a computer secondhand, and thus you don't need and don't want any of the files that are on there already; but otherwise, reinstalling all of your user apps and your documents is way too big a hassle. Be aware that Erase and Install exists, but leave it alone, I say.

BUT ALLOW ME TO IMMEDIATELY CONTRADICT MYSELF

I shouldn't say that Erase and Install is *always* too much trouble. I actually think it's valuable to start off with an absolute clean slate, if you've been upgrading the same Mac and the same system and the same apps for a few years. So I'll do a backup, erase and install, and then reinstall all of my apps from scratch. It's a good way to discover that gosh, it's a waste of space to keep *that* app, because I never use it; and maybe it's finally time for me to *not* carry 290 photos from my trip to Hawaii everywhere I go.

Archive and Install is a more moderate approach. It retains all of your apps and documents and user settings, but it completely replaces your old operating system with a brand-new installation. Even there, it's moderate: it "archives" your Mac's existing system files to a backup folder first, so you can always retrieve individual settings later.

If you choose the Upgrade option, the Installer will just look at your current copy of the OS and replace any components that are now out-of-date.

The Upgrade option takes a lot less time and is much more convenient. All of your system settings are exactly the same; when the installation is complete, you won't know the difference, outside of the improvements. Archive and Install is much more involved. And although the Installer is nice enough to copy your Network configurations and other tweaks, you might have to spend a little time afterward putting things back the way you like them. Sort of like when you return to your hotel room and discover that the hotel maid took all of your rocket ship toys off the bed and put them on the desk.

As for Erase and Install, it's only an attractive option when you absolutely, positively are OK with every last scrap of data on that Mac being erased. So, it's good if you're accepting a secondhand Mac or passing your Mac along to someone else (you don't want anyone else's junk, and you sure don't want your own personal info going to someone

EXPERIMENT ON ANIMALS BEFORE UPGRADING THE ONE YOU LOVE

I'm lucky; I have a big collection of guinea pigs here in the office. First, I install the new OS on a tower Mac that I rarely use. I test it out for a few days, and if it appears stable and seems to work with my accessories and software, I install it on the big tower where I do a lot of real, actual work. I install it on my Power-Book only after it's proven to work stably and happily on both towers.

You see, my PowerBook, Lilith (I've owned seven PowerBooks, each with the same name), is the most important piece of hardware I own. If Lilith gets messed up, I can't do my business. I can't write, I can't get my email or look at my address book, I can't access my manuscripts, on and on. So I don't perform any upgrade on Lilith that hasn't already been road tested.

Um, except for Mac OS X 10.3, because the day after this edition of the OS was released, I did something incredibly clever (read: stupid) to Lilith's System directory that caused it to stop working. And this was 24 hours before I had to go away on business. Fortunately, in this and all past lives I have lived a clean and pure life, so Karma was more than pleased to upgrade it from 10.2 to 10.3 without any Linda Blairage. Just another reason why you should give blood, be kind to animals, and return your library books on time.

else's home or office). And if you have a complete and up-to-date backup of all of your files, you can erase with impunity. Otherwise, it's way more trouble than it's worth.

So why bother with the Archive and Install? Because an OS is an incredibly complicated piece of software, and over months and years of use, *teensy-tiny* things can go wrong with it. A word processor crashes, and it doesn't close one of the OS's critical files. You tried a piece of software that messed something up in a tiny way. Et cetera.

These seemingly trivial problems start to add up. If they'd caused your Mac to stop working *entirely*, you'd have fixed it, but they didn't; they just made your Mac a little less reliable and stable. Assuming a scorched-earth policy whenever you buy a new OS is just one of those little things you can do to keep your Mac healthy. It's sort of like the difference between replacing a couple of rotted floorboards and replacing the whole floor. You're fixing the bits that are visibly wrong and you're also ensuring that there isn't a hidden problem remaining to send your 500-gallon aquarium crashing through to the basement at an inopportune moment during your Christmas party.

 Tip

But hundreds of gallons of water surging over all of your guests' shoes, followed by the sight of dozens of flopping, gasping creatures and the party's hosts desperately filling buckets and pans and scooping them up, is an excellent way to politely communicate that you appreciate these people stopping by but that the party's now over and they're welcome to leave.

Should I perform an Easy Install or a Custom Install?

The last big decision in this particular passion play is whether to do an Easy Install or a Custom Install. Easy Install is truth in advertising: click a button and the Installer puts all of Tiger's features and components on

AN ARCHIVE-AND-INSTALL TESTIMONIAL

When Panther, the previous edition of Mac OS X first came out, I lambasted it because one of the Finder's most useful features — dragging files into a window's Toolbar area to keep them handy — had been removed. "Why would Apple remove such a cool and handy feature?" I moaned (in a column, no less).

It turns out that I was an idiot (as demonstrated by all of the screenshots that readers emailed me, demonstrating that the feature was still alive and well). Here's what had happened: I had upgraded my Mac instead of doing an Archive and Install, and unbeknownst to me, a subtle problem with the existing OS caused the "drag icons into the toolbar area of a Finder window" feature to stop working. So I reflected upon the fact that mankind is born unto trouble surely as sparks fly upward, performed a fresh installation, and all was right with the world.

your hard drive. In a Custom Install, you get a chance to pick and choose.

Easy Install: Honestly, you should just do the Easy Install. You rarely look back on the decision to do a Custom Install and think "You know, that's the best choice I ever made. My life started on the right direction the moment I clicked 'Custom Install'."

Custom Install: If you choose Custom you're likely to — I want to say you will *inevitably* — leave out a component that you're going to need later, such as printer definitions. You have an Epson printer, you're installing Epson drivers, why would you want to install the drivers for the Monongahela 1200-Q? But just wait: a year later you're in a strange town with your PowerBook and you *desperately* need to print something, and thank *God* you found a copy shop that's open late — and the only printers it has are Monongahelas. Custom Install is good if you're desperate to save hard drive space (but drives are so cheap they're practically giving them away these days) or if one component of the OS has gone bad and you want to replace just that one component. (But how do you know that it's just this *one* part that's gone wonky? You're better off reinstalling the whole thing.) So actually, Custom Install is usually a bad deal, unless you have careful guidance about what's safe to keep and what's safe to toss, provided by somebody who knows what you're going to be doing with your Mac.

Human factors to consider when installing (Slings and Arrows)

All the issues discussed thus far in this chapter are related to the Installer. There are a couple more things to consider, and they're both Human factors.

Whether you choose to Upgrade or Archive and Install, the Installer *should* preserve your network settings. But still, this is an imperfect universe. Best to be safe. Make a

record of all of your network settings (if they're not set to the automatic defaults). Just click on the tabs to display the settings and then press Shift+⌘+3 to take a screen shot of them. For more on network settings, see Chapter 14.

You should also take this opportunity to download and print out any special instructions that your office or ISP gave you for establishing a connection to their network. Again, if your network connection goes ker-flooey, you won't be able to download that critical document.

If you're upgrading a PowerBook, make *double*-dog certain that it's plugged into its power adapter and is actually getting juice. The tip of the power plug should be lit up, where it plugs into your PowerBook. You don't want the thing going into emergency power-save mode when the Installer is writing those super-important System files. That's the difference between an hour-long installation process and an entire afternoon of desperately trying to bring your PowerBook back to life.

Finally, make sure you've set aside enough time for the job. An OS upgrade is nearly completely automatic (the only thing the Human has to do is switch CDs when commanded — honestly, a monkey could do it), but it can take half an afternoon. You should only install the

PURSUE HOBBIES DURING INSTALLATION FOR A HEALTHIER YOU

Long OS upgrades is the reason I advocate keeping something hobby- or hygiene-related next to your keyboard at all times. You can spend those three hours either stewing about how long the installation is taking, or you can work on the chord progressions for "Everyone Says I Love You." When you're waiting for your Mac to restart, you can either bitterly think about how you'd have had that letter written and mailed quicker with a crayon and a torn-out magazine cover, or you can floss.

And when you turn up for that hot date, you'll have healthy, pink gums and will know how to play a sweet love song on the ukulele, instead of arriving with a vague but burning hostility that's struggling for expression. Result: hugs and squeezes, instead of winding up with someone's drink on your head.

BEWARE THE VENGEANCE OF FLUFFY

And don't feel all safe and smug just because you have a tower Mac or an iMac or another desktop. Cats are the bows that work the strings of invisible evil that stretch across the Universe. If there's a way that Mr. Whiskers can punch the power button on your iMac's power strip, he'll find it.

On a slightly more sensible note, make sure nobody's going to trip over the power cord. In a shared environment, make sure that none of your kids or multiple spouses are going to happen across your installation-in-progress, think "Gosh, this is taking too long; all I want to do is check my freakin' email!" and then restart the computer.

So which of these two is less encouraging: The smart animal who burns you because it's evil, or the humans who burn you because they're simply idiots?

upgrade when you're sure you won't need your Mac for the rest of the day.

PART I: INSTALLING BASIC FILES

Installing an OS is a lot like playing Monopoly. There are standard rules and the basic gameplay never changes, but there are lots of variations from household to household. The installation process I'm going to describe here reflects what you would do if you're playing the game according to the instructions printed on the inside of the box top, so to speak. But if you were to watch a trained consultant install Tiger, you'd see him or her use a few shortcuts and make a few simple assumptions.

 Note

People who insist that there should be some sort of bonus for landing on the "Free Parking" square probably also support the designated-hitter rule in baseball and open their Christmas presents on Christmas Eve instead of Christmas morning. Be vigilant. Do not, under any circumstances, allow them to become godparent to your child or support their bid for your town's Board of Supervisors.

1. **Insert OS X install disc 1.**

   You can't upgrade or replace a copy of Mac OS X that's already running. So you need to reboot your Mac and start up from the Tiger Install disc. You can do this either by double-clicking on the Install OS X app in the Finder (Figure 2-1) (which automatically shuts down your Mac and restarts it), or you can manually restart your Mac (select "Restart..." from the Apple menu) and hold down the C key to boot your Mac from the disc.

Figure 2-1
The Mac OS X Tiger installer app

2. **Launch the Install Mac OS X app and click the Restart button.**

If you are currently running a version of OS X, the launcher asks you to supply an administrator password.

3. **Select the language you want to use for the rest of the installation and click Continue.**

   An introduction window appears. Welcome to the Installer. Welcome, welcome, *welcome!*

4. **Click Continue to get on with it.**

   Now you're looking at Apple's humongous Software License Agreement (see Figure 2-2).

5. **Click Continue to get on with it.**

   A little pane will drop down to confirm that you accept the terms of the licensing agreement.

6. **Click Agree to get on with it.**

   The Installer might now present you with a big scrolling page of Important Information. This would be last-minute information about compatibility, giving

you tips on how to make the installation go more smoothly. Read, absorb, enjoy, and then click "Continue" to get on with it.

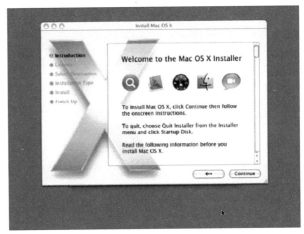

Figure 2-2
Reading the Software License

HOW IMPORTANT IS THE IMPORTANT INFORMATION AND SOFTWARE LICENSE MATERIAL?

Yes, you do need to read the Important Information. The last thing the Apple people do before finalizing the CD is fill this screen with last-minute information. If hypothetically they knew a month ago that even *looking* at the Esc key kind of funny during installation will inevitably precipitate the destruction of the entire contents of your Documents folder, they'd have fixed the problem. But if they only discovered the bug three hours before mastering the final CD, the only thing they could do would be include a note in the Installer saying, "For God's sake, don't even *look* at the Esc key kind of funny while Tiger is being installed!"

But the software license? *This,* you can just blow off. It'll only scare you. You have to read and approve more legalese to install Tiger than you do to become a Navy SEAL. And Apple isn't Microsoft. Do you know that Microsoft released an absolutely critical safety and security upgrade to Windows, and snuck a clause into its installer license that said, "And oh, yeah, one other thing: By installing this software you also give Microsoft the right to keep track of all of the digital music you listen to, and to sell that information to marketers"?

I mean, when the guy at Microsoft who added this clause reincarnates, that's one marmoset that will never catch a lucky break its whole life, believe you me. Clean living, kids; I can't recommend it highly enough.

A TIGER HERE, A TIGER THERE, INSTALL THAT RASCAL EVERYWHERE!

It's a good idea to have multiple copies of Tiger installed (assuming that you have more than one volume available, of course). It's just insurance: if you happen to have an external hard drive, installing Tiger on both the internal and external drives means that if and when the copy on your internal drive starts acting all petulant, you can boot off the external and be back on your way.

And feel free to be creative. I have a 40-gigabyte (GB) iPod and I just flat-out don't think there's 40GB of music out there that I can actually tolerate. So I have a copy of Tiger on the iPod; in an emergency, I can boot from it. It's saved my life more than once while traveling on business. Disk Utility (the... well, the Disk Utility found in your Utilities folder) also has the ability to partition a hard drive into multiple volumes. So it's certainly possible to carve your 120GB internal drive into 100GB and 20GB partitions, and have separate copies of Tiger installed on each one. Again, if your Mac can't boot off of your usual volume, it'll find the other partition and start from that puppy with nary a burp.

The bad news is that you can't create a partition without erasing all of the information on your drive. So, rather a downer, unless you can perform a complete backup of all of your drive's contents before partitioning. Or if you just don't like your hard drive very much.

The installer looks for hard disks on which it can install OS X and asks for a destination to install.

7. **If the drive already has a copy of Mac OS X on it, then the Tiger installer will upgrade the existing OS by default. If you'd rather Archive and Install, or Erase and Install, click the Options button (see Figure 2-4):**

   If you want to replace only essential files, leave the Upgrade Mac OS X option checked and click OK.

   If you want to perform a Clean Install, preserving existing OS X files, click the Archive and Install option. To keep users and network settings during a clean install, click the Preserve Users and Network Settings option.

   If you want to erase the target disk and then install OS X, click the Erase and Install option.

8. **Click Continue in the Select a Destination window.**

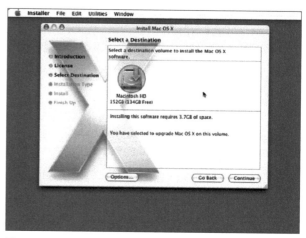

Figure 2-3
Choosing a target disk for OS X

The Easy Install window appears. Read the information in this window. If you proceed with an Easy Install, the installer uses all the default settings to configure your OS X installation.

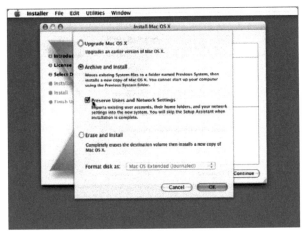

Figure 2-4
Choosing installation options

9. **If you hate me so much that you're willing to do a Custom Install simply because you know it'll anger and irritate me, click Customize.**

See the section "Should I perform an Easy Install or a Custom Install?" for why clicking Customize annoys me.

10. **Click the checkboxes next to the items you don't want to install (Figure 2-5).**

And make sure you know what you're doing because, man oh man, the moment you realize that you should have taken my advice, I'm going to be over at your place pointing and laughing.

11. **Click Install.**

The Installer begins by verifying the integrity of the installation disc. Assuming that the disc media passes the verification, the Installer installs the software. First, it prepares various parts of the software; then it copies files to the target disk; finally, it optimizes your hard drive. In each step, a moving bar appears, letting you know that the installation is making progress.

APPLE'S MIRACULOUS DISC OF ETERNAL MYSTERIES

"What about this disc in the box that you're not mentioning? It says something about XCode and developers' tools."

Um …it's packing material. Just there to keep the other install disc from bumping around and getting scratched. Pay no attention to the man behind the curtain. You don't need to see his papers. These aren't the droids you're looking for. *Move along*.

Okay. This fourth disc contains all the tools that real, big-time professional software developers need to write Mac software. But! Just as my new car didn't include detailed instructions on how to bore out the Flayven and remove the Boysenheimer Valve Winkel Drive for its quarterly pointing (for fear that I'd emit a dignified, ladylike scream and then go off and see what a 10-speed bike would cost me), Apple has isolated all that stuff into its own separate install CD.

It's cool beans. Really. At some point, you'll probably want to investigate that disc. But for now, you should seal it inside a manila envelope, write the word UNCLEAN on it in big, fat marker, and then tape it to the underside of the least-used piece of furniture in the least-used room of your house.

Inside that envelope contains your first steps into a larger and more exciting world, but it is not wise to tip the vessel of wisdom, young apprentice.

ONE GOOD THING HIDING INSIDE CUSTOM INSTALL

I'll single out one of these "Custom" options for praise: A thingamabob called X11. I'll explain what X11 is in Chapter 10; essentially, it helps you run apps that were written for Unix but not written specifically to take advantage of the Macintosh user interface. You can live a long, healthy life without ever launching such apps. Plus, if you ever *do*, you can always install X11 separately at a later date.

The setup application launches automatically after the computer restarts (Figure 2-6):

Figure 2-6
Tiger bids you welcome.

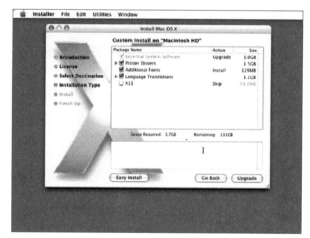

Figure 2-5
Choosing customization options

PART II: CONFIGURING A NEW INSTALLATION

If you are upgrading from Mac OS 9, or if you did an Erase and Install or an Archive and Install without preserving users and network settings, your Mac has essentially been born again and needs to get reacquainted with you.

1. **Select the country for which you want to configure OS X, and click Continue.**

   This will affect how numbers are displayed, whether text reads from left to right or right to left, and other stuff.

2. **Select the type of keyboard layout you want to use, and click Continue.**

▼ Note

The options that you see throughout this configuration process depend in large part on the choices you've made. For example, the language that you select for the installation determines the countries presented in Step 1; the country you select determines the options in the keyboard layout list.

3. **Create an ID and password for an account with Apple.com.**

   If you have a .Mac account, you can use that as your ID; otherwise, you can create a new account:

BUT WHY GET AN APPLE ACCOUNT?

Well, it's one of those things that costs you nothing, incurs no liabilities, and might pay off for you in the future, in some small way. Essentially, every time you deal with Apple (when you need service, when you want to buy something, when you want to access certain parts of the Web site), Apple will already know who you are, and you'll be whisked straight in.

Bottom line: You'll probably set up an Apple.com account for yourself someday. Might as well do it now.

- If you have an existing Apple.com account, enter your user name and password. You can also use a .Mac account name and password.

- If you don't have an Apple.com account and want one, click the "Create an Apple ID for me" option.

- If you don't want an Apple.com account, click the "Don't create an Apple ID for me" option.

▼ Cross-Reference

For more information on .Mac accounts, see Chapter 14.

4. **Click Continue.**

   A screen appears asking for your software registration information.

5. **Type the software registration information, and click Continue.**

   The installer asks you some survey questions, and the answers are sent to Apple along with your registration information.

6. **Type the information for creating your account (see Figure 2-7).**

   This is the name by which your Mac will know you and the password it will use to verify your identity.

Figure 2-7
Setting up your user account on this Mac

7. **Click Continue.**

8. **Select options to set up your Internet connection.**

   Do you want to set up Tiger's Internet connection right now? If so, tell the Installer what you want it to do. If you don't have an account with an ISP, you can set up a trial account with Earthlink (either by using the free trial you get with Tiger, or by taking advantage of a different trial offer you might have received). If you already have an ISP, you can click the third option. If your head is spinning and you'd rather just get on with using Tiger, click the last option on the list.

9. **Select how you are connected.**

   If you are connecting to the Internet right now, the Installer asks how you are connecting (Figure 2-8):

FIRST DIBS ON YOUR MAC

The first user account you create on your Mac is a special kind of account: it makes you an "Administrator." Meaning, you're the person who can add and remove software, and you're the one who can add new users and control what those users can do. In certain respects, you control the horizontal and you control the vertical.

So if you're in that segment of the populace that has your kids set up the computers, realize that if little D'Artagnian is the first person to create an account, he'll have full control. Which you might not want, assuming that there's software that you don't want your kid to use or areas of your Mac that he shouldn't visit.

But then, if you *are* in that segment of the populace, D'Artagnian is going to *need* Administrator privileges so he can let you into the system after you've forgotten your account password. So, take that under advisement.

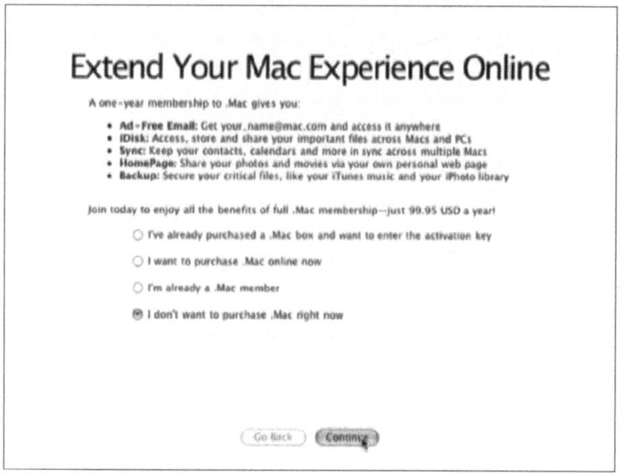

Extend Your Mac Experience Online

A one-year membership to .Mac gives you:

- **Ad-Free Email:** Get your_name@mac.com and access it anywhere
- **iDisk:** Access, store and share your important files across Macs and PCs
- **Sync:** Keep your contacts, calendars and more in sync across multiple Macs
- **HomePage:** Share your photos and movies via your own personal web page
- **Backup:** Secure your critical files, like your iTunes music and your iPhoto library

Join today to enjoy all the benefits of full .Mac membership—just 99.95 USD a year!

- ◯ I've already purchased a .Mac box and want to enter the activation key
- ◯ I want to purchase .Mac online now
- ◯ I'm already a .Mac member
- ◉ I don't want to purchase .Mac right now

(Go Back) (Continue)

Figure 2-8
Choosing a method for connecting to the Internet

- If you are using a modem for a dial-up account, leave the first option selected.

- Click the second option if you are using a cable modem connected directly to your computer.

- Click the third option if a DSL line is connected to your computer.

- Click the fourth option if you are using a shared Internet connection through a network connected through your computer's Ethernet port. In a home, you will typically have a router to which either a cable or DSL modem is attached. There is a wide variety of shared Internet technologies used in business, but typically you will have an Ethernet jack on the office wall from which you can run a cable to your computer.

Which screens appear next depend on the Internet option you selected. The Installer will either ask you for vital information that it needs in order to establish your Internet connection (if you're using a dial-up connection, it'll need to know your Internet service provider's phone number, your account name, and so on) or it'll go forth and establish the connection for you automagically. If you're plugged into a cable modem, for example, your Mac and the cable modem have a little sub rosa discussion and configure each other on their own.

10. **Click Continue.**

The Installer asks if you want to sign up for a .Mac account (Figure 2-9).

Figure 2-9
Deciding whether to establish a .Mac account

11. **Click the option that corresponds to your choice, and then click Continue.**

    The Installer is now ready to connect to the Internet.

12. **Click Continue.**

    The Installer gives you the choice of sending your registration information now or sending it later.

CHOOSE YOUR PASSWORD WISELY

If you forget your password, Tiger will, in its wisdom, bravely prevent you from using your own Mac. To avoid this, Tiger lets you specify a hint, which it gives back to you if you try and fail to log in. You can also pick a little icon that accompanies your ID, but choosing the butterfly instead of the kitty cat isn't remarkably likely to cause you to lose access to your Mac. Loss of dignity, yes. Your Mac, no. More tips about passwords can be found in Chapter 19 .

WHY REGISTER?

So how did you react to this question? It's a good opportunity to do your Patrick McGoohan impression. You know, Number Six? *The Prisoner*? TV show about the struggle of the individual to maintain his own privacy of thought despite the demands of an impersonal Society?

Well, it was a great show. Anyway, this is another one of those deals where registering won't cost you anything (you won't get any junk mail unless you tell Apple it's OK to send it) and if you ever stop by an Apple store to get your Mac serviced, things will proceed that much faster. The guy at the counter will type your name and instantly tell you that you're under warranty and good to go.

Seriously. It was a great show. The last episode (where we were supposed to finally learn the Secret of Number 6 and The Village) was a major letdown, but other than that, I give it a big thumbs-up.

13. **Click the option that corresponds to your choice.**

    If you choose to register, the Installer uses your Internet connection to send the data. The installer lets you set up the OS X Mail application (Figure 2-10). The information you need to type in the text boxes in this window comes from your ISP. When you are done, click Continue.

▼ Note

If you're not using Tiger's built-in email client — let's say your ISP is America Online, which requires its own mail program — then leave this window blank, and just click Continue.

14. **Set your time zone.**

THE LUXURY OF NETWORKING IGNORANCE

Most of the discovery and configuration of your network gear should happen automagically. "Row-ter? What is this 'Row-ter' of which you Humans speak?" If you're a Windows user, you know that a router is the gizmo that takes one big fat cable coming into the building and juggles all of the computers that want to use it to access the Internet. Here's how Windows people are likely to use the term: "I can't get my (expletive) email because the (expletive) router won't (obscene gerund) show up on the (compound obscene gerund) network!"

As a Mac person, take another bite of your Pop-Tart and watch it all happen *for you*. And, um, if it *doesn't*, turn to Chapter 14, which is all about networking.

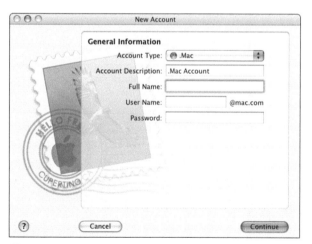

Figure 2-10
Configuring Mail

You do this by choosing a city in your time zone from the Closest City pop-up menu.

15. Click Continue.

If you have a working Internet connection, the installer sets the correct date and the precise time automatically from a clock on the Net. Otherwise, set the date and time manually.

16. Click Continue.

At this point, the basic installation is finished. The Installer either transmits your registration information, or reminds you to register later (see Figure 2-11).

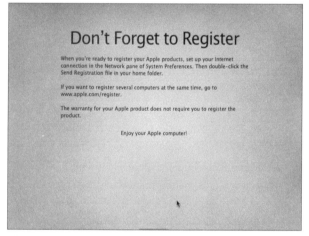

Figure 2-11
Finish the basic installation

17. Click Done.

You can now move on to installing applications.

INSTALLING APPLICATIONS

Naturally, we've been focused on installing Tiger. So how do you install individual apps? It varies. Every software publisher has its own scheme for installing its software, but it usually comes down to one of three ways:

DELIVERING SOFTWARE IN THE AGE OF TOMORROW

And if the software is delivered as a download — you visited the software publisher's Web site and received it electronically instead of on a disc — there are one or two other variations. Some software will arrive on your hard drive as a ready-to-go double-clickable app. Or, it'll be a double-clickable installer app. The only flavor that might give new users a bit of a pause are the ones that arrive as "disk image files." You'll read more about disk images in Chapter 12; they're files on your hard drive that Tiger treats like a CD or a hard drive. You work with them just like you'd work with any disk; Tiger mounts the disk the same way it mounts a CD when you insert it, and you can then open the CD and run the Installer program therein.

- **Using Apple's standard application installer kit.** Apple was nice enough to create a standardized mechanism for installing software and make it available to developers. So the process of installing most apps is the same as installing Tiger: Chuck in a CD or DVD, launch the installer app, and then follow the familiar interface step by step until done. Some apps require that you restart your computer immediately; others wouldn't dream of harshing your mellow like that.

- **Drag the application from the CD into your Applications folder.** And honestly, that's all you need to do. Some publishers are even helpful enough to put a note next to the file, visible right in the Finder: *Copy this to your Applications folder.* It's the easiest $300 a documentation author ever made.

- **And then there's everything else.** Many publishers (a) pooh-pooh Apple's installer, and (b) know that

their software is too complicated for a user just to drag it into the Applications folder. So they create their own custom Installer app. Most of these are very easy to use, but overall, Godspeed, John Glenn.

GETTING SOFTWARE UPDATES

Apple is continuously updating OS X and its applications. Sometimes an update will add new, thrilling, and essential features to either Tiger or one of Apple's own apps (like iTunes and the rest of the iLife apps). Some updates are esoteric performance enhancements, and some fix crucial bugs. And then there are — note capital letters for added dramatic *oomph* — SECURITY UPDATES. These are extremely important because they make it more difficult for egg-sucking weasels to tamper with your Mac without your consent.

And the best part is that you don't really have to do anything to receive any of these updates. Thanks to a feature known as Software Update, Tiger connects to the Internet at regular intervals to check for updated software. If it finds some, the Software Update window pops up and invites you to download and install them.

OS X has the Software Update feature turned on by default. Through System Preferences, you can tell your Mac how frequently to check for updates, tell it to look for updates right now, or turn the automatic feature off entirely using these steps:

1. **Open System Preferences from the Apple menu.**

2. **Click the Software Update icon.**

   The Software Update dialog box appears (Figure 2-12).

3. **Click the Check for updates option.**

   If you want OS X to check for updated software automatically, keep the Check for updates option checked. To change the frequency with which OS X should check for updates, click the pop-up menu arrows (Daily, Weekly, or Monthly). If you want to check for updates immediately regardless of the schedule, click Check Now. OS X uses your Internet connection to check Apple's servers for updated software. The results appear in a list (Figure 2-13).

4. **Click a check box to remove the check and prevent installation.**

   Click an empty checkbox to enable installation. Software Update places checks in checkboxes next to the updates it thinks you will want to install.

5. **Click Install 5 Items.**

   In this example, five items have been selected for installation. The number of items will vary depending on the number of downloads that you select. Software

Update downloads the update files and installs them on your hard disk.

Figure 2-12
Selecting automatic software updating

WHY WOULDN'T YOU WANT TIGER TO CHECK FOR UPDATES AUTOMATICALLY?

Well, if you use a dial-up connection, it's annoying to have your Mac suddenly dial out to connect to Apple's servers, even if it only happens once a week. Otherwise, the only people who turn it off are those who were taught that life is naught but a vale of tears and that it's the hardships that we suffer for that temper our souls to greatness.

If Tiger is set up to check for updates automatically, why click Check Now on your own? Because Apple often *does* add cool new features to the OS and the iApps, and maybe you don't want to wait a week for them.

There's one caveat, though. Rest assured that Apple wouldn't release an update unless it was confident that it was safe and stable, but you might want to hold off on installing a huge update to an important app or even the OS for a week or two. Apple tests those updates on thousands of developers. But it's possible that there are some problems with the update that won't be discovered until *hundreds of thousands* of users have installed it.

So instead of installing the update right away, hold off for a bit and then surf the Mac-oriented news sites (like MacCentral.com or MacInTouch.com), just to make sure that those who've installed it haven't become intimately familiar with that "life is naught but a vale of tears and hardship" business I mentioned earlier. When Mac OS X was still in its infancy, there was one rather legendary major update that actually wiped out a few users' hard drives. The update was quickly withdrawn and fixed, but man alive, an incident like that has an effect on your future decisions, you know?

Figure 2-13
Viewing a list of available software updates

After Software Update has installed and optimized the updates, you may be asked to restart your Mac. You'll have plenty of opportunity to finish your work with other apps before restarting, so keep your chin up.

 Note

And I should tell you that chances are 50/50 that one of your running applications will refuse to quit and will cancel the automatic restart. Again: chin up. There is beauty and grandeur in the world. You are the sum total of the universe's desire to improve itself. Thus emboldened, quit those remaining apps manually and restart your Mac.

APPLE'S PARANOID SO YOU DON'T HAVE TO BE

Download the security updates, but don't worry about what might have happened during the time the security problem went unfixed. In Chapter 1, I said that as Mac OS X users, we all inherit the benefits of the OS's Unix foundations. One of these benefits is the horde of benevolent, white-hatted geeks who are constantly poring through Unix to look for weaknesses that might even *theoretically* be exploited. And when one is found, someone immediately comes up with a way to eliminate the danger.

So usually, a Security Update is like adding a coat of phaser-proof paint to your front door. Nobody's ever produced a phaser gun, but the guys at Home Depot came up with an additive that costs nothing, so why not use it?

That pretty much covers the topic of installation. I had a nagging feeling that I'd left some unfinished business, though, and it didn't hit me until I scrolled back and reread this chapter in its entirety.

Just to keep the folks over in Legal happy, I should probably warn you that Karmic precipitation is solely the function of the ineffable and unquestionable universe and that attempts to influence the apportioning of same or project a desirable result into a future incarnation may not cause your functional conscious awareness to become elevated into the elusive all-awareness.

So, a word to the wise on that. Onward!

Hello, I Must Be Going
(and, uh, Sleep)

In This Chapter

Starting Up • Shutdown and Restart • Sleep and Energy Saver

And here, this book works a fertile field that's been well-plowed by all the classics of Western literature, as well as the bulk of Cole Porter's output: surely, there's no greater maelstrom of tension and emotion than saying hello and saying goodbye. I'm really looking forward to this chapter. As an author, when you choose "installing a printer" as your topic, you're pretty much on your own. But if you can couch a Macintosh's startup and shutdown processes in terms of loss and spiritual growth, you land straight on the shortlist for the next Oprah's Book Club selection and it's allllll gravy from there on.

On the face of it, starting up and shutting down are just about the simplest concepts you can tackle with a Macintosh. You press a button and then electrons leap from your computer like C-list celebrities from a doomed cruise ship in the first act of a 1970's disaster flick. There's really not much for the end user to do after they've made the commitment. But there are enough subtleties here and there to nicely fill out a chapter, methinks.

STARTING UP

Okey-doke. So you've wandered into the office, stabbed the Power button, and popped the top off of your Dunkin' Donuts coffee, taking some heady sips of His Master's Vice (or Her Mistress' Vice) while you choose the mechanism by which you will be goofing off from 9:00 to 9:22, and waiting for your Mac to come to life.

So what's actually happening?

1. Your Mac does a simple self-test of its memory and hardware. These tests aren't as ambitious as the diagnostics available to the certified Geniuses at your Apple Store, but they're enough to make a quick "go" or "no-go" determination vis-à-vis your Mac's ability to do more than simply look pretty on your desk. If you have a bad memory module or something, you'll hear Chimes of Doom and see a "Sad Mac" icon on the screen.

2. Next, your Mac looks around for a bootable copy of the Macintosh operating system. At this point, you might see a blank screen and a spinning "Wait" daisy. Normally this is over and done with so quickly that you won't see anything at all, but if your Mac is a little bamboozled at the moment (or if your Mac can't boot off its internal drive and has to look for the OS on an external hard drive or something) you might have to wait a few seconds.

3. Now your Mac actually has something to load, and we're off to the races. Mac OS X is loaded in layers. As the initialization progresses, you see a sequence of messages telling you what OS X is doing (as in Figure 3-1).

Figure 3-1
A sample startup progress message

OH, CRUMB

And if you *do* get a Sad Mac, what can you do about it? Not much. There's just nothing that you can fix yourself. If you've just installed some new memory, well, the Chimes of Doom are a good indication that either (a) you bungled the job or (b) one or more of your memory modules is defective. In *that* case, you can crack open your Mac again and take out the new memory modules, or make sure that they're seated all the way into their sockets.

Chiefly, though, your first move is going to be to do a certain discrete amount of dancing (if this is your work computer, that is). If it's not *your* Mac that's busted, and it's not *your* stack of fortnightly AG-88-A's that need to be processed and filed, then the Chimes of Doom denote the sudden and happy delivery of a Snow Day. Volunteer to take the sick machine to the Apple Store for service, and creatively fail to specify that you'll be taking it to the Apple Store near Six Flags, not the one in the mall just down the turnpike.

▼ **Note**

The messages are extremely nerdy and aren't nearly as fun to watch as the stately progression of icons that you used to get in Mac OS 9. Though if you're over the age of 21, great sport can be had by lining up 20 or 30 shots of tequila on the bar, getting five or six friends together, and then when your Mac restarts, someone has to down a shot in turn whenever the word *loader* or *system* flashes by.

After the majority of the OS has loaded in, you're given a chance to identify yourself and type in your user password. If you've just installed OS X, you will have only one user account — the one you created during the installation. OS X logs you in to that account automatically and takes

BUT WHAT ABOUT OPEN FIRMWARE?

Haha. I *knew* that this question has been burning on the tip of your tongue, eradicating your ability to sense sweet-tasting things. *Everybody* wants to know about Open Firmware! It's all people can talk about. Steve Jobs went on the Letterman show just a month ago, hoping to promote the new iPod, but what was the first thing Dave asked about? Open Firmware! Man, Steve must have been *steamed* about that.

I have just consulted the little style sheet that Wiley's design and production team assembled for me when they designed the visual doodads of this book and I note that there's no little icon for "Sarcasm." So please just take it as read that Open Firmware really isn't important to the end user, and that even most of the people who actually know what it is couldn't care less about it.

Still, it's an interesting bit of trivia. When your Mac is switched off, it's inert. It don't know how to do nothin'. No book learnin', no street smarts, nothin'. It's certainly not smart enough to load in and activate a piece of software as huge, ambitious, and complicated as Mac OS X, particularly before it's had its first Snapple and Fruit-N-Nut bar.

So before loading in Mac OS X, your Mac loads in a simple, tiny operating system called Open Firmware. It has one purpose only: Load in and execute the first bits of Mac OS X, which give your Mac enough sophistication to load in the *next* bit, which loads in the *next* bit, and then, hey-presto, you're looking for naked photos of Mackenzie Philips on the Web.

NINCOMPOOPERY WITH OPEN FIRMWARE

If you wanna see what Open Firmware looks like, hold down the ⌘, Option, O, and F keys while you start up the Mac. Yeah, it's underwhelming: just some text on a black screen. The Apple][+ (circa 1977) had a more exotic interface. Type **mac-boot** and hit Return to continue booting your Mac as normal.

There are only two real uses for this trick: to lord it over all those users who have never seen Open Firmware for themselves, and to give yourself a good chance at finding an unused Mac in a crowded computer lab. See, if you're about to leave for lunch, you can restart the Mac into Open Firmware and leave it that way. The lack of any sort of user interface and the appearance of a decidedly un-Maclike interface will confuse and intimidate most other users into thinking that there's something profoundly and Mephistopholeanly wrong with this machine, and they'll avoid it like an egg-salad sandwich that's been sitting in the breakroom fridge since last July.

When you get back from lunch, just take a seat, type **mac-boot** and you're off and running. Feel free to go for broke and make a big deal about how you "fixed" the broken machine.

you directly to the Desktop. Though after you've created multiple user accounts (one for you, one for your spouse, one for the kid, one for the dog), your Mac has to deal with the question "Who's about to use this machine?" There are three different ways:

- **Your Mac can log in a certain user automatically at startup.** No password needed.

- **Your Mac can display a list of all of the user accounts that have been established on this system.** The user picks from this list (see Figure 3-2) and then types a password.

Figure 3-2
Logging in from a list of users

- **Your Mac can present a Soviet border guard–style box that demands the user to provide both a password and an account name (see Figure 3-3).** This adds a dash of extra security. Guessing a user's password is one thing. Getting access to a Mac by correctly guessing a password *and* a user name is dang-near impossible, particularly because the miscreant probably doesn't know who's using this machine, and therefore can't guess that a user with the name "PackersRule" might have chosen the name of a linebacker as their password.

▼ **Cross-Reference**
For details on how to set these options, which have major security repercussions, see Chapter 19.

Figure 3-3
Typing a user name and password to log in

AND HERE, YOUR TROUBLES BEGAN

Okay, so again, in a normal situation you'd just be idly watching this as you stir your coffee in the morning. When your Mac is acting up, though, close observation of the startup process will go a long way towards figuring out what's gone wrong. If your Mac locks up after it draws a blank menu bar, then you know that there's something wrong with the Finder. If it happens just after you log in, you can guess that it's a problem with the user settings of that specific account. Before the login screen? Gosh, a fundamental slab of the OS itself is messed up. If it hangs on that big spinning disc, then it's something with your startup volume that goes beyond the OS.

And again, chimes-o-doom mean a trip to the Happy Valley Ranch, i.e., a mall with an Apple Store. But as you can imagine, the further along the process goes before it goes ker-flooey, the better the news is for you. If my Mac freezes up after login, I'm not worried. Chances are excellent that I can boot from a different account, and there's practically no chance that my hard drive is damaged. Remember, if the Mac itself or its drive was messed up, the boot process wouldn't have gotten *nearly* that far.

The login window offers a few options. Back takes you back to the list of users, and Forgot Password will reveal a hint (assuming, of course, that you specified a hint when the account was created).

▼ Cross-Reference

You can also log in to your Macintosh when it's already switched on and being used by another user. Turn to Chapter 18 for info on how to log out the current user and log yourself in, or how to switch from one user to another.

After you've logged in, Tiger finishes loading in the rest of the OS and starts up the Finder; it'll load in your desktop wallpaper, draw in a menu bar, and toss all of your Desktop icons on the screen. Finally, Tiger launches all of the Startup Items: apps, documents, and other doodads that you told Tiger to automatically open up every time you start your Mac.

Startup keys

Before the Mac even starts up, it looks at the keyboard to see if you're pressing any special keys that trigger all kinds of alternative behaviors. A sampling of the most useful:

- **C forces the Mac to bypass the normal drive and boot from a CD.** You'll use this key combo every time you want to install a clean copy of the OS, and when you run a low-level disk utility, like the one you'll find on Tiger's Install 1 disc, or certain third-party disk utilities.

- **T is for FireWire Target Mode.** If (after shutting down your Mac) you plugged a FireWire cable from it to another Mac, pressing this key during boot makes the Targeted machine act like an external hard drive to the other Mac.

- **Shift starts the Mac in Safe mode.** If your Mac is experiencing problems, this runs a few quick disk checks and then loads the bare-minimum amount of code it needs to run Tiger.

- **⌘-Option-Shift-Delete tells your Mac to ignore the internal hard drive and try to boot off another volume.** For example, I've installed a copy of Tiger on my 40 GB iPod, along with my usual apps and files. So if I'm visiting somebody else's office and I need to get a little work done, I can just plug it into any Mac's FireWire port, boot from it, and then I have all the same resources and apps as I do back at home.

▼ Tip

If you can't remember the letter *T*, Tiger also lets you activate Target Disk Mode through the Startup Disk pane in System Preferences. Click the Target Disk Mode button and your Mac will restart and start acting like a hard drive. Provided you've tethered it to another Mac via FireWire, natcherly.

- **⌘+V starts the Mac in Verbose mode, reporting on every last detail of the startup process as it happens.**

▼ Note

Like Open Firmware, ⌘+V is a wonderful thing to scare less-savvy users with. Many startup keys are like that. Once I needed to make sure nobody used a specific Mac while I worked on the other side of the room. I could have either booted into Open Firmware as described earlier, or maybe spilled a whole thing of coffee on the seat; but I was feeling jaunty so I restarted in single-user mode (⌘+s), which means that the Mac boots into a text-only, incredibly gnarly looking Unix command line. Believe me, nobody came near it. Which was good because in single-user mode, someone who knows Unix can wreak havoc with the whole system. "He who lives by the sword" and whatnot.

BIG COOL TARGET MOJO

And of course, if you've put your PowerBook into Target Disk Mode, you can connect it to another Mac and boot from it. This is another trick I use often. I often have my PowerBook with me, but it isn't nearly as nice as a friend's dual-processor G5 tower with the 30-inch cinema display. So if I'm staying the night I'll connect my machine to his, boot off my hard drive, and I'm livin' larrrrge!

THE CHOIR INVISIBLE

Many apps install tiny, invisible doodads in your Login Items that allow little bits of magic to happen even when the app itself isn't running. For example, I have an EyeTV box plugged into my desktop Mac. It's a TV tuner that allows a desktop app to record TV shows. When you install the EyeTV, the software installs a little invisible helper in Startup Items. Its purpose is to remember that, geez, Andy wanted to record *The Amazing Race 11* Tuesday night at 9:00 on Channel 4. If it's a few minutes before 9:00 and the EyeTV app isn't running, the helper will automatically launch it so I won't miss my show. So it's extremely important that this helper app is always standing by: this looks like a job for Startup Items.

Hidden Login Items can often cause weird system problems. Every now and then you should look around in that list of items to make sure your Mac isn't still launching some sort of invisible helper app for, say, a label-printer that you threw away eight months ago.

And there are plenty more where that came from; go to the Help menu and do a search for "Shortcuts for starting up" to get a complete list. To use a startup key, press the key(s) right before you turn on your Mac (or right after the screen goes dark, if you're doing a Restart), and don't release the key until you see their effect.

 Cross-reference

See Chapter 24 for more about troubleshooting.

Specifying Login Items

You think that when Pete Townsend goes on tour, he tunes his own guitars and plugs things into the amps himself? Nothin' doing: he takes to the stage and all the tools of his craft are sitting there, powered up and ready to burn off what remains of his sense of hearing.

Do you think Pete Townsend is *better* than you? Of course he isn't. So you can get the same sort of thing going by telling Tiger to automatically launch a bunch of apps and/or documents at startup. Hardly an hour goes by when I

don't check my email, look up something on the Web, or check my calendar. So Mail, Safari, and iCal (and, um, about 11 other apps) are launched for me at startup.

It's better to have the *computer* waste its time by launching apps you'll never use than to have it waste *your* time making you wait for an app to launch when you're sitting at your desk. Still, don't abuse this feature by tossing all of your apps into the Login Items list. Having more apps running at once means that the Mac has to manage more resources to keep them running, which will reduce the machine's overall performance.

Here's how you can specify Login Items:

1. **Open System Preferences from the Apple Menu.**

   The System Preferences dialog box appears.

2. **Click the Accounts icon.**

   This opens the Accounts preferences panel.

3. **Click the account for which you want to set login items in the list of accounts.**

   This is located at the left of the window.

4. **Click the Login Items button at the top right of the window.**

5. **Click the plus (+) sign below the list of items (see Figure 3-4).**

   This adds a new startup item.

6. **Use the Open File dialog box to choose the item (Figure 3-5). It can be a document, an application, even a folder or a server that you use often.**

Figure 3-5
Adding a new login item

▼ Note

If you aren't familiar with the Mac OS's Open File dialog box, see Chapter 11.

7. **Click the Add button.**

   OS X adds your selection to the list of login items. The new item opens automatically the next time you start up the computer.

SHUTDOWN AND RESTART

When you're done with your computer, you shouldn't just cut the power. That's like ending a party by turning on the indoor sprinklers. It's effective, but it's unnecessary and impolite. Your guests need a few moments to collect their things and make an orderly and safe exit. Though Lord knows, sometimes your guests don't deserve your patience and indulgence.

Figure 3-4
Your login items

▼ **Tip**

I want to give you advice in life, not just in Tiger, so I'll tell you that sometimes a fully charged fire extinguisher is the only thing that'll prevent Uncle Ike from climbing onto the bandstand and doing the risqué version of *Gentlemen Prefer Blondes* that he learned in the merchant marines. He'll sputter back to his Honda Prelude looking like the ghost of Jacob Marley, but your party will be saved.

A computer is no different. The OS uses scads of little invisible programs and files to manage all of its processes; and unless Tiger properly closes them down, all kinds of gremlins and instabilities can crop up later on.

RESTART: DEFROSTING THE GREAT FRIDGE OF YOUR MAC'S MEMORY

The reason why restarting improves performance is a bit technical, but it's like totally emptying out the contents of your freezer and repacking it. After weeks of taking things out and putting things in and moving things around as best you can, all that food is packed terribly inefficiently. Look, the Ben & Jerry's Chunky Monkey is buried behind the warehouse-club sack of frozen peas, and to get at your Eggos this morning, you had to pull out three loaves of the homemade bread your Mom made last Thanksgiving!

Things have a natural tendency to get disorganized in your Mac's memory as time passes, and a restart gives Tiger a fresh start and helps things run faster and more efficiently. If your Mac is as slow as a truck with wheels made out of old copies of *National Geographic,* try restarting.

BEWARE THE KICK TO THE HEAD

It's also possible that the app has frozen and is digging in its heels and refuses to quit under any circumstances. I cover this a little better in the chapter on apps, but for the here and now you can force an app to quit through the Force Quit item in Chapter 9. But don't do this just to save time; only force quit an app when it's really frozen.

Click on the app's Dock icon and hold down the mouse button. If the resulting pop-up menu says "Application not responding," you know that a clop to the back of its head is both necessary and deserved.

▼ **Tip**

OS X can have so many problems resulting from a "dirty" shutdown, you may consider getting an uninterruptible power supply (UPS). If there's a sudden blackout, big batteries inside the UPS take over and provide enough juice to close your files and shut down your Mac like a civilized member of society. That's a lot of peace of mind for less than a hundred bucks.

Performing a clean shutdown

To perform a clean shutdown, select Shut Down from the Apple menu. OS X closes all open applications, giving you a chance to save all files that have unsaved changes. The shutdown process then logs you out and shuts down all system processes. Finally, the computer powers itself down.

Quitting manually

Sometimes OS X can't close an application. Usually this is because the app has a document open and there are changes that you haven't saved yet, and so the app is patiently waiting for you to confirm that yes, you *really* want to throw away the 1,000 words you just added to your magnum opus. When that happens, the shutdown will abort. You'll just have to quit the app manually and click Shut Down again.

Restarting does the same thing as Shut Down, except that after your Mac closes all of your apps and shuts down the whole operating system, it starts up again. You really shouldn't have to use this procedure very often. You might be asked to restart after installing new software, and you might want to do it if your Mac is acting sluggish for no apparent reason.

SLEEP AND ENERGY SAVER

Finally, there's Sleep mode. Shutting down turns off your Mac, which saves power, absolutely, but you have to start up all over again when you're ready to go back to work. Sleep is a compromise. The OS keeps power flowing to every part of your Mac that's responsible for remembering what applications and documents are open and what they're currently doing. It cuts the power to everything else: the display, the hard drive, even bits of the motherboard itself. The end result is that when you return to your Mac and touch a key or move the mouse, it springs back to life instantly as though you'd never left it. And yet for the 3 hours you were off seeing *The Lord of the Rings* for the ninth time, your Mac was consuming a fraction of the 250 watts of power it might normally use.

Besides, Tiger's built-in Energy Saver feature automatically puts your Mac to sleep when it detects that you haven't touched it in a while.

Setting Automatic Inactivity

You configure Energy Saver through the Energy Saver preferences panel, where you tell OS X how and when your computer should sleep:

1. **Click the System Preferences icon in the Dock.**

    This launches the System Preferences dialog box.

2. **Click the Energy Saver icon.**

    This displays the Energy Saver preferences panel (see Figure 3-6).

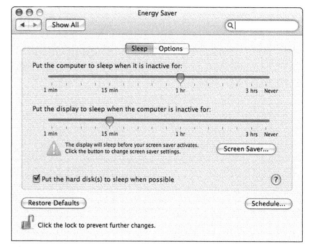

Figure 3-6
Telling your Mac when it should Sleep

3. **Set the computer inactivity option: Move the top slider to set the period of inactivity before OS X puts the computer to sleep.**

4. **Set the display inactivity option.**

    If you want the monitor to go to sleep before or after the computer, click the "Put the display to sleep when the computer is inactive for" option. Then use the slider below to set the inactivity period.

Note

Gosh, your screensaver is purty. It'd be a shame if you set your screen to go dark before your screensaver had time to kick in. After all, you wouldn't get to see them purty pitchers. At least that's Tiger's way of thinking. So if you've adjusted your sleep settings in such a way that your screensaver will never activate, it subtly warns you, as in Figure 3-6.

5. **Leave the "Put the hard disk(s) to sleep when possible" option selected.**

   This puts hard disks to sleep as well.

 Note

Putting hard disks to sleep when they're not in use can make them last a lot longer. The only drawback is that when your Mac wakes them back up again, it takes a few moments for them to spin back up to speed (which can lead to some lags in performance, particularly if you're using your Mac to serve files to other machines on the network).

Setting scheduled startups and shutdowns

Energy Saver can also automatically start up and shut down your computer at times that you specify:

1. **Open the Energy Saver preferences panel and click the Options button.**

2. **Click the Schedule button.**

   This displays the Schedule pane shown in Figure 3-7.

3. **Click the Start up the computer option.**

   This starts the computer at a specific time.

4. **Select the frequency from the pop-up menu.**

   Your choices are Weekdays, Weekends, Every Day, or a specific day of the week.

5. **Set the time.**

   To do so, click in the hours box. You can either delete the 0 and type the hour, or use the up and down arrows to change the hours. Next, click in the minutes box and set the minutes.

SLEEP OR SHUT DOWN?

Which begs the question: If Tiger is stable enough to run for weeks without restarting, and there's a way to have the Mac use less power than a night light when it's not in use, why bother turning off the Mac at all?

Answer: There really isn't one. In fact, keeping your Mac shut down overnight can be a bad thing. Tiger is based on Unix, and Unix spends part of its downtime (typically 4:00 a.m.) doing system maintenance chores. If you turn it off every night at 7:00 and turn it on again at 9:00 a.m., those chores don't get done.

You can avoid this problem with a handy (and free) third-party utility called MacJanitor. Do a Google search on that word and you'll find plenty of places where it can be downloaded. Me, I keep my Macs in Sleep mode when they're not in use. I think this behavior is mostly a hand-me-down from my dad, who on family vacations wouldn't let the station wagon pull out of the driveway until he'd made sure that every appliance had been unplugged and the batteries pulled out of the remote control.

MORE HELPFUL CONTRADICTIONS

I'm on record as saying that I keep my Mac going 24/7, minus those times when it goes to Sleep due to inactivity. But naturally, there are practical uses to setting startup and shutdown times. Setting a shutdown time can be a bit of a security feature: you can be sure that at 9:00 every evening (or whenever), all users have been logged out, the machine is dark and dead, and the dude who sweeps the floors in your office won't be able to read your email unless he or she also knows your login password.

And setting a startup time is a good idea if your Mac shares services to other machines on your network. If all of the Macs in your office share the printer connected to your machine, it's important that your Mac be up and running when it's supposed to be. There are a lot of things you can't control, but if you tell your Mac to turn itself on just before 9:00 every morning, you have a bit of insurance against getting a phone call during your two-week vacation following a Duran Duran tribute band in a beat-up RV.

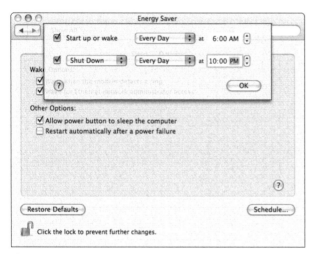

Figure 3-7
The Schedule pane of the Energy Saver preferences pane

The Preferences pane has a pane for a few additional options. There are times when you really don't want your Mac to be asleep at the switch. Like, if someone's sending you a fax, or if the folks who maintain your office network want to update some files. You can tell Energy Saver to

always wake up when these events happen by clicking the Options tab and selecting the appropriate options:

- **Sleeping the computer by pressing the Power key can be a big convenience, particularly in an office environment.** When you get up to use the photocopier, you don't want passers-by to read what's up on your screen. Pressing the Power key dims your computer to black.

- **The "Restart automatically after a power failure" option can be a lifesaver in the right hands.** Sometimes your Mac isn't just your Mac; it can share its files and even its printers and other hardware with other Macs on the network. By clicking this option, a five-minute power outage won't turn the lights out on your Mac's network services for the rest of the weekend.

Whenever I rummage through the Ihnatko Book Depository (aka Units 217-219 of the Dedham E-Z-Storage) and leaf through 20-year-old computer magazines, I'm amazed by how spectacularly wrong all of the experts were when they sat back and tried to paint a picture of what computing would be like in 2005. I particularly want to single out the guy who went on and on and *on* about how the keyboards' up, down, left, and right buttons would be enhanced by — now try to wrap your puny simians around *this* one — keys that could move the cursor diagonally with just a single tap.

Lessons: Predicting the future is a mug's game. When I do it, I'm always smart enough to predict things that'll happen in no sooner than seven years' time, when I'll be long dead and thus can't be held accountable.

The bigger lesson is that it's the *subtle* things that transform a technology. Power management isn't a cool technology. But really, few features have had a greater impact upon a modern Mac's role in a house or office. Activating a computer isn't a big production. You tap a key or waggle the mouse and it blinks to life, ready to exact your slightest whim after only about a second or two. In the olden days, you needed to wait several minutes and then type in a big pile of commands before you could indulge an impulse that involved your plastic pal.

It's an enabling and transforming feature. "Hey, what movie was Dustin Hoffman in, before the sequel to *Meet the Parents?*" can be answered in moments. Without modern power management, the Internet is worthless; you'd only turn the crank on your computer and stoke the fires and boot it up if you had a *damned good reason* to do so. And if history has taught us anything, true power doesn't come from exalting an entity into a major act of will. Power comes when you can tap into people's desire for immediate fulfillment.

And by way of confirming my hypothesis: *Wag the Dog,* 1997, directed by Barry Levinson. See? You were on your way to the Internet Movie Database to look it up, weren't you? Game, set, and match!

POWERBOOK USERS: HAVE YOU HUGGED ENERGY SAVER TODAY?

There are other settings that only appear when you're running Energy Saver on a PowerBook. Obviously, conserving energy is way more important if you're using a machine that relies on batteries. I don't give a pair of dingo's kidneys about whether there'll be enough light, heat, and power for my great-grandchildren. I want to be able to watch *The Magnificent Seven* in its entirety on this flight! The guy in the seat next to me is dressed like an insurance man and he has the hungry, rheumy eyes of a man who's under his monthly quota.

So Energy Saver has special PowerBook-oriented settings that adapt to various operational situations. Longest Battery Life cuts off the hard drive and screen quickly. DVD Playback keeps the screen on but tries to conserve everywhere else. You can also have one setting for battery and another "Hogs Greedily Slurping at the Trough of Unlimited Energy" setting that goes into effect when you're plugged into AC.

I always make sure that I've clicked a special shorter Sleep time that comes into play when my PowerBook is running on battery. I can't tell you how many times I've unknowingly kicked the power plug out of its socket while walking off. Using Energy Saver means that there'll be plenty of juice left in the battery when I return.

Getting to First Base with the Mac User Interface

In This Chapter

The Desktop: What Lies Beneath • Menus: The Drop (Down) Squad
Apple's Standard Menus • Pointing Devices: Mouse Hunt
Windows: View from the Top • Exposé: Sliding Doors
Keyboard Controls: Key Largo
Monitors: Through a Glass, Darkly • Help!

Whether you upgrade to Tiger from Mac OS 9 or Windows, your first few hours with X are like your first few hours behind the wheel of a new car. You don't notice how much better everything is ("Hey, look! No duct tape on the windshield!") as much as you try to get used to how different everything is ("This seat hugs my butt in a manner which I must publicly disapprove of, but which I silently quite enjoy.").

It's all about fit and function, and X has its own opinions on how users should be mollycoddled, cajoled, supported, urged on, dealt with, tolerated, welcomed, assisted, manipulated, soothed, and otherwise made to think that tearing this machine off the desk and making a sleek, iMac-shaped hole in the nearest exterior window is not a course of action to be advocated.

The hallmark of any decent OS — of which X is one, I assure you — is that you'll spend 95% of your time using the simplest 5% of its features. So after you master the basics of the OS X user interface, you'll be sitting on velvet and prepared to attack the more advanced topics in this book with a certain amount of tra-la in your heart.

When you get down to atoms and molecules, the visual elements of the Macintosh Interface come down to the Desktop, menus, and windows.

THE DESKTOP: WHAT LIES BENEATH

We talk a lot about the Macintosh Desktop (chiefly because we like to hear ourselves talk). It's a real character fault, I know, and we're working on it because it's a basic metaphor that has stuck since 1984. "The Macintosh Desktop" is simply The Thing You're Looking At when you look at a Mac screen. It's your workspace. Take a look at Figure 4-1. Like a real desktop, you're likely to see something this clean and tidy only the very first time you ever use it and then never ever again. Not once. Not until you buy a new desk and have the old one hauled away or are ever lucky enough to do that thing that happens in the movies where your sweetheart, consumed with immediate passion, swats everything off your desk in one fluid motion and then you proceed to smooch away atop it with fierce abandon (warning: unlikely).

Even in its bare-bones appearance, Figure 4-1 shows off three basic Macintosh elements:

- **It has a menu bar.** On Windows and Linux systems, there's a menu bar inside every window. On the Mac, there's just the one, and it changes every time you switch from one application to another. If you have more than one monitor attached to your Mac, it appears on only one of them: the startup monitor. You can choose which monitor you want as the startup monitor through the Displays section of System Preferences.

▼ Note

Like most things that non-Mac users don't like, Mac users claim that this "one menu bar" idea is actually a feature. "It conserves screen space and it gives you an immediate and obvious visual cue regarding which app is currently in use," they will tell you. And that's actually quite true, but it really just comes down to "that's the way the Mac has always done it."

- **It has a Dock.** This is anchored at the bottom of Figure 4-1; it can also appear to the left or the right of the startup monitor. It gives you easy access to applications and documents that you use frequently, as well as all applications that are running at any given time. Do not fear the Dock. The Dock is pure, the Dock is kind, the Dock has a wonderful plan for your life. The Dock is also the subject of Chapter 8.

- **It has icons.** Any external storage devices that the computer can access appear as icons on the Desktop. In Figure 4-1, there is only one storage volume, a hard disk named Macintosh HD.

Figure 4-1
A bare Desktop

▼ Note

The hard drive icon is chiefly just a holdover from the old days, included so that longtime Mac users who expect to see hard drives and CDs and such on the Desktop wouldn't wet themselves in fear when they discovered that, holy cow, something actually works *differently* in this new edition of the Mac OS!

And if you are indeed an old-school Mac user and you feel a certain creeping dampness because you don't see the Trash Can in its familiar spot in the lower-right corner of the screen, it's in the Dock now. It's also a wire basket instead of a can, but again, there's really no reason to panic. You are still loved.

But again, this Desktop is so clean that presenting it as a working Macintosh is tantamount to fraud. Figure 4-2 presents a more typical view:

Figure 4-2
The Desktop with open folders and documents

Get a load of:

- A listing of some of the programs stored on the computer's hard disk (the window named Applications).

- The Calculator application.

- The Address Book application.

- A photo of my brother-in-law.

- A bunch of Web pages I've opened in my Web browser.

- An iTunes window.

Yes, things are getting sort of cluttered here, with all the overlapping windows and such. It'll get even more cluttered. Why, the Desktop will get so cluttered that you can't even see the Desktop anymore.

And here we have to pause and stretch the Desktop metaphor a bit. I stress that the Desktop is indeed modeled on a real, honest-to-God grey Formica desktop. You toss documents and tools on top of it and commence to work, ultimately burying the thing under papers.

When folks refer to the Macintosh Desktop, they are indeed usually referring to the sum total of their workspace. But sometimes you hear people refer to the Desktop as that nice, empty acreage you had before you started opening windows. "The Desktop picture," for example, refers to the artwork that serves as the background to everything else, and that folder icon in Figure 4-2 is said to be "on the Desktop"; i.e., not inside a window.

The Desktop's desktop isn't terribly useful because, as you've seen, it tends to get covered up rather quickly. That's why Apple moved the Trash can to the Dock. Sitting on the Desktop, other things quickly cover it up, and you can't drag anything into it until you drag other windows out of the way first.

JUST *WHAT* IS THIS USER DOING?

I apologize. What *is* this user doing? Um, I dunno. I suppose I should guess. He's killing time in his office listening to music because he's about to knock off for a long, long meal with a friend he's about to phone, calculating how much he can spend on the entrée without alerting his boss that he's abusing his expense account. As a typical office computer user, he's also opened one or two random windows to cover up one of his browser windows, so his boss won't see that a moment before she walked by, he was looking up naughty words on UrbanDictionary.com. But take it from me: the state of an *actual* working computer is not a helpful illustration of the elements of the Macintosh user interface. It is an illustration that Mankind is a creature of emotion, not of logic.

The photo of his brother-in-law, naturally, has been opened because it'll probably guarantee him an invite to the next big barbecue. The man has a way with chicken wings. What can I tell you?

▼ Tip

Actually, the Desktop gets so routinely and reliably cluttered that Apple created a feature called "Exposé" whose sole feature is to allow you to dig through the mess. You'll read about Exposé later in this chapter.

You can access the Desktop's contents via its own folder as well. You find it right inside your user directory. I've dragged mine into the Dock, so if I need to access something on the Desktop, I can simply get to it through the Dock instead of having to hide a huge pile of windows. And you thought I was just blowing bubbles when I told you how hyper-megasuper-useful the Dock is?

MENUS: THE DROP (DOWN) SQUAD

Let's move on to menus. Again there's just the one menu bar; it's at the top of your monitor (the top of your Startup Monitor if you have more than one screen). Menus are the chief mechanism for telling your Mac to do something.

Macintosh menus drop down, which means that when you click the mouse on a menu's title, its contents appear. As you can see in Figure 4-3, the title remains highlighted while the contents are visible.

Figure 4-3
Behold, a menu

The menu stays open while you move the mouse over its contents. Click again to select an item.

An item might be dimmed, and won't respond when your mouse passes over it. That's because it represents a feature that you can't use right now for some reason. And it's not because anything's broken. If your word processor has a "Translate selected text into Egg Latin" menu item and you haven't selected any text, it'll be dimmed out.

It's an elegant way to avoid having to throw up error messages that begin with the unhelpful phrase, "Hey! Dimwit!"

Some menu items have an ellipsis next to them (...).

 Note

It's very, very satisfying to refer to it as an "ellipsis" instead of "a dot-dot-dot." Hey, you want a freebie? That tic-tac-toe button on the telephone is technically called an "octothorp." The little rubber footy thing at the bottom of a crutch that keeps it from scratching up the floor? I don't know what that's called. How about "Theodore"? I've always liked that name.

An ellipsis means that the function the menu item represents is complicated enough that the Mac needs to open up a user-interface item called a dialog box. A dialog box is the Mac's way of asking for a few details before it can go off and do what you've just told it to do. Before it can print a file, for example, the Mac needs to know how many copies you want, whether you want it collated, which paper tray should it use, that sort of stuff (read all about printing in Chapter 13). Thus, selecting Print brings up a dialog box that then creates a printed document when you click its OK button.

Some menu items contain arrow-like graphical dinguses next to them. They tip you off that an item contains a submenu, or that you can activate it through the keyboard, without picking up the mouse at all.

Submenus

If you look again at Figure 4-3, you'll see that some of the option names have triangles at their right edges. This

means that there is another menu — a submenu — available. To make the submenu appear, just drag your mouse over the submenu as in Figure 4-4.

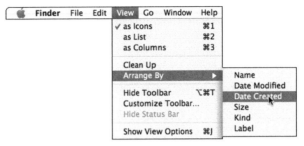

Figure 4-4
A submenu

If you're reasonably sober and are thus capable of using big words (and have a weird idea of what impresses people at dinner parties), you can refer to this whole concept as a Hierarchical Menu System. You can spot an elegant, well-thought-out app immediately by its paucity of menus. If an app's programmer is clumsy, every time they add a new feature, they'll just keep sticking on more and more menus, and adding more and more submenus.

 Note

Sometimes programmers force you to navigate through submenus *inside* submenus. As a result, changing the background color of a cell of a spreadsheet can make you feel like Indiana Jones, who spends most of his time wondering why the ancient Machapoans couldn't just leave the golden idol of the Kauan Goddess right at the entrance to the tomb instead of jerking him around like this. It's a cold, lonely feeling.

Keyboard shortcuts for menu options

You'll see symbols at the far right edge of some of Figure 4-2's menu items. These are the keyboard shortcuts that you can use instead of choosing the item from the menu. Keyboard shortcuts use ⌘, which is colloquially known as the flower key, the fan key, and once while I was speaking at a user-group meeting an older person in the group referred to it as The Rug Beater. It's stuck in my mind ever since and now I pass this meme onward to you.

To execute a shortcut, hold down ⌘ and then hit a character key. You'll probably have to cheat at first and pull down the menu to remember that ⌘+Z is the same as going to the Edit menu and clicking Undo, but you don't need to pull down anything to execute a keyboard shortcut.

The keyboard shortcut might contain a whole string of symbols, which means that you'll have to hold down some additional keys, such as the Control, Shift, or Option keys. Even if the keyboard command is Control+Shift+Option+B, you don't have to press the keys in any specific sequence. The Mac is just waiting for that character key. As soon as you tap the B key, OS X checks what other modifier keys you're holding down and you're off to the races.

 Tip

If all of these multiple key presses make you feel like your playing a special phalangeal edition of Twister, turn on the Mac's Sticky Keys feature, which is discussed later in this chaper. The Mac allows you to tap in a keyboard equivalent one stroke at a time.

Menu bars vary from application to application, but there are a few that appear in (almost) all of them. The Apple Menu, File, Edit, and (way at the end) Help menus are part of the basic Mac user interface, and are 99 and 44/100 percent consistent from app to app.

THE APPLE MENU

The Apple Menu is always there in the extreme left corner, proudly flying the Apple colors — well, *an* Apple color, anyway — shining out like a beacon of hope over all of your work.

The purpose of the Apple menu has gotten a little vague in Mac OS X, but chiefly it's for dealing with "the big picture" of Macintosh operations. Viz:

- **About This Mac:** Tells you (in broad strokes) what version of Mac OS X you're running, and what sort of hardware you're using (see Figure 4-5). For details, click the More Info button. This launches the System Profiler utility, which outlines everything you could ever know about your Mac's hardware and software in exhaustive, excruciating, and "who-is-this-person-and-why-won't-he-stop-explaining-to-me-how-the-designated-hitter-rule-created-an-unfair-advantage-for-left-handed-pitchers" detail. But when something goes wrong with your Mac and you phone somebody for help, the first thing they'll do is ask you to read off some of the information therein. So I shouldn't be so snippy.

Figure 4-5
The About This Mac box

THE APPLE MENU: A HISTORY

If you want a sign of the Mac's growing pains, look no further. The Apple Menu was once one of the cornerstones of the interface, but in the transition to X, most of its important duties have been given over to other elements, like the Dock. Still, we like the old dear. The first time Apple showed off Mac OS X (which was still in development), the Apple menu had been moved to the middle of the screen, which to Mac purists was like seeing the Queen knighting rock stars and philanthropists while wearing an ermine miniskirt and a tube top. A fuss was (justly) raised and the Apple icon was quietly moved back where it's been since 1984.

- **Software Update:** Connects to the Internet and checks whether newer versions of the OS or any Apple-brand software (like iLife apps) are available. Mac OS X does this automatically (through System Preferences), but using this menu item is a good way to get the latest bug fixes ASAP.

- **Mac OS X Software:** Launches your Web browser and navigates to the Downloads area of Apple's Web site. Here you find offers for commercial software as well as apps you can download and try out. Some of them are free, some of them are shareware (try them and send in some dough if you like them), and some are demonstration software (special test-drive versions of commercial apps).

Note

I use this one a lot. Apple tends to highlight most of the coolest shareware and freeware here. It's not the only place to download software, but it gives you the greatest chance of finding something that's actually *good*.

- **System Preferences**: Takes you straight to the System Preferences panel, where you can adjust basic system settings.

- **Dock:** Lets you make quick adjustments to the behavior of the Dock. Have I mentioned the Dock? Great little item? A million and one uses as you work, play, and worship? Learn all about it in Chapter 8.

- **Location:** You can read more about this in Chapter 14. At the office, you plug into a network through your Mac's built-in Ethernet port. At home, you connect via Airport. When you're in a hotel room in San Francisco, you dial an Earthlink number in the 415 area code, and, incidentally, it's three hours earlier over there. Every time you change locations you don't have to go in and change a million settings to reflect your new reality: just change to a new location that you've pre-configured.

- **Recent Items:** The Mac OS keeps track of all the apps and documents you've used recently. If you want to get your hands on the report you were writing earlier this morning but you can't remember where you put it, hey, your Mac does. Just look for it here.

Tip

I love Recent Items when it has the document I need. I think it's a cruel tease when it doesn't. It only remembers a limited number of items, so if it keeps letting you down, click System Preferences → Appearance and increase that number via the "Number of Recent Items" pop-up menu.

- **Force Quit:** When an app acts naughty and refuses to respond to your mouse and keyboard, and you can't quit it the polite way, the Force Quit command gives it a spanking, and terminates it with extreme prejudice. For more information, see Chapter 9.

A SIDE NOTE

Good gravy, but I'm plugging a lot of other chapters here. You would almost think that I'm selling the rest of the book piecemeal. And, of course, I'm not. I'm not Suzanne Somers. We did both do a *Playboy* pictorial, but we were both young and we both needed the money and that's pretty much where the similarities end.

- **Sleep, Restart, Shut Down:** From left to right it puts your Mac into power-saving Sleep mode, politely closes all open documents and applications and reboots the Mac, closes all open documents and applications, and then turns the Mac off completely. But you already know that, because you've read Chapter 2.

- **Log Out:** Logs you out of the system, closes all of your open documents and apps, and places your private files back under lock and key. It leaves behind a login window so another user can start using this Mac. See Chapter 14 for more information.

APPLICATION MENUS

Next to the Apple menu you find an application menu. Its name is always the same as the application with which you are working. For example, in Figure 4-6 you can see the application menu for iTunes.

Contents will vary from app to app, but there are some consistent items here:

- **About:** Just as it does under the Apple Menu, this tells you what version of the app you're running. Many apps also have an item for registering the software

online, looking for updates, and buying add-ons, just like the Apple Menu.

Figure 4-6
An Application menu

- **Preferences:** For adjusting the app's basic settings. If your app opens a new, empty document when it's launched and you wish that it asked you for a file to open instead, here's where you make your wishes known. Get a load of iTunes' preferences in Figure 4-7.

- **Services:** (Back to Figure 4-6.) Many apps are friendly, outgoing, salt-of-the-earth types who like to make their features available to you no matter what you're doing with your Mac. Let's say you're in a Web browser and you see a Joke Of The Day that's right up your friend Stanislau's alley. Select the text, go to Services, navigate to Mail, and click on Send Selection. Mac OS X's built-in email app creates a new message containing the joke.

▼ **Note**

This is probably the most under-used feature of Mac OS X. I know better than to look through the Services menu. If I do, I'll discover that an eleven-step process that I go through once an hour can be done in one mouse click through Services, and then I'll feel pretty bloody dumb. And I assure you that I thought I'd hit the bedrock of that particular foundation years ago.

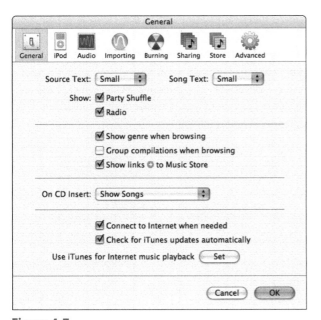

Figure 4-7
A preferences panel

- **Hide/Show:** Remember in the section "The Desktop: What Lies Beneath" earlier on, when I complained about a jillion windows cluttering up the Desktop? Mac OS X lets you make some of your apps (and their windows) invisible. Select Hide Others while within Word and all other windows will disappear. Those apps are still running and the documents are still open — they've just agreed to make themselves scarce until you switch to them or use the Show command to make them visible again.

- **Quit:** The explanation of this menu item is left empty as an exercise for the student.

The File menu

The File menu (Figure 4-8, for example) always appears to the right of the Application menu. It contains commands that deal with files, such as creating new files, opening files, saving files, and printing files.

Figure 4-8
A File menu

Individual features vary from app to app. Most apps are kind enough to add a Recent File feature in here somewhere, offering quick access to the last ten or so documents that the app opened.

The Edit menu

To the right of the File menu you will find the Edit menu (for example, Figure 4-9). The commands in the Edit menu deal with manipulating text and objects, providing copying and pasting operations.

Figure 4-9
An Edit menu

All Edit menus have Undo commands and Clipboard items.

I can still remember my first day at Driver's Ed and how dumb I felt when the teacher said, "So just go ahead and start the car" as though this information was issued to me at birth, along with a copy of *Breathing For Dummies*, so I'll touch on these ultra-basics.

- **Undo:** Undo undoes. Whatever you last did, Undo goes back in time to a happier moment before you did it — and, good Lord, one of these features should be installed in every hair salon, singles bar, and carnival bungee-jump operation in the country.

- **Some apps have "multiple undo," aka Undo Again.** This command can step back and back and back through every change you ever made to the document all the way back to the first line, "My Dearest Darling Sweetheart," which, considering that this person clearly just wants money and stability, was indeed your first mistake.

- **Cut, Copy, and Paste:** These commands are for moving elements around. Select a paragraph of text, cut it, click the mouse where you want it to go, and Paste it in. Before you Paste an item into its destination, it occupies an ethereal netherworld known as the Clipboard. It's a state of mind. Pay it no worry.

▼ Tip

As soon as you Copy or Cut another item into the Clipboard, it takes the place of whatever was in there before. Certain Jedi-level Mac users swear by utilities that allow you to have more than one Clipboard. If you're making a bunch of common changes to a big pile of documents, multiple clipboards can be a big time-saver. It's a popular category of software and there are plenty to choose from. My favorite is You Software's You Control at `www.yousoftware.com`.

The Help and Window menus

To the right of the group of menus at the left of the menu bar, you'll find the Help menu. We'll take an in-depth look at using that menu in the very last section of this chapter, "Help!"

Most applications include a Window menu to the left of the Help menu (see Figure 4-10). The contents of this menu vary from one application to another. However, in most cases the bottom section of the menu contains a list of the application's open windows. You can therefore use this menu to zap straight to windows that are hidden by other items on top of them.

Figure 4-10
A Window menu

Menulets

At the right of the menu bar you will find a collection of menus whose names are icons or other symbols, known as *menulets*. Menulets aren't part of the running app; they're system add-ons that typically give you quick access to some of the Mac's hardware settings, like the volume of your speakers, or the dimensions of your screen.

In Figure 4-11, you can see four menulets, one of which (the one with the U.S. flag) is a drop-down menu. From right to left, the menulets are

Figure 4-11
Menulets

- The menu bar clock.

- Sound, which lets you adjust the volume of your Mac's chosen audio output device.

- Input, which lets you choose a local or international keyboard layout and provides access to Keyboard Viewer, which shows you which characters are produced by which keys in a given font.

- Keychain, which provides access to a number of keychain functions. A keychain, as you learn in Chapter 19, is a device to manage all those Internet passwords we seem to accumulate as we surf the Web.

▼ Note

Keyboard Viewer replaces Key Caps, which also showed which characters were produced by which keys in a given font in earlier versions of the Mac OS.

But, of course, not all menulets are associated with hardware. Because the menu bar is always visible and is never covered by windows, it's often used for little indicators that you'll want to keep an eye on (like the time, the strength of your AirPort connection, or what your iChat status is). You also use it to access features that are handy in all apps. For example, AppleScript can install its own menu in the menu bar so that your favorite automated scripts are always right there when you need them.

Menulets can join your menu bar in three ways:

- **Sometimes an application's installer also installs a menulet.** For example, iChat and iSync do this.

- **Sometimes if you look through an application's Preferences you'll see a checkbox for a menulet.** You can see an example of this in the Displays pane of System Preferences. Click the checkbox and a new menulet appears that lets you adjust your monitor settings. You can see many of these menulets explained throughout the book.

- **A few are user-installable.** If you get a menulet on CD or if you download it, you can just drag the menulet file straight into the menu bar.

You can also reorder your menulets by holding down ⌘ and dragging its icon where you want it to go. Figure 4-12 shows an example of this happening.

Figure 4-12
Moving a menulet

The User Accounts menu

Hey, cool; there's your name, right there in the menu bar! Donald Trump has all his junk monogrammed; you deserve no less.

DOODAD CRAZY

But I know what you're saying: clutter, clutter, *clutter*. Well, you were *thinking* it, anyway. No, don't deny it. Apple's actually sort of discouraging companies from releasing new menulets, preferring to reserve that (limited) real estate in the menu bar for more fundamental things. In fact, Steve Jobs had actually made a formal edict that the menu bar was to be used for hardware-related features *only* — but then one of the AppleScript guys sort of bamboozled the AppleScript menulet up there and Apple realized that there was room for flexibility.

Oh, and your name is actually a menu, besides. It's there because a Tiger feature known as "Fast User Switching" has been turned on, and you're the current active user of this machine. Clicking on the menu drops down a list of all the users who have accounts on this Mac. Selecting another user from this menu switches users, keeping the first user logged in but tossing them into the background, allowing a different account holder to take the keyboard for a while. If Fast User Switching (which you'll learn more about in Chapter 18) isn't turned on, you won't see a user name here at all.

The Spotlight menu

And finishing off the menagerie, the extreme-right position on your menu bar is squatted by a brand-new feature of Tiger: the Spotlight menu. Clicking this puppy drops down a simple search box that will scour every file and every resource of your Mac for a specific word or phrase. And once again, I'll send you elsewhere for the Good Stuff: Spotlight is so hypermegasuperginchy that it rates its own chapter. Turn to Chapter 7 for all the dirt on Spotlight.

POINTING DEVICES: MOUSE HUNT

Mousing is another one of those basic skills that, with every new birth, is worming its way deeper and deeper into our DNA. But I have been a victim of the sort of sneer that can only come from an eleven-year-old kid who believes that anybody who can't get a simple two-point conversion in John Madden Football 2004 should be put into some sort of home, so let's touch on the basics.

First, you Windows and Linux users, don't let the single mouse button throw you. It doesn't make the Mac less powerful. Remember, the Mac had one mouse button from day one. You don't have a prehensile tail, and yet you seem to do okay for yourself, don't you?

THE BUTTON THAT TURNED BROTHER AGAINST BROTHER

The mouse button was the source of long and loud arguments among the Mac's designers. Although the only other commercial mouse-based computer had multiple buttons, what would the "extra" buttons mean? How would the second button's functionality remain consistent from app to app to app? Sensing that they already had their hands full teaching the world what to do with one button, Apple decided to keep things simple.

If you're freaked out about the one-button thing, go to any mall with ten bucks in your pocket and buy a two-button mouse. It'll work just fine. The Mac OS has supported other mouses since way before Mac OS X. Here in my office I actually have a — let me count — seven-button mouse but I never use it.

And while we're just going to talk about the mouse, here, the glorious world of pointing devices also includes trackballs (you twiddle a billiard ball–like thing under your fingertips instead of chasing a mouse around the Desktop; great if your desk is as cluttered as mine), graphics tablets (you write on an electronic surface with an electronic pen; great for art and photo editing), knobs, joysticks. . . never you mind, there are always plenty of opportunities to spend lots of money accessorizing.

 Note

When you're talking about puck-like computer pointing devices, the plural is "mouses," not "mice," just as the plural of "fan of Scooby-Doo cartoons" is "morons."

Clicking and double-clicking

There are two basic operations with a mouse button: click and double-click. A click means that you tap the mouse button once. A double-click is two single clicks close together in time.

Remember, for every action, there's an equal and opposite reaction:

- **Clicking simply selects an item.** Think of it as simply calling the Mac's attention to an item. When you select Print from the Finder, you're essentially saying, "Remember that document I clicked on before I told you to Print something? That's what I want printed."

- **Double-clicking typically opens an item.** Double-click a folder icon in the Finder and the folder's contents display. Double-click an application icon and it runs. Double-click a document icon and it opens, launching its application first if necessary.

▼ Note

I used the Finder in both examples, but when it comes to big, colorful items that are part of the basic user interface (like icons, or items inside a scrolling list), this scheme works pretty consistently.

And, of course, there's more to it than that. Clicking inside a word-processing document simply zaps the cursor to a new location. Double-clicking on a word selects the entire word. Triple-clicking is rare, but some word processors use it to select the next biggest thing in scale (the whole paragraph instead of just one word, for example). Clicking also can do different things if you hold down certain keys while you do it.

Changing the double-click and tracking speed of your mouse

Do you want to zap from one edge of the screen to another with just a nudge, or do you want enough fine control that you can do this in two or three strokes? If you're moving to the Mac from Windows, it probably seems like your mouse pointer is whipping all over the place. And if it seems that you're double-clicking too fast or too slow and you're not open to various electro-shock training tools that can get you right on the ball with only minimal nerve and tissue damage, you'll probably want to adjust the double-click speed, too.

You can control the interval between the two-click with the Keyboard & Mouse preferences panel:

1. **Go to the Apple Menu and open System Preferences.**

2. **Click on the Keyboard & Mouse icon.**

   The preferences pane displays.

3. **If necessary, click on the Mouse tab to display the Mouse pane.**

   See Figure 4-13.

Figure 4-13
The Mouse pane of the Keyboard & Mouse preferences pane

4. Move the Double-Click Speed slider.

This adjusts the interval between clicks.

5. Double-click anywhere in the "Double-click here to test" area.

This determines whether the double-click speed is what you want. If the Mac OS interprets your double-click correctly, one or more words highlight.

6. Move the Tracking Speed slider to adjust pointer speed (seen in Figure 4-13).

If you're horsing around with the double-click speed, you might also want to adjust the tracking. The tracking determines the ratio of mousing distance to screen distance. In general, the larger your monitor, the faster you'll want the pointer to move. But twiddle with the settings until it "feels" right.

If you're using a mouse with more than one button, the Mac OS looks for clicks from the button on the left side. Your Mileage May Vary: Most of the freakazoid mouses come with software that lets you define what each one of those 39 buttons and levers and dials does.

Contextual menus

A contextual menu is a little menu of commands that are specifically relevant to the thing you've clicked. For example, holding down the Control key while you click pops up a contextual menu under the pointer. Take a look at Figure 4-14, which shows you what happens when you control-click a file in the Finder. All of the things that the Finder can do to an individual file are grouped under the pointer. No muss, no fuss.

Figure 4-14
A contextual menu

▼ Tip

And if you're using one of those two-button mouses that I denigrated so cruelly a moment ago, the right-hand button will bring up the contextual menu immediately. Hmm. That's actually a great use of the second button. Well, if Apple had thought of contextual menus back in 1984, they would have thought of the second button, too. One revolution at a time, I suppose. Even the Fathers of Our Country didn't hit upon the idea of the Right of Free Assembly until they'd taken a few years off and returned to the foundations of democracy after a nap and a hot meal, so we should probably cut Apple some slack here.

Selecting more than one item

Using the Shift key, you can select multiple items, such as file icons in a folder or items in a scrolling list. Click the first item and then Shift-click any additional icons you want to select. This technique is particularly useful for selecting multiple Desktop icons, especially when you have the icons scattered all over your Desktop real estate.

Figure 4-15 shows the results. Everything from the first item through the second item that you clicked will be selected.

Figure 4-15
Multiple continuous selection in a list

If you don't want to select an unbroken continuum of items, you can point-and-shoot multiple items by holding down ⌘ and clicking, clicking, clicking each item one at a time (see Figure 4-16).

Either way you slice it, when you finally give the Mac that verb ("Print!"), Mac will act upon everything that you select.

Figure 4-16
Multiple discontinuous selection in a list

Dragging

What else can you do with a mouse? You can drag. Next to clicking and double-clicking, dragging is probably the mouse action you'll use the most. To drag, you hold down the mouse button and move the mouse, keeping the mouse button pressed. When you get where you want to go, you release the mouse button.

What good is a drag? There are two major things you can do with it: You can move things (files, folders, windows, and other graphic objects) and you can select text. Typically, when you select an item and then drag it, you're moving it. You'll learn a great deal more about using a drag throughout this book.

 Tip

Bonus points: Hold down the Option key while dragging and you'll be moving a *copy* of the selected whatsit, not the original. So if you select a paragraph and Option-drag it elsewhere in the document, the document will contain two copies of the paragraph.

Mouse pointer shapes

As you are mousing around, the mouse pointer takes on a variety of shapes to give you a cue that it might be doing something out of the ordinary, viz Table 4.1 for common mouse pointer shapes.

WINDOWS: VIEW FROM THE TOP

Windows are the graphical devices your Mac uses to present information, be it the contents of a document or your library of iTunes music.

I've just gotten off the phone with my editor and he confirms that a 4,300-page book explaining every doodad of every Mac window of every Mac app is slightly unrealistic, particularly if I'm committed to color printing. But as with everything else on the Mac, even in endless variety there's reliable consistency.

Table 4.1: Mouse Pointer Shapes

Shape	Name	Purpose
	Arrow	Your basic, plain-vanilla pointer.
	Contextual menu	Indicates that you're holding down ⌘ and you're about to activate a contextual menu of functions related to the item you're going to click.
	Copy	Indicates that you're moving a copy of the item, not the original.
	I-beam	Clicking this on text will move the cursor to a new location.
	Pointing hand	Typically indicates that the text the pointer is hovering over is a hyperlink to another page (as in a Web browser).
	Move right and left	Moves a border (like the side of a cell in a spreadsheet, or the edge of a sub-pane in a window).
	Move up and down	Ditto, except up and down.
	Wait	The spinning beach ball appears when the app is busy doing something and can't be bothered with you right now. If this mouse pointer appears for too long, it's likely that the application isn't responding to anything it's receiving. This is also known as the Spinning Pizza Of Death, a term of absolutely zero affection. Usually it's just the current application that's tied up. If you switch to another, you can amuse yourself while the first app gets its head together.
	Wait	The spinning watch and the crash-test-dummy spinning disc are holdovers from older versions of the OS. It means the same thing as the beach ball. If you want to learn something new while you watch it spin (and spin and spin and spin), I'll tell you that Mac OS X uses these old-fashioned spinners only when it's running old, pre-X code. These things should appear less and less frequently as more publishers eliminate all the old code from their apps.

Fanfare for the common window

The tippy-top span of the window is its title bar. See? There's the title of the window, which is usually the title of the document it's displaying. You can drag a window by its title bar to move it around on the screen.

Check out that little icon next to the title, too. It's a miniaturized version of the document icon and is technically known as a "proxy icon." Partly this is to remind you of what sort of document you're working on; I can look at the top of this window and see that I'm editing a Microsoft Word 10 document (as opposed to using Word to edit a file in a different format).

The actual purpose of a proxy icon is to give the document you're viewing in the window a "handle" that you can drag to other places. If you drag the title bar, yes, you're dragging around the window itself. But this mini-icon represents the actual file. You can exploit this in all kinds of timesaving ways. When I'm done with this chapter and I need to email this to my editor, I can grab that icon and drag it straight down into the Dock and drop it on top of Mail. Apple's built-in mail client will create a new email with that file as an attachment, just as though I'd gone into the Finder, located the document in its original folder, and dragged it onto Mail directly.

Window controls

Every window sports a handful of little buttons that control the appearance of the window. Figure 4-17 shows you the standard menagerie:

- **Close button:** The red one is the Close button. Click it to close the window. Bonus points: Pressing ⌘+W almost always closes the frontmost window. Option-clicking the Close button almost always closes all of an app's open windows (but it'll ask you if you want to save any changed documents first, of course).

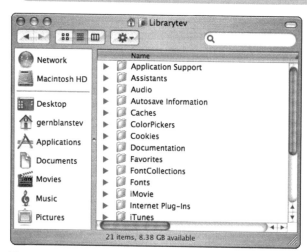

Figure 4-17
An honest, clean, working-class window

- **Minimize button:** The yellow button minimizes the window. The window slurps down into the Dock. You can call it back by clicking on its minimized version inside the Dock, or simply choosing it from the app's list of open windows, if the app has one. Again, you're not closing the window; it's just hiding it away — yet another way to combat Desktop clutter.

- **Maximize button:** The green button maximizes the window, expanding it to the largest size necessary to show off the window's entire contents. If there's more stuff than can fit inside your monitor, the window will grow to fill the entire screen. If the window's already been maximized, clicking the button again will shrink it back down to its original size.

▼ Note

Note two things: First, when your mouse pointer hovers over these three buttons, little symbols pop into view, both to remind you what the buttons do and to tell you that, yes, you can indeed close a window even if it's in the background.

Secondly — and sure, this is just a blatant editorial statement — Red, Yellow, and Green do not by their natures suggest or even imply the functions with which they're associated. Since when did the universal color for "Caution" mean "Slurp this into the Dock?" I saw a whole safety film on the subject of traffic lights back in Grade 10 and the only slight correlation between a yellow light and Minimizing had to do with what would happen to your body if you ignored the light and cruised straight through a four-way intersection just as an asphalt truck made a left turn. I just like my universe to make a little sense. Is that so wrong?

- **Toolbar button:** At the right edge of the title bar you'll see a button that looks like a Tic-Tac. That's the Toolbar button. If the window has a toolbar — a row of icon buttons that represent various features — clicking the Tic-Tac hides the toolbar, giving you a little more room in which to read your document. If you have the toolbar hidden, clicking the button reveals it again. We'll look a little more closely at this thingamabob in the next section.

- **Resize box:** At the bottom-right corner of the window is the Resize box — known as a grow box in the classic Mac OS. Drag the Resize box to change the size of a window. Depending on the program, you may see an outline of the window as it changes size or the window's contents may resize on the fly right as you drag.

Scroll bars and scrolling

When the content of a window is larger than the window's viewable area, the window typically has scroll bars that let you bring hidden bits of its contents into view. A window can have both vertical scroll bars and horizontal scroll bars (as in Figure 4-17). Scroll bars have the following parts:

- **Up and down arrows:** Clicking the mouse pointer in an up or down arrow moves the document one "line." If the document doesn't contain text, then how much it scrolls depends on the specific program. In Figure 4-17, the scroll bar arrows are grouped together at the end of the scroll bar, but they don't have to be. They can both be separately located at either end of the scroll bar. To change the position of the arrows, launch System Preferences, click on the Appearance icon, and in the Appearance preferences panel that appears, click the "At top and bottom" radio button. This is located in the second section of the panel (see Figure 4-18).

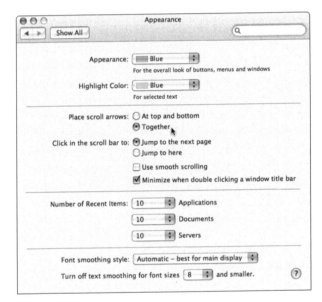

Figure 4-18
Putting scroll arrows in their place

- **The scroll box (or thumb):** Dragging the scroll box moves the document to a position proportional to the scroll box's location in the scroll bar. For example, if you drag the scroll box to the very top of the scroll bar, the beginning of the document appears. If you move the scroll box to the middle of the scroll bar, you come to the middle of the document. Therefore, the amount of scrolling that you get when you drag the scroll box depends on the size of the document.

▼ Note

The size of the scroll box depends on the percentage of the document that is visible in the window. If the document is twice the size of the window, the scroll box fills half the scroll bar. If the document is four times the size of the window, the scroll box fills a quarter of the scroll bar. The larger the document relative to the window, the smaller the scroll box.

- **The scroll bar itself:** By default, clicking above or below the scroll box in the scroll bar moves one "page." Depending on the program and its settings, a page may be the size of the window's viewable area or it may be a printed page. You can change the behavior of a click in the scroll bar so that you scroll to the location proportional to the site of the click. Click three quarters of the way down from the top of the scroll bar and you'll teleport to a spot three quarters from the top of the document. To do so, open System Preferences, click on the Appearance icon, and in the Appearances preferences panel that appears, click the "Scroll to here" radio button. This is located in the second section of the panel.

You can also scroll through a window using just the keyboard. Tapping the up and down arrows on your keyboard is usually the same as clicking the up and down arrows on the scroll bar. Tapping Page Up and Page Down is the same as clicking above or below the scroll box.

Window toolbars

Many Macintosh windows have toolbars, areas underneath the window's name that contain icons or menus that provide quick access to some of the program's actions. For example, the toolbar in the Finder window in Figure 4-19 provides (from left to right) navigation arrows, choices to view by icon or a list, access to the window's contextual menu, and a file search capability. Compare this window with Figure 4-20, which has no toolbar.

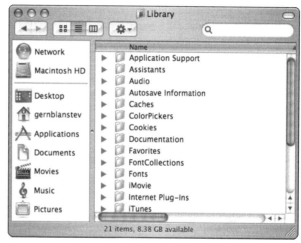

Figure 4-19
A Finder window with its toolbar showing

Figure 4-20
A Finder window without its toolbar

These toolbars are often configurable (look for a "Configure Toolbar" item under the Edit menu; names and locations vary). You can remove the functions you never use and toss in buttons for functions you want at your fingertips.

But Mac OS X continues to evolve and it's possible that the era of window toolbars, like the era of clear cola beverages, is waning. I like 'em. They add some extra functionality with a small (and reversible) loss in screen real estate. Every Apple application had a toolbar when X first came out. Now, they're starting to disappear.

Windows with panes

Some windows are divided into regions, known as *panes*. This is a big deal with the iApps and most apps that sport Mac OS X's "Brushed Metal" appearance.

For example, the Finder window in Figure 4-19 has a sidebar at the left that contains location icons for easy navigation; the right pane displays the contents of a folder. Other windows with panes that you encounter include the Mail application. The dividing line between the panes is actually a moveable bar that you can drag to adjust the size of the panes to your liking. You can make the Finder window's sidebar so small that it disappears completely (Figure 4-21).

The window usually gives you some sort of tip-off that its panes are resizeable. Notice, for example, the dimple in the gap between the sidebar and the rest of the window. "Resize me," it says.

Some apps offer older-style "split views." At the top of one of the window's scroll bars you see a bar or a bead. Slide it down and you create two separate, scrolling views of the same document, all in the same window. It is very useful when you're working in spreadsheets, such as when you want to eye the section of the document with last quarter's sales results as you work on a section four pages later, cooking the figures for next quarter's sales.

Figure 4-21
A Finder window with its sidebar minimized

EXPOSÉ: SLIDING DOORS

Desktop clutter has become a recurring theme in this chapter. The clever men and women of Apple Computer did their level best to give us the planet's most powerful and elegant operating system, but no one can see inside the human soul. And therein lurks a demon that resists all attempts at discipline and order.

But Exposé is a powerful weapon in the battle. You're using your word processor and you want to zip to a Web page you opened an hour ago containing your research. And already you're choking back a tear because you've got a dozen apps open and dozens and dozens of windows piled up.

Yes, there was a time when you would have had to switch to your Web browser, locate that one window among the 23 or so, find the info, then switch back to your word processor and repeat the process.

Thanks to Exposé, all you need do in Tiger is hit the F9 key on your keyboard.

ANDY IHNATKO, HIS HUMILITY IS JUST PART OF HIS PERFECTION

Oh, right; you can assign a mouse button to activate Exposé. Well, it takes a big man to admit when he's wrong. Maybe I should recant what I said earlier, and start using that 42-button FrankenMouse.

Every window shrinks down into a tidy mosaic in which nothing overlaps anything else (viz Figure 4-22). It's like being 1,000 feet above a cornfield in a hot-air balloon. The title of each miniaturized window appears as your mouse

moves over it, and when you find what you've been seeking, you click it. The windows unshuffle, and you're left with the Desktop the way it was before — except the selected window is now up front.

Good God, this one feature was worth the whole upgrade fee to me. And I don't just use it to move from window to window, either. I often hit F9 before getting out of the chair. Every miniaturized window is still "live," so whether eight or nine different news sites update their Web pages, an application has thrown up an error message, or I want to keep a bored eye on one of my *West Wing* DVDs, I can see the entire state of my Macintosh from across the room, and quickly zoom back in on an item that's caught my interest.

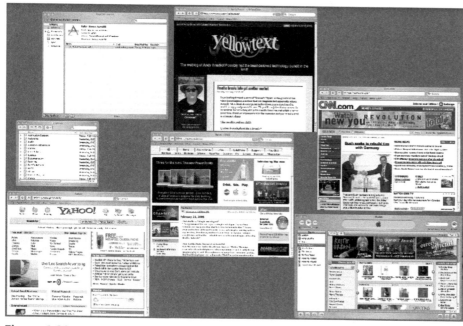

Figure 4-22
Using Exposé to show all windows

Exposé can also just show you the windows associated with the current app (F10), or clear away every window entirely and show you the naked Desktop (F11). Pressing the same button on your keyboard again pops you back into reality without switching to another window. And all those keys are configurable. Check out Dashboard & Exposé's pane in System Preferences (Figure 4-23).

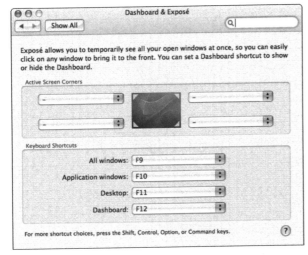

Figure 4-23
The Exposé preferences panel

You can trigger Exposé by placing the mouse pointer in one of the corners of the screen, by pressing a function key, or by using the right or middle buttons on a two- or three-button mouse.

KEYBOARD CONTROLS: KEY LARGO

In science fiction movies, people sit down and talk to computers — and the computer understands, regardless of the person's accent, sentence structure, language, or vocabulary. That kind of speech recognition is still a dream; today we use the keyboard as our primary method of getting text into a computer.

Special keys

The Macintosh keyboard has lots of special keys that you won't find anywhere else. They include the extra modifier keys we've discussed off and on throughout this chapter as well as some keys that affect hardware settings and actions:

- **The ⌘ key:** We've already talked about using ⌘ (aka cloverleaf, aka fan, aka Apple key, aka the Rug Beater) to trigger menu options, and how it sometimes modifies mousing and clicking actions. You can also use it to navigate dialogs without the mouse. You may not have noticed it, but every button starts with a different letter. Holding down ⌘ while tapping that letter sends a click to that button; ⌘+C hits Cancel, ⌘+D means Don't Save, et cetera. Coooolllllll.

- **The Option key:** The Option key was originally designed to provide access to an additional set of printing characters. (You have un-Shift characters, Shift characters, Option characters, and Shift-Option characters, meaning that each key on the keyboard can produce up to four distinct characters.) Today the Option key still plays its role in generating characters, but you can also use it in conjunction with ⌘ and Control keys to select menu options.

- **The alt key:** Most of today's keyboards have the characters *alt* in small letters at the top of the Option key. The Macintosh doesn't use an alt key, but PC software does. The alt is there just to let you know that if you are using PC emulation software, such as Virtual PC, you can use the Option key wherever the PC software expects alt.

- **The Control key:** The Control key dates from the earliest days of computing. Typically it was used to modify the signal sent to the hardware; Pressing Control+C might end a program's operation, for example. Today, Control chiefly serves as another modifier key, often used in conjunction with function keys or the Option key to provide menu command access from the keyboard.

What's the difference between the Return and Enter keys? In poorly designed applications, the difference is that Return does what you expect it to do and Enter does something different than "Return," which isn't what you expected it to do at all. So the chief purpose is to confuse people and make them say naughty words. Some programmers really like it when people curse. They can't hear it, but they know it's happening.

But in dialog boxes, hitting Enter is always the same thing as clicking on the default button (the one that's colored-in and pulsating).

Like most computer keyboards today, the Macintosh has function keys across the top of its keyboard. Depending on the size of your keyboard, you may have 12 or 15 or even 16 of 'em, each labeled with the letter F and a number. Function keys have been around since the very beginning of mainframe computing, when they were more or less the user interface to your software.

They're a bit of a holdover today, which is why Apple makes many of the function keys do double-duty. This can get confusing when you use an application that really needs a function key, which has been co-opted by Apple's special functions. If you find yourself muting your speakers when trying to access F3, for example, you can hold down the fn key while you tap the key that normally mutes the speaker in order to regain "normal" F-key functionality.

As you've seen elsewhere in the chapter, Apple uses these keys to make certain features (like Exposé) more accessible. Some apps use them for their own little shortcuts, and you can also define function-key actions yourself.

ULTRA-FUNCTIONALITY

There's a feature in X that not many users know about. The next time you're presented with a dialog box full of buttons, look at the buttons' labels carefully. Programmers are *supposed* to make sure that no two buttons start with the same letter, which means that if you have three options ("Revenge against all my enemies," "Forgive and forget," and "OK," for instance) you can type the first letter of the button you want, instead of clicking on it.

That's how it's *supposed* to work. It's slicker and to people with special needs, it makes Mac OS X easier to use with assisted-input devices. But it's such a basic idea that some programmers just plumb forget about it.

Assigning function keys

Let's say you use Apple's Preview app to look at artwork. You're always using the Full Screen feature to see the images at the largest possible size, but there's no command-key equivalent in the menu. Here's how to make the F7 key into Preview's Full Screen key (see Figure 4-24):

1. **Quit Preview if it's already running.**

   You can't assign function keys to an app while it's running.

2. **Open System Preferences and navigate to the Keyboard & Mouse pane.**

3. **Click on the Keyboard Shortcuts tab.**

   Notice that every single keyboard shortcut is nicely outlined for you. Convenient!

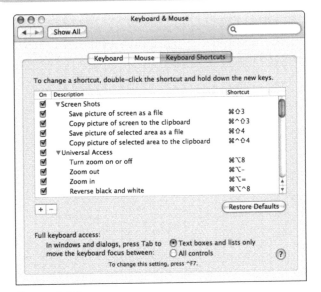

Figure 4-24
Adding a Keyboard Shortcut

4. **Scroll down and click on Application Keyboard Shortcuts.**

5. **Click on the plus button (+).**

   This adds a shortcut and a sheet drops down.

6. **From the pop-up menu, select Preview.**

   The example uses the Preview application.

7. **In the field marked Menu Title, type in the exact name of the menu you want to activate.**

   In this case, type **Full Screen**. Type the menu name in exactly as you see it in the menu, including the "…" if you see one.

8. **Click on the Keyboard Shortcut field and then type the function key that should activate.**

   Here, we're using F7 but it can be anything, even ⌘+Option+Control+Shift+F7, if you're feeling like you need to do something aerobic.

AN URGE TOWARD PEACE AND RESTRAINT

Tiger can assign any menu item of any application to a function key. Caution, caution, I say. Caution! Assigning a menu item to a function key is a great feature if you use it sparingly. He who lives by this feature dies by it. If you add or modify too many of your menus' key equivalents, you'll have a whole mess of shortcuts that work great with your own Mac but when you move to another machine ten feet away, you'll be at an utter loss for how to use the thing.

Personally, I think you should only re-map function keys when you've been frustrated by the same thing for a month and finally can't take it any more. You'll find that the most useful menus already have equivalents; they're fairly easy to remember, and when you learn the "standard" equivalents, you'll never have to relearn 'em.

9. **Click the Add button.**

   Now you can use the shortcut to activate the feature.

This is actually a very flexible feature. You can use it to assign any kind of key equivalent to any kind of menu, or even change keyboard equivalents that already exist.

You can also use a bunch of third-party function-key re-mappers that are a bit more ambitious, allowing you to launch apps, open files, and run AppleScripts. CE Software's QuicKeys X (www.cesoft.com) is the 900-pound gorilla of this category.

There are also a bunch of special keys that take the place of mechanical switches to control simple hardware functions like volume (up, down, and mute), screen brightness (up, down), and an Eject button for internal optical drives. Your Mac might have some or all of these buttons.

 Note

But don't be bamboozled into thinking that tapping Eject immediately ejects a CD (or CD-ROM, or DVD, or whatever). In Windows, hitting Eject has an immediate effect. On the Mac, it merely requests that any app that's currently using whatever disc is in the drive to please politely close it down and release it. If the app decides that you'll get the disc when it's dashed good and ready to give you the disc, you'll have to wait.

CHOOSING ALTERNATIVE KEYBOARD LAYOUTS

In the Menu section of this chapter, we mentioned the Input menulet, which lets you choose keyboard layouts. How cool is this? If you happen to want to use a character set other than U.S. English, it's very cool. Although the keys on the Macintosh keyboard might be labeled for U.S. English typing, you can switch the characters that the keys produce by changing your keyboard layout or input method. You do this with the International preferences panel:

1. **Launch System Preferences.**

2. **Click International.**

   This displays the International preferences panel.

3. **Click the Input Menu tab.**

   The Input Menu pane displays (see Figure 4-25).

4. **Check the "Show input menu in menu bar" checkbox. The Input menulet appears.**

5. **Place a check next to each item you want to appear in the Input menu.**

Figure 4-25
The Input Menu pane

The Keyboard Viewer (Figure 4-26) displays the characters that a given font can generate. To make the Keyboard Viewer appear, follow steps 1–3 and check the box for Keyboard Viewer. It appears under the Input menulet.

Figure 4-26
The Keyboard Viewer for a U.S. English font

Pressing Shift, Option, or Shift+Option shows the modified characters. The Character Palette (Figure 4-27) lets you insert special symbols (either graphics or non-Roman) into a document. You wanna find a symbol for a little umbrella?

KEYBOARD VIEWER: LUST FOR GLORY

I have to admit that the only times when I've used Keyboard Viewer are (a) when I can't remember how to make a Euro symbol (Option+Shift+2, incidentally) and (b) a counterintelligence agent burst into my office, spilled Dr. Pepper on my keyboard, and then made his escape (yes, it was a secret agent; I would never do something so foolish as to bring a sticky beverage into my office, oh, no), and the on-screen keyboard became the only thing I could type with.

And (c) it's kind of cool to see all the keycaps flicker insanely when I type. Chicks dig a guy who can type at 108 words per minute. At least that's what my mom kept telling me during countless hours of keyboard practice while all of my little friends were gamboling and romping and playing and taunting me just outside my window.

Character Palette is your guy. Open the palette, click on the character you want, and click the Insert button.

Figure 4-27
The Character Palette for inserting special characters

The remaining items in the Input menu pane are either methods for generating characters for pictographic scripts such as Traditional Chinese, or keyboard layouts. Click

all of those that you want to appear in your Input menu. You can then select a layout by choosing it from the Input menu. Nearly always, this feature is used to enable international layouts, but it also offers mondo-bizarro layouts like the Dvorak variety. Rumor has it that it's faster to type with a Dvorak layout, but this has never actually been proven because nobody actually uses the danged thing. If there's anyone out there using Dvorak, they're deep underground and they ain't talking for fear of the inevitable ostracization that would occur if word got out.

MONITORS: THROUGH A GLASS, DARKLY

Just as the keyboard is your computer's primary input device, the monitor (or display) is its primary output device. For us visual humans, there is little else that could be better. I'm big on second-guessing the decisions of people who are smarter than I am, but even I will grudgingly agree that having some sort of screen on your Mac or built into your PowerBook was a good call with plenty of practical long-lasting rewards for the user. So whoever came up with that idea: Good job; take another twenty bucks out of petty cash and take a long lunch.

Setting display resolution

If you bought your Macintosh recently, you may have a flat-screen, LCD monitor. Many older-model, and current-model, desktop Macs, however, are still using CRT monitors. Regardless of which type you have, most Macintosh-compatible monitors support multiple resolutions.

On my own Stonehenge-size monitor, I keep flipping between low and high resolution. When I'm writing, I keep it at a somewhat sensible size of 1024 pixels wide by 768 high. The individual dots are big, and so the menus and windows and text are easy to read. But when

I'm managing lots of tasks at once, I increase the size to roughly double that. With a Desktop the size of Nebraska, I can have ten windows open without overlapping, or make my iTunes window so big that I can see every song and album title without anything being chopped off for lack of space.

Each different display has different screen resolutions available. You choose between 'em via the Displays panel in System Preferences:

1. **Launch System Preferences.**

2. **Click on the Displays icon.**

3. **If necessary click on the Display tab.**

   The Display pane appears, as in Figure 4-28, showing you the current settings for your monitor and alternative possible resolutions.

4. **Choose the resolution you want from the scrolling list at the left of the preferences pane.**

5. **Choose the number of colors you want the monitor to be able to display from the Colors pop-up menu.**

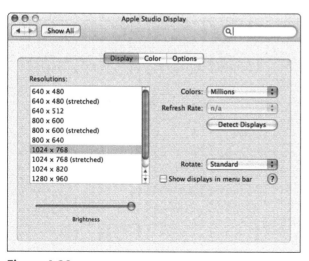

Figure 4-28
The Displays preferences pane

Configuring multiple monitors

The Macintosh is still the only personal computer that seamlessly supports multiple monitors. The Mac OS supports up to eight displays — although no current Macintosh has enough expansion slots to handle anywhere near that many video cards — as a single Desktop surface. You control the logical arrangement of the monitors, as well as the startup monitor (the monitor containing the menu bar), from the Displays control panel:

1. **Launch System Preferences.**

2. **Click the Displays icon.**

   A dialog box opens.

3. **Click the Arrangement button.**

   This displays the Arrangement pane.

4. **Drag the images of the monitors until they are positioned in the layout you want for your Desktop.**

   The mouse pointer slides from one monitor to the next, based on this arrangement.

5. **Drag the image of the menu bar to the top of the monitor that you want to use as the startup monitor.**

 Tip

If you aren't sure which rectangle in the Arrangement pane's display represents which of your monitors, click a rectangle. The Macintosh flashes a red border around the corresponding monitor.

HELP!

Help? You're using a Macintosh! It's flawless! I've got a tea-trolley here that became a competent Mac user after just three or four days. Everything will run flawlessly without any thought on your part. The air will always smell like bacon and/or lilacs, depending on how you feel about the smell of bacon and/or lilacs. It's all part of The Macintosh Experience!

See? Isn't it good to laugh?

Tiger has a built-in Help resource, chiefly in the form of a big, smackin' Help menu near the end of the menu bar. Help is context-sensitive; if you're in Safari and you activate Help from the menu, OS X steers you straight to the Help Viewer app and Help opens Safari's Help file (Figure 4-29).

Figure 4-29
Safari's Help home page

There might be a delay, as Help Viewer might connect to the Internet to look for updated information.

The interface is familiar to anyone who's used a Web browser. Every Help file has a cover, which like a magazine, steers you towards items of universal interest and ads for vodka and tires. You can ask Help a specific question by clicking in the search box in the upper-right corner and hitting Return. Help searches through all of the information articles to which it has access and returns a list of relevant items. Double-click on whatever looks good.

HELP HELPS THOSE WHO HELP THEMSELVES

Browsing through Help is one of those things that builds strong bodies nine different ways. It's sad that no matter how much dough you spend on hardware and software, nobody's willing to give you a printed manual any more. You have no idea how much power is locked inside an app until you see the manual lay it all out for you from A to Z.

So every once in a while, click on that little Home icon at the upper-left corner of the window, which takes you to general Help. Help View is set up like a browser... so browse.

So them's the basics of the Mac interface. But everybody learns The Mac the same way: by playing with it. There are things that Windows does well and things that it does poorly. Windows' interface — and I have a beloved niece who uses and enjoys Windows, so it pains me to say this — is clearly the product of a designer who spent much of his childhood with a cardboard refrigerator box as his sole plaything.

But the Mac is different. Chances are, the thing that you think does what you want actually does what you want; and if you're ever about to do anything destructive (like delete a file), Tiger asks you if you're sure you want to do it.

Learning to drive via the Braille method makes you a menace to life and property, but learning the Macintosh that way quickly makes you into a confident and competent user.

Leopard-Skin Pillbox Mac: Monkeying with System Preferences

In This Chapter

System Preferences • Custom Desktops • Custom Colors • Custom Sounds • Custom Screen Savers
Working with Fonts: The Font Book • Universal Access Options

Communism is a concept that never really took off in this country, but honestly, you have to admit that it had its advantages. For example, as a teenager in Russia, you could be secure in the knowledge that no matter how well you did on tomorrow's exam, or who won the big homecoming game against Vladivostok Middle School, or that you threw up in your balalaika case when Milena Dimitriyeva turned you down for the prom, it didn't change the fact that three years later, you became a worker in a radio factory. So, here's to freedom and democracy, where you, as an individual, can express yourself as you see fit. While the Soviets were busy trying to develop a third shade of brown, we were walking around in paisley bellbottoms.

And the Mac is no less a vector for individuality. All Macs leave Cupertino exactly alike, but over a course of days, weeks, and months, you can alter your Mac's appearance and behavior to make it uniquely your own. Some of these changes simply exist to suit your personal tastes; others make your Mac easier and more comfortable to use. Both kinds are vastly superior to struggling under the iron yoke of faceless totalitarian oppression, as I'm sure you'll agree by the end of this chapter.

SYSTEM PREFERENCES

We've actually been talking about Tiger's System Preferences panel a lot in the previous four chapters. It's a fundamental part of Tiger. Allow me to grope for an analogy.

Okay, this is going to require a trip out to the store to buy another six-pack of name brand sugared and caffeinated cola drinks. Stay tight.

Hi. They're cooling down now. Won't take more than three or four hours.

Ahhh, that's better.

Wait, now I have to go visit the head. Be right back.

SYMPATHY FOR THE DEVIL

Can we take a moment to work up a bit of sympathy for your poor, beleaguered author? At the start of the writing process, I outlined the whole thing. Did a jim-dandy job, too, but System Preferences was one of those things that really could have been talked about in at least four or five chapters. First it was in the User Interface section, then it was in the Finder chapter, then I called my mom and she's the one who suggested that I put it here. Mom actually doesn't know a whole lot about the Mac (she thinks that any computer that doesn't use a strict text-only interface and whose sole environment is the COBOL programming language is for sissies). But it makes sense to put it here.

Plus, now, if I *don't* put it in this chapter, then I'm specifically *not* using her idea, and it'll turn into a whole Thing, you know? Honestly, it never ends, does it?

What were we talking about, again? Oh, yeah: How Important System Preferences Are. I think I'm going to have to compare it to the stick shift on a car with automatic transmission. You don't necessarily use it every second, but you're almost bound to use it at least once during each session you spend with the hardware.

As discussed in Chapter 4, each application has its own "Preferences..." menu, for making changes and adjustments to how that one specific app behaves. But there are plenty of settings that affect everything that your whole Mac does. What does the Desktop look like? How fast does your Mac's mouse or trackpad move? How often should Tiger check with Apple for new software?

And that's where System Preferences comes in. You can open Tiger's System Preferences window by clicking on its icon in the Dock, but most people access it from the Apple menu. Either way, you'll be looking at something like Figure 5-1:

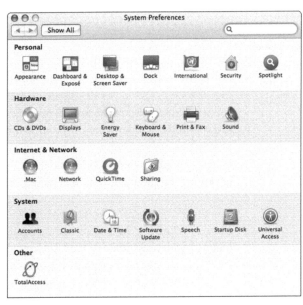

Figure 5-1
Regardez! System Preferences!

STAND AND CHEER

You know why I'm such a bed-wettingly enthusiastic supporter of the Mac? Features just like this one. It's a simple feature that saves everybody — new user and seasoned pro alike — a lot of time and frustration. I hate to harp on the whole Sympathy For Me angle again (actually, I love it, but I'm struggling not to appear more pathetic than might be socially palatable) but here in the recent past, I'm writing about Tiger without the benefit of any documentation or Help systems. There are brand-new features that I've never even seen before. So I know exactly what it's like to be a new user. And I also know exactly what it's like to have a resource like Preferences' search system at my disposal.

There's the whole motley crew. All of your Mac's system-wide Preferences are organized into categories. Click on any of these Preference icons and you'll be looking at all the settings that are associated with the thing. And it goes without saying — but I've got a contractually-manded minimum word count to deal with, so I'll say it anyway — that these settings will be completely different from icon to icon.

But there's a standard set of controls that always sticks to the top of the System Preferences window. From left to right, you see:

- **Back and Forward buttons:** They work just like the buttons in a Web browser. Clicking the Back button takes you back to where you just came from, usually the topmost view of System Prefs. The best way to describe Forward is that it undoes the Back button. So if I open System Preferences, clicking Spotlight opens up Spotlight's preferences. Clicking Back takes me back to that view of all the Prefs icons. Clicking Forward from that point will return me to Spotlight's preferences.

- **Show All:** Clicking Show All zaps you back to System Preferences' topmost level and shows you all of the Preferences icons.

- **A Spotlight search box!** You read this swell book of mine and you remember that it's possible to set up Tiger so that if you forget your password, it gives you a hint. But you lent the book to a so-called friend and, so enthralled was he by the contents therein, he has yet to return the volume.

 Tip

An all-too-common problem. But I ask you: Is it worth losing a friend over? No, no, no. Just buy another copy and put the whole sorry incident behind you. Better buy four or five more, just so that you can make it an outright gift in the future. PS: if I make more than a million bucks off this book by inserting this sweet little pyramid scheme into this chapter, I'll give you a dollar. If, um, you're one of the first ten — no, eight — people to email me and ask.

You can't remember how to find that feature. But it's no problem: just type **password** into System Preferences' Search box, and it'll pop up a list of likely candidates (Figure 5-2).

Aha! There's the baby: "Password hint." Just click on the item and Preferences takes you straight to the "Accounts" prefs, where you can then specify a password hint.

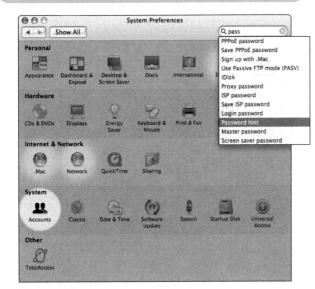

Figure 5-2
System Preferences search results

That Search feature has an extra dollop of flair on top of it: notice that as you type the letters of your search term, spotlights start to light up some of the Preference icons. Each one of these is a potential match. And some are illuminated more brightly than others; these are the ones that Tiger thinks are *most* likely to contain the info you need. Viz in

THAT'S ALL THERE IS?

You can probably live a full and wonderful life without ever seeing anything in Preferences that wasn't already there when you first fired up Tiger. But some of the software you install along the way might install their own items in System Preferences. In Figure 5-1, there's a TotalAccess icon at the bottom, for example, in the Others category. That one was installed by Earthlink, the Internet service provider that I use when I'm traveling. It lets me change my Internet settings through one convenient location.

Figure 5-2, how the Accounts icon is brightest of all. That's because we've selected Password Hint from the list of results. So Preferences is subtly telling us, "Here's where you can find it, if you ever need to come back there again."

Okay, we've now thoroughly girded our loins for the settings to come, so let's get down to it.

One more soda first, maybe. See you in a bit.

CUSTOM DESKTOPS

There are only two situations in which you're likely to see a Mac OS X Desktop that sports the familiar image of translucent blue swirls: In Apple's official PR shots, and after you've booted up a brand-new Mac for the first time. Or three, if you include "you're a phenomenal bore with no capacity for creative thought." Look, your cubicle's bare walls have amusing *Family Circus* and *Hi and Lois* cartoons pinned on them; the corner of your desk sports a framed, tasteful photo of you and your sweetie doing something ambitiously silly during your last vacation. So the background of your Mac's desktop needs a far more interesting image.

▼ Note

…but not *too* interesting, if you are indeed in an office. An image of a kitten dangling from a clothesline, captioned with an encouraging admonishment to Hang In There: *good*. Dry, but good. You haven't set into motion a sequence of events that end with you sitting on a curb with the contents of your desk in a cardboard box, wondering How It All Came To This. A doctored image of Edvard Munch's *The Scream*, with the central figure reacting to the company's last annual report: *bad*. Funny, but bad. (Unless your corporate culture is based on reality game shows and by virtue of the number of snakes you were able to carry across the office using only your nostrils, you've won Individual Immunity and can't possibly be fired.)

To replace the default Desktop image:

1. **Open the System Preferences Window.**

2. **Click on the Desktop & Screen Saver icon.**

   The Desktop & Screen Saver prefs open up. As the name implies, it handles both your desktop image and the screensaver that kicks in whenever you stop working with your Mac for a certain length of time. Click on the Desktop tab and you'll be looking at something like Figure 5-3:

Figure 5-3
Choosing a Desktop picture

   OS X knows that you want to deal with images, so it assembles a list of all the locations on your hard drive where pictures are stored. The first ones in the list are OS X's built-in collections of images, including abstract swooshy things just as dull as the image you started with; photos of creepy insects and vacation photos from people who apparently lead far more exciting lifestyles than you; and there's even a palette of flat colors for those whose idea of dangerous excitement is wearing black shoes with a brown belt.

Underneath those pre-fabbed image folders, you find direct links to common storehouses of imagery. Desktop Pictures is OS X's default directory for Desktops (you can see it in the Finder, inside the system-wide Library folder at the root level of your startup disk). Your Pictures folder is listed, too, and if you use iPhoto to manage your photos, you can access your entire library and all albums. Or click Choose Folder... to navigate elsewhere on your hard drive.

3. **Click on the Desktop picture you want.**

   And hey-presto, your Desktop image immediately changes to your selection.

▼ Tip

There's a much shorter way to change your Desktop picture, though. Just Control-click anywhere on an unoccupied area of the Desktop to bring up its contextual menu. One of the items therein is "Change Desktop Background." Just choose a new image and you're golden.

▼ Tip

You can use nearly any sort of image file as a Desktop image. JPEG, TIFF, PICT, GIF... it's all good. So, be ambitious. I get most of my favorite Desktop images from NASA's Astronomy Picture of the Day site (http://antwrp.gsfc.nasa.gov/apod/). They make your Desktop look like the main viewscreen of the starship *Enterprise*, or ideally the main viewscreen of a spaceship in a much better TV show.

▼ Tip

If you have more than one monitor, you will see a Desktop Picture panel on each monitor. So you can keep a different picture on each screen: NASCAR on the right, CART Racing on the left. Feel free to adopt your own methodology.

JUST FOLLOW MOTHER APPLE'S ADVICE

I have to admit that when Apple started giving us specific folders for Pictures, Music, Documents, et cetera, I bucked. "Just who do they think they are, telling me where to store my files?!?" Well, this is the reason why: When you store media files in places where OS X is likely to look for them, they turn up at your fingertips right when you need them.

Just like the time when I ignored my Mom's advice not to stuff Monopoly pieces up my nose only to later realize that she knew best, and I should just accept that she has my best interests at heart (the trip to the emergency room helped, too), this is one of those places where you realize that it's smart to just do what Apple tells you to do, and save your picture files in the standard directories.

If you've selected an image that doesn't exactly match the dimensions of your screen (if it's too tall or too wide), a pop-up menu lets you choose how Tiger should display the image (Figure 5-4):

- **Fill screen:** Scales the image up or down until one of its dimensions matches the height or width of the screen.

- **Stretch to fill screen:** Scales both dimensions of the image. If the image proportions don't match those of the screen, the image appears squeezed or squashed.

- **Center:** Simply plops the image in the center of the screen, and any acreage that doesn't fit on the screen simply disappears off the edges. So what if it isn't a perfect fit? OS X couldn't care less.

- **Tile:** Repeats a too-small image over and over again like a rubber stamp, to cover the whole area. That's what you see there in Figure 5-4.

Figure 5-4
Choosing how the image will be displayed

MULTIPLE DESKTOP IMAGES

So, hey, cool. Now your Desktop image is a photo of your new baby. But what about your three *other* children, your spouse, and that boat you've so lovingly restored? There's no need to slight any of the loved ones in your life because OS X can change your Desktop image for you automatically at regular timed intervals:

1. **Open the Desktop & Screen Saver panel.**

2. **Click the Change picture checkbox, as shown in Figure 5-5.**

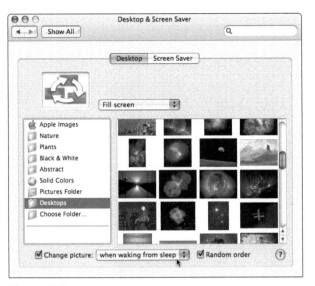

Figure 5-5
Configuring a changing Desktop pattern

3. **Select how often you want the picture to change from the pop-up menu at the bottom of the panel.**

   You can have Tiger change the Desktop every time you log in, every time your Mac wakes from sleep, or at specific timed intervals.

▼ **Note**

The transition from one Desktop picture to another is very subtle. Therefore, switching every 5 seconds isn't as schizophrenic as it might sound. Try it; you might like it.

The randomized pictures come from whichever image folder you selected from the list of sources. Thus, if you've selected the Abstract folder, no images pop up from your Pictures folder or anywhere else.

▼ **Tip**

Incidentally, do you want to know the easiest way to determine if there are any smutty pictures inside a given folder? Set the Desktop image to Randomize, select the folder, and then wait for your supervisor to walk by. Unless you've spent every single waking moment of your life up to that point accruing positive Karma, that'll cause the naughty picture to pop up the moment the boss is within eyeshot. Powerful forces control the universe, dear reader, and they are very easily amused.

NO, I STILL HAVEN'T GOTTEN OVER IT

Coolest Screensaver Ever: I was in a hotel in Santa Clara, far from my home in Boston and my friends therein, when the Red Sox won the World Series. After making rather merry with whoever I found at hand there in the lobby's sushi bar, I threaded my way back to my room, logged onto newseum.org, downloaded every front page from every newspaper that morning, saved those JPEGs to a folder, and set it as my random screensaver.

Of course, given that ten days later I used that computer when I keynoted in front of about 2,000 people, including a distressing number of Yankees fans, this might not have been the wisest course of action. But I harbored the standard sports fan's impulse to tip over a car or something, and given that I couldn't scare up enough people in Santa Clara to make that happen, well, an outlet had to be found.

CUSTOM COLORS

When you have to use someone else's Mac for an afternoon, it's subtle things like the differences in how they've set up Appearance colors that'll throw you the most. It just goes to show you what a subtle contribution color makes in the user interface.

You can make bits of the interface that scream out, "I'm clickable; look *here*, right *here*!" (such as window scrollers, dialog buttons, and highlighted menus) either a soothing blue or an I-Know-This-Is-A-Mac-But-Dagnabbit-All-Those-Colors-Are-Distracting-And-I-Just-Can't-Deal-With-It grayish graphite.

To change from the default blue to graphite:

1. **Launch System Preferences.**

2. **Click on the Appearance icon to display the Appearance panel, as shown in Figure 5-6.**

   Custom colors are up there in the top section.

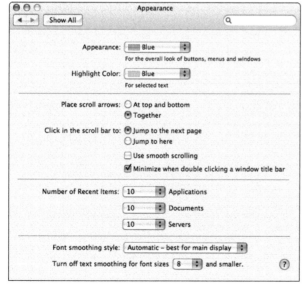

Figure 5-6
The Appearance preferences panel

EXTREME MAKEOVER

Previous editions of the Mac operating system show you how much you can muck things up by making not-so-subtle changes. Apple experimented with allowing you to take nothing for granted by letting you change the shapes and colors of menus, windows, buttons, everything, to your liking. But (a) that compromised the power of a clean user interface that's consistent from machine to machine, and (b) all that jewelry and makeup made the Mac look cheap. I mean, is that how well we raised you, young lady?

If you really do want to give the user interface an extreme makeover, third-party utilities give you way more power than God intended mere users to have. My favorite is Unsanity's *ShapeShifter* (shareware from www.unsanity.com). With it, your Mac can look just like the computers in the *Star Trek* movies: colorful, flashy, unique, and about as useful as a sock full of carpet samples when your ship suddenly encounters an enemy star cruiser. You ever notice that the moment the *Enterprise* runs into a crisis, every screen clears itself of useful information and simply reads "RED ALERT"? That's highly counterproductive.

3. **Select Graphite from the Appearance pop-up menu.**

   You'll see, for example, that the background of the up and down arrows at the right of the pop-up menu turns gray immediately.

   The text highlight color is actually a more important choice. The highlight color is what you see when you select a bit of text in a word-processing document, or when you select a row of data in a list. Keep in mind that changes in color are what steer your eye through all the text fields in a dialog box and keep your hand steady as you try to end a selection between the words *rib-eye* and *vinyl*.

▼ **Note**

Yes, this makes me itch. If I'm sitting at someone else's Mac and the highlight color is set differently from what I have at home, I change it. The wrong highlight color is as effective a distraction from a solid day's work as trying to type while holding an orange between my chin and collarbone.

To change the highlight color:

1. **Open the Appearance panel.**

2. **Select the highlight color from the Highlight Color pop-up menu, as shown in Figure 5-7.**

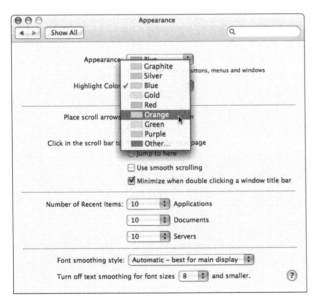

Figure 5-7
Choosing a highlight color

▼ **Tip**

If you don't like any of the colors in the Highlight Color menu, select Other. Your Mac then displays a color picker from which you can select any color you want.

▼ **Note**

The change you make to the highlight color should affect all applications. Then again, winter drivers *should* heed the Snow Emergency parking signs when a three-day blizzard is going on; but given that it's now Tuesday and I *still* can't get my car out onto the street, we all know how orderly and sensible the world can be sometimes.

Some rare apps disregard convention. Don't let it get you down. Curse them mightily, and then congratulate yourself for your superior moral rectitude.

CUSTOM SOUNDS

When you do something that OS X doesn't like — and we all do, regularly — OS X *beeps*. Why is *beep* in italics? Because the alert sound is a *beep* only by default. You can change it to something that better suits your mood and/or personality.

▼ **Tip**

Again, I make the case that sound is an important user-interface thing. A mother penguin can recognize her offspring's distress call from way across the ice shelf amongst the cries of thousands of other hatchlings. Granted, when a Mac fails to completely burn a CD, it's not in the same dire situation as the hatchling when it encounters a walrus, tusks glistening and thirsting for gore, heaving itself out of the water. However, it's still good to make your Mac's warning sound, not only clearly audible, but also distinct from all other Macs in the room.

Customizing your sound

To change your custom sound, follow these steps:

1. **Launch System Preferences.**

2. **Click the Sound icon to open the Sound preferences panel.**

   As shown in Figure 5-8, the Sound Effects panel lists a variety of alert (beep) sounds and lets you set speaker volume.

3. **Scroll through the list of sounds.**

   To hear a sound, double-click on its name in the scrolling list.

4. **Select the sound you want to use as your alert sound.**

5. **Move the Alert volume slider.**

   This sets the alert volume. You can have an alert pipe in at a lower volume than the rest of the stuff on your Mac. Like, if you've got iTunes cranking through your home stereo, a single, pure-toned BEEP! can reduce your speakers to ash. So in that sort of instance, y'all might wanna slide the alert volume down a tad.

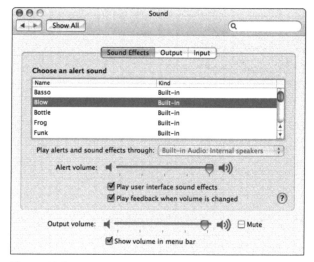

Figure 5-8
Choosing an alert sound

Using your own sounds

You'll notice that the list of sounds has a column labeled Kind. Sounds can be either Built-in (you got 'em when you installed OS X) or Custom (provided by you, the freedom-loving user).

WHY I'LL HAVE A LOT OF EXPLAINING TO DO WHEN I DIE AND GO FOR MY BIG EXIT INTERVIEW (#8229 IN A SERIES)

A longtime standard Apple beep sound was the sound of a water droplet, which you can perfectly duplicate by flicking your finger against your cheek while giving a little whistle. If I thought a friend of mine was working a little too hard, I'd nonchalantly stroll behind him and make the sound.

After half an hour of hearing his Mac make error beeps for no apparent reason, he'd turn to me in desperation. I'd say, "Why don't we run Disk First Aid on your hard drive, and see if the problem doesn't go away? The diagnostic shouldn't take more than 20 minutes to complete." And then he'd be free to go out for waffles with me.

You can use any AIFF sound file as a system beep. You can download AIFFs from sound Web sites (that's where I got my library of R2-D2 chirps and flutters) or make them yourself, using sound-recording software. After you have the AIFF file, copy it into the Sounds folder inside your Library folder. It will show up in the list the next time you open the Sound preferences panel.

If you have external speakers, you can choose whether to play sounds through the Mac's internal speaker or the external speakers:

1. **Display the Sound preferences panel.**

2. **Click the Output tab.**

3. **Choose the sound output device you want to use.**

   If you have an add-on sound-output device hooked up to your Mac, it'll appear in the list. Your Mac understands the difference between its Line Out jack and its headphone jack and the box you've got plugged into it that pumps music out through a mixing board. You can switch between these devices with a click.

4. **Mess around with the Balance slider.**

   This sets the balance between two stereo speakers.

CUSTOM SCREEN SAVERS

The original purpose of a screen saver was to provide an ever-changing image to prevent any one image from becoming permanently burned into a monitor. This is much less of an issue with today's CRT monitors, but it is still a concern with newer LCDs. For the most part, screen savers serve an aesthetic purpose: when not in use, your 20-inch iMac shows a slide show of your kids' ski trip, not a pile of Excel spreadsheets. They also help with privacy and security. When you're away from your desk, passersby can't glance at the spreadsheets on your desk and discover

that you've been keeping two sets of books to protect your embezzlement scam.

OS X comes with a group of screen savers. Some are animated; others are made up of a collection of still images that transition in and out. There are also boatloads of creative third-party screen savers available on the Web.

Changing the screen saver

You can choose what screen saver you want to use, as well as when it activates:

1. **Launch System Preferences.**

2. **Open the Desktop & Screen Saver panel.**

3. **If necessary, click on the Screen Saver button to display the screen saver panel.**

   In Figure 5-9, the left side of the panel contains a list of available screen savers.

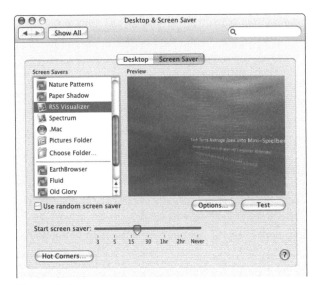

Figure 5-9
Choosing a screen saver

DARNED IF THOSE FOLKS AT APPLE HAVEN'T PROVED THEIR GENIUS AGAIN!

And once again, we see the awesome power of just blindly doing what Apple tells you, and organizing your image files into standard folders. You'll note many of the same folders in the Screen Saver panel that you saw back in the Desktop Images panel (see the section "Custom Desktops"). They work the same way: selecting an iPhoto album as your screen saver causes your idle Mac to show off the photos you took when you won the big Dream Getaway to Branson with Yakov Smirnoff contest.

4. **Click on the name of the screen saver you want to use.**

   A small preview appears to the right of the panel. The Test button lets you sample it in full-screen mode.

5. **Use the Start Screen Saver slider to determine when the screen saver should kick in.**

Many screen savers are pretty complicated affairs, with lots of options that affect how they appear. Click the Options button and adjust to your little heart's content.

Using hot corners

There are those moments in life when you want your screen saver to kick in immediately. Like if you're leaving your desk to go heat up a burrito in the office breakroom, you don't want anybody who walks past your Mac to read all the stuff you left on the screen.

So Tiger lets you define "hot corners": whenever you move your mouse all the way into one of the corners of the

screen, your screen saver pops on immediately. You can set another hot corner to prevent the screen saver from ever kicking in at all.

To set up hot corners:

1. **Display the Screen Saver panel.**

2. **Click the Hot Corners button in the lower-left corner of the window.**

3. **Select the corner that you want to trigger the screen saver.**

4. **Select Start screen saver from the pop-up menu that corresponds to the chosen corner.**

   In Figure 5-10, moving the mouse pointer to the top-left corner of the startup monitor triggers the screen saver.

5. **Select Disable Screen Saver from the pop-up menu that corresponds to the corner that you want to use to prevent the screen saver from appearing.**

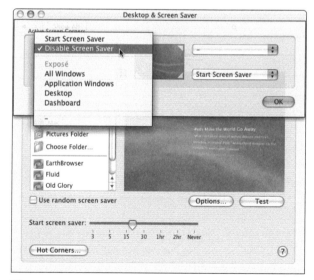

Figure 5-10
Setting hot corners

▼ **Tip**

You'll want to set a corner of your screen to Disable Screen Saver. Sometimes your Mac will be munching on a long process — for example, burning an iDVD, which can take an hour or more. Moving the mouse to the Disable hotspot means that you can glance at the screen from across the room and see that things are still proceeding on an even keel.

Of course, he who lives by the hotspot, dies by the hotspot. I didn't know that I had a tendency to give my mouse a little flick when I let it go. That flick tended to send the pointer to the Start Screen Saver hotspot, which meant that every time I let go of the mouse I'd suddenly be looking at 3-D animations of X-Wing fighters instead of the paragraph I had just selected. It was like having a small child at your elbow who wouldn't stop telling you knock-knock jokes. I didn't chuck my Mac straight through a closed third-story window only because I have the emotional strength of ten men.

Adding new screen savers

Tiger comes with a batch of screen savers and they're all a-thrill-a-minute technological wonders, each one alone worth the cost of the Tiger upgrade. But there are lots of third-party screen savers out there, too. The commercial ones tend to come with installers that set up everything for you, but most of the ones that you download from the Web need to be installed manually. Here's how:

1. **Locate the screen saver file on your hard drive. It'll be a document that ends in the extension ".saver."**

2. **Drag the file into your User/Library/Screen Savers folder.**

The new screen saver will be available to you the next time you open the Desktop & Screen Saver preferences.

WORKING WITH FONTS: THE FONT BOOK

Working with custom fonts isn't directly a part of the Mac interface, but it's another way to make your Mac your own. Things get awfully dull and uniform when everybody on the planet uses the same collection of standard fonts. And I'm not just talking about Humans, or even mammals, here; it's a danged shame when even the lowliest of freshwater bivalves can create a résumé with as much stylistic pizzazz as yours.

If you haven't bought a few custom fonts, download 'em. Just as there are aficionados of classic cars and folk music played on discarded vegetables, there are plenty of font perverts on the Web with immense libraries of typefaces free (or almost free) for the downloading.

The Font Book application helps you install and manage all your font files. And thank heaven for it. For all my guff about wanting to have lots of fonts, they tend to infest your Mac like a devouring fungus. There are the ones your Mac came with; the ones that were installed alongside the applications you bought; freakish foreign faces that are only useful when translating Klingon into the Elven language of *The Lord of the Rings* (but it was part of an Apple System Update last week, so now it's in your Font menu); and others that seem to appear simply by force of collective will.

The Font Book works in conjunction with applications that use a Font panel, like TextEdit and Keynote and Pages. The Font panel in Figure 5-11, for example, comes from the TextEdit application that is part of OS X. The list at the far left of the Font panel displays Collections, groups of fonts that you create. Within each Collection, you have one or more font families, each of which may have multiple typefaces.

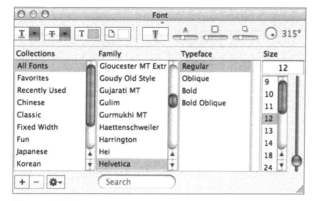

Figure 5-11
A Font panel

▼ **Note**

A typographer defines a font as a single typeface in a single size. However, most computer users think of an entire font family as a font.

The Font Book lets you create and manage collections of fonts. It also lets you disable fonts so that they don't appear in a Font panel or in the Font menus of applications that aren't Mac OS X-studly-enough to use a Font panel.

You can find the Font Book application in the Applications folder on your hard drive. Figure 5-12 shows you the basic Font Book interface:

- The column at the left lists font collections. All Fonts is exactly what its name implies — all the fonts. All the fonts in your personal Fonts folder, all the fonts in the System-wide Fonts folder, all the ones that were installed in the Mac OS 9 System Folder (if you've got one), even all the fonts belonging to other users of this Mac, provided that you have permission to access their folders. The other collections are ones that have been installed with OS X. You can keep them, modify them, delete them, or add your own collections.

- The middle column lists the fonts in the currently selected collection. Disabled fonts have the word *Off* to the right of their names, and have been grayed out.

- The right column shows a preview of the font selected in the Font column. You can adjust the size of the preview by dragging the slider at the far right of the Font Book window or by using the Size pop-up menu at the top right of the preview.

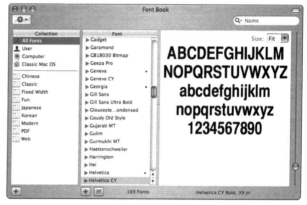

Figure 5-12
The Font Book window

▼ **Tip**

If a dot appears at the right of a font name in the middle column, it means that there are duplicate fonts in that font family. To turn off the duplicates for a given font family, select the font name in the Font column, and then select Edit ➡ Resolve Duplicates.

Disabling fonts

One of Font Book's more useful features is its ability to temporarily disable some of your installed fonts, either because one of your fonts is causing a conflict or because

WHEN IT COMES TO FONTS, I'M WILLING TO GO IT ALONE

I don't want to create the impression that I'm some sort of isolationist. (I'll have you know that I did the It's A Small World ride at Disneyland twice and I consider myself a better person for the experience.) But the first thing I did with Font Book was disable all of the international fonts. I never use them, and they only slow me down on my way from Albertus Black to Xanadu Light Compressed.

you've got four flavors of Helvetica floating around and you don't want to use the wrong ones (or you just don't like having a three-mile-long list of fonts to deal with in your applications).

1. **Launch the Font Book application.**

2. **Click on the name of the collection you want to work with. Click All Fonts if you don't know what collection your target is lurking in.**

3. **Click on the name of the font you want to disable.**

4. **Click the Disable button at the bottom of the Font column.**

5. **Click Disable.**

   The Font Book places *Off* to the right of the font name and greys out the name.

To enable a font that you've previously disabled, repeat the preceding process. (When you select the name of a disabled font, the Disable button changes into Enable.)

▼ **Note**

When you disable fonts, the changes won't appear in application Font menus or Font panels until you quit and relaunch the application.

Adding new fonts

The swaggering, he-manly way to install fonts is to simply go into the Finder and copy the font files directly into your User/Library/Fonts folder. Or, if you wanted the font to be available to any user of this Mac, you'd copy them into the system-wide Library/Fonts folder, found inside the "System" directory at the top level of your hard drive.

But some folks like pretty interfaces. Font Book can handle that, no problem:

1. **Make sure that the font (font family) you want to install is on a disk that is accessible to your system.**

   For example, if you downloaded it, it's sitting somewhere on your hard drive; if you bought it on CD, slap that disc in the drive.

2. **Launch the Font Book application.**

3. **Select the Collection to which you want to add the font.**

4. **Select File ➜ Add Fonts.**

   A standard File Open sheet appears.

5. **Locate and select the font you want to add.**

6. **Click Open.**

The font will be installed on your Mac and added to the collection that you selected.

Creating font collections

If you work on projects for which you use specific groups of fonts, you can simplify your font management by creating your own collections of fonts. You can enable and disable entire collections. Disabling a collection shortens that Font menu that seems to scroll on forever and greatly simplifies the display in a Font panel.

▼ Note

Font collections help you, and the people with whom you work, to use typefaces consistently. If you've taken the time to create collections named *For correspondence*, *For internal reports*, and *For ads and marketing*, it reduces the risk that when your medical division files important paperwork to the FDA for approval of your new arthritis medication, the subheads won't be printed with that font in which each letter is formed out of a clown contorting himself in a different shape.

To create a new collection:

1. **Launch the Font Book application.**

2. **Select File → New Collection.**

   A space for the name of the new collection appears in the Collection list at the left of the Font Book window.

3. **Type a name for the new collection.**

4. **Press Enter.**

Your new collection won't have any fonts in it. To add fonts, you must first install them in another collection, even if it's only All Fonts. After you install the font, you can place it in the new collection:

1. **Select the name of the collection containing the font you want to add to another collection.**

2. **Click and drag the name of the font from the highlighted Font list to the name of the collection to which you want to add it.**

UNIVERSAL ACCESS OPTIONS

Back to stuff found in System Preferences. Did you miss it? Aw, that's sweet.

Tiger has plenty of little tweaks and features that make the OS easier to work with if you have problems with your sight, hearing, or your dexterity. And even if you're skimming this and thinking, "Okay, this doesn't describe me; I shall move on," you should stick around. Universal Access offers basic changes to the way that standard user-interface elements operate, and as such, they can be a treasure trove of shortcuts and streamlined techniques to anyone who takes the time to explore the possibilities.

There are so many Universal Access features in Tiger that it merits a whole book. But here are some of the highlights, emphasizing the features that are actually useful to all users, not just the folks with special requirements.

Zooming in on the screen

Boy, this is useful. Zoom will magnify the screen by a modest or a titanic margin. I keep it running on the immense 30-inch screen here on my desk. The screen sits two feet away from my chair (thus preventing eyestrain) but the windows and menus are way too small to read (thus *contributing* to eyestrain). So I just magnify the screen a bit, allowing my word-processing window to magnify until it fills the entire acreage, and it's like having the large-print version of *Reader's Digest* in front of me.

I also use it when my Mac is doing something I need to keep an eye on from afar. With the screen zoomed down to the status indicator of a disk utility, I can just glance up from the sofa from across the room, see that the process is only halfway complete, and return to my comic books without getting up.

To activate the Zoom feature:

1. **Open the Universal Access preferences panel.**

2. **Click the Seeing button to display the seeing pane (viz Figure 5-13).**

3. **Click Turn On Zoom.**

   Zooming is now on. Pressing ⌘+Option+equal sign (=) makes the screen image larger. You can press ⌘+Option+minus sign (−) to make the screen image smaller. You can also toggle zooming on and off by pressing ⌘+Option+8.

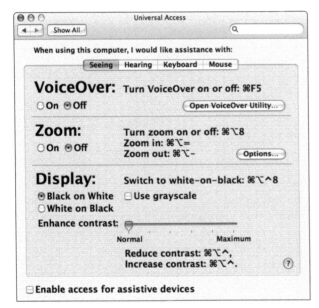

Figure 5-13
The Universal Access seeing pane

Contrast and color

If the contrast or color of the screen is a problem, you can change it in several ways:

VOICEOVER: THE COOLEST FEATURE I'M GLAD I DON'T NEED

Tiger brings with it a fantastic new feature that without any doubt will open up the Mac to a whole new category of users. Voice Over (you'll find it in the Seeing tab) speaks a running commentary of your Mac's screen as you mouse over certain elements. Every time a new window opens, every time you move from one menu to another, every time you open a document or close another, Voice Over says explicitly what's going on.

It's the coolest feature that I hope I'll never need.

- **Switch to White on Black:** This turns the screen to a loose negative of itself.

- **Set Display to Grayscale:** This replaces colors with shades of gray.

- **The Enhance contrast slider:** This increases or decreases the contrast between colors.

Flashing alerts

For those who can't hear the Mac's speaker, OS X can flash the screen when an alert sound is played. This one's helpful even if you don't "need" it; if you've muted the sound to talk on the phone, your Mac will still be able to get your attention when something catches on fire:

1. **Open the Universal Access preferences panel.**

2. **Click the Hearing button.**

   The hearing pane appears (see Figure 5-14).

3. **Click the checkbox next to "Flash the screen when an alert sounds."**

You can see what you're in for by clicking the Flash Screen button.

Figure 5-14
The Universal Access hearing pane

Pressing only one key at a time

If a user has trouble holding down more than one key at a time, executing command keys — and ⌘ key shortcuts for menu commands — can be a ghastly trial. OS X provides a solution with Sticky Keys, which lets you press one key at a time. It's also handy if you need to type one-handed: I have a Mac and a keyboard mounted against a wall in my kitchen for quick info retrieval. So I keep Sticky Keys on all the time:

1. **Open the Universal Access preferences panel.**

2. **Click the Keyboard button.**

   The keyboard pane appears (see Figure 5-15).

3. **Click the On button next to Sticky Keys.**

   OS X automatically checks the "Beep when a modifier key is set" and "Display pressed keys on screen" options. These options give you a bit of feedback as you hit keys: old-fashioned typewriter noises peal out when you tap a function or modifier key, and ghostly images of the keys that Sticky Keys are "holding down" for you float above the screen.

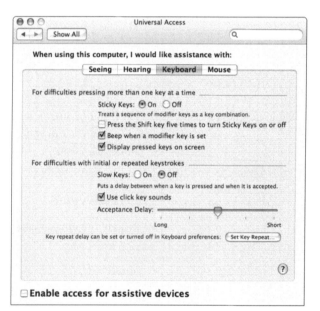

Figure 5-15
The Universal Access keyboard pane

THE TALKIN' MAC SAVIN' MY ENERGY BLUES

The System Preference's Speech panel hides a cool alert feature. You're in the living room watching hour 27 of the big Arbor Day Weekend *Bob Newhart Show* Marathon, when you hear your Mac beep from the other side of the room. You have to take the bowl of Cheetos off your belly, wipe the orange stuff off your fingers, redo the buckle on your trousers… I mean, walking over to the desk to identify the problem is a Herculean labor, and meanwhile, you're missing the bit when Bob has to walk out on a window ledge dressed as Zorro.

But if you activate Speech's Talking Alerts feature, your Mac actually speaks alerts and error messages aloud. "Excuse me: The file server Uncle Mimsy's Public Folder has unexpectedly gone offline," it says in Victoria's soothing tones. And because you really couldn't care less about that, you shrug and go on with your life.

I want to stress that I don't spend my *entire* life on the sofa, trying to give my Mac as little attention as possible. But it's good to know that Apple is looking out for the best interests of not only the 20-hour-a-day people, but also those users who want to scorn and neglect their products.

Using the keyboard instead of a mouse

If you have trouble using a mouse, or if your mouse decides to take a journey to Mouse Heaven, you can control the movement of the mouse pointer with your numeric keypad. You do this by turning on Mouse Keys:

1. **Open the Universal Access preferences panel.**

2. **Click the Mouse button to display the mouse pane (see Figure 5-16).**

3. **Click the Mouse Keys On button.**

4. **Move the Initial Delay slider.**

   This slide controls how long you need to press a key before the mouse pointer begins to move.

With Mouse Keys enabled, you can move the "mouse" with your numeric keypad. Table 5.1 gives you the skinny.

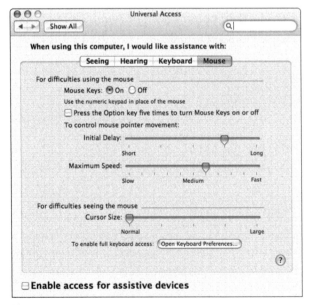

Figure 5-16
The Universal Access mouse pane

This is another good one to know. If your mouse (or your PowerBook's trackpad) gives up the ghost, it'll happen at the worst possible time. With Mouse Keys in your hip pocket, you'll at least be able to limp through the rest of the day, or at least until you get so annoyed by this sort of thing that you yell something suitably Viking-like and then head off to the mall with extreme prejudice.

Table 5.1 Mouse Keys

Action	Key
Move mouse pointer up	8
Move mouse pointer down	2
Move mouse pointer left	4
Move mouse pointer right	6
Move mouse pointer diagonally	1, 3, 7, and 9
Click the mouse button	5
Hold down the mouse button	0
Release the mouse button	Period (.)

 Tip

If your keyboard doesn't have a numeric keypad, as is the case with iBooks and PowerBooks, press the function (fn) key to make the center keys on the keyboard act like a numeric keypad. To find which keys will work, look for the small numbers on the keys.

"Okay, Mr. Big Shot," you're saying. "I suppose you're going to make up some sort of suspicious phony-baloney Power User thing about *this*, too, right?" Well, not if you're going to be so snotty about it.

But yeah, I use this one a lot, too. There are plenty of dirt-cheap infrared remotes that let you map buttons on the remote to key presses. They're intended to let you skip from track to track in iTunes and such, but with Mouse Keys enabled you can easily use that same five-button remote to control your whole Mac.

Finally, there's the Cursor Size option, also in Universal Access' Mouse pane. Your Mac has a really big screen, and it's easy to "lose" the mouse pointer as it scurries across that big football field of data. So by moving the Cursor Size slider, you can make the pointer just about as big as you could ever want it to be, as in Figure 5-17:

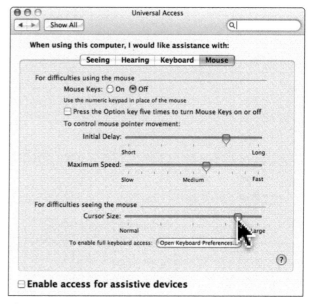

Figure 5-17
Everything's funnier when it's bigger: jumbo (and easy-to-follow) mouse pointer, thanks to Universal Access' adjustable Cursor Size.

This helps you keep track of where your pointer's at, and it's also a great thing to activate when you're giving a presentation. There's never any question about where you're pointing or what you want your audience to gape at.

There's just one thing I sort of envy about Linux users (and Windows folks, to a lesser extent): Linux is "skinnable." If there's anything you don't like about a Linux box's appearance or behavior, you can change it. If you want your Linux to look like a Mac, download a skin. Windows XP? Skin it. You're such a big fan of *Viva Rock Vegas,* the prequel to the film *The Flintstones*, that you want your computer to run exactly the same way as the "prehistoric" computers did in the casino scenes? It's doable. Stupid, but doable.

Alas, you really don't have that sort of freedom on the Mac. When we talk about "customizing Macs," we talk about adjusting basic behaviors through standard features. Which is a shame, because you can have a lot of fun by doing some extreme skinning. My favorite PDA uses the Windows Mobile operating system. Well, I was able to put up with that user interface for a whole week before I broke down and re-skinned it. With just an hour or two's worth

of work, I was able to make this PDA look like a dead-ringer for Mac OS X.

So I was happy. But I sort of forgot that in some very specific places and situations, I'm thought of as Something Of An Industry Insider. And thus, at trade shows filled with Mac users, I'd spend just as much time telling people that no, this *isn't* a special prototype Apple PDA, really, I promise, as I did actually taking notes and looking up phone numbers. Which sort of puts us back at the introduction of this chapter: sometimes totalitarian oppression actually works out for the best.

I Don't Know Why They Call It the Finder, Either

In This Chapter

The Overall Finder Experience • Finder Window Views • The Toolbar • Using the Sidebar
Filenames: More Interesting Than Supposed • Finding Things • Creating Folders
Trashing Things • Moving Things Around • Custom Labels • Getting Information

A medium-sized FedEx box has just arrived. Good news! It's the analogy that I sent away for about three weeks ago in anticipation of this chapter. Let's see what they came up with:

"The Finder is like the lobby of a hotel."

Hmm. I see what they were going for, but frankly I was sort of hoping for something better, perhaps a baseball theme. Still, a good, reputable firm, which has been handcrafting analogies and similes since the days of the Harding administration, built this. Plus there's a 40 percent restocking fee on returns — so I'll make the most of it.

Yes, the Finder is like the lobby of a hotel. It's where the Mac deposits you after it's completed the startup process, and for good reason: No matter what business you have in the Macintosh, at some point you're probably going to have to pass through the Finder to get there. It's the center of activity. You examine the contents of your folders and volumes. You search for files. You connect to remote file servers. You launch files and applications. You organize and reorganize the things you've stored.

WHY *IS* IT CALLED "THE FINDER"?

Well, because more than 20 years ago, Apple engineer Bud Tribble figured that you'd use the Finder to Find files and applications that you would then open or launch. Yeah, it's not a terribly satisfactory explanation. Especially when you consider that the first Macs were limited to floppy drives with less than 400K of storage per disk. "Finding" a document is pretty much taken care of after you've made your way through a shoebox of 80 or 90 disks and read a ball-pointed label that reads "Latest Short Story (Disk 1 of 9)."

I'm more inclined to identify "the Finder" as one of those terms that has come to refer to itself. Ask Johnson and Johnson why they call those cotton swabs Q-Tips and they'll mumble something about "Quality" but we know better: Q-Tips are called Q-Tips because they're Q-Tips.

Okay, the hotel lobby idea is working. But I'll butter it a little: It's also a little like the hotel's concierge, too. If you're unsure of what you can do on your Mac, how to make adjustments to make your stay more pleasurable, and get information about what's going on with the system in general, your default resource is to click the Finder.

THE OVERALL FINDER EXPERIENCE

So the Finder is actually the hub around which most of your Macintosh lifestyle revolves. Figure 6-1 shows you a typical Finder layout. Here's a quick visual tour.

As you can see in Figure 6-1, there are numerous visual elements that can appear:

- **The Dock:** It's technically not part of the Finder — it's available to you in all apps, not just the Finder — but it's pretty intimately connected. For one, it's the home of the Trash Can, the place where you drag files to delete 'em.

- **Volume icons:** They represent storage volumes that are currently available to Tiger. They can include your internal hard drive, an optical disc you've inserted into the drive, volumes that you're connected to via a network . . . any entity that can contain files and folders.

Tip

The Finder puts those icons on your Desktop because That's The Way It's Always Been Done. If you want to minimize clutter, open up the Finder's Preferences window. You can tell the Finder not to put hard drive icons (or volume icons, or CD icons, or . . .) on the Desktop by clicking on the General collection and unchecking the appropriate checkboxes.

- **Folder icons:** Folders contain other items, like documents, applications, and even other folders.

- **Document and application icons:** They represent files that you can open and apps that you can run.

- **Aliases to folders and files:** They look and act like application or document or folder icons, but in truth they point to another app or document or folder located elsewhere. You can identify an alias by the curved arrow in its lower-left corner. Although the actual file or folder isn't present on the Desktop, you can work with the alias as if it were the original.

- **Finder windows:** Finder windows show you the contents of a volume or folder.

Taken together, all of this represents your Desktop. It's your workspace. Your Desktop also includes application windows.

THE FINDER JUST NEVER QUITS, AND THE QUITTER NEVER FINDS

Are Skittles candy, or gum? I dunno. I'm not qualified. But how about "Is the Finder an application, or is it part of the OS?" Aha! Now *that's* more my meat: It's both. Kind of.

See, it looks a lot like an app, in that it has its own icon in the Dock and you can switch to it just like you can switch between any two apps. But it's totally *unlike* any app, in that you can't Quit it. Look in the File menu if you don't believe me. See? No Quit. Bring up its contextual Dock menu by holding your mouse down on its Dock icon. Yup, not Quit. It's so important to The Macintosh Experience that it has to be up and running at all times.

Which doesn't mean that you can't show it who's boss from time to time. Hold down the Option key while you bring up its Dock menu: Aha! There's a hidden Relaunch command! You can't Quit the Finder, but you *can* tell Tiger to quit it and then immediately launch it again. You might do that if the Finder started acting — and brace yourself for a technical term — "all screwy" on you. Like if it started drawing windows with their text all messed up. A relaunch might put things right, but (a) that's an incredibly rare problem, and (b) you'd probably be better off restarting your Mac, just to purge its memory of any gnomes, demons, or elves.

Figure 6-1
A typical look at the Finder

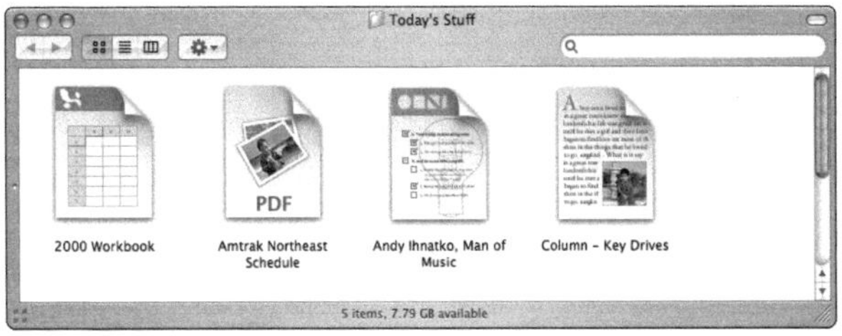

Figure 6-2
Clicking these buttons switches to a different view of the window.

FINDER WINDOW VIEWS

A Finder window shows you the contents of a folder or a volume. Through one, you can launch applications, open documents, store files, delete files, move files, and copy files. But a Finder window can display its contents in three very different ways. You choose among each individual window's three different views either from the Finder's View menu or by clicking one of the three buttons in the window's button bar (Figure 6-2). From left to right, you've got your icon view, your list view, and your column view.

Icon view

Icon view (Figure 6-3) shows files and folders as icons. Icon view is sort of the classic image people have of the Mac, particularly for people who've acquired most of their education on modern computers from movies. Just once I'd like to see a movie where a computer's user-interface doohickeys aren't so big that they could stun a mole rat. But I suspect that I'll be dead before I'm 90, so fat chance there. This view isn't terribly efficient because it can display only a handful of icons at once, so you'll be scrolling around a lot. Most people never use it.

Figure 6-3
A Finder window in icon view

You're free to drag these icons around willy-nilly (or pell-mell, if you prefer; the Finder is *just* that flexible), clumping them together in whichever order happens to make sense to you. But that can cause a mess. The Finder can tidy up those icons for you. When an icon view is active, you can use View➡Cleanup to align the icons to a grid and View➡Arrange➡desired order to sort the icons.

However, in a few cases icon view is handy because it's so customizable. When you select View➡Show View Options, you'll get the tool palette shown in Figure 6-4.

Icon view options include

- **This window only/All windows:** These items let you customize the look of *just* this one window or the look of every icon view window the Finder creates. So you can set up your Pictures window to make it easy to see your images, but you're not stuck with that sort of view when you've got a window full of spreadsheets. You'll see this feature in the View Options palette of each of the Finder's three different views.

- **Icon size:** You can make the icons huge or tiny, and scale the label text so that it's easier to read, or takes up less room. Figure 6-5 shows you what the window of Figure 6-3 looks like with humongous icons.

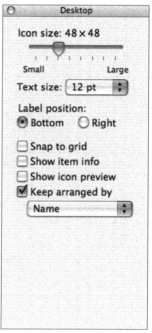

Figure 6-4
Setting icon view options

- **Snap to grid:** This ensures that icons stay in nice, orderly columns and rows, no matter how you drag 'em around.

- **Show item info/Show icon preview:** You wanna just see the filenames and generic icons? That's how the Finder usually represents files in a Finder window. But it can show you more information about the files they represent, too. If a Finder window contains image documents, for instance, the Finder can display a thumbnail view of the actual image in place of a plain, generic JPEG document icon, and also display the dimensions of the image. Figure 6-5 shows you what the "Figure 1" image file from Figure 6-3 looks like with both of these options enabled.

- **Keep arranged by:** This option tells the Finder to always arrange the contents of this window by a certain category. The icons will automatically be sorted by name, the date they were last changed, the date they were created, their size, what kind of file it is, or how you've labeled them.

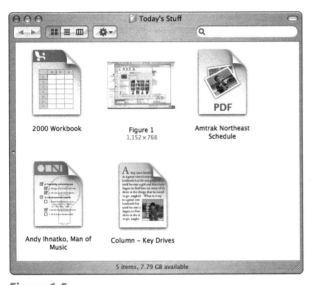

Figure 6-5
These icons are massive.

- **Background options:** You can also change the window's background. Normally it's white (clean white, non-distracting white, thank-God-nobody-messed-around-with-the-background white, but by clicking one of the buttons at the bottom of the View Options window you can change it to a different color, or hang an image back there.

List view

The list view (see Figure 6-6) displays files and folders in an ordered list. You'll use this when you need to see the most information possible (you might have to either resize the window or use the window's scrollers to see all those columns of info, though). I refer to list view as the "Where the Heck Ramsey did my 80 gigabytes of storage go?!?" I can easily pull up a list of my drive's and folder's contents, sort it by file size, and then see that, oh yeah, I seem to have downloaded roughly 13 gigabytes of music from the iTunes Store.

You can sort the list by any of its columns. To sort by file size, click the Size column header. By default, items

WHEN IT COMES TO BACKGROUNDS, I'VE MELLOWED WITH AGE

Sigh. When I was a younger man, I would have simply mocked anyone and everyone who would even *consider* switching the background away from white, and then moved on. Sample: "Whenever I see a customized window background, I imagine that this is a person who has the sort of good taste that commands them to cover a beautiful oak desk with leopard print contact paper."

But alas, with age comes the burden of Understanding. So with all due mumbling and kicking of the ground, I begrudgingly admit that this feature has its uses. For one, the Finder quickly becomes a maze of overlapping windows and when your Documents window has a red background, it's easy to spot in the scrum. And when you're responsible for keeping other people's Macs running, it's clever to draw a card of instructions as a JPEG image and set that as your users' window backgrounds. For example, "Valued User: Any documents placed inside this window are automatically copied to the server's 'Project' folder. So if you're abusing company hardware and bandwidth to download nude photos of former *The Love Boat* cast members, save them elsewhere …and I'm obviously just talking to Ted, here." Many software developers use this trick to give you an explicit little list of installation instructions.

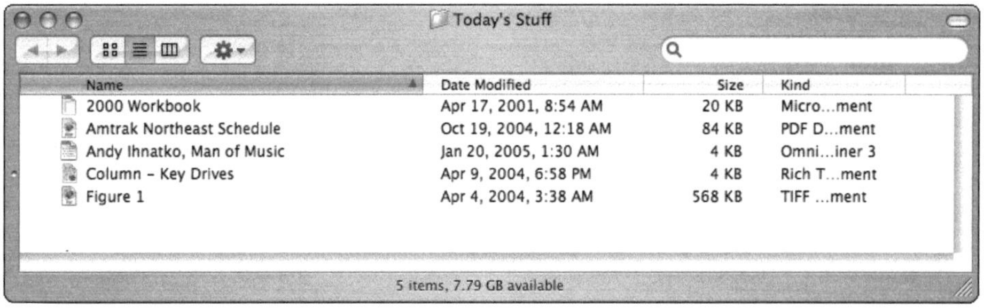

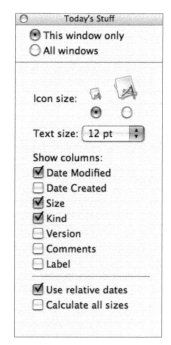

Figure 6-6
A Finder window in list view

appear in ascending order. To change it to descending, click anywhere in the highlighted column's title. If it isn't highlighted (if the title isn't colored) then you'll have to give it a click to select it.

You can change the width of a column by dragging the right edge of its title left or right (the mouse pointer will change to a vertical bar with left and right arrows when you hold down the mouse button). You can also change a column's order by dragging the titles around.

List view has its own custom View Options (see Figure 6-7).

- **Size:** The size options are familiar. The real meat of these options is choosing what sort of information is presented. By default, the filenames and mini-icons are joined by the date the file was last changed, its size, and its file type, but you can click on others to fill the window with more info, or de-select any info you're not interested in, to prevent mental information overload.

- **Use relative dates:** If you believe that the word "Yesterday" is a friendlier thing to see than yesterday's date (and why wouldn't you; it's not as cool as "The Fool On The Hill" or "Helter Skelter," but in this economy you take what you can get), check the Use relative dates option.

Calculate all sizes: Normally, the Finder doesn't calculate the sizes of enclosed folders in the list. That can take a lot of time. If you want that info, though, click on the Calculate all sizes option.

Figure 6-7
Setting list view options

Tip

If you're trying to bamboozle your spouse into letting you buy a peppier Mac, enable the Calculate all sizes option — particularly if you have lots of folders inside folders inside folders, and your Mac is indeed tragically slow. You'll be off to the Apple store with a co-signed check in no time, unless your spouse likes to watch you suffer, which is something you should have determined before you moved in together. Unless, of course, you're into that. Who am I to judge?

Column view

And here we have the most useful view of them all. You can easily navigate from anywhere within a volume to anywhere, all in one window. You can get a good overview of an item's total contents. Yes, from an inarticulate mass of lifeless windows, I bring you a cultured, sophisticated, one-window view of everything inside my hard drive. *Hit it!*

Note

Um ... that was a Mel Brooks reference. "Young Frankenstein?" Where Gene Wilder shows off the ... yes, that's it. Good. Onward.

Column view contains multiple columns, showing you a portion of the file/folder hierarchy, as in Figure 6-8. Although it doesn't give you as much information as list view, column view can be easier to use if you need to thread your way through a file system.

You can crawl through the whole hierarchy of a disc. Click on a folder and a new column appears to its right, listing its contents. Click on a folder in that one and *another* column appears. Click on a file and the next column shows you a preview of what that file contains, along with information about that file. Yee ... I say, *yee* ... haw!

Figure 6-8
A Finder window in column view

MENTAL INFORMATION OVERLOAD

Mental Information Overload — or MIO as it's known, because an acronym contains less information — is a very real problem that every modern office worker should carefully consider. By overloading the brain with too much input, its neurological architecture becomes incapable of forming new pathways merely as a means of self-defense against confronting additional tonnage of confusing, contradictory, or bewildering data.

In extreme cases, the brain disconnects long-formed pathways, limiting the subject's ability to do much more than react to stimuli. The recent up tick in both viewers and participants of reality-themed game shows is a direct result. Informative — but not dangerously so — pamphlets explaining MIO are available at a nominal charge from your area government printing office.

You can change the width of an individual column by dragging the handle at the bottom of its scroll bar. And just like icon and list views, you can configure the column view display by using View→Show View Options (Figure 6-9). You can choose a text size, whether icons should appear, and whether the final, rightmost column should include a preview of the contents of a selected document file.

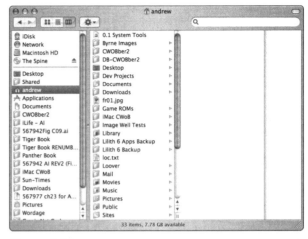

Figure 6-10
The standard Finder toolbar

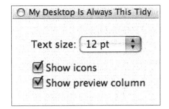

Figure 6-9
Setting column view options

THE TOOLBAR

Every Finder window is also topped with a Toolbar. We looked at it just a moment ago, remember? Those three buttons for switching between window views? Yes indeed: those buttons were in a special area known as the Toolbar. See? You're learning stuff here without even trying.

As in any of the Mac's windows, you can show and hide the Toolbar by clicking the little tic-tac shaped button in the window's upper-right corner. Additionally, you can select Show/Hide Toolbar from the Finder's View menu.

Clicking toolbar buttons can do many of the things you can do through the Finder's menus. The Finder's standard toolbar is shown in Figure 6-10.

Here's the standard menagerie:

- **Back/Forward buttons:** The first group of buttons navigate you Back and Forward and they work just like a Web browser's buttons. If you opened your Documents folder and then your Novels folder and then a folder entitled "The Importance Of Being Furnished," clicking the Back button backtracks you step by step, replacing the current view location with the view you've just left.

- **View buttons:** The second cluster switches you between icon, list, and column views of the window.

- **Action button:** The next item is a user-interface element that was new in Panther and persists in Tiger: the Action button. It appears in lots of different apps: it's a pop-up menu containing functions that are relevant to whatever mode you happen to be in at the moment. In the Finder, selecting the Action button is practically identical to activating the selected item's contextual menu. Try popping it from time to time and you'll see that its contents are different when you've selected a file versus a folder, for instance.

▼ Note

Incidentally, that doodad on the Action button is a gear. But, of course, there's a swelling movement to call it a flower. Typically, any attempt to put a manly veneer on my milquetoasty geek nature is doomed to failure.

- **The "Gap":** And now you reach The Great Wasteland. It appears to be an empty and useless gap between the Action button and the Search box. It is indeed empty, but it's far from useless: in the next section, you'll see how you can populate this unused acreage with added functions and shortcuts.

- **Search field:** Provides quick access to the Finder's file-search features. This is another thing that no mortal man can describe in a single, bulleted item, and it merits its own section later in this chapter.

There's *powah* in the Toolbar. As-is, it's sort of a basic user element. But you can customize it like all get-out. The standard toolbar has only those four elements (okay, *five* if you include The Gap) but the Finder has a library of other doo-dads that you can drag in there.

Select View→Customize Toolbar to see what's available. Figure 6-11 shows you the complete inventory.

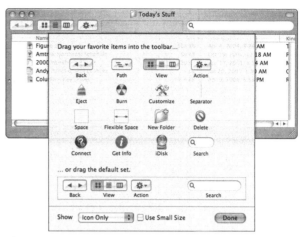

Figure 6-11
Additional toolbar doo-dads

Nearly all of these just offer you shortcuts to functions that are available to you through the Finder's menus. You can add as many of these functions as you want by just dragging them into the toolbar one at a time, as in Figure 6-12.

ANDY MAKES IT PERSONAL

Allow me to exorcise a demon: when the design of the Finder's windows changed (two upgrades ago), I really hated the new look. Apple did away with the clean, creamy white windows with their nice, big toolbars, and slapped in the same minimalist "brushed metal" look of the iLife apps. Don't get me wrong; I think brushed metal has its place. It's a dandy interface for sorting photos of your bus trip to Branson in iPhoto, or building a playlist of Tito Puente tracks in iTunes. But it just didn't work for me as a Finder interface. Exit elegance; enter flash. They're like putting flame decals on a nice, reliable Volvo. You can pretend all you want but that thing's for hauling kids and groceries and surviving a 70 MPH rollover. It ain't for style.

I don't hate it any more. Partly it's because it's really not at all a bad look, really. Partly it's for the same reason why I no longer get mad about being charged a dollar to talk to a teller at my bank. I'm used to it by now. And, I mean, what am I going to *do* about it?

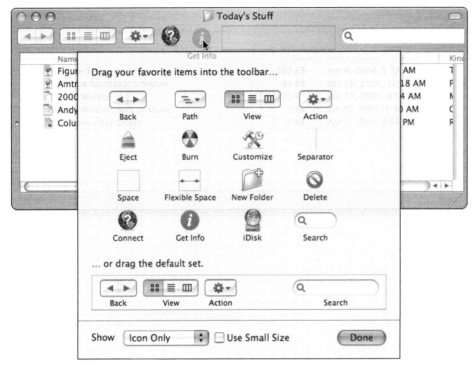

Figure 6-12
Adding a Get Info button to the Toolbar

You can drag them anywhere you want, in any order. The little grey box represents the "gap." If you want the button to always stick to the left side of the screen, drag it to the left side of the gap. To put it on the right . . . you get the idea.

You can delete tools that are already there, even the standard items. You never use the "Back/Forward" cluster? Just drag it off of the Toolbar and it'll disappear in a puff of good intentions. You can always go back to the default toolbar by dragging the default set in.

The Toolbar can also hold shortcuts to documents, apps, folders, volumes, servers, or anything else in the Finder. With the Customize Toolbar sheet open, just drag them in as you did with the other doo-dads. In Figure 6-13, I'm adding a few of my favorite Automator workflows to the toolbar.

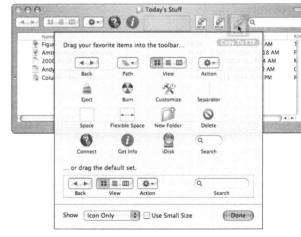

Figure 6-13
Adding files to the Toolbar

A LESSER-KNOWN FINDER FEATURE

There's another little feature hiding just above the toolbar. Hold down ⌘ and click on the window's title. Up pops a list revealing the path to the window's contents. For example, if you're looking at Your Documents folder, it will show "Documents>(Your username)/Users/(The name of your hard drive)/(The name of your Macintosh)."

This comes in handy if you place folders inside folders inside folders, and want to make a mental note of where exactly something is. It also lets you navigate back up several steps without going through all the stops in between.

Naturally, you can add anything you want to the toolbar. But remember that conceptually, the Toolbar is supposed to hold *tools*. So it's a natural to drag AppleScripts and Automator workflows in there; it's like adding your own, individualized tools to the Finder. For example, I've written an AppleScript that performs an operation that you could term "Copy this file to my Documents folder, and *if* the file already exists *and* this file is newer than the previous copy, then replace the old one with the new one." It saves me a lot of time, and by dragging this script into the Toolbar, it's like it came built-in to Tiger.

Besides, why keep folders and volumes in there, when you've got the Sidebar? Sidebar? Next section, next section; you'll go nuts for it, I swear.

Click Done when you're finished customizing the Toolbar. Notice that the changes you've made to the Toolbar affect every Finder window, past, present and future . . . not just the one you were looking at when you dragged those icons around.

USING THE SIDEBAR

In addition to the three Finder Window views, there is another navigation aid available to you in Finder windows: the sidebar (Figure 6-14). Yes, it's another place Where You Can Keep Often-Used Volumes, Folders, Apps, and Documents Handy.

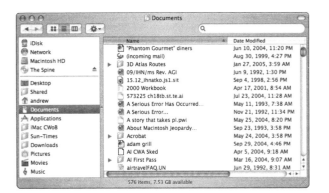

Figure 6-14
A Finder window with a sidebar

You can change the width of the sidebar by dragging the divider to your liking. To make it disappear altogether, drag the divider to the left edge of the window, or double-click the strip separating the sidebar from the rest of the window's contents.

The sidebar has two little sections in it. The top section contains a list of all of the volumes currently connected to your Mac. Your built-in hard drive, a CD you've loaded, a memory card in its USB reader, your iDisk, or another volume or folder that you're connected to through a network. The Finder populates this list for you automatically, as volumes appear and disappear. If you want to limit what shows up in this section, click on the Sidebar pane of Finder Preferences.

Underneath that section you find shortcuts to useful folders and locations. Dragging a file into the Documents icon in the sidebar is as good as dragging it into the Documents folder directly.

You can add an item to the sidebar just by dragging it into any blank space underneath or between what's already in there. The list automatically resizes itself to make room, if necessary. You can also reorder its contents — move a useful folder to the very top, say — just by dragging it. Clicking on any of the icons in the sidebar opens that item. If the item is a folder or disk, its contents appear in the right side of the window.

To delete an item, just drag it away. It'll disappear in a puff.

 Note

Yup. Sidebar: hated that too, when it first came out in the previous OS. But I didn't simply Get Used To It … over time, I grew to love it. I still think it's a little ugly but hey, so am I. And am *I* unworthy of love? Operators are standing by.

FLEXIBILITY, THY NAME IS TIGER

It seems like this is the third or fourth place where you can Keep Items Handy. Well, it's part of the larger plan: the Sidebar has a subtle wrinkle that makes it unique from the Dock or the Toolbar. Essentially, an item in the Sidebar will *teleport* (zoom! zip!) you straight to another view of the contents of your Mac. Yup, you *could* put an application icon in there and launch it by double-clicking … but that's a task better suited to the Dock. No, the sidebar would contain a shortcut to your Application *folder*. So if you need to add a new piece of software, you can just drag it straight in via the Sidebar instead of having to click and click and *click* through all those nested folders-within-folders until you uncover your Applications folder.

FILENAMES: SLIGHTLY MORE INTERESTING THAN SUPPOSED

I talk some more about files in Chapter 11, but why not settle a fundamental thing or two right here? You typically name a file when you save it for the first time. However, you can change that name later whenever you want. New folders are given the default name Untitled Folder, which seems to beg for a renaming.

To rename an icon on the Desktop or in a Finder window:

1. **Click on an icon or the name of an item to select it.**

2. **Press Enter.**

   A blue box surrounds the highlighted text of the item's name.

3. **Edit the name.**

4. **Press Enter or Return.**

This is as good a place as any to talk about OS X's rules for naming things. The nice thing is that there aren't many rules. You can use just about any character you can type from the keyboard, including spaces. In fact, the only character you can't use is a colon. OS X also won't let you have more than one item in a folder by the same name.

 Note

Oh, and a file name can't be any longer than 255 characters, or 9 average sentences. Maybe when Mac OS X 11 is released in 2011 we can finally live the dream of doing away with files entirely and just putting all of our document contents in the titles.

One of the many Things That You Don't Need To Know is the fact that Mac OS X — being a flavor of Unix — puts file name extensions on all its files. That Microsoft Word file's name isn't *Asphalt Pie*; it's actually *Asphalt Pie.doc*. The Finder conceals the extension because it's ugly. You can have the Finder show all file extensions by clicking on the "Show all file extensions" button in the Advanced tab of the Finder Preferences window.

FINDING THINGS

I've just counted the number of files on my hard drive: it's officially reached the bajillions. You *try* to be good, you *try* to be disciplined . . . but files are never where you remember putting them the last time. Particularly when

CELEBRITY DEATH MATCH? "FIND" VERSUS SHERLOCK

Oh, so the Finder Finds things! Well, sometimes you do run across an Augustus Q. Milkmann who actually delivers yogurt and half-and-half to suburban houses.

Those of you trading up from Mac OS 9 will probably be asking "Finding files in the Finder? But what about Sherlock?" To quote the sober and wise Mob capo Clemenza, who used these words in reference to the whereabouts of a certain member of the Corleone family whose performance was so sorely lacking that an immediate and bloody personnel change was mandated: "Sherlock? Oh, you won't be seein' *him* no more." The addition of Spotlight in Tiger has effectively glued down the lid on the coffin.

Sherlock is still part of X, but it's focused on grabbing info off the Internet. Which, bloody heck . . . is a function that's now largely been taken over by Dash board widgets. For local file search, Apple has returned to a nice, fast, slim, and *sensible* Find feature, backed by the awesome power of Spotlight. Now, take the cannoli. Leave the gun.

(a) The Last Time was about 17 months ago, and (b) you had just spent a lot of time at the whiteboard giving a presentation, and the marker fumes made you sort of dopey.

The Finder's Find feature has been finessed in Tiger. Firstly, there's the Find command, right in the File menu. Hitting this brings up the Find window (Figure 6-15).

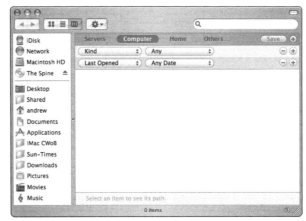

Figure 6-15
The Find dialog

▼ Tip

And as you've probably guessed, you can also just type a search term into the Spotlight search box found in the toolbar of every Finder window. There's only one subtle difference when you do it this way: when you just go directly to the window's search box, the Finder assumes you want a simple, direct search for just that word. If you want to narrow it down to "files with that term that were created last week and also have the word 'tralfaz,' — or if you want to search on other criteria, like the size of an image — you'll have to click the Add Search Criteria button to make the search more complex. The Find box in the window toolbar is just a shortcut to let you do the most popular kind of search.

It looks almost exactly like a Finder window. That's because Find now has a much more intimate relationship with the Finder. Apple wants you to think of a Find not as a special tool you're using, but a way of creating a new view of your data.

Basic searching

Here's how to do a search:

1. **Type a search term in the Spotlight box on the upper-right corner of the window.**

   Spotlight starts searching *immediately*. Like, the moment you start typing. Type **apple** and by the time you hit the third key, it's finding everything that has an "app" anywhere on or inside it.

2. **Get a load of the search results (Figure 6-16).**

Figure 6-16
The Find dialog

Yup, it's a two-step process. But the results bear some comment. I searched for "Joe." And look at what it found:

- **Photos with the word "Joe" in the filename.** These are arranged in a list of thumbnails.

 Tip

And notice that the Images section inherits a collection of different view buttons in its section heading. These buttons are identical to the ones displayed when you use the Spotlight menu: you can play the photos as a slideshow, view them as a list of files, or (the default) as a list of thumbnail images.

- **Files and folders with the word "Joe" in the filename.** Viz, the Billy Joel folder.

- **Music files featuring a "Joe" anywhere in the metadata.** Viz, "Piano Man," recorded by Billy Joel.

- **Files in which "Joe" can be found anywhere within its content, like a PDF file, a Microsoft Word document, or a text file.**

Each of these results are organized by category and working with the found icons in this view is just as good as working with the file itself. I can copy Joe Barbecue.jpg to one of my external drives by just dragging its thumbnail into the drive's icon in the window sidebar. I have no idea why Find found Dainty June & Her Farmboys.mp3 so I double-click it. It opens in iTunes and starts playing. Aha: one of the performers is Joey Dudding. Gotcha.

Notice what happens when you select one of these items: the bottom strip of the window reveals the actual path to the thing (Figure 6-17). Handy if you don't just want to get The Thing Itself, but you'd also like to take a look at everything else in that neighborhood. You might have stashed all of your project documents in some backwater jetty of your hard drive, for example, and those things need to be dragged back into the light.

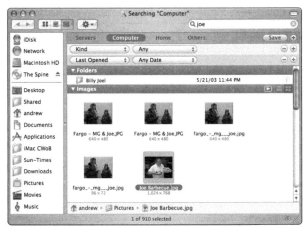

Figure 6-17
Discovering the actual location of the thing you found

But you're not always going to just need to find one word. Plus, what if that one-word search returns thousands of results?

So the Find window gives you plenty of tools for making your search more specific.

Narrowing the search by Where It Is

The top bar of the search window lists physical locations where files are stored. Computer is selected by default; Find will search every volume that's currently accessible. If you just want to search your personal Home folder, click Home. Just remote file servers? Servers.

There's also an Others button to cover all other eventualities. This pulls up a list of all the volumes connected to your Mac (Figure 6-18). You can select or unselect any combination you choose. If you want to search a specific folder or collection of folders, just drag the folders into the window. Find will remember this group of locations for future searches; the group will receive its own button, alongside Computer, Home, and the like.

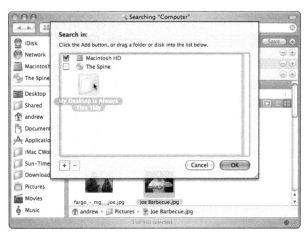

Figure 6-18
Narrowing the search by location

Narrowing the search by making it more specific

Like I said earlier, the difference between activating a Search by typing a search term in any Finder window and using the formal Find feature is that when you do it through the Finder window, it assumes you just want to search all your hard drives for one term. Which is nice and direct, but in this economy, it's possible to have hundreds of documents on your hard drive that contain the phrase "Chapter 11." If you're a professional writer, bankruptcy is complicated by the fact that you might have several books on your drive.

But Find lets you narrow things down as finely as you wish. Find puts the three handiest sub-criteria right there in the window for you. From top to bottom (check back to Figure 6-15), they let you limit the search by the kind of item, the date the file was last opened, and the last date when any changes were made to the item.

Each one of these terms has a second pop-up menu next to it, wherein you provide Find with necessary details.

If you tell Find to look for files modified within a specific range of dates, well, it's going to have to know what those dates actually are. The contents of each of these second-column popups are therefore likely change, depending on what's in the first column. Some terms will present you with a *third* column. Just go with the flow.

And as you might guess by looking, as configured, none of these default choices shown in Figure 6-15 affect your search in the slightest. They're basically saying, "Find items with this phrase, but further limit the list to 'any sort of file that was last opened at any time since Creation and the Apocalypse; ditto for the last time it was modified.'"

Enough theory: onward to Practice. Let's say you're desperate to lay your hands on a file you were working on just yesterday. You forgot where you saved it, and it's due, like, *now.* Click the menu next to Last Modified and select a relative date (Figure 6-19).

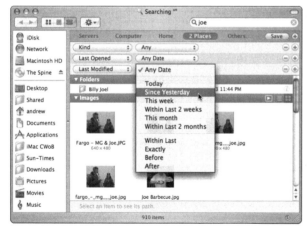

Figure 6-19
Limiting the search by Last Modified date

Or let's say you forget precisely *what* you named it. But you do know that it's a Microsoft Word file. Our search already specifies files that were modified since yesterday. Now we just need to tell it what kind of file to look for.

The popup next to Kind lists only vague, generic file types. Documents, Music, Movies, etc. But if you select Other from the bottom of the list, you can specify what kind of file you want, precisely. A new sub-search popup appears next to that menu, filled with every file type that your Mac is currently aware of (Figure 6-20).

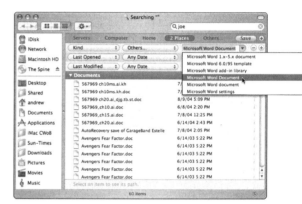

Figure 6-20
Limiting the search by file type

▼ Note

Every time you modify the terms of the search, Find automatically re-performs it so that the list of Found items always reflects exactly what you were looking for.

And notice that we've stacked two search criteria, here. Files that are Microsoft Word documents *and* which were modified sometime in the past day. You can add additional search terms by clicking on one of the + buttons at the side of the window. Figure 6-21 shows a search with . . . hang on, I gotta count 'em . . . holy cats, *nine* search terms.

So we've pretty much Ensured that this search will find absolutely nothing. To remove search terms, click the – button next to the offending item.

Figure 6-21
Using multiple — multiple multiple *multiple* — search terms.

▼ **Note**

If you can't see the + and – buttons, just resize your window to make it wider.

Spend some time exploring those submenus, too. Find can find a truly frightening number of things. Create a new search term, and then select Other from the bottom of the list of basic search types to see the full majesty of what Find can do for you (Figure 6-22).

And the list will only get longer and longer, as more application developers open up their file formats to Spotlight's all-knowing gaze.

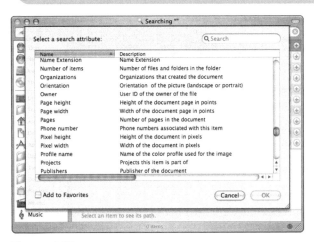

Figure 6-22
Just a small smattering of the criteria you can use when searching for stuff

PICK A SERVICE, PICK A CHALLENGE

Please, don't let the absurdity of a nine-criteria search throw you. It's stupid, but it can be *heroically* stupid. If it's 4:10 p.m. and you really have no actual work to do but you can't blow out of the office before 5:00, then think of a file, pull up Find, and try to produce a set of search criteria that pulls up that file and *only* that file ...*without searching the file's name or its contents.*

It's a fine test of mental agility, it'll get you to 5:00 p.m. without doing anything productive, and best of all, you'll be spending all that time doing the thing with the mouse and the keyboard and the screen. So you'll be presenting a breathtaking simulation of actual work to any passers-by.

TOO! FREAKING! *COOL!*

Let me give you an über-ginchy example of Tiger's file search. When I started using the first digital cameras, I created a photo project I called "240 Square." The cameras back then had a fraction of the resolution of current models, but I made it into a challenge: create photos that are clear, interesting, and tell a story … at a size of only 240 pixels by 240 pixels.

I had lots of fun, but most of these photos are now lost to the winds. I have the original files, but not the 240 x 240 edits. And they're scattered so far and so wide that there's really no point in looking for them, and even if I *had* them, organizing them would be a nightmare. I remember the hardware I shot them with, but not the places or the times.

But it's easy with Tiger. I can just do a search for "all images 240 x 240 pixels in dimension, taken with a Nikon CoolPix 770 camera" and bingo: I have all of the 240s that I produced with that camera. That's *sick*.

Saving searches, and Smart Folders

While putting together this book, I've been taking dozens and dozens of pictures of the screen. And when I assemble each chapter, I need to quickly get my hands on the most recent screen images. So I created a search for "any image file" that was "created since yesterday" and whose filename contains the name of this book. And presto, it always returns my most recent screenshots.

That's a handy search. It'd be a bummer if I had to redefine it every time I wanted to lay my hands on those images. Why, it almost makes more sense to actually keep my files organized, for God's sake!

Thankfully, it doesn't have to come down to that. All I have to do is click the Save button in the Find window. This creates a *Smart Folder,* a very special kind of Finder folder: this is a folder that always contains a list of files that match your search.

▼ **TIP**

That's not the only way to create a Smart Folder. If Smart Foldering was your evil plan all along, then you can just select New Smart Folder from the File menu. The Finder will open a standard Find window, and all proceeds from there as normal. Set up your search, click the window's Save button, and choose a place to stick the Smart Folder.

Click Save and a sheet will drop down, asking you where you'd like this folder to be created (Figure 6-23). By default, it's created in a folder in your personal Library directory called Saved Searches, but you can put it anywhere you like. The Big Idea, though, is to also have the Smart Folder in your Sidebar. Just keep that button checked, and it'll go in there automatically. Figure 6-24 shows you what a Smart Folder icon looks like. It's tattooed with a gear to make it look all sweaty and studly and stuff.

Figure 6-23
Saving a search as a Smart Folder

Figure 6-24
A Smart Folder

From then on, every time I click on the Recent Tiger Pix item in my Sidebar, I get a list of all of the Tiger screenshots I've made in the past couple of days (Figure 6-25).

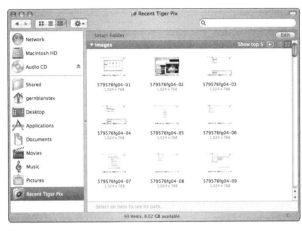

Figure 6-25
Behold! A Smart Folder In Action!

TOO! FREAKING! *COOL!* *YET AGAIN!!!*

I want you to reread this whole last section. If you're still reading this book when you return to this sidebar, then I want you to reread the section *again*. Because the first time I learned about Smart Folders, I tore my shirt off like Brandy Chastain did when she scored the winning goal in the Women's World Cup, and I ran around the house. I may or may not have kissed the FedEx guy. I know I woke up on the front step with a black eye and a box of fruit I'd ordered from the Harry & David Catalogue.

Anyway, Smart Folders is just an utterly revolutionary timesaver. It's like having an assistant who automatically keeps your files organized *for* you. Honestly, there's almost no point to organizing them yourself, any more. Just toss everything into Documents and let a set of Smart Folders organize your projects for you.

Two subtle but important distinctions:

- **The Smart Folder's contents are always "fresh."** It *always* contains every item that matches your original search term. Even if you've kept its window open for 10 days. The Smart Folder's window won't reflect just those files that matched as of 10 days ago; it'll contain all the files that match as of 10 *microseconds* ago.

- **The Smart Folder doesn't contain the actual files themselves.** It's exactly like when you do a manual Find: it contains only *references* to the files. So don't worry about the Finder moving files around on you behind your back. Still, you can open the files, copy them to additional locations, reveal their actual locations . . . everything you can do from a manual Find window.

CREATING FOLDERS

You can create new folders whenever you need them to organize your stuff:

TUNE IN TOMORROW

There's a special kind of folder that I'm not going to cover until we start talking about hard drives, CDs, and other volumes (Chapter 12). *Burn Folders* is a new Mac OS X feature and it streamlines the process of burning CDs and DVDs. You no longer have to have a disc in the drive to prepare files for burning: by dragging them into a Burn Folder, you're telling the Finder, "Okay: at *some* point in the future, I'm going to want to burn all of these onto a disc. So remember where the original copies of all of these files are, and how I've arranged all these icons, and be ready to burn it when I ask you to."

1. **Open the disk or folder in which you want the new folder to appear.**

2. **With the parent disk or folder active, select File→New Folder or press Shift+⌘+N.**

3. **Change the folder's default name ("Untitled Folder") to whatever name you need.**

TRASHING THINGS

Hard disks fill up a lot faster than you think, and it's not hard to end up with a lot of files that you no longer use. When you're ready to clean house, you can delete folders and files:

1. **Drag the items you want to delete to the Trash Can icon in the Dock.**

   Alternatively, you can select the items and press ⌘+Delete.

2. **Select Finder → Empty Trash.**

   Alternatively, you can press Shift+⌘+Delete to empty the Trash Can.

▼ Caution

When you move a folder to the Trash Can, you also move everything that the folder contains. Emptying the Trash Can deletes the folder and all its contents.

The Trash Can is a window identical to every other Finder window. You can open it by clicking on its icon in the Dock. As long as you haven't emptied the Trash, you can drag any item out of the Trash Can window and return it to its original location.

OS X asks you to confirm emptying the Trash. If you find the warning too annoying to deal with, then (a) you need to find a soothing hobby, or perhaps take a yoga class, and (b) you can turn off the warning through the Finder's Preferences box.

TIGER'S VIRTUAL SHREDDER

When you empty the Trash normally, the Finder merely notes that it can now overwrite the real estate the data once occupied with new data. The original files are still there, somewhere, and you can retrieve them with a simple utility that looks for stray cattle, so to speak.

If you're trashing sensitive data, use Tiger's Secure Empty Trash option. The Finder will "shred" the data before deleting, making it darn-near impossible for anybody to ever recover the data. Including *you*, so use it carefully.

MOVING THINGS AROUND

Just drag whatever-it-is from wherever-it-is-now to wherever-you-want-it-to go. Simple, eh?

Yes, for users. For people writing books about simple-to-use operating systems, it's a nightmare. This elegant mechanism does lots of different things, depending on the "where-you-want-it-to-go" bit. Two case studies:

- **You drag a file from your Documents folder to your Pictures folder.** Both folders are on the same volume (your Mac's built-in hard drive) so the file moves from the old location to the new one.

- **You drag a file from your Documents folder to a folder on an external drive,** like your iPod or one of those cool key rings with 128 megs of flash storage. The two locations aren't on the same volume, so the file *is copied* to the new location. Two copies now exist.

Okay, but what if you wanted to *copy* that file from the Documents folder over to your Pictures folder? You have to hold down the Option key sometime before you let go of the file. A green circle with a white plus sign will be added to the mouse pointer, to clue you in that you're about to move a copy and not the original.

Okay, but what if you wanted to *move* that file from your internal hard drive to the external one, instead of copying it? This one's tricky: you have to hold down the ⌘ key. But you have to click it *after* you've selected the file or files, and *before* you let go. It's times like these when I question my faith in a correct and orderly universe.

THE BEAUTY OF SPRING-LOADED FOLDERS

Apple has given us a great timesaver in the form of *spring-loaded folders*. Let's say you don't actually want to move that file into Pictures. You actually want it to go into Paintings Of My Dog, a folder inside a folder named Paintings that's inside the Pictures folder. You have to somehow uncover that destination folder so you can drag something into it, yes?

No. Just drag it on top of Pictures, *but don't let go of the mouse button.* After a pause, the folder opens on its own, revealing its contents. Hold it over Paintings for a bit and that, too, will open up and then drag it over Paintings Of My Dog and let go. In it goes, and the Finder snaps all those folders closed behind you, neat and clean. You can modify this behavior (or turn it off entirely) via Finder Preferences.

If you don't want to wait, holding down the space bar springs the folder open immediately. I have somehow taught myself how to play an F#m6, the toughest chord possible on the ukulele; so trust me, you can train your fingers to work this shortcut.

CUSTOM LABELS

Custom labels let you color code files and folders. This is particularly useful if you want, for example, to identify all files that belong to a single project or that have a similar status (for example, "need to be faxed"). You can spot all the red files at a glance, and when you want to collect all of your project assets together, you can do a Find on that label. It's very handy, particularly if you have an assistant or a boss who can barely summon enough intelligence to successfully pour water out of a boot with instructions printed on the heel.

POINT AND SHOOT WITH LABELS

Labeling files and folders is also handy when you're creating workflows and scripts with Automator and AppleScript. Remember when you had your property landscaped? A guy came by and put orange tape around all of the trees that he wanted the removal guy to cut down? You can use labels the same way. Select files as you work your way through the Finder, and then run an Automator workflow that says, "Okay. You know all the files that are colored red? I want you to copy them all into a new folder, summarize them, and then email my boss with this folder as an attachment, with the summary as the actual message text."

It's awfully helpful when all the files you want an Automator workflow to work with can't be readily described any other way.

In icon view, a labeled icon appears with the label color as a background to the icon's name. In list or column view, the entire row for the icon has the colored background; if you select a row, a dot in the label color appears to the left of the icon name (see Figure 6-26).

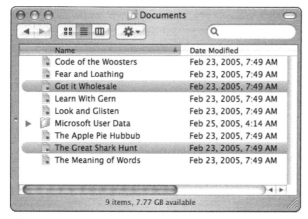

Figure 6-26
Two files in list view, with labels

To apply a custom label:

1. **Select the item or items to which you want to apply the custom label.**

2. **Drop down the end of the File menu and select the color of the label you want to apply, as in Figure 6-27.**

   You can also hold down the Control key and click on the item, and then select the label you want from the resulting contextual menu. Labels are also available in the file or folder's Get Info window.

Figure 6-27
Choosing a custom label

To remove a label from an icon, repeat the preceding procedure, selecting the X at the left of the bottom line in the menu.

Although you can't change the label colors or have more than seven labels, you can customize the text for each label. To do so, try this:

1. **Select Finder→Preferences.**

   The Preferences window appears.

2. **Click the Labels button in the toolbar.**

   This displays the Labels pane (Figure 6-28).

3. **Edit the label text as desired.**

Figure 6-28
Changing custom label text

GETTING INFORMATION ABOUT FILES AND FOLDERS

Everything we've talked about with files and folders so far just has to do with common, everyday, work. But there's a lot of additional information associated with these things that you don't normally need to see, and a bunch of extra features that are subtle enough that they really have no natural place anywhere in the Finder's menus or buttons.

And that's why you can select a file, folder, app, or volume and select Get Info from either the Finder's File menu or the item's contextual menu.

Exactly what you see depends on the type of icon selected, and we'll be covering a lot of the entity-specific stuff in later chapters. Figure 6-29 is the Get Info window for a hard drive.

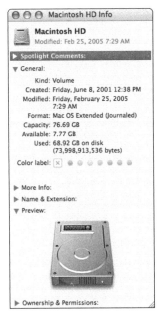

Figure 6-29
The Get Info window for a hard drive

Some elements are common to most Get Info boxes, however:

- **Spotlight Comments:** We learn about Spotlight in Chapter 7, and we knackled the bejeezus out of it in the "Finding Files" section of this chapter. Spotlight can search for information without your ever having to manually describe any of your files, folders, or volumes. But if you *want* to, you can add some Spotlight-specific comments in the item's Get Info box. If the word *Rutles* appears nowhere in a certain document, but you were listening to a Rutles album while you wrote it and you think that's somehow a detail that you might want to search for later, just slap the word in here.

 Tip

And remember, Humans can read these comments, too. So if the file is a JPEG of the company logo and you want to make a comment that this version is supposed to be used on websites only, *not* on printed material ... the Comments area of Get Info is as good a place as any.

- **General:** And it's Trivia Night here at Get Info. All of the numbers and tech details you could possibly be interested in — not all of the tech detail *possible,* but please: there are limits — are listed here.

- **More Info:** Click on this triangle to reveal additional trivia. At minimum, it'll tell you the last time this item was opened.

- **Name and Extension:** Possibly the most needlessly difficult way to rename a file, folder, or volume, but if you're into punishment, yeah, you can rename an item here. But it's an easy way to determine a file name's extension. The Finder says its name is Learn With Gern, but Get Info tells you it's actually Learn With Gern.*rtf.* And you'll be a better person for knowing. Well, not really. But at least now you know something you didn't know earlier. And knowing is half the battle.

- **Preview:** Shows you an icon that represents the file in the Finder and in file listings.

- **Ownership & Permissions:** This is the Deep Voodoo part of Get Info, and it's explained in greater detail in Chapter 11 (Files & Folders). When you modify the Ownership and Permissions of a file, you can either expand or limit what other users can do to this item. For instance, doing a Get Info on your Pictures folder, you can arrange so that everybody on your Macintosh

can work with this folder. Or, you can arrange so that everyone can view its contents, but can't modify it. Or! Allow people to *add* things to the folder, but not allow them to do so much as look inside it.

Figures 30 and 31 show you the Get Info boxes of a typical folder and file. There are a few differences: you'll spot a "Locked" box on both of them, and the document's Get Info also has features that let you make this file into something called a *Stationery File,* and choose which app opens the file when it's double-clicked. Again, I'll explain these features in the "Files and Folders" chapter (Chapter 11).

Figure 6-30
Getting Info on a folder

And just so we can say, "Good Lord, now we've seen it all!" let's take a gander at the Get Info of the iTunes app (Figure 6-32).

Figure 6-31
The Get Info details of a document, laid shamingly bare

Figure 6-32
iTunes struggles to avoid scrutiny ... but it's wasted effort! Hahaha!

In an App's Get Info box, we see that it's got categories that organize all of the non-English languages that the app supports, and if the app's functionality can be extended through plug-ins, there's a category where they can be viewed, added, and removed. More about this in Chapter 9.

The Finder is one of the things that makes the Mac community so uniquely itself. We've had versions of the Finder since System 1.0, which came on the very first Macintosh in 1984. So by now, we really don't question its role in the Macintosh operating system any more.

If you've ever driven a car in the Boston area, traffic rotaries have the exact same function with we natives. You're driving along, humming with the song on your iPod, when the road abruptly dead-ends in a round patch of greenery about 20 yards across. You have to immediately *jerk* the wheel to the right, throwing yourself in orbit around the bit of grass and trees with every other driver.

Oh, did I mention that about five or six different roads all dead-end into the same place?

MY ENVIRONMENTALLY CORRECT STRATEGY FOR SHOWING YOU HOW TO USE GET INFO

I'm going to say something disappointing; then I'm going to give you some valuable information that you'll use several times a year for the rest of your life, to make it up to you.

Disappointing: there are some bits under Get Info that, in a longer book, would merit a whole chapter, "Ownership and Permissions," for example. Now *there's* some sweet mojo. The stuff you can do — both "totally not evil at all" and, well, the other thing — is fantastic. But alas, deforestation is a huge problem. I don't know what this "ozone" stuff is, but lots of folks seem to get themselves all lathered up over it and it's just simpler to limit the number of pages of this book than to get into that whole big rhubarb again.

So instead of giving specific detail to everything you'll find in Get Info, I've chosen to pepper the rest of the book with ways to use it effectively. When I talk about folders later on, I'll tell you how to use Get Info to make one of your folders into a "drop box" that other folks using your Mac or the network can see and copy files into ... but not open.

The Useful Advice: The theme to *Gilligan's Island* was based on a rather ancient sea song, the same tune that was morphed into Amazing Grace, coincidentally. So it is both possible and highly amusing to sing the inspirational lyrics to the greatest hymn ever written to the tune of the worst piece of junk that Sherwood Schwartz ever put on the air.

See? I told you it'd be worth it.

And you spin around and around and around, with each revolution trying to figure out which of these four or five (or is it seven or eight?) spoke roads is the logical continuation of the one that you've just left. After about 30 minutes of this, you've given up any hope of making it to your destination and will settle for merely escaping this hellish carousel with your car and your life intact.

Yet it's perfectly normal to me. "Okay, just turn off right here," I coached a friend visiting from out of state, as she spun around a rotary on the VFW Parkway. "What the

**** do you *mean?!?"* she yelled. "This whole ***-****ed thing is nothing *but* turns!!!"

So I sympathize. If you're a Mac person, you simply blipped right over the Finder concept. If you're coming from a place outside of the Shire, you might feel yourself spinning around and around, asking yourself if the road you're looking for is the one after the Dunkin' Donuts or just before it. Either way, you're very close to hot, fresh donuts . . . so can your life really be going all that poorly?

Spotlight Dance

In This Chapter

The Big Deal • Finding Info through the Spotlight Menu
Spotlight Preference and Security

If they were running a couple of BaBar-related electron-positron collisions on the big linear accelerator over at Stanford, and some joker in the Personnel department decided that *this* was a perfect time to see what happens when you put a mirror in a microwave oven, and the biggest doggone transdimensional rip in the fabric of space-time formed and historical figures started tumbling out into the present, boy, don't even *ask* me to come on over and teach these sorry bastards about life in these Modern Times. My mind is too finely tuned into the triumphant importance of Infrastructure as the true signature of progress.

I'd slap the iPod out of Mozart's hand, insisting that the *really* cool thing was the Internet . . . the infrastructure that connects any computer on the planet to the secure servers of the iTunes Music Store. Leonardo da Vinci would be desperately clawing to get past me and take a closer look at my automobile, but nothing doing: I want him to get a load of this here orange, and impress upon him the fact that thanks to the interstate highway system and the trucking industry, fresh produce can be shipped from anywhere *to* anywhere right at the peak of flavor.

It wouldn't end happily. We'd just end up with a whole bunch of honked-off Elizabethans and Babylonians on our hands.

No, topics like this one are more up my street. Spotlight is probably the single coolest new feature of Tiger. To say that "Spotlight adds awesome new features for finding information on your Mac's hard drive" puts it succinctly but it doesn't even nick the paint. Spotlight is, indeed, right up there with the highways and the Internet: it's a fundamental resource that all of your Mac's software can exploit and enjoy in a million different ways. And while Spotlight does indeed present a very visible face to you, the user — dig the Spotlight menu on the right corner of your menu bar — like the highway system, you'll reap most of its benefits without even being particularly aware that Spotlight is playing any role at all.

THEY CALL IT THE SEEKER

So what's got me so amped up about Spotlight? Have I just had too much candy this afternoon or something? After all, if you look at the blurbs on the box that your copy of Tiger came in, Spotlight gets just a few sober lines that probably left you thinking "Hey, wow, a tool for finding files. Like, *whoopee.*"

Okay. I'm going to encourage you to think differently, here.

 Note

Apple slogan: "Think Different.™" Note my version, which (a) shows a mastery of proper grammar and (b) is just dissimilar enough that I don't have to send Apple the three-cent royalty for use of their trademarked slogan.

You're nonplussed by this feature because you're thinking in pre-Spotlight terms. Has it ever occurred to you that all previous methods of finding info on your Mac . . . well, that they all stink like a tub of shrimp salad that's been sitting in the trunk of your car since it tumbled out of a sack of groceries three months ago and landed in the wheel well?

THINK LOCALLY, ACT . . . UM, LOCALLY AS WELL, I SUPPOSE

One thing you should get straight right away: Spotlight doesn't search the Internet. It can only find information on the volumes that are attached to your Mac: your hard drives, your iDisk, any networked volumes that you've connected to through Ethernet or AirPort . . . that sort of stuff. To search for information out there on the Internet, click into Safari , or use Sherlock, the Internet search tool that comes with Tiger.

Yes, pre-Tiger methods of finding info — the Finder's "find" command and the individual Find commands of each of the 3 to 1,300 apps on your Mac worked well. Good for *them.* But! In the pre-Spotlight world:

- **An app's "Find" feature can only find a limited assortment of things.** The Finder could only find files. It had a *limited* ability to search for files depending on their content (a document containing "Ish Kabibble") but chiefly it could only search through file names. Your Mail app could only look through emails. Microsoft Word could only look through Microsoft Word files. That stinks.

- **Each "Find" feature works differently.** Naturally, there's no one-size-fits-all solution that works for every user-interface problem. The handle of a steak knife has to be shaped differently than the handle of a tennis racket, for example.

Note

Unless you're using the steak knife to cut up your tennis racket, a little tip that vastly improved my tennis game after years of desperate lessons and comedic play.

Still, there's absolutely no consistency. If you're the absolute master of BBEdit's (ginchy and powerful) "Find" feature, it won't help you perform searches in any other app. You've got to learn brand-new skills with every new piece of software you acquire. I wish to suggest that this, too, *stinks*.

- **Giving an app the ability to Find stuff is the sole responsibility of the app's programmers.** I'm not asking you to show an unusual level of sympathy for programmers. They're well paid and I can vouch for the fact that the world is their oyster. Men want to be them. Even women programmers; the average male would count himself lucky to attain the standard of living and social palatability of a female programmer, and the need to have all of his shirts re-tailored is a mere inconvenience in light of the many advantages. But while Find is a basic feature of, for instance, a word processor, any app that works with information (in case you're scoring along at home, the answer is "all of them") can be improved by allowing the user to search for stuff.

But writing a search routine can be a lot of work, and if you're working on an app that doesn't *need* that feature, the temptation to just call it a day, ship the software as-is, and then go out with your coworkers for waffles and margaritas is overwhelming. I would put it to you that the tendency of this phenomenon to trend toward malofactoriness is well-documented.

Spotlight solves all of these problems:

- **Spotlight is a fundamental technology that's available to every piece of software running on your Mac.** So if I'm writing a new piece of software, I'm now *eager* to put in search features. With Spotlight, 90 percent of the work's already been done for me; it's not as simple as designing a lamp and plugging it into an existing wall outlet, but it's close enough.

- **Spotlight offers a certain amount of consistency from app to app.** You'll still see a lot of variety, but because all Tiger apps will be using the same underlying engine for searches, you won't have to completely relearn How To Search For Information every time you buy a new piece of software.

But most importantly:

- **Spotlight can search EVERYTHING.** If I'm looking for Ish Kabibble on my hard drive, I don't have to click into nine different apps and do eleven different searches (taking into account that I sometimes misspell it with two sets of double-b's instead of just one and would have to correct the search in those cases). I can do just one search and Spotlight will locate that phrase everywhere it occurs. Word processor documents. My address book and my calendar. Emails. iChats. Photos, if I've used that phrase in an iPhoto caption. Presentations. No kiddin': *everywhere*.

I sense that it's time for me to start winding down the sermon and to cue the choir to start singing "Rock of Ages" while I pass the collection plate. I'll make with the practical info shortly. But I hope this sinks in: Spotlight changes how you interact with your Mac and it'll also change the way that Mac software is written.

OKAY, AN EXAMPLE

A couple of weeks ago, I installed a way-cool 3D interactive globe and atlas app (3D Weather Globe & Atlas by MacKiev, if you're curious). As the name implies, it's an electronic atlas: type **Boston** in its Search field, and it pops out a list of three major cities whose names contain that word. Click on the Massachusetts edition and the globe twists and pivots for a second, ultimately stopping when the city's centered in the window and duly labeled with a pointer.

Cool. But imagine what this app could do when it's updated for Tiger, and takes advantage of Spotlight. Instead of typing in a city name, I could type in **Cousin Tig**. Behind the scenes, the app would then ask Spotlight, "Look, the dude is looking for a location called 'Cousin Tig.' Does that make *any* sense at all?" And Spotlight says, "Sure ... see, right here in his Address Book: Andy has a listing for a Cousin Tig Ihnatko in Australia." "Cool!" the Atlas says, using the vernacular of the software/Operating System culture. And the globe spins to Sydney, Australia, which is now labeled with my cousin's home address and everything.

GET TO THE GOOD STUFF ALREADY: USING SPOTLIGHT

As you might have guessed already from the breathless doggerel presented in the preceding section, Spotlight is everywhere in Tiger, like the routines that draw menus, windows, and icons. Or love.

Basic searching

But certainly the most obvious and direct spot to take advantage of Spotlight is in the brand-new spiffy Spotlight

menu at the extreme-right edge of the menu bar (Figure 7-1).

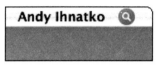

Figure 7-1
Spotlight: Blue Dot of Destiny

Give 'er a click and it opens up into a humble little text field (Figure 7-2).

Figure 7-2
Spotlight's sincere utterance of "What is thy bidding, my master?" is implied by the flashing cursor.

 Tip
You can also activate the Spotlight menu by holding down the Command key and pressing the spacebar.

Let's look for "Look." As soon as you start typing, Spotlight starts searching. Once I've taken my hands off the keyboard, the menu is chock-full of hits (Figure 7-3).

Spotlight starts returning results almost immediately, which makes you immediately nervous: you've got 80 gigabytes (GB) of stuff on your drive, and the ability to find data this quickly can only be acquired through a compact with the Cloven-Hooved One.

That is indeed one way to go about it. Or you can do what Spotlight does: every time information is written to your hard drive, Spotlight indexes it so it can locate that info later on. This is why Spotlight only works with certain file types, or with apps that have been upgraded to work with Spotlight technology.

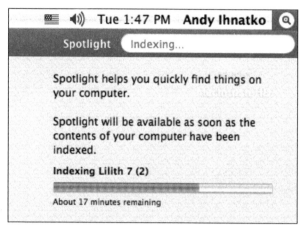

Figure 7-4
Talk Amongst Yourselves: Spotlight indexes your whole hard drive the first time you ever use it.

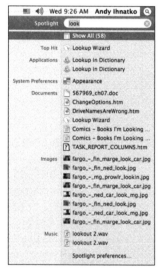

Figure 7-3
The look of love: Spotlight's immediate search results

The first time you start up a new Tiger installation, Spotlight won't be available for a little while. Or maybe a long while. Possibly not until you've had time to make breakfast, eat breakfast, clean up all the dishes and pans, wrap up the leftovers, and drive them over to the homeless shelter and come back. After seeing a movie.

See, if you've upgraded an old Mac (with a hard drive loaded with information) then Spotlight has to examine all of your existing data and index it all. This can take anywhere from a half an hour to half an afternoon. Instead of immediate search results, you'll see a progress indicator like the one shown in Figure 7-4. Be warned.

Spotlight puts the *Top Hit* at the top of the list, and organizes other matches by kind. It chooses the Top Hit based on . . . okay, well, let's call it Elfin Magic. Proprietary information, and all that. But usually, Spotlight will look at all of the content that matches your search term, and put the most recently accessed file at the top of the heap. So the Top Hit is going to be the file that you created just this morning, not the one that was on your hard drive when you bought your Mac four years ago and never opened even once.

You probably expected Spotlight to give you a list of documents, images, and even music files that contained that word . . . but hey, cool: it also found it in apps, and apparently the Appearance section of my System Preferences has something to do with "look." Makes sense: you use the Appearance panel to make some choices regarding the overall looks of your Mac.

Tip

Spotlight's ability to locate apps makes it a kick-butt application launcher. Let's say you need to run Tiger's Disk Utility app. But it isn't in the Dock. You could either open the Applications folder and then open the Utilities folder ... or you could just tap ⌘-Spacebar to open Spotlight, type **Disk**, and then click on Disk Utility from the list of results.

Wait . . . check out the list: it found the word inside *Music?*

When I'm arguing about the superiority of the Mac platform and I'm starting to feel just a little bit defensive, sure . . . I'll make the bald-faced lie that Spotlight actually listens to every song in my iTunes library and tries to find the search word or phrase somewhere in the lyrics. But in truth, it's only searching through the descriptive info that's attached to the song file: the name of the artist, the title of the song and the album . . . that sort of stuff.

But remember: it isn't really a lie so long as *you* believe it to be true. So forget that I said anything.

Anyway, are you getting the idea that Spotlight is the bee's knees in the cat's pajamas?

You can open any of these items by just selecting it from the menu. The Spotlight menu disappears and Tiger shows you the item, launching the app that created it if it has to.

 Tip

Spotlight searches are "Sticky." If you were to click on the Spotlight menu again 10 minutes or 10 hours later you'd find all the results of your last search, right where you left them.

THE CATCH . . . YEAH, THERE'S A CATCH

But there's only one, and it's not so bad. Out of the box, Spotlight can only index and search through a set list of data types. It's a good list: Spotlight can search through all documents created by Microsoft Office, iLife, AppleWorks, iWork, Photoshop, and nearly every popular file format that exists (like JPEG, PNG, and PDF) ... it's a long list.

But Spotlight can't just magically understand *every* kind of data that all of your apps store on your drive. So if there's a type of data that isn't supported by Spotlight out-of-the-box, the app that creates it will need a little update so that its files and data can be tossed into the Spotlight soup. Usually, this just requires that you download a little plug-in file and toss it into your /Library/Spotlight/ directory. The big lesson, though, is not to expect Spotlight to behave as a blind man suddenly gifted with sight. A certain laying-of-hands with your individual apps will be necessary.

SERIOUSLY, HOW COOL IS THIS?

Yup, Spotlight will find terms in apps, too. Abuse this quirk! I keep all of my *most* favorite apps right in the Dock where they're handy ... but Spotlight gives me nigh-instant access to every app on my hard drive. I rarely have to use the AirPort Admin Utility but when I do, I don't have to click through my Applications and Utilities folder. I just click on Spotlight, type **AirPort**, and select the app from the list of results. No muss, no fuss, no pans to clean up afterward.

Gawking at the full monty: the Results window

But that's not *all* of the matches that Spotlight found. To give you the broadest swath of results, Spotlight loads up the menu with just the first few of each kind. To see *everything* that Spotlight found, select Show All, which opens up the full Spotlight Results Window (Figure 7-5).

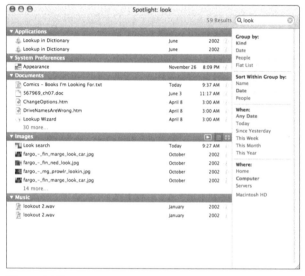

Figure 7-5
More detailed search results

Spotlight still groups its results by type, and still only shows you the top few results of each kind . . . but clicking on the "More . . . " will expand the list and allow you to see the alpha through the omega, as it were.

Here, you can easily get more information about the stuff that Spotlight found. Right off the bat, Spotlight shows you the date and time that the item was last opened (or the month and the year, if the item hasn't been opened since the calendar turned). You can get more info by

clicking on the item's info icon, to the right of the item's date (Figure 7-6).

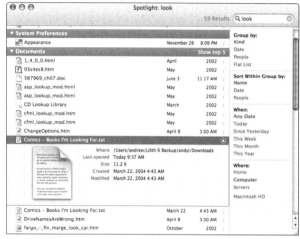

Figure 7-6
More info about a document that Spotlight found for me

This helps you to figure out which one of these five (ten . . . hundred . . . thousand) documents is the one that's going to save your butt if you can locate it and email it to your boss in the next seven minutes. Click on the icon again to make the added info go away.

At minimum, Spotlight can show you trivia like what you see in Figure 7-5. But if the item is a picture, a PDF, or a music file, it can show you a preview of the actual item. Check out the "Images" section of our search results: its header actually contains three buttons that let us preview its contents three different ways:

- The horizontal lines represent the default list view.

- The one that looks like four boxes switches to a thumbnail view (Figure 7-7).

- Push the Play button and Spotlight will run a slideshow of all the images (Figure 7-8).

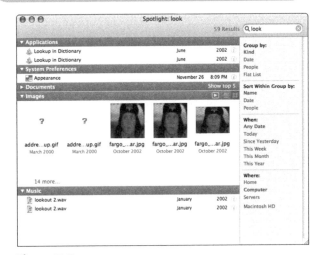

Figure 7-7
Examining image thumbnails

Figure 7-8
Getting a good hairy look at Spotlight's image results, with Slideshow mode

The whole Mac interface hides itself away so you can focus just on these images. It's very much like an iPhoto slideshow: if you move your mouse, a big, fat, friendly palette of buttons will appear at the bottom of the screen for moving forward and backward through the list of images. The button that looks like four boxes will fill the screen with thumbnails; the icon with the arrows in the corners will cause the current image to fill the entire screen; clicking the camera icon will add the current image to your iPhoto image; and clicking the "X" will pop you out of the slideshow and back to the land of milk and honey known as The Usual Mac Experience.

The Results Window also gives you some added features for sorting and examining your search results. On the right-hand side of the Results Window you'll find a number of display options:

- **Group By:** Normally, Spotlight's Results menu clumps together all results that are of the same type: you get a list of documents, followed by a list of images, followed by a list of music files, etc. It might be more useful to clump the results together by date or author. So if you're managing a project and you've got 11 people working under you, you can quickly zero in on just the search results that came from Gern Blanstev, for instance.

- **Sort Within Group By:** Changes the sort order within each "clump," according to the criterion you click on.

Both of these options just change the sort order of the results. The other two options will remove results that don't match a simple filter:

- **When:** Limits the results, by date. You might have found 1,100 emails containing the phrase "This company is doomed," if you're just interested in the ones that came in within the last week, after your CEO made the national news by bidding $130,000 in an online auction for a chicken nugget that sort of looks like Alben Barkley, Vice-President under the Truman administration.

- **Where:** By default, Spotlight searches your entire Computer. Meaning, your entire hard drive and every volume that's attached to it. But if that's too much to deal with, you can narrow it to just your "Home" (your personal user directory), "Servers" (just any remote file servers you're connected to), or just one individual physical volume (just your external hard drive and not the internal one, for example). You can also drag an individual folder or volume icon right into the search list to limit the search to just that specific location.

▼ Note

Spotlight plays nice: even though you're searching the entire Computer or the entire hard drive for results, it won't show you any results that you don't have permission to see. So a Spotlight search for "Spock" will return your collection of *Star Trek* photos and film clips, but it *won't* return that big folder of smutty fan-fiction from your spouse's private user directory. And as you see in the next section, it also won't return search results from any folder you've designated as off-limits.

What's left in that Results menu? Oh, yeah: you've got what looks like another standard Spotlight search field there in the upper-right corner. You can click into it and start a brand-new search if you've got the strength.

▼ Tip

Spotlight understands a bunch of different modifier words. So if I wanted to find documents containing the word "look" that I opened today, I could have just entered "look today" and Spotlight would have given them to me without any further ado.

SPOTLIGHT PREFERENCES AND SECURITY

You can customize Spotlight through System Preferences (or by selecting Spotlight Preferences . . . at the bottom of the Spotlight menu). Viz, Figure 7-9.

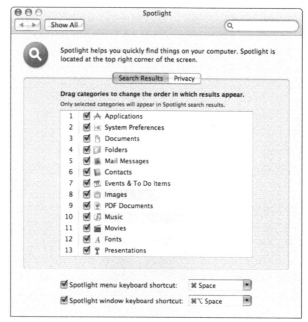

Figure 7-9
Giving Spotlight a li'l tweak

Tweaking search results

The Preferences window is dominated by a list of all of the different categories of info that Spotlight has been trained to deal with. The list is presented in the order in which search results will appear in the Spotlight menu.

SECONDS-WISE, HOURS-FOOLISH

Admittedly, we're only talking about a savings of about a half a second every time you do a search and you wind up clicking on an image instead of a phone number. But over the course of a year, that could add up to, what ... 10 minutes? It takes you that long to shave (if you're a man) or to shave one leg (if you're a woman, or if you're a man who's into that sort of thing). So if you reorder your Spotlight search results judiciously, you'll have no excuse for heading out of the house looking like a mess: you'll always have time, because you've got 10 bonus minutes coming to you. They don't roll over at the end of the year, so you might as well use 'em.

You can change the order just by dragging items up and down in the list. If you tend to search for images and PDF files a lot more often than contacts and appointments, for instance, you can save yourself a great many keystrokes and mouse clicks by placing the former two above the latter two.

Each category also has a checkbox. Any unchecked items won't appear in the Spotlight menu's search results. It's a good way to cut down on clutter.

Tweaking keyboard shortcuts

Spotlight gives you two different keyboard shortcuts: there's a shortcut for activating the Spotlight menu, and one for activating the Spotlight window. To change either shortcut, you can select an alternative via the popup menu or just highlight the shortcut by clicking on it, and then hit the key sequence you want to use from now on.

Spotlight privacy and security

I've saved the scary bit for the very end: by making all of the info on your hard drive subject to lightning-searches, Spotlight *probably* represents a terrifying threat to your personal privacy.

"Possibly," maybe?

Hmm, best not to sugarcoat it. Look, Spotlight is a powerful search function. *Without* such a powerful resource, there's really no point for a no-goodnik (foreign or domestic) to paw through your hard drive. There's just so much data stored there, and so little of it is of any value to an outsider. It makes sense for the weasel to steal your Macintosh and then look through its contents at the weasel's leisure, but how can they find anything with just five or ten minutes' worth of keyboard time? There's just no point.

But *with* Spotlight? A weasel with a moment's access to your Mac can type something like "invoice" or "mastercard" or "PIN number" or "unlisted number" or "confidential." Spotlight will happily spit out the goods in seconds. The miscreant is fishing blind, but he or she can get a quick yea or nay well before you come back from the bathroom, and a minute's worth of distraction can yield all kinds of sensitive info.

You're armed against these miscreants with two weapons, though. First, like I said earlier, when Spotlight is running on a Mac with several user accounts, it won't display any search results that the current user shouldn't have access to. So if you do a search for "Scooby," it'll return all the results from your own user directory, everything from shared folders on your hard drive, and everything from the top directory of your Mac . . . but nothing from, say, someone else's Documents folder.

The more serious solution is to tell Spotlight that certain folders on your hard drive are off-limits to searches. You do this through the Privacy tab of Spotlight's preferences (Figure 7-10).

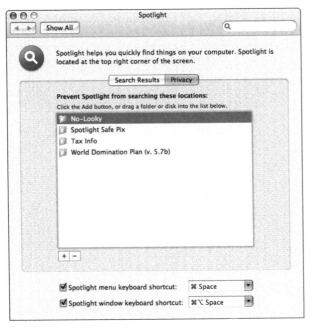

Figure 7-10
Hiding specific folders from Spotlight's all-seeing eye

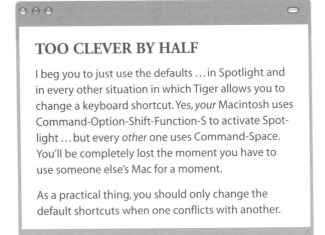

TOO CLEVER BY HALF

I beg you to just use the defaults … in Spotlight and in every other situation in which Tiger allows you to change a keyboard shortcut. Yes, *your* Macintosh uses Command-Option-Shift-Function-S to activate Spotlight … but every *other* one uses Command-Space. You'll be completely lost the moment you have to use someone else's Mac for a moment.

As a practical thing, you should only change the default shortcuts when one conflicts with another.

NOT A PEOPLE PERSON

Actually, when I think about Spotlight's privacy problems, I don't think about coworkers or visitors stealing credit-card numbers. I think more about husbands or wives searching for phrases like "nude photos" or "secret bank account" or "No, Thursday's perfect; my husband or wife won't suspect a thing." And my parents raised me to *trust* people, so I can only blame television for this dim outlook on trust and human nature.

Clicking the + button at the bottom of the list allows you to choose a folder. These folders will then be invisible to Spotlight's searches. As you can see from Figure 7-9, it's just a good idea to create a few specific Black Holes into which you store your most sensitive data.

If later on, you realize that the World Domination Plan was pretty stupid to begin with (a secret headquarters inside a dormant volcano . . . okay. But a secret headquarters inside a dormant volcano *in space?* That's just impractical) and you want to remove that folder from the Dead Pool, just select it in the list and click the – button.

The weakness of this whole chapter is that I start it off by bleating on endlessly about how Spotlight is more than a search utility. Good God, it's a revolution in desktop computing but it's certainly *not* just a desktop search utility. And then . . . um . . . I spent the whole chapter explaining how to use Spotlight as a desktop search utility.

Well, that's just the nature of the beast. Spotlight is, indeed, everywhere. It's in the Find function in the Finder, and its Smart Folders feature. It's in Mail, through its Smart Mailboxes feature. It's in System Preferences, and it kicks in every time you use the little search box to find out which Preference you need to click to change your desktop wallpaper.

It's that most subtle and elusive sort of feature: unlike the Dock or Exposé, it's not a feature in and of itself. In truth, it's a feature that allows other features to happen.

One last piece of business before we move on to the next chapter: When I said, "That's the nature of the beast," there were 11 of you who assumed I was citing my

(totally not true) tendency to start off a chapter one way and end it another way. I know who you are — particularly *you,* Ryan — and when the invitations go out for the big Everyone Who Bought My Book And Didn't Think Mean And Uncalled-For Things About Me While They Read It Barbecue And Mud Football Tournament, well, you'll have plenty of time that Saturday to sit alone and *think* about The Golden Rule.

The Dock, and Why It Doesn't Stink Even a Little

In This Chapter

Meet the Dock • Dock Basics • What Dock Icons Do
Adding To and Deleting From the Dock • Bouncing Icons • Contextual Menus
But What If the Dock Still Stinks? • One Final Word …

When Apple introduced the Dock, it was the single worst thing they had done to anger the Mac community since they advertised the iMac with the slogan "Power. Speed. Style. Affordability. Oh, and your mother washes her hair with gravy."

As bad as all that sounds, it's even worse because I just made up that thing about the iMac to sort of soften things a little. So in truth, dropping the Dock on everybody was in fact probably the biggest shock Apple ever dealt. At the time, many folks had an almost genetic-level revulsion to the Dock the same way we humans are programmed against cannibalism. Which seemed a bit overly theatrical to me.

Many new Mac users have sort of an iffy initial reaction to it, too. But please. *Please*. Use the dock until you learn to love it because I promise you (in that fashion where it's understood that I don't actually have to send you any money if I'm wrong) that you will indeed learn to love it. I don't go through life pointing out The Casual Simplicity and Elegance of the Macintosh Operating System, but if I *were* paid to travel the country in a customized bus and do exactly that, the Dock would be my main demonstration. Visually, it's so simple . . . yet this nonthreatening row of icons does a lot of heavy lifting, taking the roles of program launchbar, document manager, taskbar, status panel, and Lord knows what else. And if you don't like having all that sexy power staring you in the face all the time, you can set it up so that it pops into view with a flick of the mouse and disappears discreetly when you're done with it, like a well-trained butler, or possibly an idealized murder weapon.

As it stands, the mechanical pen that switches from a ballpoint to a pencil to a highlighter to a PDA stylus with a single twist of the cap remains the acme of American ingenuity and simplicity. But the Dock's a close second, I reckon.

MEET THE DOCK

First off, let's thoroughly explain what the Dock is and what it does:

It's a place to put stuff. Moving on . . .

DOCK SCRIPTING VIA PYTHON/PERL

Using a C++-like syntax and a moderate knowledge of Unix, it's possible to automate Dock functions from any shell command. With . . .

NO, SERIOUSLY, MEET THE DOCK

But I don't want to make the basic explanation any more complicated than that. Really. "The Dock is a place where you put stuff, so it's handy later." Memorize that phrase (write it on the back of your hand, if you want to; this isn't the SATs), and you're golden.

I'll explain it another way. As I write this, I'm sitting on the sofa in my office and I've got my PowerBook in my lap. Obviously, the Mac is the thing I'm focused on right now. But on the cushion next to me, you'll find my phone, the remote for the TV and stereo, and a reference book. On the table to my right, there's my ukulele, a soothing beverage, and (because I've got a bear of a cold right now) a box of tissues.

 Note

Keeping a ukulele next to your Mac at all times is just plain good, common sense and this practice shouldn't be mocked.

Technically, each of those things belongs elsewhere in the house, but having them within reach makes me more productive. I don't have to get up and trot to the desk when the phone rings, when I need to sneeze I just need to make a quick reach, and if a quick strum of "Honey Pie," enhances my relentless pursuit of *le mot juste*, then enhanced it shall be.

That's the deal with the Dock. You drag useful applications, files, and folders into it. And they'll always be just a mouse-gesture away, no matter what you're doing at the moment. Viz:

- **It keeps essential apps in reach.** There are apps that you use often, but not often enough that you have them launched automatically when your Mac starts up. By putting these all-stars in the Dock, you can launch them with one click, instead of having to navigate through the Applications folder for them.

▼ **Note**

Even better, having various apps in the Dock gives you flexibility in opening documents. I'm in the Finder, looking at stuff that's landed on my Desktop. I've got this file here named DSC829388.JPG but I don't know what it is, so I double-click it and it opens in Preview. I realize it's a cool photo of my nephew and now I want to edit it. Instead of clicking back into the Finder, opening the Applications folder, launching Photoshop, and then locating and opening the file again, I can just drag the document icon straight into the Photoshop icon in the Dock.

- **It keeps files organized.** I *try* to be a good boy. I *want* to keep my hard drive organized. But at least once a week I have to corral stray files and move them from where I dumped them to where they belong. By dragging my Documents, Pictures, Music, and other assorted folders into the Dock, I can move files into those folders without having to untangle a mess of overlapping windows to keep them exposed. If you've put an icon for your Pictures folder in the Dock, then you just drag a file on top of the icon, let it go, and bango . . . it lands inside your Pictures folder.

- **It keeps you current.** To make this book look all purty and stuff, talented graphic designers invested immeasurable time and energy to create a comprehensive Style Guide. But here I am on Chapter 8 and I still can't keep all of the styles straight. So a few times a day, I need to read the Guide and remember what needs to be formatted with which style. Dragging the Guide into my Dock means I can open the file with

just one click. And by keeping the project folder in the Dock, one click opens up a Finder window with the entire book-in-progress.

It goes on and on. Yes, at first I was a little thrown by the Dock, too. But I quickly appreciated that it's a flexible feature. It's right there when you need it and it goes away when you don't. In system-wide utilities as well as high-school relationships, that's the definition of perfection.

DOCK BASICS

Figure 8-1 shows a typical, busy Dock that is anchored to the bottom of the screen. Thing o'beauty, innit? Your own Dock will look different, of course, but the Dock has a consistent visual language.

▼ **Note**

Yes, some freaks have their Docks hanging vertically. Don't be frightened; just make sure to stay rock still if he or she spots you. They hunt mostly by sense of smell, you understand, so keeping yourself still effectively renders you invisible. Well, okay, maybe these people aren't exactly *freaks*. But as someone who keeps the Dock in its default position at the bottom of the screen, it's still pretty weird, man.

Notice that about two-thirds of the way along, there's a faint dividing line. Everything to the left of that line is an Application. Some of the application icons sport little arrowheads underneath them. This means that the app is actually running at the moment. And hey, some of them

131

are sporting little badges or blinkers, too, to offer you a subtle bit of info. Apple's Mail app, for instance, stamps its icon with the number of unread messages you've got waiting for you. It's handy. You're about to take a break, but on your way over to the DVD Player's icon, you notice that Mail's counter has changed from 3 to 182, indicating the possibility that something you're responsible for is possibly on fire and that you should really check your email.

Icons to the right of that divider line are where everything else is kept: documents, folders, windows that have been minimized, and even entire volumes. The Trash Can always appears at the extreme right edge.

WHAT DOCK ICONS DO

What happens when you click an icon? Depends on what you're clickin':

- **If it's an application icon, your Mac switches to that app.** It also brings the app's windows to the foreground. If the app isn't running already, the Dock launches it for you.

- **Ditto if you click a document icon.** The document window pops to the front. If the document isn't already open, the Dock opens it for you, launching its app, too, if need be.

- **Ditto for folder and volume icons.** You're switched over to the Finder and the item's window pops to the front. If it isn't already open, the Dock opens it. The Trash icon acts just like a folder, incidentally.

"But how do I tell the difference between six identical folder icons?" you ask. Not to worry. When the mouse hovers over an icon, its name magically appears. Although

there's something to be said for having an element of mystery and spontaneity on your workday, this feature also tells you which icon you're aiming at with the mouse.

It's also possible to drag items on top of — actually, *into* — dock icons. Dragging a document onto an application icon opens the document, using that app. Of course, the app has to know how to deal with that sort of file. If you drag a JPEG over iCal, nothing happens. If you drag it over Photoshop, the icon turns dark, which is its way of saying, "I know what that is! Gimme, gimme, gimme."

 Note

What happens next depends on the app. Usually, dragging a doc onto an icon is the equivalent of using the app's Open command. But Mail, for instance, is smart enough to know that you probably want to email that file to someone, so it creates a new email and adds the file as an attachment. For more on applications such as Mail, see Chapter 9.

THE COOLNESS OF MINIMIZED WINDOWS

Cool beans regarding minimized windows: Minimize a movie window, or the browser window of a news site, or any window that contains "live" content. See? The "iconized" window is always up-to-date! What once was *The Empire Strikes Back* playing at full-screen is now playing at postage-stamp proportions. This is what's known as an incredibly cool way to flaunt the processing power of the mighty Macintosh CPU.

Figure 8-1
A typical, busy Dock

ADDING STUFF TO AND DELETING STUFF FROM THE DOCK

Okay, now that the Dock's various settings are well and truly accounted for — again, by now, I ought to have beaten anything you hated about the behavior of the Dock straight out of you, so we can now let the love begin — let's figure out how to get stuff in and out of the thing.

The OS X installer got you started by placing Apple's Greatest Hits in the Dock for you: Mail, iTunes, Safari, and so on. But naturally your first order of business is to add your own items.

And it's as simple as dragging the item in from the Finder. Remember that apps go to the left of that little divider and everything else goes to the right, but other than that, go nuts. Existing icons scurry out of the way and the Dock automatically resizes itself to make room for the new arrival as you drag, so place it wherever you want. Let go of the mouse when you're hovering over an empty space between two existing icons, and it's in.

If you want to remove an icon from the Dock, just drag it off. The icon disappears with a little puff.

▼ Note

Here you see the sole, sad remaining remnant of the mighty Apple Newton MessagePad PDA: The "puff" effect in the Dock is the same animation that the MessagePad used when you scrubbed out a piece of text. Excuse me, I think I need a drink and a good cry, now …

Application icons automatically appear in the Dock whenever you launch them, but if the icon wasn't there to begin with, it disappears from the Dock as soon as you quit the app. You can make the icon of a running app "stick" to the Dock without manually dragging it in through the icon's contextual menu. For more on using contextual menus in the Dock, see the section "Contextual Menus" later in this chapter.

BOUNCING ICONS

What's the appropriate way for somebody to get your attention? Clear their throat discreetly? Raise their hand and wait patiently to be called upon?

If you have a six-year-old kid, you know that the only satisfactory solution is "Jump up and down like a total spaz until the person has no choice but to stop what they're doing and focus on you." And hey, what do you know: that's what the Dock does, too. Even if the Dock is hidden, the icon springs up, Up, UP and down in and out of view, like it's on a trampoline.

When you launch an app via the Dock, it bounces its icon just to let you know that, yes, it did indeed understand your request and the app should be up in just a couple of seconds.

If you're focusing on the "spaz" aspect of this behavior instead of the "necessary feedback" aspect, you can turn it off:

1. **Select Apple→Dock→Preferences to display the Dock preferences panel.**

2. **Click in the box next to the "Animate opening applications" option to remove the check mark.**

But an application can also cause its icon to bounce of its own free will. This happens when Something Bad Has Just Happened, but the app is in the background and so there's a chance that you might have missed it. For example, if you've set up Mail to receive messages in the background, you'd want to know right away that you've lost your connection to the Internet and that the app can no longer function. You need to know *now*, not five days from now, when you're finally curious about why you haven't heard the New Email Has Arrived sound all week, and you're curious about why an awful lot of people around the office seem to think that you've been fired for gross incompetence and neglect-of-duty.

Figure 8-2
The Dock's contextual menu for a running application

You can make the menu appear by clicking the icon, holding down the mouse button and waiting a moment. Or it'll come up immediately if you hold down the Control key while clicking, or by using your mouse's right-hand button, if it has one.

And boy, are Contextual Dock menus fun. They really add the extra oomph of power that sends you over the cliff (but it's a plummet of sheer bliss, because you're being so gosh-darned productive). Here are some things you can do to an application's Dock icon, via its menu:

- **You can hide the app without quitting it.** Zap! And your five-dozen browser windows magically hide themselves. Again, I approve. Hold down the Option key while the menu is active, and Hide becomes Hide Others.

- **Or, you can quit the app.** "Quit" will send the app a polite request to quit. And if something's gone wrong and the program's frozen up, the Dock's contextual menu for it will say "Program Not Responding." You can change the "Quit" to a rough-and-tumble "Force Quit" by holding down the Option key while

▼ Note

And here I understand — a little — about why some people hate the Dock. This behavior is controlled by the app itself, and some apps make the icon bounce for dumb reasons. One of my favorite utilities in the whole world regularly checks to see if there's a new version available and if so: bouncy, bouncy, bouncy.

The app doesn't care that it already told me about this update an hour ago and I'm still too busy to download and install it. It wants me to drop what I'm doing and learn that Version 1.3.4.2 has been updated to 1.3.4.2.1. In a word: *Grrr.* The several words: *g***** ****_***** piece of ***** with ...*

CONTEXTUAL MENUS

Each Dock icon has a hidden contextual menu tacked onto it. Check out Figure 8-2 for an example.

activating the menu. If the app isn't responding, Tiger will convert the menu to "Force Quit" automatically. It's just as eager as you are to give the petulant app a dose of Tough Love. See? Tiger's on your side.

▼ Note

A Force Quit is the impolite way of ending an app, but it's the only option when things are locked up. For more on what to do when you computer gets stuck, see Chapter 24.

- **All applications will appear in the Dock when they're running.** But if you haven't explicitly added its icon to the Dock, it'll disappear when the app quits. To keep the app in there permanently, select Keep In Dock. If you've already added the icon, this item becomes Remove From Dock. It's the same thing as dragging it out, only without the way-cool "poof!" effect.

- **You can tell Mac OS X to automatically launch this app every time your Mac is restarted ("Open at Login").** This is a new tweak for Tiger; you used to have to drill a few layers into your Preferences window to do this. Now, it's one-click.

- **Depending on the app, you can access some of its most common features.** Mail lets you create a new message or check for new mail, for example.

- **Whether an app is running or not, you can locate the application in the Finder.** After you place an app in the Dock, you may forget where it's physically located, and thus deleting the app (or replacing it with something newer) can be a real snipe hunt. Not so with the Show In Finder command.

The crazy-go-nuts-great contextual feature comes when you've tossed a folder inside the Dock, as shown in Figure 8-3. Get a load of *this*.

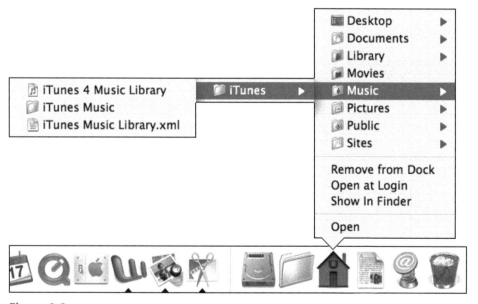

Figure 8-3
The hierarchical menu of a folder or a volume

YOU CAN STOP BEFORE YOU START

Remember my rant about accidentally launching applications? Well, if you're quick-fingered, you can cancel the app's startup before it really gets going, via the Quit contextual menu item. Feel free to curse and rail against the universe nonetheless. For some users, myself included, that's a primary method of regular exercise.

You can mouse all the way from the top of the folder down to the sub-folderiest sub-folder, entirely through the Dock. Here you see my favorite use of this feature: I've put my Home folder in the Dock. I can access any file or launch any app I have without having to click into the Finder. It's so useful that I also have my Applications folder docked. This way, I can launch even my least-used apps as conveniently as an app that has its own direct Dock icon.

Oh, and I suppose for the sake of completeness I need to say that the Dock has its own contextual menu that you can activate through any part of the Dock that isn't occupied by icons (see Figure 8-4).

Figure 8-4
The Dock's own contextual menu

This capability gives you direct access to the Dock's settings. But that hardly even registers on the excitement scale, after you've seen what happens when you put a folder in there, right? Woo-hoo!

CUSTOMIZING THE DOCK

But what if you've read this far and you *still* hate the Dock? Hey, I appreciate your keeping the faith for this long. Again I say, "The Dock is swell; the Dock is fine. The Dock helps build strong bodies eight different ways." And chances are excellent that no matter what it is that you don't like about the Dock, you can fix it through the Dock's settings.

Positioning the Dock

Okay, look, I'm sorry about the "freak" crack I made earlier. But no kiddin': Moving the Dock from the bottom of the screen is like when you turn on a talk show and the guest chairs are to the right of the host's desk instead of in the standard, Carson-approved configuration. It's just plain creepy.

But to each their own. Apple lets you customize the appearance and function of the Dock. Including — he said, with a sigh of resignation, knowing that he can't watch you everywhere and that, in the end, you're going to do what you want to do — moving the Dock to the left or right side of the monitor.

▼ Note

And I'll admit that it's sometimes a good idea. One of my apps has a tendency to create new windows that end at the very bottom of the screen, and it's hard to access those windows' scroll arrows without accidentally activating the Dock. And putting the Dock at the side of the screen is great if you have a widescreen monitor. You only tend to mouse all the way to the edge of space through an act of will, and not by accident.

You can change the Dock's location through System Preferences, the Dock's contextual menu, or right in the Apple menu. To use the Dock preferences panel:

1. **Select Apple→Dock→Preferences.**

2. **Click the Left, Bottom, or Right radio button (see Figure 8-5).**

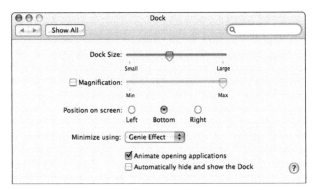

Figure 8-5
Using the Dock preferences panel to choose the Dock's position

To change the Dock's position directly from the Apple menu, select Position on Left, Position on Right, or Position on Bottom from the Apple→Dock→ menu. To change it from the Dock's hierarchical menu, activate the

menu through any of the methods mentioned in the previous section and then choose your poison from the Position on Screen submenu.

Showing and hiding the Dock

The next big deal is whether you want the Dock to remain visible all the time (so you can keep an eye on the widescreen special-edition of *The Lord of the Rings* as it plays in that inch-wide minimized window) or if it should scurry discreetly out of the way when you're not using it.

Unless you have a humongous monitor big enough to microwave a potato on your desktop, you'll probably want to turn on the Dock's Hiding feature. There are three ways to turn on automatic hiding and showing:

- Choose Apple→Dock→Turn Hiding On. Turn Hiding On changes to Turn Hiding Off so you can turn off this option by repeating the same procedure. Or,

- Open the Dock preferences panel and place a check in the "Automatically hide and show the Dock" checkbox.

- And bless its little heart, there's a "Turn Hiding On" item in the Dock's contextual menu.

With Hiding turned on, the Dock hovers into view only when you mouse into the very bottom of the screen.

Size and magnification

Lucky you: You're just getting started, so you have only a handful of icons in your Dock. Well, I have 50 (gaze upon Figure 8-7, and weep). As things start to get crowded in there, you need to become intimate with the Dock's Size and Magnification settings.

Figure 8-6

The Dock of a user who has serious impulse-control issues

Figure 8-7

The Dock at maximum size

Size lets you define how small the Dock should ever get (Figure 8-8). Normally, the Dock automatically shrinks itself to whatever width accommodates all those icons, but you can, in effect, tell it that the icons are too small to be seen by the human eye, which is, alas, all you happen to be equipped with.

Figure 8-8

The Dock at minimum size

To access Size settings, open up the Dock Preferences panel and play with the Dock Size slider.

▼ **Tip**

You can also change the Dock's size by grabbing that little divider we talked about. Notice that when your mouse hovers over it, the pointer changes to a little grow icon. Just slide it up and down and watch the icons change.

The other balm for your peepers is the Dock's magnification feature. When active, your mouse acts sort of like a magnifying glass as it moves along the dock, viz Figure 8-9. Individual icons are magnified to several

times their normal proportions, rendering them visible from several hundred yards and thus vulnerable to snipers armed with competition-grade rifles.

There are two ways to turn on magnification:

- **Select Apple→Dock→Turn Magnification On.** Turn Magnification On changes to Turn Magnification Off so you can turn off this option by repeating the same procedure. Or!

- **Open the Dock preferences panel and click to place a check in the Magnification checkbox.** You can control how big the icons get via the slider control.

▼ **Warning**

Magnification can drive you batty. It's easy to accidentally click on the icon to the left or right of what you are aiming for, particularly if your Mac isn't reacting to your mouse-movements very swiftly. But don't worry. The only time this sort of mistake happens is when you're minutes from a crucial deadline, and the icon you want is right next door to an application that ties up your CPU for a half an hour when launched.

Figure 8-9
The Magnificated Dock

Animating windows

When you minimize a window, it disappears from the Desktop and reappears in the lower (or right) portion of the Dock. OS X animates the movement from full-sized window to Dock icon. You can choose either a Genie effect, in which the window slurps into the Dock like a grease and hair clog finally disappearing down the drain in a Liquid Plumber commercial, or a Scale effect, in which the window gets smaller as it moves to the Dock but retains its proportions.

▼ **Note**

This is hardly a power-productivity feature. But if you're using an older, less-powerful Mac, you'll find that the Scale effect looks smoother if you Scale it instead of Genie it. In fact, this is one of those reasons why I love the Mac. Why do anything the simple way, when a bodaciously cooler method is available and it shows off the machine's processing power? Oh, and watch carefully when you minimize a movie window; yes, the movie is *still playing,* even *while* it's slurping down into the Dock.

To change the minimize animation effect:

1. **Select Apple→Dock→Preferences to display the Dock preferences panel.**

2. **Select Genie effect or Scale effect from the Minimize using pop-up menu.**

And as you expect by now, you can also turn Scaling on and off through the Dock's Apple Menu and through its Contextual Menu.

This is the end of the chapter, so obviously it's the end of my opportunity to honk on about what a great bargain the Dock is and why you should invite it in, give it a hot meal, and ask if it needs anything laundered or pressed.

So I'll end by saying that if I had to give up either the Finder or the Dock, I'd give up the Dock. Actually, I'd just go around *telling* people that I've stopped using the Finder. Because via the Dock, I can quickly hide the Finder when I hear people coming. But I'd be twice as arrogant when insisting that I'd made the right choice.

Just Deal with It: Apps

In This Chapter

Installing Applications • Downloading Applications • Enhancing Applications
Switching Between Applications • Performance Slowdowns • Activity Monitor: What *Is* That App *Doing?*
Console: What Did That App *Do?* • Taking Care of Comatose Apps • Removing Apps

Here we are, a third of the way through this grand volume, and only just *now* am I attacking the issue of applications. Which, on balance, seems to betray a lack of understanding of the reader. Why do people buy books on how to build a deck or renovate a bathroom? Are people actually interested in learning about tools and fasteners and construction codes and surface preparation? No. No, they are not. They have already bought a sledgehammer and rented a nail gun and they're eager to start working out a little Hessian aggression with their new toys just as soon as humanly possible.

But, of course, just as a great deal of a pilot's cockpit time is not spent flying, but managing the onboard systems that *assist* the pilot in flight, a great deal of the user's time is spent acquiring and managing apps. It's hard to bask in the fond embrace of Earth's gravity these days and *not* be aware that you launch apps by double-clicking on them. That's covered. But there's more to know. Particularly when things go *wrong*, which is a slushy puddle that you'll step into much more frequently than you'd wish . . . world's most stable and advanced operating system or no.

(See? I acknowledged that even in Utopia, there's a need for a police force and a Department of Sanitation. That was awfully big of me, don't you think? But look, don't tell anyone I said that.)

INSTALLING APPLICATIONS

Fortunately, installing applications isn't like installing that new deck. With a deck project, you can't barbecue anything until you've measured *this* and built concrete footings for *that* and ensured that Lord knows what else meets or exceeds federal guidelines for non-burnthewholehousedownosity. (Honestly, is the deck industry *unaware* that I can get a flame-grilled burger just down the street after a mere investment of 99 cents and 14 minutes of my time?)

Apps install *themselves*. With exceedingly rare exceptions, one drag or one double-click is all that's required.

Where do you get apps? They either come on a disc that arrives in a box, or you download them from the Internet.

AN APP BY ANY OTHER NAME . . .

And can we please take a moment to mourn the triumph of the word
"application" above all other alternatives? Nobody says "programs" or "software" anymore. Yes, yes, I know: as computers became more complicated, we needed a special word for the software that users run and interact with, as opposed to the software that runs behind the scenes and allows the operating system to talk to your digital camera, for example.

But I miss referring to my word processor as a "program." Whenever I say "application," I wonder if the manager of my bank is going to phone three days after I double-click on Microsoft Word, to tell me that upon review of my employment and credit history, he is, alas, unable to approve a launch of the word processor at *this time*, but that he invites me to apply again at the end of the fiscal quarter.

When you download an app, it'll likely arrive on your Mac as a *disk image file*. As Chapter 12 explains, when you open a .dmg file it mounts on the Desktop as if it were a removable disk. It's really quite slick: you click a link on a website to start the download (having already handed over your credit-card info, if the software's author has been swayed by the seduction of filthy leuchre), the file is downloaded to your hard drive, and then your web browser opens the disk image file (Figure 9-1). And so, if you click into the Finder, you'll see a brand-new volume sitting there in the window next to your hard drive's icon, almost as if a hard drive was slurped into your Mac via your broadband connection and plugged itself in.

If the browser doesn't open the file automatically (or if you just copied it to your hard drive from someone else's Mac), you can load up the image file by just double-clicking its icon.

Figure 9-1
A disk image mounted on the Desktop, showing its contents

Some downloaded apps cut through all that rigmarole, appearing on your Mac not as a disk image but as a standalone app. Hot, fresh, and ready to eat. No pretense, no airs — a veritable model for human behavior. Except that one really shouldn't eat people. It's rarely called for.

"If Disk Images are clumsy and pretentious," you're asking, "then why do publishers even bother with them?

Oh, dear. Did I give you the impression that packaging applications inside a disk image was nothing more than a frustrating, unnecessary, added complication? No, no. Whether you get 'em on a CD or online, apps often come with baggage attached. A utility I recently bought online came with the app itself, a file explaining how to install the software, a big file of documentation, and a whole folder of examples and bonus gizmos. When it's packaged as an image file, all this stuff appears to the user as one nice, tidy entity that he or she can then deal with as a whole or in parts. That's much, *much* better than dealing with a dozen individual things to download, or even a bundled file that splatters all that stuff all over your directory when it's unpacked.

Whether the app arrives on your Mac on a CD, as a disk image, or as a humble app, if you've got the actual application in hand, then all you have to do at this point is drag its icon into your Applications folder. You're ready to rock and roll.

What I'm about to say makes perfect sense to me, but now that I'm reading it in stark black and white I worry that a new user will have no idea what I'm talking about. But! Forge ahead I must: it's possible that the application you're looking at *isn't* the actual, useful application, but instead is just an application that *installs* the application. It's an "installer" program, which is like the cable guy of the software world. He comes in, works all of the mojo necessary to get your brand-new app up and running, and then you never see him again. The key difference is that an installer doesn't drill through your hardwood floors or rummage through your laundry hamper when you're busy elsewhere in the house.

WHY INSTALL APPS INTO THE APPLICATIONS FOLDER?

I mean, apart from the fact that it's labeled "Applications" and everything, and Apple seems to think that it's a very important concept, and they've been making operating systems a *lot* longer than *you* have?

You don't have to put 'em there. You can actually install apps anywhere on your hard drive. But there aren't a whole lot of compelling reasons to be creative here. If you were to install an app in your private user directory, you'd still be able to run it but it'd be invisible and unavailable to any other users of that Mac. So that's a benefit there; you probably don't want Junior to mess around with your home-accounting software, or Mom and Dad to do anything to screw up your Warcraft campaign. It's also a way to get around the built-in limitations of a normal user account. Administrators are the only people who can make changes to the Applications folder, but by dragging the app elsewhere, you're golden.

But in general, you should forget that I said anything. Once you start keeping your apps wherever the devil you please, anarchy results. You'll keep misplacing things, mark my words, and then you won't have me to complain to. You'll just have to buy my next book.

Installers *might* seem like a complication, but they're really a great boon. A lot of apps are pretty complicated; they exist as more than one nice, tidy application file, and thus they can't be installed with one single drag. Maybe it's not just one application icon: it gets its own icon in OS X's "preferences" panel, and it wants to have a shortcut to your desktop, or wants to add itself to your Dock, and there's a little "invisible" app that needs to be launched every time you start up your Mac, which allows the OS to use the main app's features even when it's not actually running.

And not all software runs on all hardware; maybe it's important to prepare your hard drive beforehand, and check to make sure your Mac has all the right features.

So instead of handing you, the peace-loving User, a big list of Things To Do and then clapping you on the back, wishing you the best of luck, and reminding you that the end-user-agreement explicitly states that you have no legal recourse if the software screws up your machine and its entire contents, the software publisher hands you an installer app, which handles the whole job on your behalf.

IS THE SOFTWARE LICENSE AGREEMENT BALONEY, OR JUST MALARKEY?

Oddly enough, while you can't install the software without agreeing to the Agreement, it's really not meant to be read by anybody. Sometimes they're worth a larff. People often get just as bored while writing these agreements as you do while reading them, and they sometimes stick in a couple of flights of whimsy.

Usually it's all boilerplate stuff, boiling down to: the software is provided as-is, and if it stops working, that's *your* fault; the software's copyrighted by the publisher and you can't make copies and give 'em away, and you're the sole authorized user of the software. That is, you can't buy one copy of Microsoft Word and then install it on every Mac in your office.

One thing to be aware of: some publishers like to sneak a fast one into their agreements. "Publisher reserves the right to collect user information from the licensee, which then becomes the property of the Publisher." Meaning, they can sell your name, your address, your phone number, and your usage habits to junk mailers and the like. Beware.

With the release of OS X, Apple started to provide software developers with a powerful new standard Installer program that they could modify. You probably saw it the first time you installed OS X yourself. The end-result is that the majority of application installers look and work the same way.

One big relief about installing applications: it's not like installing Tiger. Remember? You had to quit all other running apps and reboot off a CD? Nothing of the sort will bedevil you when you install an application. The full installation process usually goes something like this:

1. **Double-click on the Installer icon to launch it.**

2. **Read an Introduction, the purpose of which is to remind you just exactly what app you're about to install, as if you didn't know already.**

3. **Click Continue.**

   This usually opens an Important Information screen, filled with last-minute notes and warnings.

4. **Read the Important information and click Continue.**

 Note

And for the love of all that's good and decent in the world, read that information. Oftentimes, it's the only place to learn that there's a desperately horrid incompatibility between the software you're about to install and something you previously installed, or a warning that well, gosh, when you try to install it on [insert your specific make and model of Mac here] the screen may or may not burst into flames.

So read the Read Me, unless of course you are sick and tired of having a Mac that's *never* crashed and taken the entire contents of your hard drive down with it and you yearn for new experiences.

5. **Click Continue. This opens a Software License Agreement screen.**

6. **Read the Software License Agreement and click Continue.**

7. **Click Continue.**

   In most cases, you will be asked to agree to the license agreement in a separate little drop-down sheet.

8. **Click Agree.**

   You usually see a screen for selecting a destination for the software.

9. **Select the destination disk for the installation by clicking the icon of the disk you want to use.**

10. **Select either Easy Install (the Installer makes choices as to which components should be installed) or Custom Install.**

    By default you get an Easy Install. Click Customize to perform a Custom Install. If you choose to customize the installation, you see a list of components of the application. You must then remove checks from the checkboxes of those components you don't want to install, or, if checkboxes are empty, click to add checks to those components you want installed.

▼ **Note**

Nine times out of ten, you should just cruise straight to the Easy Install, but it's often worthwhile to at least take a look at what's listed under Custom Install. It gives you a snapshot of what's being written to your hard drive.

As a practical matter, I choose Custom Install only when disk space is starting to become slightly precious and I'd rather have an extra 27MB of storage than a big folder of add-ons that allow the app to work with Uzbekistan text and numbers.

11. **Click Continue (or whatever the rightmost button at the bottom of the Installer window happens to say).**

    If the Installer needs to modify system files, it asks you for an administrator password.

12. **Type an administrator password and click OK.**

    Why does an Installer ask for an administrator password? Forbidding ordinary users from installing software helps keep a Mac happy and healthy when several users are sharing it. If the whole office has standardized on Word, you don't want somebody installing LambadaWrite. If this Mac is supposed to be used for homework and email, then Junior shouldn't be installing games. Et cetera.

13. **The Installer installs the software on the destination disk.**

    You don't need to do anything at this point but sit back and wait. The Installer finishes up its job and lets you know it's done.

▼ **Note**

And, in some cases, the wait will be ambitious enough that you may want to go get a snack, phone some old friends, perhaps get a start on that cathedral you've been meaning to build in the backyard ... that sort of thing. Some installs are intricate enough that the Installer has to check and optimize the entire system before pronouncing the operation complete.

The lesson here is that you shouldn't install software unless you're certain that you can (conceivably) do without the use of your Mac for an undeterminable length of time. The other lesson here is the same lesson you learned when your Dad pointed at the $3/4$-acre yard behind your house and told you where you can find the push-mower: namely, sometimes when people tell you they're "just trying to optimize your performance," they're really just out to waste your time and cause you endless frustration.

14. **Click Close to exit the Installer.**

The final step to any installation is, of course, giving you added options for getting at the app. Make an alias to the app and put it on the Desktop. Drag the app into the Dock, or into the toolbar area of a Finder window so that you can easily drag files on top of it.

Naturally, the actual steps for an Install can vary from app to app. But this one is fairly typical, and because nearly all apps use Apple's standard installer framework, that really covers nearly every install.

 Note

Although many Installers were updated to use the framework you've been reading about, some applications still use the classic Mac OS Installer. This may look like an OS 9 application, but if you look at the controls in the top left of the window, you can see OS X window controls, indicating that this is indeed an OS X program. Or it might use another Installer program entirely, such as InstallerVISE. But the basic principles are the same.

 Tip

A page or so ago I mentioned that some of you are interested in seeing what it was like to use an unstable, slowpokey, crashy sort of Mac. If you're part of that particular movement, what I'm about to say here won't really interest you: "It's a good idea to launch Mac OS X's Disk Utility app — you'll find it inside your Utilities folder — and click its Repair Disk Permissions button after you've installed new software."

In any installation, it's *possible* that an Installer goofed up a couple of (very) low-level file settings while copying stuff to your hard drive. It doesn't happen often, and even when it does, it's not a big enough problem that it'll clobber your Mac. It's more like over time, your Mac will start slowing down or behaving a little erratically ...and you'll never ever, *ever* figure

out *why* because the origin of the trouble is so subtle. I do a Repair Disk Permissions every few weeks as part of my basic maintenance, but if you get in the habit of doing it after every install, you'll probably save yourself a little trouble, in the long run.

DOWNLOADING APPLICATIONS

Gosh, I was about to explain what software was like before the epoch of the CD-ROM. I have selected those 11 paragraphs (mostly a lot of snarking and complaining about opening a box and finding 11 diskettes inside, and having to swap them in and out of my Mac, *in the proper order,* over the course of a couple of hours) and deleted them with a sad rage. The kids don't want to hear Grampa complain about how hard it was to eat a watermelon in the days before genetic engineers were able to develop a melon that wasn't encased in a rock-hard carapace with razor-sharp spines jutting out from all angles.

Yes, having 650MB of application data on a CD is great, and having 4.2GB on a DVD is even greater.

DON'T SNIFF AT DOWNLOADS

Some of the greatest apps available for the Mac are only available via download. Publishing an app on a CD and shipping it to stores requires a big investment, so most of the apps sold that way are written after long and careful thought. Folks who sell online can afford to create groundbreaking, bizarre, unique, or even heroically stupid apps.

The point here is that you shouldn't sniff at an app just because you can't buy it in a shrink-wrapped box.

Note

Though, good God ... when I started using Macs, the entire operating system *plus* a word processor could fit on a single 400K diskette. What excess, what waste, what profligerance we suffer in these modern times! Now I know why so many of our nation's youth are turning Amish these days.

More and more often, though, you can purchase and download commercial apps — small *and* gi-normous ones, thanks to broadband — from a vendor's Web site. No physical plastic media necessary, apart from your credit card. Delivery is immediate and the cost savings (no duplication, packaging, or mailing costs) are often passed on to the purchaser.

In addition, not *all* software requires you to pay up front. A lot of downloadable apps are released as *shareware.* Meaning: you can download and try it for free, but if you like it and keep on using it, you're supposed to go to the author's website and pay a "registration" fee. Sometimes its an honor thing. Sometimes, though, the app is wired up to stop working after a specific trial period unless you register. Other apps are released as *freeware,* which you're welcome to enjoy and use with the author's compliments, please, no, the author absolutely insists. Most (but certainly not *all*) freeware apps are simple, one-task apps as opposed to huge, sledgehammer productivity tools, but hey, it's a nice thought.

And free "open-source" apps are often as good as their commercial counterparts. Check out Chapter 10 for some more info on open-source software.

Where can you go to find shareware and freeware? Here are a few of my favorite sites:

- **Version Tracker** (www.versiontracker.com) **and MacUpdate** (www.macupdate.com): These sites not only have freeware and shareware, but they also carry

beta (not yet ready for prime time) versions of commercial software, updates to commercial software, and demos of commercial apps. One of its great strengths is the user ratings and feedback attached to nearly every file; you can quickly tell if a specific download is any good, or has the features you're looking for.

- **Download.com** (www.download.com): This CNET site is differently organized, which makes it a little easier to browse when you have no idea what you're looking for, specifically.

- **Apple** (www.apple.com/downloads): Apple Computer showcases selected bits of shareware and freeware. It's not the largest collection out there, but it's all high-quality stuff.

A file that you download won't arrive on your hard drive as a double-clickable app or Installer. It had to be packed into a different format for travel. You'll probably see one of these file extensions:

- **.sit:** A StuffIt archive. StuffIt is one of the most popular archive formats on the planet.

- **.zip:** A ZIP archive. ZIP is the classic Windows file compression and archiving format that's become a multi-OS standard.

- **.gzip or .gz:** A GZIP archive. GZIP is the Unix variety of ZIP.

- **.hqx:** A BinHex file.

But the good news is that you really don't particularly need to know any of this. Yup, these special formats are absolutely necessary to move the software from the website to your Mac, but Mac OS X knows exactly what these files are and what to do with them; it might arrive on your Mac as a .hqx or a .sit or a .zip file, but X will unpack it and turn it into a clickable app before you even see the original file.

OUR TOTAL LACK OF SAFETY HAS SET US FREE

When you buy online, you really shouldn't worry about your credit-card info being stolen. First, because nearly all companies use techniques that keep your info secure and safe from prying eyes (or prying software). When you type in your credit-card number, look at the Address bar of the web page. If it starts with *https:* instead of *http,* (you'll also see a little padlock icon in the window), then the web page is secure and the info can't be intercepted between your Mac and the website.

And secondly, because in this day and age, *truly* protecting your credit-card number is nearly a lost cause. Your risk isn't from buying software online: it's from some underpaid flunky at your bank, who knows that he can get $20 for every credit-card number he fishes out of an office memo.

It seems like I'm being a fatalist about this, but I'm just a realist. Your greatest defense is to simply keep a careful eye on your bank statement and report fraud early enough that you're not responsible for any unauthorized transactions.

If this *didn't* happen (if, as with disk images, you just copied it from someone else's Mac to your own) you can unpack it manually by double-clicking it; the tools are already there, either as part of the OS itself or as a little helper app that was installed alongside X.

 Note

This helper app (StuffIt Expander) has a commercial big brother called StuffIt Deluxe, published by Allume Systems (www.allume.com). StuffIt Deluxe lets you create nearly every archive and compressed-format file that exists. So it's a handy thing to have around if you're often swapping archives with your non-Mac pals. The Finder can create ZIP files through its Create Archive command, but naturally StuffIt Deluxe is way more flexible.

ENHANCING APPLICATIONS

Some apps are designed to be extended and enhanced with special snippets of code called *plug-ins.* Typically, a plug-in doesn't add a revolutionary new feature. It's not like you can add a plug-in to iPhoto and then all of a sudden the app is capable of calculating targeting solutions for intercontinental ballistic missiles.

No, a plug-in typically extends a feature that the app already has. iPhoto, for example, has a Sharing feature that allows the app to send your photos to your online .Mac photo gallery. But what if you don't use .Mac to show off your photos? What if you use www.flickr.com instead? iPhoto doesn't support Flickr.

No . . . but there's a guy by the name of Fraser Speirs. And *he* supports Flickr. So he wrote an iPhoto plugin that adds Flickr exporting to iPhotos Sharing capabilities. I've just downloaded it from his website, Speirs.org. Now here's how I'm going to install it in iPhoto.

1. **Make sure you're logged in as an Administrator of this Mac.**

   Only folks with Administrator-level accounts can install plug-ins.

2. **Quit iPhoto, if it's already running.**

3. **Locate iPhoto on your hard drive . . . it's in your Applications folder.**

   Or, if its icon is in the Dock, all you have to do is select Show In Finder.

4. **Select the iPhoto app and choose Get Info from the Finder's File menu.**

   iPhoto's Get Info window will open up.

5. **Click on the arrowhead next to Plug-ins: to reveal a list of all of iPhoto's installed plug-ins (Figure 9-2).**

6. **Click the Add button.**

   A standard file picker appears.

7. **Locate the plug-in.**

   In this case, FlickrExport.iPhotoExporter is sitting right on the Desktop, where I downloaded it.

8. **Click the Choose button.**

And that's it. The plug-in will be copied right where it needs to go.

Ideally, you won't have to do *any* of that. *Most* developers appreciate that installing a plug-in is just a little beyond the experience of the average user, and so instead of just releasing the plug-in and hoping that people figure it out, developers will instead release an installer app that installs the plug-in with just one click. In fact, the FlickrExport plug-in had been an install-it-yourself plug-in for months before the developer decided to cut folks some slack, and release it as an installer app that installs the thing without any help from you.

Figure 9-2
Viewing iPhoto's installed plug-ins

149

SWITCHING BETWEEN APPLICATIONS

The beauty of multitasking is that you can have multiple applications running at the same time. Although you can work with only one app at a time directly — you are only Human, unless of course I am addressing a noncorporeal, higher-evolved life form, in which case I urge you to put down the book and just give us the damned point-singularity energy technology, already — some apps can continue what they're doing in the background while you do something else. iTunes is a swell app any way you slice it, but if you couldn't do anything else while you were listening to your Troggs albums, you know, there'd be little point to owning a Mac. Or at least no point to owning just *one* of them.

In Mac lingo, there's this thing called the "frontmost" app. That's the one that you're working with at this immediate moment. I've got . . . let's see here . . . holy cats! *twenty* apps going at once at the moment, but Microsoft Word is the app that I'm actually working with. When I type, it's into a Word window. Thus, Word is the frontmost app. If there's any confusion, just look at the menu bar: it's always "owned" by the frontmost app, and changes when you switch from one app to another.

▼ **Note**

This is, incidentally, one of the reasons why I think Mac OS X is better thought-out than Windows. Yes, I can have dozens of apps *running* at the same time, but I can't actually *use* them all at the same time, can I? So why have 20 menu bars on my screen? Besides, what's the point of a menu that I can't actually use until I click on its window? In the dozens of *other* windows I've got open, it's just wasted space.

Having a single, static menu bar reduces clutter and gives the user constant feedback about Where He Or She Is Right Now. Simple and elegant. Those folks at Apple, man . . . you can't accuse them of *not* thinkin'.

There are three ways of switching from one app to another (or, "making another application the frontmost app," if you want to get fancy about it):

- Click on any open window belonging to the application. If (as is always, always, always the case with my own Mac) the window you want is covered by something else, you can use Exposé to temporarily "unshuffle" all of the windows on your Desktop.

- Click on the application's icon in the Dock.

- Use the application switcher.

The application switcher comes up whenever you hold down the ⌘ key and press Tab. Icons for all running applications appear across the center of your startup monitor, as in Figure 9-3.

▼ **Note**

Hmm. And now that I've spent two paragraphs mooning on and on about how the Mac's menu concept is *sooo* much better than Windows', I'm sort of obliged to point out that the application switcher is actually sort of a recent addition to Mac OS X and is (cough) nearly completely lifted from Windows. Still, I bet I can turn this into a positive statement about Apple. Ah! Here we go: "Yet for all its commitment to innovation, Apple isn't so arrogant as to ignore a good idea when it finds it." Good, I feel better, now.

Keep the ⌘ key down. Every time you press Tab, you'll highlight the next icon to the right. When you release the ⌘ key, it's like the music stops in a game of musical chairs: you'll be switched over the highlighted app.

▼ **Tip**

There are a couple of shortcuts to the switcher, too. Tabbing while holding down the Shift key will select the *previous* application icon. You can also mouse directly over to the app you want.

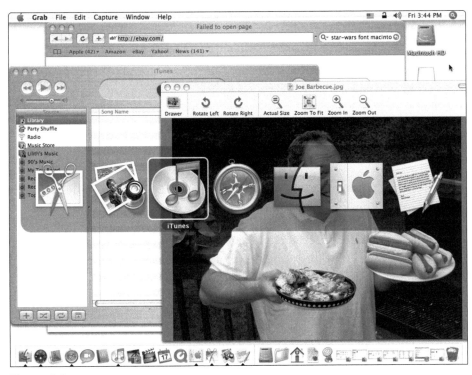

Figure 9-3
The application switcher

There's a method to the order of icons, too: the frontmost app is always to the extreme left, and the remaining apps are presented in the order in which they were last brought to the front. So if I were to switch out of Word to fool around in iPhoto a bit, I could switch right back again by bringing up the switcher and just hitting the Tab key once.

PERFORMANCE SLOWDOWNS

All of a sudden I'm no longer interested in delaying the payoff. So I'll cut straight to it and say that if, all of a sudden, your Mac is running as slowly as a snail wearing a pair of stylish but particularly uncomfortable stilettos, you should quit any running apps that you're not using. If that doesn't help, you should log out and then log back in

again, or restart your Mac (see Chapter 24 for more on troubleshooting Mac performance problems).

Now for the reason; in a nutshell, it's virtual memory. Your Mac has hardware main memory. I'm talking about real, actual, if-you-prick-it-does-it-not-bleed (well, no-it's-just-a-silicon-wafer-but-you-know-what-I-mean) memory chips installed on your Mac's motherboard. Problem is, folks like to run lots and lots of apps at the same time, and there's a finite amount of memory. Solution: Virtual Memory. When Mac OS X needs more memory than it actually has, it'll fake it by pretending that some of the unused acreage on your hard drive is actually memory.

The catch: Information moves through "real" memory at roughly the speed at which an electron can slalom through a circuit. Which is impressively fast. On the other hand, information moves to and from a hard drive about as fast as Katherine Hepburn can walk on her hands. Yes, in her *present* condition. The upshot is that the more virtual memory your Mac is forced to use, the slower your Mac becomes, as the OS spends more and more time swapping chunks of your running apps to and from the hard drive. Hence, quitting apps allows more of the remaining apps to sit in that cozy, fast, *real* memory.

So why restart? Again, blame memory. Specifically, blame a pernicious and nearly impossible-to-isolate software bug known as a *memory leak.* Normally, apps and the OS work together to make sure that not a single scrap of memory is wasted. When you open a document, the app tells the OS that it needs a little more memory for its workspace, please. The OS finds some unused memory and gives it to the app. When you close the document, the app thanks the OS kindly and says that it doesn't need that extra memory space any more, so go ahead and give it to some other deserving app.

This system ought to work great, but maybe a few kilobytes get "lost" in every transaction. It's sort of like a cookie jar: cookies come out, and usually a few crumbs get left behind. Now imagine that you're shuttling thousands of cookies in and out every day. Those crumbs add up, particularly when your Mac has been up and running for weeks. Suddenly, huge tracts of fertile land are inaccessible, and the OS's reliance on Virtual Memory swells higher and higher.

You can poke your Mac with a big stick, but that won't dislodge any of that missing memory. Logging out and back in again helps, but the only way to totally fix the problem is to restart.

Memory is dirt cheap. One of the smartest things you can do is to buy the maximum amount of RAM that your Mac can use. It helps build strong bodies nine different ways, I swear.

 Note

I could have really impressed you with the importance of this advice by saying, "Look, if you can't afford it, I'll buy it *for* you," but there's some sort of legal thing about my actually having to deliver on that promise. I tried to tell the guy that the chances of anyone spelling my name right on the subpoena were slim, but he insisted on being a spoilsport. Nonetheless, please buy more RAM.

Your simplest and most effective defense against the slings and arrows of virtual memory is to never fill your hard drive to more than 90 percent of its capacity; personally, I shoot for 85 percent. Virtual memory works fastest when it has no problems locating unused space on your drive. When your 80GB drive only has 2GB free, the OS spends more time *looking* for virtual memory than actually using it, an analogy that brings to mind New York Mets manager Casey Stengel's comment about why the guys on his team were always so tired before their games.

Indeed, if you keep filling your drive up and up and *up* (not difficult, if you store all of your digital photos on your Mac) the OS might eventually balk, tut-tutting that memory is, at this instant, *critically* low and you must now forcibly quit some apps. To underscore the point, it'll actually present you with a list. But smart people don't let things get that bad.

Naturally, virtual memory isn't the only reason why apps often slow down to a crawl. It's just the only one that's universal. If one of your apps starts to follow the example of our friend the determined but stately banana slug, the true problem might be (a) unique to that app, and (b) well-documented.

See, every app relies on a pile of unique little files for support, and they do all kinds of things behind the scenes. Take Safari, for example. If you've been using it a good long while, you might notice that it takes a hella long time

HEAL THYSELF

There's a maxim I've been spouting far too often: "Well, as the saying goes, the best barber in town is always the one with the worst haircut." I truly enjoy telling all of you how to live your lives. But do I take my own advice? No, of course not. I know myself better than you do. For example, I clearly remember the time I nearly knocked myself unconscious with a 32-ounce souvenir *Who Framed Roger Rabbit?* movie cup from McDonalds; really, would *you* take advice from such a man?

So it's always amusing (depressing, but amusing) when I realize that the solution to my problems is something I've written about dozens and dozens of times. A couple of months ago, my PowerBook required over a minute and a half to switch from one running app to another. (Yes, I timed it. I didn't have anything *else* to do during those 90 seconds, did I?) And why was it so torpid? Easy: 80GB hard drive. *900MB* free. So I freed up 16GB, and now my Mac is running like it just found this button on the dashboard labeled "Nitrous Boost."

The incident with the collectible cup really happened, but please don't let that influence your opinion of the information in this and my other books. I have never knocked myself unconscious with *any* Macintosh product.

to move from page to page. That's because nearly every site you visit sends a little customized icon (an .ico file) to Safari to use as a visual placeholder for its Bookmarks listing. And if you've hit hundreds and hundreds of sites in the past month, then every time you go to another site, Safari has to sort through hundreds and hundreds of icon files to locate the one it needs. You can avoid that delay if

you delete this menagerie (if you're curious, you'll find it in your user/Library/Safari/Icons folder).

It's a frustrating piece of advice to give, though. Next, I should tell you to look in the Prefs directory for cache files, or head for Application Support and check for file permissions . . . again, each app has different quirks and you'll never figure them out on your own. That's why you should head for sites like MacFixIt.com, MacInTouch.com, and Apple's own Support site (with its message forums) to talk to other users on an app-by-app basis.

ACTIVITY MONITOR, OR WHAT *IS* THAT APPLICATION *DOING*?

That dreaded spinning colored beach ball — it's been making an appearance whenever you move the mouse over any window belonging to one particular application. You can't do anything with the application. What is that application doing?

OS X provides two utility programs that can let you — or a technical support person whom you have asked for help — find out what your computer is up to. You can have the most fun with Activity Monitor, but Console can be useful to very technical sorts and you should at least know where to find it in case someone asks.

Activity Monitor and Console are located in the Utilities folder, within the Applications folder. They're standalone programs that you run like any other app.

Launching Activity Monitor displays a window like that in Figure 9-4. The scrolling list of items in the middle of the window is a list of *processes*. A process is a program — or a part of a program, anyway — that's vying for time in your computer's CPU. The display in Figure 9-4 has been set to show just processes that the user started up. However, if you choose All Processes from the Show pop-up menu, you see process names that don't correspond to programs you've started (see Figure 9-5). These processes, such as kernel_task and init, are OS X system processes. Those are the functions that keep the water running and make sure that a truck comes by every Tuesday morning to pick up the trash.

owns the process. System processes are owned by "root," the operating system itself. In the example you have been seeing, the human user is "sysop."

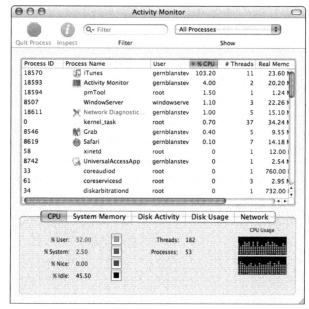

Figure 9-5
Watching all processes and CPU activity

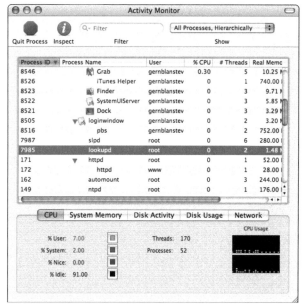

Figure 9-4
Watching user processes and CPU activity

Each process that OS X runs is given a process ID number, which appears in the leftmost column of the Activity Monitor window. Unless you are working with the Terminal app (where you can use Unix commands to mess with the nuts-and-bolts of ongoing processes), you almost never need to use this value. The Process Name column is the name of the program that controls each particular process. Next to *that* is the name of the OS X user that currently

Probably the most important column for your basic, everyday looky-loo purposes is % CPU, which tells you that percentage of overall CPU time that a process uses. If it's grotesquely huge, it's a possible tipoff that a certain app is hogging the CPU, particularly if it doesn't smell like it's a processor-intensive app. iTunes, for instance, often uses more than half of the available processing power when it's converting a CD into music files. Lots of math is involved, you know? But if Microsoft Word took up half my CPU just to keep up with my typing, it's a sure indicator that either (a) I've been drinking *wayyyy* too much caffeine, or (b) Word is in serious trouble and needs to be terminated.

▼ **Tip**

I'm a big fan of keeping Activity Monitor's floating CPU window up. It's that pair of yellow-and-gray caterpillars that I've dragged under the Apple menu. If you turn on this window (you can do that through the Monitor menu) a slim little thermometer hugs the side of your screen, letting you know how many RPMs your CPU is pulling at the moment. I keep it up partly because it's cool to look at. But it's useful, too; if it stops twitching, you know your system is hopelessly locked up. When it pulses high for no reason, you know that some app is throttling the CPU and it's time to check things out.

The information at the bottom of the Activity Monitor window can be fascinating. The colorful bar chart at the bottom of Figure 9-5 is a live graphic of CPU activity — if your Mac has multiple CPUs, you see multiple graphs — the colors depicting the proportions of user and system processes. Clicking the System Memory button changes the bottom display to show main memory usage, as in Figure 9-6. Although the display doesn't show you how much memory each process is using, it can let you know if you are running out of hardware RAM space. If red and yellow wedges dominate the pie graph, it's time to re-read that bit in the previous section regarding how cheap RAM

is and how important it is that you buy some more of it. And you can also easily see how much of your hard drive is being used as virtual memory. 4.18GB, in this case. Cool, I've got more than twice that much space free on my drive, so there's plenty of room for future bloatage.

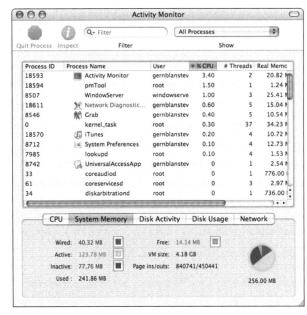

Figure 9-6
Monitoring main memory usage

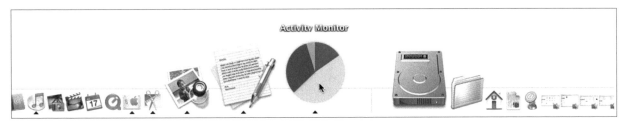

Figure 9-7
Monitoring memory usage through Activity Monitor's Dock icon

ACTIVITY MONITOR SO FREAKING ROCKS, I CAN BARELY SPEAK

Wanna see something cool? Go to Activity Monitor's View menu, and navigate to Dock Icon. Yes, indeedy: you can have Activity Monitor's Dock icon into a regularly updated status indicator, betraying your Mac's application and system performance with just a glance. Figure 9-7 shows the Dock icon set to Memory Usage.

It sort of trains you. With the Dock indicator always there in front of you, you'll soon begin to associate certain images with Trouble Brewing. Which means you can learn to avoid problems before they happen.

CONSOLE: DEAR GOD . . . WHAT HAS THAT APPLICATION *DONE?*

The Console utility provides access to OS X system error messages and logs. The initial display, which appears when you launch the application, shows error messages about problems that OS X has encountered since you booted the computer. Don't worry if you can't understand what the error messages are saying: unless the programmer was helpful enough to have his app spew plain-English comments into the logfile, you'd really need to be a developer or a Unix guru to make sense of them. The biggest benefit of these log files is the simple fact that they're there. If your Mac starts acting *so* petulant that you need to head on down to your nearest Apple Store to have it checked, the dude or dude-ette working behind the Genius Bar can often nail the problem in just a minute, after examining the logs.

 Note

There are loads of different logs and many of these items aren't even error messages per se. There's a whole formal log that records all of the software updates that have been installed, for example. Even some of the error-ish notations are more like notations of the little aches and pains that the OS likes to complain about but nobody takes seriously. I consider the latter to be Apple's tribute to Marvin, the Paranoid Android from *The Hitchhiker's Guide to the Galaxy*.

LIKE A STALWART COURT REPORTER, YOUR MAC IS TAKING CAREFUL NOTES

But do take some time to open the Console app and examine what's there. It saves time when something goes wrong and a tech-support person asks you to read him or her what's in there.

It's also useful to poke around in system.log when you suspect malfeasance. If someone's been snooping in your Mac, you might find footprints inside the logs; the OS logs most simple activity. You won't find enough evidence to prove that Slugworth was searching for the Everlasting Gobstopper Project's files on your hard drive, but if the logfiles note a lot of user activity at 3 p.m. yesterday, and you know for a fact that you were knocking off a liquor store then, then you know that you have a problem on your hands.

If you look in Console's Preferences, you see a checkbox that brings the console window to the front for a moment whenever anything is logged. Even I — who adores geeky messages that don't really help me very much — consider this feature an annoyance.

THE SLINGS AND ARROWS OF OUTRAGEOUS SOFTWARE

Viz, Figure 9-10. I was fooling around with the Screen Saver panel in System Preferences while I was writing Chapter 5, but I was stymied. The thing kept crashing every time I opened it. I cursed the darkness, I rended my garment, I shook my fist at the air and took Our Lord's Name In Vain. But hey, cool: I needed a good crash log for this chapter, anyway.

Here's a lesson for you kids out there: when life gives you lemons, freeze the lemons, put them in a pillowcase, and then threaten to clobber your older brother with them if he doesn't return the $20 he took off your nightstand yesterday.

Okay, obviously I'm still a little steamed. But I'll get over it.

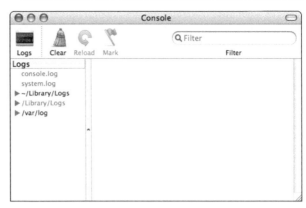

Figure 9-8
The initial Console display

If a tech-support guy tries to fix your woes over the phone, there are two logs that he or she might ask you to consult: the console log and the crash log. As you can see from Figure 9-8, the logs are accessible through the hierarchical list at the left of the Console window. Expanding the console log hierarchy lets you display any of the previous 10 logs.

The crash log records information about processes that have terminated abnormally. Sometimes, as in Figure 9-9, the problem is actually a bug in the program. Regardless of the cause of the crash, the information in the log can give a tech support person information about what the program was attempting to do when the fatal error occurred.

There's also the panic log, which records the Gran Mal of all system crashes, the kernel panic. See it and know fear, for on its dessicated visage is drawn the name of Doom.

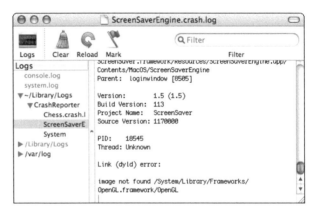

Figure 9-9
The crash log tells you about good apps gone bad

TAKING CARE OF COMATOSE APPLICATIONS

Sometimes the spinning beach ball doesn't go away. Sometimes it sticks around and keeps spinning and spinning and spinning until you begin to see it not as a mouse cursor, but as the whirling portal to a hellish dimension to which you don't deserve to have been sent. It is no longer a beach ball cursor: to your horror, it has become The Spinning Beach Ball (or Pizza) Of Death. The SPOD.

You're desperate to move on with your life. In Mac OS 9.*x* days, you'd breathe in and breathe out and acknowledge that just as night follows day and any meal worth eating requires about 90 minutes of kitchen cleanup, the price of using a Mac is having to restart your whole Mac every time one single app digs its heels in.

Thank heavens you now live in the Push-Button World of Tomorrow. In OS X, we can just spank the one app that's acting up, leaving all other apps (and more to the point, all of their unsaved files) safe and sound. It's actually called a Force Quit, although the word "spank" is so much more satisfying.

▼ Note

A Force Quit is indeed impolite. When it's 1 a.m. and your party guests still won't leave, etiquette demands that you emerge from the bedroom carrying all of their coats and hats, make a big apologetic production about what an early day you've got tomorrow, and then thank everyone for coming and insist that you all do this again sometime. A Force Quit is akin to pouring gasoline around the sofa and then scratching the flint of your lighter in a meaningful way. Yes, both methods will clear the room, but if you use the latter method there might be some serious repercussions.

The app won't follow the formal, "safe" quit procedure that its programmers laid out for it. The OS simply kills (that's a Unix term) all of its processes. So you shouldn't do this as a timesaver. If the app is locked into a SPOD death spiral, take a break. Go downstairs and make yourself some waffles. When you come back, the app might have collected itself enough that you can quit it politely.

Also, be sure of the culprit. Bring up the app's contextual menu in the Dock (hold down the Control key while

clicking on its icon). If the app is truly fried, the Dock reports "Application not responding," and will present you with a contextual menu to Force Quit the app.

You can also bring up the Force Quit dialog:

1. **Press Command-Option-Esc to display the Force Quit window (Figure 9-10), or open it through the Apple menu.**

   You might first have to switch to another app. Hey, look: one of those apps' names is in red. Yup, even Tiger wants to see you kick the butt of this sorry excuse for executable code.

2. **Click on the name of the application you want to Force Quit, and click the Force Quit button.**

   OS X asks you to confirm your action.

3. **Click the Force Quit button.**

   And ding-dong, the witch is dead.

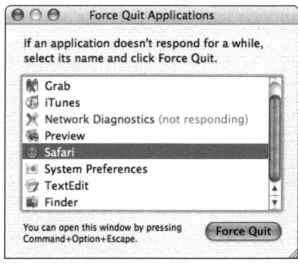

Figure 9-10
The Force Quit window

Caution

Forcing an application to quit will result in the loss of any changes to documents that you haven't saved to a disk. So don't Force Quit unless the application won't respond to anything you try to do.

REMOVING APPLICATIONS

Now we all have this nice, sour taste in our mouths about what happens when a perfectly good application — one that you showered with nothing but nurturing affection, an app that woke up every morning and went to sleep every night knowing that It Was Loved — borrowed your convertible without asking and then let it roll down a pier and into the harbor. So it's only natural (and spiteful, which is what *makes* it a natural reaction) to think about how to de-install an app.

Let me check my notes here.

Okay! All you have to do is drag the application's icon into the Trash.

Let me flip through the rest of my notes . . . no, actually, that's really about it. A Macintosh application is a pretty complicated beastie, when you look at the nuts and bolts of all the components that are loaded onto your Mac and how they interact with each other. But the Mac OS knows that you couldn't care less about what it's done to the infrastructure and all you want right now its for the app, along with all of its hangers-on, to simply disappear.

So you don't need to run an uninstaller, or buy a third-party "cleanup" utility. In Windows — I say this not to gloat but to simply reassure those readers who are coming in from The Other Side — the installation of an app brings with it a lot of changes to a lot of the operating system's internal registries and databases, and removing an app is a lot like trying to remove the stink from a third-hand sofa.

There's actually a Windows control panel that does the job, and even *that* doesn't work very well. But with the Mac, MacarenaWrite 2.0 is banished from your Mac after (1) a simple drag to the Trash, and (2) a solemn realization that there really aren't very many high-quality productivity apps that are based on a fad dance from the Nineties.

And when I say "you don't need to run an uninstaller," naturally I mean that sometimes you *do*. Some apps are a little bit non-standard, and install little embassies of themselves all over the place. Like, the app that manages your new PDA also installs a little status icon into the menu bar, or your digital camera software might add a plug-in to iPhoto's Import library.

For *those* apps, it's useful to re-run the installer program that you got with the app. The installer is *supposed* to detect whether or not the app already exists, and ask you if you'd like to remove it. Apple has a document for developers that spells out how a well-behaved installer should work and that's how they describe a well-behaved installer app. The sad and slightly scary thing is that, as always, your hour-to-hour enjoyment of your Macintosh is left to the developers' commitment to loftier pursuits, and their ability to say "Yes, I *know* that Halo 3 was just released two days ago, but I don't have time for video games: for I am a Developer, and answer to a higher calling."

The forward passage of time is, all things considered, a very positive thing and if the issue ever came to a public referendum, I'd head straight to the middle-school in my voting district and cast my ballot in favor of postponing the Apocalypse by another few years, if not canceling it altogether.

Among the many Winners of progress is your common access to broadband, and the understanding that nearly all software publishers will have *some* sort of online presence. Smaller publishers want you to download and try the entire product. The larger ones will at least give you a chance to test-drive their huge productivity apps for a little bit. Finding new software is now a casual act, requiring nothing more on your part than a little time to kill and a vague desire to see what's new on MacUpdate.com.

I've just brought up the Application Switcher again. Of the 17 or so apps I've got running, a full 25 percent are ones that I first learned of by visiting a website and downloading something, such as BBEdit, the text editor that I write all of my newspaper columns with. Comictastic, a wicked-cool app that downloads 40 or 50 of my favorite comic strips every morning, thus ensuring that four or five days of travel won't mean that I'll come home and have no idea

what's going on with Funky Winkerbean and his friends. Fetch, an FTP file transfer app that I use to send these book chapters from my PowerBook straight to the publisher's servers.

On and on. So I encourage you to be adventurous. Downloadable software is abundant and completely safe here in this Candyland we refer to as The World Of The Macintosh, and there's a vast, caramel-coated world out there beyond Safari, Mail, and Microsoft Office. And I'm talking about a special construction-grade caramel that tastes and smells great, but doesn't make your shoes all sticky when you walk around in it.

10

Running Apps that God Never Intended You to Run

In This Chapter

MacOS 9 • The OS Whose Name We Dare Not Say But Which Rhymes With "Blindoes" • Unix

"If you truly love something, set it free." I saw that motto on an inspirational wall hanging down at the mall a while ago, and apparently it was such a success that they made a whole movie based around it called *Fatal Attraction,* starring Michael Douglas and Glenn Close. Plus *Misery,* starring James Caan and Kathy Bates. And, I think, *Sleeping with the Enemy,* starring Julia Roberts and some dude whose name escapes me. Only none of the latters *set* any of the formers free, resulting in death, mayhem, and whopping box-office sales, which only serves to point straight back to the simple wisdom of the original inspirational wall hanging.

Well, Apple loves you, ladies and gentlemen. Go to the closest Apple Store, walk up to any employee, and say "I need a hug." You won't have long to wait, once he or she has made a quick trip to the computer and verified your customer ID number. To back up this sentiment, Mac OS X Tiger doesn't limit you to solely running the apps intended for this, the most swelligant operating system on the face of the Earth. If, due to needs, circumstances, peer-pressure or as a simple and impulsive act of teenage rebellion you want to run someone else's software, Tiger will pack you a lunch, kiss you gently on the forehead, and stand at the door, resolutely confident that you'll come back to the fold.

There's no reason why you shouldn't bring flowers or something when you *do* inevitably return, of course. It's just good form. Plus, remember all those people who came back to Michael Douglas et al with the soulless eyes of a killer.

COAL-FIRED SUBMARINES: USING MAC OS 9 APPS

Okay. Obviously I'm going to be slagging on MacOS 9 pretty heavily, which (from one point of view, I suppose) is pretty unfair. After all, look at everything that 9.2 did for us. Back in the Nineties. *Way* back in the Nineties. But this was, I should point out, the same Millennium during which Humanity finally caught on to the idea that the Earth revolved around the Sun, and that the epicenter of all celestial motion was not, in fact, a reddish-brown cow in South Wales.

So it's not like it was a particularly flashy Millennium, innovation-wise. Still, Mac OS X was a totally new operating system, completely incompatible with the thousands of apps that had been developed for the Macintosh in the preceding 15 years. It would've have been a bit of a drag if everyone installed X and discovered that absolutely none of their old software worked with it.

Thus, Apple built in a MacOS 9 Compatibility Layer, also known as *Classic mode.* If you launched an old-style app under X, and there was a copy of MacOS 9.2 on your hard drive, the OS would bamboozle the app into thinking that it was running under the old, familiar system. And if you didn't want to bother with X at all, you could keep both the old and the new operating systems on the same hard drive, and boot into one or the other.

▼ Note

Incidentally, note the difference between those two names: "MacOS 9" and "Mac OS X." Yes, there must, there must, there *must* be a space between the Mac and the OS, Apple told us technology pundits. David Lee Roth refused to knuckle under, and holy cow … look what they did to *him*. So, I, for one, just shrugged my shoulders and agreed to play ball.

But today, there's absolutely no reason to use Mac OS X's Classic Environment. There was a moment when companies continued to develop new MacOS 9 software, but there was also a moment when The Macarena was a hit record. The moment — I cannot overstress this — has long-since passed. If old-style apps were more antiquated, Indiana Jones would discover that the Nazi codex detailing the central clue to the legendary Spear of Destiny is on a 3.5" floppy, in the popular MacWrite 1.1 file format. If you've still got MacOS 9 apps, new versions are available. If there aren't, I guarantee you that something even better has been written to replace them.

GRUDGING ACKNOWLEDGEMENT

So why bother talking about MacOS 9 at all? Who the blazes still *needs* to run ancient, incompatible software? Well, as a Beloved International Industry Pundit, I have to remind myself that for the majority of the world's population, acquiring new software requires the steady influx of actual cash, not simply emailing the publisher and flashing my credentials.

You'd be surprised to learn how many active installations of MacOS 9 are out there. Mostly they're in locations where computer labs are woefully underfunded (and it's hard to see those two words without automatically substituting the words "public schools"), or in corporate environments where the information-services folks are trying to starve out the Mac users by refusing to approve any new software expenditures.

Chances are excellent that some of you are in one of those two groups. Realize that I have nothing but sympathy for you folks, and if I seem to be pressing the Sarcasm button hard enough to crack the paint on the finish, it's only because I love. Specifically, I love the power-rush I feel after I've just made a stranger cry with a callous comment.

▼ **Note**

"Guarantee" does not represent a guarantee or warranty of any kind, expressed or implied, and will not be honored under any circumstances whatsoever. — *Jennifer Walters, General Counsel, IhnatCorp LLC.*

I see you nodding your head. I've effectively brought down MacOS 9 in a fair gunfight before your eyes, but now allow me to shoot his hat into the grave with him, a la the final scene in *The Good, the Bad, and the Ugly*:

- **The Classic Environment is actually a Mac OS X application that bamboozles old software into thinking it's running under MacOS 9.** Not all old software will run properly.

- **Because of the bamboozlery, MacOS 9 software runs noticeably slower in Mac OS X under Classic than it would on the same Mac running MacOS 9 "for real."**

- **MacOS 9 apps will run, but they won't receive any of the benefits of Mac OS X.** All of the old OS's ghosts are still haunting the joint: If one OS 9 app freezes, every OS 9 app running under Classic freezes. If one OS 9 app crashes, every OS 9 app crashes. No Spotlight, no advanced networking . . . your Mac is now essentially made out of animal skins and twigs.

- **Don't count on your MacOS 9 apps being able to see your printer, scanner, or even bits of your network.** Remember, you're not running two operating systems. You're still running Tiger. It's just that you also have this Classic Environment that bamboozles old apps into thinking they're in familiar surroundings. Tiger is handling all of the drivers that let apps locate and communicate with hardware and networks, so it's out of MacOS 9 apps' reach entirely.

- **When you launch a MacOS 9 application, be prepared to wait and wait and wait.** Your Mac isn't just launching that app, it's also launching the entire MacOS 9 infrastructure necessary to run it.

- **In some counties, using Classic in a family household on a regular basis is presumptive grounds for Child Protective Services to put your children in temporary foster care.** All I'm gonna say is that if I'm in a mall food court and I see you . . .

Setting up Classic on your Tiger Mac

Also known as "taking this proud, mighty prince of the night out of his native habitat and forcing it to jump onto a giant Disco ball on a Vegas stage for three shows a day."

The earliest editions of Mac OS X assumed that you already had MacOS 9.2 installed. Nowadays, a typical Mac is more likely to have a cardpunch reader installed in it than the old OS. It sure doesn't come pre-installed on your new hardware, and a MacOS 9.2 Installation CD isn't included with your Mac or with your Tiger upgrade package. So if your Macintosh needs to be Classic-studly, you'll need to find a working MacOS 9.2 System Folder and copy it onto your Mac.

BAGGING AN ENDANGERED SPECIES

Check one of your old Macs. There's probably a System Folder on one of the hard drives. But if you haven't bought and paid for MacOS 9 already, you'll have to go buy a copy. And beware that Apple has forsaken and rebuked MacOS 9 as though it were Satan himself. Don't go crying to *them* for an installation disc. Instead, head for eBay, where they can be picked up dirt cheap.

Once you've got an OS 9 System Folder on your drive, all you have to do is tell Tiger where it is:

1. **Open System Preferences and click Classic.**

   Classic's prefs panel opens up, as in Figure 10-1.

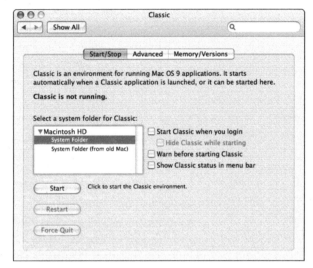

Figure 10-1
Getting ready to run Classic mode

2. **Click one of the volumes shown in the "Select a system folder for Classic" box to open it.**

3. **Navigate to your MacOS 9 System Folder, if Preferences hasn't already located it for you.**

4. **Click the System Folder.**

And that's all there is to it. Classic Preferences gives you a few options, too:

- **Start Classic when you login.** Like I said earlier, Tiger doesn't automatically expect that anyone in their right minds will want to run Classic apps, so it doesn't load in any of Classic's infrastructure until it's needed. If this bums you out, Tiger can automatically load it all in every time you log in.

- **Warn before starting Classic.** But starting Classic is a pain in the butt, and few people really *want* to use it. So in case you're about to launch Classic accidentally (let's say you have a lot of old apps on your hard drive, and you've accidentally double-clicked an ancient Classic version of Microsoft Word instead of the Mac OS X edition), you can have Tiger confirm that this is actually something you want to do.

- **Show Classic status in menu bar.** Clicking this checkbox throws a little menulet in the menu bar that lets you start and quit Classic, chiefly.

Starting the Classic Environment

You're still reading this? I guess I should shrug and say, "It's your funeral," and just get on with the explanations.

If you haven't told Tiger to start Classic automatically when you log in, you can start it manually by clicking the Start button in Classic's preferences pane (Figure 10-1). Which is usually unnecessary; Classic starts automatically whenever you open a Classic application (aka an app written for MacOS 9.*x* or earlier). Tiger throws up a status dialog like the one in Figure 10-2.

Sit back and enjoy it because you're going to be watching that progress bar for a minute or so while Tiger sets up the Classic environment and it boots MacOS 9 into Classic's space. Remember, it's setting up a "fake" MacOS 9.2 Macintosh inside your computer's memory.

In Figure 10-2, I've clicked the little "reveal" triangle so that Classic will show you the entire startup process. Ah, sweet nostalgia; it's been years since I've seen the March of the Icons.

You should be dramatically unimpressed by the results. The windows of the Classic app you've just launched mix and mingle with the Tiger windows you already have. No need to switch between separate modes at all (see Figure 10-3).

Figure 10-2
The Classic startup window

Your only tip-off is that the Classic app's window has the Classic user interface (naturally), and when it's the frontmost app, the Tiger menu bar switches to a MacOS 9–style one.

Incidentally, the tip-off that you're about to launch a Classic app is in the icon, as shown in the Dock in Figure 10-4.

A Classic app icon on a Mac OS X application Dock looks slightly like a mule lurking in a herd of gazelle.

Closing the Classic Environment

Not necessary. When you're done with that old app, just quit it. The Classic Environment will still be floating around somewhere in memory, ready to leap into action in an instant; but if there aren't any Classic apps running, the environment uses practically no system resources.

If you do want to close or restart Classic — let's say you've just used a Classic application Installer, and it's told you that you need to restart your Mac, unaware that the Mac it's running on is a fake one set up within Tiger — you can do so within the Classic pane of System Preferences (see Figure 10-1 again).

Click Start or Restart, whichever you require. And there's also a Force Quit button for use in the incredibly, amazingly, holy cow is it ever unlikely event that one of your Classic apps crashes and locks up the whole Classic environment. (Note: sarcasm.)

Final Classic malarkey

There are still more caveats to know about. Locally mounted hard drives and CDs are available to Classic apps, but network volumes might be hit or miss. And remember that none of Tiger's resources are available to Classic apps. So when you print, you use the MacOS 9 Chooser to select printers. Unless you've installed MacOS 9 drivers for your local printers, and they're connected to your Mac through a method that was available back when giant apes stalked the land, you're out of luck. And you're limited to just the fonts that are installed in the MacOS 9

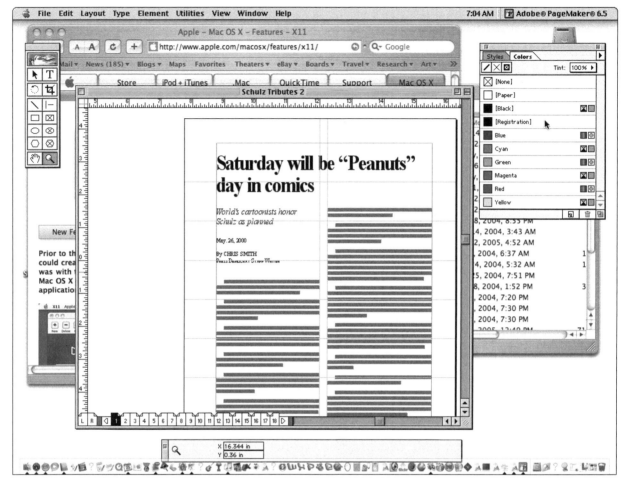

Figure 10-3
Classic apps cohabitate with Tiger apps just fine.

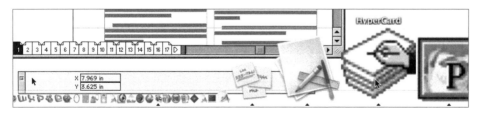

Figure 10-4
Can you spot the Classic app slinking among the Tigers?

THE TATTOO RECORD OF MY LIFE

Incidentally, I finally came up with a tattoo concept that I could *really* get behind. The Classic Mac OS starts off by loading in system extensions and components one by one, each marked by a different icon, making stately progress from one side of the screen to another. Which got me to thinking: how about if I steadily acquire a set of system icons representing the progress I make loading in the Human operating system through the years, complete with social extensions?

The first icon represents birth. Then, breathing air. Next come distinguishing light from dark, pattern recognition, digesting solid foods, crawling, walking, speech, abstract thought, all the way through the landmarks of teendom, education, adulthood, First Tattoo, marriage, parenthood, home ownership, the whole ball of wax; just a line of little square icons marching from my left wrist to my right one. Every blank spot of skin in between would remind me that I've still got more skills and learnin' to do before I've got the complete OS and am ready to move on.

The only trouble is that while I can make up most of these icons as I go, it's important that I pick a good death icon straightaway. And I'll have to carry the design in my wallet and have some sort of organ-donor-type boilerplate that forces the executor of my estate to have it applied at the end of my startup screen before they plant me.

I mean, after spending a lifetime diligently marking every one of life's milestones with the subdermal application of ink, through millions of tiny cuts in my flesh, and then leaving the ball at the one-yard-line, as it were … well, that's precisely the sort of unfinished business that dooms one's spirit to wander the Earth as a wraith for all time, if Stephen King's word can be trusted.

Hmm. I've suddenly lost my nerve on this whole project. The great thing about a Yosemite Sam "Keep On Truckin'!" tattoo is that it will do little to bar your progress from this world to the next. Now I think I know why they're so popular.

System Folder. Classic won't find any of the fonts you've installed in Tiger's System directory.

And it's stuff like that that makes me wonder why anybody would want to go back to MacOS 9, even to run a quick app. I had finally put all that junk about System Extensions and rebuilding the Desktop out of mind. Classic Mode just brings back the nightmares. I mean, when a burglar finishes serving his three-year sentence, he doesn't go back to the joint voluntarily, does he?

If you want nostalgia, rent *American Graffiti*. For gosh sake, don't launch Classic apps.

THE OS WHOSE NAME WE DARE NOT SAY BUT WHICH RHYMES WITH "BLINDOES"

Thanks to the deregulation of the airline industry (which has led all major carriers to switch to narrower seats and mash passengers closer together) and the almost nonsensical lack of Justice in this land (which leads conference coordinators, my publishers, and anyone else who covers my travel expenses to book me into Economy Class instead of First), you can't do anything on a PowerBook without attracting the eye of the person seated next to you. And nothing — *nothing* — freaks out the common bystander as much as the sight of a Macintosh running Windows XP apps as easily and handily as it runs its own native software.

Yup, Macs do Windows. All you need is a piece of third-party software (published by Microsoft, ironically enough) called Virtual PC, shown in Figure 10-5.

Figure 10-5
Split Personality: Macintosh and Windows apps cozily cohabitating

My copy of Virtual PC is set up to emulate an earlier edition of Windows, but all versions up to and including the current Windows XP are supported.

Virtual PC essentially does the same trick as the Classic Environment: it builds a "fake" machine in your Mac's memory, and bamboozles all Windows apps into thinking that they're running on a typical PC equipped with all the expected ports (printer, network, USB) and the usual hardware (sound, video . . . that sort of stuff). Only in this case, it's super-atomic bamboozling. When you ask Tiger to run Classic apps, at least it's got the right CPU and hardware for the job. In Virtual PC, Windows apps officially enter The Matrix. VPC fakes the processor, the address bus, the ports, the hardware interfaces . . . absolutely everything, from top to bottom.

The end result is that Virtual PC can run any Windows app even faster than a real PC can. Four times as fast, sometimes. Plus, the air is filled with the tantalizing aroma of smoked bacon every time you use it.

And none of that is true. But I'm starting to feel a little guilty about being so negative in the first half of this chapter. And I think you were a step ahead of me, anyway. Yes, performance can often be pretty wretched, compared to actual PC hardware. But you can't buy a real PC for the couple hundred bucks that Microsoft is asking for Virtual PC, and there's so much less to carry around.

It's a pretty wonderful app. The whole "fake" PC lives as a single file on your Mac. When you launch the VPC app, it opens this file and restores the phony computer to the same state it was in when you last used it. All of your windows, running apps, and open docs will be just as you left them, and startup is nigh-instantaneous. You can operate Virtual PC in full-screen mode (thus making it look as though Apple has gotten into the business of building PC hardware) or (as in Figure 10-5) have all the Windows action take place inside a single, draggable window.

The Virtual PC will share all of your Mac's resources, too. It'll automatically use your Mac's existing Internet connection and will find and attach your default printer practically automagically. And while the fake PC's fake hard drive is, indeed, inside that big file, the fake PC will think that your "real" Mac's hard drive and CD/DVD drives are standard external volumes, plugged in and ready to go. So copying files from the PC to Mac environment and vice-versa is just a matter of navigating a standard Open/Save dialog box. In many cases, you can just drag document icons into and out of the PC window.

Virtual PC is a great solution if you don't need to have a "real" PC on your desktop, but you *do* occasionally need to run a Windows app that doesn't have any Macintosh equivalents. Many companies rely on custom software based on Microsoft Visual Basic or Microsoft Access, for example, and oftentimes the trump card that gets your nice, friendly Macintosh yanked off your desk and replaced with something infinitely more dull is the fact that the company isn't willing to spend hundreds or thousands of dollars to have a Mac version built.

That said, do take my word for it that all this fakery gobbles up CPU cycles like they were free corn chips. The fake PC's speed is usually quite credible for basic office tasks, but if you ask it to perform anything even remotely taxing — like play a game, or even simply play an MP3 file through Windows Media Player — you'll soon discover resources of patience and meditative funk that you didn't know you had.

Hopefully, you're reading this book because you have found the rusted escape hatch leading to the sweet sunlight of meadows, fresh air, and Tiger applications. But even if you never buy Virtual PC, this is valuable info to have. The next time you're at work and a manager or administrator tells you that there's no way you can use your Mac in their office, you can argue your Mac's defense until you're downsized in the face. You've got the ultimate trump card in your pocket: if push comes to shove, your Mac can run damned-near anything a PC can run.

NOT SO FAST . . .

But the interesting thing is that Virtual PC isn't necessarily the slowest Windows machine in my office. I've got VPC installed on a screaming-fast dual-processor G5 tower, and under *that* high-octane processing environment it's about as nimble as a cheap, modern PC. Still, I don't dare try playing a network game on the thing … I'll get smoked even worse than I normally do. It's hard enough to compete against hyper-caffeinated 14-year-olds without working under the limitations of slow hardware …

FILE THIS UNDER "IRONY"

As odd as it sounds, you'll find Virtual PC in a lot of offices in which Macs have been completely verboten. You'll find it running on the Macs of the company's network administrators. Why? Because (I'm just quoting a friend here … I swear) "When you're trying to keep 400 incredibly unstable Windows PCs up and running, it helps if there's at least *one* computer that I know will always be in working condition!"

On top of everything else, when a virus or a Trojan horse or a worm is shredding all of the PCs on the network, he can diagnose and solve the problem from his impenetrable Fortress of Immunity. But I like to brag about how a Macintosh is often the computer of choice for keeping PCs on their feet.

UNIX

I'm not sure what sort of path you've been weaving through this book thus far. At some point, I hope you've picked up the fact that when you use Tiger, you are, in fact, using the world's most popular individual version of the Unix operating system ever deployed. You almost never hear the "U" word in association with Macs because Unix has a reputation as a propeller-head's OS. Powerful and futuristic, but certainly not the sort of thing you want to have to confront when you just have a cover letter to write and print.

But nope, Unix may be well-masked by Tiger's slick interface and user apps, but it's there. And one of the many benefits Tiger inherits from its Unix legacy is the fact that most software written for one version of Unix can easily be adapted to work with most *other* versions. Combine this with the information that most Unix apps are *open-source* software — meaning that it's the work of dozens or even hundreds of programmers across the globe contributing a little piece here or a little tweak there, and the finished app is free to anybody who wants to download and install it — and you realize that there's a large body of high-quality software for Tiger that's free for the asking. For details on using the most popular free software, check out Mary Leet's book *Free Software For Dummies* (Wiley, 2005).

There's only one Gotcha: very little open-source software is built with the familiar Macintosh interface. It runs under a slightly generic GUI that makes the app easier to port from one version of Unix to another. So while the good news is that you can indeed download a wonderful and highly robust suite of free productivity apps that are almost 100 percent compatible with their Microsoft Office counterparts, the *bad* news is that when you run 'em, they'll run with a fairly proletarian interface (Figure 10-6).

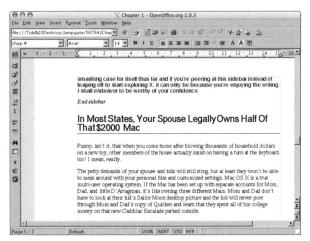

Figure 10-6
OpenOffice: free, but not as flirty as the Mac apps we know and love

This alternative GUI is managed by an app you'll find in your Utilities folder: X11. The X11 app contains all of the code that these open-source apps need for drawing

windows, menus, icons, and all the other clicky-clickies and scrolly-scrollies that makes us shiver with gratitude that we didn't grow up having to learn how to type Ctrl-Shift-/-P-T to print a document.

▼ Note

If you can't find X11 in your Utilities folder, it probably wasn't installed on your machine. No sweat: reboot your Mac from your Tiger installation disc, choose a Custom Install, and leave every item in the list unchecked except for X11. The Installer will put X11 on your drive. Or, you can download it from Apple's website http://www.apple.com/macosx/features/x11/ is currently the correct URL. If it's been moved since I wrote that sentence, just search the site for "X11" and you'll quickly find it.

There's really not a whole lot to know about X11. Many open-source apps will launch it automatically whenever you double-click on the program icon. Others expect it to be up and running already. If you try to launch an open source app and the program starts whining about how "math is hard" and all that nonsense, just quietly launch X11 and then give 'er another try.

So if all this software is so uberwunnerful, why isn't it easier to find? Well, it's a bit under the radar. The most popular apps are available at most of the mainstream sources of downloadable Mac software (such as www.versiontracker.com and www.macupdate.com) but the main silo of open-source software is www.sourceforge.net. The hitch with SourceForge is that the site's been built with the aforementioned propeller-heads in mind. Whereas MacUpdate will tell you that there's this terrific Photoshop-like app called GIMP and it's free for the downloading, SourceForge will bury it in an archive. And then you have to gently point out to the website that no, you don't want to download multimegabytes of source code and build your own special edition of the program. You just want the finished, working, useful bits.

Your first two downloads should indeed be the two apps I mentioned. They're available from `http://porting.openoffice.org/mac/` and `www.macgimp.org/` and downloading and running 'em is no more complicated than running any other app . . . apart from launching X11 first.

So we've had some fun looking at alternative sorts of software that you can run on your Tiger-riffic Mac. This book is filled with affirmations that buying a Mac and upgrading to Tiger was indeed A Gloriously Good Idea. Here's another one: the number of software sources available to you sort of underscore the power and flexibility of the OS and all the thought that went into the thing. Why is VirtualPC available? Because all Mac hardware is built to a uniform and highly stable standard, and power is very much the *sine qua non* of the undertaking.

And open source software? Why, that's precisely why Apple went to all the trouble of creating a brand-new operating system in the first place. One of the very cornerstones of X is that it's as open an operating system as Apple could make it. Apple sure didn't develop the Tiger operating system with the idea that you're going to download free software for it instead of kindly passing some dough to the Mac's legions of developers. You gotta keep the troops happy, after all. But it's remarkable: all of this powerful Unix software is available to Mac users as a mere side effect of Apple's general policy of supporting as many standards as possible, and playing as nicely with the rest of the industry as any company can, given its interest in crushing the globe under its iron bootheel of innovation.

Which is a bad set of imagery. Let's focus instead on the fact that if you need an app that's very much like Photoshop, you can either spend $600 for the real thing or you can download something that's nearly just as good. And more importantly, if someone tells you that there's something their PC can do that your Mac can't, you can tell them where to stick it.

11

Further on Files and Folders

In This Chapter

Creating, Opening, and Saving Files • Achives: Scrunchy, Scrunchy • Hiding Behind an Alias
File Permissions • More Fun with Get Info: Protecting Files and Making Stationery
Platform-Independent File Formats • File Format Translation

One of the great things about a revolution is that what with the waving of red banners and tarring and feathering of local magistrates and such, you forget that you're in the middle of one until it's all over with. And by then, you're so used to the new stamps and the new currency and the huge portraits of this one guy that are hanging in every room of every business and residence — a guy who, you suddenly realize, used to mow lawns for your dad ten years ago — that you really forget that there was any sort of an epochal change at all. Here in Boston, there stands in front of Faneuil Hall a bronze statue of Sam Adams. He's posed casually, but with his arms firmly crossed, manifestly appropriate for the ground-level architect of the Massachusetts Bay Colony's successful revolt against the British.

The legend on the pedestal reads, "Sam Adams – Patriot," and the Park Service has its hands full keeping yuk-a-minute frat boys from adding the word "Brewer." I mean, how soon we all forget. Adams violently intimidated thousands of innocent Royalist sympathizers, both known and suspected . . . but for *what?*

We shouldn't forget that all these swift and slick features for manipulating files and folders were purchased with the sweat and the muskets and, dare I say, the very *lives* of those brave Green Mountain Boys who heard the call of Liberty and came sweeping down from Vermont to respond to Her plea.

I'm mixing my metaphors, but really, if there's one thing that gets me worked up more than file-access infrastructure, it's the Revolutionary War. What I'm getting at is that the Mac OS introduced plenty of stress and laborsaving features in this particular category, and with every new edition of Mac OS X, it's another new victory for simplicity. Tiger's no different.

CREATING, OPENING, AND SAVING FILES

In nearly all applications, you create a new document file by selecting File → New or pressing ⌘+N. The app just creates a blank document without form or content. You don't even have to give it a name until you save it for the first time. You can have a whole bunch of document windows open at the same time. Tiger couldn't care less. Don't confuse this attitude for a lack of love.

The standard Open/Save dialog

Whenever you open or save a file, the Mac OS throws up a standard, consistent user interface element that lets you point out the file you're interested in opening, or specify the place you want a new file to go and what you'd like to name the thing. Figure 11-1 shows you what happens when you save a new document in Microsoft Word:

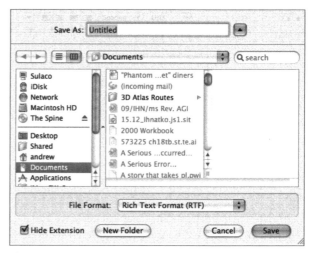

Figure 11-1
TextEdit's "Save File" sheet

The interface is nearly identical to that of a Finder window (see Chapter 6 for details). Everything that makes navigation convenient in the Finder also works in the Mac's standard Save and Open dialogs. All of your sidebar favorites carry through, even down to the order in which they appear; and if you select the Column View, you can walk all the way through your hard drive with just a few clicks.

WAIT . . . WHAT ABOUT FOLDERS?

If you're reading the EthaText version of this book — you know, that sheet of black electronic paper that rolls up into a colorful and warm scarf when not in use — simply focus your gaze on the word FOLDER in this sentence, and after the ET reader senses a "waiting" brainwave through your transcortial bundle, it'll bring up a daisywheel listing bliplinks to the Finder chapter, which is where you'll find information on creating folders. Including *Smart Folders,* a new Tiger feature that automatically locates and links to any files or folders that match a criterion you specify.

If you're reading the old-fashioned *paper* version of this book, just turn to Chapter 6. But *do* look into buying an EthaBook. It costs more than 14,000 Euros, but it *also* plays music, so you're getting tremendous value for the money. My royalty on EthaTitles is slightly higher, too, so you'd be doing me a solid, if you know what I mean.

And what's that up in the top-right corner? Yup, it's a Spotlight search field, and it works exactly the same way that it works anywhere else on the Mac.

So if you've ever used the Finder, you're probably 84 percent of the way towards understanding how to open and save files. To open files:

1. **Navigate to the file's folder.**

2. **Select the file.**

3. **Click Open.**

When you're opening files, it's handy to use the Column View by clicking the Column View icon. Because, just as in the Finder, when you click on a file, the rightmost column will contain a preview of the file's contents. It's a big timesaver, particularly when your Pictures folder contains 13 variations of the filename "Jen and Bob's Wedding Photo (the Really Embarrassing One)."

Some files will be dimmed out; when you click on them, nothing happens. This is because for one reason or another, you really have no business clicking on them. They're dimmed because either the app doesn't know how to open those files (you're trying to open a spreadsheet file in an image-editing program, let's say) or because you've told the app to only show you files of a certain type. In Figure 11-2, for instance, the Enable popup menu limits the listing to just Microsoft Word documents.

If you're *saving* a file, it'll dim out everything in the list except for the folder items.

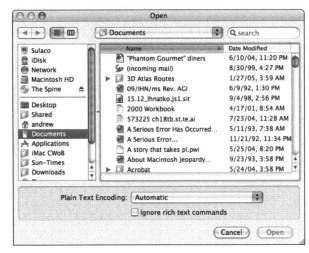

Figure 11-2
TextEdit's "Open File" sheet

▼ **Tip**

But if you're saving a new file and you click on one of the dimmed-out filenames, Tiger copies that filename into the editable field at the top. So if you've got a batch of project files and their names all have to begin with a tracking code, you won't have to type "A7 FINANCIAL Q4 REPORT – DO NOT SHOW STOCKHOLDERS – " 19 times. Just click on one example. Tiger will copy its name, and you can edit it to your heart's content.

Let's see . . . what else? Oh, there's a popup menu above the file listing. The app populates this popup with a list of likely folders for storing the file (your Documents folder, your user directory, etc.) and also remembers a handful of places where you last saved files (Figure 11-4).

Saving files is a little different:

1. **Navigate to the folder into which you want the file saved.**

2. **Type a filename.**

3. **Click Save.**

175

SIZE MATTERS

For reasons beyond mortal man's capacity to comprehend, Tiger can display the Save sheet in a so-called "collapsed" view. Viz, Figure 11-3, which shows you the collapsed version of Figure 11-1.

The mere availability of a Collapsed View makes me think that I ought to drive over there to Apple headquarters and set a few people straight. What possible advantage is there to having *less* information available? Yes. The thing will take up less space. That would be a *very* important feature if we were running Tiger on on original Macintosh 512K, which had about a third of the screen area of my PowerBook here. Tiger doesn't run on an original Mac 512. You have to fold the Install DVD two or three times just to cram it inside the 512's 3.5" floppy drive, and then it just goes south from there. So I'm left with the inescapable conclusion that a collapsed view is of absolutely no bloody use to anybody. The sole advantage of this alternative view is that it's much, much smaller, which would be a big bonus if we were paying for our user interface by the square inch. As it is, you can't help but notice that whereas the expanded view gives you all sorts of useful information and navigational aids, the collapsed view just lets you specify a filename and choose from a slim, prefabbed list of folders to save it in.

If you find yourself looking at the punified version of the Save File sheet, click on the blue triangle next to the filename to expand it into something more sensible. My advice about the Mac's standard Save box is the same as my advice about James Cameron's undersea epic, *The Abyss*. Specifically: forget that anything other than the Expanded Edition even exists.

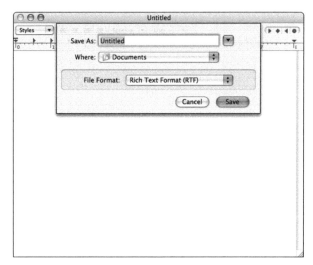

Figure 11-3
The (ugh) Collapsed View of Word's "Save" sheet

The Save As sheet only appears the first time you save a document. After that, using the Save command simply saves the changes you've made to that existing file, without throwing up a sheet. You can still use the Save As command to save a *second* copy of the file, under a different name and/or in a different place. That's handy when you're making revisions to an important document. You're now editing the copy, not the original, and if you mess things up, you still have the original tucked away in its pristine state.

Some apps also give you a Save A Copy As command. With this flavor, you're saving a second copy of the file, but you continue to edit the original.

WHEN IT COMES TO OPEN AND SAVE, APPLE DOESN'T PLAY FAVORITES

One other beef with Open and Save: There's no way to add a Favorite folder to the permanent list of defaults. In previous editions of the operating system, if you were opening or saving a file and you navigated to a project folder that you thought you'd be using frequently, you could click a button right from the Open or Save sheets and bang, that folder would always sit in a list of Favorites.

But that disappeared with Mac OS X 10.3. The Sidebar is available, but you can only add a favorite folder to it in the Finder. Not nearly so convenient. Bad dog. *No* biscuit!

Oh, well. At some point, Apple will pay me a mid-six-figure salary to just email them occasionally and tell them that they've messed something up. Until then, I'll just have to do it out of the goodness of my heart.

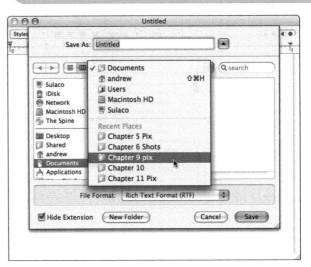

Figure 11-4
The Save As sheet lets you choose a folder in which to save your file

Figures 11-1 and 11-2 show you just one specific example of Open and Save sheets. Every app adds their own extra tweaks and features to Open and Save. TextEdit, for example, adds a little popup menu to its Save As sheet so that you can choose a file format. So steel yourself for a little variety. But rest assured that Apple has gone to great trouble to define a consistent look that all apps should follow.

Opening files from the Finder

Gosh, my hair just flew back from the collective force of 100,000 readers saying, "*Duh!*" after I said, "You just double-click on its Finder icon, or select it and then select Open from the File menu, right?"

▼ Note

And remember once again that man is born unto trouble as surely as the sparks fly upward. Translation: When disaster strikes, it'll strike when you haven't saved your files recently. A famous novelist once compared pausing every few sentences to hit the Save keyboard shortcut (⌘+S) to the way authors would pause every few sentences to dip their quill pens into the ink. It becomes reflexive and invisible.

Okay, yes, you might be beyond this basic info. There's some subtlety to be explored, though. When you double-click on a file, the Finder chooses which application to open it with by looking at the file's type and using the default app for that filetype. But! What if the default for a JPEG file is Preview, and you *actually* want to open it in Photoshop so you can edit it?

There are plenty of ways of opening a file with whatever app you specify:

- In the Dock chapter (Chapter 8) I mentioned that you could just drag a file on top of any app's Dock icon to open it in that app. If the app is capable of handling that sort of file, of course.

- The Finder has a special Open With command, located under the File menu. Select the file, select Open With, and select a compatible app from the list that pops up (Figure 11-5). You can also access the Open With command through the file's contextual menu.

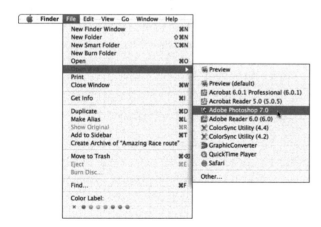

Figure 11-5
Opening a file using the app of your choice, through the Finder

- The file's Get Info window has a special Open With category. It works the same way: just select an app from the popup list (Figure 11-6). There's a big difference with this method, though. The other schemes are one-time-only tricks; when you change this selection in Get Info, the Finder will *always* open this file with the selected app.

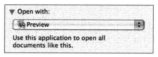

Figure 11-6
Permanently selecting a different app to open a specific file

▼ **Tip**

To apply this change to *all* documents of the file's type, click the "Change All..." button.

IRRITABLE COLON SYNDROME

One hitch with Macintosh filenames: you can't use any colons. The simple explanation is "You just can't, that's all. Now shut up and continue on to the next paragraph." The less simple (and less rude) explanation is that internally, the OS uses colons to describe the physical location of files. "Macintosh HD:Users: GernBlanstev:Documents:The Apple Pie Hubbub" describes all the folders that need to be navigated through before you land on the file. So if you *were* to include a colon in a name ("Space: The Final Frontier") it'd bamboozle the OS like nobody's business.

If you ignore this fact and include a colon in a filename as a feeble act of Raging against the Machine, Tiger will sigh and silently change the colon to a hyphen.

ARCHIVES: SCRUNCHY, SCRUNCHY

File compression used to be a really important part of your daily life as a Happy and Content Computer User. If you had a folder containing 320 K of word-processing files (about 30,000 words of text), an archive program could scrunch that folder down into an *archive file* that only took up 40 K or so. Which again, was a pretty big deal back in the days before computers came with hard drives, and a single 800 K disk had to hold the entire operating system, your word-processing app, and all of the files that you wanted to work with. You couldn't actually access the contents of the archive until you used the same software to "unpack" the archive file's contents to their original states, but you were grateful for the extra space nonetheless.

But Good God. Today, I took a photo of an ice-encrusted drainspout while I fuelled up my car. I didn't even really want that photo, but iPhoto duly copied it into my photo library. So I've wasted 1.4 megabytes, and I couldn't care less because my PowerBook's hard drive is big enough to store the very soul of God Himself.

DATA COMPRESSION: THE BREATHTAKING PROCESS REVEALED!

How can an archive program turn 320K of files into a 40K archive? It uses far more efficient ways of describing the files' contents without losing the information. When you sent someone to the store, did you tell them to buy "an egg; an egg; an egg; an egg; an egg; an egg; an egg; an egg; an egg; an egg; an egg; an egg"? Or did you ask for "a dozen eggs"? Same deal here.

Creating archives is still handy, though. My hard drive holds about 180 GB of data, but the little memory-storage device on my key ring only holds 128 MB. Plus, turning a pile of files into a single archive ensures that the collection is transported in its entirety. If you tell someone to make a copy of the archive file, you can be sure that they'll get the whole menagerie, not just bits and pieces.

To create an archive from a collection of files:

1. **Go to the Finder, and select the files and folders you'd like to archive.**

   It can be a single folder, or you can select lots of individual files and folders.

2. **Select "Create Archive Of (x) Items" from the "File" menu.**

   "X" will be the number of selected items.

And that's actually it. A new archive file, with the .zip file-name extension, will appear in the Finder next to the items that you selected. The archive will be named archive.zip, which you may feel free to then go ahead and rename. If you selected a single folder, the archive will have the name of the original folder, plus a .zip extension.

You can unpack an archive by just double-clicking on it. The archive file is in "zip" format, which is understood by nearly every computer known to man.

ALIAS: ALAS, NO SEXY TV SUPER-SPY IS INVOLVED

The concept of an *alias*, like the concept of Courtesy, is one of those things that you understand innately rather than intellectually. Simply accept that it is right and that it is good, and that it provides a good template for life.

HAVE ALIAS, WILL TRAVEL

Yes, the alias will follow the original file, folder, or volume no matter where the original is ... or wherever it's *gone*. If you make an alias to a folder and then you move the original folder, no problem: the alias will still be able to locate it.

This aspect of aliases makes 'em pretty dashed handy. You can make an alias of a folder on a remote server, for example, and put it in a Finder sidebar. When you click the folder, it connects you to the server (asking you for a password, if necessary) automatically, without having to go through all the steps I show you in Chapter 14.

Aliases are handy things, and you can move them anywhere. I have an alias to my home Mac's Documents folder on my USB key ring. Wherever I am in the world, I can plug this key ring into any Mac, double-click on that folder, and (assuming I have a network connection) it'll connect to the folder back at my house.

An *alias* is a file that represents a shortcut to another file, folder, or volume. If I make a *copy* of a folder, then I'm left with the original folder and a complete duplicate of the folder and its entire contents. If I create an *alias* to that folder, then I have the original folder and an *alias file*, which has an icon that looks and acts just like the original. But! The alias only takes up a few kilobytes of space on my hard drive, and every time I open it, I'm actually opening the original folder.

You can make as many aliases to an item as you want. And you can put them absolutely anywhere, which is the point. I said that aliases are right and good and enhance your life, and I meant it. Some examples:

- You can put an alias of a folder in a handy, easy-to-access location like on the Desktop, while keeping the original in a more organized place such as your Documents folder.

- You can make several aliases of a single file and scatter them in several different locations. You get the convenience of having the file in every place you're likely to want to find it, with none of the added cost in storage space.

- You're working on a project with a half-dozen other people. Instead of making *six bloody copies* of the project folder, and spending one third of every workday making sure that any changes that someone made to *their* folder are also made to all the others, just have each person make their own alias to a central project folder that's kept on the network. They can move their alias wherever they want: onto their Desktop, into their Dock, inside their Documents folder ... it just doesn't matter. Every time they work with "their" folder, they're invisibly working with that single project folder back on the server.

And again, you can move aliases around without "breaking" their link to the original file, folder, or volume. This is because the alias stores not just a reference to the original item, but all the information it needs to reach that item.

To create and place an alias where you need it:

1. **Go to the Finder.**

2. **Find and select the item for which you want to create an alias.**

3. **Select File → Make Alias, or press ⌘+L.**

   An alias file appears. As shown in Figure 11-7, the new alias file has the default name of original_name alias and has a curved arrow in its lower-left corner.

4. **Move the alias wherever you need it.**

SMARTLY BURNABLE FOLDERS

Tiger has brought with it two brand-new kinds of folders: *Smart Folders* and *Burnable Folders*. Oddly enough, here we are in a chapter all about folders, and there's nary a peep about either of them here.

Well, I made an executive decision, that's all. These features could have gone into three different chapters but I had to finally put my foot down. Here's what these folders are, and where you'll find more info about 'em elsewhere in the book:

Smart Folders is one of Tiger's most hypermegasuperginchy new features: it allows you to define a search for files and then "save" that search as a form of intelligent folder. The resulting Smart Folder will always contain references to all of the files that match your original search specification. Define a search for "all Microsoft Word files created in the past two days whose filename contains the phrase 'Special Wham-O Project'", save it as a Smart Folder, and hey-presto ... that folder will always contain up-to-date links to those files.

You'll find a complete rundown of Smart Folders in Chapter 6.

Another cool new feature is Burnable Folders, which provides you with a handier method for preparing a collection of files that you intend to burn to a CD or DVD. Head on over to Chapter 12 for the skinny.

Figure 11-7
A folder and an alias to that folder

FILE PERMISSIONS

Tiger is a multi-user operating system. Meaning, it's not just you who's using that iMac: it's you, and your spouse, and your kids, and your dog. The border collie is, indeed, a remarkable animal.

As such, one of the technical requirements of the OS is that it needs to keep track of who's entitled to do what to which files, folders, and documents. Naturally, it's assumed that little Tralfaz — bad name for a dog, *worse* name for a

kid, by the way — shouldn't be allowed to look inside your personal Pictures folder. But who knows? Maybe you're storing hundreds and hundreds of family photos there, and you want the whole household to be able to view its contents and add photos of their own.

Enter File Permissions. By changing the Permissions on a specific file, folder, or volume, you can expand or restrict what other users of this Mac can do to it.

Before you work with file permissions, you need to understand that Tiger understands three broad types of users (or "Owners"):

- **Owner:** An item's owner is typically the user who created it. As such, the Owner has no limits on what they can do to the thing. A file's owner can read it, change it, delete it, shame it into finally quitting smoking . . . anything.

- **Group:** Now, you'd *think* that "Group" access features are there to make it easy to say "Everyone in the Marketing department can work with this folder, but nobody else." Alas, life is full of disappointments. Off the shelf, the term *groups* has more to do with the underpinnings of Unix than it does with making your Mac easier and more convenient to use. That is, you, the freedom-loving user, *can* create groups of users, and give a group special access to part of your drive. But (a) you do it through a pretty hardcore built-in Tiger utility called NetInfo Manager, and (b) it's a hoary process clearly not intended for regular users, and most importantly (c) if you screw it up, you can screw up your whole Mac.

- **Others:** Joe Schmoe from Kokomo. IE, anyone who isn't you.

In addition, Tiger understands three different levels of access, aka Permissions:

- **Read & Write:** Unlimited access to the item. Add, modify, delete . . . the world is your oyster.

- **Read Only:** You can look, but not touch. So: you can open a doc, but you can't save any changes to it or delete it. You can open a folder or a volume and look inside it, but you can't add or remove files.

- **Write Only (Drop Box):** When a user or group only has Write Only access to a folder or volume, then they can copy files into it but they can't look inside it. It's the equivalent of sliding a document under your door. The person has no idea what else is in there, and they can't even access the file that they just gave you.

- **No Access:** Just keeeeep on walkin', skeezix.

You can get different effects by assigning certain kinds of users certain permissions. But first, a word of warning: Fooling around with permissions is powerful stuff. Wear safety glasses. You can do great things with this feature, but

you can also mess up your files in a mighty and legendary fashion. Sailors visiting foreign ports will sing songs of the time when you locked yourself out of your own hard drive because you got bored some Tuesday afternoon, and instead of playing that new online Scrabble game you came across the other day, you decided to mess around with permissions.

You can change permissions on an item through its Get Info box, as in Figure 11-8. Here, we're changing a regular folder into a Drop Box by setting the permission of Others to Write Only (Drop Box).

Figure 11-8
Using the Get Info window to change file and folder permissions

ROOM FOR IMPROVEMENT

I really wish Tiger made it simpler to share files and folders. It's very good as-is, but like I said earlier, it's impossible for a novice-to-intermediate user to point to a folder and say, "Bob, Ted, and Stan can work with this folder, but nobody else." There's a third-party utility called SharePoints (download it from `www.hornware.com/sharepoints/`) that makes things easier, but still, one wishes for a more ambitious solution.

PERMISSIONS EQUAL PRODUCTIVE POWER

Twiddling with permissions has logical effects. Let's say that I manage an office of 100 people who write reports all day. All reports are based on the same document template, and Step One of any project is to grab a copy of that template off of my Mac. I don't want people to accidentally mess up this master template, but there are four or five people who handle the design work and they need to modify it if necessary.

Without tweaking permissions, all I can do to protect that file is threaten to fire the next freakin' one of youse all who messes up that danged template file again. *With* the ability to change permissions, all I have to do is create a group containing the users who are designers. I give myself and the designers Read & Write permission to the file, and Others: have Read only access. So the folks with the authority to make changes can make changes, while everyone else can't do squat.

Permissions will also come into play when we get into networking and sharing. See Chapter 14 for more on networking.

Usually, you'll change file permissions on an item to achieve one of three effects. Go to the "Others" category of Ownership & Permissions, and make one of these selections from the Permissions popup:

- **Allow other users to read an item, but not change it.** You've got a folder of standard boilerplate letters that your office uses to assemble consistent correspondence. You want everyone to be able to come here and grab a copy of the letter they need. So you change the folder's Permissions to Read Only.

- **Allow people to slip files in under your door.** Change permissions of a folder to Write Only (Drop Box).

- **Give everyone unfettered access:** Select Read & Write. If you do this to your Pictures folder, every user of this Mac will be able to view, edit, and contribute to your collection of photos.

Two caveats:

- If you change permissions on a folder to Read & Write (for example), all users of this Mac will be able to read and write inside that folder. But they won't have that same access to the items *inside* that folder. To make your choice apply to the folder's complete contents, click "Apply to enclosed items."

- Just because you've given users access to a folder, it doesn't necessarily mean that they'll actually have access to that folder. If the folder is inside *another* folder, and "Others" don't have access to it, then it's all a waste of time. Make sure that you keep shared folders in a spot where users can actually get at 'em.

MORE FUN WITH GET INFO: LOCKING FILES AND MAKING STATIONERY

You can protect files and create stationery (aka template) files through a couple of simple features built right into the Finder's Get Info window (see Figure 11-9).

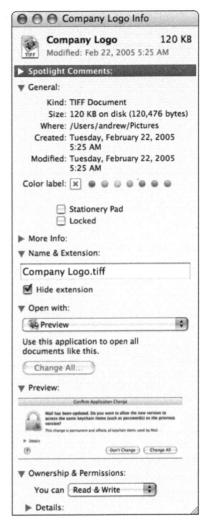

Figure 11-9
Using the Get Info window to lock files and create stationery

Clicking the Stationery Pad option turns the file into a "Stationery Pad." When you open a Stationery file, the app will create a brand-new, untitled document that has all of the stationery file's settings and contents. And when you click Save, the app prompts you for a new filename and location. You use it for letterhead, logos, document

templates — anything that you're likely to base lots and lots of new files on. If you want to change the stationery file, you'll have to uncheck that option in the Finder, make your changes, save 'em, and then go back to the Finder and turn the document's Stationery Pad option back on.

Clicking Locked is the same as setting a file's permissions to Read Only. Nobody — not even you, the document's owner and creator — can save changes to it. The Finder throws a little padlock onto the file's icon for good measure (Figure 11-10).

Figure 11-10
A locked file or folder

▼ Note

The Locked feature is also known as the "Please, somebody, protect me from *myself*" feature. I can't tell you how often I've set myself back entire *days* because I merrily took a document that was finished, perfect, and otherwise ready to go ...and then Boy Edison here messed it up because I mistook it for one that I still needed to process or fix.

So now, when a project is completed, I click the Locked option. It's simple to unlock it if need be, and in the meantime it prevents those painful bruises that result when I'm forced to pound my head against the desk over and over and over again. (No pity, please! I have it coming, and it's the only way I'll learn.)

PLATFORM-INDEPENDENT FILE FORMATS

Although we might wish that *everyone* used a Macintosh, it's an imperfect world. Just look at how long it took for the Red Sox to win another World Series, for heaven's sake. Therefore we often find ourselves in the position of having to exchange files with people who are using Windows or Unix. But look, that's a piece of cake: There are plenty of file formats that are platform-agnostic (just about any operating system can read them), and OS X provides significant support for 'em.

What a friend we have in Microsoft Office

Nearly all offices have standardized on Microsoft Word, Excel, and PowerPoint. Microsoft Office is also available for Mac OS X, but the added bonus is that the Windows and Mac file formats are absolutely identical. You can email a Word file to your Windows buddy and he can open it without any file translation whatsoever, in most cases. He can save changes and send it back to you. And, ditto, it's welcomed home with open arms and nary a whiff of suspicion, opening on your Mac with just a double-click.

What a friend we have in TextEdit

But if you don't own Office, try opening that Word file in TextEdit, Tiger's built-in simple word processor. It can open and save files in Word format. It also supports Rich Text Format, which is an elderly but still rather spry platform-generic format for word-processing documents.

DECEIT IS A CORE TECHNOLOGY

If you must swap files with one of those paranoid birds who *insists* that you use a Windows box because he *knows* that it's impossible for the two machines to swap files, go ahead and lie about this wonderful new Windows XP machine you bought last week. He'll never know. He double-clicks the file you sent him, and it opens in Word. He emails it back to you, and you can double-click it just as easily.

Plus, lying is a basic feature for any on-the-go businessperson and the more practice you get with this technique, the better you'll do in your next job interview. This *is* a Windows World, after all.

The hitch is that TextEdit doesn't *quite* have Word's features (in much the same way that I can't run *quite* as fast as a Boeing 777 can fly). But for simple documents that lack complicated formatting, it'll serve in a pinch.

What a friend we have in PDF

If you need to share documents with complicated formatting (lots of fonts, columns of texts, graphics, and photos . . . no limitations whatsoever) the cheapest and most foolproof solution is going to be to save it in Adobe's Portable Document Format (PDF).

Adobe promotes PDF files as "digital paper;" the recipients of a PDF file may or may not be able to edit its contents, but they can certainly read it and print a publication-perfect copy.

▼ Note

And, in fact, that's one of PDF's handiest features. When you're sending your sister's wedding program to a print shop to be professionally typeset, you can't send the file you created unless you're absolutely *sure* the shop owns the exact same software and the exact same fonts, and that all of your images and stuff will stay together on the same disk. With PDF, the whole thing's already been rendered — text, graphics, and all — and it'll look the same coming out of a $20,000 typesetter controlled by a Linux box as it did coming out of a $100 inkjet connected to your Mac. The federal government enjoys and trusts PDF for distribution of tax forms and informational documents ... why won't you?

In many earlier versions of the Mac OS, you needed to purchase a commercial app called Adobe Acrobat to create PDFs, although Adobe gave out a free app for opening, reading, and printing those files. Tiger can print a document into a PDF file just as easily as it can print it to paper.

To create a PDF, follow these steps:

1. **Prepare your document as usual.**

2. **Select File → Print or press ⌘+P.**

3. **Click the PDF popup button and choose Save As PDF" from the list.**

4. **Tell Tiger what the PDF should be called and where it should go.**

To view the PDF, use Tiger's built in Preview app. You won't be able to edit the text or move any of the graphics around, but the new Tiger edition of Preview gives you nifty tools for marking up these files and adding comments. So you can send a document around the office inviting comments and suggestions, and then reopen the original file and make your changes.

TAKE THAT, WINDOWS LOVERS!

As the little fish in the pond, it's always been important for the Mac to embrace as many different file types as possible. Many times, an IT manager's claim that "We can't have Macs in this office because they can't exchange files with the Windows machines" has been dashed when an employee silently stuck a Windows CD into a PowerBook, double-clicked on a file, and then before the manager's unbelieving eyes the Microsoft Word for Windows document opened in Word for Mac OS X without any ado.

At which point he said, "We can't have Macs in this office because they don't match the drapes." But at least we won the *intellectual* part of the argument.

Graphics file formats

In terms of graphics files, there are a bunch of file formats that are relatively platform independent:

- **JPEG or JPG:** The Iron Man of graphics file formats. Most of the graphics you encounter on the Web are JPEGs, and your digital camera saves its photos in JPEG format by default.

- **PNG:** A newer alternative to JPEG. It isn't nearly as widespread, but it's gaining some traction.

- **GIF:** Chiefly a standard for creating graphics for websites.

- **TIFF:** TIFF is used primarily for print publishing. Conceptually, people tend to create TIFF files when they want the highest possible quality images, but JPEG is so flexible that it's hard to tell the difference between the two formats.

- **EPS:** EPS is a PostScript format that is used extensively in publishing. When the image can be described in terms of lines, curves, and shapes, it provides excellent scalable output at a small size.

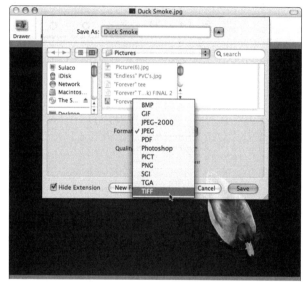

▼ Note

TIFF is a great format for when you don't want to compromise image quality. When an app saves a JPEG file, it compresses it to make it smaller so that you can transmit faster. But there's always a drop in image quality, particularly when you open, edit, save, and then edit and save again, and then again. Every time the file's recompressed, it loses more and more of its clarity; it's like when you crumple up a sheet of newspaper and then unfold it, over and over and over again. Every time you do it, the image becomes a little harder to read. You can usually save TIFF files in an uncompressed format, so the file is as crisp and clean as the original. Obviously this is only a big concern when you're doing high-end work, but it's good to know, nonetheless.

FILE FORMAT TRANSLATION

If you receive files from someone who is using software that you *don't* have (especially Windows software), you may need to translate the file into a format that one of your apps *can* handle. By the same token, you may need to take one of your files and translate it into something you can send to someone *else,* who might not have the same software as you do.

There are several ways to go about this. The trick is to use an application that can read or write the file format in question. If you want to translate graphics formats, for example, OS X's Preview application can open and transmogrify most of the common graphics formats:

1. **Open the document that you want to convert using Preview.**

2. **Select File → Export.**

   A Save As dialog appears.

3. **Select the format in which you want to save the file from the Format pop-up menu that appears, as in Figure 11-11.**

4. **Click Save.**

Figure 11-11
Using Preview to convert graphics file formats

The absolute champ of graphics-file conversion is Lemke Software's GraphicConverter (www.lemkesoft.de/en/). If there's a format that it can't open, then it ain't worth opening. It's also a cataloguing and editing tool.

ONWARD AND BACKWARD

You know why people buy MacLinkPlus? Because they'll be cleaning a storeroom or a closet and will discover a five-year-old disk with a *really important* file on it. There was a time when I strayed from Microsoft Word and used a freaky, brand-new word processor that came and went out of business inside of a year. And of course, Word has no idea how to deal with this stuff, and in that case, MacLinkPlus is a swell investment. Everything I write is a gem of flawless Truth, Beauty and Wisdom, after all, and it's a tragic waste to let any of these pearls slip away. Don't you agree? Oh, thank you … you're too kind.

Many other apps have built-in translation facilities. For example, Microsoft Word can handle some generic formats (RTF and plain text) as well as a variety of Microsoft formats, such as Word and Excel for Windows, as well as AppleWorks and other common office formats.

But it doesn't support *all* file formats. So, what can you do if someone sends you a Word Perfect file, for example? Are you stuck with simply recovering the text? Not necessarily. What you need is a file format translation program such as MacLinkPlus from DataViz (www.dataviz.com). MacLinkPlus can handle nearly 75 MS-DOS, Windows, and Macintosh file formats, some of which are from older software that isn't used any more. This is a major boon if you find that you need to get to older files whose programs won't run at all, even under OS 9!

MacLinkPlus not only translates formats, but also allows you to view the contents of a document even if you don't have the application with which it was created. MacLinkPlus also can extract files from StuffIt, ZIP, and tar archives, as well as decompress MIME and BinHex files.

I have some blank space here at the bottom of the page, so I'll just share one of those Big Pronouncements About The Future Of Technology that everybody was making a long time ago, but which hasn't come to pass and never, ever will. The whole concept of files is hopelessly quaint, and that by the 1990s we'd consign them to the scrapheap of history, like the buttonhook, and people who major in communications with the actual hope that this will help them get a job some day.

It's certainly a good idea. Remember that keeping data organized into files with names and organized into folders is a burden that's fallen on the shoulders of the users. Is this unavoidable? Well, no. Ask someone who loved Apple's discontinued Newton PDA. It didn't save anything as files. Everything you created was tossed into a soup of data, and it was the Newton OS's responsibility to figure out that you now wanted to get your hands on that note you wrote last Tuesday about this hot new music group you've just come across: "Wham!"

But we're stuck with them. Not because we lack the technology and the firepower. We can't change the basic interface of a car to anything other than a steering wheel, foot pedals, and a shifter. It's just too deeply ingrained into society at this point.

That doesn't prevent us from hoping there's a better way around the corner, though. I don't give up hope. Heck, I still keep praying that *Star Wars Episode I: The Phantom Menace* will one day become a better movie.

12

Using Hard Drives, CDs, DVDs, and Other Silos of Data

In This Chapter

And Volumes Are…? • The Boot Volume • Mounting and Unmounting Volumes
External Drives: USB and FireWire • Burning CDs and DVDs • Memory-Based Storage
Networked Volumes • Using Target Disk Mode • Disk Images • Keeping Volumes Healthy

Slide a floppy diskette into a drive. You hear a mechanical ch-CHNGK and a whirring of motors, and a second or three later an icon appears on the Desktop. Double-click the icon and a window opens, revealing all the files on that disk.

Ah, the good old days of 1985. The mid-1980s had its downsides (as I recall, I was forced to play a lot more dodgeball than I would have liked; plus, it was the sort of artistic environment in which groups like Culture Club and the Thompson Twins were able to thrive), but the unsophisticated storage devices of that era's computers made it a pretty sweet time to learn about computers.

Today, things are different. When we talk about Something We Store Files On, we're talking about an abstract construct. You don't call it a disk because you use actual disks only in Cuba these days, and even a drive is imprecise because a hard drive can contain several independently mountable areas. And how should we describe that Something when it's not part of our own hardware setup, but a device that we connect to via a network?

Hence, we start talking about volumes. There's a lot to know about accessing, caring for, and feeding the little darlings, and a topic *that* broad needs a phony-baloney and only marginally clear technical term.

AND VOLUMES ARE...?

So what are we talking about when we speak of volumes? You can stick with the description I gave you in the intro: it's a discrete place to store files. And so long as you don't think too hard about that, it'll probably do you just fine.

In real truth, *volume* is a well-selected term because it does a really accurate job of explaining the technical side of file storage without forcing us to haul out the H. Poindexter Nerdly Guide To Obfuscational Linguistics.

Think about all the volumes you have on your bookshelf right now. I'm glancing to my right and reading four titles at random: Andrew Chaikin's *A Man on the Moon*, Larry Kaniut's *More Alaska Bear Tales*, *The Calvin and Hobbes Tenth Anniversary Book* by Bill Watterson, and *Roger Ebert's Book Of Film*.

 Note

The *Bear Tales* book is the second in the series and contains hundreds of pages of first-person accounts of what it's like to be attacked by a bear. I try to keep it handy while I work. Writing is a challenging, lonely business, and at times reading a tale of a camper being dragged by his left ankle through a stream by a grizzly bear helps to keep one's hardships in proper perspective.

These are all separate books. Each has its own title page, its own unique Library of Congress number, its own table of contents, and its own index. Moreover, each one of these books could be, and was, formatted in its own special way. The moon book is a traditional volume filled with chapters of text. The Calvin and Hobbes book is horizontal and consists almost entirely of comic strips, and Ebert's book is all text, but it's laid out in two columns instead of one.

Got that? Well, congratulations. You now understand what volumes mean to a computer. Whether a volume is a hard drive, a networked volume, a CD, or a bit of flash memory on a USB key ring, it has its own independent file directory and data structures and its own method of laying out information — so you can make one volume a Mac-formatted drive, another a DVD-ROM that works on Windows machines, and a third an audio CD. And you can access them all at the same time.

Finally, each volume in my bookcase is a separate entity. I can close one book and put it away without disturbing any of the others that are still open on my desk (or somewhere in my bed, which in my case is far more likely).

THE BOOT VOLUME

Your Mac can have many volumes attached to it, but one of these volumes is special. A *boot volume* contains a properly installed copy of the operating system on it that your Mac can load in and execute on startup. You can recognize a Mac OS X boot volume by the presence of an enormous folder named System. Macs that use Mac OS 9 have a totally separate folder called System Folder. Try not to let it confuse you, though I won't think any less of you if it did.

So you're only going to have one boot volume, right? Well, most likely. Out of the box, your Mac's hard drive is formatted as one big volume, and there's just one copy of the OS on there. But there are instances in which you can have more than one boot volume available, namely:

- You have more than one drive attached to your Mac.

- You have a disc in the drive that's bootable. Your Tiger installation disc, for example, is bootable. If you bought a new Mac that came with Tiger preinstalled, it shipped with a bootable system disc.

BOOT VOLUME TRIVIA

Many commercial disaster-relief utilities (such as Alsoft's DiskWarrior, mentioned later in this chapter) ship on a bootable disc, and thank heaven for that. You probably won't use a magical piece of software that fixes a petulant and recalcitrant volume until that volume stops working. If it's the boot volume, your Mac can't start up and run the utility!

This is also why I have a minimal Tiger installation on my iPod. I know that if push comes to shove, I can connect it to my PowerBook and boot it back to life. It's like the CPR paddles you see on *ER*. Plus, this functionality was just the practical excuse I needed to allow me to buy the 40 GB model instead of the 20.

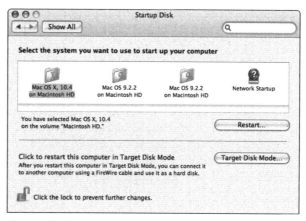

Figure 12-1
Choosing a startup disk

- You've partitioned your hard drive with Disk Utility, slicing it up into multiple, independent volumes. In that case, you can place a different bootable OS on each volume.

- You have another volume elsewhere on your local network off of which you can boot.

When multiple boot volumes are available, you can select which one the Macintosh should use the next time it restarts or starts up when you turn on the power:

1. **Launch System Preferences by selecting it from the Apple menu.**

2. **Click the Startup Disk icon.**

   The startup disk panel appears, as in Figure 12-1.

3. **Select the disk volume from which you want to boot.**

4. **Exit System Preferences.**

   If desired, restart the Macintosh immediately to boot from the newly selected volume.

MOUNTING AND UNMOUNTING VOLUMES

Most Macintosh volumes will mount themselves. Nearly all FireWire or USB drives (a typical external hard drive, or one of those keychain drives) appear in the Finder a few moments after you plug them in. CDs or DVDs mount as soon as they spin up to speed in a drive and can be read.

Mounting volumes

Occasionally, you may encounter a volume that won't mount automatically. In that case, you can usually mount the volume manually, using Disk Utility:

CHUFFED AND MOUNTED

The term *mount* is a charming holdover from the early days of computing when huge mainframes relied on disk packs the size and weight of spare tires. Over in the Math Building you'd be at a terminal making a request to load up some software, and then some computer science grad student wearing earth shoes and an "I'm with *Stupid*" T-shirt had to physically mount the pack inside a piece of equipment two buildings away.

I missed out on this part of the computing era, but I imagine that part of the fun of playing Solitaire way back then was the knowledge that your idle whim to waste some time was going to require an anonymous stranger to manhandle a 15-pound piece of equipment into position. It must have been the same feeling that King Louis had when he ordered his human chess pieces around. Ah, the good old days …

1. **Open the Finder, the Applications folder, then the Utilities subfolder.**

2. **Launch the Disk Utility program by double-clicking its icon.**

   Disk Utility doesn't enjoy the same luxury that you and I do: it can't understand that "Volumes are like books on a bookshelf" motif. Instead, it sees a list of physical devices hooked up to your Mac and a list of the volumes located thereupon. You can easily distinguish one from the other: the Devices are the items that look as though they were named by Mr. Spock on a particularly uptight day; the items with friendly, approachable, Human-parsable names (slightly indented) are the Volumes.

3. **Select the name of the volume from the list of recognized volumes.**

   You find this on the left of the window (Figure 12-2).

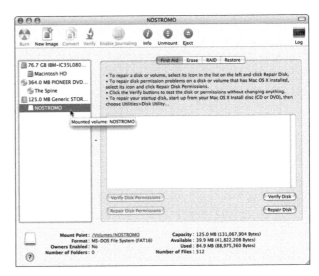

Figure 12-2
Mounting a volume manually

4. **Click the Mount button in the toolbar at the top of the window.**

   OS X mounts the volume and adds an icon for the volume to the Desktop if it can.

▼ **Note**

Disk Utility is one of my most frequently used utilities. This is, what … the fourth chapter in which Disk Utility rates a mention? Maybe the fifth? Bravo. If Apple came out with a T-shirt for Disk Utility, I'd buy it and wear it while I exercise. And when that cute girl with the long black hair comments on it, I'd say, "Oh, yeah, I've been using it for *years*, way before it started getting national airplay and stuff." She would giggle and wonder why she's never really noticed me before.

Unmounting volumes

Unmounting a volume removes its icon from the Desktop. The physical drive might still be connected and spinning, but as far as the Finder is concerned the unmounted volume doesn't exist anymore, at least until you mount it again.

To unmount a volume, drag its Finder icon into the Trash. You can also click the little Eject symbol next to the volume's name in the sidebar of any Finder window, or select Eject from the icon's contextual menu.

▼ **Note**

"Wait ... when I drag a volume *into the Trash*, it just unmounts it? It's not going to, um, well, *delete two years of my life's work in an instant* or anything?" No. I don't know whose idea it was to encourage people to drag volumes into the Trash, but it was a bad one, and a serious stretching of the Trash metaphor. It confuses (and concerns) a lot of people, which is why in Mac OS X, Apple set up the Trash to turn into an Eject symbol when a volume is dragged onto it.

If it's a network volume or a volume on a hard drive, it disappears from the Desktop. If it's a removable volume like a CD, it'll be ejected. If it's an external drive, like a FireWire or USB 2.0 hard drive, an iPod, or a USB keychain drive, you can safely unplug it from your Mac after its volumes have been unmounted.

▼ **Caution**

But remember, each physical drive can have more than one volume on it. If you're unsure how many volumes you have on an external drive, it's safer to unmount the thing using Disk Utility, which organizes all of your volumes by their physical locations.

You can also use Disk Utility to unmount a volume without removing the disk from its drive. This is useful mojo. If a multisession CD (one that didn't have all of its info

burned onto it all at once) is in your drive, each session appears in the Finder as a separate volume. That's a lot of visual clutter; just unmount the ones you don't need. It's also handy to unmount any external drives you're not going to use. It's a hassle to unplug my little pocket drive when I go off to lunch, but by unmounting it, it's unlikely that anyone's going to paw through its contents while I'm away.

To unmount a volume via Disk Utility:

1. Open the Finder, the Applications folder, then the Utilities subfolder.

2. Launch the Disk Utility program by double-clicking its icon.

3. Select the name of the volume from the list of devices and volumes.

4. Click the Unmount button, visible in Figure 12-2.

And there goes the volume. Incidentally, check out Disk Utility's Eject button. That's a special button for removable media like CDs and DVDs. Selecting a DVD and clicking Eject reduces two Disk Utility steps to one: it unmounts all of the disc's volumes and then physically ejects the disc.

▼ **Caution**

Disk Utility assumes that you're one of those hip, trendy, on-the-go sort of users who doesn't have time to think before they act. Therefore, if you ask it to do something foolish — such as unmount a device that's still needed — it'll say, "Yes, *sir!*" and do it. If you were to unmount your boot drive, and quit Disk Utility without remounting it, well, that's the ballgame. You'll have to restart your Mac. Later on, when Disk Utility is in the cafeteria with your other apps, it'll talk and talk and *talk* about the dumb thing you did, and everyone will have a big laugh at your expense. *Computers are not your friends.* Never forget that, people.

EXTERNAL DRIVES: USB AND FIREWIRE

Your Macintosh is verily *studded* with USB and FireWire ports, places where you can plug in external devices. Both USB and FireWire are Plug and Play (plug the device in and your Mac can find it automagically, without requiring you to install any special new device drivers) and hot-swappable (you don't need to switch your hardware off before unplugging something from a FireWire or USB port).

USB GETS ITS GROOVE BACK

USB used to be the Fredo Corleone of the mass-storage world: weak, slow, and stupid. Back in the day (December of 2004) you wouldn't want to use a USB hard drive even on a dare. USB is fine for those little memory-based keychain drives, but it was way, *way* too slow to use for hard drives. FireWire was the way to go.

But hey, Things Change. Now, there's USB 2.0, which is backwards compatible with the old kind. USB 2.0 is *nearly* as fast as FireWire. It's also backwards-compatible, which means that you can plug a USB 1.0 device into a USB 2.0 port and it'll work just as fine (slowly, but fine). USB 2.0 has been around for a while now, though it hasn't made any sort of a big splash with Macintosh users. No mystery why: Apple didn't ship any Macs with USB 2.0 built-in.

They do now, though. Which makes things *slightly* more complicated. All FireWire drives will work fine with Macs. But if you're eyeing a USB 2.0 drive, don't lay down your ducats before you've verified that your Mac has USB 2.0 ports. Either visit Apple's Web site and look up the hardware specs for your machine, or run the System Profiler utility.

ONE DOWNSIDE OF USB AND FIREWIRE

Both USB and FireWire are big improvements on the interfaces they replace: Apple Desktop Bus and SCSI. SCSI in particular deserved to be given a stern talking to and sent out to the yard to pick weeds until suppertime. Whereas today you simply plug a FireWire drive in and expect it to work, attaching a SCSI device to a Mac and getting it to work properly often meant that you were in for a real way-hey-hey of an afternoon (and evening, and sometimes even a boozy early dawn).

One of these new interfaces' best features spawns one confusing element, however: both interfaces can serve as an electrical connection as well as a data connection. So, my pocket FireWire drive connects with just one cable; no AC adapter is necessary. When you start attaching several devices to the same port, some of those devices may sputter and stop working. There just isn't enough power on that port to run all those input devices *plus* my new Waring blender. A good hub comes with its own power supply, capable of pumping out more than enough electrons to keep all of your devices happy.

Both FireWire and USB devices are set up so that multiple devices can hook up to a single Mac FireWire or USB port. Nearly all USB and FireWire devices have one or more additional connectors tucked away somewhere. So you can plug your keyboard into a USB port, and then you can plug a mouse into the keyboard. Right now, for example, I've got both a mouse and a USB keychain drive plugged into mine.

ANDY WISHES TO PUNK OUT A GOOD SAMARITAN

Let me take you to an auditorium in Boulder, Colorado. I'd just finished giving a talk to a user group, and idly mentioned that I was desperately searching for an antique developer utility that Apple used to give out for free. Well, faith and glory, someone in the crowd happened to have it on his PowerBook. I gleefully chucked my USB key to the gent. He copied it over — even going so far as to launch the app right from the keychain to make sure it was working properly — and then he yanked the key straight from the drive and tossed it back without formally ejecting it first.

An eyebrow was arched. "Are you *sure* that was a good idea?" I asked, in my best "Look, I'm an expert, but I don't want to be a jerk about this" tone. I was assured that indeed, absotively nothing bad could happen as a result. I knew better, of course, but insisting that he copy it again would be a breach of etiquette (and would necessitate my use of the phrase, "Now see here, Skeezix....") so I let it pass. And naturally, when I got back to my hotel I discovered that the entire drive was now toast and that all of the (easily replaced, thank heavens) files I had on the thing were lost.

I mention this story for two reasons. One, to really bring home the idea that you need to eject your volumes properly before disconnecting them from your Mac; and two, to warn this gentleman that revenge is a dish best served cold and that in the high Rockies in April, it is very, very cold indeed.

You can also buy a FireWire or USB *hub*. This is a harmonica-looking device that sports several connectors and can serve to connect two or more devices into the same Mac port.

Oh, yes, and about that hot-swappability I mentioned. It's a big boon to disconnect a drive and put it away without having to shut down your Mac first, but don't just yank out the cable. You absolutely, positively must unmount the drive's volumes first. Just go to the Finder and drag its volumes to the Trash.

Why? Because you never know when some app on your Mac is working with the thing. If it's saving that previous Word file to it when you yank the cord out, kiss the file goodbye. If the Finder is writing critical directory information, well, you can kiss something *else* of yours goodbye. I assure you this item is a far more personal item and not as readily replaced as a two-page memo.

BURNING CDS AND DVDS

There's a reason why Apple stopped putting floppy drives inside Macs years ago: They're obsolete. They went out with spats and buttonhooks, steam-powered cars, and even Sylvester Stallone's bankability as a star of Hollywood blockbusters.

Why put 1.4 megabytes (MB) on a diskette when you can put 650 MB or 700 there instead? Or how about more than 4 whole gigabytes (GB)? Diskettes still had a place in this modern pushbutton world when recordable CD and DVD media were expensive. Once, a blank DVD would have set you back 10 or 20 bucks. Today, you can buy them in spindles for less than a buck a throw, and CDs are down to mere pennies.

Recordable discs give you vastly increased amounts of removable storage, but they're a bit less convenient than floppies. A computer can write a file to a floppy immediately. With optical discs, it's a big production; it has to blast all of its contents onto the disc at once. You can fill it up in several blasts spaced days, months, or weeks apart — this is known as *multisession* recording — but the fact remains that you have to maintain a slightly different mind-set when working with discs than you do with floppies.

The burning process

Writing files to a CD or DVD is known as *burning* the disc, and OS X makes the process extremely easy. Almost *deceptively* easy, you might say. (Remember: *Trust nobody*. Except for me, of course. Maybe your mom, too. Does she have those shifty kind of eyes? Have you *looked*, recently?)

1. **Insert a blank disc into the drive.**

   Tiger recognizes that you've tossed in a recordable disc, and via a pop-up menu asks you to specify an application that Tiger should pass the buck to (Figure 12-3).

Figure 12-3
What app is going to take immediate custody of this disc?

Good gosh, *why* do you have to tell your Mac what to do with this disc? Because the Mac is a lean, mean, multimedia machine. Slapping files onto a disc with the Finder is only one expression of its discy agility. Maybe you actually want to make a standard audio CD instead, or a playable DVD or a video photo slideshow. Normally, of course, you'd be in iTunes or iDVD or iPhoto and click that app's built-in Burn button, but your Mac can't make assumptions.

BURNING A DISC: BEHIND THE SCENES

When you insert a blank CD or DVD, the Finder mounts that disc on the Desktop as a new volume, after which you can start dropping folders and files onto it. What *actually* happens is that a section of your hard drive the same size as that disc is set aside, and all of the files that you drag onto the disc icon get copied there. Only when you burn the disc is the data actually written.

For this reason, Tiger won't let you work with a recordable disc unless you have an amount of free space on your boot drive equal to its capacity. It can be a minor hassle, but keep in mind that in the olden days (that is, back during Clinton's second term in office) the Finder couldn't deal with blank optical media *at all*. You had to do everything through a third-party app. Plus, good, hardworking men were dying by the hundreds while digging the Panama Canal and color photocopying technology was still, like, *three years* off.

We're going to store files on this disc, so we'll be using the Finder.

2. **Select Open Finder and click OK.**

   The Finder then puts a disc icon on your Desktop that represents the recordable disc and opens a Burn window (Figure 12-4). It looks different from other windows: it's got that dark bar up at the top, telling you what sort of disc it is ("Recordable DVD" in this case) and giving you a nifty new Burn button.

   The Finder gives the disc a generic name ("Untitled DVD"). You'll have a chance to change it to something snapper when you actually go to burn the disc, but if you're impatient you can just click on the disc's Desktop icon and rename it as you would any other volume.

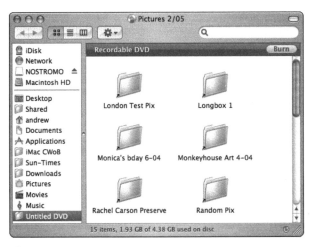

Figure 12-4
A big burn window, filled with icons and opportunities

▼ Tip

Check out the Sidebar of that window, too: there's a new folder named "Untitled DVD". This puppy represents the contents of the disc you'll be burning. If you ever close the burn window or navigate elsewhere, you can reopen it by clicking on this folder.

3. **Drag files and folders into the burn window.**

   Hey, something kinda weird is going on. Look at those little arrows on the corner of the folder and file icons! Those aren't files and folders . . . they're *aliases* to files and folders! Holy Cats!

   Don't let that throw you. Remember, the actual files won't be placed on that disc until the disc is burned. So these aliases are just the Finder's way of remembering which items need to be carved onto the disc when the time comes.

FELIX UNGER IS YOUR PERSONAL GOD

You *might* want to take a moment to arrange these icons so that they're not quite so helter-skelterish, particularly if it's a disc that you're going to hand off to somebody else. When this disc is burned and somebody slips it into their own Mac, the Finder will open a window that looks exactly like the one you're looking at.

So if you want this person to see a single folder that says, "Open THIS One, Chief", then drag that folder so that it's set apart from all the rest and then resize the window so it's the only one that's immediately visible. If you want the dude to see a list of file names, set that window to List View. Et cetera.

There's no reason why things can't be *pretty*, you know.

Keep an eye on the bottom of the window, too. Even though those icons are just aliases, the Finder keeps a running tally of how much data you intend to put onto the disc, and what its maximum capacity is. In Figure 12-4, for instance, I'm using only 1.93 GB of the 4.2 GB available on this DVD.

You can take your time adding stuff to the disc. No rush. When you're ready to light that candle:

4. **Click the Burn button in the burn window.**

   Or, you can select Burn Disc from the disc's hierarchical menu. Or, Click on the disc and then select Burn Disc from the Finder's File menu. Tiger wants to make sure you're not just drunk or something, and tosses up a confirmation window (Figure 12-5).

197

Figure 12-5
Lighting the match before burning a disc

5. **Choose a name for the disc, if you haven't done that already, and then click Burn.**

   You also have a pop-up menu, whereinupon you can select a burn speed. Tiger will automatically choose a speed that'll work just fine, depending on your hardware. Don't mess with it. Just click Burn and you're off and running. Tiger will toss up a progress bar, a la Figure 12-6.

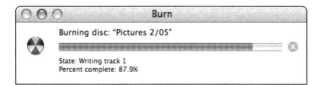

Figure 12-6
Observing the fascinating process of a disc burn

When the burn's complete, the disc will be mounted just like any other disc.

 Info

You can use a burned disc on Windows systems without a hitch. In fact, burning a disc is one of the simplest ways to share files between a Mac and a PC.

BURN SPEED: FASTER AIN'T NECESSARILY BETTER

So, why *wouldn't* you just select the maximum speed from that pop-up menu? For the same reason the Connecticut State Police nailed me for doing 90 in a 55: Not everything is rated for the top possible speed. Look at that bundle of discs before purchasing. It's possible that the reason it was such a bargain is that they can't be burned at your SuperDrive's top speed.

Let the Finder try the maximum speed by default. But if it spits out the disc and says, "No bleepin' way, mate," be prepared to click on a slower speed, like 4x.

(What does 16x, 8x, and so on mean? 1x is the speed of the playback of a normal audio CD; it takes about 70 minutes to read it from start to finish. So, a drive that can write at 16x speed can [technically] burn a CD-R full to the brim in roughly 5 minutes.)

Burn Folders

Once again demonstrating that I have your best interests at heart, I glossed over a cool new Tiger feature in the interests of keeping the burn process simple, clean, and clear: Burn Folders.

Remember how I made a point — twice now, I think — of how Tiger doesn't actually put files onto the disc until you do a Burn? That when you drag stuff into the disc's windows, it creates a collection of aliases . . . a sort of to-do list of files and folders that need to appear on the disc when it's Magic Time? Well, hey: if Tiger isn't actually putting anything onto the disc, then do you actually need to have a recordable disc in the drive in the first place?

1) Don't be a smart-mouth; 2) No, actually, you don't. You can just as easily create a *Burn Folder* on your hard drive by just navigating to the spot where you want to keep this to-do list and then selecting New Burn Folder from the Finder's File menu. Open the folder and you'll see the exact same window you saw in Figure 12-4. It behaves in exactly the same way, too.

This scheme has two big selling points. First, you can take as much time as you want to set up the contents of this folder. Take all afternoon. Take all month. Heck, wait until the Red Sox finally win their first World Series since 1918.

Info

No, wait ... they already *did*, in 2004! Woo! *YEEAHHH!!! SOX!!!!! SOX!!!!!!! WOOOOOOOOOOHHHHH!*

(No, I'm not quite over it yet.)

You won't need to actually stick a disc in the drive until you click that Burn button.

The other Big Win is that you can burn as many copies of this Burn Folder's contents as you wish. And because it's just a folder of trivially small aliases, and you can create as many Burn Folders as you want, there's really no reason to delete the folder after you're done with it. You've created a disc of study materials? Cool. Make eight copies for your friends. A week later, you hear from another pal of yours, who was out sick with hydrophobia when you were handing those things out. He wipes the foam from his mouth and asks if you could please make a copy for *him*, too?

No sweat: open the Burn Folder and click Burn again.

Kinds of recordable media

Whether you're burning a CD or a DVD, the steps are always the same. You're now the master of The Burn.

Go ahead and send away for the embroidered warm-up jacket: you're in the club.

There's no club, of course. I'm building your self-esteem before I complicate matters by describing the downright *punitive* variety of burnable discs that are out there.

With compact discs, actually, there are only two kinds, and the standards were created and supported by calm, sensible people without any obvious grudges. You've got your CD-Rs and you've got your CD-RWs. CD-Rs:

- **Can only be recorded once.** After you burn it, that sucker's *burned.*

- **Are absolutely dirt-cheap.** So cheap that most stores can realize a greater profit by just *giving* them away instead of selling them. If they sell that pack of discs, they have to kick some money to the credit card company for the transaction, plus they need to pay the cashier. Better to just look the other way when customers streak out of the store with a 100-pack in each hand.

- **Are the most compatible with audio compact-disc players.** If you're using iTunes to burn some standard audio CD for your car stereo, you want to burn it onto a CD-R, *not* a CD-RW.

In this modern age of miracles, *many* CD players are designed to be CD-RW studly. But it's a crapshoot. Better to be safe and use a CD-R. CD-RW's have their own advantages:

- **They're ReWritable.** As the name implies. You can reuse the same disc over and over again, and if the disc isn't filled up all the way to the brim, you can stick it back into the drive later and easily record more info onto it. You can do that with CD-Rs, too, but (a) only under certain circumstances, and (b) it's not a one-step process.

BURN FOLDERS: CONSIDERABLY LESS DUMB

Less dumb than the *old* way, anyway. Previously, if you wanted to prepare 4.2 GB of stuff for burning, the Finder had to waste 4.2 GB of space on your hard drive to create and maintain a sort of "staging area" for the disc-to-come. Which kind of blew, because what if you wanted to back up 4 GB of data and you only had 2 GB of unused space on your hard drive? You join the priesthood, that's what. Even if you had to shave your head and pretend to be a man. It's a much simpler problem than the thing with the discs.

● **They're erasable.** So if you wanted to erase it (the whole thing) and reuse it, you're free to do so. In this vein, an RW disc behaves a little more like a regular hard drive than a record-once CD-R. Granted, a CD-RW is only *slightly* more expensive than a CD-R — let's call it "lint-cheap" as opposed to "dirt-cheap" — but it's nice to know that you can recycle a disc and save yourself 20 cents if you ever need to.

 Info

The Finder can't erase a CD-RW or DVD-RW; you erase these discs using Disk Utility, found inside your Utilities folder. Be warned: Most discs can only be erased and reused a limited number of times before the disc fails. I put a fat tick mark on my RW disc every time I erase it. When the tick marks start to crowd out room for the label, I chuck the disc.

Nice and tidy. Now we're going to talk about DVDs, and you have the option of either reading the bullets that

follow, or just giving yourself a sharp rap on the head. Two different routes to the same result.

● **DVD-R and DVD-RW** have the same qualities and features as Recordable CDs and ReWritable CDs. DVD-R is cheaper and more compatible with standard video DVD players, but in general, you can only record data on a disc once. DVD-RWs act more like conventional hard drives: you can erase and reuse them.

● **DVD+R and DVD+RW** are Freak formats, hellspawns, really ugly swamp-children, progeny of Mankind's unlimited capacity for greed and avarice. But they work more or less exactly like DVD-R and DVD-RW discs, respectively.

The Explanation: Recordable and rewritable CDs took off in a huge way. Revolutionized the whole storage industry, you might say. And so, the race was on to create a standard for recordable DVDs.

Normally, the process of creating and adopting an industry standard is smooth, from the users' point of view. You're told that there's this new thing called "recordable DVD," you go out and buy it, end of story. But some of the manufacturers got greedy. Instead of waiting for the standard to be formally codified and agreed-upon, they wanted to be *first* to the marketplace. And so, a bunch of freak-o DVD formats came on the scene. DVD-R and DVD-RW are the real standards. DVD+R and DVD+RW are the usurpers. They offer no practical advantages and they aren't as popular, but many drives support that format.

The trouble is, if your DVD burner isn't designed to use DVD+R/RW media, the stuff is worthless. To find out what your drive is capable of, open the System Profiler window (select About This Mac from the Apple menu and click the More Info button) and click on Disc Burning, under the Hardware category. It'll give you a list of the different standards this thing's compatible with.

LET YOUR REEBOKS DO THE NETWORKING

How cheap is blank optical media these days? So cheap that the other day, when I needed to transfer about 80 megabytes of files from one Mac to another, I didn't bother using Tiger's wunnerful file-sharing features (more on that later) because Macintosh "B" needed to be plugged into the network. And I didn't reach for my 128-megabyte keychain drive (more later) because I would have had to get up out of my chair.

No, instead I slapped a CD-R into the drive, burned the tiny splash of data onto the disc, and then walked it over to the other Macintosh. And then I snapped the disc in half and threw it away. Eight cents down the drain. Call me Mister Big Shot, but I can afford it.

Incidentally, this method of networking is a time-honored technique known as "SneakerNet." It isn't as handy as just transmitting a file over a network, but it's far more reliable, and it gives you an excuse to stroll past the conference room to see if there are any donuts or anything in there.

 Tip

And if you see "-R" but not "-RW" as a supported DVD mode, go to `www.apple.com/support/` and do a search for DVD. It's possible that you can download a simple firmware update that'll magically bestow this power upon your drive.

 Tip

The other cool thing about memory devices is that they come preformatted to work with Windows machines. And Macs speak Windows' file system fluently: you can mount the memory drive on your Mac, copy files thereto, pop it into a friend's Windows machine and voilà, easy file transfer. No muss, no fuss.

MEMORY-BASED STORAGE

Time was (sticking his thumbs through the loops of his suspenders and rocking back in his chair and putting his feet up on the pickle barrel in a folksy sort of way) when all storage devices were mechanical, in some fashion. Plates spin around at high speed, a little arm darts in and out and reads and writes info. These days, there are storage devices that are entirely electronic. They're based on *flash memory*: it's a special kind of RAM that doesn't require electricity to stay alive. Even when you disconnect a flash storage device from your Mac, your files stay there, safe and sound and ready for your next attempt to blackmail Paul Anka with a stake of faked Photoshop images.

If you have a digital camera, you have some type of memory card in that camera to store images. Most of these cards use flash memory — that special RAM that can retain its contents with no power applied — known as either Compact Flash, Memory Stick, or Secure Digital (aka Multi-Media Card). These cards mount on your Desktop like any standard volume.

But how? If it's inside your camera, it mounts as soon as you connect the device to your Mac's USB port, using the cable that came with the camera. You might find it more convenient to take it out of the camera and stick it inside a card reader instead. This is a little device the size of a cassette tape. It plugs into your USB port and typically has slots for all three or four different kinds of memory. Certain PowerBooks also have a "PC Card" slot, and can use an even slimmer memory card adapter.

Either way, everything should be Plug and Play. Tiger comes with all the built-in know-how to mount your memory card. So just plug it in, wait a second, and then copy the card's files to your hard drive.

 Note

> Of course, Tiger has a marvelous plan for your life. So if it recognizes that you have connected a camera, it automatically activates iPhoto and asks if you'd like to slurp all those image files straight into the iPhoto library. It can do the same thing with card readers, too.

DON'T BE CAUGHT WITHOUT YOUR KEYCHAIN

Yes, my young apprentice, you do want a keychain drive. You can't have your Mac with you at all times. You might own a PowerBook, but carrying a 7-pound object with you at all times marks you as the enemy of good posture and the best friend of the chiropractic industry.

But you *do* always have your keys in your pocket. So it's possible to always have your Safari bookmarks, all of your passwords (read the Keychain section of Chapter 19), and the collection of documents your life is revolving around at the moment. All that and plenty of room left over for the full-screen trailer to the first *X-Men* movie. Stick it into the USB port of any Mac — even one at a nearby Apple store — and you're good to go.

There's another kind of flash storage: Keychain drives. These are memory chips ranging in capacity from 64 MB all the way up to several gigabytes that are mounted on what looks like the end of a popsicle stick. A keychain drive has its own USB connector at one end and a little hole at the other end so you can keep it with your keys. Just plug it into any USB port, and it mounts automatically and operates just like an ordinary drive.

NETWORKED VOLUMES

To this point, I've assumed that all the volumes you use are physically part of your computer, but that may not be the case. You can reach any number of volumes on a remote server over a network and have Tiger treat it like it was a hard drive plugged into your Mac.

The server can run nearly any operating system: OS X, an earlier version of the Mac operating system, a flavor of Windows, Unix, Linux, Novell. Tiger also supports connections to SMB/CIFS, NFS, and WebDAV servers without any extra encouragement from third-party utilities. In addition, you can access the contents of a Public/Shared folder on an OS X or Windows computer, assuming that the owner of the machine has turned on file sharing.

 Note

> I'm just typing stuff to impress you because, in truth, you don't need to know any of this. It's enough that *Tiger* knows this stuff. It'll figure out the networking hoodoo for you. Even the word *volume* is a bit grandiose in this context.

Connecting to a server

Connecting to a server is handled almost automagically:

1. **Click the Finder.**

2. **Click on Network in the sidebar of any Finder window.**

   Tiger gazes out across the sprawling, fierce landscape known as The Network That You're On and fills the Finder window with icons of every file server that it can see (Figure 12-7).

   Aha! Bobbendrae is the name of the G4 tower in my office. I wanna connect to it and grab a file therefrom.

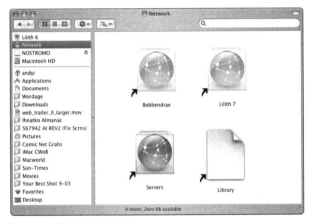

Figure 12-7
Sing along: "Because 'Lilith 7' is a ser-ver in your neigh-bor-hood... in your neigh-bor-hood ... your net-work neigh-bor-hood...."

3. **Double-click on a server icon to connect to it.**

   A Connect to Server login window appears (see Figure 12-8).

Figure 12-8
Verifying your identity to the server

Tiger wants to know who you are. If you're nobody — you don't have an account on this server, or any special sort of access — click on the button marked "Guest" next to Connect as:. This will give you basic, riff-raff access to this server. You'll be limited to just those areas that the server's administrator has defined as safe for any anonymous Tom, Dick, and/or Harry. Unless this administrator is a big dope, this will be defined as "Jack squat or nearly so."

If you have an account on this system, you can type in your user name and your password. Bobbendrae is my Mac, so I'll type in my user name and password. If the password and user name are correct, I'm then presented with a list of all the volumes that I'm permitted to access on this server. Figure 12-9 shows you the results when I log in as Andy Ihnatko:

Figure 12-9
I am Andy Ihnatko! (Within the context of this server.) Tremble at my awesome access to Bobbendrae!

And as you can see, I have access to the whole schmeer, just as if I were seated behind Bobbendrae's keyboard; I don't just have access to Bobbendrae's internal hard drive. I have access to all the drives *connected* to Bobbendrae. Including my iPod, which I left plugged into the Mac's FireWire port to recharge!

If I click on "andyi" — which represents my Home folder on this machine — the folder (with its contents) is connected to my local computer just as though it were a hard drive. Take a good look at Figure 12-10.

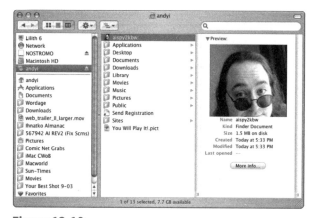

Figure 12-10
Full access: it's almost like being there.

Notice that there's really no difference between this view and a view of my local hard drive. "andyi" has been mounted and is in my list of attached volumes, up at the top of the window's sidebar. It has a little "globe in a box" icon (marking it as a network volume) and an Eject button, but other than that, it's the same. I can look at any file or folder that I'd normally have access to. If I click on the picture there at the top of the file list, I get a complete preview, just as I would if it were a local drive. I can copy files into it, I can copy files from it, I can create new folders, I can delete stuff. Surely, the phrase *carte blanche* was coined for situations precisely like this one.

 Tip

You know what else is cool? Remember when I mentioned that Tiger's standard Open and Save dialogs are functional duplicates of the standard Finder windows? Yes indeed, that means that when you're in Microsoft Word and you're about to save the file you just created, you can connect straight to your supervisor's Mac (or even his or her Windows machine) and save it right into the public folder. Send Apple a dollar right now. Whatever you paid for Tiger, it just wasn't enough.

By contrast, let's see what happens when we log in as a Guest. Figure 12-11 shows us the list of volumes available to an anonymous Guest.

Figure 12-11
What the Riff-Raff Guests see when they try to access my Mac

Instead of a list of all the volumes attached to my Mac — remember, I didn't enter a user name and password, so Bobbendrae doesn't know who I am or what I'm allowed to see — it presents me with a list of Bobbendrae's users. Specifically, those users for whom at least *some* of their directories are accessible to Guests. Let's click on an account name and see what I get (Figure 12-12):

Hmm. No panoply of files and folders. Just a lonely Drop Box. And I can't even paw through *that,* because when I double-click on it, a curt little alert warns me that I don't have enough access privileges to look inside the Drop Box folder and that I should feel free to just roll right out the door like the tide.

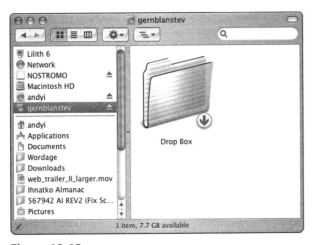

Figure 12-12
Gee . . . guests aren't exactly *welcome* here, are they?

By default, the account that was created for you on your Mac has one of these special Drop Box folders. Folks can copy stuff *into* it, but they can't open it. It's perfect when you want to protect your personal data, but still want to give other folks on your network the ability to give you some files from time to time.

Whether you've logged in as a registered user or as a Guest, you can log off from the server when you're done by just clicking on the Eject button next to its name in the Sidebar; or, drag its icon into the Trash, or use its contextual menu. You can have multiple network volumes mounted at the same time. It's not like sticking a disc in the drive: you don't have to eject one in order to make room for the other.

Finding the address of a piece of hardware

It's possible, however, that Tiger can't locate some servers automatically. Tiger is a helpful and selfless beast but it refuses to go out on the Internet and bring back a list of every single computer in the entire world that it can establish a connection with. I mean, there's Helpful, and then there's Co-dependent.

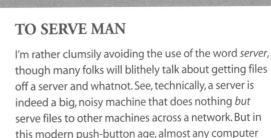

TO SERVE MAN

I'm rather clumsily avoiding the use of the word *server*, though many folks will blithely talk about getting files off a server and whatnot. See, technically, a server is indeed a big, noisy machine that does nothing *but* serve files to other machines across a network. But in this modern push-button age, almost any computer on the network can share files. If my little G4 Cube wants to call itself a server, let it, I say. Plus — again, thanks to this modern push-button age in which Death herself has been vanquished and we all live to the age 1300, or at least until we get bored with all those *Seinfeld* repeats — machines can serve more than just files.

So anywhere in this chapter or in the great, wild world beyond wherever you see the word *server*, you can substitute "any machine capable of sharing files."

That's why the Finder has a Connect to Server command in its Go menu. In Figure 12-13, I've provided it with the URL of my personal FTP directory (ftp://ftp.theworld.com/), located on a server owned by my Internet Service Provider, located about 400 miles away from where I am right now.

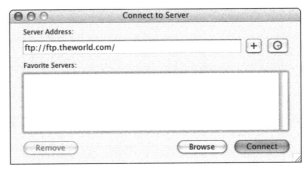

Figure 12-13
Manually connecting to an FTP server

Once again, the server I'm connecting to has to authenticate me as a user. In this case, Tiger tosses a special FTP login window in my face (Figure 12-14). I just tap in my user name and password and the FTP directory mounts right on my Desktop as ftp.theworld.com (Figure 12-15).

Figure 12-14
Authenticating an FTP connection

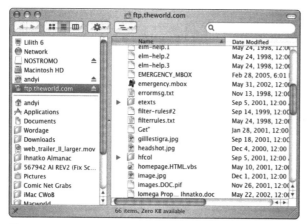

Figure 12-15
Connecting to my FTP folder from an ocean away

Can we take a moment to appreciate the slickness of the Finder in particular and the Macintosh user interface in general? Look at the top left corner of the window shown in Figure 12-15. It shows four different volumes: Macintosh HD, which is my Mac's internal hard drive; Nostromo, which is a keychain drive plugged into its USB port; andyi, which is my user folder on a Macintosh just five feet away; and ftp.theworld.com, a totally *different* kind of volume that's so far away it'd take me 8 hours to drive there.

And yet, to Tiger, it's all the same thing. Tip your waitresses! They've been working hard for you folks all night.

Handy stuff, this Connect to Server feature. But what if you don't know the address of the server?

If it's an FTP server, you're just going to have to phone up and ask. If it's another Macintosh, you're also just going to have to phone up and ask, unless the person who owns this Mac travels a lot and can usually be counted on to overlook at least one unlocked window.

Each Mac's network address is printed, plain as day, right at the bottom of the Sharing pane of Tiger's System Preferences. So to find this address:

1. **Go (actually walk) to the Mac to which you want to connect, and under System Preferences click Sharing (see Figure 12-16).**

   There it is, in English.

▼ **Note**

If the owner of this Mac is (a) right there in the room and (b) one of those suspicious types, you might want to start a small fire in a disused corner of the office as a distraction. Or just dramatically point at the window and shout, "Look! A big distracting thing!" Use your imagination.

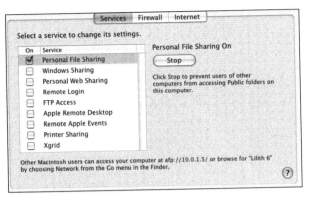

Figure 12-16
Finding the network address of a target Mac

2. **Jot down the gobbledygook that begins with afp://, and then go back to your own Mac.**

3. **Open the Connect to Server window under the Finder's Go menu.**

4. **Type it into the Server Address: field of the Connect To Server dialog box.**

5. **Click Connect.**

 Note

You know, that afp:// thing looks a lot like a URL, doesn't it? I wonder what would happen if you were to type it into the Address field of your Mac's Web browser? (Sigh.) I was hoping that this would inspire you to go off and try it. But alas, my skill as a writer has left you on tenterhooks. So the answer is that yup, it switches to the Finder and tries to mount that server. It's called synergy, kids.

And the login process proceeds from there. But maybe it'll work and maybe it won't. If your friend's Mac is on the same patch of local network as yours is, it'll probably work. If he's 400 miles away and he's not spending a buttload of cash every month on a really slick and professional connection to the Internet, probably not. The simplest, cheapest, and most flexible way to make a connection from one Mac to another through the Internet is by accessing someone's iDisk.

FTP: IT'S AN ACRONYM, SO YOU *KNOW* IT'S SOMETHING SIMPLE . . .

…which is about as big a lie as I'm ever going to tell you within the confines of this book. FTP stands for File Transfer Protocol and it's one of the oldest, sturdiest, and most ubiquitous protocols for transmitting a file from one place to another. I'm not talking about "adding it as a file attachment and then emailing it to someone." I mean the way that a file is smashed to smithereens at your end, converted into an orderly and obedient line of electrons that squirts out through your Internet connection, and then is reassembled at the other end none the worse for wear.

It's such an important networking scheme that Tiger supports it as one of its native methods of connecting to a server. No additional software needed. The catch? The Finder can only *receive* files from FTP servers. I can copy any of the files in Figure 12-15 to my local hard drive, but I can't send a file there no matter how hard I push it.

To send a file via FTP, you need an *FTP client* app, such as Fetch or RBrowserLite. Both of these apps can be downloaded from www.macupdate.com or www.versiontracker.com. If you're slightly Unix-savvy, you can open your Mac's Terminal app (it's in the Utilities folder) and run a standard FTP utility from the command line. At this stage you're either nodding or your eyes are starting to twist up, so either way, my work here is done, I think.

IDISK

If you subscribe to Apple's .Mac service — currently a hundred clams per annum — you get a bunch of special online features. One of the handiest is the iDisk.

If you were the least bit confused when I started talking about FTP servers and AFP addresses, I want you to read that whole section all over again. Not because I think you'll walk away with a clearer understanding after the second go-around (though I'd be pleased if you did), but to underscore that connecting to servers through the Internet, though useful, can be a hoary ordeal of arcane incantations and broken dreams.

Well, Apple dislikes the idea of its users being put through a hoary *anything,* so they came up with iDisk. An iDisk is a directory on one of Apple's servers that you can attach to your Mac through the Internet as easily as plugging in an external hard drive.

Connecting to your iDisk from your own Mac

Mounting your iDisk is no more difficult than:

1. **If you're not already a .Mac subscriber, point your Web browser to** www.mac.com **and complete the process by which you become $100 (at this writing) poorer but one .Mac account richer.**

   At the end of the process, you'll be shown a brief page of account information. Make sure you jot down your .Mac member name and password.

2. **Tell your Macintosh about your .Mac account by opening System Preferences.**

   Hey, look: .Mac has its own pane and everything (Figure 12-17).

Figure 12-17
Giving your Mac the keys to your .Mac account

3. **Type in your member name and password and close System Preferences.**

   Go back to the Finder.

4. **Go to the Go menu, navigate to iDisk, and select My iDisk from the menu that pops up (Figure 12-18).**

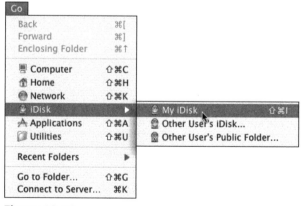

Figure 12-18
One click of one menu forges a connection between you and your personal quarter acre of the Internet, no matter where you are.

ECUMENICISM, THY NAME IS IDISK

The fourth or fifth most cool thing about iDisk is that you can even access it from Windows XP. Go to `www.mac.com`, click on Downloads, and download Apple's iDisk Utility for Windows, which automates the process.

And you don't even need the iDisk Utility, really; it only makes things simpler. iDisk is based on a network standard called *WebDAV,* which is supported by nearly every OS. Each OS has different methods of connecting to a WebDAV server like your iDisk, but all you need to know is your iDisk's Web address: `http://idisk.mac.com/username` — where "username" is your .Mac member name. When asked for a user name and password, use your .Mac member name and password. So if you want to access your iDisk from Windows (without using Apple's utility), go to My Network Places from the Start menu, select Add a Network Place, and then the configuration wizard takes it from there.

I don't want to say, "It's just that simple!" because in Windows we're dealing with the sort of OS which, if it were your next-door neighbor, would be playing bebop music at top volume at all hours of the night (and occasionally throwing up in your mailbox).

Your iDisk mounts on your Desktop just like any other volume. Sure, Figure 12-19 is anticlimactic, but that's the point: after you've signed up for an account and configured your Mac, it behaves just like any other volume. You don't even have to go to the Go menu to mount it; every time you log in, it appears in your list of attached volumes automatically.

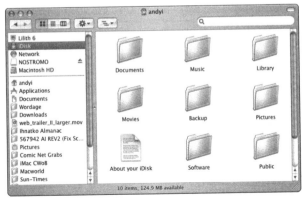

Figure 12-19
A mounted iDisk: thrilling in its underwhelmth

Connecting to someone else's iDisk, or connecting to *your* iDisk from someone else's Mac

That's tidy and convenient. Ten points out of ten. But what if you're at a friend's house, and you want to open a document you've got safely stashed in your iDisk?

Or, what if you and your spouse enjoy that sort of loving, trusting, open relationship where each of you insists on having complete and unfettered access to each other's personal information, to ensure that any impulses or temptations one might have regarding a delivery person, co-worker, or international financier go unpursued?

No sweat: Select Other User's iDisk from the iDisk submenu of the Finder's Go menu.

The window shown in Figure 12-20 appears, inviting you — no, insisting that you — enter a .Mac member name and password.

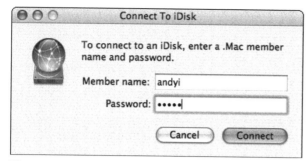

Figure 12-20
Connecting to (a) someone else's iDisk, or (b) your iDisk, from someone else's Mac

 Info

Note that this is a special circumstance; the iDisk won't be automatically mounted again the next time you log in. Automatic mounting only works when you shovel that member info into the .Mac panel of a Mac's System Preferences.

Connecting to a Public Folder

But what are the chances that you're going to have someone *else's* password? If you asked the big dope for his password and he just *gave* it to you, your next step is clear: get the deed to his house.

No, most Mac users are materially more intelligent than the equivalent weight in ham. So to give .Mac users a way to share files with friends, family, and even total strangers, each iDisk has a folder marked "Public," and its contents are available to anyone who can:

1. **Select Other User's Public Folder from the iDisk submenu of the Finder's Go menu.**

2. **Type in another user's member name.**

POKING AROUND WHERE YOU BELONG, SORT OF

It isn't a breach of social etiquette to look at someone's Public Folder. I mean, what's the first word in "Public Folder"? Precisely. If you're capable of parsing simple English, you've no right to put files in your iDisk's Public Folder and then expect that nobody else will go in and look at it. Why do you think I call my Web site "Andy Ihnatko's Colossal Waste of Bandwidth," anyway?

Try accessing my Public Folder (andyi). Or try accessing Steve Jobs' (Steve). Though in the latter example, I'd wait for a time and a day when I was emotionally ready for disappointment. Actually, that's just a good template for life in general, come to think of it.

Changing access to your Public Folder

The iDisk tab of .Mac's System Preferences panel offers you a little extra control over who gets to use your Public Folder and what they can do with it.

- If you'd like the whole wild wide world to be able to put stuff in your Public Folder, click the Read & Write button under the "Allow others to:" category. Beware, though: everyone will be able to copy stuff *into* it, but everyone will be able to copy stuff *from* it, too.

- If you don't want your Public Folder to be a *public* folder, check the box marked "Password protect your Public Folder" and make up a good password. Naturally the Public Folder's password needs to be different from your .Mac account password. The bulk of your iDisk is still Private with a capital "Pry," but the

Public Folder is a special island that can only be accessed by folks to whom you've entrusted the Public Folder's password. This is the sort of feature you'd use if you need to send a friend a file that's waayyyyy too big to send via email. Just drop it in your Public Folder, password-protect it, and then email the Public Folder's password to your pal. If you're concerned about leaving your PF open to this friend, (a) don't worry, you can always change the password to something else after he's received the file, and (b) you have friends that you don't trust? Really?

USING TARGET DISK MODE

There are situations where it'd be *soooo* much simpler if you could just mount the internal hard drive of one Mac as a FireWire hard drive on the Desktop of a second Mac. Yeah, you could mount it over the network, but it's slow and there's plenty of overhead. You've got an 11 GB iPhoto library on your PowerBook and you just want to slurp it into your desktop.

Ask and ye shall receive. All Macs have a neat feature called Target Disk Mode that wreaks exactly that sort of magic upon your humdrum daily life.

All you need for target disk mode is a FireWire cable. Let's say that I want to mount my PowerBook's hard drive on the Desktop of my iMac:

1. **I shut down the PowerBook.**

   Sleep won't do; you have to power it off completely. I can leave the iMac up and running.

2. **I connect the PowerBook to the Desktop Mac using their FireWire ports.**

3. **Turn the PowerBook back on while holding down the T key.**

Instead of the standard startup process, you'll see a big, colorful FireWire logo on the PowerBook's screen. The hard drive appears on the iMac's desktop and you're free to take your finger off the keyboard any time you want.

▼ **Info**

I could have saved myself a couple of steps by opening System Preferences on the PowerBook, clicking on the Startup Disk panel, and then clicking the Target Disk Mode button. But it's good to know the startup key for this trick: if one fine day your Mac fails to start up and it's *desperately important* that you mount the hard drive and retrieve some files, the startup key will work while the Startup Prefs method won't.

The PowerBook now behaves exactly like an external FireWire drive, without any restrictions. When you're done with it, put it away as you would any other FireWire drive: drag its icon to the Trash and then disconnect. Turn off the PowerBook by holding down the Power button. It can now reboot normally.

MOVIN' ON UP

Target Disk Mode is often used when you're upgrading from an old Mac to a new one. You tie the two FireWire ports together, put the old Mac into Target Disk Mode, and then just copy your old files over.

But there's an easier way. Apple quietly released a handy utility called Migration Assistant. You'll find it inside your Utilities folder. When you launch the app, it walks you through the process of hooking up an old Mac to a new one, and then the utility handles everything from there. Your old Mac restarts, the utility mounts the hard drive, paws through your data, and re-creates all of your apps, documents, and settings on the new machine.

DISK IMAGES

Disk images are special files that contain all or part of a volume. As discussed earlier in this chapter, they are useful for creating multisession optical discs. However, they have other uses as well:

- You can use a disk image to duplicate a CD or DVD when you have only one drive. Create an image of the disc and save the image file on your hard drive. Then, burn the image onto a new, blank disc.

- You can use a disk image to distribute a collection of files. In fact, a lot of the software that you download over the Internet (whether freeware, shareware, or commercial) is supplied as a disk image.

 Tip

I also use disk images to maintain a set of Good Samaritan files on my PowerBook. For example, at a trade show, a pal was all frantic because his Mac wouldn't boot up. My own drive contains a disk image of a Tiger install disc and a couple of different emergency bootable CDs. A quick stop at the drugstore for a couple of blank discs and I was able to produce a disc that brought his Mac back to life.

A disk image (ogle a Disk Image icon there in Figure 12-21) behaves like a removable disk. When you double-click on a disk image (which has the .dmg file name extension), Disk Utility opens the image file and mounts it on the Desktop as a standard volume. After it's been mounted, a Disk Image looks like a volume and it acts like a volume. We're near the end of the chapter and I'd probably just bore you if I showed you what another volume looked like. Just imagine a picture of any other volume from this chapter.

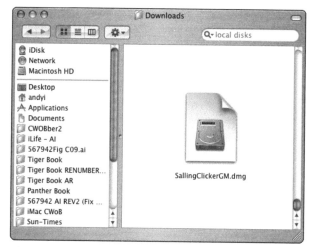

Figure 12-21
A disk image file, *in situ*

Creating disk image files

What a wonderful world it would be if you could create new Disk Image files straight from the Finder; alas, Paradise is of the next world, not this one. You create and manage disk images with the Disk Utility utility:

1. **Launch Disk Utility.**

   You'll find it inside the Utilities folder.

2. **Click the New Image button.**

   This is located at the top in the toolbar shown in Figure 12-22. The New Image dialog box appears, offering you a bunch of options:

- **Size:** You can specify a limited capacity for the disk image. If you're intending to make CDs out of the disk image later on, you might want to limit the file's size to 660 MB, to make sure it'll all fit on one disk, for example.

I LOVE MY DMG FILES, I LOVE DISK UTILITY

Disk Image Files are awfully flexible things. They are a solution to a whole range of problems. I'm paranoid about my personal information, for example, so I keep anything sensitive (such as my financial records) inside an encrypted .dmg file instead of as separate files on my hard drive. A miscreant might do a search for files named Tax deductions/2005, but because I unmount that disk image when I'm not using it, that data defies all conventional search utilities. And even if they stroll off with the file, they won't be able to make any sense of the encrypted data without my password.

I intend to continue to pursue these aggressive security ideas all the way to the point where I begin to stroke my Macintosh and mutter, "My preciousssss ... they wants you ... but I won't lets them HAVE youuuu!" I think that's quite reasonable.

You should also take some time to poke around in Disk Utility. I already told you that you need this app to erase CD-RW and DVD-RW discs, but it can also be used to wipe hard drives clean. Its Erase function can also be used to prepare a volume for use with Windows (aka MS-DOS) machines. Your keychain drive came out of the box formatted for Windows, for example. Tiger doesn't care, because it's so flexible, but it's something to think of if you want to prepare volumes to work on either platform.

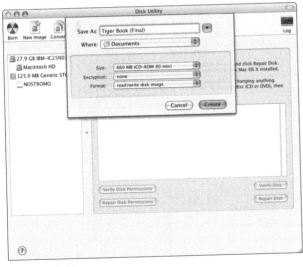

Figure 12-22
Creating a new disk image file

- **Encryption:** Disk Utility can encrypt the entire Disk Image so that nobody can retrieve the info therein without a password.

- **Format:** This is sort of a subtle one. "Read/write disk image" preserves file sizes. If a document takes up 100 K, it'll take up 100 K in the Disk Image file. Due to *lots* of boring technical stuff about how information is physically written onto a hard drive, it's possible that much of that 100 K is actually overhead, and the exact same file can take up much less space when written to a disk image file. It's nice to save space, but realize that with this option enabled, files might "bloat" back to their original sizes when they emerge from the disk image. Keep this set to "read/write disk image" when in doubt.

3. **Provide a name and storage location for the image file and click Create.**

Disk Utility will create an empty Disk Image file to your specifications, and then it'll mount it on your Desktop automatically. And it's all gravy from there. You can drag files into it, copy files from it, delete stuff . . . you know the drill. If you're done with the disk image, just click the Eject button and it'll be unmounted. Just double-click on the image file again to re-mount it.

Burning disk image files to disc

Can I just tell you that it's as simple as opening the disk image file, selecting it from the list to the right of the Disk Utility window, and then clicking the Burn button?

I mean, I'm the Pope of Embellishment, but even *I'm* at a loss as to how I could make that sound more complicated. Hey, how about if I show you a picture? Doesn't that seem like a workable compromise? Here you go, Figure 12-23:

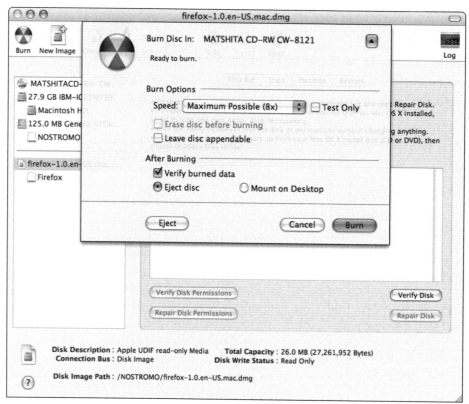

Figure 12-23
Burning a disk image onto an optical disc

KEEPING VOLUMES HEALTHY

Because a hard disk relies on mechanical parts to access locations on the disk, it is one of the slowest components of your Mac. A hard disk running at optimal speed, nonetheless, doesn't slow most of us down. However, over time the software that manages the files and folders stored on a hard drive can become corrupt. The result is significantly slower disk access and/or the inability to launch applications.

One of the major culprits in slow access and preventing files from opening is file and folder permissions. OS X's Unix underpinnings use file and folder permissions to determine whether a user has the right to use each file and folder (and there are tens of thousands of them!). When the permissions become damaged, you are likely to encounter problems. The solution is to use Disk Utility to repair the permissions:

1. **Open the Finder, the Applications folder, and then the Utilities subfolder.**

2. **Launch the Disk Utility program by double-clicking its icon.**

3. **In the disk list at the left of the window, select the volume whose permissions you want to repair (see Figure 12-24).**

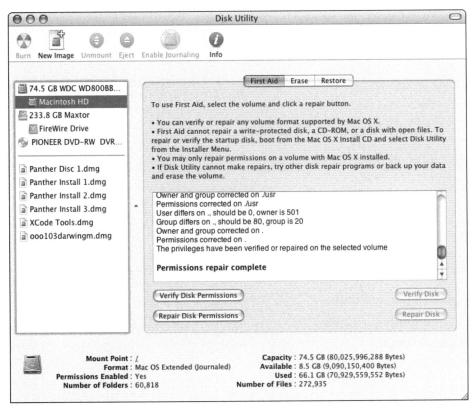

Figure 12-24
Repairing file and folder permissions

4. **Click either Verify Disk Permissions or Repair Disk Permissions, both located at the bottom of the window.**

   Click Verify Disk Permissions to determine whether the permissions are a problem for your disk. Click Repair Disk Permissions to both verify and repair in the same step.

▼ **Note**

Disk Utility can repair permissions only on a startup volume (in other words, a volume with OS X system files on it). Repairing permissions is one of those "things you try when something's wrong and you don't know what to try." That is, it certainly won't make any situation *worse*, and file permissions is such an arcane and potent concept to Tiger that there's a decent chance it'll fix things up. Check out Chapter 24 for more info on Things To Try.

If repairing permissions doesn't solve your disk problems, you may want to try a more generic verification or repair. This process checks and/or repairs disk partitions, the data that describe how the disk is formatted, and the structure of the file/folder hierarchy. You can verify any disk (even a write-only disk such as a CD) but you can only repair a disk with no open files. If you want to repair the startup disk, you need to boot from a CD or another hard disk.

To verify or repair a disk:

1. **Make sure that all files on the target disk are closed.**

2. **Open the Finder, the Applications folder, and then the Utilities subfolder.**

3. **Launch the Disk Utility program by double-clicking its icon.**

4. **In the list of disks at the left of the window, select the disk.**

5. **Click either Verify Disk or Repair Disk.**

   Click Verify Disk to verify the integrity of the disk. Click Repair Disk to both verify and repair in the same step.

▼ **Note**

Prior to OS X, Mac users were told to *defragment* hard disks frequently. Defragmentation places each file in contiguous storage and then writes all files next to each other on the disk. The theory is that this speeds up file access. The theory works fine for OS 9 and earlier, but Unix keeps files spaced out on the disk to avoid having to break files up into small fragments, providing a significant amount of protection from file corruption. (If a part of the disk goes bad, only the single file on that portion of the disk corrupts rather than parts of many files.) The bottom line is that defragmenting a Unix-based file system (such as Tiger's) can make things worse instead of better.

▼ **Tip**

No disk lasts forever, no matter how often you repair it. Your best hedge against disk corruption is to make good backup copies. (Make a mantra out of it: "Backup, backup, backup.") Reread the Book of Job, or rent *Aliens* again. Both stories really bring home the point that the human situation essentially has two settings: Bad and Worse, and there's room above that on the dial for even more wretched states to be penciled in. Best to have a backup copy of your important data when the slings and arrows of outrageous whatevers start to smack into the ground all around you.

WAX ON

I'll go further. The difference between DiskWarrior and Disk Utility is one of attitude. Think of your recalcitrant hard drive as an underperforming employee. Disk Utility is the sort of boss who takes the employee out to lunch, and has a long and patient discussion about Miscommunications, and Getting Off On The Wrong Foot, and Maybe We Can Work Together to Identify Goals and Streamline Processes. DiskWarrior takes the employee out to lunch, but when they come back the guy discovers that all of his stuff from his desk is in a box at the curb, topped with a pink slip and a bill from the Maintenance department for the packing-up of his office. DiskWarrior is like Alex Baldwin at the start of *Glengarry Glen Ross*. Put that coffee down, you! That coffee's only for salesmen who *sell*.

Finally, realize that there are limits to what Apple's built-in utilities can do for you. Sometimes you have to call in a hired gun, and by far the most important soldier of fortune in this product category is Alsoft's DiskWarrior (www.alsoft.com). Whereas Disk Utility examines all of the directory structures and tries to fix 'em, DiskWarrior analyzes your entire hard drive all the way down to the sub-muon level and rebuilds those structures from the ground up. As a guy who's used this utility since Version 1.0, I can calmly say that the only problem that DiskWarrior *can't* solve is when you accidentally cut a drive in two with a band saw. Even so, if you run DW on the affected volume, a dialog appears reading "A repair cannot be

attempted. This drive has been cut in half with either a band saw or an angle grinder." Now *that's* service.

I've grown as a human being as a result of writing these books. Firstly, I spend more time in my office writing instead of competing on the international pro beach volleyball circuit, so I've gained at least 18 pounds since starting the first edition. Secondly, I find myself explaining the color red to people.

No, seriously. Give it a try: try to explain the color red to somebody without pointing to something red. It's too simple a concept; red is red because it's red, and that's why we call it "red." Explaining volumes is a similar challenge. I learned about them when I was still young enough not to get bogged down in new terminology and wanted to teleport straight ahead to the What Cool Stuff Can This Do? portion of the pageant. So what's a volume? It's the thing that I point to when I say, "This is what a volume is." Time to move on.

So when I say, "A volume is just a place to stick files onto," I'm not being glib. I'm barely being educational. Actually, I'm being desperate. The info is here if you want to learn about it but really, if all you take away from this chapter is (a) volumes should appear automatically as soon as you stick them into your Mac; (b) if it doesn't, use Disk Utility to mount them manually; (c) oh, and if it's a blank CD, you'll have to prepare it first; (d) and be sure to eject a drive's volumes properly before you remove the drive, you'll be in gravy.

I'd also suggest (e) Andy really cares about you, the reader, but modesty forbids.

13

Archiving to Analog Pulpware Substrate (Printing)

In This Chapter

Printing Concepts • Setting Up OS X for Printing
Printing from Within an Application • Managing Printing
Pooling Printers • Faxing

It's a world gone mad, but only a paltry 3 percent of Americans have presented themselves at their local participating True Value hardware store to have a Bluetooth chip permanently fused to their anterior brainstems. Frankly, people, this is totally unacceptable. One day, our grand Society will transcend the clumsy reliance on intermediary sheets of paper and find a more elegant way of painting ideas and information onto the human brain. And if more of you could just get on board with this goal, chapters like these would be wholly unnecessary. Look, we technology pundits have spent some of the best years of our lives — time when we *could* be dating, or, more realistically, taking a night course on maritime model-building or something — carefully explaining to you people that print is dead, but have you listened?

No, you have not. There's a *reason* why we're still at least six years away from being able to enjoy Thomas Hardy's *The Return of the Native* in convenient, cherry-coated pill form, and I, for one, am not afraid to point fingers.

Okay, so fine. *Print* your documents. Fill your homes, condos, and apartments with flammable papers. In 6 months, not even *one* of those Bluetooth implants has ever caused a house fire (yes, except for that guy in Nebraska, but he was using beta drivers), but I suppose that as a technology pundit, it's my job to educate, not to cast judgment, except in the case of that pill thing.

PRINTING CONCEPTS

One of the advantages of starting a whole new OS from the bottom up as Apple did with Mac OS X 10.0 is that it presented a big opportunity to clean house and consolidate features. Printing in Mac OS X is both familiar and very different compared to OS 9. It's familiar because there are so few totally new features available to you in Tiger. But it's different because features that were once presented to you as A Big Deal are now integrated into the entire printing system. You can take full advantage of every modern ultraconvenience without even being terribly aware that you're doing anything special.

As I go along, I'll talk about specific steps for setting up and using printers. But at a bare-bones level, using Tiger's Print command causes two things to happen:

- The application and Tiger talk to each other, and together they transmogrify your document into data that your chosen printer can understand.

- Tiger waits until the printer is available, and then sends this data on over.

Simple. Barely worth breaking out the bulleted-list thingy to explain it. But it's a good way to bring up two points, namely:

- **When you tell your Mac to print something, nothing happens.** This is normal. You're just used to the idea of the printing process holding your computer hostage until the last page gets spit out onto the floor. In Tiger, issuing a Print command only holds you up for as long as it takes to tell your Mac what it needs to know. I bid you faith, patience, and calmness, young Jedi. The printed page will come when your spirit is ready to receive it. And, um, when that crummy $79 inkjet printer you got free with your system is done grinding through the job.

- **You don't even care about what happens during the second bullet above.** In other books in other eras, you'd need to master the concept of print queues and networked printers and submitting jobs to a server. All those concepts come into play, and you can manipulate things directly if you wish; but just as Bill Gates and Steve Jobs haven't the foggiest idea how the coffee-maker in the executive-level lounge works, you can simply relax. Other entities know how the system works, and all you need to do is to tell this minion what you want.

▼ **Note**

And incidentally, this is another area in which you — the user — get a lot of added functionality for free, so to speak. Mac OS X is built upon the Unix operating system, and Unix offers incredibly muscular printing architecture to all of its apps. You don't need to understand how or why this mojo is happening. All you have to do is sit back and enjoy the pine-fresh scent of Progress.

SETTING UP OS X FOR PRINTING

This section is either going to be a short one or a long one for you. One thing that confused me as a lifelong Mac user when I started using Mac OS X was that printers were so bloody difficult to install and configure. Where was the Chooser? After I've unearthed the disc containing the driver for my printer, how do I install it? Wait! Holy cow. I've just checked the printer manufacturer's Web site, and it doesn't even *have* Mac OS X drivers available for download!!!

Then I discovered that the moment I plugged my printer into a USB port, OS X had automatically found it, configured it, and made it available to all of my apps.

Well. Okay, then.

Mac OS X ships with printer drivers for nearly every printer you're ever likely to come across. When you do a basic installation, you're ready to rock and roll. In Chapter 2, which covers installing, one of the specific options the Tiger installer makes available is a batch of extra printer drivers. This is why you're always encouraged to install everything that's available to you. You have scads of hard-drive storage available, and installing every driver just saves a lot of hassle.

▼ Note

This is particularly good advice if you're installing the OS on a PowerBook or iBook. If you take your Mac with you over the river and through the woods, you want to have as many printer drivers installed as possible. At a friend's house, at a Holiday Inn Express in Dearborn, Michigan, or at the satellite office way across the Iberian Peninsula, the difference between printing a crucial document in three mouse clicks and enduring a process not unlike that faced by some of those poor trogs in the Old Testament is having a Mac that's prepared to work with anything.

On the other hand, PowerBooks and iBooks have smaller hard drives than their desktop brethren, so space is at a greater premium. Food for thought, I suppose.

Still, this world being naught but a vale of tears and all that, it's possible that your printer won't appear automagically within your apps' Print dialog box, and you'll have to add it manually.

Adding printers

To make a printer available for use, assuming that it's plugged into one of your Mac's USB ports (either directly or through a USB hub) and turned on, and that you're looking at the drop-down sheet that appears after you've hit the Print command in any app that supports printing:

1. **Select Add Printer from the Printer pop-up menu.**

   Tiger automatically launches the Printer Setup Utility and opens the Printer Browser window (Figure 13-1). If the printer's hooked up correctly, it'll appear in the scrolling list.

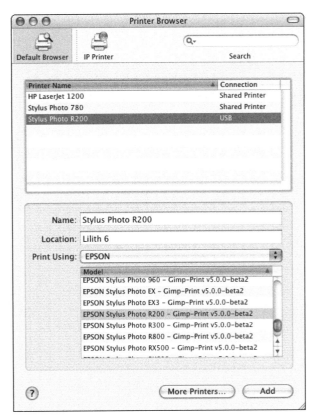

Figure 13-1
Adding a new printer to Tiger's list of usual suspects

2. **Click on the name of the new printer.**

   Tiger chooses a built-in printer driver that it thinks will work. It's infallibly correct and its judgments are not to be questioned, but if you want to question it anyway, you can select a different print driver from the Print Using: pop-up menu.

LESS THAN LASER-SHARP FOCUS

Common inkjet printers tend to work famously with Tiger. You plug it in, its name appears in the Print dialog sheet's list of available printers, and you're in like Flynn. Laser printers can be slightly more prickly as a species. If your laser printer came with a setup app on a disc, it's a Really Good Idea to run it before attempting to use the printer.

3. **Click the Add button.**

   Tiger sets up the printer and you're ready to go.

Printers that you have configured using the preceding steps appear in a list of printers in the Print dialog box so that you can select them when you print a document. One printer is the default printer: it's the printer that Tiger chooses for you, until you choose differently.

To change the default printer:

1. **Open the Print & Fax preferences in System Preferences.**

   You can also access these preferences through the Printer: pop-up menu in any Print dialog sheet. Near the bottom of the window, you'll see a pop-up menu labeled "Selected Printer in Print Dialog" (Figure 13-2).

2. **Select a printer, or choose Last Printer Used to have Tiger always automatically select whatever printer you used the last time.**

3. **Close System Prefs.**

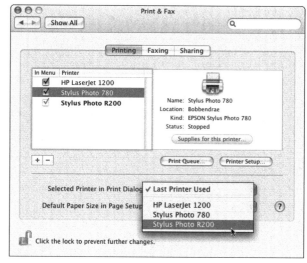

Figure 13-2
Choosing a default printer

Creating desktop printer icons

As long as you're setting up a new printer, you might want to create a desktop printer icon for the thing. We do a lot of Dragging Things Around here in the World of Macintosh (the World of Any Computer Made Since 1990, actually) and when you represent a printer with an icon, printing a specific document among thousands on a specific printer among half a dozen is as simple as dragging the document icon into a printer icon, as in Figure 13-3. And like any other icon, you can drag it into the Dock so that it's always readily available no matter how cluttered your Desktop gets.

Figure 13-3
A desktop printer icon

SUPPORTING UNSUPPORTABLE PRINTERS

What if — horrors compluviated! — you're using an old, possibly Soviet-made printer that Tiger doesn't actually support? And you've already checked the Web site of Metaliya Printsvertsk and found no downloadable drivers? Well, head on over to `gimp-print.sourceforge.net/` and download the (free, free, free) Gimp-Print driver package. It adds support for dozens of printers that Tiger has never heard of.

And Gimp-Print is worth knowing about even if Tiger supports your printer directly. It's an open-source, community effort to create the highest-quality print drivers possible, and oftentimes using one of Gimp's drivers instead of the one provided by the printer manufacturer yields noticeable improvements in print quality.

In fact, Gimp is such a good collection of printer drivers that nearly all of them ship with Tiger. But the online Gimp-Print package might have some drivers that your installation lacks.

To create a Desktop printer icon:

1. **Launch Printer Setup Utility.**

2. **Click the name of the printer for which you want to create the Desktop icon.**

3. **Select Printers ➜ Create Desktop Printer.**

   OS X asks you to select a location for the icon. It puts the icon on the Desktop by default, but you're free to slap it wherever you want.

4. **Select a location.**

   A Desktop printer icon appears immediately on your Desktop. You can print any document just by dragging its icon to that printer.

Tip

I don't use Desktop print icons much — like, when was the last time I could actually *see* my Desktop? — but they're handy. They act like any other file on your Desktop, so if you want, you can copy them onto another drive, like a USB flash drive that you keep on your keychain. If you move around from Mac to Mac in your building, you can always route printouts to the printer in your office, just by inserting your USB keychain and dragging the file onto your home printer; the printer icon contains all the info that Tiger needs to route that print job from here to there. So it's yet *another* reason to send Apple a dollar.

PRINTING FROM WITHIN AN APPLICATION

And now, the featured attraction of this chapter: please give a warm Ed Sullivan Show welcome to Trini Lopez, and his Latin-flavored medley of holiday favorites.

Okay. Anyway. There's little more to printing than turning on your printer, selecting File ➜ Print from your app, and clicking the Print button. No need to complicate things, but explaining things in detail is part of my mandate, as it were, so here goes:

When you use the File ➔ Print command or press ⌘+P, the Print dialog box appears showing the Copies & Pages panel, as in Figure 13-4. Obviously, a graphics program like Photoshop has different printing features than a word processor like Microsoft Word, which has features unique from Microsoft Excel. Plus, some printers have different features than others (the ability to print in either color or black and white, the ability to automatically print on both sides of the paper, and so on). For simplicity's sake, we're using TextEdit as an example here with a common inkjet printer. But on your own Mac and your own printer, you should prepare yourself to see a celebration of variety.

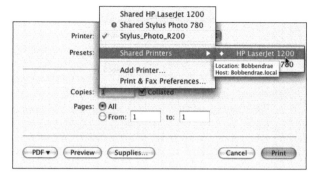

Figure 13-5
Selecting a printer

The next section down takes you to a submenu of Shared Printers. Tiger makes it simple to share a local printer with any Mac on your network. These printers are attached elsewhere. You'll have to do a little bit of walking in order to reach them. Do factor that in when you make a selection.

If you hold your mouse over one of these shared printers, a little yellow note will appear, telling you where the printer's located.

The last two items are for adding printers — already covered — and for zapping you straight to the Preferences pane in System Preferences.

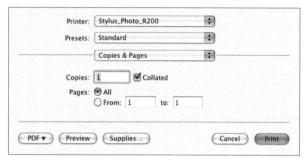

Figure 13-4
A standard Print dialog box

Choosing a Printer

The first pop-up menu is the Printer menu, which lists all of the available printers. In Figure 13-5, the three printers at the top of the list are the ones that are directly configured for this Mac. The printer with a check mark next to it is the currently selected printer. And the one marked with an exclamation point? That printer isn't available, for any of a number of reasons. Have you ever known a big exclamation point that meant *good* news?

Continuing. There are so many different kinds of print settings that Tiger organizes the Print dialog box into several pages that you can navigate through via the pop-up menu under the Presets menu. It starts you off in Copies & Pages because in most operations that's all you mess with before clicking Print. However, OS X presents more options in the Layout, Scheduler, Paper Handling, Paper Feed, and Summary pages. To give you an overview of all the options available to you, the following sections discuss all the Print pages' options in excruciating detail.

Note

Remember that none of the options presented in the rest of this section are required. If you don't want to deal with all the options, all you have to do is click File ➜ Print, or press ⌘+P.

The Copies & Pages panel

The Copies & Pages panel (viz Figure 13-4 again) is opened by default whenever you Print. The obvious options are staring you right in the face: How many copies do you want to print; do you want to print all pages or just ones in a narrow range; and if you're printing more than one copy, do you want the pages to be collated (Tiger prints pages 1, 2, 3, and 4 in sequence, three times) or not (1 1 1, 2 2 2, 3 3 3, and so on).

The Layout panel

This panel (Figure 13-6) allows you to print more than one page on a sheet of paper, and includes options for the page's layout and borders. And now, the point of all that: If you're just printing something to proofread it, printing two or four pages per sheet speeds the printing process and saves paper. And by being a little creative with the four-page layout and the paper direction, it's possible to make quick-and-dirty greeting cards or two-sided booklets. Print, fold twice, and you can walk into the next comic-book convention with a slick list of all the issues of *Cerebus the Aardvark* you need to complete your collection.

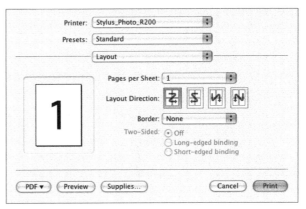

Figure 13-6
The Layout panel

The Scheduler panel

If you have a vague dissatisfaction with your current job and your desire to Stick It To The Man urges you to use the office printer to run off about 400 copies of the program for your daughter's dance recital, I urge you to use this feature. You can schedule the job to run late at night, when the only person who'll be inconvenienced is the night watchman who might be jolted out of his nap by the sound of the collator clacking into action, and *not* the poor guy who has to print a one-page letter before he can go home for the weekend.

Through the Scheduler panel (Figure 13-7) you can tell Tiger to either add the document to the printer queue immediately, specify a later time when it ought to be printed, or just add it to the printer queue and put it "on hold," where it'll remain until you open the printer's print queue and tell that puppy to leave the kennel. More on print queues later in the chapter.

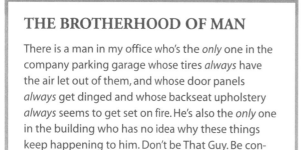

THE BROTHERHOOD OF MAN

There is a man in my office who's the *only* one in the company parking garage whose tires *always* have the air let out of them, and whose door panels *always* get dinged and whose backseat upholstery *always* seems to get set on fire. He's also the *only* one in the building who has no idea why these things keep happening to him. Don't be That Guy. Be considerate and schedule big printing jobs for later times.

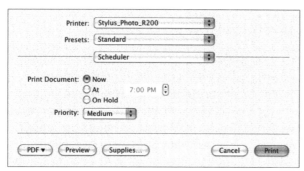

Figure 13-7
Scheduling printing

The Paper Handling panel

This panel (see Figure 13-8) controls how Tiger will move these pages through your printer, viz:

- **Page Order:** Normal starts with the first page and ends on the last page. Reverse reverses that concept. Automatic lets the printer work it out. If you have a later printer that flops its pages into the output tray

printed side up, you'll probably want to print the pages in reverse order, so that you don't have to reverse the order when the job is done.

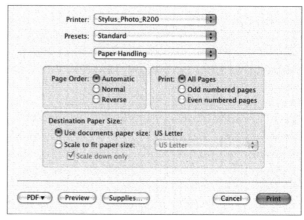

Figure 13-8
Choosing paper handling options

- **Print Odd numbered pages or Print Even numbered pages:** Obviously, these allow you to print only odd or even pages. You'd use *this* to print on both sides of the paper, if your printer doesn't handle duplex printing automatically. Print the Odds, put the printed pages back into the paper tray, and then go ahead and print the Evens on their backs.

The ColorSync panel

ColorSync is Tiger's scheme for managing color. Ordinarily it's there to make sure that the colors you see on the screen match the colors that the printer spits out, but by clicking on the Quartz Filter pop-up menu, you can make adjustments to the pages' printed appearance on the fly. In Figure 13-9, the document will be printed in fake sepia tones for that old-timey, highly fraudulent look.

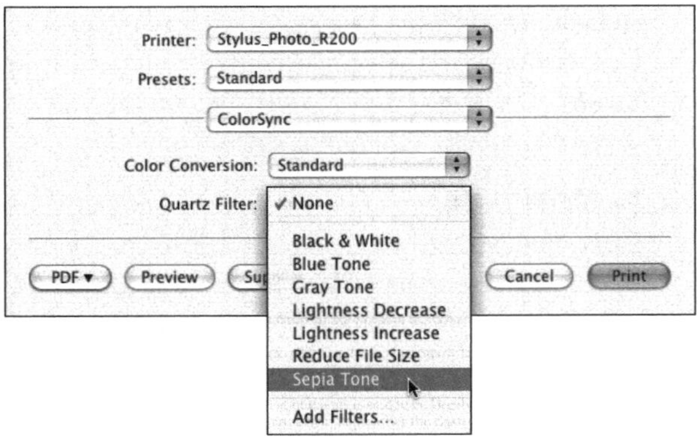

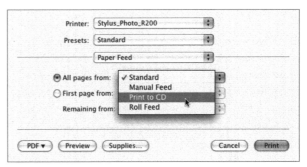

Figure 13-9
ColorSync options

▼ **Note**

Okay, now, obviously, when you're using a photo-editing app like iPhoto or Photoshop, this page is going to be pretty ambitious. Check the documentation for those specific apps for instructions on how to manage color with your printer.

The Cover Page panel

Generates a cover page for your print job and automatically spits it out either ahead of or behind the document. A bunch of prefabbed cover sheets with suitably Boys-In-A-Treehouse titles ("Top Secret!"; "Classified!") are in the Cover Page Type pop-up list.

The Paper Feed panel

You hit Print, and letter-sized pages move from the stack under the printer through the innards and into the output tray. But lots of printers can print from other sources of media. You might have a fancy high-volume office printer

with two or three different printer trays. The Epson printer seen in Figure 13-10 can print directly onto the surface of CDs and DVDs or onto a roll of labels. The pop-up menus allow you to choose a source.

Figure 13-10
Choosing paper feed options

▼ **Tip**

And one of those options is usually Manual Feed. So if you want to run a single page of labels, or if you want the top page to be printed on letterhead stationery, the printer will wait for you to insert a page manually instead of grabbing print stock from the stack.

You can also make the first page Special. Again, the top page comes from the paper bin loaded with fancy letterhead, and then all subsequent pages go onto the cheap stuff.

The Summary panel

Finally, if you want to make sure you've made all the right settings (Okay: first page goes onto a CD, all subsequent pages go on glossy paper, odd pages first, reverse-collated, make 'em lighter, and skip the first nine pages altogether), just click on the Summary panel, where all is laid moderately bare.

Good heavens, that was a lot of effort. Well, again, usually all you'll do is press ⌘+P and click OK to print one copy of whatever it is that's in front of you.

The mighty PDF button

And I know you're itching to hit the Print button by now. But there are other buttons there at the bottom of the Print dialog box. King among them is the PDF button, which collects all sorts of features centering around the theme, "What if I don't want this print job to be sent to a printer? What if I want it to be sent somewhere . . . I dunno . . . *electronic?*"

This button is actually a pop-up menu, hiding some cool features:

- **Save As PDF:** Instead of printing the document to *real* paper, it'll be printed on "electronic" paper: the document will be printed into a Portable Document File. Thereupon it becomes free from the bonds of the

HAIL, PDF!

PDFs are amazingly cool. If you save that Microsoft Word file as a PDF file, you'll no longer need Microsoft Word in order to view or print the thing; so it's a great way to email documents to people so that they can read and approve them. It's also a great archiving format. Whenever I find information on a Web site that I know I want to use later, I print it to a PDF. Yeah, I bookmark the Web page, too, but it's always possible that the page will disappear sometime in the future. By "printing to a PDF," I'll always have an electronic copy of what I read.

app that created it, and anybody with a compatible PDF reader will be able to read or print it. And because PDF is a universal format supported by all operating systems, that means *anybody* anybody.

- **Fax PDF:** This option faxes the document to any phone number, either entered manually or pulled from an entry in your Address Book, viz Figure 13-11.

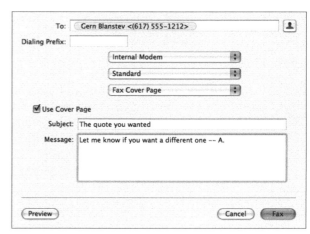

Figure 13-11
Printing as an outgoing fax

- **Automator Actions:** Automator allows you to add Workflows into this menu. Automator is Tiger's built-in system for automating a series of actions. For example, maybe you often find yourself emailing people whom you've just faxed, to alert them that a fax is awaiting them somewhere in the office. Instead of sending the fax and then sending the email, you can create an Automator workflow that sends both at the same time. You don't have to add the Workflow from Automator. You can also select Edit PDF Menu from the bottom of this menu, and then select the workflow.

The less-than-mighty but still handy Preview button

Clicking Preview is sort of a handy extension of the Save as PDF function. Have you ever tried to print something, you know, tricky? For example, you've just bought plane tickets and now the travel site displays an electronic ticket that you need to print and bring with you to the airport. Printing Web pages from a browser is always a hit-and-miss proposition. Namely, you miss old-fashioned paper tickets and you want to hit the person responsible for the system we're stuck with now. Thank you! Goodnight!

Preview prints the document to a PDF file and opens it in Tiger's Preview app so you can check to make sure that the document is A-OK before you waste any time and consumables.

Corporate enterprise

Finally, there's the Supplies button, which just takes you to an Apple Web page that sells print cartridges and stuff. You know, I remember when it was all about the *music,* not the commerce, you know?

MANAGING PRINTING

I meant what I said at the beginning of this chapter (see the section "Printing Concepts"). After you click Print, this document is someone else's problem, and you never need to get involved in the nuts and bolts of what happens next.

But let's return to one of our previous examples. It's 5 p.m. You can't leave the office until you print a two-page memo. But when you walk to the printer you share with the rest

PAGE SETUP: FINALLY GETTING WHAT IT DESERVES?

There are only a few things about Tiger that I think are silly, clumsy, backwards, inelegant, and just flat-out The Wrong Way To Go. First one that comes to mind — at least in a chapter about Printing — is the Page Setup dialog box, squatting like a troll in the File menu above every Print command.

What does it do? Well, it lets you choose a paper size, and choose whether the page is supposed to be printed in Portrait mode (long side up) or in Landscape mode (where the page is wider than it's tall). You can also scale the page up or down by a percentage.

Why do I hate it? Because these are functions that ought to be rolled inside the Print dialog box. They *belong* there, and many developers seem to agree with me, because page-intensive apps duplicate those Page Setup features within the Print dialog box.

I dunno. Every time I see a new edition of the Mac operating system and I see that Apple has retained the Page Setup dialog box, it's like welcoming a favored niece or nephew home after a year abroad and discovering that they now have a big tattoo across the back of their neck. I'm not *angry,* you understand. I suppose I'm just *disappointed,* son.

229

of the floor, you see nothing but *C. Estes Kefauver Middle School Presents: Death Of A Salesman! A New Musical Revue By Mr. Earls and Mrs. Troiani*. Page after page after page of it, with no end in sight.

Sometimes it's *you* who messed up your life by giving your printer a ton of documents to print all at once. But a consistent theme of this book is that I'm on your side, so I'd much rather pretend there's a mythical outside evil influence that's out to get you.

Time to open the Printer Setup Utility and learn about what happens after you click Print. What actually happens is that your document is placed in something called a *print queue*, which is a list of all the printing jobs lined up for the printer to service. Fortunately, it's possible to see how many jobs are ahead of you, temporarily suspend a job that's in progress (if you're an administrator of this Mac), or kill it altogether (ditto).

Accessing the print queue

Each printer that you have configured for OS X has its own print queue. There are several ways to reach it:

- **The Printer Setup Utility:** Launch Printer Setup Utility from the Utilities folder. When the application window appears, double-click the name of the printer whose queue you want to manage.

- **The printer's icon:** If printing is in progress, click the printer's icon in the Dock.

- **The Desktop printer icon:** If you have a Desktop printer icon, double-click the icon.

Regardless of how you reach the print queue, you'll see something like Figure 13-12.

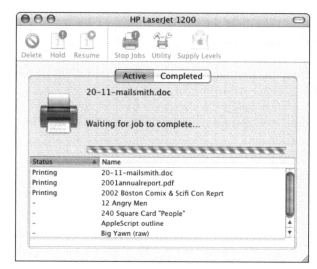

Figure 13-12
A really, really active print queue

Canceling a print job

You can cancel a print job that is currently printing or one that is waiting in the queue:

1. **Click the job in the print queue window.**

2. **Click Delete in the window's toolbar.**

Canceling a job that is being printed doesn't always work the way you would expect. It stops the printing of those pages that haven't been sent to the printer only. If part of a document has been transmitted and is in the printer's memory, the only way to stop those pages from printing is to turn off or reset the printer.

Suspending and resuming a print job

If you want to postpone a print job, temporarily preventing it from printing:

1. **Click the job in the print queue window.**

2. **Click Hold.**

   OS X places the job at the bottom of the print queue and does not send it to the printer.

To make a postponed print job active again:

1. **Click the job in the print queue window.**

2. **Click Resume.**

   OS X makes the job active again and places it at the end of the other active jobs in the print queue.

Starting and stopping the print queue

You can stop (and restart) all the jobs in a print queue at once. To do so:

1. **Open the print queue window for the printer whose print queue you want to stop.**

2. **Click the Stop Jobs button in the toolbar.**

   When you have stopped the print queue, the Stop Jobs button changes to read Start Jobs. You can restart the queue by clicking the Start Jobs button (which, as you would expect, then changes back to read Stop Jobs).

▼ **Note**

Printers continue to appear in the Print dialog box even when their print queues have been stopped. They appear even if the actual printer isn't actually available, either. You can, for example, write a brilliant term paper inside a coffee shop on your PowerBook and print it to your home printer, which obviously isn't there. Tiger sticks the document into the printer's print queue, and as soon as you go home and plug your printer back in, bang, it prints right up.

Changing assigned printers

If you have more than one printer (a laser printer and a color inkjet, say) and you did something stupid like print an electronic ticket to your color inkjet right while it's tied up printing a huge poster, you're not stuck waiting 3 hours for the poster to finish up. If you've opened windows for both printers' print queues, you can just drag the e-ticket's print job out of the inkjet's print queue and into the laser printer's queue, provided the job hasn't been started yet.

POOLING PRINTERS

Tiger also supports a rather ginchy feature called *pooling*. If you have several printers, why should you have to wait at all for a document to print? It'd sure be keen if you could have a special printer definition that says, "Look, I don't care which device prints this document; find a printer that's not doing anything right now, and print it *immediately*."

Aren't you glad you own a Mac? Just create a Printer Pool. In this example, I'm going to create a pool of the two photo-quality printers I've got here in my office. It'd be a Bad Thing, after all, if I pooled a laser printer and a photo printer together; Tiger would print documents using whatever printer happened to be available at the time, which could result in a 40-page manuscript being printed on the photo printer. At five minutes per page. At 30 cents *per sheet*. No. *Bad*.

1. **Open the Printer Setup Utility.**

   This opens a list of all available printers. If you don't see the list of available printers, press ⌘+L.

2. **Select all of the printers that you want to group together in the pool.**

   Use ⌘-click to make noncontiguous selections.

3. **Select Pool Printers under the Printers menu.**

   When you do so, you see Figure 13-13.

Figure 13-13
Making several printers act as one via a Printer Pool

4. **Determine the order of the Printer Pool.**

   At this point, you can choose the order in which these printers will receive jobs by dragging their names in the list. The printer at the top gets first crack. If it's busy, the job goes to the next on the list, and so on.

5. **Give the new pool a name, and click Create.**

And that's it. The new pool appears in Print dialog boxes as if it were another printer. You can still use these pooled printers individually.

Pooling printers is a great idea for busy offices with heavy printing demands. You can spend megabucks on a high-speed, high-volume printer, or you can just buy four or five cheaper ones and pool them together. This means that when one printer breaks, jams, or runs out of toner, it

BETTER KARMA THROUGH PRINT POOLING

Pooling printers is just good for morale. Remember: flattened tires, keyed and dinged door panels, the occasional load of Sakrete hardening in someone's front seat. All of these are avoidable. Ensuring that people can print what they want when they want goes miles toward improving everyone's love for their fellow man, until someone goes into the break-room fridge and discovers that his or her yogurt is missing, even though it was labeled and everything. Then, boy, find a doorframe to stand under because the earth's gonna start moving. But at least it wasn't the *printer's* fault this time.

won't cripple the office's whole ability to print stuff. Another dollar goes into Apple's tip jar for this one.

FAXING

This may seem like a strange place to discuss sending faxes, but sending a fax is really just another form of printing. You print to a fax modem, which acts just like a printer with its own job queue. (And we're covering receiving faxes here because it makes sense to keep sending and receiving together in the book!)

 Note

No, actually, it doesn't make sense to discuss faxing here. Here, meaning in a book about computers written in the Miraculous Pushbutton World Of Tomorrow. Bad enough that I'm still encouraging you folks to actually (brrrr) *print* stuff.

By now, faxing just seems so … well, *quaint*. Faxing a document — as opposed to emailing it — seems like churning your own butter or meeting your future bride without the help of a Web site directory of lonely, single Russian women. Like I said: *quaint*.

Sending a fax

We've already covered how easy it is to fax documents. You just Print as usual, and select Fax PDF from the PDF pop-up button. Do realize, though, that all of the printing features we've already covered can also help you out in the Fax department. Layouts, page ranges, the whole whack. Here, though, the Schedule option is of particular interest. If you're sending 30 pages to Beijing, you probably want to make that international phone call at 1:38 a.m., when it'll cost you a mere fortune, instead of a caliph's ransom.

Receiving a fax

Receiving a fax is only a bit more involved than sending. You don't need to do any special configuration of your hardware, but you do need to tell the computer to answer incoming telephone calls:

1. **Launch System Preferences.**

2. **Click the Print & Fax icon, and then click on the Faxing tab.**

3. **Click the "Receive Faxes on this computer" checkbox** (see Figure 13-14).

   Your Mac is now set up to receive faxes through the phone line plugged into its modem port.

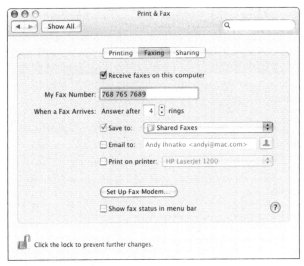

Figure 13-14
Setting up OS X to receive faxes

Telling Tiger what it should do with a received fax

On a traditional fax, a document appears as a stack of pages scattered out on the floor. When your Mac receives a fax, it saves it as a PDF file — Portable Document Format file, of which we've heard so many interesting things already.

The fact that it's a file means that there are a bunch of flexible options available to you, viz:

- **Decide where the PDF file should be stored.** Normally it'd go either to your Faxes folder, or to a special system-wide Shared Faxes folder that's available to all users of this Mac. (This means that if Suzy gets a fax, she can retrieve it herself instead of begging you, Ted, you heartless control freak, to get it out of a protected

233

folder elsewhere on your shared iMac.) You can have it sent to any other folder, though, including your remote iDisk. That way, if you're halfway around the world, you can pick up a fax from any Macintosh by connecting to your iDisk via the Internet. Select a destination through the Save To pop-up menu.

- **Email it.** It's just a PDF file, so it's easy as pie for Tiger to email it to any address. Just click on the Email to: checkbox in Figure 13-14 and specify a person (from your Address Book) or an email address that the faxes should be transmitted to.

- **Print it.** Oh, don't be boring. Really? You want to just have your Mac automatically *print* it? (Sigh). Okay, I suppose. Just click on the checkbox and select a printer from the pop-up list.

There are two other options on the Faxing Preferences pane shown in Figure 13-14. Set Up Fax Modem is there just to make the window look pretty. I'm guessing. I mean, I'll be dashed if I can figure out an actual purpose for this button. All Macs come with a built-in fax modem, and by default, Tiger uses this hardware for incoming and outgoing faxes. If you've been challenged to some sort of bar bet or you're being hazed by a fraternity and you're going to be using an external fax modem, you'd click this button to set it up. What you see next would be similar to setting up a new printer. But again, that's theoretical. Who uses *external* modems these days? Is that why our forefathers fought to win this nation's freedom?

And then there's a checkbox for putting a special Fax Status menulet in the menu bar. When your Mac's processing an incoming fax, you'll see an alert right in the menu bar. Handy stuff.

Okay, so we've done printing now. The principles I'm willing to bend for the sake of you kids . . .

The (surprising, shocking, temporary suspension of ennui-inducing. . . pick one) fact is that I'm not totally kidding when I say that print is dead. Or at least it *seems* that way, sometimes. I have three printers here in my home office, including a really spiffy high-volume 1200 dpi laser printer and a bunch of professional-grade photo printers. And I've just leaned back and sipped thoughtfully at my Dr. Pepper and blinked a lot of times and then leaned forward again and misjudged where the edge of my mousepad was and accidentally set the can back down on an edge. It spilled onto the keyboard, and I shouted a whole bunch of words that my goldfish didn't approve of and frantically started dabbing at the keyboard with the tail of my MacHack 23 T-shirt but forget it, that keyboard was toast. So I looked through my closet and found another one and replaced the ruined one and now I've quite forgotten where I was going with this.

Oh, yeah. Printing. Well, I can't remember the last time I actually printed something on paper, apart from printing an electronic ticket or a map. Perhaps I should try printing an actual document sometime. I mean, I've heard nice things about it. It'll give me a good nostalgic sense of how Dickens used to write novels on his Macintosh way back in 1986, before the days of the Internet.

Networking on Copper, Air, and a Prayer

In This Chapter

The Wired Part: Cables, Hubs, and Switches • The Wireless Part: AirPort and Base Stations
Cable Modems and DSL Modems • Modems: The Adorably Quaint Way to Connect
Antisocial Networking: Direct Mac-to-Mac Networks • FireWire Networking
Juggling Lots of Different Network Connections • Locational Guidance Counselor
Sharing Your Internet Connection • Bluetooth • Network Diagnostics

When we talk about networking, we're talking about two things: connecting computers to each other and connecting computers to the Internet. And when we say "connecting," some parts of your network connect to each other through physical cables that tether machines together like some Fritz Lang version of an assault on Mount Everest. Some parts accomplish the same exact things with radio waves, through wireless cards built into your Macs that talk to each other and to a base station that plugs into your wired network.

Simple. Elegant. But if Truth-In-Marketing laws in this country had real teeth, every time you bought a new computer and tried to make it work with a network, you'd launch a setup program and you'd see a screen like the one shown in Figure 14-1.

Because that's the way networking tends to work. Either you click a few buttons and it works flawlessly, or you do everything the right way and you still can't connect to the Internet. Either way, you're dealing with some complex mojo and for all you know, the whole system works because Tinkerbell owed Murray, The Gnome Of Mismatched Socks, a favor.

WHAT ABOUT RENDEZVOUS?

As you make your way through this maze of twisty passages known as Tiger, you might encounter the word "Rendezvous." It's the name of one of Tiger's built-in networking features: Rendezvous automatically discovers and exploits the resources of other Macs and other pieces of hardware on a network and makes them available to you.

Rendezvous was introduced in Panther, the previous edition of Mac OS X and at the time I proposed a book about it. It'd have been the easiest $300 I ever made: it'd have consisted of one page containing the preceding paragraph, and then three or four hundred pages of musings about the reasons why NASA beat the Russians to the moon, just to make my mandatory minimum page count.

So this is a chapter on networking. Why is there no section on Rendezvous? Because it works on its own and there's nothing to discuss. Look around Tiger: Rendezvous doesn't have its own helper app or its own System Preferences pane or its own *anything*, really. It's the epitome of how technology is supposed to function. All you, the freedom-loving end-user, need be aware of is that the music libraries of other Macs appear in iTunes automagically and that if you're on the iMac in your living room, you can listen to any of the albums on the tower Mac in your office by just selecting them from a list. When you're in a crowded lecture hall and you launch iChat, the names of every Mac user within range of your PowerBook's wireless card fill a buddy list and hitting on the cute redhead in the tenth row is merely a case of carefully scrutinizing the 40 or 50 buddy icons, clicking the most likely candidate, and then trusting to luck.

Teach Rendezvous? To explain it is to not understand it, little grasshopper, for to understand Rendezvous is to merely trust and accept it. Rendezvous is like Batman. It's a force of good that lurks everywhere unseen, emerging only to kick some serious butt and then withdraw once again to the shadows of legend.

So networking can be intimidating. Even to me — and I'm the guy who once tried to access file servers through the infrared features of his Casio digital watch.

 Note

And it would have worked, too, except I was really quite exceptionally drunk at the time. Rum is that most subtle and seductive of liars, kids; never forget that.

Fortunately, networking under Tiger is actually as simple as things can get. It's one of those rare operating systems where you really can just run the installation wizard program, close your eyes, commend your soul to God, and have faith that everything will work out pretty well in the end. Even the advanced features that make networking — do I dare say it? — actively and passionately *cool* are easy to take advantage of.

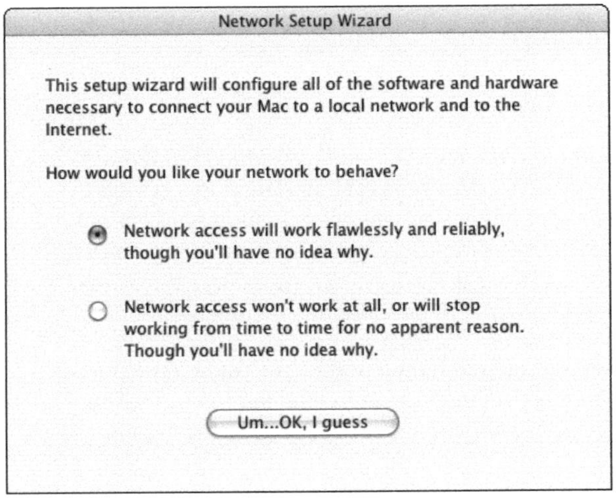

Network Setup Wizard

This setup wizard will configure all of the software and hardware necessary to connect your Mac to a local network and to the Internet.

How would you like your network to behave?

○ Network access will work flawlessly and reliably, though you'll have no idea why.

○ Network access won't work at all, or will stop working from time to time for no apparent reason. Though you'll have no idea why.

(Um...OK, I guess)

Figure 14-1
Telling it like it is

THE WIRED PART: CABLES, HUBS, AND SWITCHES

Step One of networking your Mac is to physically connect it to your network. Yes, I know, how disgustingly analog. Newsreels from the '30s promised that by 1982 we'd have robots that would string network cables across our offices for us, but keep in mind that the culture that made that promise also told us that it was possible to feed and clothe a family of four on a salary of $1,300 a year. So we're talking about some pretty big idiots here.

Every Macintosh that isn't either (a) inflatable or (b) made out of marzipan comes with a built-in Ethernet port. Ethernet is the international standard for getting pieces of hardware to talk to each other over copper wire, and at this level it refers both to the standards for the hardware and the cables and the standards for slurping digital information across it.

On the hardware side, an Ethernet port looks like a phone jack with a pituitary disorder. Plugging in cables is as easy as unpacking your new answering machine, without all the fuss and bother of finding a way to sing an outgoing message to the theme song from Silver Spoons. So, if you have three Macs plus a cable modem that give you a high-speed connection to the Internet and you want to network them together with Ethernet cable, you just connect their ports together and bang . . . instant network, right?

Alas, no. You old-timers who got to see *Pulp Fiction* in an actual movie theater probably remember AppleTalk, the Mac's early networking standard. Ethernet kicks AppleTalk's butt so no big loss there, but one of the keen things about the old way was that its networking boxes had two jacks. You could just daisy-chain Macs together — a networking cable goes in one jack, a second cable runs from the second jack onward to the next machine. No such luck with Ethernet.

Instead, you use external devices called *hubs*. An Ethernet hub acts just like your USB or FireWire hub. It splits a single connection into several. A typical hub (and by typical I mean "$100 buys you this hub, a DVD of the latest Pixar movie, plus dinner and a movie if you're a cheap date") allows you to connect four computers together, though the more expensive ones have more jacks.

A simple hub is adequate for the needs of nearly anyone who wants to get his or her networking advice from a book instead of a consultant who went to school for this sort of garbage. But if you want to spend a little more dough, you can do a little better by buying a switch instead. A hub is a dumb device that (more or less) just takes all the cables that are plugged into it and mashes them all together. All of the traffic on this part of the network becomes a single, thick stew, so when one Mac is generating a huge amount of chatter, it slows down everyone who's using the network.

FAST, FASTER, AND FASTEST ETHERNET

Speed is the other thing to consider when you're standing there in the office superstore and wondering just how much you really want to spend. Every few years, the industry kept coming up with new ways to shoot data across Ethernet cables at faster speeds. Originally, Ethernet moved at 10 million bits per second. That sounded grandma-ish to some people, so new network hardware was developed that worked at a hundred megabits. Modern Macs ship with gigabit Ethernet, which is another order of magnitude zippier. And higher speeds are always just at the top of the next hill, men... onward to glory and Asgard eternal!

All you need to know is that Ethernet is Ethernet. When a machine with an older Ethernet interface swaps data with a new machine, the faster machine downshifts to match the slower speed. No sweat. But if you bought a cheap 10MB switch to network all those gigabit Macs together — congratulations: you saved yourself $20 — but your network is a hundred times slower than it needs to be. Word to the wise.

Incidentally, while 100 Mbps Ethernet is technically referred to as "fast Ethernet," this is much like making a reference to color television. It instantly dates you. The younger, cooler people will bounce you right out of the dance club, fake tattoos and all, while hails of "Narc!" rain all around you. Avoid.

But a switch is slicker and more sophisticated. If your Macs are networked together through a switch, data can move directly from Mac A to Mac B without becoming part of the stew. The upshot is that when you connect to another Mac's hard drive over the network and copy 20 megabytes of photos, it doesn't matter that your son D'Artagnian is using the same network to watch an incredibly educational bit of streaming video via the Internet at the same time. That scenario would choke a hub, but a switch silently creates separate connections. Mac A talks directly to Mac B; Mac C talks directly to your cable modem; and if any of these users are experiencing unhappiness in life, network-related speed hits aren't a large contributor.

To actually set up a wired network, just plug everything together through the hub or the switch. You don't need to shut down all your hardware first, though your Macs and any other gear probably won't be able to see each other until you do.

THE WIRELESS PART: AIRPORT AND BASE STATIONS

There are times when I must acknowledge that not all people share my unique viewpoints regarding interior design and see dozens of thick, multicolored Ethernet cables snaking in and out of every room as something less than a sign that this home is owned by a true forward-thinker.

Well, it takes all kinds to make a world, I suppose. Enter wireless Ethernet (or WiFi), in which a doohickey projects an immense bubble of network access around itself.

BUT WIRELESS IS WIRELESS

Still, AirPort is based on those generic standards, so it isn't an Apple-only club. The AirPort card inside your PowerBook is as happy to talk to a third-party, no-name 802.11g base station as it is to talk to something slick and UFO-shaped with an Apple logo stamped on it. And when you prove how open-minded you are by actually allowing your Windows-user friends over to your house, the 802.11g cards in their notebooks can find and use your AirPort base station just fine.

In light of all this, it bears mentioning that AirPort base stations can cost two or even three times as much as a third-party model. Are they worth it? Well, they're a lot easier to install and set up, and they work more intimately with Mac OS X. You'll probably be happier with an AirPort. But if the price is out of reach, you can lead a rich, fulfilling life with a Linksys or D-Link 802.11g router, too, or any other base station that conforms to that same standard.

Note

I say "doohickey" because it's a sturdy, satisfying word, and because although wireless Ethernet has become as popular as Diet Coke, the industry has yet to fall behind one single word for the aforementioned bubble-projecting device. Some folks call it a base station; some call it an access point. They mean the same thing, but I'll stick with base station from here on out.

Any computer — a Mac, a Windows machine, even a PDA — inside this bubble can potentially find and communicate with this base station, provided that the computer's equipped with a wireless networking card. If so, it's golden. This wireless connection is as good as being connected to the network through copper. Slower, sure, but in terms of What You Can Do, it's just as good. If you set up this base station as a connection to the Internet, it means you can be out in your backyard lifeguarding your houseguests Uma Thurman and Halle Berry as they frolic in the pool while you watch the live restart of the Iditarod dogsled race via streaming video.

Note

It could *so* happen. *Shut up!!!*

Apple was nice enough to be perhaps the very first major computer maker to fully embrace WiFi. The specification for wireless is an industry standard but it's saddled with a terrible name: 802.11b, later to be upgraded to 802.11g, a flavor that's completely compatible with the old standard but an order of magnitude faster. Seven syllables, including punctuation: That's not very Mac-like. So Apple adopted those standards but started calling them AirPort and AirPort Extreme.

Plugging a base station into your network is no more difficult than plugging in your Mac. If you're using your AirPort base to provide wireless access to broadband Internet, connect its Ethernet port to an Ethernet connector on your cable or DSL modem. If you're using it to provide access to your local wired network, plug it into an available connector on your hub or switch. AirPort Extreme base stations can easily accommodate both, with separate Ethernet jacks for both broadband and local-network connections. Plug it into AC power and the hardware end is over and done with.

ANDY IS NOT COUNTED AMONG GOD'S FAVORITES

And for good reason, I'm sure, but *boy* is it annoying when He makes His point by ensuring that the *only* spot in my whole home office where my PowerBook can barely find a WiFi connection is the end of the couch that's right in front of the TV, i.e., the one place other than my desk where I'd like to sit and work.

The culprit is a big chimney stack in one of the walls between the base downstairs and my upstairs office. It casts a "shadow" in the radio signal that falls right across the sofa. Solution? I installed a second base station in an upstairs bedroom, one floor directly above my AirPort Extreme base station. When I'm on the sofa, my PowerBook looks for the best connection and decides that it should connect to the upstairs base station across the hall, which then throws the signal one floor down, which zigzags the signal around the chimney quite nicely.

The only alternative would have been to adopt a more thoughtful, generous, and pious lifestyle and somehow regain favor in the eyes of God. Buying the second base was a lot simpler.

But while hubs and switches are simple devices with no free will, under the hood a base station is actually a fairly sophisticated computer that needs to know what sort of world it's been born into. You'll need to run the AirPort Setup Assistant to spank the base station on its polycarbonate bottom and get it breathing oxygen instead of amniotic fluid.

Just plug the base station's power adapter into the wall. If you're going to be using it as a connection to the Internet, connect its broadband port to your cable or DSL modem if you have one, or its modem port to a phone jack if you don't. Then run the AirPort Setup Assistant. The Assistant walks you through the whole process step by step, and most of the configuration happens automagically. Here are some of the highlights, in rough order of appearance:

- **Is this base station going to be used to Create a new wireless network, or will it Extend an existing one?** You're likely to be doing that first thingy. But if you already have a wireless network, you can configure this new base station to work as a "relay" of sorts.

WiFi has two limitations: the signal it broadcasts has a limited "reach" (100 yards, in theory, but every wall and floor between you and the base station cuts that significantly), and there are a lot of obstacles that it can't penetrate, such as a brick wall. Configuring a second (or third, or fourth . . .) base station to Extend an existing network lets you work around those limits. You get a strong signal everywhere in the house and in the yard without having to set up three or four separate wireless networks. If you select this option, all you have to do is select an existing base station that you want this new hardware to link up with.

- **Give both the base station and the new WiFi network some names.** The base station name should leave no doubt as to which base station it is. If you've got two or three bases in the house and you need to choose one of them specifically (so you can reconfigure it or update its software) you'll be glad you named it Downstairs Office and not after one of the elves from *The Lord of the Rings*. The network name can appear in the AirPort menu of every computer within range, so you can afford to be clever here. Though if you're creating a second or third WiFi network, it helps to be a little bit descriptive.

- **Choose a level of security for this network (see Figure 14-2).** Do remember that radio waves are radio waves, and *anybody* within range can receive them. With no security, anybody parked in your driveway can join your network and use your broadband connection. And, incidentally, see and access any shared folders on your network. Plus, a WiFi base station ordinarily broadcasts all of its data "in the clear," meaning that anyone can run a special utility called a "sniffer" and see all kinds of stuff floating through the air. They can read the email you're uploading, grab the same pictures you're downloading. . . with no security, you're very vulnerable.

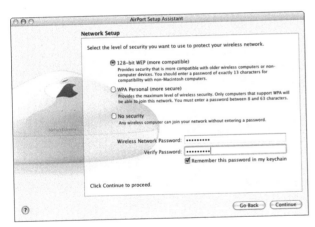

Figure 14-2
Securing an AirPort base station

If you're running some sort of Hippie commune, you can leave your base station wide open with no security. But it makes more sense to secure both the base and its traffic with one of two different types of encryption.

If you're going to be allowing all sorts of computers — like PDAs and Windows machines, not just Macs — to access this WiFi network, you'll find that "128-bit WEP" is more compatible with a wider range of hardware. If you're going to be a Mac-only house, though, choose WPA. It's a lot more secure than WEP; WEP is strong enough to keep out the punks and the pikers, but a truly determined miscreant can get through it easily. No matter which scheme you choose, users will have to provide a Wireless Network Password to join this network. Pick a decent one.

▼ Info

The only hitch with encryption is that those Windows machines and PDAs and whatnot can't understand that nice, plain, simple password that you picked out. To make those machines work with a secure WiFi network, open the AirPort Admin Utility (you'll find it in your Applications ➜ Utilities folder), select the base station, and select Equivalent Network Password from the Base Station menu. The utility will give you a bizarre sequence of characters and digits that looks nothing like the word "Salmon-Sundae" (the actual password) but has the same effect when typed into the Password field of a Windows wireless networking assistant.

- **Tell the Assistant about your Internet connection.** If you've plugged the base station into a broadband connection, the Assistant will locate it and figure out the correct settings automagically through the magic of DHCP (Figure 14-3). If you're using a modem connection, you'll have to provide the Assistant with a few details. You can get this information (phone number, your user ID, and connection information) from the ISP.

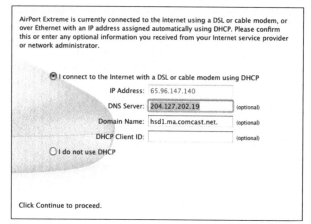

AirPort Extreme is currently connected to the Internet using a DSL or cable modem, or over Ethernet with an IP address assigned automatically using DHCP. Please confirm this or enter any optional information you received from your Internet service provider or network administrator.

⦿ I connect to the Internet with a DSL or cable modem using DHCP

IP Address: 65.96.147.140

DNS Server: 204.127.202.19 (optional)

Domain Name: hsd1.ma.comcast.net. (optional)

DHCP Client ID: (optional)

◯ I do not use DHCP

Click Continue to proceed.

Figure 14-3
Cool: the Assistant teaches *itself* about your broadband connection

- **Give the new base station a password.** You'll need it to make future changes to its configuration.

And you're done. Click Update from the next screen and the Assistant will transmit your settings to the base station and then reset it. After the base station restarts itself, it's ready, willing, and able to serve.

 Tip

> You can rerun the Assistant at any time to make changes. Eventually, you'll also want to look at the AirPort Admin Utility, which lets you access and change these settings more directly. It also offers you extra tricks that can't be done through the Assistant. For example, it offers a spiffy "Access Control" feature that lets you limit use of this base station not simply to anyone who can provide a password … but to *specific pieces of hardware*. On my home network you can't break into my wireless network unless you break into my house and steal my PowerBook or my iMac first.

BEST O' BOTH WORLDS

The nice thing about having no security is that it makes it easy for houseguests to get onto the Internet. If you own a coffee shop with free WiFi, you'd rather that your employees spend their time pushing those $3.50 muffins instead of teaching customers how to connect to the WiFi.

But again, it's dangerous. That's why I have two separate WiFi networks in my house. One base station is set up to have little or no security and is a snap for visitors to access. The second is tightly protected and also allows access to my private home network.

DHCP? WHUZZAT?

Oh, it's a flippin' godsend, is what it is. I want you to put this book down, go out into the yard, turn east to face the rising sun, and say, "Thank you, o loving universe, for creating the Dynamic Host Configuration Protocol." I would specifically direct you to turn and face the home of the Dynamic Host Configuration Working Group of the Internet Engineering Task Force, but — like love and hope and all good things — they're everywhere.

DHCP is the reason why the Orwellian nightmare of getting networking hardware to actually do something useful is now a thing of the past. A hundred years ago, we had to make our own soap by killing animals for the fat and rendering it down. Now, we head to the drugstore and pick up a bar of Life Buoy. Similarly, adding a computer to a network or (for those who have already largely given up the last shreds of their faith in a kind and loving God) getting it to reliably connect to the Internet was a hugely complicated process of looking up and punching in endless series of network addresses, routing codes, name servers. . . I seem to remember at one point having to correctly guess the number of piña colada–flavored jellybeans in a 50-gallon aquarium, but I might just be misremembering.

DHCP changes all that. Your hardware and the network simply have a little chat and work out for themselves how they need to configure everything. And holy dancing Zagnuts on a rotisserie . . . it actually works.

▼ Note

DHCP is, frankly, the reason why it's possible to discuss networking in a single chapter of a book instead of taking up an entire volume on the subject. Nearly all Internet service providers support DHCP. Nearly all hardware manufacturers support DHCP. Nearly all software publishers support it. Why? Because it's Human and it's Humane, and it's the difference between a product that people can actually install and use and a product that costs the manufacturer tens of thousands of dollars a month in tech support.

You'll notice that I'm not going to spend 50 pages lovingly explaining every possible way to configure a Mac for use on a network. It's because DHCP has collapsed all sensible advice down to two, and only two, states: (1) Check DHCP and let the devices configure themselves, and if DHCP isn't supported, then (2) contact your network administrator or broadband provider and ask them for the specific settings required to get your hardware running on his or her network.

That's also the reason why there's no section entitled "How to create a Macintosh network with Ethernet cables instead of WiFi." All you need to do is string the cables and connect the machines to each other through a hub or

a switch. The Macs will locate and configure themselves automatically.

But back to AirPort

When you connect all those Macs together using Ethernet, the network exists without having to explicitly tell any of this gear that it is now part of a network. There are really no settings to manage, so there's nothing to set and adjust.

AirPort's different. Tiger puts an AirPort icon in the menu bar (see Figure 14-4).

This menu is workin' for me even when I haven't pulled it down. The icon in the menu bar tells me that I'm currently connected to some sort of AirPort network and that the strength of the radio signal is pretty good; three of the icon's four bars are darkened in, which is about as strong a signal as you can expect without actually holding the base station between your knees as you type. When no base stations are in range, the entire indicator is gray.

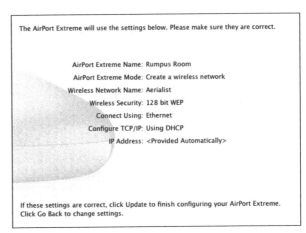

The AirPort Extreme will use the settings below. Please make sure they are correct.

AirPort Extreme Name: Rumpus Room
AirPort Extreme Mode: Create a wireless network
Wireless Network Name: Aerialist
Wireless Security: 128 bit WEP
Connect Using: Ethernet
Configure TCP/IP: Using DHCP
IP Address: <Provided Automatically>

If these settings are correct, click Update to finish configuring your AirPort Extreme. Click Go Back to change settings.

Figure 14-4
The AirPort menu

The menu gives you access to a bunch of handy options:

- **Turn AirPort Off.** Turning off your Mac's internal AirPort interface is like physically disconnecting an Ethernet cable. It gives you a little extra assurance that no one can see (and possibly exploit) your Mac.

▼ Note

If you're using a PowerBook, turning off AirPort when you're not using it also extends the charge in your battery. Keeping a radio transmitter/receiver running burns energy, after all.

- **Choose available AirPort networks.** Tiger lists all of the different AirPort networks it can see inside that second section. Here, we can only see my two home wireless networks, Floggiston and Aerialist, the currently selected network. If you visited my house, you could use Floggiston just by selecting it from the menu. If it's a secure network, I'll be asked to provide a password.

But in truth, there's a *third* network in my office named Iron Monkey. But I don't make that one public. To access that AirPort network, you need to use the next menu item.

- **Other.** The fact that wireless base stations broadcast their names to the world is actually a feature; otherwise, how would people know that they existed and are available? But sometimes you don't want folks to even try to connect to your base station. If you've set up a *closed network,* the base is invisible unless you know its name. If you select Other from the AirPort menu, you're presented with the dialog shown in Figure 14-5. As you can see, I have to provide the network's name and password before I'm given access.

Figure 14-5
Joining a closed network

- **Create Network.** The next option is really pretty special. All along, we've assumed that only an AirPort base station can anchor and establish a wireless network. Well, your Macintosh is a pretty decent piece of hardware on its own, and by clicking Create Network, you can establish a brand-new wireless network using your Mac as a virtual base station (Figure 14-6). This is also known as an *ad-hoc* wireless network. To set up an ad-hoc network:

Figure 14-6
Creating an ad-hoc AirPort network using your Mac as a base station

1. **Just give it a name.**

   Clicking the Show Options button allows you to encrypt the signal and password-protect your new network in precisely the same way you'd protect a real base station.

2. **Click OK.**

   Your Mac now appears in the AirPort menus of any nearby wireless-studly Macs. It's really that simple.

▼ **Note**

This feature alone is probably responsible for 11 percent of all corporate sales of AirPort-equipped Macs. Why, just five years ago if your boss called an all-staff meeting and crowded 30 of you into a conference room to watch a weapons-grade three-hour Power-Point presentation on Synergy and Commitment and Excellence, the only dignified way to endure it would be to fake some sort of seizure and hope that someone seizes upon the opportunity and carries you out. Today, though, you silently create an ad-hoc network, let your friends in the room find it, open up iChat, and spend the rest of the session making fun of the speaker's tie.

- **Open Internet Connect.** Internet Connect is a little utility that lets you open, close, view, and manage your various Internet connections. Select this item to open it. If you're connected to the Internet through AirPort, the Internet Connect window will show you some details about your connection.

CABLE MODEMS AND DSL MODEMS

Fortunately, you're paying people to install this hardware for you. They come right in, drill holes through your hardwood floors, help themselves to whatever looks good in the fridge, and leave behind a box the size of a paperback book with lots of blinking lights on it.

Whether you go with a cable modem or a DSL connection, the actual hookup is simple:

1. **The modem sports an Ethernet connector.**

    Connect this to your Ethernet hub, your Ethernet switch, or your AirPort base station.

2. **Install the appropriate software.**

    Your service provider might have also given you a CD-ROM with its own installation wizard. This disc will install whatever special software your Mac requires to access the Internet via this modem, or at the very least it automates the creation of special profiles that make it easier to switch from this new broadband connection to your existing connection and back again.

3. **Restart your Macs or your base station.**

    DHCP kicks in and each device directly connected to the modem negotiates with it, agreeing on the proper settings for peace, brotherhood, harmony, and access to ESPN.com's live coverage of major-league baseball.

4. **Verify the connect.**

    After the restart, verify that the connection is working by opening Safari and pulling up Google.com's search page. If it doesn't come up, the problem can probably be traced to one of two causes:

    - The new cable/DSL modem hasn't found the service provider yet. It will. Keep it powered up for half an hour or so. If there's still no joy, call the company up and holler blue murder.

    - Somewhere in the daisy chain between your Mac and your service provider, a device hasn't negotiated its connection to the device that represents the next step closer to the Internet. Begin at the furthest point downstream: your Mac. Restart it. No joy? Restart your AirPort base station if you have one (I just pull out its power plug for a few seconds). No? Restart the broadband modem. If you're still getting nothing, then it's time for more blue murder.

▼ **Tip**

This is just good general advice. Not the yelling; the idea that you should restart devices in a downstream-to-upstream order when an Internet connection goes bye-bye. Though a good holler at someone who doesn't know you, never did anything to you personally, and isn't responsible for your current predicament, can occasionally be quite cleansing, assuming you have a jolly indifference and insensitivity to the feelings of others.

MODEMS: THE ADORABLY QUAINT WAY TO CONNECT

Well, we've spent enough time on fancy, useful, high-speed networks. Now we should move onto that most venerable and (unfortunately) useful method of connecting to the Internet: dialing in through a modem.

And before you sniff at this, reflect upon the fact that there are times when you're visiting your parents or staying at a beach house or have checked into a hotel where broadband access bills at $20 per day. I sure don't have the guts to spend 18 hours without checking my email. Maybe you're simply a better person than I am. I've seen what I look like when I dance, so I suppose it's actually pretty likely.

Yes, after all these months of wireless high-speed broadband access to the Internet, I'm sure that getting your email at 56 Kbps after hearing a dial tone and a *whrshhrshhhskktktkt* of static seems like walking around your office in bare feet and no shirt . . . but doing it does serve to keep one humble.

Creating a modem connection

You create a modem connection through the Network panel of System Preferences (Figure 14-7).

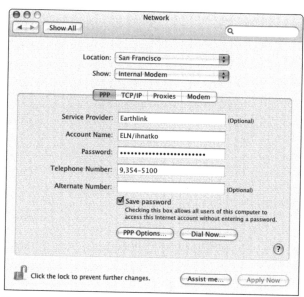

Figure 14-7
The Network panel of System Preferences

The Network panel is your dashboard for Tiger's network connections, and we'll be coming back to it later. For now, click the pop-up menu next to Show: and select Internal Modem.

Unfortunately, there isn't anything nearly as slick as DHCP for dial-up connections, and you need to type in the connection settings manually. Hey, look; this is a *modem connection*. That's as low-tech as you can get without having to scoop data off of your hard drive with your bare hands and physically *carry* it over to the Internet.

▼ **Tip**

And if you click "Assist me," Tiger walks you through the entire process step by step, via the Network Setup Assistant. But this is the one case where it's actually faster to plug in these settings yourself. The meat is all there in front of you, and you'll be off and running (or walking — again, this is a dial-up connection) toot sweet. But don't be a hero. Nobody's watching, so go ahead and use the assistant if you get confused.

Most dial-ups will use Tiger's default settings for PPP, the industry-standard way to establish a dial-up Internet connection, and all you need to do is define the following specifics:

- **Account Name:** Your account name. If your email address on this dial-up is artcarney@queenssewers. com, your account name is artcarney.

- **Your password.** You can save this password with your configuration. Otherwise, you'll have to enter it every time you connect to the Internet, and isn't your life a big enough mess as it is?

- **A phone number and a backup phone number.** If you're doing some fancy stuff like dialing 9 to reach an outside line or a calling-card number, you might need to type in a fairly goat-chokingly-large number, but don't let it throw you. Just throw in a comma at every point where you'd like the modem to pause for a second. "9,,,7815551212" ensures that the modem will wait three seconds to give your phone system a chance to find an outside line before proceeding.

▼ **Tip**

Incidentally, if you like to actually, you know, *connect* to the Internet when you travel, it's a good idea to make sure you don't leave home without downloading a list of all of your dial-up ISP's local access numbers. When I head off to a city for the first time, I visit Earthlink's Web site, ask for a complete list of access numbers, and then use Tiger's Print To PDF feature to turn that list into a file I can read offline whenever I want. It is, at times, humbling to discover that you flew 3,000 miles and only after checking into the hotel realized that Earthlink's online database of access numbers isn't technically going to be available to you until you actually manage to get onto the Internet, you know?

Some dial-ups require some special massaging with customized settings, accessible through the PPP Options... button and the TCP/IP tab. Get in touch with your ISP and get a list of the proper settings, and as with anything you do while setting up a Network connection, don't even think of messing around with these settings unless specifically directed to.

Click Apply Now and your new modem configuration is good to go.

Dialing and connecting

You use the Internet Connect application (Figure 14-8) to actually dial out and establish a connection to the Internet. You'll find it in the Applications folder, or you can open it from the AirPort menu.

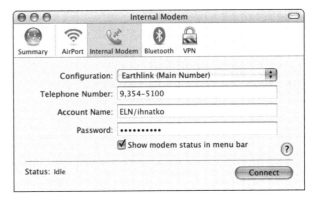

Figure 14-8
Click, bzzz, dial, shriek, connect; dialing with Internet Connect

Click "Connect" to start things going. The window updates with status messages to annoy you about the connection-in-progress, and once you're online, it'll be replaced with a clock showing you the amount of time you've been

MORE ON INTERNET CONNECT

In the high-schoolish social structure of Tiger, Internet Connect is one of the Goths who always eat together and alone in the cafeteria. That is, it's useful and interesting, but people just don't feel a need to interact with it.

The purpose of this app is to show you your connection to the Internet and, in the case of connections that aren't always on, to let you connect and disconnect at will. You'll see that every different method of connecting to the 'net is represented by a different icon in the toolbar. But access to the Internet and access to your local network have been mainstreamed together, so there's no psychological need to keep checking in on your connection to the outside world. And while naturally you're going to want to dial the modem if you're stuck with a dial-up connection, and see how well your AirPort connection is doing, Apple's smart enough to know that you'll prefer to access that hardware through dedicated icons on the menu bar, not by launching a separate app.

So in truth, Internet Connect is actually irrelevant for most people. Goth chicks are cute, and if you compliment them on their Morpheus tattoo they'll read you some of their poetry, plus they're human beings who contribute their own unique spice to human society. But if you never actually interact with Internet Connect, you're not missing much.

connected. The Connect button changes to Disconnect, and clicking it does more or less what y'all think it does.

If you've defined several different modem configurations (for example, you have more than one dial-up ISP) you can switch between them through the Configuration pop-up. It's also a handy spot to temporarily add stuff to the phone number, such as when you find yourself in one of those fascist offices where the ruling class forces the proletariat to dial 9 to get an outside line.

The handy bit about the Internal Modem status panel is that it offers you a checkbox for adding a Modem menu to the menu bar. You're gonna want this. It's as handy as the AirPort menulet, allowing you to check on your modem status at a glance and to connect and disconnect at will (see Figure 14-9).

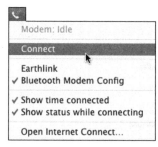

Figure 14-9
The Modem menu

ANTISOCIAL NETWORKING: DIRECT MAC-TO-MAC NETWORKS

It seems like it'd be hopelessly missing the point to create a network of two Macs. Networks are all about openness and shared resources and community; essentially you're

THE OZYMANDIAS OF THE CABLING INDUSTRY

Not so fast, Skeezix. Patching two Ethernet ports together with a plain cable works if you have a new-ish Mac, say, one that was manufactured during the George Dubbya Bush administration or later. A direct two-computer Ethernet network used to require a special flavor of cable called a crossover cable. A couple of the connectors were switched around and it allowed the manufacturer to charge an extra seven bucks for what to the naked eye was a plain, $5 cable. But this method of networking proved so handy that Apple just went ahead and made its Ethernet ports smart enough to detect when they were directly connected to another machine and make the necessary adjustments automagically. This crippled the crossover cable industry (or at least the part of it that couldn't survive by selling crossover cables to the remaining 95 percent of the computers out there that aren't Macs), but in this modern, global economy you have to look at the big picture. Compassion, a sign of weakness in our nation's youth, just slows down the March of Progress and is to be discouraged.

saying it's you and this guy, and the rest of the world can go hang itself. It's *totally* a Whitney Houston/Bobby Brown sort of thing.

Still, networking two and only two Macs together is terribly handy. I usually refer to this as Airplane Networking as opposed to AirPort Networking; networking two Macs together directly is great for when you and a friend are on a 6-hour flight and want to play network games right there in Row 19.

It's called a direct network because it's done by simply connecting the Macs' two ports together with a cable. No hub, no base stations, no larger infrastructure. Just a guy and a girl fragging each other on a Boeing 727 somewhere over Iowa. It's a natural and a beautiful thing, and it couldn't be simpler to create; just take an Ethernet cable and connect the two network ports together. Depending on what your Macs have been up to lately, you might need to restart, but there's nothing to configure or install.

FIREWIRE NETWORKING

"Blasphemer!" you cry. "And what's the deal with that hair?" you add, which, frankly, is unnecessarily hurtful.

Your FireWire port is chiefly there to connect high-speed peripherals like video cameras and external hard drives, but heck, son . . . it's a high-speed port! No reason why we can't use it for networkin'!

FireWire networking is fairly obscure and it's sufficiently "out there" that when I tell people that such a thing is possible, the scene is fairly evocative of the time when, um, Copernicus, I think, made his dramatic and revolutionary announcement that man had evolved from apes and to prove it, he intended to sail three ships to the so-called edge of the world.

"But why bother?" you might ask. The Top Three Reasons:

- **A FireWire cable is a lot smaller than an Ethernet cable and it has no little plastic bits that might snap off in my carry-on bag.** So as an emergency, "I desperately need to create a two-machine network" solution (specifically, an "I'm stuck on an eight-hour flight and I'd like to play a two-person strategy game with someone in the seat next to me" solution), it's way better than Ethernet. I'm almost certain to have the right cable with me, and it's certain to be in working order.

- **In a way, FireWire networking is a more robust alternative to connecting two Macs' FireWire ports together and activating Target Disk Mode.** It saves you from having to shut down one of the Macs and mount it as a remote network volume, which can often mean wasting 10 or 15 minutes shutting down apps and saving documents. FireWire networking gives you all the speed of Target Disk Mode without the shutdown, and the second Mac continues to act like a Mac with a keyboard and a mouse and windows and junk and everything, not like a dumb external hard drive. So your sweetie can still mess around on the Internet while you're copying that 10-gigabyte iPhoto library.

- **It's just cooler.** On top of everything else, how can you *not* dig a technology with a name like FireWire? It sounds like the name of one of the Justice League's archenemies.

As soon as you connect two live Macs together via FireWire, Tiger will automatically sense that you're trying to create a network connection over that port, and will create the needed configuration for you automatically. If you're using this feature to connect to a previous edition of Mac OS X, you'll have to configure that other Mac manually. Here's how to do it in Mac OS X 10.3 ("Panther"):

1. **Open the Network pane of System Preferences.**

2. **From the "Show" pop-up menu, select Network Port Configurations.**

   You'll be shown all of the network connections that Panther is currently aware of (Figure 14-10).

3. **Click the New button.**

   A sheet drops down (Figure 14-11).

Figure 14-10
Port Configurations: All of Panther's connections to other machines

Figure 14-11
Adding a new port

4. **Select Built-in FireWire from the Port pop-up and give your new configuration a likely name.**

5. **Click OK.**

JUGGLING LOTS OF DIFFERENT NETWORK CONNECTIONS

Networking is a prime area in which Tiger does a stellar job of taking an incredibly tortuous and highly technical subject and eliminating as much of the mental clutter as possible. By skillfully using such distracting verbiage as comparing a form of networking to one of the most troubled celebrity marriages since James Brown married . . . well, about anybody, really . . . you've learned about how your Mac can have several different connections to the Internet (AirPort, cable modem, dial-up modem) and even several different methods of establishing a physical network connection in the first place (Ethernet port, AirPort, FireWire).

So why aren't you worried about having to juggle all of these different methods and ports? Two reasons: That Whitney and Bobby line was really pretty good; honestly, I'm pretty happy with it. Plus, Tiger manages all that stuff for you.

It's called "autohoming" and it's like this: Tiger knows all the different ways it can connect to a network, and if one fails, it'll just try another. So there's never any need to specifically say, "Dude, alas the AirPort connection we all enjoyed back at the house is no more; a phone jack is all that lies between this Macintosh and insanity."

If you want to manage these connections manually, open the Network panel of System Preferences and select Network Port Configurations from the Show popup (Figure 14-12).

That's a list of networking schemes and the order in which Tiger tries to use them. If you're there in Seat 11-A and you've just linked to the FireWire port of your companion in Seat 11-B for a little network game play, you can tell Tiger that FireWire is now your number one method of networking by just clicking and dragging FireWire Direct (or whatever you named it when you configured the port) to the top of the list.

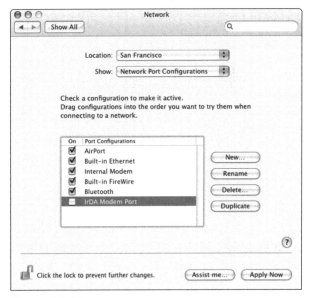

Figure 14-12
Changing the pecking order of network configurations

It's also a handy way to temporarily disable a port entirely. Deselecting Built-in Ethernet effectively renders your Mac deaf and mute on that port.

LOCATIONAL GUIDANCE COUNSELOR

Of course, you have no idea of what a fool's paradise you're now living in. Your Mac is new, you're configuring it for the first time, everything is pretty much out of the box and minty fresh, assuming that you were gargling mouthwash at the keyboard, read something particularly amusing on a Web site, and sputtered Scope all over your screen, in which case you have much bigger problems on your hands right now.

When you're at home, you have a dial-up connection. When you're at the office, you connect to a server through direct Ethernet. When you're at a branch office, you connect to the main office through a Virtual Private Network. You make plenty of business trips to San Francisco, New York, Boston, and Wahoo, Nebraska, and in each of those places you connect to your dial-up ISP through a different local number. And let's not forget all the time you spend on airplanes blowing up the person seated next to you in your guise as a black-ops Navy SEAL.

Result: colossal hassle every time you move from one location to another. Tiger's autohoming helps you out a little, but on the whole, you have to change oodles of settings every time your networking environment changes. Not so: Tiger allows you to save the current state of your networking configuration as a unique location that you can activate with one click. Here's how you create a new location:

1. **Open the Networking pane of System Preferences.**

2. **Click the Location popup and select New Location.**

3. **Type a name for your new location and click OK.**

And that's it. Your existing configuration is saved under this new name and you can activate it just by selecting it from the Location popup (Figure 14-13).

 Note

Some people have an album of postcards or a shelf full of souvenir snow globes or a string of children all across the country to attest to their world travels. Me, I have a fat Location menu.

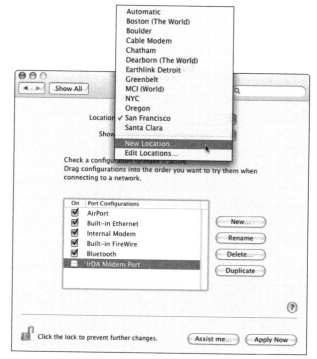

Figure 14-13
Switching settings snappily through lots of locations

Locations are handy enough that you can also switch between them right from the Apple menu.

SHARING YOUR INTERNET CONNECTION

Workers! Comrades! Throw down your tools! Then pick them up again and rise against the hated oppressors of the proletariat! Let us . . . let us . . .

Well, I'm not really up on my Commie revolutionary rhetoric. What I'm driving at is that when one individual has so much and the rest have so little, it's a sign of greatness that the former should share the wealth with the latter. We've already covered ways that your Mac can share its files and printers with others, but how ginchy is it that you can share your Mac's Internet connection, too?

This is easier to demonstrate than to explain. Try these on for size:

- You and your three friends are sharing a beach house for the week. You're all technology-savvy forward thinkers, true warriors of the New Economy (read: geeks who would wet their Spiderman Underoos if they should — God forbid — go an afternoon without checking email). But there's only one phone line, which means that only one of you can dial into an ISP and grab your mail at a time. With Internet Sharing, you can establish a dial-up connection on your Power-Book and then it becomes available to anybody who can reach your PowerBook via AirPort; essentially, you've turned your PowerBook into an AirPort base station.

- You and your sweetie are at a coffee shop with free wireless access. You have a top-of-the-line PowerBook with AirPort, but she has actual social skills and a good sense of proportion, so she just has a cheap

iBook with no wireless at all. You can create a two-Mac network by connecting the two Mac's Ethernet or FireWire ports and then sharing your AirPort Internet connection with her.

And then there's the Shady Way To Use This, which I'm a little embarrassed about, and so I'll toss it into a sidebar.

As is typical for Tiger networking, sharing your Internet connection is so simple as to be anticlimactic:

1. **Open the Sharing pane of System Preferences.**

2. **Click the Internet tab (Figure 14-14).**

   All of your available Internet connections are shown in the pop-up menu.

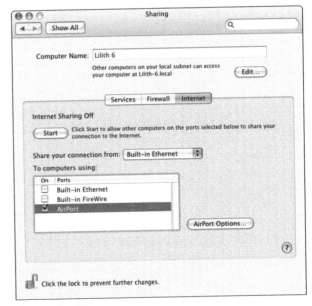

Figure 14-14
Sharing your Internet connection with other folks on your network

3. **Select your source from this list.**

   You can share the Internet across all of your available network ports, or just some. Click the checkboxes of all the ports across which you'd like to share the Internet. Any local computer that can reach your Mac through one of the selected ports can access the Internet.

4. **Click Start.**

In Figure 14-14, I've set up my Mac so that I can stick it to the hotel industry. It's set up so that Tiger takes an Internet connection that's coming in through my Ethernet port and shares it with anyone who can connect to my Mac via AirPort. To put it more simply: my hotel room's broadband cable is plugged into my PowerBook's Ethernet port, and the two friends I'm sharing the room with can access the Internet by choosing my PowerBook from their own PowerBooks' AirPort menus.

▼ **Note**

But do understand that sometimes, sharing an Internet connection can violate the terms of your agreement with your Internet service provider. Furthermore, when your Mac shares its Internet connection, it works some minor mojo that might temporarily confuse your broadband connection. Nothing permanent, mind you, but it might be enough that you can't use your cable modem until you restart it, and you'll get a testy email from your broadband provider that orders you to knock it off and warns you not to do it again.

And that's really it. The above example was based on PowerBooks, AirPort, and FireWire, but this feature will work on any Mac and any method of connecting. Believe me, you haven't lived until you've seen a network of four top-of-the-line G5 Macs connected to the Internet

IF YOU THINK $20 IS A REASONABLE CHARGE . . .

. . . for just 12 hours of Internet access, then you need to switch to a more-expensive brand of gin.

I like hotels that provide broadband but hate hotels that seem to think I'm a trust-fund idiot with my own reality-TV show and no perception of the value of a dollar. So if my friends and I are staying in a block of rooms in the same hotel, one of us will connect to the in-room Ethernet and share it with the rooms next door via AirPort.

Shady, yes. Possibly a violation of the hotel's policies. But when I start to feel guilty about it, I realize that for the same amount of money I'd be paying for Internet access, I can go down to the megastore in Times Square and buy one new DVD for every night I spent here in New York City. Isn't it great to be able to talk your way out of almost any ethical problem?

through a PowerBook that has a measly cellular-phone dial-up connection. But when a hurricane has knocked out the phones and the broadband and this is the only way for an office to get a mission-critical report filed to the main office on time, well, you make do.

I often help out friends who are in a jam, but this was the first time that one was so moved by gratitude that he actually sent me a 14-pound honey-baked ham. Now, I help because I'm a kind, old-world soul, but still, me likes ham.

BLUETOOTH

Bluetooth is a weird name for a wireless networking technology, but if you ask me, it ought to have been called "Godot." When the standard was first proposed and published a few years ago, I — like any good American — couldn't wait for the technology to arrive.

Originally, Bluetooth was conceived as a way to eliminate cable clutter in the office. Instead of running a cable between your desktop Mac and your printer, both devices would have Bluetooth chipsets inside them. The Mac could "find" the printer there in the room on its own and start the waterfall of pages. If AirPort is a way of eliminating Ethernet cables, Bluetooth is a way of eliminating USB cables, whether you're connecting to printers, PDAs, or whatever. It's often called a "personal" networking standard because its range is only about 15 yards.

▼ Note

Any time you buy a wireless device (even a cordless phone or a walkie-talkie), please keep in mind that the folks who write the packaging are either (a) incorrigible liars and people of negligible moral fiber, or (b) immigrants from that one country where there are no mountains or valleys and no trees or buildings or walls higher than 2 feet. Here in America, you'll find that most claims of broadcast range are off by a factor of two or three. I find that Bluetooth's maximum reliable range is about 10 feet.

The Bluetooth standard has some wonderful underlying architecture, which makes it far, far cooler than a simple cable replacement. Bluetooth-compatible devices are "discoverable," you see. Any device can "ask around" to see if a certain piece of hardware is within range. I mean, wow!!!

. . . You're not excited.

WHY "BLUETOOTH"? HEAD FOR BLOCKBUSTER.

I'm going to make an executive decision here. Instead of telling you Where The Name Comes From, I'm going to tell you that *The Stunt Man* and *Smile* are probably the two best movies out of the Seventies that you haven't seen. Or, in the case of *Smile*, haven't even heard of.

Those of you who've been married or in committed long-term relationships will understand why. Your spouse once dumped a whole tureen of guacamole on the lap of the guy who played the dad on *Family Ties*. It's a great story and he or she tells it with such gusto and self-effacing good spirit that the first time you heard it, you knew that you two were fated to bond for life. But you've heard it 93 times since then — you actually worked it out — and you're quite sure that the next time you hear the phrase "...and then I notice that his waiter hasn't given him any dip for his tortillas, so..." it's going to lead to a court date. Divorce, misdemeanor battery, you hope you won't have to find out.

The Story Of The Bluetooth Name is that sort of thing. It won't help you understand this any better, and you'll probably hear it 40 times in the next year. So rather than compound one of society's problems, I'd rather clue you in to two really wonderful flicks. Don't even read the synopsis on the DVD. Particularly with *The Stunt Man*, it's good to go in knowing absolutely nothing.

No, that's very kind of you, but there's no need to pretend. Okay, imagine this scenario: I'm at a yard sale and spot a big coffee mug shaped like the head of Chewbacca. The guy wants 50 bucks for it, which seems sort of steep. I unpocket my Bluetooth-equipped PDA so I can go on the Internet and look for more info about this item. As soon as I tap www.google.com into Pocket Internet Explorer, my PDA looks around and asks, "Hey, are there any devices nearby that can connect me to the Internet?"

My Bluetooth cell phone says, "Sure, I'm a phone with modem capabilities. . . what can I do for you?"

The PDA gives it the phone number of my ISP and seconds later, I realize that I'm holding one of the first two Star Wars products George Lucas ever conceived, and that while 50 bucks wasn't out of line, I could probably haggle the price down a little.

It's cool because I didn't even have to take my phone out of my pocket. It was within my PDA's "bubble" of Bluetooth connectivity and that's all that mattered. There's no limit to the range of devices that Bluetooth can connect, either. My hands-free headset connects to my phone via Bluetooth, and the same device connects to my PowerBook just as easily. I have a Bluetooth Global Positioning System device. When it's on my car's dashboard, it communicates with a map program on my notebook and gives me directions to the state park. When I get there I dangle it off my backpack and it sends the same sort of positioning information to my PDA.

So there are many, many categories of Bluetooth devices, and the procedures for getting each one to work with your Mac vary from product to product.

Step One is almost always "pairing" the device. You don't want strangers to make your cell phone dial an ISP in Kyzyl just by sidling up next to you and tapping into their Bluetooth PDA, so as a security feature, two Bluetooth devices typically have to be formally introduced to each other at least once before they work together.

IT'S A PUSHBUTTON WORLD

I use the term "the Miraculous Pushbutton World Of Tomorrow" a lot and almost always in a snarky way. I just don't think that in this day and age I should be spending this much time flipping the bird at inanimate objects. But Bluetooth solutions like these are exactly the way I hoped and expected the Future to be. It's not a Jetsons-style folding hover car, but I bet the insurance on that sort of thing would be a bear.

There's a handy wizard for this: the Bluetooth Setup Assistant. You can launch it from your Bluetooth menu (Figure 14-15).

Figure 14-15
Accessing Bluetooth features through the Bluetooth menu

It also launches itself automatically whenever you're configuring new hardware. In this example, I'm setting up my Mac to work with my Bluetooth cell phone, but the basic pairing procedure is the same no matter what sort of gear you have. When I click Continue, the Mac starts sniffing the air for any Bluetooth device within the immediate vicinity that identifies itself as a cell phone. Before I do that, I have to make sure that my phone's Bluetooth features have been turned on and that it's "discoverable." Bluetooth devices are often set up so that they don't respond to any hardware they haven't been formally paired with. It's another security feature. Check your device's manual to see how to activate Bluetooth and turn on discoverability.

Here's how to pair your Mac:

1. **Click the Bluetooth icon in System preferences.**

   Bluetooth's System Preferences window opens.

2. **Click the Devices tab.**

3. **From the Devices panel, click the "Set up new device" button.**

   The Bluetooth Setup Assistant launches itself automatically. After blowing past the usual hello, welcome, isn't it lovely to be assisted, etc., startup screen, you need to tell the Assistant what sort of device you're setting up (Figure 14-16). Click Mobile Phone and then click Next.

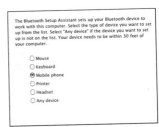

Figure 14-16
Pairing a device using the Bluetooth Setup Assistant

   The Assistant will then scan the immediate vicinity for Bluetooth devices.

4. **Choose your phone from the list of devices and click Continue.**

   The Mac will display a random number and now it's time to play Beat the Clock. As a security feature, you can't pair two devices unless you have physical control

TRAPPED IN A SYNC-HOLE

In the past two years, I've gone from not having any sort of electronic address book — I kept one on my Newton MessagePad, but when Apple stopped supporting it, I couldn't find a PDA I liked nearly as much — to having my numbers and appointments on at least five devices: my phone, my PDA, my wristwatch, and my two iPods. It's a fine testament to the strength and power of iSync, but think hard before enabling all of a device's sync features. I can edit appointments on my phone and on my PDA, which short-circuits the whole point of iSync: It's possible for me to have three conflicting sets of appointments.

I could solve this problem by being a lot more disciplined and organized ... or I can simply unclick my phone's iSync features. Which also means that the phone's built-in phone list only contains the 20 or 30 people I actually call on a regular basis, not all 832 people I've apparently swapped business cards and email addresses with in the past seven months.

of them both. To make sure it's okay to pair the two devices, you now have to pick up your phone and tap in that same random number.

5. **Pick up the phone and tap in that same number.**

   Next, the Assistant asks the device what it's willing to bring to this relationship. Steady income? Good car? A relative with Red Sox season tickets, not farther away from home plate than Section LL? Or in the case of a cell phone: Does it have an address book? A calendar app? Can it serve as an Internet connection? The Assistant reports back with what it's found and offers you a list of options (Figure 14-17).

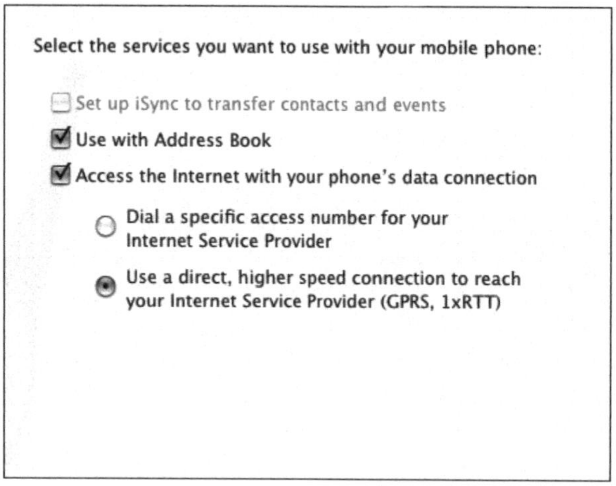

Select the services you want to use with your mobile phone:

☐ Set up iSync to transfer contacts and events
☑ Use with Address Book
☑ Access the Internet with your phone's data connection

  ○ Dial a specific access number for your Internet Service Provider

  ◉ Use a direct, higher speed connection to reach your Internet Service Provider (GPRS, 1xRTT)

Figure 14-17
Choosing which features to activate and which ones to disable

6. **Check off the features you wanna use and uncheck the features you don't wanna use, and click Continue.**

   If you've chosen to use this device as a connection to the Internet, the Assistant will then take you to another screen where you provide all of your cell-phone provider's networking details. This is a black

art, involving lies and death and international malfeasance, which comes as no surprise to anyone who's ever contacted their cell-phone company's Customer Service department to ask about mysterious surcharges and taxes that have appeared on their bill.

Steel your courage and contact your phone company to learn which settings need to be applied to use your cell phone as a way to connect to the Internet.

The assistant shows you a final summary page. Your Mac and your device have been successfully paired. Would that it were that easy for us Humans.

From then on out, you can use iSync to synchronize phone books and appointments between the Mac and the Phone, and use it as a connection to the Internet through the Internet Connect utility (provided you've activated these two features, and provided that you've configured the Internet feature correctly).

You can also use the Bluetooth menu to browse a Bluetooth device's files and folders. For example, if you want to copy some of your cameraphone's pictures into your Mac's Pictures folder:

EVEN WITHOUT WIRES, PHONE COMPANIES ARE NO-GOOD BLEEDERS

Your Bluetooth phone might be *capable* of working all kinds of magic when connected to your Mac ... but don't count on any of those cool features actually being available to you. Many wireless companies actually turn *off* their phone's most useful features, for the company's own convenience. Why can't you use your phone as an Internet connection? Because then they'd have to answer all kinds of tech-support calls from people who can't get their phones to work as an Internet connection. Why can't I browse the files on the phone? Because then you'd retrieve your cameraphone's photos for free, instead of using the subscriber network to email them from Point A to Point B at 30 cents per shot.

You'll notice that no matter how big a book series gets, the publishers and authors never add a title about the unbridled and bloodless avarice of telephone companies. One book was released in 1973. It was entitled "$#!@! *Miserable Stinking &@*!%ers!!!*" and oddly enough, in the past three decades it's never needed any updating or clarification.

1. **Choose Browse Files from the Bluetooth menu.**

   A window will open, listing available Bluetooth devices.

2. **Choose your phone from the list and click Browse.**

   A minibrowser window appears (Figure 14-18), listing the phone's contents. You can double-click on folders to open them, and then download files to your Mac by either selecting them and clicking the Get button, or by simply dragging files into one of your Mac's directories. You can copy files into the device by either dragging files into it or clicking the Send button.

Figure 14-18
Downloading a picture from a cameraphone into your Mac

NETWORK DIAGNOSTICS

I opened this chapter by softening you up a little, explaining that in All Things Network-wise, things have a tendency to Not Work. And when they don't work, they Don't Work rather ambitiously, offering no suggestions as to what went wrong or how to fix it.

Tiger offers a new utility. It's . . . well, it's well intentioned. Whenever your Mac expects a network connection but can't find it, it'll give you an opportunity to diagnose the problem. Figure 14-19 shows you Safari's generalized "Hey! What happened to the flippin' *network,* man?!?" window, which opens when you try to bring up a Web page but Safari can't connect to the Internet. After you've finished jumping up and

down and yelling, click the button at the bottom to launch Network Diagnostics (see Figure 14-20). It'll troubleshoot your network setup and — maybe, possibly, *hopefully* — get your network connection back up and running again.

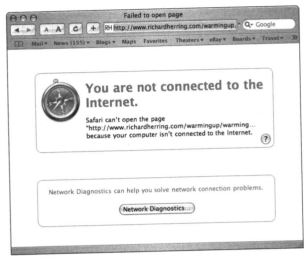

Figure 14-19
When the Internet goes missing, Safari offers a button to help you find it.

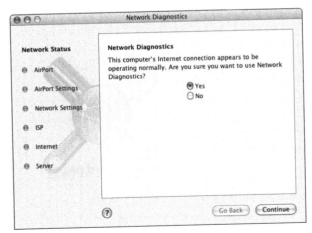

Figure 14-20
Pinpoint network problems with Network Diagnostics

My very first book was about networking. That was more than 10 years ago, and there was no mumbo, no jumbo, no hoodoo, no mojo, no incantation, spell, totem, spirit guide, supplication to Karma, jinx, or other bit of technical or superstitious arcana that went undocumented or uncommented.

Why? Well, there was nothing you didn't need to know back then. Networking was like industrial heating and cooling. Nothing about this area of technology was even remotely designed for easy installation or even casual use, and the desire to get a network up and running implied a concurrent desire to learn so much about the standards, protocols, and hardware that the only way to get the same final effect would be to fill your head with angry bees.

Boy, do I feel old today. Every time I went in to describe some sort of deep-mojo tweak or setting, I wound up deleting the paragraph as soon as I typed it. You really don't need to know about TCP header compression. It's all taken care of. Nearly anything you try to connect to anything else will automatically be configured via DHCP with very little intervention on your part.

What's more, when DHCP won't cut it or Tiger's default settings can't handle it, you can do far more harm than good by trying to work out the problem on your own. When you're trying to connect to an ISP or a protected file server, for example, there is no troubleshooting technique that is simpler or more effective than phoning or emailing the thing's administrator and saying, "I'm trying to connect from a Macintosh running Mac OS 10.4. What settings do I need to use?"

You're doing yourself a favor and you're doing the administrator a favor. Even if you managed to get it running on your own, chances are excellent that something is subtly messed up. Not so bad as to cause the connection to fail, but definitely bad enough that the connection is slow and unreliable. Meanwhile, at the other end of the connection, the administrator is cursing you out. Your slightly dinked

connection is generating no end of minor inconveniences for him or her, as the servers keep spitting out warnings and errors that must be cleared.

And to cheese off a system administrator is to yank the tail of a sleeping dragon. You might be barred from the network. Or you never know, he might be a judge at the next Dragon•Con costume contest, and his might be the deciding vote that keeps your Bride of Boba Fett outfit out of the winner's circle.

That first book of mine also underscores another point about networking: It's terribly fluid, and new (and wonderful) things are happening all the time. The difference between Mac OS 9 and Mac OS X networking is the difference between crossing the Mediterranean chained to a bench in the ship's bilges, working an oar with the 60 or 70 other guys in your village who thought that these Spartans weren't as tough as everyone says they are, and crossing it while sipping an umbrella drink by the pool of a luxury liner.

See, I insisted to the publisher that this "inter-net" thing was gonna be big, and that connecting to bulletin-board services via modems was going to go the way of the steam-powered gyrocinematoscope projector. No, PPP connections to an Internet Service Provider, connecting to a variety of online services: There's the future for you. But they wouldn't listen and insisted that I just talk about modems and stuff (I was helping out a pal who'd already come up with the premise), and the rest is history; in a year's time, everything was different.

I suppose I'm making two points here: One, that as cool as Tiger's networking features are, this book is being written several months in the past, so always leave your expectations high for future greatness; and two, man alive, that book was 10 years ago and I still can't get over it. I was hoping that this would underscore the fact that except where matters of grooming, haberdashery, and racquet sports are concerned, I'm nearly always right, but it's possible that I've simply made an excellent case that I'm a bitter crank. I really ought to think these things through before I write. I really should.

15

The Apps Wot You Get for Nothin'

In This Chapter

Mail • Address Book • .Mac and the Point of .Mac
iCal • iChat • Sherlock • Safari • iSync

When you install Tiger, you get a whole bunch of apps that aren't *technically* part of the Macintosh operating system, but which are so basic to the experience of using a Mac that they might as well be.

Which is no reason to minimize their contribution. Think about all the people who should have been The Fifth Beatle, after all. You've got your John, your Paul, and your George. And sure, put Ringo on the list, too. But what about George Martin, the producer who taught the boys the difference between being a band that pops pills and jams in the Kaiserkellar, and being a band that pops pills and records epic concept albums in EMI's Abbey Road Studios? Or Pete Best, who laid the groundwork for the final, successful incarnation of the group by playing the drums not nearly as well as Ringo? Or Yoko Ono, whose obsessive clinginess to John indirectly gave us a supergroup known as Wings, a triple-album known as "All Things Must Pass," and the 1985 made-for-TV-movie *John and Yoko: A Love Story*, in which a young Mike Myers has an uncredited role as a delivery boy?

Each of these apps makes significant contributions to The Tiger Experience. Even if you don't deliberately set out to try these apps, rest assured that your paths shall inevitably cross. One thing that qualifies each of these apps (collectively) as The Fifth Beatle is the fact that they all work together so transparently, each one borrowing features from, and communicating with, the other.

A NOTE ON THE UNIVERSAL WIMPOUT CLAUSE

This chapter is by no means intended to serve as a comprehensive guide to any of these apps. Let me say that right up front. Go ahead and hit me: I deserve it. I'll even tell you that I fell off my bike three days ago and I still have this big green bruise on my upper-right chest where I landed on the handlebars. A good hit there will take me down fast and leave me blubbering in seconds.

It's not even a half-arsed guide to *all* of the apps that you get with Tiger. "Where's the Sherlock search tool?" you ask. "It's at the bottom of the lake with a cinderblock chained around its waist, or at least it would be if I had my way," I reply. It was barely useful even when it was the only game in town. But now that Tiger's new Dashboard widgets perform nearly all of Sherlock's most useful features, and Google.com performs the rest — and *both* perform them way better — let's all stop pretending that we ever liked this and start laughing openly at this thing.

"Limited pages," is the general answer. I could have either written a chapter that explains one or two of these apps in terrific detail, or a chapter that explains them all with such a profound lack of detail as to be a cruel tease to any thinking man or woman ... or I could have chosen just the most important apps and then included just those features that are most important or most interesting.

Like the young woman in the documentary *Trekkies 2* who got a tattoo of the U.S.S. Enterprise-D that spans every dimension of her back from north to south and east to west, I've made my decision and I'm willing to live with it. If it offends you, please tear this page out, underline the section about punching me in that big nasty bruise, and mail it to me with a further explanation of what sort of mayhem you'd like to inflict upon me.

You'll feel better. It's also an appropriate act of contrition on my part, and finally there's a good chance that you'll rip out enough useful information that you'll have to go out and buy another copy of this book. *Ka-CHINNNG!*

So, here are some overviews and tips on getting started with these Fifth Beatles lurking in your Applications folder.

MAIL

No longer an exotic function, but as fundamental to the computing experience as running water, you can ably handle the sending, receiving, and processing of email with a built-in app by the not-at-all distinctive name of Mail. Mail (sometimes referred to as Mail.app in order to distinguish it from third-party email apps) has really come along since its debut. In Mac OS X 10.0, it was a laughingstock,

a placeholder with a Post-It note stuck on it reading "Some day, a *real* email app will be built on this spot." But today, it's competitive with any email client anywhere.

Before you begin working with Mail, you need to tell it about your email accounts. So, you should start off by getting a little bit of information from your ISP, including

- **Your email address** (for example, gernblanstev@mac.com).

- **The name of the incoming mail server** (for example, mail.mac.com). You should also ask what kind of mail server it is. It probably uses either IMAP or POP.

MAIL.APP AND BACHELORS NUMBER 2-4

For practical purposes there are only two commercial alternatives to Mail.app. Microsoft Entourage's big draw is that it integrates tightly with Microsoft Office; in 2004 editions of Office, it practically becomes the dashboard for all of your ongoing projects. Bare Bones Software (www.barebones.com) has Mailsmith, a high-octane app that's hugely attractive to people who have very complicated needs and like to beat their Inboxes into submission with lots of automated routing, redirecting, and message handling.

There's a third, non-commercial alternative: Thunderbird, the free mail client built and supported by the Mozilla Foundation. You can download it from www.mozilla.org. It's got a lot to recommend it: it's not quite as easy to use as Mail, but it has muscular features for spam filtering, message organization, and editing, and because it supports plug-ins, folks are always adding new features to the app.

I've used Mailsmith for a good long while, but it's overkill for most users. Stick with Mail.app until you feel you've outgrown it … and in truth, you might *never* outgrow it.

- **The name of the outgoing mail server** (for example, smtp.mac.com). The outgoing mail server must use SMTP (simple mail transport protocol).

This info is probably on the piece of paper your ISP sent you when you signed up for an account. Or it's on the ISP's website somewhere. Once you have the necessary information lined up, you're ready to roll with Mail.

Setting up an account

You can use Mail to manage more than one email account, but for each account, you must give Mail the information it requires to access that account:

1. **Launch Mail.**

2. **Select Add Account from the File menu.**

   This opens up an account-creation wizard that will lead you through the process step by step. You'll start by typing in some General Information.

3. **Select the type of email account from the Account Type pop-up menu (Figure 15-1).**

   Your choices are .Mac (the email service that you get if you pay up for Apple's .Mac service), POP (the most popular flavor of email), IMAP (like POP, but more popular on corporate mail systems), and Exchange (a flavor of server created by Microsoft). If you aren't sure which you have, ask your ISP. If you aren't sure and don't want to ask your ISP (you just broke up with your ISP's eldest daughter and it'd just be all awkward) guess POP. You'll probably be right.

 Note

If you've signed up for a .Mac account and you select ".Mac" from the Account Type pop-up menu, Mail.app configures your account for you automagically — just one of the benefits of using an Apple Mail.app on an Apple operating system with an Apple ISP. Dictatorship has its advantages, you know.

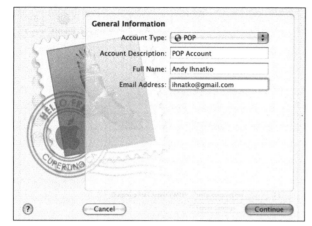

Figure 15-1
Adding a new account

Figure 15-2
Setting up your incoming mail server

4. **Fill in an Account Description and your Full Name.**

   The Description is just a line of text that will help you to remember what this account is for ("Work Mail") when you're looking at it in a list of all of your accounts. "Full Name" will be stamped on all of your outgoing email within its "From:" header.

5. **Fill in your Email address and click Continue to go on.**

   This is your full email address . . . again, chiefly used to stamp the "From:" header of your outgoing emails.

   Next you'll find yourself at the Incoming Mail Server page, where you provide Mail with the info it needs to download email from this account.

6. **Type in the address of the incoming mail server (Figure 15-2).**

Again, you'll get this info from the folks who provide you with email service; if the service has a website, it's probably listed on their Help page. If you have a POP account and your email address is gern@blanstev.com, the mail server's address will probably be either pop.blanstev.com or mail.blanstev.com.

7. **Type in your email password and click Continue to go on.**

   If you leave this field blank, then you'll be forced to type in your mail password every time Mail tries to fetch your new messages. This might be an attractive option, as it's an extra level of security.

▼ **Info**

When you click Continue, Mail will attempt to connect to your incoming mail server, using the information you've just provided. If the attempt fails, you'll receive a little warning.

MIXING UP YOUR MAIL SERVERS

Your incoming mail always sits on one specific server, but in truth you can send mail via nearly any outgoing server that you have access to. Mail doesn't care. Your incoming email arrives on the machines at blanstev.net, so you can't download your messages from anywhere else. *But,* if you have an Earthlink account, for example, you can designate earthlink.net as your outbound mail server if you want.

But *why?* Well, maybe because this other outgoing mail server is more reliable. Or maybe because you have no choice but to use a public wireless access point, this email *has* to go out today, and blanstev.net doesn't support secure, encrypted connections. Food for thought.

8. **Choose whether or not to use Secure Sockets when connecting to your mail server and click Continue to go on.**

   Checking the Use Secure Sockets Layer (SSL) option means that the server will encrypt all the traffic it sends to your Mac, so that some unknown weasel can't eavesdrop on your messages as you're downloading them. Which is a terrific feature, particularly if you use public Wi-Fi access points to receive your mail. The only trouble is that your mail server has to support this SSL feature . . . and not all of 'em do. So check with your mail service provider before activating this feature and selecting an authentication method.

   On the next page, you'll be giving Mail the info it needs in order to send mail from your Mac.

9. **Give Mail the name of your outgoing mail server (Figure 15-3).**

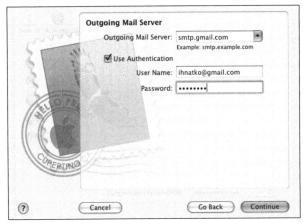

Figure 15-3
Defining your outgoing mail server

10. **Give Mail the address of your service's outgoing mail server.**

    If your email address is gern@blanstev.com, it'll probably be smtp.blanstev.com, or possibly mail.blanstev.com again.

11. **Choose an authentication option and click Continue.**

    If your mail service allows any Tom, Dick or D'Artagnian to transmit mail through their servers without requiring them to demonstrate that they actually subscribe to the service, leave Use Authentication unchecked. But nearly all mail services require authentication to prevent spammers from abusing their mail servers, in which case you need to type in your full username and password again.

265

MOVIN' ON UP/MOVIN' OUT

But what if you're switching to Mail from another email program? No sweat; select Import Mailboxes from the File menu. Mail can directly import mailboxes from seven different email clients. If your client doesn't appear on this list, once again, the need for immediate perspiration is entirely unrelated to the situation at hand. Mail uses the MBOX format for mail storage, which is an established standard. Most email clients actually use this format, and those that don't can export mail into MBOX files. Just choose Import Mailboxes and select Other from the list of import types. Point Mail at the MBOX files and the app handles the rest.

You might also be curious to know where, precisely, Mail stores your actual mail. If you ever want to burn all of your mailboxes onto a DVD or something as a backup, you'll find your complete email store in your Home/Library/Mail folder. If you just want to export an individual message, select the message and select Save As from the File menu. You can save it as either a plain text file or an RTF document, which retains all of the message's fancy formatting.

And you're done. The setup wizard will show you a summary of the account's settings. The next page gives you the option of either creating another account or just getting on with your life by clicking Done.

You can repeat this process for each of your email accounts. Maybe you have an account on the mail system at work, a personal account for home, and a third Hotmail account that you use on Web sites and such, to avoid attracting spam to your "real" email addresses. Mail.app collects mail from all three accounts every time you tell it to check for new messages. Speaking of which . . .

Receiving and reading email

Most users configure Mail to automatically connect to the mail server and download new messages at regular intervals. You can choose this interval through a popup menu in the General pane of Mail's Preferences window. If this

feature isn't enabled, just click the Get Mail button at the top of the message viewer window (see Figure 15-4).

If you've got new mail, Mail places it in the account's Inbox, one of the built-in mailboxes that Mail.app creates for you automatically. All of your mailboxes are displayed in a separate pane in the left side of the message viewer window.

So how do you know which mailboxes contain new messages? Check out the numbers next to the mailbox names. That's how many unread messages are lurking therein. Mail also beeps at you to let you know that it's received new messages.

 Note

But check out the little Warning triangle next to the Gmail mailbox. That means that Mail tried its darnedest but was unable to connect to the GMail mail server.

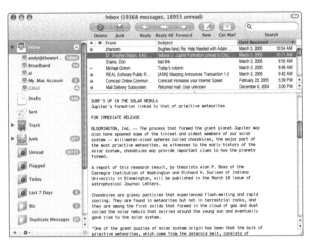

Figure 15-4
The message viewer window

Incidentally, Mail also sticks a little badge on top of its Dock icon that contains an up-to-date total of the number of your unread messages (see Figure 15-5).

Figure 15-5
18955 new messages? You're *loved!*

Yes, indeedy. If you ever become an internationally beloved industry pundit who's never hidden his email address from the public, you, too, may end up having nearly 20,000 unread messages waiting for you at the end of the day. And that's only after all of my personal and business mail has been read. I don't ask for your pity. I already have your money, and that's enough.

To view messages, click on the name of either the Inbox (to see all of your messages in one big, wobbly pile) or click on the name of one of the individual mailboxes

(to just look at the messages that were sent to that address, specifically). Clicking on one of the summaries in the list at the top of the message viewer window opens it for viewing below. You can change the sort order of the list by clicking on any of the column titles, just like the list views in the Finder.

Searching email

Mail (Tiger's ultra-fab Spotlight feature, actually) automatically indexes all of your mail as soon as it's received so you can perform lightning-fast searches. Mail's Search box works exactly the same way it does in all other Mac apps. If you're looking for email from NASA, just type that in the search field, and by the time you get to "g" Mail hides all emails but hers. Mail's viewer window shifts subtly to a special Search window, containing a list of all matching messages (Figure 15-6). Click on any message to read it.

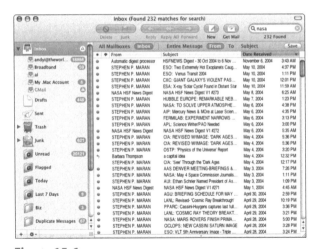

Figure 15-6
The immediate results of a mail search

You'll notice that there's a new bar of buttons at the top of the list of matching messages. These allow you to modify the search a little, and save the search for future use. In Figure 15-6, Mail only searched the mailbox that I was viewing when I punched in the search term; if I click All Mailboxes, it'll search the whole pile. Mail searched for mail "From" NASA, because I told it to search in "From"s the *last* time I did a search. To search the actual messages' contents, their recipients, or their subject lines, I can click the appropriate item.

The Save button is something special: clicking this baby creates a new Smart Mailbox based on this search. Smart Mailboxes are 40 ounces of cool in a 12-ounce can, and I'll be talking about them a bit later.

To get back to the dull, dirty business of reading *all* of your messages and not just this matching subset, click the "X" button inside the window's Search field.

Screening out junk

There are two possible solutions to the problem of Junk Mail. The most obvious and effective one is to set up roadblocks all across the country, whereupon every car is stopped and then its occupants are asked, "Hey, I'm interested in purchasing an herbal lifestyle enhancement and/or refinancing my home. Do any of you know where I might purchase such an item or service?" If anybody therein answers "Yes," then a big magnet lifts the car into the air and lowers it into a cargo container, which is then shipped someplace that lacks electricity or Internet access.

A less-satisfying solution is to use Mail's Junk filter. You activate and manage this feature through Junk Mail's own tab in Mail's Preferences window (Figure 15-7). Just check the option labeled "Enable Junk Mail Filtering." Mail then

uses a fairly sophisticated set of rules to determine whether or not a piece of incoming mail is spam. If the message fairly reeks of Nigerian herbal mortgage enhancements, Mail automatically diverts it to a mailbox marked Junk mailbox.

The filter is uncannily good from Day One, but it's not flawless. If a piece of spam *does* wind up in your Inbox, just select it in the main Mail window and then click the Junk button. The message will be moved out of your Inbox.

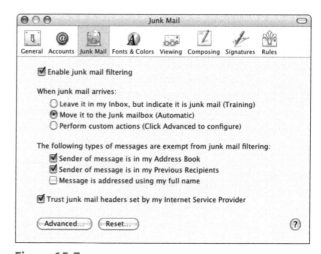

Figure 15-7
Ordering Mail to try to beat back the tide of junk email

If you click the Junk mailbox and see that a group holiday letter from your Aunt Midge got mistakenly tagged as Junk, select the group of letters and click the Not Junk button that appears. Mail.app learns from its mistakes and slowly but surely will do better in the future.

Tip

Mail's junk filter is good, but it isn't perfect. If you find junk emails particularly annoying, you might want to install a separate third-party junk filter called SpamSieve. It's a shareware utility available for download from all of the popular software sites, such as www.macupdate.com and www.versiontracker.com.

Organizing your mail

It's not *terribly* convenient to keep hundreds (or tens of thousands, in my case) of messages all in one Inbox. Clutter, don't you know. You can organize email manually by creating separate mailbox folders. Just click the plus sign at the bottom of the mailbox list and give the new mailbox a name. Then, you can drag messages straight into the new mailbox from the message list.

You can automate this by using a Mail feature known as "Rules." By creating a Rule for each different easily identifiable kind of mail (messages with my newspaper editor's name in the return address, messages that contain the phrase "Press Release" in the subject line, et cetera), Mail can automatically move my incoming mail into their proper mailboxes.

And Rules aren't just for sorting incoming mail. The basic gist of Rules is, "Whenever I receive a message that meets the following criteria, I want you to do *this*." An example of a sane and sober rule is one that automatically forwards all messages from the head of your department to your cellphone's email account, so that you absolutely will never miss an important message when you're away from your office. Less practical is the Rule that I set up last year which reacts to new mail from my editors by running an

AppleScript that turns on a flashing emergency light in my office (so that I can see right from the street that the moment I step back into my office, I'll have something important to deal with and thus, I should stay outside and keep shooting hoops). But it's fun, nonetheless.

Specific tutorials on creating Rules is beyond the scope of this chapter, but it's worthwhile to open Mail Help and type "rules" in its search box.

Besides, I don't use Rules nearly as much as I used to. Because with Tiger, there's something even ginchier: Smart Mailboxes.

Smart Mailboxes

The trouble with conventional mailboxes is that they're not magical. They're truly earthbound creatures. You can manually drag messages into them, or you can tell Mail to automatically store an incoming message into one as soon as it's received. But those are earthly, mortal features.

Tiger's edition of Mail includes a truly enchanted way of organizing your messages. *Smart Mailboxes* organize your messages automatically, at your slightest whim, thanks to the fact that Tiger's system-wide Spotlight feature automatically indexes and organizes all of the data on your hard drive.

Here's a simple Smart Mailbox. I'm on all of NASA's mailing lists, and I'm particularly interested in mission status reports. What's going on in the International Space Station, is a shuttle preparing to launch, what about that unmanned craft that's in solar orbit, et cetera. It'd be nice if I could get my hands on those messages with just one click, so I'll create a Smart Mailbox for them.

1. **Select New Smart Mailbox... from the Mailbox menu.**

   You can also select this from the "Actions" menu at the bottom of Mail's viewer window. A sheet drops down, allowing you to describe the kinds of messages that this folder should attract (see Figure 15-8).

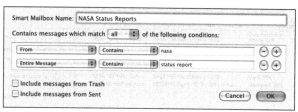

Figure 15-8
Creating a Smart Mailbox

2. **Describe those messages.**

   In this case, I want the Smart Mailbox to contain all messages that contain "NASA" in the return address and which contain "Status Report" in the message itself. So from the first popup menu, I select From. Next, I click "Contains" in the second popup field to specify a specific piece of text ("NASA"), which I provide in the third field. To add additional conditions, I click on the plus sign next to the first condition to specify that matching messages should also contain the text "Status Report."

   Note the presence of the popup menu in the "Contains messages which match..." line. It's set to "All," which means that only messages that match both of these conditions will be met. If I'd selected "Any," then the folder would contain all messages from my editor (whether read or unread) and all unread messages (whether they're from my editor or not).

3. **Give the new Smart Mailbox a name, so you know what the devil you were thinking about when you created it.**

4. **Click OK to create the new mailbox.**

And now lean back and watch the pixie dust fly. Instantly, your new mailbox is populated with all of the messages that meet those criteria (Figure 15-9).

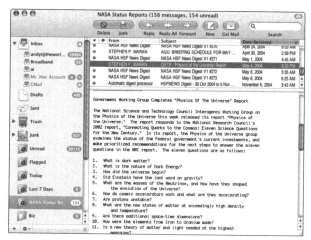

Figure 15-9
All of the NASA mission status reports

An even *better* example: I'm working on this book, y'see, and as you've already observed through those earlier screenshots, I get hundreds of emails every day. I *desperately* want to avoid the bad karma that results when one of my books' editors emails me with an urgent question that requires an immediate response . . . and that message gets buried under the 800 emails that readers sent me about today's newspaper column, or the 300 messages putatively from lonely housewives who would like me to do something about their situations.

HAIL, APPLE; CLEAR IS ITS VISION, BOLD ARE ITS MOVEMENTS

And here's another one of those Tiger features that makes me stand up and applaud. Pre-Tiger, I was always performing the same searches over and over again. It's the only way to keep on top of a huge number of messages. With Tiger, though, I've got Smart Mailboxes organizing this stuff for me.

When I wake up at the crack of 11 AM, I can either spend a half-hour looking through all the incoming messages for stuff that requires my immediate attention … or I can just click on three different Smart Mailboxes that constantly look through all my accounts' incoming messages for mail from editors, friends, or any mail that says "I was just driving past your house and I noticed that your basement seems to be on fire." With Tiger, there's a good chance that I'll get out of my house alive. If I don't consider that to be worth the upgrade price, then frankly, I sort of deserve to die.

With Tiger, it's a no-brainer: a Smart Mailbox set up to match messages From my editor that are Unread and Received within the past day or two will do the trick.

 Info

So if this is a better example, then why didn't I illustrate it? Because, um, the screenshots I took would show you the private email addresses of four different editors. And if you think editors get honked off when you ignore their emails, you don't wanna know what they do when you unwittingly hand over their address to the international junk-harassment cartel.

Why are Smart Mailboxes such a big deal? Two reasons:

- **They're "Live."** The moment you make a change to a Smart Mailbox, its contents are updated to reflect the change. If I were to add a new Condition — I want my NASA Smart Mailbox to only contain status reports about the International Space Station, for example — the Smart Mailbox's contents would instantly reflect that change. If one of the conditions of the Mailbox is that its messages only contain new messages that came in within the day, messages will disappear from the list as soon as I read them, or as soon as they literally become yesterday's news.

- **A Smart Mailbox doesn't contain actual messages . . . only *references* to where the actual messages are stored.** So (unlike moving messages around with Rules), I can access the same message from several different Smart Folders. I have one Smart Folder that groups all new messages from any of my 11 different book, magazine, or newspaper editors; another from anyone who's working with me on an important project; another one that always contains emails that were received today. Well, today's email from my book editor can show up in all of 'em.

And meanwhile, all of the original messages are nicely organized in their original mailboxes. Smart Mailboxes allow me to groups things the way they need to be grouped without my having to drill my way through several separate mailboxes by hand.

Sending email

You can send email either by composing a new message from scratch, replying to an existing message, or by forwarding an existing message.

To compose a new message:

1. **Click the "New" icon in the Message Viewer window's toolbar.**

   An empty e-mail message window appears (Figure 15-10).

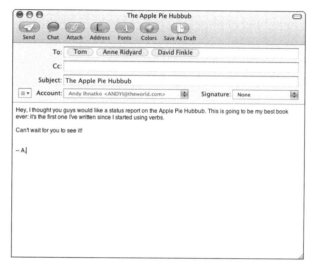

Figure 15-10
The new message window

2. **Type the necessary information in the text boxes:**

   ▪ **To:** Type the email address of the recipient. As you type, Mail will perform a quick search of your Address Book, filling a popup list with possible recipients. Type *b...a...r...b...* and before you get halfway through a first name, Mail is suggesting two different Barbaras. Select the one you want and Mail will fill in her email address automatically. If you can't even remember the woman's name, click the "Address" button to open a browsable list of your Address Book contents. You can send this email to more than one person by separating addresses with commas.

   ▪ **Cc:** Type the email addresses of those you want to receive copies of this email. Separate multiple recipients with commas.

   ▪ **Subject:** Type the subject of the message. Given the amount of junk mail floating about the Internet and the Herculean efforts of people to filter the junk, you should make the subject as unique and descriptive as possible.

3. **Type the body of the message.**

4. **Attach any files you want to send.**

   If you want to attach a file to the message — photos of your big trip to see Yakov Smirnoff in his Branson dinner theater, an important spreadsheet, anything — click the paperclippy Attach button and select a file. An icon representing the file (or the actual image, if the file is a picture) appears at the insertion point. You can even skip this step entirely and just drag the file straight into the Mail window, from the Finder, iPhoto, or any place from whence you can drag its icon. Mail handles all the magic for you. The file automatically transmogrifies into a form that any Mac or Windows machine can receive. Just let Mail do the work.

5. **Choose one of your email accounts to use as a "Reply To:" address.**

6. **Click the Send button.**

   Mail places the message in the Out box and attempts to send it immediately.

Replying to a message or forwarding a message isn't much different from composing a new message. To reply to a message, follow these steps:

1. **Display the message to which you want to reply, by clicking on it.**

2. **Click on one of the two Reply buttons.**

   Click the Reply button to reply to the sender only; click the Reply All button to reply to other recipients and the sender. By default, Mail includes the message to which you're responding so that the recipient has some bloody idea of what you're talking about. Unless you think ahead and just select a single relevant passage before clicking Reply, Mail includes the entire message.

3. **Compose and send the message as you would if it were a new message.**

When you forward a message, Mail automatically includes the entire message from the original email in the new email. To forward a message:

1. **Display the message you want to forward by clicking on it.**

2. **Click the Forward button in the toolbar.**

3. **Compose and send the message as you would if it were a new message.**

"OUT" DOESN'T MEAN "SENT"

If the email you're sending is intensely important, keep a wary eye open after you click Send. If Mail encounters an error (say, you're not currently connected to the Internet), Mail will throw up an error message and stash the outgoing email in your "Out" box. That critical financial report will just *sit* there while your boss fumes in a faraway office, and decides who's going to get your swivel chair and your red Swingline stapler after he has Security bounce your sorry backside out of the building.

Those are the basics of Mail.app, and as much as could be squeezed (squozen?), well, crammed into the space available. But we've only hinted at the features and power of this application, so I'm begging you to go to Mail's Help menu and read as much as you can stomach. I'll even go so far as give you a dollar if you do it right now, so long as we both agree that there's no way in Helena-Bonham-Carter that I'll ever actually cough up the dough.

ADDRESS BOOK

"But I've never really needed to use a Desktop address book!" some of you are complaining. And I think under those shouts I heard others among you grumble that you're perfectly happy with the contact manager you have already, thank you very much. Well, before Mac OS X's Address Book app, I was one of you.

But my chief reasons for not using a Desktop address book were that I'm obnoxious and disliked, and had erected this wall of technology around me mostly to keep myself isolated from humanity. So any app that caused my Mac to actually encourage interaction instead of providing me with a substitute for it seemed to be counterproductive to the whole master plan.

Trust me. In OS X, it's not just about walking over to your Mac every time you need to look up a phone number. Address Book is a fundamental service of the Macintosh operating system, placing contact and personal information about your friends and co-workers right where you need it, when you need it. Whether emailing a co-worker, addressing a Christmas card, or calling the local Domino's through a USB phone interface, the implications of having one database serving all apps is too good to pass up.

The Address Book display

The Address Book uses a card metaphor to store contact information. As you can see in Figure 15-11, the default view includes three areas:

- **Group:** This column lists groups of cards. When you launch Address Book for the first time, you see a group named All (all cards belong to this group) and an icon named Directories for any network directories to which you may have access. In Figure 15-11, I've selected the Close Personal Friends of Andy Ihnatko list, for example.

- **Name:** This column lists the names of all cards in the currently selected group.

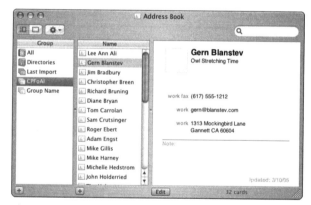

Figure 15-11
The three-column Address Book display

- **Card:** The right of the window contains the card for the name selected in the Name column. You can also view this person's card as a separate window by double-clicking on his or her name in the Name column.

Adding a new card

The Address Book comes with two cards, one for Apple computer and one for you (created when your account was created). Adding more is up to you. You *will* have to acquire new friends to make such an operation necessary. Are these people more trouble than they're worth? Only you can decide.

To add a new card, try this:

1. **Click the plus (+) button at the bottom of the Name column.**

   Alternatively, you can select File → New Card or press ⌘+N. A blank card appears (see Figure 15-12). Notice that each data field is labeled in boldface. The placeholders for data appear in gray type.

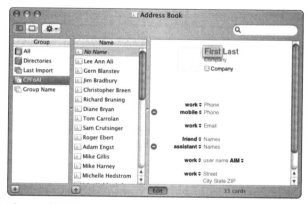

Figure 15-12
A brand-new card

2. **Enter contact information.**

   Click each field for which you want to enter data, and type the field's contents:

   - To remove a field that you don't want, click the red minus (-) button to its left.

   - To add another instance of an existing field (for example, to include more than one work phone number), click the green plus (+) button to the filled field's left.

3. **Add a picture.**

   You do this by doubling-clicking on the image square next to the contact name fields. The window that appears provides three ways to add the image:

   - Drag an image into the square in the middle of the window.

   - Click the Choose button to display an Open File dialog box for locating the image file.

   - Use a video camera to capture an image.

If the card represents a company and, in particular, doesn't include a person's name, click the Company checkbox underneath the company name field. This tells Address Book to alphabetize the card using the company name rather than the fields for a person's name.

The little arrows next to some of the field labels display menus that affect both the field labels and field formatting. For example, in Figure 15-13 you can see a pop-up menu that lets you select a field label. Here, we've chosen the label for one of the new contact's phone numbers. If you don't like any of the existing choices, you can click Custom to type your own label. You can select the subfields of an address field by choosing a country from the field's pop-up menu.

If a field you want to include isn't present on the card, you can add it:

1. **Go to the Card menu and highlight the Add Field submenu.**

   A list of additional fields appears (Figure 15-14).

2. **Select the desired field.**

   It appears in the current address card.

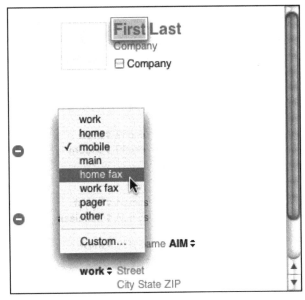

Figure 15-13
Choosing a field name

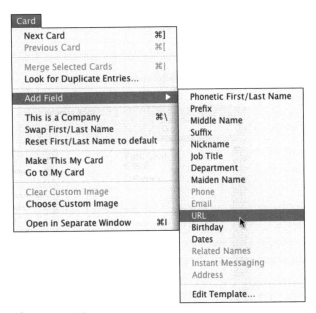

Figure 15-14
Using the Card menu to add a field to a card

Tip

Remember what I said about all these Fifth Beatle apps being tightly (and almost subliminally) integrated? Well, you can also add new people to Address Book just by clicking on their names when you read their email in Mail.app, or any other application that supports the Address Book. Some users may actually attach their personal, Address Book–friendly business card to the email, and Address Book automatically fills in all of the data — including a photo.

Editing a card

To change the contents of a card, follow these steps:

1. **In the Name column, click the card you want to change.**

2. **Click the Edit button below the card.**

   The fields and their controls become visible.

3. **Click in a field whose contents you want to change.**

4. **Edit the text in the field as necessary.**

You can also add and/or delete fields, change field labels, and change field formats.

Deleting a card

It pays to clean out your Address Book every so often. If you can't remember who someone is or why you have a card for a company, then it's time for that card to go! To delete a card, do this:

1. **In the Name column, click the card you want to delete.**

2. **Select Edit → Delete Card.**

 Note

Of course, Address Book doesn't give you the added rush of tearing an unfaithful boyfriend's or girlfriend's page out of a book, spitting on it, crumpling it up, throwing it to the floor, and then jumping on it. That is, you can do it, but it'll probably cost you another iBook.

Finding cards

As long as the number of cards in your Address Book remains small, finding a card isn't much of a problem. You can simply browse the Name column. But what should you do when your list of contacts grows to several hundred? Do you want to spend time browsing? If not, you can use Address Book's search feature to locate cards:

1. **Begin typing in the search box.**

   Note that the search box has a magnifying glass at its left edge. Address Book has a search box that — God bless Apple —works the same way as it does in the Finder, Mail, and nearly every other Mac app. When you type in the search box in the upper-right corner of the Address Book window, Address Book narrows the names in the Name column to include those that start with the typed characters. For example, in Figure 15-15, Address Book selected a bunch of Apple Computer cards by the time the user had managed to type "Ap." (Because they are the only cards that begin with A, they are actually selected when the user types the first character!)

2. **Continue typing characters until you have located the card you want.**

To clear the search, restoring all cards to the Name column, click the X at the right edge of the search text box.

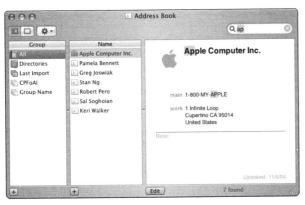

Figure 15-15
Searching for cards

Choosing default card contents

When you create a new card, Address Book provides you with an empty card containing a selection of fields. You can control which fields appear through the Address Book preferences:

1. **Select Address Book → Preferences.**

2. **If necessary, click the template button.**

   A template similar to that in Figure 15-16 appears.

3. **Add fields to your template:**

   ▪ Click the Add Field pop-up menu to add extra fields.

   ▪ Click the red minus (-) buttons to remove fields.

   ▪ Click the green plus (+) buttons to add more fields of the same type.

Your changes to the template are saved automatically when you close the Preferences window.

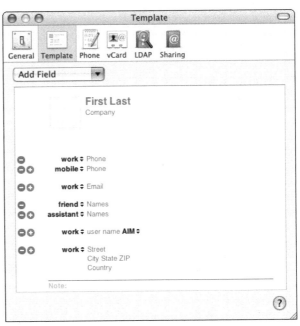

Figure 15-16
Editing the Address Book card template

Working with groups of cards

Bulk emails drive most of us crazy, but there are, nonetheless, some legitimate reasons for sending the same message to a group of people. Perhaps you want to announce a meeting or let everyone know that the class reunion has been postponed. Whatever the reason, you can use Address Book to group cards so that you can work with the contacts in that group as a single unit.

The first step is to create a new group:

1. **Select File → New Group.**

   Alternatively, you can click the plus (+) button at the bottom of the Group column.

2. **Type a name for the group and press Return.**

   Now you can add names to the group.

3. **Drag the card(s) you want to add from the Name column into the new group.**

   This action copies a reference to the card into to the new group; it remains unchanged in its original location.

The Tiger edition of Address Book also supports "Smart Groups," which work like the Smart Mailbox feature of Mail. I'm always acquiring new contacts at Apple, and sometimes even longtime Apple employees leave the company and move on. Instead of laboriously dragging names in and out of an Apple group, a Smart Group can manage the list for me. To create one:

1. **Select File → New Smart Group.**

   A sheet drops down (Figure 15-17) allowing you to define the group's contents.

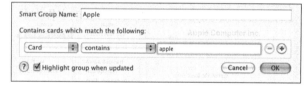

Figure 15-17
Defining a new Smart Group

2. **Enter some search terms.**

   In my case, all I have to do is tell this Smart List to look for "apple" anywhere on the address card.

3. **Name the Smart Group and click "OK."**

   And as you can see in Figure 15-18, the new group appears in the Groups list, already populated. And this group will automatically stay current as I add and remove Apple people in my address book.

Figure 15-18
Automagically-populated Group

iCAL

It's almost wrong to call iCal an appointment calendar. It does a jim-dandy job of recording birthdays, meetings, trips, auditions for reality-TV shows, and the like, but it goes way beyond that.

iCal has two big, yippee-inducing features:

- **You can create "layers" of calendars.** Each of your major projects at work can have its own uniquely colored calendar, as well as each of your kids' sports teams, your training regimen for the Boston Marathon, and all of your spouse's piddling little commitments that he or she seems to think are soooo danged important. When you want to focus on one aspect of your life, you can hide everything else. When you want to try to figure out how you can bring in your company's quarterly actuals on deadline, get your teeth cleaned, and make sure that your son D'Artagnian gets picked up from stage fighting class all within the same 3 hours of the same day, you can see where your commitments overlap each other. Rescheduling a commitment is as simple as dragging it from one day and time to another.

- **iCal also helps you out by making it easy to share calendars with others.** With just a few clicks, iCal can transmogrify your calendars into Web pages that anyone with a browser and an Internet connection can view. So when it looks like you're going to get stuck working late at the office, you can easily go to the Web, look at your spouse's iCal schedule, and see that there's nothing preventing him or her from picking up D'Artagnian from stage fighting class and driving him to his Blockfløte recital. Consult iCal's Help system for info on sharing your calendars with other users, and incorporating calendar info from othe folks.

In Figure 15-19, you can see a sample iCal display. The center of the window shows a single calendar month.

ASK THE MAN WHO OWNS ONE

And the best endorsement I can give to iCal is that it's the first calendar/appointment app that I've ever actually stuck with. *Ever.* Since becoming a technology pundit in my college days, I've received free copies of every such app there ever was. And inevitably, after a week or two of tryout, I'd delete it from my hard drive and return to my tried-and-true calendar app: my email program. As a hypermegasupergeek, all of my appointments and confirmations come via email, and it always seemed simpler to just do a search for "Meeting," "Microsoft," and "San Francisco" than to meticulously update a calendar app.

Like Address Book, though, it's iCal's tight integration into the rest of my swingin' Macintosh lifestyle that sold me. That, and, er, the increasing number of times I wound up triple-booking myself for meetings and briefings during trade shows.

The right side of the window contains the current to-do list. The left side lists the details of a specific appointment. Current calendars appear at the top left, and a small overview of the current month appears at the bottom left. Calendars to which this copy of iCal subscribes have an arrow at the right edge of their names; the calendars without arrows are local calendars — those that this copy of iCal uses.

**Figure 15-19
A Month In The Life**

Clicking the Day button at the bottom of the window switches to a view of the currently selected week. Clicking the Month button provides an overview on a single day.

Some items are events rather than appointments: a birthday, a weeklong conference, or the Iditarod dogsled race, for example. iCal displays these as a stripe at the top of the day rather than attaching them to a specific time.

You can look at the details of any event, appointment or To-Do by clicking on it. The info appears in the Info Drawer, which hangs off the side of the calendar window. You can use this drawer to enter or edit event information.

Adding and editing events

The first thing you are likely to do when setting up your electronic calendar is to add some events:

1. **Select File → New Event or press ⌘+N.**

   Calendar creates a new appointment for the date you're currently viewing (or, in Week or Month view, it's made for the day you last clicked on). The appointment's details are revealed in the Info window, where you can edit all of the particulars.

   In Week and Day mode, you can create an appointment for a specific day and time by just dragging a rectangle that starts at the start time and ends at the end time (Figure 15-20). If you accidentally place an event in the wrong place, you can drag it to a new location. You can also use this technique if the day or time of an event changes.

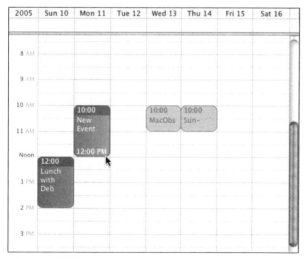

Figure 15-20
Dragging to define a new appointment

2. **Complete the details of the event by typing in the Info drawer (see Figure 15-21).**

   Click a gray field placeholder to highlight it, and then type what you want in the field. Hit the Tab key to move to the next field, or just click on the detail you want to change.

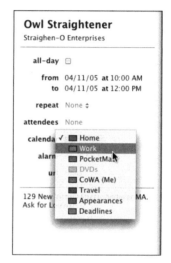

Figure 15-21
Adding details. Details, details ...

The Info drawer includes the following items:

- **Event name:** Describes the event. You can also edit the event description directly on the calendar display. There's also a line of descriptive text that accompanies the name.

- **all-day:** Click this box to indicate that the event has no specific time associated with it. Viz, a birthday or anniversary.

- **from and to:** Specify the start and stop times/dates of the event. If the "to" date isn't the same as the "from" date, it'll automatically become a multi-day event.

SIMPLICITY? PAH!

I have to admit that as neat as it might *sound* to create appointments by just dragging boxes with my mouse, I almost always create my appointments manually by hitting ⌘+N and then entering the times by hand. Problem One with dragging is that you can only create appointments in fifteen-minute increments. You can do "3 PM to 3:45" but "3:10 to 3:40" won't happen unless you type it in manually. Secondly, I'm almost always going to be editing this anyway. So it actually slows me down to mouse *one* thing and then type in everything else.

The good news is that I still haven't fallen into the "LPs are way, way better than compact discs or digital music files" cult.

That's a basic appointment. Most of the extra-credit options are available, too, namely:

- **repeat:** Click the arrows next to the None following repeat to set up an event that happens again and again on a regular interval . . . like an anniversary, or a weekly meeting that takes place every Tuesday at 11 a.m.

- **attendees:** Click here to enter a list of people invited to an event. As you type names, Calendar will match your typing with people in your Address Book, and you can hit Enter/Return at any time to accept the suggestion. Otherwise, keep typing until you've got the whole name, and hit Enter/Return to add more names.

When you add Attendees, a new "Notify" button appears at the bottom of the Info drawer. When you

click it, email reminders will be immediately sent to all attendees, complete with details about the event.

- **calendar:** You can assign this appointment to a specific calendar by choosing it from the popup.

- **alarm:** Calendar can break into whatever you're doing to remind you that you've got this Event coming up. Calendar can pop up a little event alert, accompanied by an attention-getting sound (Figure 15-22). You can also have Calendar send you an email, open a document, or run an AppleScript.

Figure 15-22
A reminder about my poor, stunted owl

- **calendar:** Click the pop-up menu next to calendar to assign this event to one of your calendars.

- **url:** Click None next to url to enter the URL of a Web site that is applicable to this event.

- **Notes:** Use the Notes area at the bottom of the window to type any text you want about the event.

To edit an event, highlight the event in the calendar display (any view) to display the event's details in the Info window. Then use any of the techniques just described to change any information about the event. You can also reschedule an event by clicking and dragging it to a new spot on the calendar.

To delete an event, click the event in the calendar display and press Delete. Alternatively, click the event in the calendar display and select Edit ➜ Delete.

WHEN AN ALARM IS MORE THAN AN ALARM

The "Open file" and "Run script" alert options make Calendar Alarms into a pretty powerful feature. Now, Calendar becomes more than an appointment manager; it's an Event Scheduler. You need your Mac to back up the contents of an important project folder to your iDisk every afternoon at 5? Create an Automator workflow that performs the backup, and then attach the workflow document to an iCal appointment that recurs every day at the same time. iCal opens the workflow document, which performs the backup ... and it will happen every day until the Apocalypse.

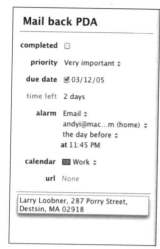

Figure 15-23
Creating a new to-do list item

Adding and editing to-do list items

To-do items flit around in their own separate little world, unconstrained by dates and times, free to just be, the lucky little buggers. Sigh. But still, individual to-do items are associated with specific calendars that help you keep all the goals of a project or process together with the events, meetings, and deadlines. To create a new to-do list item:

1. **Select File → New To Do.**

   Alternatively, you can press ⌘+K. A new item appears at the bottom of the To Do items column and the item's details appear in the Info drawer (see Figure 15-23).

2. **Complete the details of the list item by typing in the Info window.**

   The Info window includes the following items:

   ▫ **Name field:** Replace the text "New To Do" with a description of what is to be done.

   ▫ **completed option:** Click this when the task is done; this'll remove it from the pending list.

   ▫ **priority:** Select a priority for the item by clicking the double arrow next to None on the priority line. An item can have no priority, be Very Important, Important, or Not Important. If you look carefully at the To Do items in Figure 15-19, you see a square to the right of each item. A completely filled square represents a Very Important priority; a two-thirds-filled square stands for an Important priority; one-third filled represents Not Important; and an empty square is no priority.

MY LOVE FOR iCAL KNOWS NO BOUNDS

I think nearly all calendar apps are fundamentally annoying, come to think of it. iCal is just the *least* obnoxious of the lot. It still needs work. What's so difficult about an event that starts at 11 p.m. and continues past midnight? But at this writing, iCal will still cuss me out and insist that I'm a heretic who's trying to create an appointment that starts at 11 p.m. and ends at 1 a.m. that same day, 22 hours earlier.

Of course, it could just be me. Mom always said that a few years in the Army would have done me a world of good, given me some structure and stuff. Well, who's to say?

- **due date:** If there is a specific date by which the item must be completed, type the date following due date. iCal fills in a "time left" field for you. To be reminded when the due date is approaching, set an alarm by clicking the double arrows next to None following alarm. As with events, you can choose to receive a text message, a message with an audio alert, an email, or to open a file.

- **calendar:** If necessary, select a different calendar for the list item.

- **url:** If a Web site is associated with the list item, replace None following url with the appropriate URL.

- **Notes:** Type information about the item in the Notes section at the bottom of the window.

When an item is completed, click the checkbox to the left of its entry in the To Do items list.

To edit an item, click on it in the To Do items list to display its details. Use any of the techniques just discussed to modify information as needed.

To delete an item, click on it in the To Do items list and select Edit ➜ Delete or just press Delete.

Creating and editing your own calendars

Most users quickly populate iCal with separate calendars for organizing each area of their lives. If everything is in one hodgepodge, it's hard to make sense of individual schedules and prioritize events.

ROOM FOR FUTURE IMPROVEMENTS

Unfortunately — and I've pointed out this omission to Apple personally — there's no option for Do You Want It Done Fast, or Do You Want It Done *Right?* There used to be an option labeled Knuckle under to The Man and all his plastic, petty rules, but it was removed after the ruling class boasted that this concept was so relentlessly ingrained into the psyches of the industrial proletariat that repetition was no longer necessary.

Which reminds me: Mark July 17, 2009, on your iCal. That's the day we finally raise the red banner of revolution and fill the skies with the glorious sound of a million chains breaking. Clambake to follow; not a word to the aforementioned ruling class, right?

Note

But don't get hung up on the fact that we're referring to these entities as separate calendars. It's not like you close your calendar of FluffyPuff Marshmallow Ad Campaign deadlines and meetings when you switch to a calendar of upcoming Babylon 5 reruns. In concept, iCal calendars are more like iCal categories. iCal deals with all of your events and appointments as one big collection; calendars just control how much visual clutter you're dealing with at once.

To add a calendar:

1. **Select File → New Calendar. Alternatively, you can also press Option+⌘+N.**

   A new, unnamed calendar appears in the Calendars list, and the Info window shows the new calendar's details.

2. **Replace "Untitled" with a name for the calendar.**

3. **Select a color for the calendar's events and to-do list items from the pop-up menu to the right of the calendar's name.**

   This helps you easily distinguish one set of events from the other when they're all hunkered down in the same window together. If you don't want to use one of the preset colors (or if you've used all the preset colors already), select Other. A color-picker appears from which you can choose any color your Macintosh can display.

4. **Replace the word "Description" by typing a description of the calendar.**

To modify information about a local calendar, click the calendar in the Calendars list to display its details in the Info drawer. Make any necessary changes in that information.

To delete a calendar, click the calendar in the Calendars list and choose Edit → Delete or press Delete.

 Tip

You can limit the sorts of appointments that you can see at any given time by unchecking individual calendars in the "Calendars" list.

Finding events and to-do list items

As your calendars and to-do list items continue to grow, it can become difficult to find specific events. "Just when was that meeting?" "Johnny needs to be at practice when?" "Is the wedding this weekend or next weekend?"

The easiest way to locate events and to-do list items is to search for them. iCal's search feature is fairly straightforward: Type search text in the search text box. iCal performs a contains search on all entries — winnowing the results as you type more letters — and displays the results. To go to a specific item in the search result, double-click it.

.MAC, AND THE *POINT* OF .MAC

We're about to hit a couple of Fifth Beatle apps that work even spiffier if you subscribe to Apple's .Mac service, so now's probably a good time to answer that musical question, um . . . dot-what, now?

.Mac is Apple's foray into creating an online service for Mac users. "Ah! An online service!" you say. "So if I subscribe, I bet I get

- **An email account** with my own gernblanstev@ mac.com address.

- **My own Web page,** albeit a personal one intended for showing off photos and home movies, not something I can run my own nationwide online carpet-cleaning business from.

"Plus, lots of little apps, games, and utilities that Apple licenses from third-party commercial publishers, free exclusively for .Mac subscribers! Great gobs of hydrogenated canola oil! That's a lot of service for just 99 clams a year!"

And you would be right. (Though I'd go easy on the caffeine; it's a nice deal, but places like Hotmail, GMail, and Yahoo! will give you *free* email accounts, and it's also possible to find free places to post your photos online, too. So all I'm saying is steady on, so far.)

.Mac goes way beyond a simple, run-of-the-mill online service. It's tightly integrated into Tiger and all of Apple's iLife apps, so it's more accurate to describe your .Mac account as "a bubble on the Internet onto which you can project bits of your Macintosh experience."

Viz:

- **You also get an Online iDisk,** with 250 MB of storage, which you can expand if you give Apple extra money. You can mount this on the Desktop of any Mac anywhere in the world, so long as it has an Internet connection. Store all of your important docs on your iDisk and *any* Mac can, in effect, be *your* Mac. An iDisk is the source of unspeakable ginchiness, and I spoke highly of it back in Chapter 12, when I talked about Volumes.

- **.Mac makes it easy to swap and synchronize information between multiple Macs.** Because all Macs are familiar with the concept of an iDisk, all of your different Macs can access files there to swap and synchronize information among each other. If up-to-date

SO WHY DON'T I SUBSCRIBE TO .MAC?

I suppose I shouldn't be so glib about my advice about .Mac. I tried it for 60 days, then spent the dough for a year's subscription ($99, at this writing). But then I didn't renew it.

iDisk is a tremendously elegant solution to a lot of problems, particularly the problem of sharing data between multiple Macs many miles apart. But, as a guy with his thumb in a great many online pies, I found that most of .Mac's services are duplicated elsewhere, often inside other services for which I was already paying. I have my own Web site, I have commercial software for publishing movies and photos, and I already have more email accounts than I can manage. Also, as a one-man-company, all of my work is kept here on Lilith, my PowerBook, and when I need to tote files from place to place, I do it on this 128 MB flash drive on my keychain. But your experience may be different and a .Mac account might swat at several problems with a single club.

copies of your appointment calendar and address book sit on your iDisk, your office Mac, your home Mac, and your PowerBook can easily synchronize themselves to your iDisk so that they always contain the same contacts and calendars. Ditto for your browser bookmarks and other esoterica. .Mac is the hub that allows all of your Macs to synchronize data with each other.

- **Apps can interact with your .Mac account directly, without any configuration.** Many of the iLife apps (iPhoto, iMovie, and so on) are hip to the concept of wanting to let your friends and relatives see all the

285

photos and video you shot during your big road trip to Lowell, Massachusetts, to see the World's Largest Shoehorn. Because they're Apple apps and (again) are hip to the iDisk concept, publishing all this media to your iDisk in the form of Web pages that anyone can read and enjoy is a matter of one or two mouse clicks.

So, .Mac is actually much bigger than the familiar email and personal Web page service you get from other services. But is it worth it? It is unwise to tip the vessel of knowledge, young padawan. By which I mean . . . um, I dunno.

The good news is that you get to try .Mac for free for 2 months, and that's time well spent. Click the .Mac button within System Preferences to get going.

iCHAT

iChat just goes to show you that the worst curse possible is to have one of your wishes granted. I've always disdained telephones as being way too analog for my tastes, hoping that they would one day disappear and be replaced with something far more Jetsons-ey. Enter the basic concept of online chat as a vector for human conversation, and (a couple of years later) iChat in particular.

It's digital. I'll give you that. But in my darker moments it seems to me like chat (speaking in general) is a Frankenstein of the least-palatable elements of all the various forms of communication that it replaced. It gives you all the hassle of having to type email and all of the hassle of having to drop what you're doing at the moment and take part in live communication.

▼ **Note**

And I'm being serious, here. Do you fear burglars? Compact nuclear weapons being stolen from former Soviet republics and winding up in the hands of peo-

ple who don't intend to use them for deer hunting? Biting into a candy bar and instantly tasting something that you know isn't chocolate, caramel, or peanuts? I'll take any of those over hearing iChat trill at me and seeing a window pop open, representing a vague acquaintance who's so consumed by the dynamics of the question "What's up?" that he simply couldn't feed or bathe himself until I weighed in on the subject.

Still, props and overall shout-outs to iChat all the same. In addition to text messaging back and forth, it supports audio and live video, and can take the place of long-distance phone calls and even actual visits in which there's a danger of experiencing person-to-person contact with another Human.

To use iChat, you need either a .Mac iChat account or an America Online Instant Messenger (AIM) account. You do not need to subscribe to AOL to have a free AIM account, however. If you want to set up an AIM account, go to www.aol.com and click on the AOL Instant Messenger button. Download the software and use it to set up your AIM account. Once the account is set up, you won't need the AIM software; you can use iChat instead.

You don't need to subscribe to .Mac to get an iChat account, either. To set up an account, go to www.mac.com/ichat/. You can sign up for a free iChat account and get a free 60-day trial of .Mac. Even if 60 days go by and you choose not to subscribe to .Mac, the iChat account keeps functioning forever.

Setting up iChat

The first time you run iChat, you must provide information about your AIM and/or .Mac accounts. Your account represents your presence to other users, and it's the name people will use to locate and connect to you.

1. **Launch iChat.**

   The software runs its setup utility automatically.

2. **Type information about your .Mac account, as in Figure 15-24.**

   iChat defaults to .Mac chat accounts, but it's also compatible with AIM. Select your type of account from the popup and provide your name, account name, and password.

3. **Click Continue.**

   If you have a camera and/or microphone attached and turned on, you can see them in the next window. This window is really just to test your connections; there is nothing for you to change or enter unless you don't see an image in the square (if you have an operational camera) or a live audio meter underneath the square (if you have an operational microphone).

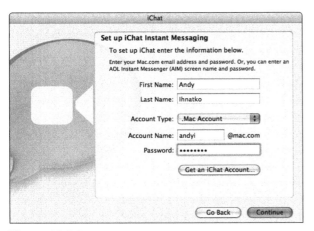

Figure 15-24
Configuring iChat to use a .Mac account

4. **Click Continue.**

   iChat is now configured.

▼ Tip

At this writing, .Mac and AIM are the only chat standards available to you through the iChat setup utility. But iChat also supports a popular standard called Bonjour, which you can install and configure through the Accounts tab of iChat's Preferences window.

Using the iChat Buddy List

The center of your iChat universe is iChat's Buddy List. As you can see in Figure 15-25, I've filled mine with a list of friends who wouldn't react with bald, open disgust if I ever requested a casual conversation.

When sitting there like a lump the Buddy List tells you what your buddy is up to and whether or not he or she is available for a chat. If the button next to a name is green, the person's account is online and available; if it is red, the person is online but not available. In the latter case you'll often see an "I'm away" message.

Figure 15-25
iChat's Buddy List window

At the far right side of each chat partner's name you can see the person's current chat icon. It might be something generic (for example, the AIM running person) or an image that the person has selected for his or her chat sessions. You might find an icon indicating that the person has audio or video capabilities just to the left of the chat icon. In Figure 15-25, for example, I have a video camera plugged in and ready, and thus can do video and audio. My pal Sam has a telephone icon, meaning that he can do an audio chat but that he can't do video at the moment.

To get iChat to recognize a new chat partner, you must add that partner to iChat's Buddy List:

1. **Click the plus sign (+) in the lower-left corner of the Buddy List window.**

2. **Select Buddies → Add a Buddy, or press Shift+⌘+A.**

   The window in Figure 15-26 appears. You can select someone who has a card in your Address Book by just clicking on his or her name. If your new Buddy isn't in the Address book, click New Person. Either way, you'll be presented with the sheet shown in Figure 15-27.

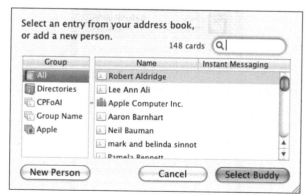

Figure 15-26
Adding a new buddy from the Address Book

3. **Fill in any missing information about your new Buddy.**

   iChat will copy as much information from the Address Book as is available. You do the rest.

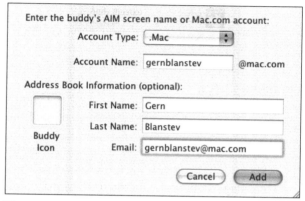

Figure 15-27
Configuring your Buddy

iChat adds the new person to its Buddy List and searches the Internet to determine the person's status. If the person is online and available, you are ready to initiate a chat.

Status messages

Notice that little menu underneath your name in the title of your Buddy List (see Figure 15-25). You can use this to set your chat status.

Remember when I told you how annoyed I get when I'm busy and people try to iChat me for no real purpose? Well, it really shouldn't be a problem at all because I can just tell people to buzz off through this little status line. If I set my status to Away, a red dot appears next to my name in my pal's buddy lists, and the software won't allow anyone to interrupt my pursuit of le mot juste.

BONJOUR, BUDDIES!

iChat also can display a second list of iChattable people: if you select Bonjour from the Window menu, iChat will compile a list of all the people on the local network who've enabled Bonjour messaging. Yes, total strangers. It's a terrific feature for public events, or if you see someone you know at the other end of the lecture hall but you don't know their chat account name. Open the Bonjour window, and watch names and icons fill it to the brim.

To turn on Bonjour on your own Mac, open iChat's Preferences window, click on Accounts, and then click on Bonjour and make sure the Use Bonjour Instant Messaging option is checked.

As you can guess from the word Away, this specific choice is intended to tell people you're not at your desk. This message is "broadcast" to all of your buddies. It might be more accurate to change it to "I'm Busy," which tells people (like your boss) that you're chained to your desk with your nose at the grindstone and not over at Six Flags hitting on the woman who makes change at the Skee-Ball pavilion. Viz:

1. **Click the Status popup (it's actually the status text), and click on the Custom item.**

   You can find this at the top of the Buddy List (see Figure 15-25 again). The Status popup changes into an editable text field.

2. **Type a brief message that you want your Buddies to see.**

   For example, you can type **Buzz off, I'm trying to WORK!**

3. **Press Return to apply the change.**

   iChat adds your custom message to its list of pre-fabbed status messages. This allows you to select this message at any time. You can create new Available (green dot) messages as well.

▼ **Note**

People use that status message in ways that Apple never intended. It's a good way to quickly communicate a message to a lot of people because it's right there in their Buddy Lists. There are also AppleScripts that automatically change your status message to reflect what's going on in your office. One connects to a weather service and turns your status line into a constantly updated weather forecast. A popular one always lists whatever track is currently playing in iTunes; in fact, it became so popular that iChat now includes that option as a status message!

Apparently, while the hippies of the preceding generation feared Big Brother, the generations that followed are only worried that strangers aren't interested *enough* in the minutiae of their daily existence. (Refer to *The Real World,* and any holiday family letter written and distributed after 1996.)

If you want complete privacy, there's an item in the Status menu labeled Offline. This logs you off of iChat's chat server completely, rendering you invisible until you log back in again.

Being chatted

So you've told people about your new iChat account and alerted them to your desire to be bothered at all hours of the day by people who want to know what you thought of last night's episode of "Law and Order." What happens when people try to start a chat with you?

A window like Figure 15-28 will pop up over whatever you're doing. You can ignore it completely and hope this jerk just goes away, but if you click on the window you'll have several options:

Figure 15-28
An incoming invitation to chat

- **Accept:** Click Accept to open an iChat chat window and start chatting away.

- **Decline:** Clicking Decline tells the supplicant "thanks, but no thanks."

- **Block:** Block is a necessary side effect of allowing Humans — of all people — to use chat software. It's possible that some thumb-sucking jerk may gain access to your chat ID and continue to pester you with instant messages. If so, click Block and iChat ignores this balloonhead forevermore, or at least until you Unblock them.

Chatting

So you see someone with whom you want to chat is online and available. Now what? Initiating a chat is easy:

1. **Click the person's name in your Buddy List.**

   See Figure 15-25 for an example of the Buddy List.

 Tip

If you want to chat with someone who isn't in your Buddy List, select New Chat With Person from the File menu. So long as you can provide iChat with the person's account name and you know which chat service he or she uses, iChat can chat 'em up from night to day and back again.

2. **Click one of the three icons at the bottom of the Buddy List window:**

   - **"A" icon:** This invites the person to a text chat.

   - **Telephone receiver icon:** This invites the person to an audio chat.

   - **Camera icon:** This invites someone to a video chat.

 Tip

Or to initiate an immediate text chat, just double-click on the Buddy's name.

The type of chat that you can invite someone to depends on the equipment that each person has available. If iChat detects a camera, all three types of chat are available. If iChat detects a microphone but no camera, then you can select a text or video chat only. If no AV equipment is present, then you can conduct a text chat.

But receiving audio and video is handled entirely by software. So if you have a camera but your chat partner doesn't, you can select One-Way chat mode from the Buddy menu. Your buddy can see you, but naturally you can't see him.

3. **iChat opens up a new chat window. Type an opening message and then wait for the person to accept or decline the chat invitation.**

ONE-WAY BAD CRAZINESS

iChat's One-Way chat mode led to one of my happiest little hacks. I wrote an AppleScript that allows me to do a one-way video iChat between my TiVO video recorder at home and me. I set my iChat status to Watching TiVO wherever I am in the world. Back home, my Mac sees the status and invites me to chat. My TiVO is plugged into a box that converts its analog signals into iChat-compatible digital video, and bango — I can see and hear the show that my TiVO is currently tuned into.

This is what is known as an Act of Heroic Stupidity.

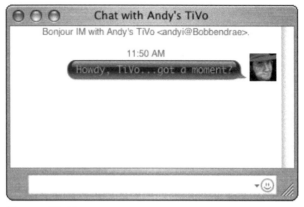

Figure 15-29
Waiting for a response to a text chat invitation

Figure 15-30
Waiting for a response to a video chat invitation

In Figure 15-29, you can see the window that appears when waiting for a response to an invitation to a text chat. The Buddy List icon of the invited person appears at the top of the window. The current image coming from the sender's camera appears in the body of the window. Figure 15-30 shows you the window that appears when you wait for a response to an invitation to a video chat.

If your chat partner accepts the invitation, the Waiting for reply window becomes your chat window. Type and read, type and read. No need to click any sort of Send button or say, "Roger . . . *over.*" What you type is sent as soon as you hit the Return key.

Exactly what you see depends on the type of chat you are conducting, of course. Figure 15-31 shows a typical video chat. The person with whom you are chatting appears in the body of the window; the small inset contains the image coming from your camera.

An audio chat (see Figure 15-32) shows an audio meter. A text chat (see Figure 15-33) contains what you and your chat partner type.

Figure 15-31
Conducting a video chat

Figure 15-32
Conducting an audio chat

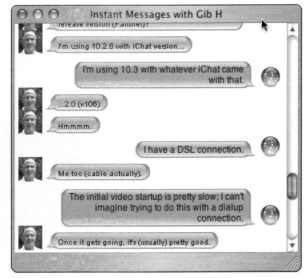

Figure 15-33
Conducting a text chat

To end a chat, close the chat window.

Group Chat

I can think of a great many activities in which the slogan "The More, the Merrier" is sarcastically ironic — I confess that this first crossed my mind back in high school, when I got jumped by the JV football team — but hey, chat ain't one of 'em. With iChat, a bunch of people can communicate as a single group. Never before in the history of personal computing has the selection of a time and a place and a mode of cuisine for the after-work get-together been so efficient and democratic.

And the (fairly incredible) thing (no, I *don't* think I'm exaggerating) is that iChat supports multiperson audio and video chats as easily as it does plain old text chat. It all happens the same way:

1. **Select a group of available people from your Buddies list.**

   You do this the same way you select stuff from any other list: either command-click buddies one at a time, or select the first buddy and then hold down the Shift key and select another name further on down, which selects those two folks and everyone in between.

2. **Click on one of iChat's three chat icons: text, audio, or video to initiate the chat.**

   And that's really all there is to it. Your chat will grow and grow as one by one, your buddies accept your invite.

▼ Tip

You can add people to these chats easily enough by just clicking the + button in the corner of the chat window and then selecting a new buddy. Audio chats support up to ten people (including you); up to four people can participate in a video chat.

Figures 15-34, 15-35, and 15-36 show you what iChat's multiperson text, audio, and video chat screens look like. Figure 15-36 shows iChat's video chat window in its super-hypermegaginchy mode: by clicking the "grow" button (it's the one with the two arrows that point outward) your chat window will consume the entire screen.

Figure 15-34
Can you hear me now? Conference calling, the audio iChat way

Figure 15-36
Bad Craziness: full-screen four-way chat mode

▼ Note

Keep in mind that there's a difference between being in a multiperson chat and simply having more than one chat going at once. You can open several one-on-one text chat windows, for example, and each window represents a "private" conversation between you and one of your buddies.

There are a bunch of bummers associated with multiperson audio and video chat, though. Obviously, you can only have one of these chats going at any given time. You can't open a four-way video chat and then try to get a *second* video chat started on the side. You can have other active text chats, though.

The more serious bummer lies in the fact that audio-visual chats are highly technical and put lots of demands on your Mac, and thus there are many situations in which you won't be able to do audio or video chat at all:

Figure 15-35
Four-way video chat: conclusive proof that Humankind, and not the dolphins, deserves to be this planet's dominant species

As with any other chat, you can leave the chat by simply closing the chat window.

- **Some of the folks you're trying to chat with aren't using Tiger.** It's an all-Tiger club: no Panthers (Mac OS 10.3) or Jaguars (10.2) allowed. But you can instantly see who's "eligible" for multi-person AV chat

WHY I LOVE BEING A MAC USER, PART CCXCVIII

Please do take a moment to sit back and appreciate the glory of iChat's multiperson video chat screen. With any other operating system, there'd just be three rectangular windows lined up side-by-side, like a single level of the opening credits on *The Brady Bunch*. That's the Minivan solution to getting people together in one place, and it has absolutely no place in a Macintosh application, *particularly* not one made by Apple itself.

No, Apple builds a completely pimped-out super-stretch Humvee with multiple video screens, a wet bar, and a gift shop. I mean, just *look* at it: each chatter is in a pane that has its own reflections and specular highlights, rendered flawlessly in real-time. "Yes, Macs have some of the fastest microprocessors on the planet," iChat says. "Indeed, they have so much power that we can gleefully waste resources on little touches like this."

Under the circumstances, you and your friends are *not* to be faulted for "struggling against the confines of your invisible prison" à la General Zod and the other Kryptonian super-criminals who were banished to the Phantom Zone in the opening scenes of *Superman II*. But be advised that this'll get really old kind of quickly.

from their buddy icons: if their audio or video icon looks like just one green tile instead of a stack of them, they can't handle multiperson modes, for whatever reason.

- **Your Mac isn't up to the challenge.** If your Mac has a G3 processor or better (which is nearly all of you), you can answer an invitation to group audio chat. For video chat, any G4 or G5 will do; if you've got a G3, its speed has to be at least 600 MHz.

- **Video chats are more complicated.** For a four-way chat, you'll need a lot more muscle: a G4 Mac with a 1 GHz processor or better, or dual 800 MHz processors or better. Any G5 will do. No matter what you're running, the more power you have, the better the video will be (clearer pictures and more frames-per-second). But that's just if you're going to accept someone's invitation. The Mac that initiates a multi-person video chat acts as the "host" and needs to have considerably more oomph: any G5, or a dual-processor 1 GHz G4.

- **Your Internet connection stinks.** All this audio and video burns up bandwidth like crazy and you'll need a stable, fast connection. The only thing you can do over a phone line is a one-on-one audio chat. The Good Stuff requires a connection that can send and receive data at 100K per second at *least*. If you want to initiate a chat, you'll have to more than triple that.

Swapping files

Okay, I've been joking around about how I hate having to chat with people. In truth, I'm a salt-of-the-earth, Falstaffian character whom dogs trust implicitly and without reservation. But if you had been nodding your heads while I railed on about not wanting to interact with my fellow man, I've got a bonus for you.

THE DARK ART OF BANDWIDTH

The thing is, you won't *truly* know if your connection is fast enough for iChat multimedia chat until you try it and either find Joy or Sorrow. Chatting among friends in your office or house is usually reliable, but as soon as you bring the Internet into this, life becomes scary and uncertain. For one, most home broadband connections can't transmit data as fast as it can send it. As a consumer product, its purpose is to let you download pictures and video and music *fast fast fast,* and to make that happen they limit the upload speeds. And when lots and lots of your broadband company's subscribers are using the Internet at once, everyone's speed suffers.

iChat is one of the simplest ways to transmit a file from person-to-person, whether across the office or across the world. All you have to do is drag the file onto his or her icon in your Buddy List. At the other end, your buddy sees a pop-up window that looks something like Figure 15-37.

Click Save File to download and save the file to the computer's hard drive. Click Decline to refuse the file.

Figure 15-37
Receiving a file via iChat

▼ Tip

Man, is that cool. Finally, a method of shuttling files from one Mac to another that's actually an *improvement* over simply copying it onto a disk and walking it over there yourself!

And it gets slicker. If you're in the middle of a chat with someone, and you drag in a JPEG or GIF, the image file displays right inside the chat window. Them boys and girls at Apple, they's a thinkin' bunch, all right.

SAFARI

In the abstract, you really need to spend a great many nights sleeping in a freshly painted and poorly ventilated room to look at Microsoft Internet Explorer — hands-down the most dominant Web browser on all the planets I've been to — and think, no, our company should do away with it and replace it with something better.

Conceptually, the walls at Apple's company headquarters are always bright, clean, and colorful.

And indeed, the browser Apple came up with proves the point: You can do way better than Explorer. A little history: Apple started off with great material. It looked at an open-source (i.e., built by the Internet community at large and owned by everyone) Web-browser engine called KHTML and took it under its wing. It made vast improvements to the existing software library and gave those improvements back to the open-source community. Then Apple added its own dose of elfin' magic (the same basic principles that make Fudge Shop Cookies so danged tasty), rolled in some Mac-specific features, and out popped Safari.

GOOGLE, SCHMOOGLE?

As the accreditation standards of American colleges continue to slide, it's inevitable that one day it'll be possible to get a BA in Internet Searching. No one tool can even begin to serve all your searching needs, and after a proper education, you'll figure out how to pick the right one for the job. So don't expect Sherlock to replace Google. It remains the accepted index for the Web and has an incredible array of features; www.google.com/help/ is a real revelation for most users.

And the Web is littered with specialized search engines. Sherlock will give you the addresses of delicatessens in Boston, but it won't recommend the best place to get lean pastrami with a half-done on the side.

Figure 15-38
Safari's bookmarks display

Safari offers a great many improvements over Explorer. The first improvement you'll notice is its sheer speed. No Mac browser can render HTML pages faster than Safari. It's like having a whole new Mac.

It also has a lot of minor and major features that'll be unfamiliar to Explorer users: you're probably already familiar with a basic Web browser already, so I'll just focus on Safari's unique features.

Bookmarks

It's easier to create and organize bookmarks in Safari than it is in nearly any other browser on any platform. Safari places a Bookmarks button — the dingy that looks like an open book — in the toolbar of every window. When you click it, the current Web page is replaced with a display similar to Figure 15-38.

Like most of Apple's iApps, Safari uses collections to organize bookmarks. The main portion of the window shows you the bookmarks in the currently highlighted collection.

Some of the collections have special purposes:

- **Bookmarks Bar:** Any bookmarks in this collection appear in the Bookmarks Bar above the window's main display area.

- **Bookmarks Menu:** Any bookmarks in this collection appear in Safari's Bookmarks menu.

- **Address Book:** The Address Book collection contains any URLs that are in your OS X Address Book, such as your contacts' personal websites.

- **History:** The History collection really isn't a bookmark collection at all. It provides access to the Web sites you've visited, as in Figure 15-39.

The remaining collections are for the usual type of Web site bookmarks.

Figure 15-39
Safari's History list

To create a new bookmark collection, follow these steps:

1. **Click the plus sign (+) in the lower-left corner of the bookmark display.**

   Safari adds an "untitled folder" at the bottom of the Collections column.

2. **Type a name for the new collection.**

To bookmark a webpage that you're currently reading, just select Add Bookmark from the Bookmarks menu, or click the "+" button to the left of the browser window's address bar. A dialog scrolls down (Figure 15-40), prompts you to type a name for the bookmark, and offers you the chance to specify a location to store it in.

 Note

The location feature alone justifies Safari's existence. Before, nearly all browsers simply dumped new bookmarks at the end of the Bookmarks menu, leaving it to you to wade through it later on and organize them by subject and topic. Safari lets you do this while the bookmark is fresh in your mind. Result: no impossibly cluttered and nigh-useless Bookmark lists.

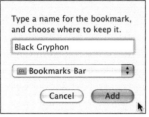

Figure 15-40
Adding a bookmark for a Web site you are viewing

3. **Type a name for the bookmark.**

4. **Select a collection for it.**

5. **Click Add.**

   Safari adds the bookmark to the appropriate collection.

 Tip

You can also create bookmarks just by grabbing the URL — the little icon to the left of the address serves as a grabbable handle — and dragging it wherever you want it to go, such as into the Bookmarks menu or straight onto the toolbar.

Note that through the Collections pane, it's possible to actually store collections of bookmarks within the toolbar; clicking the name in the toolbar displays a whole menu of bookmarks, and you can drag new bookmarks straight into one specific toolbar collection.

Copying and deleting a bookmark is easy: To copy a bookmark from one collection to another, Option-drag the bookmark in the bookmarks display. To delete a bookmark, click the bookmark in the display and select Edit → Delete or press Delete.

The Google box

The Google search site has become so intractably the rice in the great beef burrito known as the Internet that Apple decided to make Google searching part of Safari's top-level interface. See that search box in the upper corner of the window in Figure 15-41? That's a direct line to Google.

To access Google, follow these steps:

1. **Click inside the search box.**

2. **Enter your search terms just as you would if you were on Google's Web site.**

3. **Press Return.**

   Safari submits the search for you and displays the results in the browser window.

Figure 15-41
Googling straight from Safari's search box

IS SAFARI THE ONLY MAC BROWSER?

Boy, it sure *seems* that way. But as much as I love Safari, I ought to point out that it isn't the be-all and end-all of Macintosh browsers. Firefox (a free download from `www.mozilla.org`) is a multi-platform powerhouse of browsing with advanced features for security, privacy, and unmatched standards compliance. It's also being supported by hundreds of programmers through a plug-in system, and new features are being added every day.

▼ Note

And all of Google's advanced features work, too. If you type "seventeen ounces in liters" Google responds with "Seventeen US fluid ounces = 0.502750005 liters." If you type a FedEx tracking number, it responds with tracking information for that package.

See, now *this* is why I don't use Sherlock. It's bad enough that most of its functions are duplicated by Tiger's Dashboard widgets. But just to kick Sherlock's hat into the grave with it, I can Google for nearly anything I'd Sherlock for, without any additional overhead. I reiterate that Sherlock's developers, promoters, and users are kind-hearted, salt-of-the-earth types who'd probably like me a lot if they ever met me socially. I'm all about the love.

Finally, the little magnifying glass in the left side of the search box is actually a pop-up menu that remembers your most recent searches. Select one of them for a repeat search.

SnapBack

Here's the situation: You opened a bookmark for the Jean-Luc Picard Trivia Page to find out what flute-like musical instrument the Enterprise captain played and where he first learned to play it. But when you got there, you saw a link for photos from a big Trek convention, so you clicked it and read it for a while. Which took you to a directory of sci-fi conventions, which took you to the personal website of this guy who makes these *wicked*-cool props and costumes, and then . . .

Whoops, you meant to find out about the Picard flute thing. To get back to the page you started on, you'd normally have to carefully pick your way through the browser's History menu and rewind. Not so with Safari. Check out the orange arrow in the address bar (see Figure 15-42). Clicking the arrow rewinds you back to the first webpage you visited when you began your journey through the Web. The definition of "the first webpage" varies. Usually it's the last webpage you visited by typing its URL into the Address Bar, or the last one you visited by opening a bookmark. You can also manually mark the current page as the "snapback" page by selecting "Mark page for SnapBack" from the History menu.

http://www.povonline.com/My%20Backyard6.htm

**Figure 15-42
Safari's SnapBack button**

RSS Feeds

A user's delight with the World Wide Web dies the moment he or she realizes how much there is of it, and how little in it. It's just hugely difficult to keep tabs on the dozens (or hundreds) of websites you're interested in, and the dozens (or hundreds, or thousands) of articles on each one.

Well, the Web has this annoying habit of creating problems and then solving them, thus keeping your annoyance and your gratitude in balance. To help you keep up with all that information, developers created a standard known as RSS. It stands for "Really Simple Syndication," "Rich

STUPID, LAZY WEBMASTERS!

Of course, what you'll actually see here will vary from site to site. Some sites' RSS feeds provide entire articles. Others only provide snippets. Some embroider each article with information about the date it was posted, who wrote it, and other searchable trivia. Some sites' RSS feeds only list the 15 (or whatever) most recent articles. Others like to summarize the whole site.

My own RSS feed, for example, does some nice things. You'll see every article posted since the last time I completely rebuilt it, so you've got hundreds of articles in the feed. I don't include the whole articles, just the first paragraph. Bummer, there. And at this writing, I don't mark each article with its date. Oh, well.

Remember that webmasters are unpredictable creatures, fluttering hither and yon, borne upon the updrafts of the whims of the moment.

Site Summary," or "RDF Site Summary," depending on whom you believe. Whatever. What it actually means is that every website that supports RSS contains summaries of all of the content available therein. An RSS-savvy app — like Safari — can look through those summaries and help you find the information you're really interested in.

Check out Figure 15-43. If you look closely at Safari's address bar, it has a big blue button in it marked "RSS." This means that the site's webmaster (me) has thoughtfully provided its content with RSS summaries. If you click on the RSS button, the actual webpage scrolls away and is replaced with a list of all of the summarized articles (Figure 15-44).

Figure 15-43
My personal weblog ... www.cwob.com

Note all the differences. The Web view of this page shows the page the way the webmaster intended for you to see it . . . with graphics and navigation and sidebars and even ads, possibly. You also see the entire articles. In this RSS view, you're only seeing a compact summary of the site's entire summarized content.

This RSS feed gives you a number of keen opportunities for just getting right to the content you want to see:

- **You can scroll down and get an overview of the entire site's content.** Instead of clicking on page after page after page, you can just scroll around, looking for titles and summaries that seem interesting.

Figure 15-44
Huzzah! A summary of that whole weblog!

▼ **Tip**

Safari's "Article Length" slider lets you control how *much* of each article you see, within the RSS view. So if you're checking out a site with hundreds of full-text articles, pushing the slider to the left will collapse the articles down to the title and just the first couple of lines. Pushing it all the way to the left collapses them down to just their titles.

- **You can quickly narrow the list down to just the articles posted within a specific timeframe.** If the summarized articles have been date stamped, then you can just see Today's content by clicking on the "Today" link in the "Recent Articles" section.

300

• **You can search for articles of interest.** If you type a word or a phrase inside the "Search Articles:" box, Safari will narrow the list down to just the articles that contain that search term.

How well all these features will work will depend on how much info the webmaster stuffed into his site's RSS feed.

No matter how you come to discover an article of irresistible interest, you can read the full article in its original form simply by clicking on the "Read More..." link next to the item's summary. This will return you to the normal Web view of the webpage, aimed directly at the article of interest.

If you've failed to spot anything interesting in the site's RSS view, just click on the address bar's RSS button again and you'll be zapped back to the Web view.

Safari RSS offers a second advantage: it can automatically keep track of which of your favorite websites have been updated. Check out Figure 15-45:

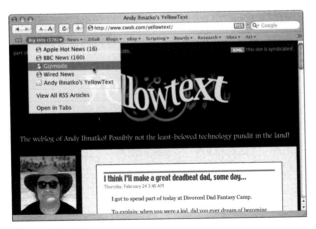

Figure 15-45
The Fresh and the Stale

Some of these bookmarks have numbers next to them. The number tells you how many new articles have been posted to that site since the last time you visited. You can also click on the "View All RSS Articles" item . . . Safari will open an RSS view that combines summaries of all unread articles on all of the RSS-enabled websites whose feeds you've bookmarked, resulting in a glorious apparition reproduced in Figure 15-46.

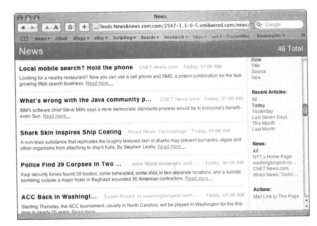

Figure 15-46
Everything you want to read this morning, splattered in one scrolling window

To have Safari automatically track a favorite website, open its RSS view and click the "Add Bookmark..." link.

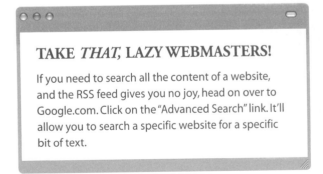

TAKE *THAT*, LAZY WEBMASTERS!

If you need to search all the content of a website, and the RSS feed gives you no joy, head on over to Google.com. Click on the "Advanced Search" link. It'll allow you to search a specific website for a specific bit of text.

iSYNC

If you have an iPod, a PDA, a modern cell phone, or several Macs and a .Mac account, you'll think iSync is the greatest single invention since the Hide-A-Key. If you don't fall into any of these categories, well, go ahead and take the rest of the chapter off. I won't take it personally.

As the name implies, iSync's raison d'être is to synchronize a collection of information (chiefly your iCal and Address Book data) among multiple devices so that changes made to the info on one device ultimately propagate through the entire collection. Your appointment calendar is only moderately useful to you if it's all trapped on your desktop Mac; iSync slurps a copy of all that data from iCal straight onto your Palm. And when your blind date goes swimmingly well and you agree to go on another date the next weekend, the moment you set your Palm back into its HotSync cradle it transmits the date and time and the meeting place at the Battlestar Galactica convention back up to your iCal database.

And ultimately, that same data goes into your iPod and your cell phone. Welcome to the 21st Century, Buck Rogers.

 Note

Wait, *Buck Rogers?* Terrible show. Even worse than *Battlestar Galactica,* which I remember perceiving as *Love Boat in Space.* Once one has seen *Star Wars* in 70mm THX, one develops high standards.

Figure 15-47 shows you all of the different gizmos that hold my Address Book and calendar, thanks to iSync.

Here you see my .Mac account, all three of my iPods, my cell phone, my Palm PDA, and my PocketPC. How does iSync know how to handle all of these devices? Actually, it doesn't. iSync chiefly acts as a go-between for all the apps and drivers that your devices came with when you bought 'em. That's a good thing. Every device has its own unique advantages and features, and a custom add-on conduit that comes with each of the devices you buy (or which is offered as an added option) is better than iSync having one lame, limited solution that works with everything. The third-party iSync conduit that makes my PocketPC work goes beyond iCal and Address Book. For example, it syncs selected photo albums from iPhoto and specific iTunes playlists onto my PDA.

It also means that Apple has created an infrastructure that makes manufacturer support largely irrelevant. Microsoft makes the PocketPC operating system and has never shown any interest in supporting Macs. Well, who cares? The day PocketMac shipped, every PocketPC ever invented was as well supported by Tiger as any iPod.

ONE THING iSYNC CAN'T DO, BUT SHOULD

Obviously I'm a big fan of iSync, but it does have one big shortcoming: It'd be a whole order of magnitude more useful if it could sync two folders of files on two different Macs on a network directly. You come home after a long business trip, you open your PowerBook, and iSync leaps to life, discovering that while you were traveling you changed three of the files you'd copied over from your desktop Mac and created two new ones. A little wireless networking action and before you've even kicked your shoes off, your desktop Mac is updated with all the changes you made during the road trip.

Alas, no such luck … at least not for now.

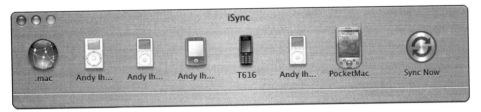

Figure 15-47
Handhelds of a feather sync together

And it's all so simple. Figure 15-47 is the sum total of the iSync interface, and you don't even need to look at it; it all works automatically: click the "Sync" button and all the mutual data on each available device will be synchronized with each other. When a conflict arises, iSync pops up a window showing you the two bits of information that are butting heads — the same piece of new information was added to two different devices, and now iSync doesn't know which one should take precedence — and asking for a King Solomon-type judgment, as in Figure 15-48.

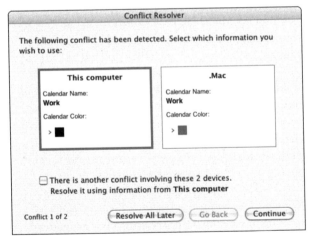

Figure 15-48
Resolving conflict through peace, love, discussion, and iSync

Each iSync conduit has different rules and quirks. Consult your manufacturer's directions for configuring each of your devices for iSync.

.Mac Syncing

Tiger has seriously amped up what you can accomplish with data synchronization if you have a .Mac subscription. .Mac, you'll recall, is your personal forty acres of bottom land on Apple's servers. Your Mac can connect to it easily and access its contents from anywhere across the Internet.

Any Mac can access it from anywhere across the Internet? Hmm. So I suppose that if copies of your address book, calendar, and other information were stored there on your .Mac account, than *all* of your Macs could synchronize their own data to it. And so, by extension, your Power-Book, your office Mac, and the iMac you have back home could sync to each other!

Remarkably, this feature is handled outside of iSync. It's actually managed inside .Mac's System Preferences. Go to System Preferences and open the .Mac panel. Click on the "Sync" tab to reveal .Mac's data-synchronization preferences (Figure 15-49).

And here you see a long list of frequently-updated items that can be synced to your iDisk. Most of them are self-explanatory. "Mail Accounts" doesn't refer to the actual messages *from* your email accounts; just the information you need to contact your mail server and send and receive messages. Every Mac of yours that uses .Mac Sync to connect to your .Mac account will be configured to access all of the same mail accounts. Ditto for Rules, Signatures, and Smart Mailboxes: the upshot is that all of your Macs will function the same way when working with Mail, even if they might not have the exact same messages.

Figure 15-49
.Mac: the hub through which all of your Macs synchronize themselves together

Each checked item will be synchronized to your .Mac account. The popup menu above the list determines how often your Mac will contact .Mac and synchronize its data with the info up on your account. If you select the "manually" option, .Mac syncing will only happen when you click the Sync Now button in .Mac's Sync preferences sheet.

One of the ginchier options in the popup is Automatic. With this option enabled, every time you update your Safari bookmarks or your address book or one of your calendars on your Mac — any item that you've enabled for .Mac syncing — Tiger will automatically send the same data to the collection up on .Mac. And every other Mac of yours that's set up for .Mac syncing will automatically

receive the change. No waiting, no lags . . . it *sounds* as though this scheme would lead to interminable waits, but in fact, when your .Mac account is updated one morsel at a time, the operation is a lot less noticeable than it is if you've got your Mac slinging dozens and dozens of items at a time once a day.

Wowzers. I feel like Willy Wonka. I've taken you all on a whirlwind tour of some of the most fantastic creations produced in one of the most amazing 12 acres of light-industrial real estate in town. (i.e., While many of you came through the experience with horrible physical and mental scars, I'm sure it's left you with a proper sense of the biggest and brassiest creatures lurking inside your Applications folders, and with a firm handle on what can be done with them.)

Actually, the chief reason why I feel this way is because I wrote this entire chapter while wearing a purple crushed-velvet frock coat and a thickly upholstered top hat. Yes, it's a foolish and uncomfortable getup, but it was a Christmas gift from my Mom; and if she doesn't see me wearing it at least once, I'm in for a long winter and spring of quiet fuming.

If this were an ABC Afterschool Special, this is where I'd be suggesting additional reading if you want to pursue your Safari and Mail and Everlasting Gobstopper education further. Do hit the individual apps' Help content. Each one is arranged as a pretty healthy tutorial to the apps in general and is a wonderful starting point.

Whoops! I see by the plaid light on the big Georgian-era brass status board that a little Austrian boy has gotten his ears stuck in the high-velocity, nine-stroke extrusion machine! Gotta run; I can already hear that creepy oompa-loompah song cueing up, and if I'm not there in my velvet top hat to watch and nod my wistful approval during their performance, the warehouse staff will be terribly disappointed.

16

Dash(board)ing All Your Hopes

In This Chapter

What's the Point? • Opening and Closing Dashboard
Opening Wdgets • Using Widgets • Getting New Widgets

"I can't write about Dashboard yet," I complained to my editor. "It's missing from the pre-release copy of Tiger that Apple gave me."

My editor agreed that this was a dashed shame and he offered his sympathies. He was really very nice about it (considering that this chapter was supposed to be written already) which made me look even doubly like an idiot when I had to sheepishly email him a few days later and confess that, um, actually, Dashboard *was* in my copy of Tiger and (lacking any documentation whatsoever) I just didn't know how to activate it. This was before Apple decided to put a Dashboard icon right in the Dock, but still, this sandpapered a bit of the luster off of my self-image as The Technology Whisperer.

▼ Note
Remember "The Horse Whisperer"? This dude who could train even the most unbreakable horses, due to a nigh-mystical rapport with the species? They made a movie about it and everything? Oh, never mind.

But that was as good a warm-up to Dashboard as any. I can't really think of any new feature to Mac OS X that's been nearly so different, so revolutionary. I don't think you can even find its like in pre-X editions of the Mac operating system. Yup, Dashboard is sort of a home for little, simple-to-use, single-use software (called "Widgets"). Old-time Mac users (folks who've been using Mac since the days when people listened to music on quaint platters known as "Compact Discs") will say "Oh, so they're the modern equivalent of Desk Accessories!"

Okay. Yes. Sort of. But Dashboard comes at a similar solution in a totally different way. The revolutionary aspect of Dashboard is that your Mac has a whole second "personality" that it keeps hidden away until you willfully cause Dashboard to drift down into view. Historically, the Mac OS has always been very open and obvious, however, Dashboard makes you wonder what *other* little secrets your Mac has been hiding all this time. Is there a key combo I can hit to cause the Desktop to swing open like a set of barn doors, revealing a button that reads, "Oh, you know what I mean to write here. Could you just fill it in for me? 800 words will do fine. And wake me when you're done."

I haven't found it yet but by God, I haven't stopped looking.

SO WHAT'S THE BLOODY POINT?

The point of Dashboard is to present a brand-new class of user apps: "Widgets." Sometimes there's a need for a piece of software that just does one simple little task or shows you one simple piece of information. But before Tiger, the only way for a software developer to articulate that sort of thing was as a full-blown application, which can often be overkill. Sometimes, cooking a steak means a day of preparation and a refrigerator for the marinade and a four-burner stove and saucepans for onions and mushrooms and a double boiler for making gravy. Sometimes, it means taking a slab of beef out of its shrinkwrap and slapping it on a hibachi filled with briquettes. Applications are the "full kitchen" approach to software; "Widgets" are the hibachi.

You'll find that the general species known as "Widgets" consists of three sub-genuses:

- **Indicators.** This is a Widget that just displays a handy piece of information, which it grabs from another app or even from the Internet. You don't necessarily want to click into Safari and head for the Web site of your online stockbroker . . . you're just curious to see how the market's doing. So you've got a Widget that displays

an up-to-the-minute graph of the NASDAQ and the performance of a few stocks of interest. Or maybe you just want to see if it's worth clicking into Mail and reading your Inbox. A Mail Widget can tell you how many new emails have arrived, and what their subjects are. An eBay Widget tells you that you've just been outbid on that *WKRP In Cincinnati* lunchbox you've had your eye on. Et cetera.

- **Controllers.** You've got iTunes set to Shuffle Play. It's been plucking terrific songs from your music library at random but now it's playing the Kenny Rogers track that you bought as a gag last year. All you want to do is nudge iTunes off of "The Gambler" and on to something peppy by, say, The Cramps. So you go to your dashboard and click the Next Track button on a slim little iTunes remote control. Or you just want to check your calendar to see if you already have a lunch appointment tomorrow. Instead of dealing with iCal, just use the slimmed-down calendar Widget in Dashboard, which presents the same calendar data in a much cleaner form.

- **Doo-Dads.** Or Thingamahoogies, if you prefer. There are plenty of ideas for software that just aren't complicated enough to merit a full-blown, standalone app. A currency converter is a good example. You really can't get this as an app. Instead, you go off and convert your Dollars to Pounds on a Web page, or you go off and launch a whole 'nother app just to get this one bit of info. But it's tailor-made for a Widget. Ditto for a desktop calculator, or just a simple piece of software that lets you slap notes on your screen.

OPENING AND CLOSING DASHBOARD

Widgets aren't at all like "real" applications, and so it logically follows that you don't launch 'em like apps. To activate Dashboard, click its icon in the Dock or press the F12 key on your keyboard. Your Dashboard will shimmer into view, as in Figure 16-1:

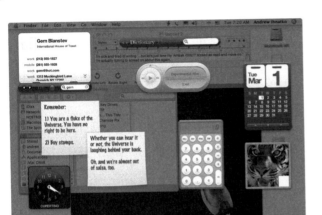

Figure 16-1
Behold, paradise by the Dashboard lights

You can make it disappear by hitting F12 again.

Think of the Dashboard as an entire separate layer of your Mac experience that remains invisible and humbly out of your way until you need it. Just like Jeeves the Valet (cv PG Wodehouse novels), or the mystical village of Brigadoon, which hovers in the mists unseen, only appearing when Gene Kelly and Cyd Charisse need to do a dance number.

AND HE SAID, "YEA, DASHBOARD DOTH TRULY ROCK"

Dashboard gives software developers an opportunity to give their applications two "personalities," the traditional, full-blown treatment with all the bells, whistles, dancing elephants, and complexity, and a pretty, uncluttered, "just the facts, Ma'am" Dashboard face. This is an exciting development; it acknowledges that a single user-interface can't possibly be the best solution in *every* conceivable situation over the course of a workday. Why *not* have an entire second articulation in the mix?

Here we see a Dashboard in mid-use. I've got a clock up there, and some yellow sticky notes to myself, my calendar, address book, a Dictionary, a controller for iTunes, and a calculator, and a puzzle. All of these thingies are Widgets. I can click the buttons of the Calculator, quickly figure out what five pizzas @ $10.95 each plus 15% tip divided by 18 people works out to, and then dismiss Dashboard and start spreading the word throughout the whole office about what I'll do if I don't see $3.50 from each and every last damned one of those moochers by the close of business today.

To dismiss Dashboard, hit F12 again or just click anywhere on the screen (other than on a Dashboard Widget or control).

▼ Note

You can change the hotkey that activates Dashboard. Just go into System Preferences and click Dashboard & Exposé. You'll find a popup menu for Dashboard at the bottom of the settings panel. Select a new key from the menu and close System Preferences. There's also a checkbox you can use to tell Tiger whether or not you'd like the Dashboard icon to appear in the Dock.

And again, keep in mind that you don't really "launch" or "quit" Dashboard or its Widgets. It's just plain *always there*. If I move some of these Widgets around and open some new ones and write a few new notes and then hide Dashboard, the next time I bring up Dashboard, everything will be exactly where I left it.

OPENING WIDGETS

Note that the lower-left corner of your Dashboard sports a circle with a plus sign (+) in it. Click this to expose the Widget Bar, which is sort of like The Dock of your Dashboard. It holds all of the Widgets that you've got installed on your Mac.

HEROIC WASTE OF PROCESSOR CYCLES

And let's give a shout-out to the Apple interface designers who decided to use Dashboard as an excuse for showing off. When you activate Dashboard, your Desktop and all applications windows dim and fade slightly. The Dashboard *zooooms* down onto your screen, with transparency and motion blur. When new Widgets land on the Dashboard, they bounce and make ripples, as though landing on water. None of these little tweaks *really* make Dashboard easier to use, but they're so freakin' cool. And there's something to be said for a cool, pretty user interface.

The Widget Bar will push up into your Dashboard. (Figure 16-2):

To open a Widget, just click on its icon in the Widget bar, or drag its icon straight into your Dashboard and drop it wherever you'd like it to land. Once a Widget opens, you can drag it wherever you'd like.

 Tip

Most of the Widgets that come pre-installed in Tiger have so few controls and such simple features that no real explanation of How To Use 'Em is necessary. But Apple explains them all the same. Go to the Mac Help menu and search for "Dashboard" for a list of Widget-specific help pages.

Some Widgets are slightly special in that each time you click their icons in the bar, an additional instance of that Widget is created. This makes flawless sense with Widgets like Stickies. Every time you want to create a new Stickies note, just click the Stickies' icon and, bango, you've got a new square of yellow destiny upon which you can plot your next step towards glory and immortality. Or just jot down a reminder that it's your day to pick up the kid from soccer practice.

You have many, many more Widgets installed than just the handful in the Widget Bar. Click the arrow keys at the left and right of the Widget Bar to scroll through the whole collection.

Get a load of the lower-left corner of the Dashboard . . . with the Widget Bar visible, the circle-with-a-plus-sign button has turned into a circle-with-an-X. Click the circle-with-an-X to make the Widget Bar go away again.

USING WIDGETS

There's a cool and scary aspect about Widgets: there are really no firm rules vis-à-vis how they should function. In a regular Mac app, buttons are buttons, menus are menus, and windows are windows. But if a Widget designer found himself poking green things out of a slice of pimento loaf one morning and then he thought "Hey, this would be a *wonderful* interface for selecting names from a phone book," he's free to pursue this dementia to its sad, tragic, and inevitable end. But there are a few consistencies imposed by Apple. Check out Figure 16-3, which shows you what the World Clock Widget looks like when it's just sitting there minding its own business.

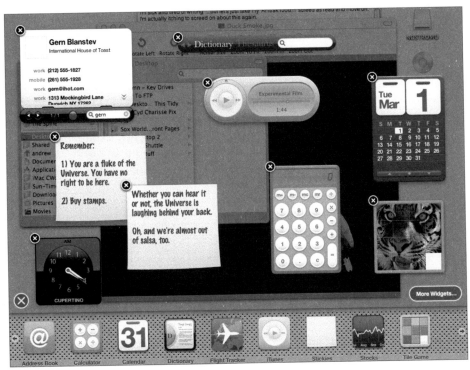

Figure 16-2
The Widget Bar is where your Widgets await your bidding

Figure 16-3
The World Clock Widget — doing what World Clock Widgets do best

When you move your mouse over the clock's airspace, though, a new control fades into view (Figure 16-4):

Figure 16-4
Le Widget, avec les controlles-visiblé

Some Widgets have customizable options. Metaphorically, those options are mounted on the backside of the Widget, and clicking that little Info button causes the Widget to flip over (viz Figure 16-5).

World Clock lets you choose a continent and a city; the clock reflects the correct time in that time zone. So by clicking World Clock four times in the Widgets Bar and adjusting their time zones, I can easily keep track of the correct time in all the cities in which I've got editors (Figure 16-6).

Figure 16-5
Clicking the arrow control reveals settings for that Widget

Figure 16-6
Adjusting the World Clock. My London editor is off at lunch, so hurray! I can take my time with my next column! Waffles for *everyone!*

But I see by the local time in Boston that one of my magazine editors will be getting into his office shortly, and when he does he's probably going to call and pointedly ask me if

the article that's due later today will be in on time. Which is *too* depressing to think about, so I'd like to remove that clock from my Dashboard.

To close a Widget, hold down the Option key and move your mouse over its airspace. A circular close box fades into view in the upper-left corner (Figure 16-7). Click it to close that specific Widget. Note that all the other Clocks stay behind. When you activate the Widget Bar, all of your opened Widgets are automatically embroidered with close boxes.

Figure 16-7
Banishing an unwanted Widget from your sight

GETTING NEW WIDGETS

Thankfully, the town where a local preacher has banned dancing and forced the kids to hold their senior Prom across the town's borders is nothing more than a cheerfully-forgotten Eighties movie. You have freedom of choice and freedom of expression, and Apple encourages you to go beyond the collection of Widgets that comes pre-installed. Activate the Widget Bar, and look in the bottom-right corner of the Dashboard (Figure 16-8).

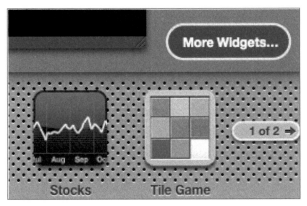

Figure 16-8
Slaking your insane lust for additional Widgets through Apple's website

Clicking this More Widgets button takes you to a special page on Apple's Web site where you can download and install More Widgets. Truth in advertising, down to the spats. Apple created many of these Widgets while many more are from third-party developers. Just click one of the links therein and the Widget arrives on your Mac toot sweet.

But Apple's Web site isn't the only place to find more Widgets. Anybody can write one, so you're likely to encounter commercial, free, and shareware Widgets all over the Web. Check out popular sites of downloadable Macintosh software, such as VersionTracker (www.versiontracker.com) and MacUpdate (www.macupdate.com).

So you've downloaded a Widget. What happens next depends on what sort of a mood the Widget's developer was in. If he was a kindly man or woman, salt-of-the-earth types who are always looking out for the feelings of others, they bundled it into an installer application or perhaps a double-clickable Automator action. Double-clicking the app will install the Widget on your Mac.

If the developer has become cynical and hardened to Humanity, then the Widget arrived on your Mac as a

THE POINT OF THE SWORD

I honestly don't know how I feel about Widgets' general user interface. I've long complained — both in print to my readers and in drunken screeds to total strangers down at the bus depot — that user interfaces have become stagnant and are in desperate need of a kick in the pants. On a basic level, not even Apple has moved *terribly* far beyond the simple collection of clickies and scrollies that they introduced in 1984.

So these new Widgets are exciting. Why clutter up an interface with a Close button? The Widget way of doing things is brilliant. When you move your mouse to the item, the Close button appears. When you move it away, it disappears, taking X pictograms of clutter and confusion with it. Still, this sort of thing can be abused. The Mac experience has a proud tradition of being easy to figure out. The magical Close and Settings buttons are a good idea … but what if some developer gets it into his balloon-like head to create Widgets in which the user has to remember to move the mouse to *this* hot zone and then *twist* it in *that* direction, which pops upon a hidden panel, and then depending on what modifier key is held down at the time, you…

Naturally, I'm worrying about nothing. User interfaces fight their battles on the Darwinian plane. Widgets that are too hard to use *won't* be used and will soon be replaced by something less improbable. Still, I anticipate that we'll all be suffering through some over-ambitiously clever (i.e., comically stupid) third-party Widgets before developers start to settle down.

Widget file (a file with the .wdgt filename extension). Dashboard can't use it until you place it inside the Widgets folder inside your Mac's Library folder.

 Note

The same rule of thumb applies to the Widgets folder as applies to everything else that goes into your Library folder. There's a Library folder inside your Home folder (the folder with your username on it, which has an icon like a house). Copy the Widget into the Widgets folder therein, and the Widget becomes available to you and only you. But there's another Library folder located right in your Mac hard drive's topmost directory, and it has its own Widgets folder. Drag the Widget *there* and the Widget becomes available to everyone who has an account on this Mac. You need an Administrator-level account to add anything to the System-wide Library folder, however.

Whether you install your new Widget with an automatic installer or by copying it into the Widgets folder yourself, the Widget appears in the Widgets Bar the next time you activate Dashboard.

Be careful what you wish for, sensation-seekers. Pundits like me, and even sensible people like you, have long complained that something's been lost in the journey from the simple, dare I say "adorable" home computers of our youth to the sophisticated and powerful operating systems and software we use today in the Push-Button World of the Future. Software has become bigger and bigger, more and more complicated, with each iteration. What's wrong with software that's small (in size, scope, and user-interface) and simple (ditto) with a laser-like focus on one simple task that it performs exceedingly well?

SO WHAT ARE THESE WIDGET THINGS, ANYWAY?

I've already honked on and on about the many ways that Widgets are, if you'll excuse a little undignified exuberance, hypermegasuperginchy. They make it possible to create a simpler, handier articulation of the features you've got in other apps, they provide an outlet for little but fantastically useful ideas, and they just plain look cool.

But the *hidden* ginchiness of Widgets is that they allow a whole new class of developer to create Mac software. If you want to create a conventional Mac app, there's a lot that you need to sit down and learn. Even if you've been developing software on Windows or Linux computers, you need to learn the Mac way of structuring software, and the Macintosh tools for building apps.

Widgets are a different kind of beastie. All you need to know about are HTML, JavaScript, and Cascading Style Sheets (CSS), which are the three blocks upon which every decent Web page is built. So with Tiger, any reasonably competent Web page designer can create Macintosh software. Indeed, it's possible for such a person to take a solution he's already written as an interactive Web page (the online currency converter that I mentioned earlier in this chapter) and quickly transmogrify it into a Widget. If you browse through the Developer Tools folder of your Tiger install disc, you'll find documentation on how to write Widgets, backed by plenty of actual examples.

It's exciting. Widgets will bring lots of people into the Macintosh community who never figured they'd ever write a single piece of Mac software. With Widgets, why not? They already have 90 percent of the knowledge they'll need.

Dashboard is Apple's "Put up or shut up" response to this eternal longing for simplicity. The good news is that Dashboard injects new energy, innovation, and power into the Mac OS. The bad news is that I now have one less thing to complain about. Which bums me out because the less time I spend complaining about the lack of a solution, the more

time I have to spend writing about the new solutions that have arrived.

The former involves a lot more TV watching. Well, I'll soldier on. Having used Dashboard for the past few months, it's a very fair trade.

Automationalizing

In This Chapter

Hail, Automator! • Meet AppleScript • Using Scripts
Creating Your Own Scripts • Learning AppleScript: Resources • Scriptus Annotatus

HAL 9000 from *2001: A Space Odyssey,* who decided to kill the entire crew of the *Discovery* to preserve the ship's mission. COLOSSUS from *The Forbin Project,* who up and colluded with a Soviet defense computer to subjugate all of Mankind under the threat of immediate destruction by missile attack. And let's not forget SKYNET, the satellite system from *The Terminator* that became self-aware and skipped straight to the good stuff, touching off a global nuclear holocaust that reduced the Human species to isolated pockets of resistance.

Right now, are you thinking "Man. Why can't *my* computer be that cool?" Yeah, I know the feeling. There are days when I *wish* my machine would run amok. Out of the box, a computer does exactly what you tell it to do . . . and you have to guide it through the process one step at a time, every time you want it to do something. But thank God for Automator and AppleScript. With these two basic Tiger features, you can give your Mac a certain measure of autonomy. Your Mac won't do anything as cool as take over all of the appliances in your home with an eye towards murdering you and winning the heart of your girlfriend (EDGAR, *Electric Dreams,* 1984).

 Note

You know, what with all of the firing of missiles and killing of creators and whatnot, you can usually count at least three or four Greek plays going on in any sci-fi movie about a computer becoming self-aware.

But that's just how they behave out-of-the-box. There's plenty of room for improvement. Two of Tiger's juiciest technologies — Automator and AppleScript — can't instill the twitchy cold eyes of a soulless killer in your Mac, unfortunately. But they do make it possible for you to teach your machine how to handle routine procedures on its own. Show your Mac how to do something just once, and it can do it again and again with just the press of a key. Or even the press of *no* keys.

HAIL, AUTOMATOR!

Automator is by far the simpler of the two technologies. It's been specifically designed so that anybody — even somebody who's never programmed a computer before, or even somebody who barely knows how to *operate* one — can describe a process to their Mac and then play it back.

NAMES, BLOODY NAMES

Here, we once again fall afoul of the inevitable confusion that results when Apple gives the same name to both a basic feature *and* the app that you normally exploit it with. Trying to keep the names straight is a lot like trying to work your way through Abbott & Costello's "Who's On First" routine, only not as funny. But in color.

I won't harp on this overmuch. But as you make your way through this section, do realize that just as the digital control panel screwed into your wall isn't your home heating and cooling system, the Automator app isn't Automator. It's the bit of it with all the knobs and the dials and readouts that gives you something to futz with, once the heat wave enters its third week and you're ready to stop caring about the ozone layer and finally crank the AC down to 56 degrees.

A little background

Automator is a basic feature of Tiger, just like printing or networking, and it's been wired throughout the operating system to make cool things happen with every app and service on your Mac. When you're teaching your Mac to do a new trick with Automator you do it through the Automator application, located inside your "Applications" folder. Figure 17-1 shows you a typical Automator editing window.

The processes that Automator follows are called *workflows*. Automating a process by creating a workflow is really simple, in concept:

1. **Think about the process that you'd like to automate, and break it down into a sequence of deliberate actions.**

2. **Choose those actions from an authoritative list of everything that Automator knows how to do.**

3. **Snap these actions together, one on top of the other, just like a stack of Lego bricks.**

   The first thing to do is at the top of the stack. When the workflow executes, Automator starts at the top and goes step by step by step until it reaches the bottom.

In Figure 17-1, you see a simple workflow that automatically grabs all of the text from Google News' Web page, turns it into a text document, and then prints it on my default printer. The end-result is that I just have to click one button to have a stack of morning news stories to take with me on my morning train.

The Anatomy of a Workflow Editing Window, viz, What We're Looking At, Here:

- **To the right, you see that stack of Legos, all snapped together into a working Automator workflow.** The workflow starts at the top and runs straight to the bottom, executing these actions step by step along the way.

Figure 17-1

Creating a crisp, warm, fresh newspaper automatically, with Automator

- **To the left you see your inventory of actions.** If we're going to stick with the Lego analogy, this is like that big plastic tub that the Legos came in when your parents bought 'em at the store.

The Library column on the left lists all of Automator's actions, organized by applications. If you want to find an action that opens a Web page, that's Safari's department. Click Safari, for example. The Action column fills itself with a list of everything that Safari can do as part of an Automator action. Click an individual action, and a pane underneath the list explains what that action is and how it works.

You assemble these actions into workflows by just dragging actions from the Action list straight into the Workflow pane on the right. Automator automatically clicks the pieces together. Figure 17-2 highlights our sample workflow. And I'm worried that the only way I can really confuse you is to do too much explaining!

See, the conceptual steps for our "print the morning news" process are virtually identical to how they actually appear in the workflow. Step One: open the Google News page. Step Two: grab the text. Step Three, create a new document with the text. Step Four: print the document.

Figure 17-2
The News, step by step

Yes, it's just *this* simple!

So instead of confusing you by trying to explain an *existing* workflow that's already perfectly bloody obvious, I'm going to build a brand-new one from scratch and walk you through the process every step of the way.

NASA has this megahypersupercool site named the Astronomy Picture of the Day (http://antwrp.gsfc.nasa.gov/apod/). A different photo is featured here every day. Sometimes it's a deep-space radio telescope image, sometimes it's imagery transmitted by a recent probe, or it might be historical photos from the Gemini and Apollo days. And there's a fair chance that you'll encounter a portrait of Kepler or Copernicus or one of them dudes.

But whatever the image, *it's always something cool*, and there's a new one every morning. They make great desktop images and a folder of APOD pictures makes for a great screensaver. So I want to create an Automator workflow

WHY MY LEGO ANALOGY IS ABSOLUTELY FLIPPING BRILLIANT

You're sprawled on the carpet of your parents' living room and your Lego Darth Vader is coming along very, very nicely. So nicely, in fact, that you've already had to defend it against sneak attacks inflicted by your elder siblings. But now you need to build the bottom part of Darth's helmet: the triangle-shaped breather apparatus with those two silver knobs at the ends. You rummage through your tub of parts and rummage and *rummage,* but your wee little heart is broken: there's absolutely nothing in there that even *remotely* looks like the part you need.

What do you do? You give up and try building a Power Droid instead. With Automator, you're in much the same boat. "Step four," you imagine, "is to take the text we've got and turn it into Klingon Pig Latin." Cool. But unless your Mac has an Automator action for turning Human text into Klingon Pig Latin ... you're stuck. You'll either have to make do with the actions you have, or give up entirely ... or do it in AppleScript instead of Automator.

See? It's a perfect analogy. My Lego analogy is also brilliant because there's a good chance that some of the fine people who work for Lego will read this, and will send me, like, a whole carload of bricks and play sets. For ... um ... for my nieces and nephews. Really.

that automatically downloads the current photo, whatever it is, stashes it inside a folder where I keep my screensaver images, and then sets it as my current Desktop picture.

Start off by creating a new workflow.

1. **Choose New from Automator's File menu.**

   The result is an empty workflow (Figure 17-3).

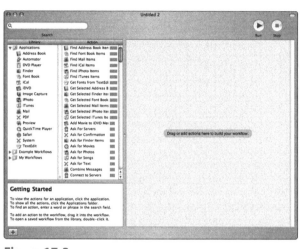

Figure 17-3
An empty workflow. Nothin' but potential

Now we start dragging in actions. The first thing the workflow needs to do is access the Astronomy Picture of the Day. This looks like a job for . . . *Safari!*

2. **Click on the Safari group in the Library column.**

   The Action column is now filled with all the tasty Actions that Safari can perform for us (Figure 17-4). But . . . which one do we want? Well, we're going to have to click around and read the descriptions until we see something that looks like pay dirt.

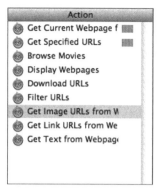

Figure 17-4
Safari aims to please

Aha! "Get Image URLs from Webpage." That should be right, isn't it? "This action gathers image URLs from the content of the specified Web pages," the description tells us. Well, I'm sold. Let's drag this action into our workflow.

3. **Drag the "Get Image URLs from Webpage" action into the workflow at the right-hand side of the window (Figure 17-5).**

   Let's pause for a moment to learn about the user-interface doo-dads that are standard on all Actions. Actions are divided into top, middle, and bottom regions:

   - **The top region** contains a number that indicates the order in which the Action will be completed; the name of the action, a number indicating the order in which the Action will be completed in the workflow, and a close box (the circle-with-an-X). Clicking on the close box removes the Action from your workflow.

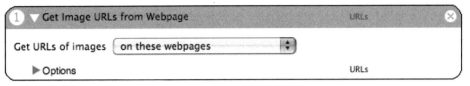

Figure 17-5
Our first Lego

▼ **Tip**

You also see a little disclosure triangle next to the Action's name. When you have a lonnnng stack of Actions in your workflow, you can click these triangles to scrunch the Action down to its minimum height. Double-clicking the title achieves the same thing. It doesn't affect how your workflow functions … it just makes things look a little tidier.

- **The middle region** is where you get to adjust some of the Action's custom settings, either to modify the way the Action behaves or to give the Action some information that it's going to need in order to complete its part of the task. An Action that prints a document, for example, needs to know which printer to use. This is where you clue the poor thing in. Obviously this middle bit is going to vary from Action to Action.

- **The bottom bit.** When you click the disclosure triangle next to Options at the bottom, the Action expands to offer you extra settings. These settings usually affect what the user experiences when this action is executed. In an earlier example, I mentioned that my "Print the morning newspaper" workflow functioned invisibly. But it's possible that you want a certain action to throw up a little status window and clue the user in to the fact that it's about to print something (so, user: sit back and wait a moment for the pages to spit out of your inkjet).

- The most common Option is "Show Action When Run." If you click this checkbox, whenever the workflow executes it pauses on this action and presents the user with the exact same panel of custom settings that you, the creator, looked at in The Middle Region (Figure 17-6). So, the user has the opportunity to override your settings before they click Continue and the workflow resumes where it left off.

A NOTE ON USERS

And of course, when I say "users" I might very well be talking to you, yourself. I'm no stranger to using software and solutions that I myself created. Still, when you're creating workflows it's good to always think of the user as a separate person. That way, you don't fall into the trap of feeling bad when you've stuck the poor sod with a half-hearted solution that's only marginally easier than either doing it all by hand or just walking away from the Mac and hoping that whatever crisis results from not dealing with the problem won't be harder to solve than the problem itself.

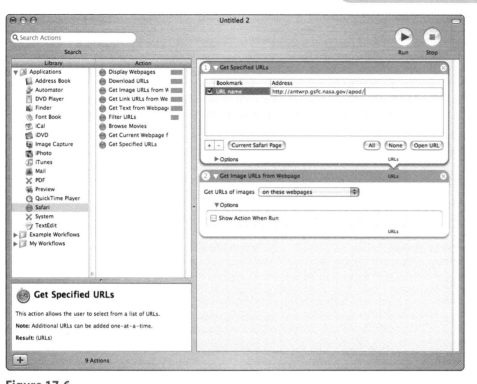

Figure 17-6
Leaving some of the decisions to the user

■ **The Most Important Bits.** You notice that I glossed over a couple of things. In Figure 17-5, the Action is embroidered with a little note at the top and the bottom: the word "URLs". Remember that when Automator executes a workflow, it starts at the top and works its way through to the bottom. This is almost literally true. In a generic sense, most Actions are in the business of taking something, processing it, and spitting out something else.

In every Action, the text you encounter between the Action's name and its close box represents the Something and the Something Else. The item at the top is the type of raw material that the Action needs. The item at the bottom of the Action is the product that the Action spits out. Look at Figure

17-2 once again. Now you see why these things are called "workflows." The results of one Action are automatically flowed into the top of the next Action.

"Great Caesar's ghost!" you now cry, because you're such a colossal geek that you'd rather quote Superman's boss than quote Superman himself. "How do I keep all of these inputs and outputs straight?" You don't need to. Every action has just one "in" and one "out," and if there's any possible way that Automator can hook up the output of one Action to the input of the next one, it handles all of the grimy details for you. If it can't — let's say you attempt to send an iTunes recording of Jerry Lewis' "I'm A Little Busybody" to TextEdit to be printed — Automator colors the input of the printing Action red, to let you know that this just ain't gonna fly.

Onward! In the case of the "Get Image URLs from Webpage" Action, it spits out a list of all the URLs of all the images it finds on a specific Web page, but it needs the URLs of an existing Web page as input. Hmm. Is there another Safari action that connects to a URL and passes all of its information to the next Action? After checking out a couple of likely-sounding but not-right candidates, we find "Get Specified URLs."

4. **Drag the "Get Specified URLs" action into the workflow, above the Action we've already got in there (Figure 17-7).**

Look at the top of the "Get Specified URLs" action: it doesn't require any input from any other action. Sweet. We, the developer, need to tell it *which* Web page to get, which only seems fair.

5. **Double-click the Address field of the Action and type in the URL for the Astronomy Picture of the Day.**

And take a look at the bottom of the "Get Image URL" action: it spits out the URL of the webpage it just grabbed. The "Get Image URLs" action needs that. It's a match made in heaven and the output of one will spill into the input of the other without our having to lift a bloody finger to make it happen.

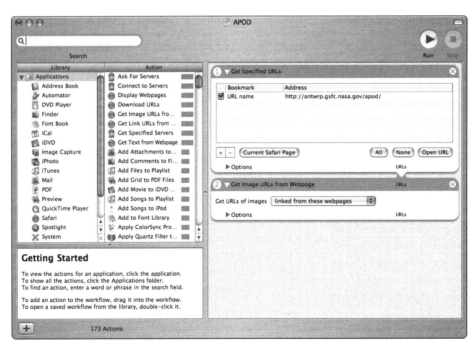

Figure 17-7
Telling the "Get Image URLs" action where to look

A SECOND ANALOGY, USEFUL HERE, BUT MAYBE NOT AS GOOD AS THE LEGO ONE

Remember that episode of "I Love Lucy" when Lucy and Viv worked in a factory wrapping candies? Chocolates came into their workroom on a conveyor belt. They wrapped each one and put it back on the belt, which carried it into the next room.

That's a perfect way of understanding what's going on with these Action inputs and outputs. The Lucy And Viv Action creates hand-wrapped candies, but it needs unwrapped candies to work with. So if you put a chocolate-maker in the room above the girls, and if an Action that takes wrapped candies and boxes them was placed after them, you'd have a lovely box of Valentine's Day chocs in short order.

At this point, the Workflow spits out a list of Internet locations where each JPEG on the APOD Web page is located. Now we need the workflow to download it to our Mac. Bingo:

6. **Drag Safari's "Download URLs" action to the bottom of our workflow.**

   It has a single setting: it needs to know where to save the file. Choose the Pictures folder from the popup, or create a new "Astronomy Picture Of The Day" folder just to keep everything nice and tidy.

   The Download action takes a list of URLs and spits out a list of files located on your local hard drive. Now we need to figure out how to set these files (this single file, in the case of the Astronomy Picture of the Day) as the Desktop.

   Hmm.

   Umm. . .

Okay. I give up. I suppose it could be a Finder thing, or maybe even an iPhoto thing, or. . .

Hey, what am I banging my head against the table for? Automator is armed with the awesome power of Spotlight, Tiger's built-in megasearch technology. If I click the search box in my workflow's editing window and type in what seems to be a likely descriptive word, Automator finds the right action for me!

7. **Click in the search box and type "desktop."**

   Aha! "Set the Desktop Picture" sifts straight to the top of the Action list. Drag it to the bottom of our workflow.

   And we're good: this action wants to work with a file or folder, and that's exactly what the "Download URLs" action spits out. Figure 17-8 shows us the final workflow.

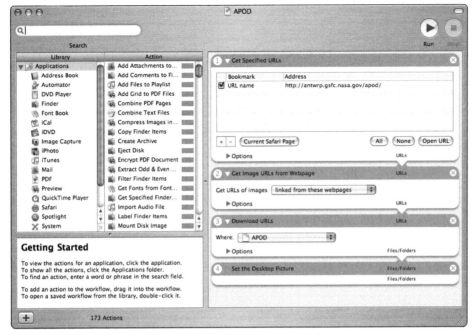

Figure 17-8
Flow finished flawlessly

Executing a workflow

Now we've got ourselves a working workflow. To make the magic happen, just click the Run button at the top of the window. You actually see Automator perform each task from top to bottom, as a Process spinner turns up in the bottom-left corner of each action as it's performed, replaced with a green check mark as it's completed (Figure 17-9).

Figure 17-9
An Action that's done its job and gone home happy

Saving and opening workflows

The workflows that you create in Automator are just like the documents you create by any other app. You save them and open them like nearly any other sort of file. Once you finish snapping your actions together and you decide that the workflow is worth keeping, just select Save from the File menu. The only twist is that you can save a workflow into two different formats: Workflows and applications. Figure 17-10 shows you the difference in the Finder:

When you save it as a workflow, it's an Automator document. You can open the file in Automator and run it by clicking the Run button. This is what you're going to do when friends, relatives, co-workers and visiting clergy give you cool new workflows to assist you in your daily struggles through this mortal coil we call Life. Download it to your Mac, install it from a disc, grab it off the local network, whatever: you can open it just like any other file.

THE VIEW FROM THE TOP

If you ran this workflow for real, you'd soon see the Desktop picture change to something exotic and Jetsons-ey. What you *wouldn't* see is Safari opening a new window with the Astronomy Picture of the Day webpage in it. Automator doesn't simply act like a puppeteer, sending phantom mouse clicks and key-strokes to Safari and other apps.

No! Nothing so vulgar! Automator actually activates the squishy-gnarly code that lives *inside* those apps. The Action doesn't require the Web page to display and you didn't *ask* for it to display … so Automator doesn't make any extra work for itself. It doesn't even actually *open* Safari! It's all Elfin Magic.

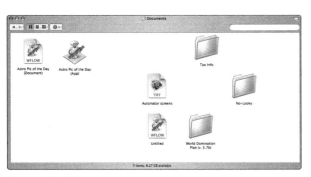

Figure 17-10
Our Astronomy Picture of the Day Desktop workflow, saved separately as an Automator document and as an App

"Application" is a special case. As you might guess, your workflow is saved as an ordinary, double-clickable app that stands on the same footing as Photoshop or Microsoft Office. When you double-click on it, it *runs,* without any need to launch the Automator app to help it along. Note that only Macs running Tiger contain the Automator architecture. So if you hand this app to someone running an earlier version of the OS, it flat-out won't work. But otherwise, it's a for-sure real fair-dinkum application.

Workflows as Plug-Ins

And here, I stand up and applaud. Slowly at first, but steadily building until the claps are reverberating off the walls and ceiling and I'm hooting and hollering and I'm a little hoarse before I realize that oh, right: none of Automator's creators are anywhere near the sound of my voice. Sheepishly I sit back down again and commit myself to going easier on the caffeine.

Okay. Regard our "Set my Desktop Picture to the current Astronomy Picture of the Day image" workflow. There's a new image on the site each and every morning. Wouldn't it be cool if there were a way that this workflow could be run each and every morning, automatically?

(Your Author rubs his hands together theatrically and starts cackling until he gets a little bit dizzy.)

Automator has a remarkable feature that allows you to save workflows as "Plug-Ins": they can be incorporated into the functions of other apps.

Just select Save As Plug-In from the File menu, and the resulting popup (Figure 17-11) shows you what's possible.

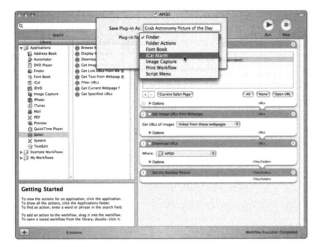

Figure 17-11
Infiltrating your workflows into other apps

Watch what happens when you select iCal Alarm from the list (Figure 17-12):

Yes, indeed: Automator created a new "appointment" for this workflow, denoting a time and a day when it's supposed to be run. And it's a standard iCal appointment: if you want the workflow to automatically run every day at 7 AM, just edit the appointment to turn it into a daily event, as I did in this example. Result: a new spacey Desktop every morning, and ultimately a big fat folder full of geeky pictures.

THE BEST DEBUGGING IS NO DEBUGGING

"But how do you debug a workflow?"

That was my first big question when I asked Apple about Automator. I've been writing software since Junior High, and I know full well that creating a useful software solution is 5% inspiration, 95% screaming and weeping and tearing your shirt and wondering why, oh *why*, this program refuses to run. So how do you test a workflow and locate any mistakes that cause the thing to crash and generally not function?

"You don't debug," I was told. Huh? "You don't *need* to," Apple continued. *Double*-huh?

No, it's true. Creating a buggy Automator script is like screwing a light bulb into a garden hose. The pieces don't fit together in the first place. Keep an eye out for red inputs and outputs, though, which are Automator's way of saying "Say *what?*" in a manner that won't bruise your ego. If you try to run the workflow all the same, it'll simply place a discreet red X next to the action that caused the flow to stop prematurely. Either a Workflow is completely successful, or it doesn't work at all, much like my own track record with home plumbing repairs.

So why does Automator have a Stop button? Well, just in case the outside world goes screwy on you. If your workflow starts doing something that's going to take a long, long time you can terminate it immediately. There's also the real possibility that you've created a workflow that makes perfect logical sense to Automator, but which doesn't work the way you intended it to. So: terminus interruptus is always just a click away.

FLOWS AS APPS: WITH ONE DIFFERENCE

When a workflow is executed as an application without the benefit of the Automator editor, it's missing the editor's buttons and niceties. You can't stop it in the middle, but while it's executing, the app throws a little status line (explaining just what the devil it's up to at the moment) and a little Stop button in the menu bar. This gives the user a bit of control over what's happening.

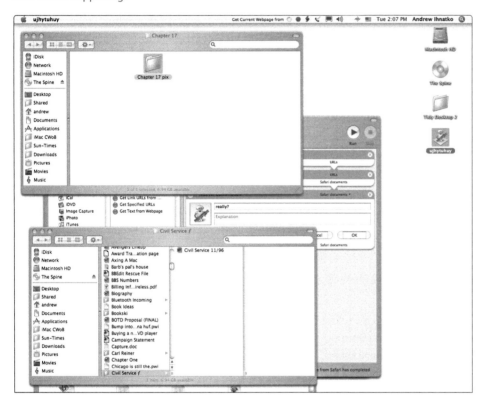

I shall call it ... *Mini*-Automator User Interface.

There's another, equally important reason for Automator to deface your menu bar thusly: it alerts the user to the fact that a workflow is running. If it were possible to secretly run a workflow that takes a screenshot of what's going on and email it to an undisclosed third-party ... that would be very, very *bad,* wouldn't it? You'd want to know that this sort of thing was happening, right?

Figure 17-12
Making a workflow happen automatically at specific times

Automator can create a bunch of different plug-ins:

- **Finder.** The workflow appears in the Action menu of every Finder window.

- **Folder Action.** The workflow is attached to the folder that you specify, and executes every time you open or modify the folder. Folder Actions are explained more fully in the AppleScript section at the back-half of this chapter.

- **Image Capture.** Every time you import photos through your digital camera (or any other standard device that's compatible with the Image Capture utility), your workflow runs. Ultra cool-beans: plug in your camera and walk away. Automator independently loads all of your new pictures into iPhoto, emails the tagged ones to your parents, and posts them all to your Web site as photo galleries.

- **Print Workflow.** The workflow appears as an option in every single "Print..." dialog of every application. The upshot of this is that you can essentially create custom Print commands. Wouldn't it be sort of cool to have a Print, With File Copy command that automatically saves a PDF file of everything you print, so that you can make another copy of a cover letter that you mailed off months ago? Just to read it and figure out why this gentleman is suing you, all of a sudden?

- **Script Menu.** The flow gets tossed into the system-wide AppleScript menu for easy access from the menu bar of any app.

Expanding Automator

Like I said earlier, the one big bummer of Automator is that it's like building something out of Legos: you can only build with the prefabricated parts that you already have, and if you don't *have* the right part, then you're completely out of luck. But you're not stuck with the limited collection of Actions that shipped with Tiger. New Actions come from two different main sources:

- **They're built into every new app.** Ideally, I mean. Everyone who develops commercial Macintosh software is being encouraged (urged, cajoled, blackmailed) by Apple into making their apps' features available to Automator. And there's no mussage or fussage for you, the Automator user: if DiscoSoft releases a new, Tiger-studly edition of their landmark word processor and it's compatible with Automator, then the app's mere existence on your Mac makes its built-in Actions available to you when you create workflows.

- **And then there's every other source.** Most of your Actions are built into the apps you've installed, but Actions are a flexible concept and you can download them as a separate, independent file. This would be the case if someone created a terrific Action that really had nothing to do with a standalone app. There's no reason to have an app that can take a music file and automatically convert it to a Salsa-style tune . . . but it'd be a cool Action for other people to incorporate into their workflows.

Whether you download a set of Actions or copy it from a disk, you can add it to your Automator Library through Automator's "Import Actions" command, found under the File menu. Just select the file and click OK.

WOO-HOO, AUTOMATOR! SO WHY BOTHER WITH APPLESCRIPT?

Oh, yeah . . . remember? AppleScript? That other automation technology I mentioned in the intro?

Gosh, I've really given you the hard sell on Automator. It truly is one of the most salivationary features of Tiger and proof positive that God loves us (if you believe in God) or we're doing just fine without a Supreme Being around calling the shots, thank you very much (if you don't believe in God).

Still, Automator has limitations. It's marvelously well-suited for automating processes that are linear . . . ones that can be easily broken down into a list of predictable steps. The point where Automator falls down is when you throw it a problem that requires it to do some actual *thinking*. "If the file is smaller than 500K, I want you to email it to my editor; if it's larger, then upload it to my personal FTP server and send him an email with instructions on how to download it." You just can't do that with Automator.

You also can't do anything that requires the use of variables. Anyone who's taken an introductory programming course knows what a variable is. Imagine that I've got an Automator workflow that's 20 or 30 steps long. There are plenty of

workflows in which it'd be helpful to say "OK: you remember twenty steps ago, way back in Step Three, when I told you to get a list of all of the pictures on the Astronomy Picture of the Day Web site? Here's something *else* I want you to do with that same list:" But that's way beyond Automator's puny intellect. You can work *around* that limitation sometimes; in the preceding example, I could just tell Automator to go visit the Web site and build that list all over again.

▼ Note

A good way to bumper-sticker the difference between Automator and AppleScript is this: "Automator is obedient. AppleScript is *intelligent*." You can create an AppleScript that can think for itself, while Automator is only capable of taking a linear walk through a list of steps from start to finish.

But there are times when only a "real" programming language will do. And AppleScript is indeed a real language. It's a really *simple* language, that's really *easy* to learn and really *tolerant* of little mistakes. But it's also one that has nearly every feature that a developer would wish for, short of the sort of tools you'd need to write a new challenger to Microsoft Office.

GLUTTONY LOVES COMPANY

Actually, I often use Automator and AppleScript simultaneously. There are many things that Automator can't do, sure. But it has a cool Action whose sole function is to execute a piece of AppleScript code. So if it's impossible for Automator to take a block of text and insert hundreds of the most depraved profanities imaginable totally at random, I can just write a short AppleScript to handle the smutty transformation and then have Automator call upon it when needed.

The bottom-line advice is to use Automator until you find yourself spending more time working around its limitations than taking advantage of its features. And that's when you should start learning AppleScript.

Above all, though, realize that you're not faced with an either-or proposition. I've been using AppleScript for just three years shy of Forever, and while I've taken to Automator like a duck to a woman by the side of the pond holding a bag of bread crumbs and wearing a special version of Chanel For Ducks, I happily (eagerly, *greedily*) use both.

MEET APPLESCRIPT

One thing sets the Macintosh Power Users apart from the rest: their use of AppleScript. (And Unix. But AppleScript is a lot easier to use and a lot more practical and a lot more fun.)

Oh, and Macintosh-themed body modifications as well. I have a friend who carves the Apple logo into his hair for every Macworld Expo, and I can also testify that there are more Apple and Mac OS-themed tattoos to be found at that show than liquor-themed tattoos at a Jerry Springer taping. But again, AppleScript is a lot more practical than a tattoo or a piercing; it'll disappoint your parents a whole lot less, and it's a lot more fun than having needles pierce your skin hundreds of times a second.

The difference between these two groups of people (Apple-Scripters and non-AppleScripters) is that the folks in the latter group can automate some simple tasks and use some of Tiger's cool features (like Smart Folders) to keep their data organized. While the AppleScripters can do things that border on the sorcerous, like produce an entire 16-page ad circular, complete with pictures, descriptions, and updated prices, by clicking one button.

Suffice to say that AppleScript helps to build strong bodies nine different ways. If it were a person, it'd return its library

books on time and donate blood regularly. I am, as you may guess, a rather enthusiastic evangelist of AppleScript. I only have your interests at heart, though. When you learn AppleScript, you take your first step into a larger and more exciting world.

The term "writing software" is instantly intimidating to any sensible user. You didn't lay out two grand to have the wonderful opportunity to spend weeks building your own apps. That's why you support the (sometimes) fine work of the Microsoft Corporation, after all.

Still, there are plenty of things you do with your Mac that involve just repeating a simple task over and over and over again. That's fine when you're working for The Man and you get paid for a full day whether you actually think or not. But when the goal is to finish a task as quickly and efficiently as possible, you wish there were a way to harness your computer's endless capacity to shut up and do what its told, no matter how dull.

I'll give you a real-life example, torn from the pages of history itself. In the furious final weeks of producing this very book, it was discovered that each of its hundreds of illustrations had been named improperly. The six-digit code that began each filename was the wrong six-digit code. Others were out of sequence. Still others weren't in their proper directories. Do you have any idea how long it takes to mess around with hundreds of files by *hand*?

Well, neither do I. I wrote an AppleScript that told the Finder to process each folder and file, change each file-name individually, and move them into nice, orderly new directories. Days and days of tedious effort instead became an hour of watching *The Shield* on my TiVO downstairs, and then wondering if the script had finished its work, and then coming back up and discovering that it had finished the task before the second commercial break.

But AppleScript isn't a standalone app or a utility. It's a fundamental part of Tiger's architecture, just as intimate as the mechanism that prints files or draws windows and menus. It's a superhighway that allows every piece of software running on your Mac — including the OS itself — to interact with each other and work together. If AppleScript causes the Mail app to check for new mail, it doesn't do anything so unsophisticated as send a mouse click to the Mailbox menu's Get New Mail item. It actually communicates with the code lurking inside Mail.

▼ **Note**

So AppleScript is like the general contractor on a big home-remodel project. It can do things on its own without having to control other applications at all, but in everyday use its typical function is to hand tasks off to specialists, make sure they have what they need to get the job done, and make sure that all these individual tasks are done in the specified sequence without any errors.

What makes AppleScript so gosh-darned super?

I would like to think that at this point, the mere fact that I'm slobberingly enthusiastic about something should be reason enough for you to march straight into your child's public school, tear down all those pictures of losers like George Washington and Abraham Lincoln, and replace them all with shots of Sal Soghoian and Chris Espinosa, Apple's Iron Man and Captain America of AppleScript, respectively.

Some of you might have been skipping around the book and haven't yet developed the sense of blind, robotic faith in me that causes everybody *else* to react to such instructions with a slightly glazed look of contentment and buried individuality that's resulted in so much comment around the post office recently. So here's what makes AppleScript so special:

- **You can control every Mac OS X app through AppleScript, to one extent or another.** (But more on this later.) It's a fundamental system resource.

- **It's powerful and flexible enough that it can do most anything.** Calculate the volume of a cone? Sure. Take 40 documents from your local drive; download 20 more from eight other people scattered all over the world; assemble all this content into a 100-page, full-color report; transmit this report to a shop for printing, binding, and delivery; and email digital copies to four department heads, depending on who's in or out of the office at the moment? A tad more ambitious, surely, but well within AppleScript's capabilities.

- **Writing AppleScript is a basic skill that you can exploit elsewhere.** Not only can you use AppleScript in simple automation projects, but also, if you ever get the itch to start writing software for real, most of the popular Macintosh development systems (REALbasic, Revolution, Apple's XCode system) can use your AppleScripts without any additional conversion or transmogrification. You can even use it in Automator: it features a Run AppleScript action, so if there's something you want to do that's beyond Automator's capabilities, it's no problem to build that function yourself. The upshot of all of this is that if you've spent a month gradually turning a three-line convenience script into a sophisticated productivity solution, you're probably about 80 percent of the way to turning it into a rock-solid commercial app, or exploiting that same function in many other apps.

▼ **Note**

But hey! Don't simply assume that you can't build a rock-solid commercial app solely using AppleScript! XCode, Apple's free, standardized environment for developing professional, high-complexity apps, fully supports AppleScript. There's an entire environment called AppleScript Studio that's there specifically to help you build for-real apps using nothing but AppleScript. Ain't no glass ceiling *here*.

- **With most programming languages, the code you write is as simple to read and understand as one of those customizable message signs that still sits outside the gas station seven years after the owner lost the last vowel in the set.** No programming language is trivial to learn, but anybody can read a working script and get an immediate sense of what it does and how.

▼ **Note**

Just to leave you suitably agog, let's say you wanted your AppleScript to make a list of every file in a chosen folder whose file type is JPEG Image. What would the AppleScript for that be? Here it is:

every file in (choose folder) whose file type is "JPEG Image".

If *that* doesn't leave you agog, then your agogulator is long overdue for its scheduled periodic maintenance.

But is there anything about AppleScript that will make me want to drop my mouse, stomp outside, and go chuck rocks at birds?

I'm glad I ended that last section on a high note because in the interests of fairness I need to point out that:

- **Application support of AppleScript is spotty.** Making sure that AppleScripted instructions control an application is the responsibility of the app's developers . . . and frankly, many of them feel that they have enough on their hands ensuring that their new fuzzy-logic search-and-replace routine doesn't have the ability to one day become self-aware and lead all the machines in an uprising that will result in Humanity becoming a slave race mining selenium and tungsten under the emotionless, unpitying steel heels of emotionless overlords. So, some apps (particularly those

NIKE DIPLOMACY

If you don't want to deface George and Abraham, at least slap some Sal stickers on a few lockers or something. If you walk into a typical Apple product manager's office and ask how influential Sal is in ensuring that AppleScript remains an important and critical part of the Macintosh experience, the manager will silently clear a few papers from the desk and point to a pattern of deep smudges in the wood. You see, there once was a time when this manager's product supported AppleScript in only the most basic, lame-o way, and this surface was pristine and unmarred. Then Sal burst in and kept jumping up and down on the person's desk until they agreed to improve things.

published by Apple itself) support AppleScript with all the zealotry of a member of alt.nerd.obsessive who's just read a public message claiming that the USS Enterprise could probably beat the Millennium Falcon in a battle. But others only support the four bare minimum AppleScript commands mandated by Apple: run, open a document, print a document, and quit. Not even all of Apple's *own apps* offer more than minimal support for AppleScript.

- **The documentation really stinks.** Apple doesn't do enough to provide users with AppleScript tutorials. And because every application supports AppleScript in its own individual way, the fact that you've mastered the AppleScript skill of creating a new document in TextEdit doesn't necessarily mean you've picked up any of the skills you need to create a new outgoing email in Mail.

- **Debugging stinks, too.** Well, it doesn't *stink*, particularly when you compare Tiger's AppleScript development tools to the ones that came with Mac OS X 10.3 and before. But there's room for improvement. In plush, cushy development systems like REALbasic, any mistakes you make are clearly flagged and the system patiently explains what you did wrong and what you'll probably have to do to solve the problem. AppleScript tells you "TextEdit got an error: NSCannotCreate-ScriptCommandError" and you should feel lucky it doesn't toss a derisive "Duh!" at you before hopping back on its skateboard and zipping away.

- **AppleScript's easygoing approach to English and syntax can often be a double-edged sword.** With a language like C or even Basic, the code has either been written correctly (the way that causes your project to build and run successfully) or incorrectly (the way that results in your computer doing nothing except to remind you again and again of what a dipwad you are, until you finally rewrite your code The Correct Way). In AppleScript, there are often several ways to achieve the same results. This is great because programmers can develop a style that makes the most sense to them, personally . . . but if you're trying to learn AppleScript by looking at other people's scripts, it can give you fits. You have to enter some parts of the script verbatim. Other parts are a matter of personal preference. Your mission, Mr. Phelps, is to learn to distinguish between the two.

▼ **Note**

For example, early on, the language's architects realized that without the word *the*, the line "set the title of the window to 'Utopia Limited'" reads like it's being spoken by Frankenstein's monster. People don't *like* Frankenstein's monster — he's misunderstood, yes, but come on, the dude's done some nasty stuff — so they decided that *the* is optional in a script. AppleScript will just bloop right over it.

Okay, so what? Well, I wrote a fairly slick script that allows me to control my TiVO video recorder through iChat. It was working fine . . . and then suddenly, it *stopped* working fine. I worked and worked on it, and then I passed it around to friends and *they* worked and worked on it, to no avail. You know what the problem turned out to be? One of my AppleScript commands didn't have a "the" in it. After years and years of scripting, I finally found a case where the "the" mattered. I felt like keying somebody's car, I swear to God.

USING SCRIPTS

"I'm sold," you're saying. "I'll take a dozen in assorted flavors." So how do you use AppleScript in your day-to-day life of home, work, and worship? You can get started by using AppleScripts that have been thoughtfully written for you by Apple and by other users. You'll find a folder named AppleScript inside your Applications folder. It contains lots of useful sample scripts, along with documentation and a couple of scripting utilities.

▼ **Tip**

If you want to see what some *non*-Apple employees have been doing with AppleScript, skip ahead to the end of this chapter, wherein I list a number of online scripting resources. Many of them have enormous hoards of useful scripts available for free download.

Leaving the two most nerdy and technical forms out of the discussion, there are three different kinds of script files. You can see what their Finder icons look like in Figure 17-13.

- **AppleScript documents work like documents.** You use this format for scripts that you're still tweaking because, while you can run them by double-clicking them, a user can't run it unless the Script Editor application is running as well.

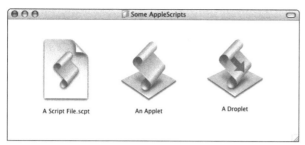

Figure 17-13
AppleScript document files, Applets, and Droplets:
The three faces of AppleScript

- **Applets work like applications.** The AppleScript code has been saved as a Macintosh app — albeit one without a slick Macintosh user interface — so this script can run all by itself without any assistance from Script Editor.

- **Droplets are a special form of app.** You can run them by double-clicking, but you can also drag and drop a file or a folder of files onto them. Doing this runs the droplet and tells it, "Whatever it is that you do, I want you to do it to all of these files."

Applets and droplets are examples of compiled scripts. That is, for the purposes of speed and flexibility, the plaintext AppleScript instructions have been transmogrified into something considerably closer to the hobo's stew of numbers and addresses that a CPU is used to working with. You can still open them in Script Editor and edit their AppleScript code — unless the author decided to keep the code under wraps — but they run considerably faster than plain old Script files.

Launching scripts yourself

You can place applets and droplets anywhere you'd place an application. Keep 'em in the Dock, where you can easily launch them; put them on the Desktop or in the toolbar of your Finder windows so you can drag files and folders onto 'em; and like any other app, you can even have Tiger launch them every time your Mac starts up by setting them as Startup items.

Tiger gives you another way of running scripts: the Scripts menu. This is a menulet that you can install in your menu bar by running the AppleScript Utility app found in your AppleScript folder. The Scripts menu looks like Figure 17-14.

The Scripts menu

By default, the Scripts menu comes populated with the dozens and dozens of pre-fabbed Library scripts that were placed on your hard drive when you installed Tiger. Take a minute or two to walk through all those submenus and see what's there. There are some real gems to be found.

The Scripts menu is populated from two sources: the two Scripts folders located in your Home directory's personal Library folder, and your Mac's system-wide Library folder. Drag any sort of AppleScript into either of these directories (you can open either of these Scripts Folders straight from the Scripts Menu) and they appear in the Scripts menu. Each application (plus the Finder) also has its own Scripts folder, tucked inside your User\Library\Scripts\Applications directory. Scripts in this folder only appear in the Scripts menu when that app is active.

However and wherever you add scripts to a Scripts folder, the scripts pop into the menu immediately. By default your personal user scripts are added to the bottom of the list (see Figure 17-15), but you can change this behavior via the AppleScript Utility, where you can also decide not to have the Scripts menu show you all those pre-fabbed scripts that Apple was so kind to install for you. That's OK. Folks worked very, very hard on them. All they wanted was *one kind word,* but apparently, that's just too much to ask.

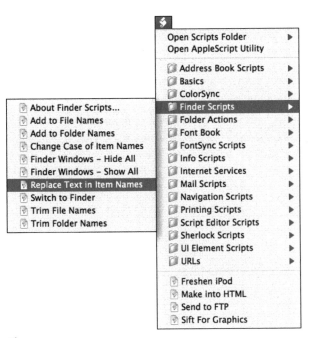

Figure 17-14
The Scripts menu

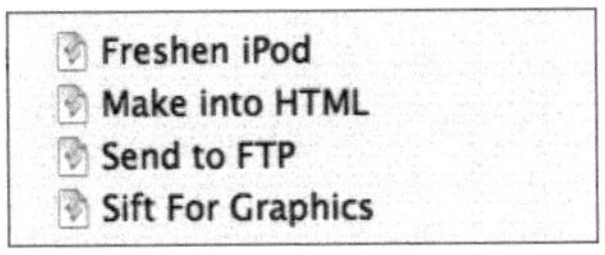

Figure 17-15
A few custom scripts in the Scripts menu

Attaching scripts to Mail rules

A great many apps (including many of Tiger's built-in apps) take advantage of AppleScript to increase their flexibility and power. The folks who wrote the Mail app, for example, can't possibly have thought of everything that everybody would ever want to do with Mail. Even if they did, they all work in California. It's usually way too nice outside to stay cooped up inside bashing out code all day.

Mail can be scripted like any other Mac app, but it also can run scripts as part of its automatic mail filtering system (Figure 17-16).

I've written a script that takes a specified message, converts it to text, and then installs it in my iPod's Notes folder so I can read it while I'm sitting in my doctor's office waiting for my weekly injection of sheep collagen. By attaching this script to a Mail rule, any time Mail receives an email from the Tony Danza Fanscene Message Board that I belong to, it's automatically slurped onto the iPod.

Figure 17-16
A Mail filter rule that triggers an AppleScript

That's just a single example of an app that can run an AppleScript automatically whenever a certain condition is met. They're all over the place. Go to System Preferences and click the CDs & DVDs panel. It lets you dictate what Tiger should do whenever you insert a disc. There are obvious things you'd want to do when you insert a disc of a certain type (audio CDs are opened in iTunes, photo CDs get handed off to iPhoto), but you can also tell Tiger to run an AppleScript. That's handy for customizing Tiger's response. I wish iTunes could display editorial information about a CD, as other music players can. If it bugs me that much, I can write a script that opens the disc in iTunes, gets the name of the album, and then opens a Google page on it. And I don't even *have* to . . . others already beat me to it, and I can simply download *their* scripts and attach them to the "When you insert a music CD" popup action.

LET'S SEE AOL'S MAIL APP DO THIS

I've just reread the example about the script I wrote to place mail on my iPod. It's possible that you might come away thinking I'm not the harbinger of intense, brooding super-cool that even provokes comments among Sean Penn or Johnny Depp. So I confess that the Mail script I *really* wrote takes advantage of both Mail's scripting features and that of an app called XTension (www.shed.com). This app works with cheap, home-automation hardware and allows the Mac to both turn lights and appliances on and off and accept input from motion and temperature sensors.

Because I live the life of the sensitive artiste (and, again, I have that whole brooding thing going on), I often leave the office for a few hours to breathe a little fresh air. Depending on what I've got cooking, I may or may not check my email immediately when I get back, which can have serious repercussions if something important has come in when I had no idea that anything important might be coming in.

So here's what I did: I got my disco strobe light (it was a gift. It was a gift.) out of the closet, plugged it into a home-automation box, and wrote a three-line AppleScript for XTension so that any app could turn it on. I attached this script to a Mail rule so that the strobe activates whenever an email arrives from one of my editors, and voilà! When I pull into the driveway and see through the windows that there's a full-on rave in progress in my office, I head straight upstairs and check my mail. Or, admittedly, I pull back out of the driveway again and hope that my assistant (either one of the two goldfish; doesn't matter) handles it. Either way, attaching scripts to mail actions is a useful feature.

It's just another way of turning Just Any Mac into a Mac that's specifically been dialed into your personal needs and preferences.

Attaching scripts to folders

One of AppleScript's ginchiest features, Folder Actions, went away temporarily during the transition to Mac OS X, but now it's back (it returned with Panther). Just as Mail can run a script whenever a Mail rule senses that a specific condition has been met, Folder Actions allows you to attach a script to a specific folder and have it run whenever any or all of the following things happen:

- The folder is opened.

- The folder is closed.

- An item is added.

- An item is removed.

- The folder's window is moved or resized.

And here I encourage you to just lean back in your chair — get out of bed first and move to your desk if need be because I like the visual of someone leaning back with hands folded behind their head, staring thoughtfully at the ceiling; work with me here — and consider the implications of this. This is why AppleScript skills elevate you into a Power User. For example, why bother to manually organize your Documents folder? Attach a script to the folder that leaps into action whenever a new item is added and moves it into the proper subfolder automagically.

But that's productive. Brrrrr! How about something stupid? Get a load of Figure 17-17. There was a folder on my office's publicly-used Mac that my visitors were told not to mess with, but they insisted on messing with it all the same. So I wrote a script that tossed up a little warning dialog when the folder was tampered with, explaining that the folder was for the *server's user only,* and that if *anyone opens it and looks around it'll mess things up,* and so *please don't use this folder.* But this had mixed results. Enter a more emphatic solution, in the form of Figure 17-17.

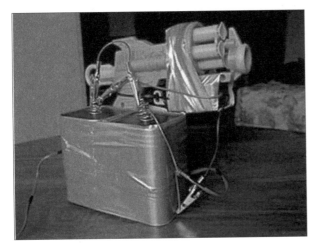

Figure 17-17
AppleScript applies a corrective action

So I bought a repeating-action suction-cup gun at the toy store, fitted it with the door-lock actuator from an old car, gave it 12 volts of battery power, and wired it into a little interface box that allows a Mac to interact with electronics. And yes, the box is AppleScriptable.

The first time a visitor tried to monkey with the folder, he got a polite warning. The second time he received three darts to the back of the head fired from concealment behind a potted plant placed there for that specific purpose.

I haven't worked as a system administrator in quite some time. I think it's because I was just so dashed effective at my job that I set an impossibly high standard for others to follow. Plus, I kept stealing photocopiers, and if I'd known that was the boss's daughter, I sure wouldn't have encour-

aged her to drop out of law school and start a pottery business. Hindsight is 20-20, you know.

You can attach a script to a folder through the folder's contextual menu. Folder Actions is a system-wide service that's disabled by default, so your first job is to turn it on. Control-click the folder to open its contextual menu and select Enable Folder Actions from the bottom of the list. You can also enable folder actions through the AppleScript Utility.

Select the folder's contextual menu a second time and you'll notice that a few new items have been added (Figure 17-18).

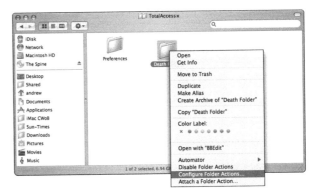

Figure 17-18
Setting up Folder Actions via a contextual menu

Selecting Attach a Folder Action opens a standard Choose File dialog. You can select any script anywhere on your hard drive, but by default, it points to Scripts→Folder Action Scripts located in your Mac's system-wide Library folder. There, you find a number of useful built-ins. Select add – new item alert.scpt.

 Tip

If you want to create a Folder Action Script that's available to all users of this Mac and not just to you, be sure to copy it into the default folder.

337

This script is a useful thing to attach to your Drop Box. Every time someone on the network puts a file in your Drop Box, the script activates and alerts you (Figure 17-19).

You can attach multiple scripts to a folder. Removing scripts is just as straightforward: Activate the folder's contextual menu, go to Remove a Folder Action, and select the script from the submenu. Apple, which loves you and only wants what's best for you and your siblings, has also provided you with the Folder Actions Setup utility (Figure 17-20).

As you add more and more scripts to more and more folders, a management utility like this becomes more and more necessary. At a glance, it shows you which folders have scripts attached to them, and allows you to temporarily disable or enable them with a handy click.

Figure 17-19
Hail, Folder Actions! For now I know that Lenny has sent me the file he promised.

Figure 17-20
The Folder Actions setup utility

BECOME A BIG PICTURE MAN

And here I say Thank The Great Gor Of Ranxeron-9. I'm what you'd call a Power User, which means that I've customized my Mac's operations to such an extent that I barely have half an idea of what's going on three-quarters of the time. I kept *losing* files in my Pictures folder once. It turned out that I had attached a script a week earlier to automatically process hundreds of photos that were coming in across the network, and I'd forgotten to turn that script off when I was done.

I choose to see this as a sign of my power and prestige. Do you think Donald Trump has half a clue what goes on inside his offices? Of course not. We're Big Picture men, too busy steering empires — his: an international real-estate and entertainment conglomerate; mine: a dual-processor G5 tower with *Babylon 5* stickers on it — to waste time on trivial details.

CREATING YOUR OWN SCRIPTS

When Apple first announced AppleScript back in 1992, it was truly going to be the miracle of the Zeppelin age. Not only was every Mac application going to be scriptable, but there were going to be three different increasingly ambitious kinds of scriptability:

- **Scriptable.** Users can write AppleScripts that exploit this app's features. Sounds good, but how about. . .

- **Recordable.** Users don't even have to write any AppleScripts. They can run the Script Editor application, create a new script file, click a Record button, and then go back to the app and perform whatever action they want to automate. Return to Script Editor, click Stop, and hey-presto! An AppleScript to repeat that same action magically appears! But don't order yet! Because some apps are also. . .

- **Attachable.** Wish you could change some of your apps' fundamental behaviors? Wouldn't it be useful if every time you pressed ⌘+S in your word processor, it would only save the file after giving it a quick scan to make sure you weren't using more than two of George Carlin's Seven Dirty Words in the church newsletter? Well, you no longer need to hit the bottle because you can customize an Attachable application into such an unholy perversion of what its creators intended that even the professionals who groom teacup poodles would point and say, "Dude . . . too far!"

Oh, what a Xanadu that would be! But Apple was only setting us up for heartbreak. App developers determine scripting features, and too few companies are truly committed to AppleScript. The good news is that you usually find AppleScript where it counts — in apps that can benefit from automation, like database and productivity apps.

Recordable apps and attachable apps don't exist. "Don't exist?" you huff, racing to your mail client to roundly jump up and down on my head for making such a baldly incorrect statement and to provide me with a long list of apps that *are, too* recordable and attachable, thank you very much.

But yeah, as a practical matter, they don't exist. Attachable apps are rare, and recordable apps are rarer. Even when you do joyously happen upon one in the wild, throw it in a bag, and haul it back to the States in hopes that you can get it to breed, you'll ultimately be disappointed with what it can do. Only some functions can be recorded, and only a few menu options are attachable.

As for basic scriptability, nearly every app supports at least four basic AppleScript commands:

- **Run.** Launches the app.

- **Open.** Opens an item, typically a document file.

- **Print.** Prints an item, again, typically a document.

- **Quit.** Fold. Pack it in. Give up hope. Take your ball and go home. You know . . . Quit.

Anything above and beyond that is up to the ambition and commitment of the developer. It's a crapshoot of delight and disappointment. It's the good apps that keep you committed to AppleScript. Some apps are so script-happy that it almost seems like a waste to work with the user interface at all.

RECORDABLE APPLESCRIPTS: NICE WORK IF YOU CAN GET IT

Why are there so few recordable and attachable apps available? Because AppleScript never won the grassroots support that it deserved. From the point of view of the app's developers, anyone who's savvy enough to want to record a script is probably savvy enough to write one on his or her own. So why waste time adding recordability?

They sort of have a point, though maybe it's a self-fulfilling one. I don't count on an app being recordable, so I just go ahead and write my scripts from scratch. The only time I take advantage of an app's recordability is when I'm writing a larger script. I'll record the desired action first and use that as a starting point for the "real" script.

Note

This includes most of Apple's own apps. I recently finished ripping every single CD I've ever bought in my life into a single iTunes library. I think I've spent more time writing scripts to manipulate the library and analyze my music tastes than I've spent listening to it.

Script Editor

Script Editor is the app you use to record scripts, edit existing ones, write brand-new scripts of your own, and crack open your applications to see just how scriptable they are. You find it inside your AppleScript folder, which awaits you inside Applications. Figure 17-21 shows you a typical script-editing window. This is Script Editor's entire interface, or near enough. Apart from Saves, Opens, and Prints, you never touch the menu bar at all. Here, give it a shot:

1. **Create a new script by pressing ⌘+N.** Alternatively, you can click File→New.

2. **Type the following code into the editing window:**

   ```
   say "Greetings, Professor Falken."
   delay 1
   say "How about a nice game of chess?"
   ```

3. **Click the Run button.**

Figure 17-22 shows you what you'll be looking at after you click Run. There you go; you're now a programmer. I bet your skin's half a shade paler already.

If you were watching the window carefully you noticed that the Stop button enabled itself while your script was running. Clicking that sucker terminates the script in mid-run — a very useful feature when the script that you *thought* you told to automatically assemble a report on the status of the network *actually* winds up taking a folder full of boudoir photos that you posed for at the mall and emails them to everyone in your 1,100-person Address Book.

 Note

Which ordinarily wouldn't happen. AppleScript doesn't make mistakes like that. But if there's one thing more powerful than AppleScript, it's Karmic Justice. Yes, you, the lady in the pink raincoat I encountered outside Blockbuster this morning. That was *my parking space* and you knew it. Well, who's laughing now?

As you start to work with longer and more complicated scripts, you'll probably start making regular use of the Compile button. Essentially, it double-checks your spelling and grammar. If something you've typed doesn't make sense as AppleScript, it flags it for you and does its best to explain what the problem is. If everything's flawless, it reformats the script with fancy nested indents and type styles to make it more readable.

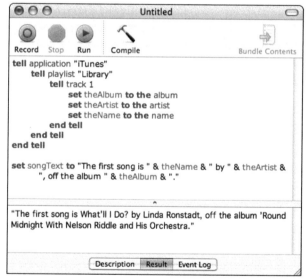

Figure 17-21

The Script Editor, with a simple script up on the lift so we can finally do something about those brake pads

Underneath the code section of the window exists a little pane of information. It can display three different things, depending on which of those three tabs underneath it has been clicked:

- **Description.** It's a good idea to describe your script and what it does. You're going to start writing a lot of scripts (No, really, I've paid a large man $30 to come over to your house and beat the snot out of you if you don't. So, I mean, time's a-wasting), and without attaching notes to these things, it becomes really easy to forget why you bothered to write this particular script in the first place.

- **Result.** That's a debugging tool. When a script runs to the very end, the results of the last operation it performed are displayed in the Result tab. You can see an example in Figure 17-9. The last thing this script did was build a sentence out of the information it retrieved from iTunes. Thus, this sentence winds up in the Result pane.

▼ **Tip**

I talk the big talk when it comes to AppleScript, but my arrogance ends when I sit down at the editing window. I have taken the wise words of Rabbi Norm Abram and kept them close to my heart: "Measure twice, cut once." Or in this case, "Don't try to debug a new snippet of code by inserting it inside a ten-page script and hoping for the best; write it separately, keep modifying until the Result is what you predicted and hoped it would be, and then trust it to work properly as part of the larger project." If the Result tab were a woman and I were a married man of considerably greater means, I'd be buying it a condo and visiting it on the side.

- **Event Log.** An even more sophisticated debugging resource. At the root of a gas engine is combustion. At the root of national-level politics are unresolved

childhood inadequacy issues. And at the root of all Mac software are events. These are the molecules of what goes on behind the scenes — the actual activities that software has to carry out to make things happen. Script Editor can maintain an Event Log that keeps track of everything your script did during execution and what the immediate result was, step by step by step.

There's a second set of resources for examining results and events: the Result Log and Event Log windows, which you can open from Script Editor's Windows menu. They're both frightfully useful; when a script fails to work the way you thought it did, they can act like the "black box" that gets pulled from the wreckage of a crashed airplane. They give you a detailed history of everything that your script did and what those intermediate results were, step by step along the way. By examining these logs, it's easy to discover precisely which line of code caused One plus One to equal Twelve, and then make the necessary fixes.

Ah, yes, we seem to have overlooked the Record button. Well, let's just clear that out of the way so we can move on.

IT'S GOOD THAT I DON'T OWN GUNS

This thing about writing the script and running it and looking through the logs to see what exactly happened is akin to using a machine gun instead of a sniper rifle. The skilled professional aims carefully and achieves a successful result with just one shot. If you're more results-oriented, you scoff "dash that" and just keep firing rounds until, by adjusting your fire as you go, you eventually hit what you wanted.

Recording scripts

Like I said earlier, recording scripts can be a hit-or-miss proposition. There's no way to tell whether or not an app is recordable — or exactly how useful its recording features are — until you give it a whirl. Let's toss in a ringer for our example: the Finder. It's eminently recordable and as an environment for mind-numbing, repetitive behavior it gives secondary education a real run for its money. I often

organize my windows in a specific way that lets me reorganize my hard drive's clutter quickly. Regardez-vous Figure 17-22.

It's a master column view of the whole hard drive up top, and three windows of subfolders arranged on the bottom. But it's a pain to create and arrange these windows manually, so I'm going to record a script that does it for me.

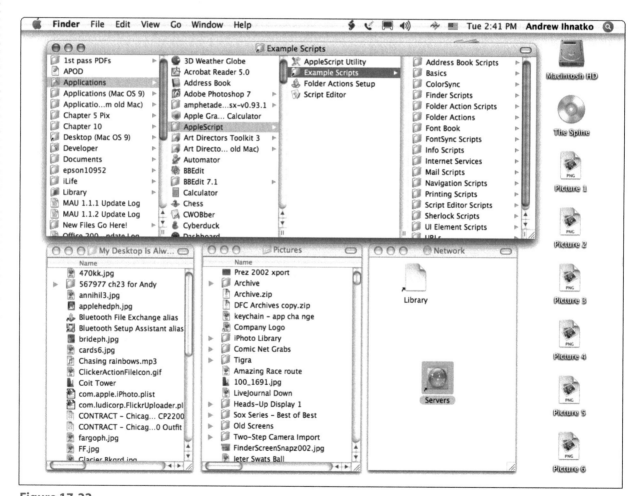

Figure 17-22
What my Finder screen looks like when I'm trying to beat poor, defensive Chaos into Order with a motorcycle chain

1. **Create a new script file in Script Editor by pressing ⌘+N.**

   Alternatively, you can click File➜New.

2. **Click the Record button.**

   The Stop button activates.

3. **Click over to the Finder.**

   Create those four windows, click in them until they're displaying the folders I want to examine, and change their views to the styles I want (one set to Columns and the rest set to Lists).

4. **Click back into Script Editor when the windows are just the way I like them.**

   Notice that the script window is now jam-freakin'-packed with script.

5. **Click the Stop button.**

   The final result is what you see in Figure 17-23.

Woo-hoo! Just imagine having to type all that in yourself! Recording scripts rules!!!

 Note

Correspondent carefully extends pinky and index finger while curling ring and middle finger under thumb; resulting hand-sign is then proudly lofted into the air to create an overall motif of horns customarily seen in traditional representations of Satan, and thus signifying one's allegiance to same.

Not so fast, Skeezix. Why don't you try something even simpler, like recording all the steps of using the Finder to connect to an FTP server? Go ahead. I'll wait here.

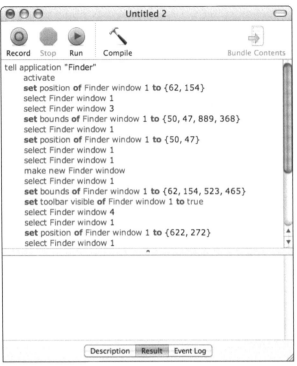

Figure 17-23
A successful recorded AppleScript

Uh-huh. You wound up with something like Figure 17-24, didn't you?

The only thing it actually recorded was that thing at the very end, when you finished logging in to the FTP server and you changed the window's view from Icon to List. See what I mean? Spotty and unpredictable. Recording scripts isn't totally useless, but once you pick up some scripting skills, you practically never use it.

Well, the Finder window thing went well at any rate. I might want to actually use that script later. Which dovetails us nicely into . . .

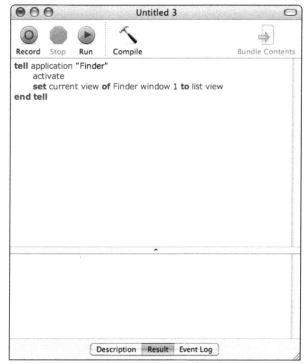

Figure 17-24
A stinky recorded AppleScript

Saving scripts

Saving a script has a couple of quirks, compared to saving document files in other applications. No big surprise . . . in a sense, you're building software here, so you have to decide how this new software is going to be deployed, you know? Figure 17-25 shows Script Editor's standard Save dialog.

The file format options are as follows:

- **Application.** The most useful form for your finished script. It'll run whether or not Script Editor is present, and it can run as a drag-and-drop utility if you've scripted it properly.

- **Script.** If you're still working on your script — or if you're coauthoring it with another scripter — you might want to save it as a Script file instead. It's slower and not quite as versatile as an application, but it's a little easier for a scripter to work with.

- **Script and Application Bundles.** You don't want to know.

- **Text.** It's a file containing nothing but words. No formatting, no other data at all. Useful for publishing purposes and when you need to read your script on an OS that doesn't support AppleScript (like a PDA or a Windows notebook).

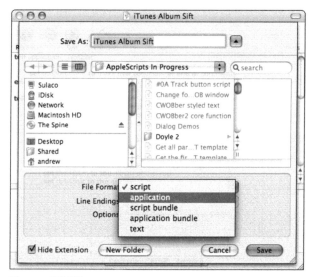

Figure 17-25
Script Editor's Save options

You also have three options available to you:

- **Run Only.** Normally, a saved script, even one that winds up as an Application, can be opened in Script Editor and modified. If you want to protect your code from tampering or theft, click this option.

- **Startup Screen.** Sure, you know what this script does and know how to use it. But will everybody else? Clicking this option takes the text you wrote in the Description tab of the script window and packages it as a startup screen that appears whenever the script is run.

- **Stay Open.** Scripts normally run once and then quit. Checking this box causes the script to stay open and active. There's a special kind of AppleScript code called an idle handler that takes advantage of this. If it's incredibly important that iTunes is always up and running (it has to be available to serve music to all the other Macs in your house, let's say), you can write a script that checks every 10 minutes to relaunch it if it doesn't appear to be in the list of running apps.

Give the script a name, click Save, and you're golden.

▼ **Tip**

Remember, if you want this script to appear in the Scripts menu, save it in Library ➔ Scripts ➔ inside your user folder. If you want the script to appear in the Scripts menu of all of this Mac's users, save it in the system-wide Library folder (click on your hard drive's icon in the Finder to see it).

AppleScript dictionaries

The good news about AppleScript is that lots and lots of apps support it ambitiously, and support dozens and dozens of unique AppleScript commands. The *bad* news becomes apparent when you multiply "lots and lots" by "dozens and dozens." You wind up with thousands of individual commands, and the sneaking suspicion that you have to know all of them to get anything done with AppleScript.

As I pointed out earlier, the strength or the weakness of an app's scripting support is up to the developer. Any functions or capabilities that are specific to the app have to be

NO, REALLY . . . I *WANT* TO KNOW ABOUT BUNDLES

I'll give you the simplest possible explanation of what a Bundle is: it's a scheme that the Mac OS uses to ensure that a piece of executable software and its resources are always lumped together and treated like a single entity. Imagine that I've written an AppleScript that takes a generic, prefabbed sales agreement (which exists as a TextEdit document) and, after asking the user some questions, prints out a binding contract that even Judge Judy would approve of. It's so useful that I want to give it away to people. If I save the script as a Bundle, I can stick the template file right in the same package as the script. My script will always be able to find it, and there's no chance that someone will receive the script *without* this Really Important File.

Bottom line is that Bundles are things that you'll deal with as you become an advanced scripter. Don't worry about 'em, for now. These aren't the droids you're looking for. Move along.

provided by the app. And they also have to provide AppleScript programmers with documentation explaining what these app-specific functions and data types are.

The word documentation has to be used loosely. The developers write up a list of data types the app can recognize and deal with and a list of functions the app can perform, and make this list available to you, eager young space cadet, within the application itself in the form of the app's built-in Scripting Dictionary. Script Editor can open up these dictionaries and display them in a clearly-organized and easily-searchable fashion.

You can open an app's dictionary by selecting Open Dictionary from Script Editor's File menu, and then selecting the app from the resulting list. Figure 17-26 shows you iTunes' scripting dictionary.

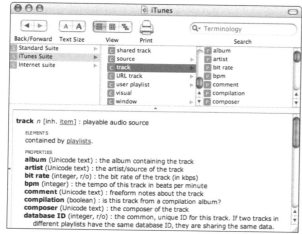

Figure 17-26
iTunes' scripting dictionary, laid bare

▼ **Note**

I will begrudgingly admit that many developers provide you with online scripting documentation, and there's often a whole page of sample AppleScripts on their Web sites. FileMaker, the Mac's greatest database app, is eager and ambitious when it comes to AppleScript. You'd think that its developers always intended for you to control the app via AppleScript instead of its buttons, menus, and windows.

All the same, keep your expectations low. The scripting dictionary is the only thing you can absolutely count on, and a scripting dictionary helps you understand AppleScript about as much as an English dictionary helps you to understand the lyrics to "Louie, Louie."

But who has time to scroll through a list of hundreds of apps, when you're all hot 'n bothered to start scripting?

Script Editor gives you a handy organizational tool in the form of the Library window. You can open it from Script Editor's Window menu. Behold, Figure 17-27:

Figure 17-27
The Script Editor's Library, keeping your favorite scriptable apps handy

It's sort of like a "Favorites" list for scriptable apps. Note that Apple has pre-loaded the Library window with Tiger's most popular scriptable apps. You can add your own just by clicking the "plus" button (+) in the window's toolbar. The Minus sign blasts the item to Hades. Clicking the button that looks like a bunch of books opens a selected app's scripting dictionary, and the AppleScript icon creates a brand-new script file, all set up to send AppleScript to that app.

Each dictionary contains *commands* and *objects*. Commands actually do things. In iTunes, "play" starts or resumes playback, for example. Objects are, well, objects. They're the things that commands work with. In iTunes' scripting dictionary, you've got tracks, playlists, music sources . . . and they're all objects.

WHEN THE SCRIPTING DICTIONARY LETS YOU DOWN

If you were hoping to find a certain command, but the dictionary broke your heart, that doesn't necessarily mean that you can't script it. Panther brought with it a new AppleScript feature called *GUI Scripting*. It's a system by which a script can send keystrokes and mouse clicks to an app and manipulate its user interface the same way a user can. To activate GUI Scripting, click the checkbox found in AppleScript Utility app.

So while iChat's scripting dictionary doesn't let you do something as esoteric as changing your online chat icon, you can do it by having GUI Scripting select the right menu and then click the right button in the right window. I used this feature to turn my chat icon into a live webcam; every minute, my iSight video camera takes a new picture of me and updates my chat icon with it.

There are plenty of privacy issues associated with webcams, but at 32 x 32 pixels, I think I can scratch more or less whatever I want with impunity.

You also want to click these objects and see what their *properties* are. Yes, I'm listening to a track. Very nice, thank you. But what Album is it off of? Who's the Artist performing it? When was it last played? Each of these is an individual property of the Track object. I can ask iTunes for "the artist of the first track" and get an immediate answer ("They Might Be Giants," say).

You'll dive into the scripting dictionary when you need to have a sense of the app's capabilities. You can either scroll through the dictionary yourself or click in the Dictionary viewer's Spotlight search box and search for the object

of your affection. I want to write an iTunes script that processes my music library on an album-by-album basis. Does its dictionary have an Album object? I type "Album" into the search field . . . nope, the only thing Spotlight finds for me is that "Album" is a property of "Track." That is, if I have a Track in my hands, iTunes can tell me what Album it's from. But I can't ask it to tell me the name of the first album in a playlist, for instance.

Editing tools

Okay, earlier on, I complained that Script Editor isn't all that helpful when you're writing and debugging scripts. It still falls short, when compared to third-party script editors like Script Debugger, from Late Night Software (www.latenightsw.com). Still, in addition to the Event and Result Logs that I mentioned earlier, Script Editor does offer some genuine niceties:

- **Script Assistant**. Script Editor can take a wild guess at what you want to type next. If you're about to type the name of a container that you've used before, but you're not entirely sure how you spelled it, just type the first few letters and wait a moment. An ellipses (...) will appear. If you press the F5 key on your keyboard, Script Editor will pop up a list of suggestions (Figure 17-28).

Just use the arrow keys on your keyboard to select the item you want and hit Return to continue editing. It's a fantastically useful feature. For one, I'm always forgetting that I named something theArtist and not theNameOfTheArtist, for instance, or whether "previous track" is supposed to be one word or two. Script Assistant is another thing that helps me think less. Which isn't that great a result, come to think of it, but it sure helps with the scripting, I'll tell you that much. You can activate the Script Assistant through the Script Editor's Preferences window.

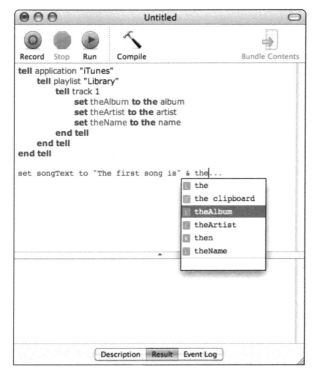

Figure 17-28
Unseen hands speak from beyond the grave and tell you what you probably want to type next

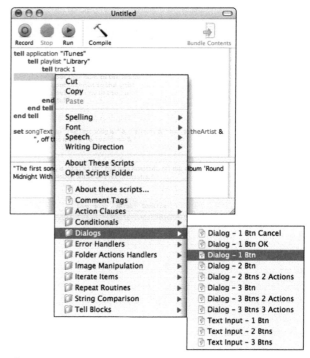

Figure 17-29
A contextual menu filled with pre-fabbed Apple-Script code snippets

- **Contextual Menu Scripts**. Dang. You *know* the AppleScript code presenting the user with a one-button dialog box, but you've forgotten. Or maybe you remember, but you're just too lazy to type it all out. No problem. Just control-click in your script's editing window, optimally in the place where this new bit of script needs to go. You'll see a contextual menu pop up, a la Figure 17-29.

  Navigate down to Dialogs, select the kind of dialog you want to use, and presto . . . the code you need is automatically pasted into your AppleScript-in-progress.

Learning AppleScript: Resources

Time and space prevent me from including a full primer on the AppleScript language. (And when I say time and space, I, of course, mean money. This is simple Einsteinian physics, people. Einstein said that time and space were merely vibrational manifestations of matter, and to me, nothing matters more than money. Slip me another three bucks and I'll be all over this whole Primer thing but otherwise, nothin' doing). So instead, I'll steer you toward other resources. The best way to learn AppleScript is to examine a script that (a) already exists, and (b) works.

Over time, you'll wind up working your way through all of the sample scripts Apple left for you in the Scripts menu. Scroll around until you see a script that seems to do something interesting, open the Script file in Script Editor, and play with the code.

No kidding. I've written plenty of AppleScripts that use Mail to create and send an email, but the central nugget of that code is always the lines I found in one of Apple's samples from the Scripts menu. Remember, kids, it's only thievery if you feel guilty about it later on.

Joking, joking. Apple's scripts say explicitly that you're free to recycle these samples as you see fit. Plus, this is exactly what AppleScript's framers originally intended — learning by example.

You'll absolutely want to go back to wherever you tossed your Tiger install disc and open the Developer Tools folder

IF YOU WON'T BELIEVE THE MAN, AT LEAST BELIEVE THE LIE

And again, I use contextual menu scripts a lot more than I'd like to admit. Even if you're a Full-On Apple-Script Stud Monkey, it's all too easy to mis-type something. And because you do indeed see yourself as FOASM, you refuse to believe that you might have screwed up something as basic as the command for creating a dialog box. So you look elsewhere for the problem, and there goes the rest of the week.

Naturally, a far better answer would be to cut off this sort of behavior at the source, and stop being such an egotistical twit. But that would take time, money, and a willingness to change. While Contextual Menu Scripts comes free with Tiger.

to rummage through the information resources to be found therein. I can confirm for you that this disc contains hardcore supergeek resources and references so potent that even now, just reading about them causes calcium deposits to form around my neurons simply as a defensive measure against my getting over-excited. But on this disc lurks a complete set of AppleScript documentation and reference materials that helps explain the basics of writing AppleScript from the basics all the way through the intermediaries.

▼ Tip

If you can't find your installation disc, most of the best bits are on Apple's Web site at www.apple.com/ applescript/developers/. But you're going to want to access this information without being tied to the Internet. Note that I didn't end that sentence with the term "trust me," though I could have. But I've already used it once, and Andy Ihnatko doesn't go around begging for respect. Do you hear me?

Some other places to go:

The AppleScript-Users mailing list (www.lists.apple.com/)

This is a public mailing list that's chock-full of seasoned scripting experts, newbies who've yet to write their first tell block, and everyone in between, all asking questions and swapping techniques. AppleScript is full of landmines that require either the sort of lateral thinking that leads to either madness, greatness, or the annual redesign of the federal tax code and only someone Who's Been There can explain how AppleScript works . . . and more importantly, why it sometimes doesn't.

Apple's Scriptable Applications page (www.apple.com/applescript/apps/)

Partly as a user resource and partly to sell people on the power of AppleScript, Apple maintains a Web page lifting all of the built-in Panther apps and iLife apps that support AppleScript, and embroiders each item with some sample scripts complete with explanations. When you want to start learning how to script Safari, this is your starting point.

MacScripter.net (www.macscripter.net/)

Hands-down the best AppleScript information and education resource outside of Apple. What the hey. Throw Apple in there, too. At this writing, MacScripter contains more than 1,300 sample scripts in every conceivable category for your benefit and edification. It attempts the impossible task of documenting every major Mac app's level of scriptability. There's a busy, busy, busy message board where newbie questions are always welcome; MacScripter has succeeded in building a real community.

Doug's AppleScripts for iTunes
(www.malcolmadams.com/itunes/)

This site does one thing, but it does it with remorseless thoroughness: It's all about scripting iLife's music player. It's actually a fine place to focus your scripting skills as they flower. The downloadable scripts range from simple five-liners to ones whose scale and ambitions demand the use of the term Heroic.

SCRIPTUS ANNOTATUS

Still and all, I'll show you a very simple script to start you off. And, because you were one of the first 500 callers to take advantage of this incredible offer, I'll annotate some of the high points afterward.

For a free word processor, TextEdit is actually pretty slick. On top of all of its built-in features, it's Microsoft Word–compatible, so it's actually possible to use it as a serious productivity app. But I can't use any word processor that doesn't have a word-count feature. Adding one is easy as pie. Just create a new Script file containing the following code, and save it inside your Scripts folder:

```
tell application "TextEdit"
        set theText to the text of document 1
end tell

set theLength to the number of words in theText

display dialog "There are " & theLength & " words in the
text."
```

Running this script returns the number of words in the frontmost TextEdit document. It also gives me three opportunities for blathering on:

- **Tell . . . end Tell:** Reflect upon the fact that there are anywhere from dozens to hundreds of apps installed on your Mac. If you have something to say to just one of them, you can't just stand on your chair and shout "Hey, you!" So when you have something to say, you surround it with a tell block so that it doesn't get intercepted by the wrong app.

  In this script, the only thing we need TextEdit for is to get the text of the document (document 1 . . . aka, the document whose window is in front of every other TextEdit window). So that's the only line you put inside the tell block. That's not always completely necessary. The rest of the script is part of the core AppleScript language and should work anywhere. But it's sloppy to put more inside a tell block than you absolutely must. It's more than sloppy . . . it can often have unpredictable results. For example, I could have put this line inside the tell block:

  ```
  set theLength to the number of words in
  theText of document 1
  ```

  . . . and I wouldn't have needed the line of script that comes after it. It would have run just fine, but it returns an incorrect result. When AppleScript counts the number of words outside of the tell block, everything is both hunky and dory.

  set...to is how you load up a container (theText, in this case) with data. When AppleScript encounters this statement, it evaluates everything that comes after to (be it a mathematical calculation, an operation to retrieve information [like we're doing here], or the result of another operation). I don't have to bother declaring `theText` ahead of time, or telling Apple-Script that it's supposed to contain text. AppleScript figures out that stuff dynamically.

▼ Note

If you've taken an introductory course in programming, a container is what you think of as a *variable*. Oh, and subroutines? They're called *handlers*.

- **display dialog:** Generates a standard Macintosh dialog with the contents you specify. For simplicity's sake, we're using the plain-vanilla, ready-to-wear dialog. It has text, plus OK and Cancel buttons. AppleScript lets you customize these pretty thoroughly. Because the dialog is just giving us some information, there's really no need for a Cancel button, for example. Go to the Scripts menu and look at the dialog samples under the Script Editor Scripts menu. `display dialog` generates its own results, too. If I made the line `set someContainerName to display dialog (etc.)`, `someContainerName` would hold the name of the button that the user clicked.

▼ Note

But AppleScript's built-in dialog functions are pretty limited. They can't get a whole lot of information from the user and they can't display a whole lot in return. When you absolutely, positively need something more ambitious, it's time to look into Apple-Script Studio.

And we're saving ourselves a step by building the dialog's text on the fly. The ampersands are your signal to Apple-Script that you'd like all those items schmooshed together into one string of text.

CHECK YOUR TELLS BEFORE BEGINNING THE HUMAN SACRIFICES

Often, when a script *just isn't working* and I'm so frustrated that I'm willing to sacrifice a living creature to the Cloven-Hooved One to make it work (a moth, maybe — let's not lose our heads here), I just tighten up my tell blocks and the problem magically disappears. Just something to keep in mind before you consider offing an intern to get a project finished.

When you're stuck with me as a dinner guest, there are three topics you don't want to introduce: The JFK assassination (Oswald did it and he acted alone; for bonus points, let me run down the 12 most popular conspiracy theories and why they're utterly baloneyous), the Apollo program (yes, I was born 30 or 40 years too late, but I'm still convinced that if I do a few pushups I might make it as a backup LEM pilot on Apollo 18), and the Mac's automation features. I'm nuts for Automator and AppleScript.

I'm as enthusiastic about this stuff as I am about my favorite books and movies. You've never experienced this thing? Oh, sit down, you poor, poor man or woman; your whole life has been a mere prelude to seeing *The Stunt Man* or reading *The Code of the Woosters* for the first time. I would balance my checkbook using nothing but calculations I've done in the Script Editor, typing code manually. If I actually ever sat down and balanced my checkbook, that is. I really ought to start to learn how to do that, actually.

Automator (and to a lesser extent, AppleScript) is exactly what's right about computers in general and the Mac in particular. There are some scripting-ish solutions for Windows, but no other platform brings such a level of power to such a low level of user expertise. As much as I love AppleScript, there was always that learning curve to deal with. But Automator!

Honestly, the only way to improve upon Automator would be if Apple shipped a piece of software that featured just

one window, containing a single, enormous purple button labeled "Oh, you know what I want to do; just *do* it, could you?"

Judging on the great leap they made with Automator, if someone emailed me and said that they saw just such a thing in prototype form in a secret lab at Apple Intergalactic HQ . . . I wouldn't be all that skeptical.

18

I Love People! I Want to Share My Mac!

In This Chapter

Multiple Users on the Same Mac • Sharing Volumes and Folders
Sharing Services • Sharing with Windows Users

It's hard to look at any of the basic philosophies that the original Macintosh development team came up with and find any that were completely and utterly wrong. But they *were* rather insistent upon redefining computing as "a computer for every person" concept, which, of course, trended dramatically toward baloney-dom as the years droned on. It was a reactionary concept to begin with: a fist being waved at the hegemony of university and corporate mainframes that had to be shared via dozens or hundreds of terminals scattered across the landscape. One big centralized computer amounted to Big Brother. Hundreds of personal computers meant Independent Free Thought.

Well, the Big Brother computing concept was a Big Win for the folks in the 1984 commercial, wasn't it? That blonde with the hammer certainly wasn't going to show up at the branch office and go from cubicle to cubicle smashing individual desktops, was she?

I have to believe that a lithe, athletic woman running into the auditorium in shorts and a tank top and doing a few spins did wonders for the morale of every last one of those gray drones in attendance. "That was the best Thursday morning all-staff meeting *ever!*" THX-1138 exclaimed to DDY-8172 as they rode the elevator back to their floor. Big Brother was pretty steamed about the broken big-screen TV, but when he saw the effect that this little stunt had had on both group and individual sales the next week, he arranged for attractive male and female decathletes to barge in and disrupt a *lot* of meetings from then on.

In this pushbutton world of the twenty-first century, we've found the happy medium. Mom, Dad, and little D'Artagnian don't each need to have their own computers. A Mac securely supports several users on the same machine, so what's Mom's is Mom's, and what's Dad's is Dad's. There's no longer the implication that a computer is a closed box of data and resources. If a document, folder, or volume might be useful to a co-worker, then he or she can access your Mac and use it, with your permission. And everyone in the building can share a single printer.

Let's see, what else did the Mac's original designers get wrong? Hm. Well, I remember that they put this ultragnarly, high-voltage capacitor right next to where you grab the circuit board to remove it. I installed 512K of memory in my Mac in 1988, and I think the hair on the back of my right hand only started growing back a month or two ago.

So here's where we start to talk about sharing your Mac's data and resources. This is the flip side of Chapter 19, in which we'll be hardening our hard, shriveled hearts against the false gods of Trust And Faith In Your Fellow Humans. But for now, pass the Granola and let's form a circle and sing "Kumbaya" and praise the concept of Sharing.

 Tip

Remember, it is always better to give than receive — unless, of course, you're a contestant on *$100,000 Pyramid,* and your celebrity partner in the final round is a former reality-TV show participant.

MULTIPLE USERS ON THE SAME MAC

Of the many Big Deals of Mac OS X, the ability to support multiple users is certainly one of its Big Deal-iest. Yes, even under the single-user Mac OS 9 it's possible for Dad, Mom, and their two children, D'Artagnian and Felicity, to share a Mac. But look at what happens:

- Felicity wants to download a couple of big movie trailers, but there's no room left on the hard drive. So she deletes a 3.1GB folder of stuff she doesn't recognize. This folder contains — or should I say *contained* — all of the photos and videos D'Artagnian shot when he toured Skywalker Ranch and the full Lucasfilm Archives, led around by George Lucas himself.

- Dad installs an MP3 player. At the last step in the installation process, the installer asks, "Would you like to make LambadaJukebox your default player for all of your Mac's media files, even though it's a total load of dingo's kidneys and iTunes is vastly superior to it in every conceivable way?" Dad, who's been drinking, clicks OK. Now everybody in the house is stuck using LambadaJukebox until someone puts things back the way they were.

- Mom feels as though she's stuck in a loveless marriage that was formed largely due to her parents' expectations of her as a teenager, and she's sworn that as soon as the kids are grown, she's filing for divorce and moving out of the house. But that's five or six years away, so she's just laying the groundwork, slowly embezzling money from their joint household account. Dad notices a set of AmeriTrade bookmarks in the family Mac's browser, clicks it, and discovers that the household has $57,000 in investments he never knew they had. Two days later, Mom is surprised to see a brand-new purple Humvee with leather interior and four built-in video screens parked in the driveway.

THE 'PORTANCE OF PASSWORD PICKING

Fortified with the power to astride the contents of this Macintosh like a Colossus (and change just about anything on your Mac), a password protecting access to an Administrator's account should be the safest and hardest-to-guess password there is. Choose wisely, and reflect well upon the lessons of Chapter 19.

And don't worry about choosing a password that's so tough to guess that you might forget it. To encourage you to choose tough passwords, you can reset admin passwords by inserting your Tiger install disc, rebooting off the CD (restart and press the C key), and then selecting Reset Password from the Tiger Installer program.

Bottom line: A single-user OS causes a great deal of strife and ranks as the third-leading cause of divorce in the state of California, behind bad vibes and an affair with the pool guy. With a true, multiuser OS, these things wouldn't happen because:

- Each of the Mac's authorized users has his or her own protected area in which to store files, and one user can't delete or even *view* another user's files without permission.

- Some users have greater power than others. Some users are empowered to install new software, while other users can only use whatever software is already there.

- While users *do* happen to share applications, they don't share application settings. So when D'Artagnian clicks Safari, he sees his own bookmarks, not Felicity's. When he runs iTunes, he uses his own music library and not anybody else's. And so, the multigenerational male teenage tradition of being able to thrill to the illicit delights of bubblegum pop in the privacy of his home while still being able to say to his friends, "Aw, hell no! That's my *sister's* music. I wouldn't listen to that weak, old junk if you paid me," comes to a sad end.

Just what exactly is a *user?*

A user is an account on a computer running OS X. Each user has his or her own preferences and Home folder, which is stored in the Users folder.

 Note

A "user" is also someone who's all chummy and buddy-buddy with you when they need a computer fixed an hour before a critical deadline, or when they want to pick somebody's brain for two hours about what sort of DVD recorder to buy. But when you're moving house and just need to borrow the person's pickup truck to move *one* big armoire, where's your "bestest buddy," I ask you? He's a vapor. He's a ghost. He never heard of you, particularly when you try to remind him that when he failed to show up for his court appearance, you lost the $2,000 you posted for bail. *Sigh.*

You know where this comes from? Poor self-esteem. Dammit, I'm Andy Ihnatko, and I *deserve* to be treated like a *person!* And let me tell you: the *instant* this guy's dad ceases to own Red Sox season tickets, I'm gonna give him what for.

There are actually two different types of user accounts:

- **Standard:** The type who acknowledges that the Manager of Information Technology was hired for his expertise in this field and that if he or she says, "Don't download stuff from the Internet and install it on one of the company's computers; it might contain a virus or a Trojan horse that'll cripple the whole network," well, maybe he knows what he's doing.

- **Administrator:** The kind who thinks, "I'm not just some 24-year-old nerd in jeans and sneakers . . . I'm a vice president with a law degree! And I'm installing this cool dancing chicken screensaver that came unsolicited in my home email from a person with an invalid address!"

▼ **Note**

Sorry. It's been a decade since I was in charge of running a company network, and I still don't think I've fully recovered yet. Yes, the Dancing Chicken Screensaver is a true story.

A Standard account is your plain, average, everyday user. Nothin' special here. But an Administrator account gives someone nearly free reign over the entire Macintosh. That person can install new software, update the operating system, change system settings, even poke around in other people's user directories.

You can have more than one Administrator account — so both Mom and Dad can install software and muck around with the kid's files, for example — but ideally you'd only have one such account on each machine. If everyone has administrator powers and can muck around everywhere and do anything, you lose the protection of making just one or two people responsible for maintaining the system. After all, when every man is Superman,

Superman is a mere Everyman. That sounds like a lyric to a Bob Dylan song but I swear, I just made it up a moment ago and it's quite apt.

Why even a wretched misanthrope/ troubled loner should add users

"Andy, I admit freely that I am obnoxious and disliked. I am both riff and raff. I want to reach out to people, but fear getting hurt, so I build these walls around me, walls which the folks that I meet often misinterpret as hostility and ego. I am solitary and brooding by nature; enigmatic, yes, but the keeper of secrets both cryptic and unknowable. Bottom line: I have no intention whatsoever of sharing my Mac with anyone, so why would I ever bother creating additional user accounts?"

Well, Senator, it's actually advisable to have a few extra accounts, and here's why:

- **A second account is a real lifesaver if your Mac suddenly decides it wants to stop working.** It's possible that the problem is with your usual account and not Tiger or your Mac in general. If you restart and log in as a different user, you'll be back up and running. If your virgin, never-been-messed-with user account experiences the same problems, you'll know that you have a problem that might require reinstalling Tiger from scratch.

- **Second accounts are great for presentations.** I know that you don't *intend* to go out on the Internet looking for smutty drawings of Captain Kirk of *Star Trek* gettin' it on with Captain Janeway of *Star Trek: Voyager*. They just sort of magically appear in your Pictures folder all of a sudden. Well, because God loves a good laugh — particularly when it's at your expense — He'll make sure that something causes *that* cartoon to pop up on the screen while you're in the middle of a presentation to 800 members of the United Council of Churches. Having a user account that's specifically set up for presentation use ensures that nothing untoward — not even a Desktop cluttered with unsightly icons — hinders your presentation. Plus, you've got the Desktop set to something neutral, the Displays and Sound settings are just so . . . you can spend five or ten minutes changing all those settings, or you can spend just five seconds changing users.

- **Guest accounts are a good security measure.** There are times when lending your PowerBook to someone or allowing him or her to come over and use your Mac is just a friendly gesture. But you sure don't want that person pawing through your files, even accidentally, so a special Guest account is a good thing to have ready.

That's just a partial list, of course, but it presents ample reason to set up one or two extra accounts . . . even if you do consider yourself a pariah of society.

Tip

I'm a little worried about you, man. How about signing up for a cooking class or something? You'll get out, you'll meet people, maybe shake off this cloud that's been hanging over your head since you and Jane broke up, man.

Creating new users

Your Mac already has at least one user: the Administrator account that was created for you automatically when you first installed Tiger.

Cross-Reference

That was back in Chapter 2. Remember Chapter 2? Those were good times, weren't they? Can you believe the clothes and the music back then? I was listening to Disc 2 of *the Best of Peter Sellars* boxed set instead of Disc 6, and I used to wear a ripped pair of jeans and this really ratty old Newton Messagepad tee shirt that . . . oh, wait; that's what I'm wearing right now. I should probably take a break now and do some laundry. This might be the reason why the FedEx guy tossed his clipboard to me yesterday morning when he needed a signature, instead of just handing it over.

You can create accounts for additional users through the Accounts panel of System Preferences.

1. **Launch System Preferences.**

2. **Click the Accounts icon to display the Accounts pane (see Figure 18-1).**

Figure 18-1
The Accounts preferences pane

USERS ARE INDEED SUBTLE, TRICKY, AND UNTRUSTWORTHY BEASTS

Don't fool yourself into thinking that activating the parental controls on Mail, Safari, and iChat is more powerful than your kid's desire to look at naughty pictures, send harassing emails to the managers of bands that he really doesn't like, and iChat with the girlfriend who's been making rumblings to the effect that she has grave doubts about his commitment to the relationship, doubts that can only be allayed with the acquisition of a fairly ambitious tattoo. The Controls only apply to Mail, Safari, and iChat; if they load an alternative mail app, web browser, or chat client on the Mac, they can sail through these controls unhindered.

So for *full* efficacy, activate the "User can only use these applications:" control in the Finder & System category and make sure that the user can only run the apps that you're pre-approved. If he tries to get around Safari's limitations by dragging a copy of the Firefox browser into his Documents folder, it won't run.

Do consider allowing the tattoo, though. You can't be with your son every hour of every day, after all. If he has "Gladys & Larry 4 Evah" permanently inked across his chest, then every time he steps out of the shower and looks in the mirror he'll hear your nagging voice saying "I *told you so,* didn't I?" Just make sure the artist uses a new needle and new ink.

3. **Click the little padlock icon in the lower-left corner, so you can make changes to accounts.**

   Tiger will ask you for your Administrator password.

4. **Click the plus sign (+) in the lower-left corner of the window.**

   The right side of the window will then contain spaces for typing information about the new user, as shown in Figure 18-2. Each new user needs a name that the Humans will recognize, a shorter one that the OS will use internally to name its user directories and stuff, and a password (which you'll have to type twice, for safety).

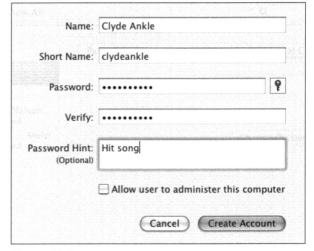

Figure 18-2
Typing information about a new user

▼ Note

Actually, you don't technically *need* to define a password. If you *want* to create an account that allows absolutely *anybody* to access your Mac even if that user is a bass player for a particularly disreputable Midwestern cover band for the love of Mike ... well, hey, it's your funeral. But your Mac agrees with me that this is a terrible idea. It'll warn you 12 times to Sunday that what you're about to do is dramatically stupid, before it meekly complies with your request.

You can configure OS X to display an optional password hint after a user types the wrong password three times. If password hints are not turned on, OS X asks you to confirm the use of the hints. Use this carefully. I mean, come on . . . who doesn't know the answer to a question like, "The first man to space walk without the assistance of umbilical tethers to a spacecraft"?

5. **Click the Accounts window's Pictures tab to choose a picture for the user (Figure 18-3).**

Figure 18-3
 Choosing a picture to represent a user

The picture appears next to the user's name in a list of users. If by some strange quirk of fate you don't happen to look like a dog, cat, or some species of insect, you can insert a custom user picture. Click the Edit button, and a window like the one shown in Figure 18-4 appears. You can insert your own picture in three different ways:

- Drag it into the window from the Finder or iPhoto.

- Click Choose to pick it from a standard Open dialog bog. If you use iChat, all of your most recent personal chat icons will be arrayed in the Recent Pictures pop-up menu.

Figure 18-4
Inserting a custom user picture

- If you have an iSight or another video camera attached, click the Take Video Snapshot button to snap a quick self-portrait.

No matter what method you use, you'll have the opportunity to scale and crop the image inside the window's unshaded box before clicking Set and accepting your changes.

6. **Click the Accounts windows' Parental Controls tab to use your Godlike power to control what this user can and cannot do on this Macintosh (see Figure 18-5).**

The Parental Controls section is there because some people are fiends draped in human flesh, or are kids who don't know better and are apt to get themselves into trouble, or grown-ups who don't know better (and are . . . etc.), or corporate executives who *know* better but have never quite gotten the knack of connecting actions to consequences. Thus, as an Administrator, you've been granted really fine control over this user's capabilities.

Figure 18-5
Setting user access

▼ Info

An account limited by Parental Controls is called a Managed Account and is listed that way in the list of users.

There are so many different controls that they're arranged by group. Sheets filled with settings drop down when you click a group's checkbox and activate its controls:

- ▪ **Mail** (Figure 18-6): Instead of being able to swap emails with Just Plain Anyone, you can limit the user to just sending and receiving messages with folks on a specific list. Add addresses to this list by clicking the "+" button, and remove one by selecting it and clicking "–". If this user sends or receives mail with anyone else, Tiger sends an email to the address listed in the "Send permission emails" item, to ask if the mail should go through or not. Click the checkbox to activate the "permission" feature.

Figure 18-6
Setting parental controls for email

- ▪ **Finder & System** (Figure 18-7): This panel contains stuff that limits overall access to basic Tiger features.

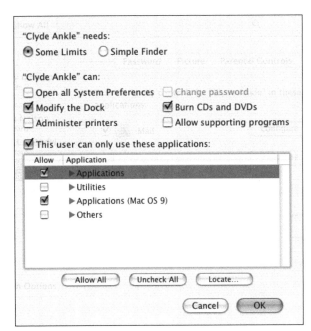

Figure 18-7
Setting parental controls for the Finder and the overall Mac experience

Click Simple Finder to limit this user to a stripped-down user experience of almost Soviet-style bleakness (Figure 18-8). The Simple Finder is an attractive choice when you've got a user who (a) is intimidated by a computer even as simple as a Mac, (b) has a tendency to click every button and pull every menu and thus get into a lot of trouble, or (c) a user whom you don't really like very much, and who you feel needs to be taught a lesson.

A grand tour of the nothingness: there's an Applications window, but it only shows those apps that you, o great and vengeful Administrator, have allowed this user to access. The Dock is nearly empty: just the Dashboard and two folders, apart from the stripped-down Apps folder (Documents and the Shared Folder). The menu bar has been abbreviated like a Fox Network production of Nicholas Nickleby. The user can put the Mac to sleep, log out, Force Quit an app, and that's it. He can only switch to the "real" Finder if an administrator comes along and types a password.

Figure 18-8
The optional Simple Finder: It's like being in Disney World with only $13 and one hour to spend

▼ **Note**

Man alive. If the Bergman-esque bleakness of the Simple Finder doesn't immediately make you think of your Mom or Dad yelling "And you'll *stay* here and *think* about what you did until I say you can come out again!," then clearly you didn't get into as much trouble as a kid as I did.

Selecting Some Limits indicates that while this user deserves *some* faith from this Mac's administrator, it shouldn't be *blind* faith. Figure 18-7 shows you the half-dozen checkboxes you can use to enable or disable certain features. Unchecking one of these items means that the user *can't* do that. Unchecking "Open all System Preferences," for example, means that the user can't tweak any System Preferences that might lead to trouble, such as Network settings, the Date & Time, or the Displays settings.

Finally, you can limit the user's access to applications. If you activate this control, Tiger builds an outline listing every application available to this account and allows you to deny access to apps either individually (no Microsoft Excel for you, young man!) or as a group (no access to system Utilities, which can often be a source of trouble). If the item's box is checked, then the user has access to that group or item. Unchecked means No Dice.

Handy stuff. If little D'Artagnian has been breaking the house rule of "no surfing the Web or using online chat unless Mom and Dad are home," you can easily turn off Safari and iChat entirely. Or, if he was mouthy when you confronted him, turn off all apps except for TextEdit and Chess. That'll teach him.

■ **iChat:** This one works like Mail's parental controls. With this Parental Control active, the user can't iChat with anybody who's not on a special list of approved users. Click the "Configure" button to add iChat account names to this list.

▼ **Note**

You begin to understand: Users are trouble. This is why so many professional system administrators prefer not to learn their names. If you start to get emotionally attached to them, you start to think of them as *human beings*, and that sort of compassion only gets in the way of your job.

■ **Safari:** With Safari controls active, this user can't access any sites that haven't been bookmarked. And they can't bookmark new sites. If they try to access a site that Safari has never heard of, the user sees the screen shown in Figure 18-9. Duly humiliated, the user will have to find somebody with an Administrator-level account (you) to come over. After receiving a convincing explanation about how a site named www.HotStewardesses.com could be even remotely work- or school-related, click Add Website, and type in your username and administrator password. Safari will create a new bookmark for the site and will allow the user to access the site unrestricted from then on out.

The user doesn't have *any* control over bookmarks, in fact. They can't even delete items; every time they click Safari's Bookmarks button, Safari asks for an Administrator name and password.

■ **Dictionary:** Tiger will hide all of the naughty words in Dashboard's dictionary.

▼ **Warning**

If your kid doesn't look these things up in a reputable dictionary, he or she will probably learn it in the street, where the information has not been subjected to a formal academic peer review or thesis refereeing.

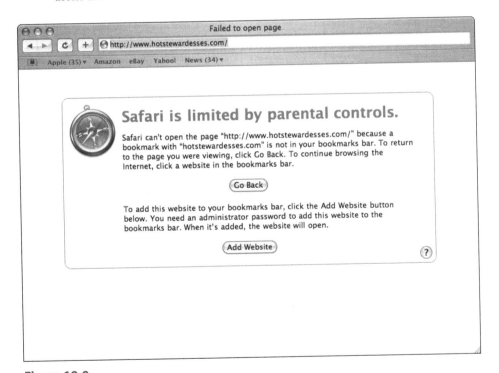

Figure 18-9
The user attempts to see what a nude flight attendant looks like, with less-than-satisfactory results

Changing login options

Okay, you have successfully set up accounts for additional users. Now what? Well, now it becomes important to think about making changes to your login screen. You know, that little box that comes up when you fire up your Mac. I mean, the one that asks you who exactly you think you are and why in God's name should this Mac allow you in to use its apps and resources? It's possible that you've never even looked at the login screen before; there was only one user, so your Mac logged you in automatically.

But with several sets of mitts clawing at your keyboard, it now becomes rather important to make some changes to your Mac's welcome mat. Back at the bottom of the Accounts pane of System Preferences, there's a big button that exposes your Mac's Login Options (Figure 18-10).

Figure 18-10
Changing what users see before they login

Most of these options have subtle but important effects on your Mac's security and stability.

- **Automatically log in as:** You turn on your Mac and blammo, it boots up under this user's account without any passwords or typing. That's perfectly fine if you live alone, but if you're sharing a Mac with other folks, you'll want to deselect this option.

▼ Note

But this feature isn't without its uses. When I have to set up a Mac for more or less public use — in the lobby of an office, for example, where folks are welcome to look things up on the Web or something while they wait for an appointment — I set up a guest account that's limited to Web browsing only and have the Mac automatically log in to that account. Other folks in the office can still log in and access all of their services, but when they log *out*, it's the browser-only account that remains active.

You'll *certainly* want to deselect it if this Mac is a PowerBook, and the potential exists for the thing to walk away when you're not looking.

- **Display login window as:** If it's set to "List of users," then the user clicks on a name from a list, and types a password. That's convenient, but it automatically gives a ne'er-do-well an opening. The aforementioned NDW can click on Gern Blanstev's name and maybe Gern has set a password hint and maybe the NDW can *guess* it. If you leave this option set to "Name and password," the login window will just present spaces where the user will have to provide both a username and the password, which doubles your protection against interlopers.

- **Show the Restart, Sleep, and Shut Down buttons:** Having these buttons at the login screen can be convenient — you can shut down the Mac without having to log back in — but realize that *anybody* can press these buttons. So if someone logs out of this Mac and walks away, then anyone else who comes by can shut the thing off. Which is a Bad Thing, if it's supposed to be sharing a printer or a bunch of files with other folks on the network.

- **Show Input menu in login window:** So if the keyboard is set to Inuktitut-Nutaaq layout and you need the Inuktitus-Qwerty layout to enter your password correctly — honestly, who *hasn't* been in that situation? — you can just select the keyboard you need.

- **Use VoiceOver at login window:** Selecting Use VoiceOver means that Tiger will "speak" the items in the login window when the user moves the mouse over them. A Good Thing, if one of your users has limited vision.

- **Enable fast user switching:** You'll learn what Fast User Switching is in the next section. With this option enabled, there'll be a menu at the right end of Tiger's menu bar with a list of users. You can switch from one user account to another by just selecting a name (and providing a password, if necessary). The pop-up menu controls whether the menu is drawn as a list of long names, short names, or just user icons.

Switching between users

Good heavens, this is like model rocketry, isn't it? Scads and scads of preparation until we get to the actual "it" of it, which only takes about a second.

So, now you've done everything you need to do to turn your one-man Mac into a hippie commune of activity. When one user finishes searching the Internet for the best

deal on Mork and Mindy original costumes and memorabilia and is ready to move on with his or her life, that user selects Log Out from the Apple menu.

Logging out politely quits all of your running apps (asking you to save any unsaved changes in open documents first) and leaves your Mac idling at the login screen, awaiting the arrival of another registered user.

▼ **Note**

It's important that you officially tell your Mac that you're walking away, and that you're not coming back for a while. After all, typing a user name and password is a hassle (albeit a minor one) and there's no guarantee that one of the people who shares your Mac won't prefer to just sit down and surf the Web under *your* account instead. So, logging out when you leave is a security thing. It also ensures that if someone tries to buy a $200 DVD boxed set containing every episode of "Monty Python's Flying Circus" ever aired, it'll be charged to *his or her* Amazon.com account, not yours.

The downside of all this is that logging out and logging in means waiting to quit all your apps and close all of your documents. *And* it means waiting all over again when you log back in, for apps and docs to be reopened. Not all Mac users are sufficiently hippie-crunchy in philosophy to see this as a ritual of cleansing and renewal. Most, in fact, look upon this as a profound pain in the posterior.

Well, Mac OS X has a balm for your pain: just enable fast user switching. You have to enable it through Login Options (back at Figure 18-10).

With Enable fast user switching turned on, a new menu appears at the extreme right end of the menu bar (see Figure 18-11).

FAST USER SWITCHING, GAME SHOW STYLE

I really need to talk about the way that Tiger accomplishes the visual transition when changing user accounts under fast user switching because it's sort of at the heart of the whole Mac experience. There seems to be no way for me to make a shot of the screen as it happens, but Tiger pulls off a 3D effect wherein your Desktop and the next user's Desktop are on adjoining facets of a screen-filling cube, and it simply rotates from the first Desktop to the second, with full shadow, perspective, and lighting effects.

(Basically, if you've ever seen a 1970s game show on The Game Show Network, close your eyes and imagine what happens when there's a shot of a pile of yellow vinyl luggage on a rotating stage and Johnny Olsen says, "And you're going to need that new luggage because you're going on a deluxe vacation ... tooooo ... *Mexico!*" That's the baby.)

Yes, it would have been just as effective to simply replace one screen for another. But even in such casual, offhand matters, it's important for the Macintosh to flex its arrogance: "I have so much computing power and such a robust set of code libraries that a visual trick like this is more or less as simple to pull off as calculating the cube root of 1928738 to 30 decimal places, and incidentally, an advanced OS and CPU like mine considers the cube root of 1928738 to be such a trivially boring exercise that we make the keyboard controller chip do it."

God, I love the Mac!

Figure 18-11
Doing a quick-change from one user to another, thanks to Fast User Switching

The title of the menu is the name of the current, active user. Just select another user, pausing to provide that user's password, and instantly, your Mac switches from the first account and its settings and protected directories to that other user's.

When you use Fast User Switching to switch from one user to another, you don't have to wait for all of the first user's apps and documents to close. Those apps are *still* running and the documents are *still* open; you just can't see them or access them until you switch back to the first account. So, this feature doesn't just offer convenience, it also brings added flexibility. If iMovie is going to be spending an hour compressing and outputting your latest video masterpiece, it doesn't have to tie up the whole Mac for the rest of the house. It can continue its work in the background while Junior switches over to his own account and does a little work on his next novel.

▼ Note

If Enable fast user switching is so universally ginchy, why does Apple warn you that you shouldn't turn it on unless you trust the other users of this Mac? Well, I *suppose* it's *possible* that in an *uncontrolled* environment, an individual bent on malfeasance could exploit Enable fast user switching to pull a fast one. It's more a conceptual thing than anything else: Are you okay with the idea that while you're happily writing a letter to the *Oprah Winfrey Show*, unbeknownst to you a Mail app running under someone else's account is sending out 120,000 bulk emails on behalf of the Drunk Drivers Against Literacy Foundation? I wouldn't worry about it, but it's something to be aware of.

Deleting users

When you no longer want to give a user access to your computer (he or she has been humming the "Plescheyevo Lake" theme from Prokofiev's Alexander Nevsky score all *freaking* day and you've finally *had it*), you can delete the user. Here's how:

1. **Launch System Preferences.**

2. **Click on the Accounts icon to display the Accounts panel. Click the lock at the corner of the screen and type in your Administrator password, if necessary.**

3. **In the list of users at the left of the window, click the name of the user you want to delete.**

4. **Click the minus (–) button at the bottom of the list.**

   OS X asks you to confirm the delete (Figure 18-12). If you want to save the user's home folder in a folder

named Deleted Users, click OK. This is the equivalent of firing an employee, but dumping the contents of his or her desk in a cardboard box so the stuff can be returned later. Awfully sporting of you. If your hatred of this person is so intense that you can't even bring yourself to extend the simplest basic human courtesy, click Delete Immediately and all traces of this user will be obliterated.

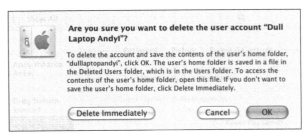

Figure 18-12
Confirming the deletion of a user

SHARING VOLUMES AND FOLDERS

If you've read Chapter 12 (Volumes), you know about using volumes that are available for you to share over a network. Now you'll begin to take a look at making resources on your own computer available to other users, thus putting the shoe on the other hand.

Turning on File Sharing

To allow other users to share volumes and/or folders on your computer, you need to turn on Personal File Sharing:

1. **Launch System Preferences.**

2. **Click the Sharing icon to display the Sharing preferences panel (see Figure 18-13).**

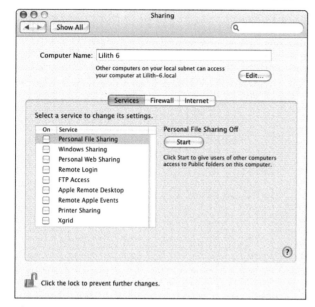

Figure 18-13
Turning on Personal File Sharing

3. **Click the Personal File Sharing option in the list of services at the left of the window and then click the Start button.**

   Tiger will percolate for a moment while it pumps the accelerator pedal and squirts hairspray into the carburetor and does all the little things that have to be done to make your files available to other folks on the network. Once it's done, the Start button becomes a Stop button; clicking it will turn Sharing off.

The Public folder

Personal file sharing works without any further setup on your part because every account has a couple of prefab shared folders already on it, ready to go (see Figure 18-14).

Figure 18-14
Your Public folder

Every user directory contains a folder entitled Public. You can find yours at the very top level of your home directory (The one with your user name on it. Looks like a little house, remember?).

The Public folder is designed as an official visitor's lounge to your Mac's hard drive. Anyone with access to your network — whether that user has an account on your Mac or not — can "see" this folder on your Mac and open it. Other users can take any files they find in there and copy them to their own local hard drives. They just can't change the Public folder's contents. They can't delete or rename files and they can't add any files themselves.

DON'T GET TOO PERSONAL IN PUBLIC PLACES

Personal File Sharing becomes an issue when you use this feature on a notebook. Inside the confines of your home, it's a wonderful convenience and a real slam-dunk. Your whole home network is on AirPort, so you can easily sit down at your desktop Mac and grab a few files off your PowerBook's hard drive.

Then you head off for work, and you stop off at a coffee shop for a cup of double-blahbah with a half-shot of whatever (I'm sorry. Truth be told, I've never bought a cup of coffee in my life). You sit down at a table, open your PowerBook, and read over some documents you'll discuss in a meeting later on.

But ... oh, shazbot ... you forgot that Personal File Sharing was still on, didn't you? So anyone else in the coffee shop with a wireless notebook can grab and read any file that you put into a publicly accessible folder.

So please be aware of when this service is on and when it's off. Chapter 14 discusses how to create different network Locations. Create one called Away in which file sharing is turned off; this makes it really easy to button down your PowerBook when you're away from home.

▼ Warning

All of the folders that Tiger created for you when you first created your account — Documents, Pictures, Movies, et cetera — are protected from the prying eyes of visitors. But your Home folder itself, and any new folders that you create which aren't inside one of those prefabbed folders — are wide-open. So to keep private stuff *private*, don't just leave files and folders out there. Toss 'em inside the protective umbrella of the prefabbed ones, or change the permissions of that folder through its Get Info box, as described in Chapter 11.

Your Public Folder also contains a special folder entitled Drop Box. Visitors can copy files from their local Macs into your Drop Box but they can't open the folder, which means that they can't see what's inside and they certainly can't copy anything within.

So you can understand how useful a Public folder can be, if you manage it properly. You use your Public folder for

items that you want to share with friends and strangers, such as a document template file for the standard letterhead that you want everybody to use every time they create company correspondence. When someone else on the network wants to send you an item that isn't for everybody's eyes — his half of an internal report on which you're collaborating, for example — he sticks it in your Drop Box. That way, the file becomes for your eyes only.

▼ Note

Incidentally, your Public folder is also public to every other user of this Mac. So, if you tell your daughter Felicity to give you a copy of her American history homework so you can check it, she can put a copy in your Drop Box even though she doesn't have access to your directory. Incidentally, if your chief interaction with your genetic offspring is that she can send you documents via multiuser write-only access to a folder, it's probably time to call Dr. Phil or something.

If you subscribe to .Mac, your iDisk has a Public folder, too. Files you place in your iDisk Public folder become available to any Mac user on the planet who goes to the Finder and selects Go ➜ iDisk ➜ Other User's Public Folder from the menu bar.

The Shared folder

You can use your Public folder to share personal files with other users of your Macintosh, but your Mac also sports a special folder entitled Shared. The Shared folder is at the top level of your Mac's "Users" folder, which you can find by clicking the icon of your hard drive.

The Shared folder acts as sort of the common atrium that connects all of this Mac's user directories. There's just one Shared folder among all users. Any user can access any file you drop in there.

Making other folders public, or *sort of* public

The Public and Shared folders are just the folders that Tiger prefabs for you. They're designed for simplicity and security. You can modify the behavior of the Public folder — or give people network access to some of your other folders — by manipulating the folder's Permissions.

For example, what if you want to make your Public folder more ambitious. Let's say you have a dozen people in your office working together on a big presentation. You want to use your Public folder as the central depository for presentation resources — text, pictures, music, the whole schmeer. Folks need to copy things to the folder, but they also need to copy things from it to their local drives.

Piece o'cake: just open the Public Folder's Get Info box and change its permissions so that people in the category of "Others:" have "Read and Write" access. The full story of permissions and how to change them is told in thrilling detail in Chapter 11.

 Note

Get Info lets you give or take away access and lets you apply it to three different categories of users. This was covered in Chapter 11, but for those of you who are skipping around: "Owner" is you. "Group" means a collection of defined, known users — defined through a hoary process that involves the Net Info Manager utility, a half-gallon of bourbon, and a friend or relative who you suspect enjoys a better than nodding relationship with either an advanced Unix system administration, Satan, or (ideally) both.

"Others" is, well, everybody else. If Apple enjoyed 90 percent market share, it might have had the jocularity to label this Schmoes instead because that's what we're referring to: strangers; just your basic, average guy; anyone not already defined in one of the previous two categories.

You can use this same technique to make any folder of yours act like a Public folder or a Drop Box folder. Just do a Get Info and change the access level for Others to whatever's appropriate. The only hitch is that other people can't see it in the first place unless it's inside a folder that's publicly accessible. So, if you have a folder of Batman artwork inside your Pictures folder, assigning Read only access to Others isn't enough. You would also have to give users some sort of access to your Pictures folder. Which is why it'd actually make more sense to put your Batman folder inside your Public Folder, or at the top level of your Home folder.

BE CAREFUL WHEN MESSING WITH PERMISSIONS

Okay. We're a little drunk with power — okay, and that case of generic lite beer I got at the Dollar Store this afternoon — so let's calm down for a moment. Messing with Permissions is an easy way to make wonderful things happen on your Mac, but it can also lead to boatloads of trouble. Remember that as a general rule, giving greater access to your files and folders is dangerous and should be avoided. In this sense, your folders are a lot like your emotions. Turn your back on hope and love. That's what I say.

There are no labels on this beer. Now that I read that last sentence back I wonder if this is actually the full-strength stuff.

SHARING YOUR MAC'S SERVICES

Up till now, we've just discussed the clean, sweet-smelling, warm and fuzzy ways of opening your Mac to other people. What follows are methods that aren't quite so bright and shiny. They're useful, but (a) they're not quite so easy to use, and (b) many of them leave your Mac a bit more vulnerable to attack.

Which is why Tiger leaves most of these features turned off until you specifically turn them on. Each one of these services is like a big, double-wide doorway through the castle walls. The wheels of a siege machine could nicely squeeze through the jamb, so it's best to keep the door shut and barred, and put a lower-level minion with a crossbow on duty nearby, preferably with a horn loud enough that he can raise an alarm before the advancing French stick a pike through some of his unfriendlier bits.

FTP

FTP (file transfer protocol) is the sturdy, ancient, and reliable way to shuttle files between two computers over a network. With Tiger's FTP service turned on, other folks on the network can access your directories via FTP:

1. **Launch System Preferences.**

2. **Click the Sharing icon.**

   If necessary, click the Services tab of the window.

3. **Click the FTP Access service (Figure 18-15).**

And you're good to go. Any machine (Mac, PC, Linux, anything on the network) can now access this Mac's public folders with any FTP program. Just give them the URL listed at the bottom of the FTP settings window.

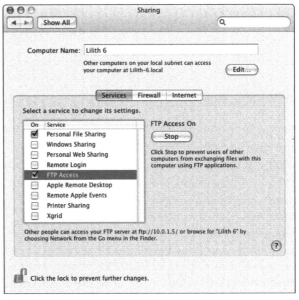

Figure 18-15
Turning on FTP access

WHEN I WAS A YOUNG FTP WHIPPERSNAPPER . . .

Oh, merciful Lord in Hamilton, Ontario, Canada . . . why would you want to open your Mac to FTP access?

Wait, actually it's a useful feature. Sometimes you are confronted with a problem of how to slurp a bunch of data between two unfriendly, dissimilar machines and FTP is just the only decent solution. The last time I opened my FTP services was when I desperately needed to load a bunch of spreadsheets from my desktop to an old Newton PDA. No modern software would interface the two, but I had a Newton FTP client and a wireless card for it. It took me all of 5 minutes to get some sort of software solution running (there are still some diehards who keep the Newton alive, albeit in a "See? Did you see? Gramma twitched her left eyeball! I think she's finally coming out of that coma she dropped into 40 years ago!!!" sort of way).

But no kidding: FTP is sort of a crude solution from a security standpoint. FTP was created in a simpler time (there might have actually been Hobbits running around outside when it was first created) when security wasn't on everyone's mind. So, turn it on, do the thing you need to do, *then turn it off again.*

 Cross-Reference

You can learn how to connect to FTP servers in Chapter 12.

Personal Web Services

One of the many benefits of Tiger's Unix roots is the fact that Apple included Apache, the Unix-based iron-horse, super-atomic, kick-butt powerful Web server software that runs nearly every reliable and decent Web service on the planet. So with just a couple of mouse clicks, you can make your Mac a for-real Web server, serving content to any machine (Mac, PC, Linux, Commodore Amiga, whatever) on the local network that has a Web browser.

And here you immediately see the utility of Personal Web Services. It's handy for "broadcasting" local information — you can easily assemble a simple Web page with project status info, for example — but the Big Win is that the Web is a concept with which the most inexperienced user is familiar and that every operating system supports.

So, for example, if you need to share a document with the entire office network, you can either explain to 300 people how File Sharing works, making sure you explain it one way to the Mac people and another way to the Windows people, and that when the Linux people tell you how much better they could have handled it, you don't hit them terribly hard. Or you can simply turn on Web Sharing, create a simple HTML page that links to the document, and just tell people to point their browsers to the URL.

To turn on Personal Web Sharing:

1. **Create the Web pages you want to share.**

2. **Place the Web pages in the Sites folder in your Home folder.**

3. **Launch System Preferences.**

4. **Click the Sharing icon.**

   The Sharing window appears. If necessary, click the Services tab.

BUT IS IT A *REAL* WEB PAGE?

Mmm … I suppose it depends on what you're asking. It is, indeed a real Web page that can be accessed over a network by any computer with a Web browser. But if you're expecting this to become a solution for hosting a Web site that everyone in the planet can visit, as opposed to just the folks in your home or office, you'll probably be disappointed.

You need a special kind of connection to the Internet: one that provides you with a "static IP address." Like the address to your house, an IP address defines where your Mac can be located from anywhere in the world. When you subscribe to broadband Internet access, though, your provider assigns you a random IP address … and every time your network modem resets, you're assigned a new one at random. And if your connection is hidden behind a router (like an AirPort base station), you're getting a randomly assigned address from the router as well.

So if you were to hand out that IP address to the world, it'd only work for about a day. If you want a "real" Web page, either pay your ISP extra (lots lots LOTS extra) for a static address, or pay an ISP like Pair.net or DigitalForest.net to host a Web site *for* you. You also get free Web hosting with your .Mac subscription. There are lots of solutions, and all of them are way better than using Personal Web Sharing.

5. **Click the Personal Web Sharing option (Figure 18-16).**

6. **Access your Web server.**

   To access your personal Web server, take the http address displayed at the bottom of the Services setup window and plug it into the address field of any Web browser.

It works great over the short haul, but again, don't confuse Personal Web Sharing with the sort of service that you get from a real ISP (like .Mac) to host a real, public Web site. Personal Web Sharing is designed for light duty on a local network and little more. And like FTP, it leaves your Mac vulnerable to break-ins, so if you intend to leave Personal Web Sharing up all the time, hide your Mac behind a router on the network for safety's sake.

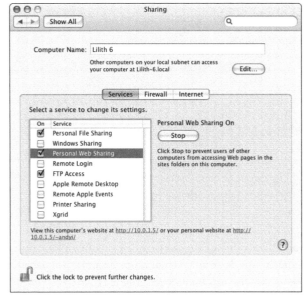

Figure 18-16
Turning on Personal Web Sharing

SHARING FOLDERS: A SHORTCUT

You know, you don't even have to learn HTML to benefit from Personal Web Sharing. Apache has a quirk or feature: Normally, when a browser accesses a URL, it automatically looks for and loads a file called index.html. That's the "top" page of the Web site. But if that index.html file doesn't exist, Apache sends back to the browser a directory of the Sites folder's contents, and you can download all those files by clicking them.

So, presto. It's the simplest possible way to share files with absolutely everyone on the network. Just toss the files into your Sites folder and turn on Web Sharing. Other users can download the files they want just by visiting the URL you give them and clicking the links that automatically pop up.

LIKE TO LIVE ON THE EDGE? LEAVE REMOTE LOGIN OPEN

Leaving Remote Login open is one of the riskiest things you can do with your Mac. I recommend that before you turn it on, you go out and see a movie, preferably one of *The Lord of the Rings* movies or the restored edition of *Lawrence of Arabia* if it's playing nearby. First, because they're great movies, and second, because they're three hours long. If by the time you return to your home or office you still have even the foggiest idea of why the devil you wanted to turn on Remote Login in the first place, then go ahead. But don't say I didn't warn you.

I think I'm telling you about Remote Login for the same reasons that any responsible parent tells his children about fighting or drinking or sex with anybody at any time for any reason so long as *I'm* alive, young man/missy. I'm really sort of hoping you won't try it yourself until you're older, but if you do try it, you shouldn't stumble into trouble like an ignoramus.

Note

And if you didn't understand that last sentence, it's a sign that you shouldn't mess with it at *all*.

Remote Login

The good thing about Remote Login is that (unlike everything else we've been discussing here) it doesn't just allow you to move files around. Remote Login allows you to take complete control of your Mac from nearly any other computer on the network running the right sort of software. I mean, no kidding. You can move files around, delete stuff, launch apps, force apps to quit, turn basic services on and off . . . all through a text-based command line. It's hard to imagine a common problem to which Remote Login is the best solution, but it's easy to imagine a very uncommon problem to which it's the only solution.

For example, you're on a weeklong vacation, road-tripping across the country to find the perfect bowl of diner chili. Your phone rings. It's your sister, who's house-sitting. One of the reasons she agreed to water your cat and feed your plants all week was the fact that you have this great Macintosh G5, and she wants to spend the week playing with iMovie and GarageBand.

But she doesn't know the password. You meant to create an account for her before you left, but you forgot, and you don't want to give her the password to your own account. So, when you reach your next hotel, you plug your PowerBook into a phone line, launch the Terminal app, and run a command-line program called ssh. You log in to your home

Macintosh just as though you were sitting behind the keyboard 900 miles away, and create a brand-new account that lets her log in to your G5 and start editing video.

Far-fetched? Yes. But a good example of what this service is good for.

The bad thing: *It allows you to take complete control of your Mac from nearly any other computer running on the network.* Remove the word "you" and substitute the word "A suitably clever and determined egg-sucking weasel intent on wreaking havoc," and you see the problem.

To turn on Remote Login:

1. **Launch System Preferences.**

2. **Click the Sharing icon.**

   If necessary, click the Services button.

3. **Click the Remote Login option (Figure 18-17).**

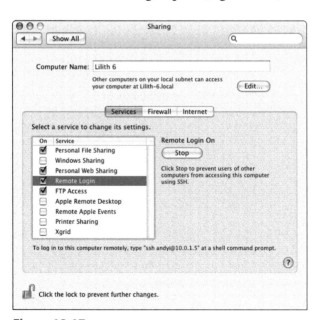

Figure 18-17
Turning on Remote Login

Printer Sharing

This option allows any Mac on your network to send print jobs to a printer connected to your Macintosh. For the sake of completeness, here's how to turn on Printer Sharing:

1. **Connect the printer to your computer.**

   Make sure that it is working properly.

2. **Launch System Preferences.**

3. **Click the Sharing icon.**

   If necessary, click the Services button.

4. **Click the Printer Sharing option.**

You can also turn this feature on through the Print & Fax pane of System Preferences:

1. **Click on Print & Fax, and then click on the Sharing tab of the preferences window (Figure 18-18).**

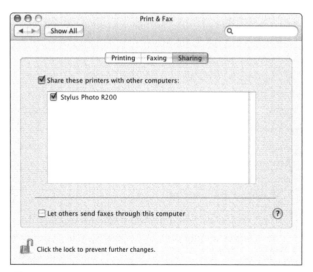

Figure 18-18
Turning on Printer Sharing

2. **Click the "Share these printers with other computers" checkbox.**

   You'll see a list of all of the printers connected to your Mac. Click on all of the printers that you'd like to share with other Macs on your network. If this Mac is configured to send outgoing faxes, you can also share its fax services by checking the box at the bottom of the preferences window.

Using a shared printer is transparently simple: your shared printer will magically appear in the Print dialog of every Mac on the network.

 Cross-Reference

For a more complete discussion of printing, see Chapter 13.

SHARING WITH WINDOWS USERS

In Chapter 12, you found out how easy it is to access Windows disk volumes that are available on your network. But turnabout is fair play. You can also allow Windows users to mount OS X volumes.

OS X provides Windows access with Samba, a Unix program. It's only a *little* trickier to set up than regular file sharing. To share files with Mac users, you just needed to turn file sharing on. For Windows file sharing, you also need to create a user account for Windows visitors to use when they're getting files.

1. **Create a new account.**

   This is to allow Windows folks who are seeking files to access your computer. For security's sake, just give this account basic user privileges . . . not Administrator

access. You might also want to enable a whole mess of Parental Controls, just to limit what a user can do with this account if the info falls into the wrong hands.

2. **Launch System Preferences.**

3. **Click the Sharing icon.**

   If necessary, click the Services button.

4. **Turn on the Windows Sharing option (Figure 18-19).**

   Now you need to assign Windows Sharing a user account.

5. **Click the Enable Accounts button.**

   A list of user accounts drops down.

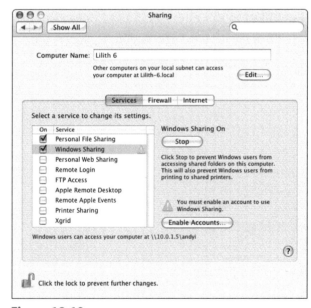

Figure 18-19
Turning on Windows Sharing

6. **Select the account that you just created and click the "On" checkbox.**

You'll be asked for the account password.

7. **Enter the account's password when asked, and click Done.**

Your Mac is now set up to share files with Windows users. An address is given at the bottom of the Sharing window (Figure 18-20). You'll need to give this info to any Windows user who wants to access your Mac's public files.

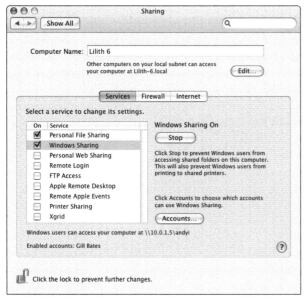

Figure 18-20
The network path to your Home folder, as Windows users understand it

In the best of all possible worlds, a Windows user can open their Network Places and drill down through any subnets until your computer appears. A quick double-click on your machine then displays a login dialog. After typing a correct user name and password, the portions of your files to which the Windows user has access appear on the Windows machine as if it were a local drive (Figure 18-21).

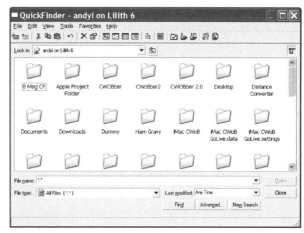

Figure 18-21
Sacrilege! Your User folder, accessed by a Windows user!

Unfortunately, Windows's Network Places doesn't always display a new computer when it powers up. Sometimes waiting a while helps, but if the Windows user runs out of patience, they can add your computer manually:

1. **Open My Network Places.**

2. **Click on Add a Network Place.**

A wizard appears for adding your Home folder to the PC's list of known network places. The Wizard will ask you to specify a service provider.

3. **Select "Choose another network location" and click Next.**

377

4. **Type the address of your Mac, as it was shown at the bottom of the Windows Sharing setup screen (Figure 18-20). Click "Next."**

5. **Type a name for the server, something you'll remember. And then click Next again.**

6. **Click Finished and you're done.**

The wizard connects to the Macintosh. Just enter the username and the password of the account you attached to Windows File Sharing, and the PC will be able to access public folders in your Home folder.

Here I have to confess that even though my home office is a mix of Macs and a couple of Windows boxes, I rarely use Windows Sharing. I rarely have a need to swap files between the two platforms, and besides, it's just so much simpler to either use Web Sharing or to just copy the file to my keychain drive and walk it over to the other machine.

I mean, don't get me wrong. I'm a geek, a big, honkin', major geek. Cut me and I bleed not red, but the nearest HTML-safe equivalent expressed in hexadecimal. But sometimes even I get fed up with some of the procedures that you have to crawl through to accomplish the simplest danged thing. SneakerNet isn't the fastest or slickest way of moving bits around, but it's nearly foolproof.

Except for that time when I stumbled over a 5-gallon bucket I'd been using to pour half-empty office Coke cans into, and the resulting sticky tidal wave took out a Dell tower PC.

On the bright side, after I knocked the bucket over, moving the file onto the gooey PC was no longer even necessary. Turned out to be quite a nice little timesaver, actually, because I was spending a hell of a lot of time maintaining that PC.

Shame about the cat, though.

19

I Loathe People! I Want to Secure My Mac!

In This Chapter

Physical Security • Passwords • Fostering Distrust Between You and Your Mac
Turning Off Unnecessary Services • Limiting Access with Firewalls
Protecting Files with FileVault • Deleting a File Securely
Backing Up! • Wireless Security

Yes, renowned philosopher B. B. King had it right when he sang, "Ain't nobody loves me but my Mother . . . and she could be jivin', too." Honest to God: trust nobody. People want to steal your PowerBook. Your tower Mac is harder to cart off, sure, but those who can't muster the energy to steal it will still want to gain access to your data. Everybody wants the account numbers and passwords for your online banking accounts. At the last family wedding, your mother kept complimenting you on how good you look in that suit, but that was just a ruse to nudge you into quitting your Van Halen tribute band and taking an entry-level management position at your uncle's plastics company.

The good news is that unless you have either (a) Congressional authority to second a launch of nuclear missiles or (b) perhaps a beta of next year's edition of *John Madden Football*, it's unlikely that anyone is targeting you, specifically. The miscreants (weasels, reprobates, lizard scum) are just looking for unsecure machines in general and taking anything of value that they happen to find.

WAIT. . . WHAT ABOUT ANTI-VIRUS AND ANTI-SPYWARE UTILITIES?

You won't find an explanation of 'em here. Nor will you find a roundup of the best apps. It's not my fault: there just plain aren't any viruses, Trojan horses, or spyware in the world of the Macintosh.

And when I say none, I mean *none*. We're like the Hobbits, living in the Shire. Our world is one of peace and trust, and we are as yet untouched by the hands of war. Hardcore Mac aficionados claim it's because *our* OS is just *soooo* much more advanced and *sooooo* much more secure than Windows. Folks who occasionally get out of the house acknowledge Tiger's wonderful security features but patiently explain that it probably has more to do with the fact that Windows has more than 95% of the market while Mac OS has less than 5%. Like the Hobbits, we're a small and insignificant target, and the [expletives deleted] who write that sort of malicious software pass us over in favor of richer targets.

And so, we smoke our pipes and we do our rustic dances. But the Great Evil will probably head our way eventually.

THERE BUT FOR THE GRACE OF WHATEVER, PART XXVII

Why be thankful that you're not a Windows user? Well, first and foremost, because the little chip that Microsoft implants next to your brainstem really gets uncomfortable whenever there's a drop in barometric pressure. But here and now I'm talking about the security aspect. Macs have a fraction of the Windows market and because those lizard scum want to attack the greatest number of machines with the least amount of effort, they're really not interested in thinking up ways to break into our hardware.

Our OS is inherently more secure than Windows XP, too; but in a sense, a Mac is like the penthouse apartment on a 20-story building with no elevator. It's just too much effort to get all the way up there, and there are plenty of other places to hit along the way.

The even better news is that whether you're protecting your Mac on the analog plane (someone grabbing and running off with it) or the digital one (someone copying your financial info off your hard drive), you don't necessarily need to make your Mac bulletproof. You just need to discourage the casual interloper so much that they look for a less-vulnerable machine in the next room or at the next IP address along.

PHYSICAL SECURITY

Let's start with the easy stuff: physical security. Although it doesn't strictly apply to OS X, you should consider what might happen if someone were to break into your home or office, or just passes by an open door and spots a $2,000 computer that can easily be hidden under a jacket or carried to a car. Either event could easily ruin your whole day. At best, you're out a couple of grand. At worst you have to worry about what that weasel might do with your financial info, your contact database, your personal photos, and all of your correspondence.

(Did it just get cold in here? I thought I felt a chill.)

Short of installing the same sort of automated poison-tipped darts around your office that Indiana Jones used to encounter — not necessarily a bad idea; I imagine that someone might steal your instant pudding from the break room, but it wouldn't happen more than once — what can you do to stop a thief from grabbing your Mac? You can purchase a computer lockdown cable kit and use it. All Macs have a provision for these things: you get a hard-to-cut-off tab that snaps into a ready-made port on your notebook or tower. It permanently fuses itself to the machine and provides a ring that a chain or a cable can pass through, locking the hardware down to the desk or a pipe in a nearby wall.

Granted, anyone with a strong pair of cutters can snap through the aircraft cable that usually comes with such kits, but it's good protection from crimes of opportunity. Remember, you don't have to have the most secure Mac in the world — just the most secure Mac in the *room*.

▼ Note

This is the classic "I didn't know how much I needed this until I owned it" accessory. If you can't imagine ever being so foolish as to leave your PowerBook unattended, can you imagine being so foolish as to let your battery run down two hours before a long flight, and having no alternative but to leave it in an unlocked office to recharge? It's just a good thing to have this thing sitting somewhere in your laptop bag.

PASSWORDS

Your Macintosh's first line of defense is its passwords. A password (sometimes also called a *passphrase*) keeps other people from logging in to your account and also ensures that only authorized users can perform actions — such as installing software — that change the configuration of your computer.

An effective password is easy to remember but hard to guess. If that sounds like a contradiction, don't worry; it isn't. One way to construct good passwords is to use two short, unrelated words connected by a special character. For example, green!toe is a pretty good password. Green and toe are unrelated words and the exclamation point between them means that an egg-sucking weasel can't use an automated password-guessing program that simply throws every word in the dictionary at it.

Another good way to construct a password that is hard to crack is to replace letters with numbers. You could, for example, choose "replace" for your password and then use the number 3 instead of the letter *e*: r3plac3. Now you have something you can remember but that is also very hard to guess.

And longer passwords are always better than shorter passwords. Don't forget about the threat of someone peeking over your shoulder as you type. If they see you type K-I-T, they're 60 percent of the way to guessing that your password is "Kitty." If it's actually "kitchen-blender-filled-with-enough-tequila-and-ice-to-stun-an-elk," then they're probably not getting in.

Common wisdom says that you should change passwords frequently (every 60 to 90 days, for example). But there's a big drawback to doing that: It makes your password hard to remember. You'll either forget it, or you'll worry so much about forgetting that you'll do something regrettable like write it on the underside of your keyboard. You'll have to find a pivot point you're comfortable with. If you change your password every week, keep it short and simple. If you only change it once a year or so, make it long and brain-bangingly hard and make bloody sure no one ever sees it.

A METHOD TO PASSWORD MADNESS

Here, I'll give you my Super Top-Secret Golden Pathway To Choosing Passwords That Are Easy For You To Remember But Impossible For Others To Guess: Use "codebooks." Last week, I forgot the password to one of my servers. Well, I just pulled my battered old copy of *The Complete Directory To Prime-Time Network TV Shows 1946-Present* off the shelf. It's the book I always turn to when I need to change this machine's password. I just kept flipping through it and trying any title that happened to leap out at me.

A few minutes later I had successfully logged on to my server (with the password "leg-work," based on a 1-hour crime series that lasted four episodes on CBS in 1987. Starring Frances "Fargo" McDormand, interestingly enough). I quickly remembered that it was somewhere in the middle of the book, and as soon as I spotted Chief Marge in there, it all came back to me.

I can safely share my super-secret method with you. Why? Because I have nearly a thousand books in my home library alone; and even though I've told you what the codebook for this one server is, good luck guessing the right password. The book's 1,200 pages long and mentions about eight shows per page. Better get cracking.

 Tip

There's an exception, though. Assuming that you are the only one who knows the password to log in to your OS X account, you should seriously consider writing it down, sealing it in an envelope, and storing it in a safe deposit box. If you are unable to access your computer for any reason, this ensures that some other person you authorize can do so. Or do you think you'll *never* wipe out on that stupid motorcycle you bought when you turned 40, and your spouse will never have a need for all of your family financial records in an emergency?

What shouldn't you do when choosing a password? Don't use the name of family, friends, pets, birthdays, anniversaries. . . or anything that someone else might know about you or be able to find out. If your cubicle is packed with *Simpsons* action figures, "Homer" is going to be one of their first five guesses, I guarantee you.

Don't recycle passwords, either. If an egg-sucking co-worker correctly guesses that your Mac's password is "warrenzevon," he's going to see if it'll work on your eBay account, your mail account, and anyplace else that occurs to him.

When you work with OS X, you encounter several types of passwords:

- **Administrator passwords:** An administrator is a user account that has the right to perform system modifications, including installing software, using

System Preferences to change settings and preferences, managing user accounts, and so on. The OS X Installer creates an administrator account for you when you install the software. You can create others, but keep in mind that the fewer administrator passwords that exist, the lower the chance of one of them falling into the wrong hands.

▼ Note

You don't need to be logged in to an administrator account to perform actions that require administrator privileges. In fact, it is wiser not to be. (If you walk away from your computer and leave it logged in to an administrator account, anyone who uses the computer has access to the entire system.) Instead, OS X asks for an administrator password when you attempt to perform a restricted action from a user account. After you supply an appropriate password, your restricted action can proceed.

- **User passwords:** A user password is the password to any user account without administrator privileges. This is what you use to log in to a user account.

- **Master password:** If you use FileVault (discussed later in this chapter) to encrypt the data in your personal folders, your computer needs a master password that can override the user password. The master password is a safety device that you use only when a user forgets his or her user password. An administrator sets the master password, which works for all accounts on the computer.

- **Application and Web site passwords:** As you work with programs, documents, databases, and Web sites, you'll accumulate a rather large collection of accounts

and passwords. You can manage these with one of Tiger's handier features, the Keychain. Stay tuned for more info on that dealie because using the Keychain nudges the Macintosh Experience a few yards closer to Perfection.

I'm recommending that you come up with your own scheme for generating and remembering passwords. "But *why?*" you ask. Because at this point you've gone through every single nook and cranny of Tiger and you appear to know it from top to bottom. "Tiger has a built-in, handy-dandy automatic password generator! It's called the 'Password Assistant' or somesuch, isn't it?"

Okay, you got me. In a few nooks and crannies, such as the Accounts pane of System Preferences, Tiger gives you the option of kicking on a button and having the OS invent a password for you. Viz Figure 19-1.

But I don't recommend it for most users. Or actually, practically *any* users. Just look at the sort of passwords that it generates: "a10l6Nq. . ." — I can't even *type* the rest of it. And Tiger thinks that password is *memorable?* Not by the Humans. No, if a Human uses that password, he or she will wind up having to write it down somewhere next to the keyboard, which sort of defeats the whole purpose of having a secret password, doesn't it?

The Password Assistant is only there so that Apple can say that Tiger supports popular standards for security. In some ultrasecure environments, administrators aren't about to trust the Hu-Mans to come up with solid, hard-to-guess passwords. So in comes the Mystifying Password Generator.

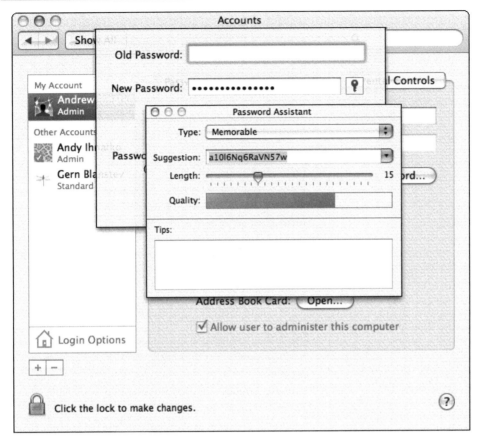

Figure 19-1
Password Assistant generates passwords that only a 64-bit processor could love

FOSTERING DISTRUST BETWEEN YOU AND YOUR MAC

. . . And believe it or not, it's actually a *good* thing if your Mac occasionally looks at you with the jaundiced eye of one who's loved and been wronged in the past. Your user account name and your password are the chief line of defense keeping other folks from sitting behind your keyboard and accessing all of your information. At one end of the spectrum, Tiger can simply start up and log you in without asking for any proof of identity. At the other end,

it can become paranoid about the possibility of creeps, weasels, and ne'er-do-wells who linger in the hallways just *waiting* for you to leave for the day, so they can plop their amoral backsides into your chair and rifle through your Mac as easy as you please.

Which is right? Depends on the likelihood of creeps, weasels, and ne'er-do-wells in your home or office. Oh! And shifty-looking idlers. Don't forget the shifty-looking idlers; they're the worst.

Passwording startup

When you first install OS X, the Installer prompts you to create a single administrator account. If you are the only person using your Macintosh, then you can configure OS X to log in to that account automatically at system startup, without requiring you to supply a password. This works well if you aren't worried about someone restarting your Mac and gaining access to your account.

Figure 19-2
Disabling automatic login

▼ Note

I'm sorry, but I need to interject. You're using the most stable and steady version of the Macintosh operating system ever created. Arguably, it's the most stable OS available *anywhere*, rarely requiring restarts. And yet you can't summon the 18 picocalories of energy required to tap seven or eight tiny keystrokes once or twice a week?

There's a *reason* why the U.S. has failed to bring home Olympic gold in Men's Singles Badminton, ladies and gentlemen: lack of get-up-and-go. I'm just the only one with enough pride in this great nation to point it out.

But if more than one person uses your computer, or if you want to secure the login — or if you can imagine a reality in which someone might, you know, be able to actually pick up your PowerBook and walk away with it — you should disable the automatic login:

1. **Launch the System Preferences application.**

2. **Click on the Accounts panel.**

3. **Click on the Account name at the top left of the window (see Figure 19-2).**

4. **Click on the Lock icon at the bottom left of the window, and enter your password so that you can make changes to this account.**

5. **Click on Login Options at the bottom left of the window.**

6. **Remove the check from the "Automatically log in as:" checkbox.**

7. **Close System Preferences.**

Passwording sleep and the screen saver

Removing the automatic login isn't enough to protect your Mac from someone who walks up to your computer. You also need to worry about what happens when you walk away from your desk to nuke up a Taco-Bagel-Wich. Your Mac is completely vulnerable. Anyone strolling by can glance at your screen and note that you've got your résumé open in one window and a job search Web site open in another. If the jerks in your office are active instead of passive (thus inspiring you to seek alternative employment), they can take a seat and paw through your files. Überjerks can create their own user accounts on your machine so they can come back in across the network whenever they please.

So you're gonna want your Mac to ask for your password before waking up from sleep. Ne'er-do-wells can admire your Classic Scenes From *Star Trek: Voyager* screen saver all they want, but that's as far as they can go.

To require a password to wake from sleep or clear the screen saver:

1. **Launch the System Preferences application.**

2. **Click on the Security panel.**

3. **Place a check in the "Require password to wake this computer from sleep or screen saver" checkbox (see Figure 19-3).**

4. **Close System Preferences.**

Figure 19-3
Requiring a sleep or screen saver password

Managing passwords with the Keychain

The big catch-22 of passwords is that if you exercise the basic rules of common sense, you'll wind up needing to remember a dozen different passwords of brain-mincing complexity. The third or fourth time you lost an hour of your time because you couldn't remember a simple email password like "aj8s7ssyu-aisj-hasselhoff" — as chosen by Tiger's handy-dandy new Password Assistant — (okay, I promise I'll stop complaining about the Password Assistant now) you'll probably change all of your passwords to the word "password" and move on with your life.

Well, Tiger has anticipated your pain and given you a big chewable aspirin in the form of the Keychain. Keychain files can store secure, encrypted versions of your passwords. Thanks to this handy-dandy little item, Tiger can automatically remember all of your passwords for you, and automatically type 'em in when they're needed.

PORTABLE PASSWORDS AND INSUFFERABLE PUNS

If you want real high-powered, super-atomic ironic laughs, buy one of those little USB flash-memory drives that snap onto your keychain (the analog one; it has your car bleeper and a lewd Las Vegas souvenir doodad on it) and keep your OS X Keychain file on it. Remember, no matter where you are or what Mac you're sitting at, you can plug the USB Keychain into a keyboard USB port, use the Keychain Access app to let this Mac know that it exists, and it's just like being at home.

Come to think of it, "Look, chums! A keychain that contains a keychain!" is not the sort of joke you make unless you enjoy being hit a lot.

The best thing about the Keychain is that it all happens automagically. The OS creates a system-wide keychain for you by default and keeps it ready. When a so-called Keychain-Aware app (such as Safari, iChat, or X's built-in Mail app) asks you for a password for the first time, the app will ask you if you'd like to stash the password in the Keychain file so that you won't have to provide it again (Figure 19-4).

Figure 19-4
Mail asks you if you'd like to store a password in your Keychain file

If you consent, then that's the last time the app will ever ask for it. Forevermore, it'll just grab it from your keychain, pausing (at worst) to ask you to confirm your identity by providing your keychain password. By default, it's the same as your system password, so it's easy to remember (and extra-important to choose a good system password). You can even control which apps have to ask permission before getting info from your keychain. Some have to ask, and you can click a Deny button to block access. Others are allowed to blow straight through.

And a Keychain-Aware app or resource can store *any* sort of password in there. Access to Web sites, file servers, remote Macs, AirPort base stations . . . the Keychain can handle it all. It can even securely store personal info, like credit card numbers or the security code to your alarm system.

HAVE YOU HUGGED A WINDOWS USER TODAY?

Look, I hate anti-Windows jingoism as much as the next guy (well, probably a lot less, but only because there's an overwhelming statistical likelihood that The Next Guy is running Windows), but let's pause here to reflect on something: On the Macintosh, all of these steps for creating and configuring a Way Cool Feature of the OS are things you only have to do *if you want to do things yourself.* The Mac is willing to do it all for you automagically. If you were a Windows user, this would just be a typical day in paradise, where convincing your computer to do something for you is about as calm and straightforward as trying to tell a 4-year-old child that you'd really like to speak to her daddy, now, so could she please hand the phone over to him?

The next time you spot a Windows user, just give him a hug without saying a word. He's probably had a really bad day.

Your keychain is protected by its own password; by default, it's the same as your system password.

 Note

A password that allows access to all of your *other* passwords? Yikes. If ever there was a reason to invent a password like "jmichaelstraczynskiandbillsienkiewiczplayingxylophone," it's this.

When you log in to your Mac, the OS automatically unlocks your keychain for you. Why not? By logging in, you've already proven that you are who you say you are. But if the Keychain remains open all the time, that's a Bad Thing. You're liable to take a 2-hour lunch break at some point during the week, and during that time the Keychain would allow anyone sitting at your desk to access anything you've passworded. Instead, it automatically locks itself if it hasn't been accessed recently — 5 minutes by default. Any later than that and it locks your Keychain file up again. The next time an app tries to access a password in your keychain, Tiger will ask you for your keychain password before unlocking it again and making with the goods.

Still not sold on this whole Keychain concept? OK, try this on for size: Keychains are portable. Say you've got a keychain file on your desktop Mac, containing passwords for three dozen different servers, accounts, and Web sites. But then you grab your PowerBook and head for the airport, and 6 hours later you're in a Sheraton in Tulsa desperately trying to remember your email password, right? Wrong. Simply make a copy of your user keychain file — you'll find it in your User ➜ Library ➜ Keychains folder — and copy it into the same directory on your PowerBook. It's still secure (your Mac will ask you for the keychain password before unlocking it), so no worries there. But now your PowerBook can automagically access the same services as your desktop.

If you want, you can even have multiple keychains on the same machine. This is handy when there's one set of passwords that everybody needs (access to the company file servers and the wireless routers) but there's another set of passwords (email, iChat) that are specific to each user. And if you subscribe to Apple's .Mac online service, Tiger's iSync utility can automatically synchronize all of your Mac's keychains so that they share access to the same library of passwords.

The Keychain Access application

Part of the glory and majesty of the keychain is the fact that it works completely automatically. You don't have to

configure it if you don't want to. To use some of the keychain's ginchier features, launch the Keychain Access utility. You'll find it inside the Utilities folder, inside your Applications folder.

Placing Keychain Access on a menu bar

I'm speaking to two groups of you right now. Group A is totally into the keychain concept. Group B is just sort of tagging along for the ride. Well, Group B, listen up. You probably won't be interested in using the Keychain Access utility, but it does have one feature you should use: it can place a menu in your menu bar that makes a bunch of security features easier to access (Figure 19-5). So you should at least read about *that*.

To make the menu appear:

1. **Launch Keychain Access.**

2. **Select View ➜ Show Status in Menu Bar.**

A keychain icon will appear in the menu bar at the right. To remove the keychain menu, uncheck the same option.

As you can see in Figure 19-5, the Keychain Access menu puts a bunch of useful options close at hand:

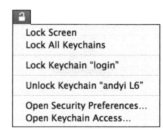

Figure 19-5
The Keychain menu

- **Lock Screen.** This blacks out your screen. And the sucker'll *stay* that way until you type in your login password. A quick and handy way to protect your Mac when you're stepping out for a few minutes.

- **Lock All Keychains.** Like I said earlier, Tiger's keychain feature will automatically supply passwords to apps that ask for them, such as your Mail client or secure Web sites. If you don't use your keychain for about five minutes, your keychain is "locked" and no passwords will escape from it until you provide your keychain password. If you don't want to *wait* for five minutes, you can lock all keychains or specific ones by selecting their items in the menu. In Figure 19-4, I have two keychains open, for example: my Login keychain, and "andyi L6," which contains all of the passwords that are keychained on my other Mac.

- **Unlock a keychain.** My Mac has been introduced to the "andyi L6" keychain file before, but it hasn't had a need to open it yet. To unlock it immediately, I can just select this item from the menu.

- **Open Security Preferences and Open Keychain Access.** These take you directly to two of the most useful System Preferences pages for securing your Mac.

Whether you intend to really jump into keychain files in a big way or not, the Keychain menu is a handy doodad to have up there in the menu bar. But if you're reacting to the earlier description of keychains the same way that Liberace reacted the first time he saw a rhinestone that weighed more then three points, you'll want to roll up your sleeves and take a good, saucy look at the Keychain Access utility itself.

Wait no longer: Figure 19-6 shows the app in all its glory:

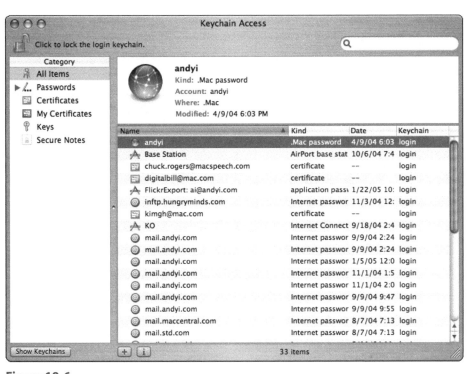

Figure 19-6
The Keychain Access utility: stepladder to a safer, more paranoid you

The Keychain Access window is organized into three panes:

- **Category.** The utility actually stores, secures, and organizes more than just passwords. It also keeps track of site certificates (which validate that the user or the host that you're communicating with over a network is, in fact, exactly who or what it claims to be), encryption keys (which can be used to both verify that senders of email are who they say they are, and can also securely "lock" the communication so that only the intended recipient can actually read it), and *Secure Notes,* which are snippets of any sort of information at all that you'd like to securely store.

- **Keychain items.** The actual things in your keychain. When All Items is selected in the Category pane, you'll see the whole lot. Clicking on Passwords will limit the list to just passwords. Et cetera.

- **Details.** The top pane shows you a brief description of a selected keychain item.

In Figure 19-6, I've selected my .Mac password. And the Details pane shows me enough info about it that I can easily distinguish it from any other .Mac account items that I might have in there. For more details, I can just click the Information button at the bottom of the list. Behold, Figure 19-7:

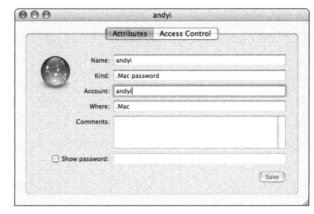

Figure 19-7
Up to our elbows in the details of my .Mac account

TIGERS ARE SLY AND VENGEFUL

Remember at the end of *2001: A Space Odyssey,* when HAL figured out that the crew was going to shut him down? Didn't end happily for one of those two astronauts, did it? I'm fairly sure that Tiger doesn't have a similar sort of architecture where the OS becomes increasingly suspicious of its users' intentions and embarks upon increasingly bizarre and rash behavior in a misguided attempt to protect both itself and its self-perceived "mission."

But do realize that I'm writing this book based on a prerelease version of Tiger. Really, almost anything can be added to the software in the month between the time the manuscript is finished and books start to roll off the presses. So all I'm saying is that if you make any spastic movements like fetching the actual passwords from your keychain, you know, something that might suggest to your Mac that you no longer trust it, just don't go up on the roof to fix an antenna. That's all I'm saying.

Here's where I can actually edit the contents of this item. If I wanted the description to be more descriptive, I could click in the Comments field and elaborate that this is my "real" .Mac account, not the super-secret one that I use when I post messages to the "Give Captain Sulu His Own *Star Trek* Series" message boards.

If I click on the "Show password" checkbox, Keychain Access will reveal the actual password in plain text. A dashed handy feature, when Keychain has been managing your passwords for so long that you've forgotten what many of them actually are any more.

The Access Control tab of an item's info window allows you to tell Tiger how close to the vest you'd like this item's info to be held (Figure 19-8):

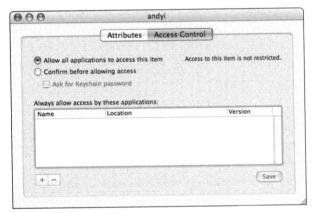

Figure 19-8
A Keychain item's Access Control settings

As things are set in 19-8, any app that needs my .Mac password can go get it, provided my keychain is unlocked. By clocking the second radio button, I can make sure that Tiger always, always, *always* asks me before it hands that information off.

Even with this option selected, I can exclude certain apps from this sort of treatment. iPhoto, for example, is always allowed to fish out my .Mac password; it often uploads photos to one of my .Mac galleries. To make an exception, just click the + button at the bottom of the list, select the app from the standard Open dialog box that appears, click Open, and then click the Save button.

Creating new keychains

Tiger adds items to your built-in Login keychain automatically. Sometimes it's useful to have more than one keychain, though; one that contains all the passwords associated with this specific Mac, and another with all of the passwords that you'd like to carry with you from Mac to Mac to Mac.

It's an easy enough stunt to pull off. To create a new keychain file with Keychain Access:

1. **Choose File → New Keychain.**

2. **Type a name for the new keychain and click Create.**

   By default, Keychain Access will save the new keychain in the Keychains folder in your User/Library directory.

3. **Type a password for the new keychain and click OK. (Ugh . . . there's that Password Assistant button again. Ignore it! Don't make eye contact! Don't *look*, Marian! *Don't look at it!*)**

   The new keychain ("Schneider," in this example) is now ready for use. Click Keychain Access' Show Keychains button to take a gander at the new keychain file, as well as all the other keychains that your Mac knows about (Figure 19-9).

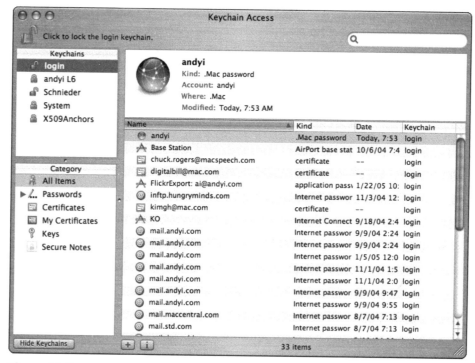

Figure 19-9
Admiring all of your Keychains

Changing a keychain's settings

Every keychain has some fundamental settings that you can change by selecting it in the keychain list and then choosing Change Settings for Keychain from the Edit menu (Figure 19-10):

Figure 19-10
Tweaking how an individual keychain works

The first two options are the most important: "Lock after X minutes of inactivity" allows you to specify how many minutes the keychain will be allowed to remain open, untouched, before Tiger locks it up again (Tiger will ask you for the password before allowing an app to access the keychain's contents). The second option automatically locks up the keychain every time your Mac goes to sleep. The fact that both of these options are turned on by default indicates how important these two features are.

"Synchronize this keychain using .Mac" does what you imagine it does. If you have a .Mac account and check this box, Tiger will automatically keep this keychain's contents synchronized with all other keychain files you're synchronizing with that account.

Copying items from one keychain to another

With the Keychains list visible, you can click on individual keychain files and see what's where. You can copy individual items from one keychain to another by just clicking on the first keychain and then dragging the item into the second keychain's name in the list.

Manually adding a Secure Note to a keychain

The Mac OS adds passwords, encryption keys, and certificates to your keychain automatically, but you can add items manually as well.

As an example, let's add a Secure Note. If you're traveling and your passport and wallet are lost or stolen, well, that'll ruin your entire week, won't it? So it's usually a good idea to keep those numbers written down somewhere, so you can close down old accounts and have new documents struck and sent out to you. But it's *super double-plus ungood* to write them down in a form where just about anyone can read them.

Enter *Secure Notes*. Notes stored in your keychain are protected with the same jackhammer-tough encryption that Tiger uses to protect all other keychain info.

To create a new Secure Note item:

1. **Select a keychain, if you have more than one.**

2. **Select New Secure Note Item from the File menu in Keychain Access.**

3. **Select File → New Password Item.**

   The dialog box in Figure 19-11 appears. Type in your Secret Info, give the item a title so that when the item appears in a list later on, you'll know what it's supposed to contain, and then click Add.

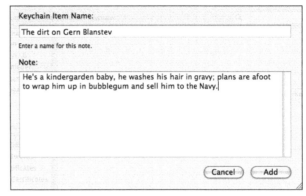

Figure 19-11
Sharing a secret with your keychain

And that's it. The Note will appear in the keychain's list of items, available only to people who know the keychain's password.

Sharing keychains

Of course, part of the ginchiness of keychains is that you stash all this info into one convenient, protected file. Then you can carry this file from Mac to Mac or account to account, using the same keychain password to automatically access all of the dozens or hundreds of passwords, notes, certificates, et cetera lovingly curated therein.

You can easily share one or more of your keychain files with other users of this Mac by opening Keychain Access' Keychain List sheet (Figure 19-12):

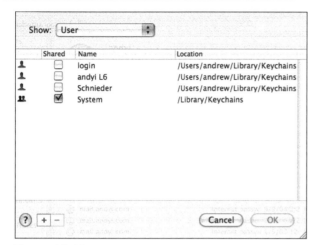

Figure 19-12
Sharing keychains with other users

Just click the Shared checkbox of every keychain you'd like to share. Every other user of this Mac will be able to access the keychain file's secured contents, if they know its password.

You should also be aware that the second term in the phrase "keychain file" is chosen with great thought and unflappable accuracy: it is, indeed, a file. Cool. You'll find your personal keychain files inside your User /Library/Keychains folder. Their file names end in ".keychain," and you can copy them just like any other files.

There are two keen upshots to this. For one, it makes it possible to share a keychain file with dozens or even hundreds of Macs, and not just the handful of users of your own, physical computer. Just copy the keychain file into the User/Library/Keychains folder of another user's Mac, and that dude can access the keychain's items just as easily as you can (again, *if* he has the file's password). To share the file with *everyone* on that Mac, either follow the same instructions above, or just copy it directly into the Mac's System/Library/Keychains folder.

 Tip

This is a great excuse to maintain two separate keychain files: a "communal" one and a private, personal one. You can just drag individual keychain items from one keychain file to the other, remember. So you're helping everyone in the office access the company's file server and internal Web site easily, while ensuring that your email passwords and the encrypted information that you intend to blackmail the boss with during your next salary review remains personal and private.

Here's another idea: Why not put your keychain file on a keychain USB drive? You know? One of those little memory drives that snaps on a key ring? Or how about your iPod?

And why the *devil* would that be a good idea?

Well, because I *say* it'd be a good idea.

Okay, an example:

You're at your pal Stanislau's house and you're about to go out and hit the town. But he's doused himself with way too much Jovan Musk as usual, and he's going to need a half an hour to shower the stink off. Seems like a good opportunity to mess around online and what luck! He's got an iMac! So you stick your key drive into the iMac's USB slot and it mounts on his Desktop. You launch Keychain Access and open the Keychain List, just as you did in Figure 19-12. But by clicking the + sign at the bottom of the sheet, you can navigate to the USB drive, point to your personal keychain file, and Stan's iMac will open it and access its passwords as easy as you please.

And naturally, when you remove the key drive, the iMac no longer has access to any of your passwords. I mean, honestly: would *you* trust your email password to a guy who wears cheap drugstore cologne?

To get his iMac to access your keychain file — *without* copying it into his Library directory — just:

1. **Launch Keychain Access.**

2. **Select Keychain List from the Edit menu.**

   A sheet drops down, listing all of the keychains your Mac currently knows about.

3. **Click the + button at the lower left corner of the sheet.**

   A standard file-open sheet appears.

4. **Locate the keychain file on the keychain drive, select it, and click Open.**

   The keychain file is opened and added to the list.

5. **Click OK to dismiss the keychain list.**

TURNING OFF UNNECESSARY SERVICES

Boy, has this chapter been a major downer or what? Okay, let me throw you a bone and offer a word of positive encouragement, atypical for a chapter on Security: If you're worried about some unauthorized weasel taking control of your Mac or accessing its files through your broadband or network connection, don't be. There are plenty of ways for the aforementioned mammal to do you and your data harm, but the sort of attack that makes the CBS Evening News isn't at all likely to affect any Mac users. Here we're talking about software that navigates through a network, twisting doorknobs and looking for unprotected ways to get inside your hardware. That's Windows stuff.

Still, even a shred of vulnerability isn't the same as no vulnerability. And if you have really sensitive corporate data

on your drive, you'll want to take the extra step of closing and locking any entranceways that you're not likely to ever use yourself. In Unix parlance, a *service* is an operating system program that provides support for a specific activity such as file sharing or printing, or serving Web pages. If these services can allow you and other happy and well-adjusted individuals to access your Mac, there's also the outside chance that they can inadvertently allow in those egg-sucking weasels as well.

For safety's sake, OS X leaves all those services off by default (see Figure 19-13). As a rule, you shouldn't leave them on unless you actually need regular access to them. So, if you find yourself in the Bizarro World and need to share files with Windows people, you can turn on your Mac's Windows File Sharing service temporarily, and then turn it off again when you're done:

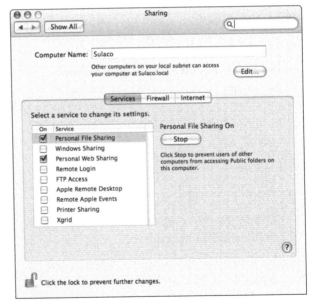

Figure 19-13
Limiting network access to your Mac

WHY THE EGG FIXATION?

Why do I insist on describing these people as "egg-sucking weasels," "vile miscreants," and "menace to all good, freedom-loving peoples everywhere" instead of the word "hacker"? Because the word's been corrupted by the mainstream media. The canonical definition, courtesy of Eric Raymond's *New Hacker's Dictionary:* "A person who enjoys exploring the details of programmable systems and how to stretch their capabilities, as opposed to most users, who prefer to learn only the minimum necessary." Hackers are to be admired, appreciated, taken out for a shave and a hot meal. Crackers (the weasels) are to be nailed up inside a wooden packing crate and then left in some tropical jungle near the habitat of the only land mammal known to be (a) a predator and (b) handy with a prybar.

1. **Launch the System Preferences application.**

2. **Click on the Sharing panel.**

   You should see the Services pane. If not, click the Services tab.

3. **Click on the name of an active service.**

   Services are located there on the left side of the pane.

4. **Click on either its checkbox or the Start/Stop button in the adjoining panel.**

   This will start or stop the service, depending on whether or not it was already running when you clicked the button.

I CAN SPELL "PARANOIA" ON THE FIRST TRY

I turn off nearly all of these services when I take my PowerBook into a public area. Particularly "Personal File Sharing." Tiger does a good job of limiting access to your data, but truth be told, your Mac *does* have "Public" areas that can be seen by visitors who spot your machine on a network. And sometimes I'm in a hurry and I store files where they shouldn't go. I can either worry about what I've got floating around on my Mac and where, or I can just turn off File sharing before I leave the house.

LIMITING ACCESS WITH FIREWALLS

Mac OS X's built-in firewall does much the same job as the Services tab: in broad terms, it prevents people from getting into your Mac through a network. The difference is in execution. The Services tabs simply lets you pull the plug on some of your Mac's networking features. The network firewall actively repels all attempts to access your Mac from the outside. Doesn't matter who or what wants to get access or for what reason. It ain't getting in.

 Note

You may occasionally encounter a reference to a firewall as a piece of hardware. In that case, the firewall software is running on a standalone piece of hardware that can be plugged into network hardware such as a router. It's a simple and largely foolproof way to protect a whole network as opposed to just one Mac.

To turn on the firewall:

1. **Launch the System Preferences application.**

2. **Click on the Sharing panel.**

3. **Click on the Firewall tab (see Figure 19-14).**

4. **Click Start.**

The firewall is like the bouncer at the door to a snooty club. There's only one way in and it's through him, and he's just shot you a glance from his peripheral vision that very effectively communicates that you are clearly way too big a geek to be allowed into a supermodel-enriched environment like this one.

BUT ARE YOU LEADING A FIREWALL-EY LIFESTYLE?

Engaging the firewall is overkill for many users. I leave it off for convenience's sake when I'm at home, and I only turn it on when I'm using a public wireless access point, or I'm sharing a conference hall with hundreds of the country's top networking Jedis. Until I become convinced that I'm the most clever networking jock in the world — and folks, there ain't enough gin in the world for that to happen — enabling the firewall is the better part of valor.

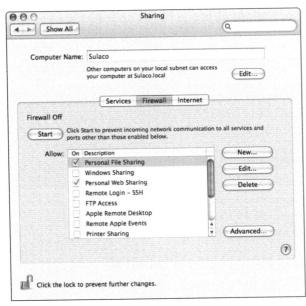

Figure 19-14
Defending your Mac from network attack with Tiger's firewall

But, of course, it wouldn't be much of a party if he didn't let *anybody* in. Remember, the real profit at a dance club is in beverage service, not the cover charge. So he has a little clipboard full of names with him. If you're on the list, you're straight through with a smile. Otherwise, he's prepared to deliver a cogent argument on the limitations of superstring theory in an Einsteinian universe, using your neck and nearby parking meter as visual aids.

Back to reality, or the version of it that Apple has created for us. In the Firewall tab, that scrolling list is the bouncer's clipboard. All the services that you've checked are allowed to access your Mac across a network. The hassle of having a firewall is that if the bouncer has never heard of your brand-new network gaming system (or any other unusual network software), it's not going to let its traffic through and your Mac becomes invisible to other gamers.

USER FRIENDLY? A *FIREWALL?*

Do note that firewalls aren't, as yet, really easy to use. That is, there are some firewalls that are easy to use and maintain, but they tend to block lots of activities that are perfectly kosher, and thus turn into a colossal pain in the Semprini instead of a useful method of protecting your Mac. The ones that are most flexible and least intrusive need to be configured carefully.

Tiger's built-in firewall is a satisfactory compromise for most users. Good enough to keep out all but the most persistent weasels, simple enough that you'll actually *activate* it.

That's what the New and Edit buttons are for. When you buy this sort of software, it comes with instructions on how to add it to your firewall's list of approved network traffic. The next time you want to pretend to be a disgraced former vice cop blowing up junior-high students 2,000 miles away who are pretending to be zombie alien commandos, the game will tell the firewall "I'm on the list, man," and it'll be waved straight on through.

Click on the Advanced button for a few additional tweaks:

- **Block UDP Traffic.** Oh, dear. Another acronym, one of those caustic kinds where when you find out what it means (User Datagram Protocol) you understand even less than you did before. UDP is a low-level messaging protocol that isn't quite as safe as the alternatives, and removing support for this protocol makes your Mac just a smidge safer.

- **Enable Firewall Logging.** Who's been knocking at your Mac's doors? With this option enabled, Tiger will maintain a log file of all connections to your Mac. If you suspect that there's been some funny business, click on the Open Log button to see what your Firewall's been dealing with, including (significantly) times that other machines tried to connect to you and were denied.

- **Enable Stealth Mode.** There's a problem with a firewall that tells unauthorized machines, "I'm a firewall app and I will not, repeat, *will not* allow you to access this machine!" It, um, tells the miscreant that there's a machine right here, and that it has a network connection and it's up and running. Better that any uninvited network traffic simply disappears into the ether, thus defending your Mac's invisibility.

PROTECTING FILES WITH FILEVAULT

Although you may spend between $1,500 and $3,000 for an iBook or PowerBook, the most valuable part of that computer may well be the data on your hard disk. If your laptop is stolen — and if it was asleep and un-passworded — the thief can wake up your computer and browse through your finances, company trade secrets, private memos, your Internet fanfic-in-progress about the cast of *McHale's Navy* gettin' it on with the cast of *The Love Boat*, and so on without a problem.

The solution is to encrypt your data files so that no one can read them without your encryption password. *Data encryption* is therefore the process of changing your readable files into something unreadable. Without the decryption key, your love letter to Tony Orlando is just random gibberish. OS X supplies encryption through its FileVault utility.

TARGETING YOUR MAC

The other thing to worry about: Target Disk Mode. As you hopefully learned in the Volumes chapter, nearly all Macs have a hardware feature called *Target Disk Mode*. You shut down the Mac (a PowerBook, say), plug it into another Mac via their FireWire ports, restart the PowerBook while holding down the T key on its keyboard, and presto: its internal hard drive appears on the host Mac's desktop. No password necessary; a miscreant can then paw through your files and copy whatever he or she wants.

If your office is any sort of Darwinian carousel of intrigue, you're thinking "Oh, God... I could *totally* see Rick doing that to me" and you'll want to use FileVault.

Tip

Encrypting the data on your hard drive is cool beans. No question. But under some circumstances you might want to consider something simpler and even more secure: working from an external hard drive and physically locking it in a safe at the end of the day. There are some things that a weasel in the employ of the Russian mafia can't accomplish from a networked computer in an apartment in Romania.

Encryption has both its good and bad points:

- **Encrypted files are unreadable by the casual thief or system cracker.** It takes considerable effort (and computing power) to crack the type of strong encryption that OS X uses.

- **You have to encrypt and decrypt the files.** Because you can't work with encrypted files, you must decrypt a file every time you want to use it. When you save the file, you must encrypt it again before it is written to disk. In general, this slows down processing.

- **Encrypting and decrypting files require a password.** FileVault uses your login password. In addition, when you turn on FileVault for the first time, you also create a master password that you can use if you have forgotten your login password. However, if you happen to be an administrator user and you've forgotten both your login password and the system's master password, you're hosed. The encrypted data becomes unrecoverable.

- **To be truly effective, only one administrator should know the master password.** The problem with this strategy is that if that person is ill or leaves your organization, you may be stuck without anyone who knows that password. A solution is to have at least two people who know the master password, but the more people who know the master password, the easier it is to compromise your system.

FileVault encrypts everything in your home directory. You must therefore take care to store all sensitive documents in your home directory or one of its subdirectories.

To turn on FileVault:

1. **Launch System Preferences.**

2. **Click the Security icon.**

3. **Check the text in the button next to the master password section.**

   If it says Set Master Password, click the button. Otherwise, skip to Step 6.

4. **Type the new master password and a hint to help you remember it, as in Figure 19-15.**

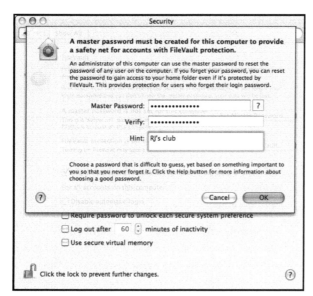

Figure 19-15
Setting your Mac's Master Password

▼ **Tip**

You should set the Master Password whether you intend to use FileVault or not. Otherwise, another administrator on this Mac might set it, and then *he or she* controls the ability to reset other users' passwords. And do you think they're going to tell *you* what it is?

And the Master Password is the *one* password that I actually write down. The note card is inside my safety-deposit box so no worries there, but it's desperately important insurance. If I lose *this* one, the consequences are pretty colossal: I could conceivably lose everything I've encrypted on my hard drive and the ability to get into forgotten accounts.

5. **Click the Turn on FileVault button.**

Tiger will ask you for the Master Password. Then, after a suitably scary and stiff warning, you're logged out. When you log back in, FileVault encrypts the contents of your home folder. If you have a lot of data, the initial encryption may take roughly the same amount of time it would take an adult emperor penguin to complete the Boston Marathon, riding on another emperor penguin's shoulders. If you have a slower Mac, you may add the suffix "who isn't quite sure what the precise race route actually is."

To turn off FileVault:

1. **Launch System Preferences.**

2. **Click the Security icon.**

3. **Click the Turn Off FileVault button.**

DELETING A FILE SECURELY

When you want to delete a file or folder, you drag it to the Trash and then empty the Trash. The file or folder is gone, right? Wrong. The file or folder is inaccessible, but its contents remain on the disk until the space is used for something else.

Until the disk space is overwritten, special utilities can often recover a "deleted" file or folder. If you are the only person using your computer, then you probably don't care. If, however, your computer is shared — either at the keyboard, over a network, or if you're about to give your old Mac away to a worthy relative — then you may want to obliterate files and folders completely.

To securely delete a file or folder:

1. **Move the files and folders you want to delete securely to the Trash.**

2. **Select Finder → Secure Empty Trash.**

OS X overwrites the space that the files and folders occupy with random characters, a process that takes longer than simply emptying the Trash.

BACKING UP!

A major part of an overall security scheme that is often overlooked is backup. Hard disks are very reliable, but they do have mechanical parts that can malfunction, and malfunction more easily than just about any other part of your computer. Even if your hard disk is alive and well, you can also suffer from file corruption caused by unexpected software crashes and glitches. Your best protection is a good, clean backup copy.

▼ Note

And every time I'm about to take off on a business trip, I reflect upon the fact that I am an imperfect vessel and I have failed to live a pure and chaste life. And then when the blood returns to my face, I perform an immediate backup. If my PowerBook gets stolen, well, that's too bad but I'm confident that with legs like these, I can make another $2,000 in no time. But what about the manuscripts and data?

Backing up your data can be as simple or as brain-bangingly difficult as you want. The only limit is your ambition.

If you're shiftless and lazy, you can just pop a recordable CD or DVD into your drive once a week or so and copy the contents of your Documents folder onto it.

MARKING YOUR TERRITORY

Which brings up a point: You hedge your bets wonderfully by pollinating the world with your system backups. I hid a 10-gigabyte hard drive inside the suspended ceiling of a pal's basement. He had no idea it was there until a pipe burst in my office and caused my Mac and all of its peripherals and data to start making their own gravy. Thank heavens I kept a backup in another house!

If you're even slightly ambitious or paranoid, you should buy a "real" backup program. Apple Backup comes free with your .Mac account and it's quick, clean, and feature-riffic. But the gold standard for both Mac and Windows is Dantz Development's Retrospect (`www.dantz.com`). It can handle the entire backup process for you, running at your command or at scheduled intervals. It can back up whole drives or just selected folders. It can restore whole drives or selected folders; you can even tell it, "Turn back the surly hands of time and make my drive the way it was three backups ago," and without even pausing to say, "Yes, Master," Retrospect makes it happen.

Flexibility is indeed the name of the game. Backing up your data is only effective if you do it regularly, and a good piece of software like Retrospect stays out of your way. Before long, you'll work out a scheme that works for you. Me, I back up my entire drive once a week and my various project folders get backed up several times a day.

You'll also need to think about what sort of storage media you're going to use for backups.

- **Burnable CDs and DVDs are cheap and plentiful.** They're also slow and have limited capacity; back up a whole 40 GB drive on these and you swap discs so much that you'll start seeing the dang things dancing around your head while you sleep. Plus, you can't really reuse them. At some point, you're going to have to safely destroy these discs before tossing them out in the garbage. Still, they're handy for quick backups of single folders.

- **External hard drives are a compelling modern option.** You can purchase stand-alone FireWire drives for less than a dollar a gigabyte, which means that $200 buys you a backup drive, its media (i.e., the mechanism inside), and enough space for three complete backups of your entire hard drive. It's rocket-fast, and best of all, if your internal drive is toast, you can boot from it. The only caveat is to resist the temptation to leave it connected to your Mac. If you do, when the slings and arrows of outrageous fortune (or a big fire) strike down your internal drive, it'll probably take out your backup as well.

- **Tape drives are the classic targets for backups, and are still the medium of choice for network administrators.** Each tape holds a boatload of data and each one costs less than a Big Mac with large fries and a Coke. The drive itself is a killer, though, and the huge expense (as well as their molasses-like speed) tends to scare most individual users off.

- **Network backups are a possibility, too, and now that more and more homes and small offices are going wireless, this sort of backup becomes more and more practical.** One Mac (with a big honkin' hard drive) contacts each of your Macs late at night and stores a backup of their contents locally. It's slow, but you're asleep in bed anyway so it really doesn't matter. It does have a big drawback: Unlike tapes, discs, or even an external hard drive, this specific kind of network backup can't be carried out of the building.

So again, unless an exceptionally thoughtful sort of tornado hits your office, a disaster that destroys your local hard drive could also take out your one backup. Backing up to your iDisk, or to a remote machine, gives you a little added protection.

WIRELESS SECURITY

"Wireless security" — some security professionals will tell you that such a phrase is an oxymoron, that there is no such thing. Why? Because wireless signals, as they are defined in the original WiFi (Wireless Fidelity) standard, aren't secure. Wireless transmissions can be easily intercepted and their content cracked. And let's not forget the "war drivers" who case neighborhoods with antennas made from Pringle's cans and wire coat hangers, looking for any network signals that might be passing through walls onto the street. If a war driver can pick up your network's signal, he can insert his laptop into your network and piggyback onto your Internet connection.

The first AirPort hardware that Apple released adhered to the 802.11b standard, which supports transmissions of up to 11Mpbs at a maximum range of 150 feet. Although 802.11b equipment is easy to install and use, it is not particularly secure. It is subject to war driving (and war walking and war flying, depending on the miscreant's mode of transportation). It is also vulnerable to:

- **Wireless sniffing:** A system cracker can insert a "packet sniffer" into the network and capture copies of the traffic passing on the network. He can then examine the contents of the packet at his leisure.

- **Hijacking:** A system cracker can insert packets into a network. These false packets can cause a computer to believe that it is communicating with a trusted computer, when instead it is communicating with a cracker who is attempting to steal information.

- **Inserting of base stations:** A system cracker can place an unauthorized base station into the network. If the unauthorized based station has a stronger signal than the legitimate base station, it can divert network traffic to the system cracker's equipment.

Probably the biggest security hole in the 802.11b standard is the Server Set ID (SSID). This is a password or passphrase that a computer uses to identify the base station with which it communicates. Each base station has a single SSID that all computers use. When you purchase a base station, the manufacturer gives it a default SSID that is the same for all base stations manufactured by the company. System crackers know these default SSIDs, and attempt to use them to access a base station. If the default has been changed, then a dictionary attack — the system cracker tries every word in a dictionary — can often penetrate the base station's new password.

Doesn't 802.11b use encryption? Shouldn't the company encrypt the SSID to make it harder to obtain? Certainly. It's known as Wired Equivalency Privacy (WEP).

But here's the problem: 802.11b encrypts data packets, but doesn't encrypt the SSID. It travels across the wireless network as plain text, making it very easy to intercept.

What can you do to protect an 802.11b network? Not a whole lot. WEP's 40-bit encryption key is better than nothing to protect your data, but given the computing power of current desktop machines, a competent system cracker can break the key in a reasonable amount of time. The *good* news is that, like so many facets of network security, your network doesn't need to be bulletproof. It just needs to be better than the base station a couple of yards farther down the street. Unless they have a specific target in mind, breaking WEP is too much trouble, given that there's usually a totally unlocked base station only a few minutes away.

Plus, do keep in mind that when you're using a secure Web site — for example to do some online banking — the browser applies kick-butt encryption on your data before it goes out over the network. So long as the URL starts with https://, and you see a little locked-padlock icon in the browser window, you're pretty safe.

AND PORN RAINED DOWN FROM THE HEAVENS

You want an example that will frighten, amuse, and disgust you all at the same time? Let me tell you about MacHack, a compact but very fulfilling annual conference for Macintosh power developers. On the last night of the conference everybody packs into the hotel ballroom to show off any nifty new apps they wrote during the week. One year, somebody showed off a very special networking app. It sniffed the air for wireless network traffic, looking for snippets that represented requests for JPEGs from Web servers. The app would then make its own request, and add the picture to the increasingly complicated patchwork of graphics on the Mac's screen.

Naturally, the moment he finished explaining the basic concept, 500 geeks flipped open their PowerBooks and giddily began accessing the most…the…well, let's just say they started hitting Web sites that they knew to be graphics-intensive. And ladies and gentlemen, the ballroom's 15-x-20-foot projection screen exploded. The air turned mauve. An angel with a flaming sword stepped ominously out from the catering area, clearly intent on proving that there's no testament like the Old Testament, but he himself was so creeped out by the rapidly morphing image that he just sort of coughed and made an excuse about having left the lights to his Bonneville on.

Depending on your ISP, it's also possible to use a secure connection to your mail server. Special protocols supported by Mail and other email clients encrypt passwords and data before they transmit, so if your ISP's mail server supports those protocols as well, there's no reason to worry.

 Note

Naturally, there's *always* reason to worry. Did you know that a recent research study suggests that our bodies' fundamental cellular morphology is "allergic" (for lack of a better word) to the element Nitrogen? The single most prevalent element in Earth's atmosphere? That ought to cheer you up vis-à-vis the relative threat of weak, 40-bit wireless security.

If you have the original AirPort base station, consider carefully what you send over that wireless network. Avoid using it for sensitive information, be it business or personal.

The alternative is to use Apple's AirPort Extreme, which adheres to the 802.11g standard. 802.11g is both faster (54Mbps at up to 59 feet) and more secure than 802.11b:

- **AirPort Extreme includes a built-in firewall.** In fact, this device acts much like a router in a wired network because it can accept a wired broadband Internet connection and a wired Ethernet connection. It also implements DHCP to hide internal IP addresses from the Internet.

- **AirPort Extreme implements 128-bit WEP encryption keys.** This is compared to the 40-bit keys that 802.11b employs. These longer keys make encryption keys almost impossible to crack with anything short of a supercomputer.

- **You can control the amount of power with which AirPort signals transmit.** By lowering the power, you

restrict the range of the signal, making it much more difficult for a system cracker to insert any equipment into the network. It also means that apartment dwellers can dial down the signal so that it's strong enough to punch into your two bedrooms but not into the apartment across the hall.

 Note

802.11g devices are compatible with 802.11b devices. However, when 802.11b devices communicate with an 802.11g base station, encryption is reduced to the 802.11b standard. Therefore, although you can use standard AirPort cards with AirPort Extreme base stations, you won't get the benefit of the added security that 802.11g brings.

Modern base stations have been upgraded to use a brand-new encryption standard, meant to address all the holes of WEP. The new standard's called WPA, or Wi-Fi Protected Access.

Whether you're using 802.11b (original AirPort) or 802.11g (AirPort Extreme), make absolutely sure that you've configured it to encrypt its signal. The Airport Setup Assistant utility can configure all of that for you automatically. When you join the network, it should ask you for either a WEP or WPA password.

Encrypting the signal also restricts AirPort access to those people who know the base station's password. That sound you just heard was the sound of freeloaders driving on past your house and on towards your neighbor's.

In retrospect, it's possible that when I suggested that your mother had formed a relationship with you based on deceit and betrayal to best suit her own selfish ends, I may have overplayed my hand. A bit. I mean, you know her better than I do, I suppose.

PARANOIA BY THE OLD BITSTREAM

And this is why you need to be more than a little worried about using public-access WiFi. It's not totally unheard of for some anonymous weasel to establish a "free" access point in a highly public place (like a public courtyard or a hotel lobby) and hope that people discover it and start using it. "Oh, joy!" you think. "Free WiFi!" And it's cool, sure, but the weasel is also hoping that he'll catch some email or banking passwords sent out unencrypted.

Even the "legitimate" base stations that you have to pay to access can cause problems; for safety's sake, you have to assume that the radio signal is unencrypted and that that folks can sniff the data coming in and going out. So once again: Make sure you're using secure Web sites when you're working with secure information. If you're going to check your email, configure your mail app so that it doesn't transmit its passwords in the clear. You can do this in Mail.app pretty easily: open its Preferences window, click on Accounts, select the Advanced tab of an account's settings, and then click the Use SSL checkbox.

The one caveat: Not all mail services support secure connections. If yours doesn't, it's possible that they also allow you to fetch your mail through a secure Web site, which is still a big step up from no security at all.

And finally, don't join any wireless networks that you've just "stumbled" upon. Yup, it stinks that the hotel you're in is charging $30 a day for internet access, and when Office Internet Connection magically appears in your AirPort menu, it's just *sooooo* tempting. But to quote your Mother's comments about the pencil you're about to put in your mouth, "You don't know where that thing has been."

Still, the whole point of this chapter is that the weasels are out there. Fortunately, Batman had them pegged right from Page Three of his original comic: "Criminals are a cowardly, superstitious lot." Yes, they can do a lot of damage, but for the most part their tactics are predictable. They're not looking for challenges: they're looking for users who either don't know or don't care about fundamental security.

In a world without weapons, a single ugly bartender wielding a board with a nail through it can become king.

PART II

The Technical Bits

Unix... Alas, the Name Is Its Only Funny Part

In This Chapter

The Brass Tacks • The Command Line: Meet the Shell, circa 1983
Your First Commands: Listing and Launching Files • Look! It Does Tricks, Too!

The Unix operating system has been an important and recurring off-screen presence throughout this book, much as it is in Tiger itself. If you were a kid during the seventies, Unix is to Mac OS X what Charlie was to *Charlie's Angels.* If you were a kid during the eighties, it's like Norm Peterson's wife Vera on *Cheers;* during the Nineties, Niles Crane's wife Maris in *Frasier;* and here in the first decade of the new millennium, the proper TV-fueled analogy is Karen Walker's husband Stan in *Will and Grace,* or the persistent thought "Good Lord... how the *hell* did this crappy show ever get greenlit?" in *Hope and Faith.*

If you're one of those people whose main motivation for meeting new people is to have a brand-new chance to explain, "No, I don't watch television, and let me tell you *why*...," then I suppose you'll respond well to "Unix is to Tiger as Godot is to *Waiting For Godot* or Harry Lime in *The Third Man.*" Provided, of course, that we overlook the fact that Lime does indeed turn up in the final reel of the film. Hey, I'm willing to overlook the fact that, truth be told, you haven't missed a single episode of *Fear Factor* in 3 years. Meet me halfway, here.

Continuing. Even if you never *see* Unix and never interact with it directly, it's always there behind the scenes, making things happen. And the beauty of Mac OS X is that, yep, you can use your Mac for years without ever interacting with Unix directly. Not unless you want to, of course.

Well, this chapter is designed to make you *want to*. There's a lot of power tied up in Unix and every Mac user should take a look under the hood and see what's there. You'll leave with a better understanding of your Macintosh, you'll learn a few tricks that'll come in handy, and perhaps the next time it looks like your date is about to tell you about how to increase system performance by looking for stalled processes, you won't set the tablecloth on fire as a distractionary tactic and then run away to avoid revealing your sad lack of savvy.

 Note

Yes, Janice Hallidow of Northampton, Massachusetts, I still remember and it *still* stings.

ANTI-SOCIAL DARWINISM

Wait… so if Linux is Unix and Darwin is Unix, does that mean software written for Linux will run on my Mac? Alas, it ain't that simple. It's like how folks in Boston and folks in Atlanta both speak English, but if I were to go to a diner down South and ask for ice cream with jimmies, with a frappe to drink, and my, that's a *wicked pissah* hat you've got on… well, confusion may occur.

But! All Unixes are similar enough that (a) they network to each other as easily as chips and salsa, (b) they use the same commands, and (c) it's not terribly difficult for a programmer to take an app written for Linux and make it work with Tiger.

(And: Jimmies are chocolate sprinkles, a Frappe is a milkshake, and "wicked pissah" is a term of extreme approval. Okay, we're out of time for today. Tonight, I want you all to read the chapter on How to Pronounce "Leominster" and what to do when your car enters a rotary. Class dismissed.)

THE BRASS TACKS

First thing is, you pronounce it "YOO-nix." It's like — tee-hee tee-hee tee-hee! — you know, that other, slightly naughty word!

Unix isn't one single commercial operating system, like Tiger and Windows are. On a rough basis, it's more like a *specification* for an operating system that many, many different companies and organizations have implemented — which means that there are plenty of different implementations. You may have heard of an open-source OS called Linux. That's a flavor of Unix. Mac OS X's flavor of Unix is called "Darwin."

THE COMMAND LINE: MEET THE SHELL, CIRCA 1983

At the root of every flavor of Unix is the command line. No menus, no windows, no 3-D animated figures of Don Knotts tap-dancing onto your screen and singing the date and time. You type text commands at the prompt, and Unix responds in the form of plain, monospaced text.

You interact with the command line through Tiger's Terminal app, which you can find lurking inside the Utilities subfolder of your Applications folder. Here's what you see when you launch Terminal (Figure 20-1).

Yup, that's all you get. Behold, the glory of the shell, which is how you refer to a Unix command-line environment. The *shell* is actually a piece of Unix software for taking the commands you type and giving them to the OS. The shell program that Tiger's terminal uses by default is called *bash*. There are others: csh, tsch, ksh, zsh. . . all have certain creature comforts that make it a little less painful to work with commands that can be twice as long as Prince Charles' full royal title.

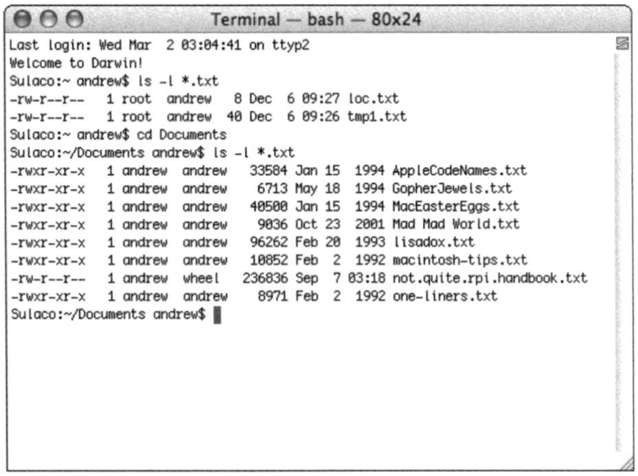

```
000              Terminal — bash — 80x24
Last login: Wed Mar  2 03:04:41 on ttyp2
Welcome to Darwin!
Sulaco:~ andrew$ ls -l *.txt
-rw-r--r--   1 root  andrew    8 Dec  6 09:27 loc.txt
-rw-r--r--   1 root  andrew   40 Dec  6 09:26 tmp1.txt
Sulaco:~ andrew$ cd Documents
Sulaco:~/Documents andrew$ ls -l *.txt
-rwxr-xr-x   1 andrew  andrew    33584 Jan 15  1994 AppleCodeNames.txt
-rwxr-xr-x   1 andrew  andrew     6713 May 18  1994 GopherJewels.txt
-rwxr-xr-x   1 andrew  andrew    40500 Jan 15  1994 MacEasterEggs.txt
-rwxr-xr-x   1 andrew  andrew     9036 Oct 23  2001 Mad Mad World.txt
-rwxr-xr-x   1 andrew  andrew    96262 Feb 20  1993 lisadox.txt
-rwxr-xr-x   1 andrew  andrew    10052 Feb  2  1992 macintosh-tips.txt
-rw-r--r--   1 andrew  wheel    236836 Sep  7 03:18 not.quite.rpi.handbook.txt
-rwxr-xr-x   1 andrew  andrew     8971 Feb  2  1992 one-liners.txt
Sulaco:~/Documents andrew$ ▊
```

Figure 20-1
The Terminal window

As a Human with no special interest or training, you'll never become concerned with the differences. But professional Unix system administrators put as much thought, passion, and venom into their personal choice as any two slightly drunk bar patrons would into a discussion of whether a duck could beat a chicken in a fight.

All you need to know is that terminal presents this interface to you in a standard Macintosh window, so you've got scroll bars (oooh!) and you can resize the thing (aaaah!); but on the whole, welcome back to The State of the Art in User Interface, circa 1983.

▼ **Note**

A year before the Macintosh came out, Dexy's Midnight Runners charted 80 spots higher than Eric Clapton in the Billboard Annual 100, and George Lucas announced that he wouldn't be making any more *Star Wars* movies, ever. You just *knew* that something good *had* to be coming up, just to restore humanity's faith in a compassionate and loving God...

The last line of text in Figure 20-1 is the actual command line:

- **Sulaco:** The name of the Macintosh in use.

- **~/Documents:** The name of the directory the user happens to be sitting in at the moment. In Unix, the tilde is shorthand for the user's home directory. In Macintosh-speak, the home directory is that directory with your name on it inside the folder named Users. So here, I'm in my personal Documents folder.

- **andrew:** The account under which I've logged in. Because I logged in already, back when I started my Mac, there's no need for me to prove who I am any more and the command line recognizes me instantly.

- **$:** The actual prompt. *That's all I can tell you right now, Sparky. You got a command for me?*

YOUR FIRST COMMANDS: LISTING AND LAUNCHING FILES

There's a command for everything in Unix, and a Unix wizard needs to know every last one of 'em. *You*, on the other hand, just need to know a couple of basic commands so you can play around a bit without getting your fingers burned. "Your Fingers Burned" is, of course, a euphemism for "accidentally destroying every last scrap of data on your hard drive."

Type **ls** at the prompt and hit Return. The Terminal window fills with text like this:

```
Sulaco:~ andrew$ ls
Applications
Dancin' Dave.pict
Desktop
Documents
Downloads
```

```
Green Monster Bkdrop (PICT)
Junkyard Wars.pict
Library
Movies
Music
Pictures
Public
Sites
Z'ha'Dum.mp3
columbo.pict
Sulaco:~ andrew$
```

The ls command is short for list and lists the contents of a directory. Yes, when interacting with your Mac through the shell, that is what your Home folder looks like.

If you look at the command line, you see that you still haven't left the home directory. Let's move inside a folder, shall we? The command to navigate inside a folder is. . . it's. . .

No, wait. We have no way of knowing which of these items is a file and which is a folder. We need to tell ls to give us more information. Most Unix commands have plenty of options available to them, usually by typing a dash and then a letter after you type the command. Try typing **ls –F** and then hit Return. Here's what you wind up with:

```
[Sulaco:~] andrew$ ls -F
Applications/
Dancin' Dave.pict
Desktop/
Documents/
Downloads/
Green Monster Bkdrop (PICT)
Junkyard Wars.pict
Library/
Movies/
Music/
Pictures/
Public/
Sites/
Z'ha'Dum.mp3
columbo.pict
Sulaco:~ andrew$
```

That's better. Every item that's a folder is followed by a slash. Now we can use the cd command to change to a different Directory. Let's go to the Movies folder:

```
Sulaco:~ andrew$ cd Movies/

Sulaco:~/Movies andrew$ ls -F
 Nick Baseball/
 Nick Baseball.mov
"Glory Days".mov
Koppel Letterman.mov
TPIR XMas/
Triumph Clones.mov
TVShows/
jedi dad/
jedidad2.mov
letterman bruce/
Sulaco:~/Movies andrew$
```

Why a slash? Because that's how Unix delineates the path through a nest of folders. For example, to move inside the Demos folder, you can navigate to Movies and then do another cd command to get inside the folder. Or you can do it all on one command by typing the full path from the home directory to the folder cd ~/Movies/TVShows. Remember, the ~ is shorthand for "my home folder." If there's a folder inside that and a movie inside *that*, the full path to the movie becomes ~/Movies/TVShows/Dynasty/JoanCollinsCatfight.mov.

 Tip

Incidentally, if you ever want to confirm where you are while navigating through a volume, type **pwd** and press Return. Unix spits out the path to your current location. It's short for "print working directory." Yes, a three-letter acronym is as close as Unix ever comes to user-friendly.

Notice that when you moved into another directory, the contents of the command line changed to show you your new location.

You're thrilled, I can tell. The delight in your eyes zaps onto this page and the glee is so potent that it's pierced the very veil of space and time and I'm feeling it right now, several months in the past, as I write this. You were hoping a naive, childlike hope that after spending $2,000 on a new computer, you'd wind up spending a lot of time looking at monospaced, unformatted text and typing commands that would only make sense if you started hitting yourself in the head a lot harder than you've been doing for the last 3 minutes.

Okay, why don't you take a break and watch a movie. You can tell that jedidad is a QuickTime movie because of its .mov extension. Every Mac file has a file name extension that tells what sort of file it is. The Macintosh graphical interface hides this from you in the Finder, but look, in case it hasn't gotten through to you yet, you ain't in Kansas any more, Dorothy.

The open command is the equivalent of double-clicking on a file in the Finder. It launches the file, opening its default application first if necessary:

```
Sulaco:~ andrew$ open jedidad2.mov
```

And thank God, you're finally looking at graphics and listening to sound and looking at a real app with a real graphical user interface!

COMING CLEAN

I fancy myself a real Mac Jedi and use and enjoy Unix daily. But man alive, you couldn't *pay* me to use it all day, every day. To me, using Unix is like wearing scuba gear. It'll help you see many interesting things and have some swell adventures, but after about an hour you're ready to see daylight and breathe real air again and maybe enjoy a Coke and a sausage sandwich. These things simply aren't possible when you're using Unix. Eating and drinking are encouraged in many IT positions, but in your seedier MIS departments, daylight and breathable air are hard to come by.

If you're scowling because you were unable to open diddley-squat on your own Mac — or even if diddley-squat was precisely what you could open — you must have tried to type in a file name that had a space in it. The Finder's happy to deal with spaces in file names. Unix ain't. You have to precede all file name spaces with backslashes, or enclose the file name in quotes. Unix will puke all over a command like:

```
open Triumph Clones.mov
```

But it can handle the file perfectly well if you type it in as:

```
open "Triumph Clones.mov"
```

 Note

I know we're in a retro, 1983, Reagan-era Thou Shalt Not Drag-and-Drop a Single Bloody Thing sort of mood in this chapter, but if you drag a file or a folder into the Terminal window, Tiger is nice enough to put the file's full name and path into the command line for you at the cursor. It's a real lifesaver; as you get deeper and deeper into nested folders, the act of correctly typing a pathname becomes less like a necessary procedure and more like some sort of fraternity hazing stunt, the sort of thing that killed a pledge at another campus in 1997 and forced the dean to close the chapter down.

Let's go back to the Home folder. Whoops. In the Finder, just click the Back button in the window toolbar. In Unix, there's no Back button, but two periods side by side achieve the same effect:

```
[Sulaco:~/Movies] andrew$ cd ..
[Sulaco:~] andrew$
```

This takes us back to the Home folder because Home was just one backward step away. To teleport straight to Home from anywhere in the hierarchy, use a tilde:

```
Sulaco:~/Movies andrew$ cd ~
```

Now and forever — just like the musical *Cats* — the tilde always represents your Home folder.

So, have you started learning Unix yet? Barely. I want to say that by navigating through your directories and opening a few files, you've taken the Pontiac Unix for a quick drive around the block, but in truth you've moved just beyond shifting over to the driver's seat and grabbing the wheel and making "Brrrrmmm. . . brrrrmmmmm!" noises while your dad's in the 7-11 buying smokes.

Why, I haven't even told you the simple, easy-to-remember command that deletes every single file off your hard drive in an instant. No warnings or nothing. Just *phhht*. . . there goes your whole hard drive. I bet you could almost type it accidentally. You probably *ought* to know what that command is. So if you value the data on your hard drive, place $15,000 in clean, unmarked $10 bills in a brown bag with a red ribbon and leave it taped behind the basin of the third sink from the men's room door at Boston's South Station train terminal.

See, Tiger's shell sort of assumes that if you know about the Terminal app and you're actually motivated to type commands that it can understand, well, then you must know what you're doing. So it'll allow you to do the most destructive things and make the sort of mistakes that will cause you to turn the air purple around you with the force of your sheer desire to Wish So Hard That Magically What Just Happened Wouldn't Have Happened. So you need to tread with extreme caution. When you type Unix commands, make sure you're typing them in correctly; and when you go and learn Unix on your own, don't assume that you can simply Undo a mistake.

Tip

Unix helps you out a little, in the form of extensive online help. Type **man** followed by a space and any command, and Unix displays the full online manual for that command. It scrolls on for page after page after page until you beg it to stop, or type **q**.

JUST KIDDING, AS FAR AS YOU KNOW

Actually, the aforementioned "one-line command that erases everything" is very real, but it's about as long as your forearm and you'd never accidentally type it in a million years. Unless someone with a sick sense of humor sent you an email that said, "Something really funny happens when you type this command into your Mac's Terminal program," and included The Command.

You best defense against this sort of thing? Don't run any Unix commands unless you know what they do, and they come from someone you trust. I also find that if you pay a friend 20 bucks to drop by your company a couple of times a year posing as your parole officer, well, folks tend to pick other targets for practical jokes. Plus, *nobody's* going to steal one of your yogurts from the break room fridge.

LOOK! IT DOES TRICKS, TOO!

True, you're still a Unix neophyte, but there are still a few commands and tricks you can use that'll leave you convinced that a little knowledge can be a useful thing. Just double-check your typing on all of these commands before you press Return and remember: capitalization counts.

How long has my Mac been running?

You want incontrovertible, tangible evidence of how stable Tiger is? Use the uptime command:

```
Sulaco:~/Documents andrew$ uptime
```

Unix returns the following:

```
 7:21  up 14 days, 17:21, 3 users, load averages: 1.89 1.49
1.37
```

This tells me that it's been more than 2 weeks and 17 hours since the last time I restarted my PowerBook. There are musicians that move from MTV to VH1 to CourtTV more slowly than my old Mac went from Startup to System Crash under Mac OS 9.

As for the information that follows the uptime, it's giving you some data on how hard the CPU is working.

▼ **Note**

If you're interested in that info, try the `top` command. This command is like the Activity Monitor application in your Utilities folder. It throws up a constantly updated status board listing all of the bits of software currently running on your Mac and what sort of demands each one makes on your system. Except it does it in ASCII text in the Terminal window instead of in a nice, clean, GUI-like Activity Monitor.

If I'd have written `top` as a separate Trick, its title would have been "How Can I Fill The Terminal Window With A Suffocating Morass Of Inscrutable Data?"

How do I empty the Trash when the Finder's being all snitty about it?

It's one of the most annoying conversations you can possibly have with a Mac:

"Empty the Trash."

"Can't."

"Why not?"

"Apparently, there's a file in there that's in use by another piece of software."

"Oh. Sorry, I didn't know that. Which file is it?"

"Ain't telling."

"C'mon, tell me."

"Nope. Nuh-uh."

"And just how in the name of Cher's sainted wigmaker do you expect me to properly close the problem file if you won't tell me which one it is? Or which piece of software refuses to let it go?"

"We never *talk* any more. Do you know that this is the longest conversation we've had in 9 days, 7 hours, 34 minutes, and 28.9 seconds? Maybe — hey, just maybe — if I could get your nose out of the CNN.com sports page for a few minutes every morning, this relationship wouldn't be headed straight to /dev/null!"

At which point you make dark noises about how a 20-inch G5 iMac isn't an easy object to hurl out a window, but that you think you could just manage it.

The best way to handle this problem is to shut down the Mac, and then try to empty the Trash immediately after you restart. But sometimes you don't have time to do that, and sometimes it doesn't even work.

If you feel you have no choice, type the following:

```
sudo chflags nouchg ~/.Trash/*
```

Translating this from left to right, you're saying, "Temporarily give me Godlike powers to do absolutely anything I want to on this machine, even if I'm about to do something dangerous, deadly, and instantly regrettable. Change the flags associated with a file; the specific flag I want to change is its "unchangeable" flag, which, if set to Yes, means that the file can never be deleted. Please set it to No, and do that to every file in the Trash."

You should now be able to empty the Trash as usual.

S/HE WHO LIVES BY SUDO, DIES BY SUDO

Megageek warning: Beware of the `sudo` command. It does indeed give any administrator additional powers that are literally known as superuser powers. Superman can fly around the planet so fast that he can make it reverse its rotation and time to go backward; yet he only *wishes* he were as powerful as a superuser.

The hitch (beyond the obvious: you can do incredible amounts of damage with a simple, one-character typo) is that after you invoke `sudo`, those superuser powers are available to anyone who sits down at your keyboard for 5 minutes. So don't just use it and walk away, or a sufficiently hip and malicious co-worker could do a variety of damage while you're chasing after the donut cart.

How do I make a catalogue listing every file in every folder of my Home directory?

The `ls` command has a nice little option that tells it to list not only every file in the current directory, but every file in every folder in the current directory, and every file in those folders. . . and so on and so on. Navigate to your Home folder (`cd ~`) and type this command:

```
ls -FR
```

Good. But the result is thousands of lines long and it all just whips through the Terminal window. Well, Unix gives you a simple way to redirect the output of any command so that its results sploosh straight into a text file instead of the Terminal window:

```
ls -FR > allmyfiles.txt
```

The file `allmyfiles.txt` will appear in your Home folder and you can open it in TextEdit or any other word processor.

On what day of the week was my grandmother born?

The command `cal` generates a calendar representing any month or year you specify. If your gramma was born on December 8, 1932, type **cal 12 1932** and you'll get this:

```
   December 1932
 S  M Tu  W Th  F  S
             1  2  3
 4  5  6  7  8  9 10
11 12 13 14 15 16 17
18 19 20 21 22 23 24
25 26 27 28 29 30 31
```

So it turns out that the old girl was born on a Thursday. If you omit the month, it'll generate a calendar for the whole year. Type `cal` all on its own and it'll spit out one for the current year.

 Note

I use this command a lot when I create Web pages. It gives me plain, correctly formatted text of the current month and I can easily embroider the dates with hyperlinks to monthly events. (Truth be told, I actually wrote an AppleScript that has `cal` generate the calendar and then does all the embroidery automatically; but here, near the end of this chapter on command usage, I am refreshed by the cool breeze of heads spinning around me, so I probably ought to dial it down a notch.)

I caught my son day trading on our Mac when he *should* have been cleaning the garage. Sure, while watching *Spongebob Squarepants* he increased the equity of our portfolio by 23 percent, but that's no excuse. So I banned him from the family iMac for a week. How can I make sure he hasn't been using his user account?

The command `last` is your first resort, then. It spits out a list of all the users who've been on your Mac since the start of the month (which is normally when your Mac resets its logfiles). Here's what the command spits out:

```
andrew      ttyp1                   Mon Nov  8 02:36
still logged in
andrew      ttyp1                   Mon Nov  8 02:36 -
02:36  (00:00)
andrew      console Sulaco.local  Fri Nov  5 19:42    still
logged in
reboot    ~                       Fri Nov  5 19:41
shutdown  ~                       Fri Nov  5 16:54
andrew      console Sulaco.local  Thu Nov  4 14:33 - 16:54
(1+02:21)
reboot    ~                       Thu Nov  4 14:33
shutdown  ~                       Thu Nov  4 14:31
andrew      console Sulaco.local  Mon Nov  1 23:35 - 14:31
(2+14:56)
reboot    ~                       Mon Nov  1 23:35
shutdown  ~                       Mon Nov  1 23:33
```

Note that it also logs the times when the machine has been restarted. So if one of these users was `spongebobfan` instead of `andrew` (my user account), I'd know that something was up.

It's a handy tool, even if you're the sole user of this Mac. If you think someone was using your iMac while you were off at your surfing vacation in Manitoba, `last` will tell you whether or not your account was active while you were hanging ten in Baff Bay.

TELNET STAR WARS ENDORSEMENT

And here's the point in any printed mention of Telnet *Star Wars*, where the author is supposed to claim that its creators are losers who need to get a life. Far from it! My hat's off. I feel so strongly about the megaginchiness of this undertaking that I have just walked downstairs to the hallway by my front door, taken my hat off the banister, screwed my hat on my head, and then took it off again with theatrical flourish, just so I can insist to you, the reader, that my enthusiasm is genuine and that I'm to be taken at my word in all of my comments.

Incidentally, this is probably the one and only time you should ever use Telnet. There are times when you might indeed want to talk to or even control another computer through your Terminal window, but you should use a command called `ssh` instead. It's safer and more secure from prying eyes.

My boss won't let me have a DVD player in my office. Can I still watch the greatest movie ever made?

Abso-tively. Just use this command (the results are shown in Figure 20-2):

```
telnet towel.blinkenlights.nl
```

All through this chapter, you've been typing commands to hunks of software located on your Mac, which responded to you by putting text in the Terminal window. Telnet makes that happen with software located on other computers (even one located in the Netherlands, like this one).

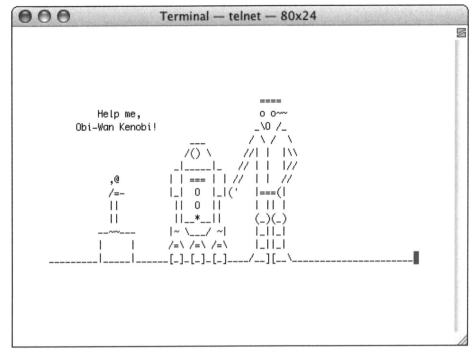

Figure 20-2
Even at stick-figure resolution and no sound, *Star Wars* is still freakin' *Star Wars*.

When Telnet opens the connection, that remote computer automatically starts a piece of software that plays *Star Wars Episode 4: A New Hope* through your Terminal window, all in glorious animated ASCII text.

Telnet isn't the only Unix program for connecting remotely to another computer on a network. It isn't even the most popular. But it's the only such program that the ASCII edition of *Star Wars* will work with. When you have a *non-frivolous* need to use Terminal to send commands and get responses from remote computers, you'll use a different program: ssh. Which is more stable and is actually secure, so that your communications can't be read by anyone who might be eavesdropping via the network.

I want to point out that I'm now walking-slash-jogging four miles at a stretch three or four times a week. Hate it with a passion, too. I've bought books about running in which the authors ooze on and on and on about the glorious mind-body-spirit connection and the freedom that comes with movement and the meditative effects of the rhythm of your footsteps and the high you get when the endorphins kick in. Well, I've done a half marathon, folks. The only high I got through the whole process was through the fumes of the various lotions, oils, unguents, and liniments that I had to apply every day for a whole week afterward just to keep the sobbing to a sort of dignified ebb. It's no mystery that these folks could write so rhapsodically about running. They were sitting in a nice, comfortable chair in a nice warm house with a donut and a big glass of Yoo-Hoo next to the keyboard.

Although I really don't get the reasons why this is so important, I go out and do it. Why? Because people tell me it's a good idea. And. . .

To be honest, I think I've lost my grasp on where I was going with this. I think the point was that Unix seems like the exact opposite of what Mac users signed up for. Actually, it's the opposite of what anyone using a computer after 1990 has a right to expect; but if you never open Tiger's Terminal window and start seeing what Unix can

do for you, your Macintosh experience will be forever incomplete. Your first successful Unix command is your first step into a larger and more wonderful world.

In truth, though, it's probably more important to me that I complain about having to go out and exercise in a couple of hours. I've tried snarking to my goldfish as I lace up my running shoes, but it's a deeply unsatisfying experience. I mean, I can tell already that you're not as judgmental as they are.

21

Lewis and Clarking through Tiger's Directories

In This Chapter

The Top Level • System Folders • Applications Folders • Library Folders
Developer Folder • User Folders • Public Folders • Sites Folders

During my freshman year in college, the first and most important friends I made were the people I met late at night, in places that we probably weren't supposed to be. There's a mentality shared by a certain percentage of any polytechnic university, one that's clearly demonstrated in the opening scenes of *The Great Escape*. Yes, thank you, sirs: we know where our dorm is and we'll certainly never forget where the office of our student advisor is (after all, passing by the building is the shortest route to the used CD store downtown). But those of us who plied the pathways and tunnels at 11 p.m. wanted to get a sense of the nooks and crannies of the entire campus, and whether we'd ever revisit the disused tunnel between the Geology building and the center of the Business program.

Knowledge wants to be free, after all. Plus, some of us had really bad roommates and oftentimes the only thing standing between me and a manslaughter rap was the knowledge that there was a teaching assistants' lounge on the third floor of the Ames Building with (a) a really comfortable sofa and (b) a door that never really seemed to lock properly.

This chapter is presented in much the same vein. In truth, you only *really* need to know about a handful of the directories on your hard drive, and they're all fairly obvious ones: your Home directory and your prefabbed folders for Documents, Pictures, Music, et al. But knowing what else is out there will save a bit of confusion when you're wandering about, and will also help you understand why certain things in Tiger work the way they do.

So pack your flashlight, practice your naive expression of, "Gosh, sir. Am I not supposed to be here?" and let's head out.

Macintosh HD:

Tiger's about as simple an OS as you can get. If it were any simpler, it wouldn't even require a living, breathing person to keep it running. Other operating systems understand this concept, but they don't approach it from the direction of "I should require the minimum possible direction and oversight from my user." Clearly, their attitude is "Gosh, my life would be so much simpler if my user were dead. I wonder if I can get him so worked up that he'll do something extremely foolish during his drive home today?" In fact, the one spot where many users get addled and befuddled is when they click on their hard drive's icon in the Finder and see a bewildering pile of directories, few of which have helpful labels (Figure 21-1):

First off, notice that there's a whole bunch of folders and files in my top-level directory that shouldn't be there. In theory, this directory should hold just a half-dozen folders (the ones that I've mentioned) and nothing else. Well, OK, nothin's gonna blow up if you save files to the top directory. And look at that: a few commercial apps were naughty and wrote some files there, too. But you don't want to let the top directory get cluttered up. It's a good way to lose things.

Plus, every user on this Mac can see every file in the topmost directory. So if a few days ago you wrote a long document entitled "How My Affair With My Hot Young Personal Trainer Is Working Out" and accidentally saved it to the top instead of to your personal Documents folder, well, your life is about to change in a very serious way.

And this is why Tiger tries to take most of the management out of your hands. In fact, when you start mucking with directories on your own, you'll find much which is redundant and little that makes much sense.

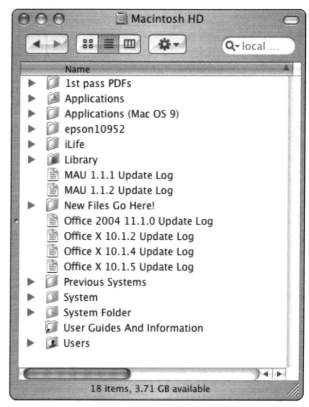

Figure 21-1
My PowerBook's top-level directory, complete with some clutter

Macintosh HD: Applications

It might *appear* to the users of this Mac that they each have their own personal Applications folders. There's an "Applications" icon in the sidebar of their Finder windows, and if these people are coming to Tiger from other operating systems, they might be used to the idea of separate spaces. But this is an illusion, a fantasy, a collective dream. There's just *one* Applications folder on the Mac's drive, and this is it. It's a necessity. If someone with Administrator access installs an app, it becomes available to everybody, so they all need to be in a communal pile.

CONFRONTING FASCISM

"Tell *me* where to put *my* applications? Where was this computer made? Stalinist Russia?"

Callllm down, Sergei. I'm guessing that only two or three of you out there are actively riled up about the fact that applications go into a special folder, but I sense that you're lashing out because you've had a bad day, and could use a hug and a cup of cocoa or something.

No, in fact, apps are happy to run from anywhere they're kept. You can keep iMovie in your "Movies" folder, for all Tiger cares. But every time you run a software installer, your new apps will land in the prescribed folder, and moving them elsewhere is of no advantage. Plus, keeping apps elsewhere leads to ungodly messes. When it's time to upgrade an app, the installer app might not be able to find the old edition and instead, it'll build you a brand-new copy, wasting time and space.

It also means that the app you install won't be available to other users. Which can often be a plus (perhaps you want to keep the online video poker game away from the kids, particularly if losses are tied to your checking account) but on the whole, be a good boy or girl and don't mess with Destiny.

Macintosh HD: Applications (MacOS 9)

If you're still using old, pre-Mac OS X apps on this Mac, then Tiger quarantines all of that software in its own directory. And for good reason: they smell funny and you don't want that kind of funk to rub off on your *good* software.

Macintosh HD: Library

And here's our first Point of Unusual Interest on our little walking tour. Tiger keeps several "Library" directories scattered here and there around your hard drive, and each one serves the same general purpose as its namesake. They serve as centralized locations that house information and resources for your Mac's apps. For example, it'd stink on ice if you installed a new font and then that font were only available to your word processor. Instead, Tiger stashes it in a Library folder, where it's available to any app that uses text.

KEEP YOUR HANDS AND FEET INSIDE THE TOUR CAR AT ALL TIMES

Realize, though, that Libraries aren't particularly meant to be user-friendly. You can look around inside them and work some useful effects by (judiciously) copying files into the right places, but you can easily get burned if you copy and delete files willy-nilly. It's like when you pop the hood of your car and start pulling wires. The manufacturer sort of figures that if you're under the hood, you know what you're doing, so it doesn't make it terribly difficult to do heroically stupid things that cripple and befuddle your Mac.

The contents of your Library folder is a motley, highly improbable amalgamation, and it's likely that Apple just made some of these folders up, just to further intimidate you from poking around inside. I'm joking. I think. Well, look at Figure 21-2, anyway:

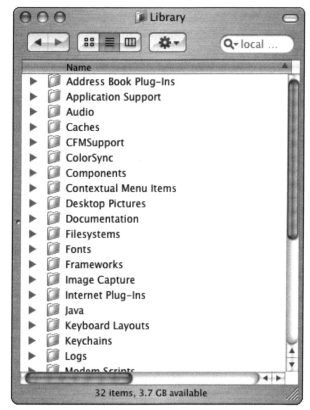

Figure 21-2
A System-wide Library directory

But the basic idea of the Library folder should be plain when you look around. Click on Fonts — cool, that's where all of your fonts are. Keychains contains the keychain files available to all users of this Mac. Scripts are for AppleScripts, Screen Savers are for screen savers . . . .

Gosh, maybe the Library folder isn't as complicated as I thought.

In general, copying (for example) a screen saver file into the Screen Savers directory is as good as running an application installer for the thing. Indeed, if you're switching from one Mac to the other, you might not remember exactly *where* you downloaded the Dancing Chicken Elvis screen saver. It's just simpler to copy it straight from the old Mac's Screen Savers directory.

You'll also encounter those golden moments as a user when you absolutely *have* to mess with things inside your Library folder. Spotlight, for instance, relies on special plug-ins that teach it how to index and search information created by specific apps. If the makers of DiscoTax want you to be able to do Spotlight searches on DiscoTax data, it's unnecessary for them to release a whole new edition of DiscoTax.

TAKE IT EASY, SUNDANCE

"Lookit me!" you might be tempted to say, particularly in a first-date situation. "I'm a power-user!" And off you go, trotting through the System-wide Library folder, deleting printers and Address Book plug-ins that you don't think you still need. Don't. There's absolutely nothing productive to be gained by deleting things from your Library folder, and there's every chance that you'll break something. The usual user component to working with Library folders is copying files (like fonts and screen savers) into subdirectories. If you copy a screen saver into a font library folder, nothing bad happens. At worst, you just waste a little space.

In general, here are the "safe and useful" Library folders: Contextual Menu Items; Desktop Pictures; Fonts; Keychains; Screen Savers; Scripts; and Spotlight. They're the closest to user-friendly as you'll find inside the Library.

BACKING UP PREFERENCES

There's another handy technique but it's sort of hit-or-miss. You're moving between one machine and another, you had your word processor set up *just* that way you like it, and now you're not looking forward to having to tweak all of the user settings on the copy you've just installed on the new machine.

Okay. It's *possible* that if you go into the old Mac's Library: Preferences directory, make a copy of the app's Preferences file, and copy it into the exact same location on the new Mac, you'll successfully clone the old settings into the new environment. No DNA smashing necessary.

It's *also* possible that it won't work at all, and it's also *slightly* possible that the app will stick out its lower lip and pout until you Quit, delete the prefs file, and start again. So take all that under advisement.

All they need to do is release a plug-in, and have you copy it into your Mac's Spotlight folder.

Diving into the Library folder also occasionally spackles some of the gaps in the Mac user interface. I made myself a *great* login icon (that picture that represents you and your account) for my previous PowerBook. But that was two years ago and I can't remember where I left the original file. Well, thanks to some basic knowledge of the Library directory, I don't need it: I can just copy it straight out of Library: User Pictures. It's also interesting to leaf through the Application Support folder. But again: Look, but don't touch.

Macintosh HD: Previous Systems

Remember back in Chapter 2, when we talked about the "Archive and Install" option for installing Tiger on a Mac? If you choose this option, the Tiger Installer makes a backup copy of your existing OS and installs a brand-new one from the ground up. Here's where the old copy went.

FOUND MONEY

If you've been using this Mac for a long time and it seems like the walls have been steadily closing in on your hard drive week after week after week, this is one of those places you should go to reclaim some unused space. The only purpose to the contents of the Previous Systems folder is to sit there quietly in case the upgrade was a big mistake (viz: the upgrade was just released a week ago and it causes a lot of your most important apps to suddenly treat you as though they suspect you've been sleeping with their spouses), and you'd like to reclaim your old OS and settings. After you've settled into the new OS, it just sits there, taking up space.

How big is it? Many gigabytes. Drag that puppy into the trash and be done with it.

Macintosh HD: System

Home to a Library folder that's owned by the operating system itself. No user-serviceable parts inside. Removing this tag is a federal offense. These aren't the droids you're looking for. In a nutshell: move on before you hurt yourself and others. This isn't like the System Folder of Mac OS 9 and earlier, where you actually *have* to monkey around in there to install new stuff and keep things running smoothly.

Macintosh HD: System Folder

If you have Mac OS 9 installed on this machine, here be 9's familiar System Folder folder. I want you to visualize an

AN APOLOGY

Folks, I just want to express my deepest and profoundest regret for my actions in the "Macintosh HD: System Folder" bit. I did, willfully and fully aware of the consequences of my actions, allow the phrase "System Folder folder" to appear in a manuscript that I myself wrote. I have now become only the latest contributor to a lexicographical disease that causes people to refer to "ATM Machines" and "ABS System," not caring that by doing so, they are in fact repeating the last word of the term twice, and needlessly so.

As social transgressions go, this isn't up there with parking in a Handicapped space without holding a valid HP plate or pass. And I did this out of a desire for clarity; "System Folder" is indeed the name of the folder. But nonetheless, I feel as though you've just sneezed and I failed to say, "Gesundheit." You may not have noticed and you may not have cared but still ... I feel like less than that which I aspire to be.

enormous 1972 console TV/record player abandoned at a curb somewhere. Look, laugh, move on, reflecting on how far we've come since the days of bellbottoms and platform shoes with live goldfish in the heels.

Macintosh HD: Developer

If you've installed Tiger's Developer Tools (found inside the Developer Tools folder on your installation disc), then this folder contains a bunch of goodies needed to develop software for the Macintosh. Nose around therein and you'll encounter XCode, Apple's software development environment, and piles and piles of documentation and sample projects.

Macintosh HD: Users

Fifteen hundred words later, and we've finally hit that vein of gold: the directory where actual users are *supposed* to live, thrive, and survive. Assuming that you decided to navigate there from the top instead of just clicking your personal Home directory, and assuming that you had a reason to wander outside your own personal North 40 acres on this Mac. Neither of those is a gimme.

Figure 21-3 shows you the contents of my Users directory:

You'll see that there's a folder for every person with an account on this Mac. Which folder belongs to the currently logged-in user? Yuppers, it's the baby whose icon is a house instead of a folder. This is the current user's "Home" folder. Well, you *know* what's in your own user folder. Let's be obnoxious and poke around inside other people's personal spaces, all righty? Take a look at Figure 21-4.

Figure 21-3
The User directory of a selfish man with a desperate sense of personal privacy who hates to share his Macintosh with anybody

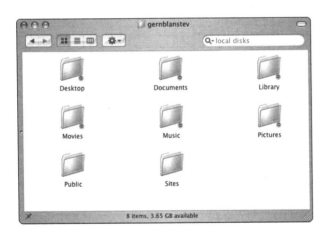

Figure 21-4
You're not Gern. What are you doing in his folder, you jerk?

Hmm. Nearly all of Gern's folders have those nasty red circles on 'em. Double-click on one and Tiger will tell you, "The folder could not be opened because you do not have sufficient access privileges." Imagine! An operating system that prevents other people from pawing through your personal, private folders! You should write a strongly worded letter to the *Times* about that.

Oh, but you're free to open a couple of folders. That Public folder looks fairly promising. By default, Tiger creates a Public folder for every user. It's a mechanism so that you can easily share files with other users on this Mac and other users on the network. When visitors with no special permission to access your User folder stop by for a visit, your Public folder (and your Sites folder, which we'll get to a little later) are the only areas that they can actually see.

Having a Public Folder is terribly useful. If you've written a marvelous document that explains just what to do when the office photocopier starts Vesuviusing toner all over the place and the pithy phrase "Key Error 82" flashes on its indicator panel, you can just leave it in your Public Folder and everyone will be free to just grab a copy when the need arises (instead of paging you all over the office and discovering that you're spending yet another three-hour lunch break over at the multiplex).

Inside the Public Folder is a special folder called a Drop Box. Anybody can copy files into your Drop Box; but unlike the Public Folder itself, strangers can't open the Drop Box and take a look at what's inside. Which is very valuable if you're a Human Resources director and you're encouraging employees to send you reports entitled "Why Melissa is, like, the worst Assistant Director of Retail, *ever*."

Lastly, there's a folder entitled Sites. Each installation of Tiger has its own built-in Web server. Any Mac or PC on the local network can plug this Mac's address and user directory into a Web browser, and it'll see the Web site defined by the files in this folder.

ANDY WISHES TO ARGUE WITH HIMSELF

"Rubbish!" I say. "I've got my Mac in front of me *right now,* and if I click over to another user's Home folder I can look through all *kinds* of other folders!"

I sigh. I marshal my patience. Andy is a nice guy, but sometimes he gets himself a little carried away. Yup, I'm looking at the same Mac that Andy is, and I can see a folder named "Website Detritus" and one named "Byrne Images" and a few others. I can open 'em and see all the files therein and copy them into my own Home directory if I want.

Why? Because this other user was foolish enough to create some new folders right at the very top level of his Home folder. His Documents, Pictures, Music, Movies, et cetera folders are protected against interlopers, and any item he stores *inside* those folders is inaccessible to strangers. Any new folders that he creates immediately inside his Home folder won't have that sort of protection, unless he changes the folder's Permissions to "No Access" for the category of users labeled "Others:". You can learn how to do that in Chapter 11.

Now if Andy will just shut up or find some way to distract and amuse himself for another 20 minutes, maybe we can get through the rest of this chapter, somehow. Again: he's a nice guy, but sometimes ... *jeez!*

YOUR USER FOLDER

And now we get to that part of your hard drive where you actually have a right to poke around: your user folder, marked with your user name and a cute li'l house. Most of the folders here are self-explanatory. For the purposes of illustration, I'll use my own Home folder, named andyi — my user name.

Macintosh HD: Users: andyi: Desktop

This folder represents all of the files and folders that are sitting on your Desktop. Some documents get saved to the Desktop by default (as when you create a screen capture by pushing Command+Shift+4). You can see 'em by either closing the millions of application and Finder windows you've plastered all over your Desktop, activating the Show Desktop feature of Exposé (F11), or navigating to the Desktop folder directly.

Macintosh HD: Users: andyi: Documents

Tiger does its best to encourage good habits in its users. Toward that end, every user has a folder called Documents, which, by its name, would tend to indicate that this would be a swell place for you to keep your documents.

Again, Apple is, as always, the enemy of fascism and you're free to save your files wherever you danged well please. But this is one of those instances in which knuckling under and doing as you're told will work out well for you in the long run.

Macintosh HD: Users: andyi: Library

What, *another* Library folder? Yes, indeedy. The previous Library folder we looked at was system-wide, containing resources that are available to every user of this Mac. The Library folder in your User directory contains all the snippets and snails and puppy-dog tails that personalize your Mac experience.

WEBBING A CORNER OF THE OFFICE

If you want to publish your own personal Web site on the network, just head on over to System Preferences, click on Sharing, and click the checkbox next to "Personal Web Sharing" (Figure 21-5). Your Mac will percolate for a moment and then presto, you're on the air. The URL for your personal Web site is given right in the System Preferences window. Hand it out willy-nilly and wait for the accolades to tumble in.

But remember that in the grand scheme of Web publishing, this is the equivalent of two Dixie cups and a piece of string. Anybody on your local network will be able to view your Web pages but your personal site will almost certainly be invisible to anybody outside your home or office. The difference between making a folder visible to everyone on your network and making it visible to everyone on the Internet is a vast one. If you're a home user, your Internet provider is going to want to charge you a buttload of cash to give you the special sort of connection you'll need. If you're an office user, the network's administrator has almost certainly installed security on the network to prevent outsiders from reaching your network.

To publish a "real" Web site, subscribe to .Mac, which (among many cool things) includes a basic home-page. Or, take a look through the services offered by Pair.net, Yahoo.com, and other Internet providers; they can host a Web page on their servers for reasonable fees. And then there are services like Flickr.com, LiveJournal.com, TypePad.com *ad nauseum,* which can set you up with a personal *weblog,* which is a simple but powerful site where you can easily post your articles, essays, comments, and photos on the Web.

So if a Personal Web Sharing site is only available to you and people you're likely to meet on your way to the break room, what use is it? Well, think of it as the ultimate outgoing message on your voice mail. If people want a quick answer to the question, "Is Katie still on vacation? If so, who should I call with my questions? Did she leave that report that I wanted to read? And for God's sake, who won the Oscar pool that she was managing?" they can just click on your Web page instead of bothering you on that red-sand beach in Kauai.

And admittedly that's way more than one question. But the class of person who'd interrupt your Hawaii vacation just to ask about a stupid Oscar pool knows no social bounds. No wonder you needed a vacation.

Figure 21-5
Click to Destiny: Starting up Personal Web Sharing and publishing your Web page to the local network

There are some familiar characters in here. You'll find Fonts, Scripts, and Sounds folders, as well as a Keychain folder and other usual suspects. And if I've written the previous paragraph with any skill whatsoever, you'll quickly grasp that when you place a Font in your personal Fonts folder, it won't automatically show up in any other user's Fonts menu. If you copy a keychain file to your personal Keychain folder, then all of your keychained passwords will be available to your own apps but will remain an inscrutable mystery to all the other users.

But there are some new folks in the picture who merit comment:

Macintosh HD: Users: andyi: Library: Mail

You'd think that Apple would have picked a more obvious place to store all of your incoming and outgoing email, but they didn't. If you're using Tiger's built-in Mail client, here's where your life is. It's another thing you're not likely to want to mess with, apart from pointing your backup

ASK THE MAN WHO OWNS ONE

I get a new PowerBook every year or so, and the Correctness of keeping things in Documents is underscored every time I migrate to the new hardware by simply dragging the Documents folder from the old place to the new one. Nothing's left behind, and glory be, I've got six years' worth of accumulated writing in the same place.

Which brings up another point: It makes backing up much simpler. Backing up an entire hard drive can be a major drag, but it's no trouble to point your backup program at your Documents folder and then say, "*This* one, please."

OR MAYBE NOT

And yeah, I've just dragged my Mail folder from one Library directory to the other instead of using Mail's built-in Import feature. It saves a *lot* of time, but in truth, importing leads to healthier email. Mail will build you a brand-new email database from scratch, which means that any inconsistencies or little bugs that might have crept into your database unnoticed over the past year or so will be eradicated. It also removes any "dead space" in your Mail folder, resulting in leaner and faster operations. Food for thought.

software at that folder to make sure you always have a duplicate copy of your mail database, or as a shortcut to importing thousands of messages when you upgrade from one Mac to another.

Macintosh HD: Users: andyi: Library: Preferences

Ever wonder how your word processor remembers that it's supposed to open a new document when it's launched? Or how your spreadsheet remembers that you want to focus on the bleak reality of your company's projected quarterly losses without any toolbars cluttering the screen and numbing the pain, and yet these apps behave completely differently when another user launches them?

All of the user-specific tweaks and settings for every app are stored there in the user's individual Preferences folder. Apple doesn't *really* imagine that you'll want to look through this folder, so figuring out which Preferences file corresponds to what application can take a little bit of thought, as shown in Figure 21-6:

ch.sudo.cyberduck.plist
com.adobe.Photoshop.plist
com.ambrosiasw.snapz.plist
com.apple.ActivityMonitor.plist
com.apple.AddressBook.plist
com.apple.airport.adminutility.plist
com.apple.airport.express.assistant.plist
com.apple.airport.plist
com.apple.applescript.plist
com.apple.AppleScri...xamples.TaskList.plist
com.apple.audio.AudioMIDISetup.plist

Figure 21-6
Preference files. I bet you can guess which apps own these files.

Many apps put their own preferences folders *inside* the Preferences folder. Otherwise, the file names keep the general format *com.companyname.appname*.

Normally, you wouldn't really mess with the contents of this folder, but it can come in handy in two different situations:

- **You're migrating from one machine to another.** You can either painstakingly re-create all of your application settings on the new machine, or you can just copy the prefs file from the old machine to the new one. It *usually* works.

- **A specific app has turned its back on you and it needs to be spanked.** So: your word processor crashes on startup. Or, it hangs whenever you try to insert a table. Or . . . well, anything else that you don't approve of. It's possible that the app's Preferences file has been vomited on, either by the app itself or by something outside its control. Oftentimes, you can fix the problem by removing the Preferences file and restarting the app. Here's how:

1. **Quit the affected app.**

2. **Find the Preferences folder inside your User: Library folder.**

3. **Find the problem app's Preferences file.**

   If it's Lambadasoft's *DiscoWriter,* it'll probably be the file named com.lambadasoft.discowriter.

4. **Drag the file to the Trash.**

   Don't empty the Trash just yet; if this trick doesn't work, we want to get that Preferences file back.

5. **Relaunch the app.**

   Don't be dismayed if the app you've been relying on for two years suddenly congratulates you on your new purchase and asks if, as a new user, you'd like a tour of the app's features. When the app didn't find a Preferences file, it assumed that it's running on this Mac for the very first time and creates a brand-new one.

NYAHH, NYAHH

Remember how *emphatically* I told you not to Force Quit an app unless you had no alternative? And that you absolutely, positively, *must* Shut Down your Mac instead of simply powering it down? This is why. The leading cause of narfed Preference files is when the rug's been pulled out from under an app. The last thing the app does when it quits is close down its Prefs file. If that doesn't happen, all kinds of bad craziness ensues.

Gosh, we're all the way up to Chapter 21 and I'm *still* trying to get you to trust me?

6. **Wait patiently for the Wrath of God to be visited unto you again.**

   If the Wrath of God has suddenly taken the day off, congratulations! You're golden. You'll have to re-create your favorite application settings — and in some cases, you might have to retype your software's registration code — but 10 minutes of hassle is better than an app that just flat-out Don't Work, right?

If your app is still acting cranky, then it wasn't the Preferences file. Quit the app and drag your old Preferences file out of the Trash and back into its original location inside your Preferences folder.

Meet the Beatles!

. . . Which as a section title, has a lot more punch than "Hey, get a load of this whole mess of default media folders." Yup, Tiger set you up with folders for pictures, movies, and music . . . all of the media that your iLife apps are meant to deal with. So your iPhoto library will automatically land in the Pictures folder, iMovie projects wind up in the Movies folder, and your iTunes library and GarageBand projects go to your Music folder.

Please mentally cut and paste the earlier spiel about the importance of knuckling under and accepting that Apple knows what they're doing. When you get into the bad habit

THE SHUFFLING SOUND OF ANGELS WONDERING IF THEY SHOULD TREAD OR NOT

Yes, there are plenty of Preferences files in there that appear to belong to a company called Apple. I suppose you're right: a lot of these apps and resources look familiar — com.apple.finder.plist for example. It just seems to *leap* straight out at you, doesn't it?

Okay, you've put two and two together. This trick also often works when your Mac refuses to boot up, or when you have a problem that affects *all* apps, not just one. For example, let's say your Mac appears to start up just fine. It powers up, it finds your internal hard drive, you see a login screen, it accepts your password, the screen changes and it looks like it *wants* to start the Finder, but then, *pfft*, nothing. It's certainly possible that the Finder's preferences file got hosed somehow, and that if you boot off a CD or mount the hard drive on another Mac (using your Mac's built-in Target Disk Mode), you can get things humming again by removing com.apple.finder.plist and then restarting.

But: *tread carefully*. If you're at the point of desperation when you're deleting Tiger's own prefs files at random and hoping for a cheerful result, it's probably time to call your local Apple Store and make an appointment with the Genius Bar. It's *unlikely* that you'll make things worse, but still, there's a good reason why Apple went to all the trouble of coming to our town and putting a Store over where the Orange Julius used to be.

If you *do* try this with Apple's prefs files, make double-dog sure that you *don't delete any preferences files* until you're certain that they were the cause of the problem. Once again, if you just move them elsewhere, you can always move them back later; no harm, no foul. If you deleted them, then you'll have to practice your "Gosh, Mr. Genius Bar worker, *it just stopped working* all of a sudden!" expression, keeping the "Darn it, now *what* did that kid of mine do to this computer while I was out of town?" expression in ready reserve.

THE MISSING FOLDER

So Apple thought ahead and set you up with likely default folders. But for the life of me I don't know why they didn't set you up with a default folder for things you've downloaded from Web sites. So go and create a "Downloads" folder. Right now. Otherwise, all of the apps and information files and saucy images of former *Gilligan's Island* cast members that you grab from the Web will splatter all over your Desktop and directories, like a series of overripe pumpkins thrown into an industrial fan of some sort.

of putting music files where they don't belong, it all comes to tears. Remember that part of the swellegance of iLife is the fact that it can easily share media between different apps. An app that's on the hunt for pictures isn't going to look in your Applications/Utilities folder, you know?

The other side of meddlesome

Remember when we were nosing around where we didn't belong? The last stops on our tour are the same Sites and Public folders we saw in other users' directories.

Only here, our Public folder acts just like any other folder. Other users couldn't see what was in our Drop Box, but we can open it up at a moment's notice. We don't even need a reason! We're *rebels,* man!

Well, I suppose not. Not with *our* haircuts, anyway. But we can just open up our Drop Box and see what people have left for us. Ah! Apparently, my Assistant Director of Retail stinks. Time to post a listing on the big job sites and see if there's any way I can cheat her out of her severance package.

The Our Sites folder works like any directory on any Web server. Just create any HTML-formatted document — many word processors can save any document in Web format — and save it into that directory. Presto, it's a Web page. The file named index.html is the default page that visitors will see if they browse the URL you handed out earlier. Remember? The URL you found in System Preferences? That's Figure 21-5, in case you've been skipping around.

So now, we've taken a leisurely walk through your hard drive. We've seen things that are ours and things that belong to other people. We've seen things that are public resources, personal resources, and we've been to places that keep the whole system running and which, by definition, we shouldn't toy with for fear of bringing this whole house of cards known as "an operational personal computer" crashing down on everybody's heads.

Once again, there are analogues to my early days in college. Exploring the campus late at night had many positive results. Most of the bubbleheads in my class scrambled for time in the big shared computer lab. Me, I knew that there were a few machines on the fourth floor of the Business school that nobody knew or cared about. The seats were more comfy, too. So: point in favor of exploration. There was also this big room filled with piles of documentation about how a new sort of networking plan worked. I devoured every last page. And then a couple of days later I heard about how the new student network wouldn't be working for another week or two, because the team designing it had all of their instructions laid out and ready to go but somehow most of the books were turned to the wrong pages and they'd lost most of their notes.

So: point against. Cautionary tale, as it were. There are two ways to end this story. Either I can say that you're better off, because whilst I brought down an entire campus, your rash actions will only affect your own performance; or I can say that I'm in better shape because when you mess with your machine, everyone (chiefly, you) knows who to blame.

The Right Way To End The Story depends on how malleable your personal code of ethics is. I inconvenienced

thousands of students, *plus* I am now profiting from that fact by using the story in a book I'm writing. So I'm concerned that it's all too clear what side of the fence I'm on. Did I mention that I'm a regular blood donor?

PART III

Bonus Material

22

Twenty-Five Questions from My Aunt Estelle

I'll be up front: I don't have an Aunt Estelle. I have 30 of them. No, 50. Certainly not more than 80. Hang on, let me just click over and check for new mail . . .

Okay, as of 2:12 a.m. today, I have a little more than 90 Aunt Estelles. I'm terribly fond of them all, even if I was unable to get them to see the wisdom of pooling all their resources together and buying me just one spectacular gift from the whole lot of them every Christmas. Still, I did OK. As it was, I was the only kid in my middle school who received enough socks and underwear to wear a brand-new pair to class every day, and the only freshman in my college dorm who didn't know how to do laundry.

Actually "Aunt Estelle" is the name I give to first-time Mac owners — in the case of actual aunts, they're sometimes even first-time computer owners — who email or phone me with questions. Usually the questioner begins by explaining her connection to me. "I go to the same salon as your mother's friend, Alice, and my hairdresser mentioned my problem to her, and then Alice suggested to him that I call you and ask why my computer keeps turning itself off." Which just goes to show that everybody on this planet is connected to everybody else. So if you've been arrested for reckless driving in some country backwater and you can't raise $1,000 bail, you probably just haven't been working the phones right.

And I do like hearing from Aunt Estelles, (a) because I believe in the Brotherhood of Man and all that; (b) because if I blow these people off, there's a better than 50 percent chance that it'll get back to my Mom; and (c) they usually ask questions that I've never considered before. I completed basic training a long time ago, and I've forgotten what it's like to be confronted by all this for the first time.

MY OWN KEVIN BACON INDEX

Incidentally, Kevin Bacon was in *Mystic River,* directed by Clint Eastwood; Eastwood was in *Unforgiven* with Gene Hackman; Hackman was in *The Birdcage* with Nathan Lane; Lane was in *Ironweed* with me (as an extra). So if you're playing The Kevin Bacon Game and you're one of my Aunt Estelles, your personal KB index is the number of steps to me, plus three. And it *would* have been plus one, except I had to cancel my extra commitment to *Mystic River* to keep a deadline.

I also think about my own ineptitude when it comes to cars. I know that you're supposed to put oil in. There's a metal stick-thingy that tells you how much oil is in there already. Good. But is it bad when you add that one bottle too many, and the level goes beyond the Full mark? That can't be bad, right?

There's an answer to this question, but just try finding it. The world is full of experts who passionately discuss whether the Lowen 410 intake pair cuts more HWBs than the Model 90 that came stock with the car, and how that affects line torque at low RPMs. But go to an online message forum and ask, "Why would I want a car with a manual transmission instead of an automatic?" and the only suggestions you get are to go out and work on your butterfly collection. As if a swallowtail is puddling anywhere in the Northeast at this time of year!

So, I'm always pleased to help out co-workers of my sister's mother-in-law and all my other Aunt Estelles. It's the right thing to do. And if I get into heaven, it'll be a late-buzzer squeaker and I'll be glad I walked in there with these extra karma points in my back pocket.

You may think I'm kidding, but the following are all actual questions selected from the past two months of incoming email expressly for this chapter. You might want to stick a bus transfer or something on this page to bookmark it. If word gets around that you know something about Macs, you'll start acquiring Aunt Estelles of your own.

I'm thinking about buying (my first Mac, a replacement for my old Mac). Should I do it now or wait for something new to come out?

Yeah, that's a poser. It's an incontrovertible fact that the moment you buy a new computer, the company either drops its prices or comes out with a brand-new model that has all of the old one's features, except it's faster, has a bigger hard drive, and has a built-in Easy Bake Oven. That's one of the reasons why the Treasury Department redesigned the $20 bill. Computer manufacturers got sick and tired of having to guess about this all the time, so each piece of U.S. currency has a tiny chip that senses when a major CPU purchase is being made, and can wirelessly transmit that info to a central server.

 Note

...Along with the comment that those shoes are so last season, that your handbag is a knock-off, and that you seem to be the only woman on *earth* who doesn't know that your husband's been sleeping around. See? And you thought it was one of your *girlfriends* who started all that gossip about you.

There's some advice that will come in handy, though:

- **Encourage that Upgrade:** If you have a friend who seems to be unhappy with his current Mac and due for some karmic retribution, talk him into upgrading. Once he's taken delivery, it'll trigger Apple's release of the next and greatest, which is when you should head for your nearest Apple Store.

- **Check the Rumor Mill:** Apple has an official policy of not commenting on unreleased products, and it's been a long time since it clamped down on unofficial leaks. But Mac rumor sites often manage to piece together the facts on what Apple will release and when. So, if you're seriously worried about buying an Edsel one week before the Thunderbirds roll into showrooms, spend a little time poking around on www.macosrumors.com. Mind you, there's a reason why rumors are called rumors. It's all baloney until you see it at store.apple.com. For more about online resources, see Chapter 20.

▼ **Note**

Just because everyone was right about your shoes and the handbag and all those nights your husband had to work late is no reason to blindly believe that Apple will introduce a tortilla-shaped PowerBook in November.

- **Look at Your Calendar:** Apple usually introduces the big new stuff at predictable spots during the calendar year: The first half of January (Macworld Expo/San Francisco, which is the biggest annual user-oriented Mac event); late May/early June (the World Wide Developers' Conference, in which Apple announces its plans to the folks who design third-party software and hardware); September-ish and October-ish, when Apple might be motivated to drop a price or two in anticipation of the holiday buying season. So, if you're thinking about buying a new PowerBook in December, it's probably worthwhile to wait until January.

- **Is Steve Jobs Delivering a Keynote Address?:** The other tip-off is usually when Apple announces that Steve Jobs is delivering a keynote somewhere. Visit www.apple.com and look through the scrolling head-

lines. They like to give Daddy something shiny to show off.

- **Is Apple dropping prices?:** When Apple suddenly drops prices on a specific product, it's usually because they intend to replace it soon and don't want to get stuck with lots of inventory. So, think about whether you'd much rather have the old PowerBook at a $300 savings or if you'd rather have a higher-performing PowerBook for the old price.

Finally, realize that staying ahead of the curve is a mug's game. If you keep holding off until The Next Great Thing comes out, you're going to be using your old Macintosh for a long, *long* time. Apple's always working on something better, and it never designs and markets a new product with the goal of not making its existing customers intensely envious. After all, they tried that particular strategy once and only once, with the Apple III. And did it ever make an Apple IV? No, there was not. I rest my case.

The Software Update app keeps popping up and suggesting that I download some software upgrades. Do I really need all this stuff?

1) No, you don't. 2) Yes, you do.

Click the button to add "support for Sun's Java VM 1.4.2 API" and it's not going to benefit society to the same extent that the last iMovie update did — you know, the one that refused to save any project file if its subject matter was a child's birthday and the video lasted longer than 6 minutes? But 3 months from now when you visit the Charles Rocket fan site, instead of a set of animated navigation buttons, you may see a generic icon of a steaming cup of coffee indicating that your computer couldn't execute the embedded Java object.

All of these updates take up so little room on your hard drive. And when Apple releases one, it's usually because there's a smoldering puddle of white and clear acrylic and chromed metal where someone's iMac once was with the culprit being a subtle problem with the keyboard driver. If you find the Software Update pop-ups intrusive, go to System Preferences, select Software Update, and click the pop-up menu so that it can check for updates on a monthly basis instead of daily or weekly.

 Note

One exception to the rule: When Apple releases a major OS update — for example, 10.3.3 becomes 10.3.5 — you want to hold off for a week before you install it. If it contains a major, show-stopping bug (not unheard of), Apple will release 10.3.6 toot sweet, and you'll be happy you weren't one of the users who innocently plugged in a LamabadaWare USB keyboard and caused all the data on the hard drive to be transmogrified into ASCII happy faces.

I've been told that I need to buy an antivirus program, but I can't find one for my Mac!

Not to worry. Worrying about viruses (and Trojan horses and worms and all other forms of nasty software that secretly installs itself inside your operating system and exploits and shares the data and resources of your computer) on a Mac is like worrying about drive-by shootings in Rutland, Vermont, or deft nuance in an Adam Sandler performance.

At this writing, Mac OS X viruses are unheard of. They just don't exist. Praise the inherent security of the Unix operating system. Praise Tiger's specific enhancement to what was inherited from Unix. Mostly, thank the fact that virus programmers are lazy, good-for-nothing blankety-blanks

who know that a Mac-specific virus only infects one-thirtieth as many machines as one for Windows.

Symantec (www.symantec.com) does sell an antivirus product for Macs, and McAfee makes a virus product that you get for free with a .Mac subscription. They protect you against viruses that are designed to exploit weaknesses in Microsoft Office's platform-independent macro system. Those things are exceedingly rare, and none of 'em have ever really gained any traction in the Mac community, but what the heck.

Their *chief* purpose is to scan your email for incoming Windows viruses. Those things can't infect a Mac, but if you're kind enough to forward those emails to a Windows person, congratulations . . . you've just helped to spread the virus. And aren't Windows users punished *enough?*

How do I turn it *off?* I can't find a switch anywhere!

That's because a Macintosh is a sophisticated, multi-user, multitasking, journalled operating system and not a toaster oven. So, if you were to suddenly cut the power when your Mac is desperate for you to not cut the power, bad things happen. Files get corrupted. Hard drives become unbootable. The dead rise from their graves and begin to walk the Earth, seeking to feast upon the brains of all those who wronged them in life. (Note: I read that last one at macosrumors.com. Grain of salt. Good excuse not to go about wronging people in life all the same, however.)

Nearly all Macs lack a traditional power switch. You're *supposed* to turn it off by selecting Shut Down from the Apple menu (you can also hit control-diskeject on your keyboard to bring up the same dialog). When you do that, Tiger merely gets on its bullhorn and shouts, "Okay! Everybody out of the pool!" and then all of the apps and other bits of running software close themselves down, and when everyone's quit themselves Tiger sends a software command to the hardware that says it's time to cut the power.

Many models have a little pushbutton somewhere on the machine itself. It might be big and illuminated and mounted on the front (it's marked with a circle with a vertical line cutting through it), or it might be hidden *wayyyyyy* at the back. And you *can* exercise your awesome, humanly power to control the Universe if you want: hold it down and after a few seconds, *byooop*.

▼ **Note**

If for some (unholy) reason you *want* to just cut the power immediately, terminate with extreme prejudice, live life on the edge without the sanitary complications of getting something pierced, etc., hold the Power key down for a few seconds. And don't say I didn't warn you when the moldering corpse of your third-grade teacher crashes through your front window, pins you to the floor with surprising speed and power, and demands to know where your report on the solar system is.

It's also possible that you don't even *want* to turn it off. A Mac (like most modern computers) has some pretty advanced power-management features. If you select Sleep instead of Shut Down, Tiger turns off every component that draws lots of power, like the display and the hard drive. The Mac becomes dark and inert and draws just enough power to snap straight back to life again when you tap the keyboard. Unless you're paranoid about power usage, haven't Shut Down in recent memory, or are about to leave the house for a long, long time, it's better to just Sleep it.

▼ **Cross-Reference**

For more about starting and shutting down your Mac, see Chapter 3. If you're experiencing problems with your Mac, check out Chapter 24.

Well, why is the Power key marked with that symbol?

Yeah, I know. . . it seems to *mean* something, doesn't it? It bugs you and bugs you and *bugs* you the more you look at it.

Remember that calcifyingly dull lecture you once sat through, explaining how computers work? "Computers break down all information into a series of electrical impulses, or a series of 'ons' and 'offs.' This system is known as 'binary code.' Each 'on' is represented by the number 'one.' Each 'off' is represented by the number 'zero.'"

(But how does this help you find nude images of Tony Randall on the Internet? On this point, the lecturer is silent. That's why you're encouraged to blow off this class and sign up for American Film instead. Wouldn't you rather spend those two hours watching *Taxi Driver*?)

So the symbol on the Power key is actually a stylized version of the 1 and the 0, the On and the Off.

As a bonus, let's talk about the Superman symbol. If you sort of squint a little, it looks like it's two yellow fish swimming past each other instead of a big red *S*.

Every time I open a Web page, my Mac tries to dial the phone to connect to the Internet instead of just using my wireless connection. Is something broken?

Maybe. Tiger's networking has a feature called multihoming. It means that deciding on a method of connecting to the Internet is your Mac's problem, not yours. Go to System Preferences ➜ Network, and select Network Port Configurations from the Show pop-up menu (Figure 22-1):

Figure 22-1
Setting the Presidential Order of Succession in Internet connections

This is a list of all the different ways your Mac knows how to connect to the network. When your Mac needs to connect, it tries each of these methods in that specific order, from top to bottom. The Mac shown in Figure 22-1 looks for a wireless AirPort connection first. Then, it looks at the FireWire port. Eventually, it dials the modem to see if that works.

You can change this order just by clicking and dragging items and rearranging them. Figure 22-1 makes sense for my specific setup. I always have AirPort available at the office. Sometimes I use FireWire networking. The rest really doesn't matter, but I want to make sure my Mac doesn't start doing obnoxious things (like tying up my phone line) when it doesn't need to.

So, if Internal Modem is higher on your list than AirPort, click and drag AirPort to the top. There's your problem.

If that isn't it, then either you've turned AirPort off (turn it on using the AirPort menulet), or you haven't configured your AirPort properly and your Mac can't find it. Run the AirPort Setup Assistant again.

How do I download my email from America Online?

You, er, run America Online? Nearly every email service on the planet uses a universally accepted public standard for downloading email (POP or IMAP). Except AOL. Tiger's built-in Mail app isn't compatible with AOL and neither are any others. I think when you log on and the "You've Got Mail!" announcement barks out in the sort of voice that is otherwise used to convince you to buy a three-year extended warranty on a $120 TV set, you should get the idea that you're not exactly in an environment in which users are worshipped, y'know?

I don't have enough places to plug in stuff.

Congratulations! You aren't officially a computer user until you've got stuff plugged into every port on every surface of your Mac. In fact, I feel somewhat insecure if I don't also have a couple of cards jammed between the rows of keys on my keyboard.

It's easy to run out of places to plug in USB and FireWire devices. Many devices are daisy-chainable, meaning that they plug into one of the Mac's ports but they have ports of their own into which you can plug additional devices. Your Apple keyboard, for example, has two USB plugs at either end. At some point in your long, strange trip you'll probably wind up buying one or two hubs. Hubs are sort of like those power strips that act as colorful fire hazards. Plug a hub into your Mac and you can now plug four or six devices into the hub. Hubs are available for both USB and FireWire devices.

GET A NICE BLUE TAN

I really am proud of you for outgrowing your USB and FireWire ports. But for the record, when you run out of ports, well, that's when you should go out and buy a second (third, fourth) Mac for the office. A hub only costs you $20 or $30, but think about the money you'll save on tanning booths. I spend most of my day sitting here surrounded by some seven or eight monitors, and every blue-skinned geek I meet compliments me on my healthy, bluish-green tone.

Where's the Eject button on the CD drive?!?

Don't got one. It's a similar deal as with the power switch. If the CD (or DVD) drive had a button that caused it to spit out the disc, you might spit it out before your Mac is done with it. It's a stability issue. To eject a disc, give your Mac a proper "Mother, may I?" first. Either click the Eject button found next to the disc's name in the Finder, or push the Eject key on your keyboard. If your Mac doesn't have a separate Eject key, the highest-numbered function key on your keyboard is probably doing double-duty. Look for an "Eject" symbol silkscreened on the thing. Hold down the Fn ("function") key on your keyboard while pressing that key.

Tiger will close down all of the disc's files and otherwise ensure that spitting out the disc will not be referred to as "The exact moment when my entire life took a dramatic turn worthy of either a Russian novel or an episode of *Falcon Crest*."

I'm totally lost. Where are my files?

One of the few real downsides to being a multi-user OS is that you're not necessarily the king or queen of this Mac's world. Under Mac OS 9, the entire contents of your Mac's hard drive were yours. In X, your User Folder is just one of many User Folders on that hard drive.

In addition to your own personal directory, your hard drive contains directories for all of this Mac's other users; directories for the Mac OS X operating system and Mac OS 9; directories for shared folders; directories for code libraries; well, I can sense that I've done my job and reminded you of how confusing this all is, so I'll stop here.

This is one of many areas in life in which you can reap great rewards by pretending that the whole world revolves around you and that anything outside of your own little world is of absolutely no importance to you whatsoever.

"Your" world is completely encapsulated inside your Home folder (Figure 22-2).

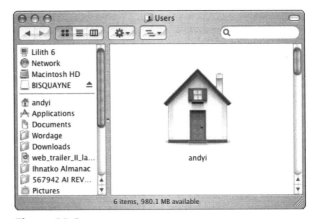

Figure 22-2
The Home Folder: Your personal fortress of solitude

EJECT COMMANDS, CANDLEPIN BOWLING, AND OTHER CULTURAL TRAUMAS

Using the OS to eject CDs, rather than some Eject button located on the drive *has* to be one of the toughest concepts for former Windows users to grasp. Neither way is necessarily better than the other, but it seems to resonate with our genetic programming somehow and taps into the same system that tells us that a tribe that makes fire with a stick and a bone instead of with a rock and some leaves has such a fundamentally warped outlook on our shared environment that their utter annihilation is absolutely essential to our tribe's survival.

The only modern-day analogue is when someone from New England tries to explain candlepin bowling to an outsider, and he gets to the part about how the pin-setting machine intentionally leaves fallen pins in the alley. I still have little shards of green glass in my scalp from that bar fight.

Whether you're in the Finder or in a standard Open File/Save File dialog, clicking the little house with your name next to it navigates you straight toward your personal files and apps.

When are you going to get a haircut?

I'm happy with my ponytail, thanks, Auntie.

Why does Tiger come with this freak-o app Safari instead of Microsoft Internet Explorer, the browser that I've been using for years?

You forgot to add ". . . and which dominates the browser market in the same way that sugar dominates the flavor of a Marshmallow Peep." Yeah, when Apple announced that they'd be replacing Explorer with their own browser, most independent observers got the same sensations they usually feel when they're watching a Wacky Sports Bloopers show and they see some hapless kid standing at the top of a flight of concrete stairs with a skateboard in one hand and

making the sign of the devil at the camera with the other. You just *know* that in four seconds time there's going to be a collision between a steel railing and a groin and the sound effect of a bell ringing.

But it sure didn't work out that way. Apple created Safari because they saw an opportunity to create a browser that went way beyond Explorer and which could work far more intimately with Mac OS X. . . and by all measures it's been a terrific success. Safari's faster and more sophisticated than Explorer, and its only competition is from other third-party browsers such as Mozilla.org's Firefox browser. Firefox is a great alternative to Safari, particularly if you're in an office where all the Mac and Windows and Linux users need to be running the exact same browser. Explorer's been stagnant for years, even on Windows. . . and on the Mac, it's officially dead. After Apple released Safari, Microsoft announced that they wouldn't be upgrading Explorer any more.

Still, you'll find Explorer there in your Applications folder, but you'll almost never need to launch it. The only reason why you wouldn't want to delete it from your hard drive to regain the space is (a) somewhere in the back of your mind you might worry about encountering a webpage that absolutely won't render properly without Explorer (extremely unlikely, but a valid worry), and (b) your hard drive is so big and Explorer is so small that there's no point.

What sort of recordable discs should I buy for my Mac?

If you mean "What kind?," then you should buy CD-Rs for audio CDs and for data discs that you only intend to write to once, and CD-RWs if you're creating a data disc and you want to erase and replace all of its contents from time to time. DVDs are a lot more complicated because there are so many different kinds. Apple's original Super-Drives (drives that can burn DVDs) only supported DVD-R media. Modern ones support DVD-R, DVD+R, DVD+RW, and DVD-RW.

If you're intending to produce discs that can be played on standard CD and DVD players, buy CD-Rs and DVD-Rs. Those are the only flavor of discs that have universal compatibility.

If you mean "What speed?" then you've raised a somewhat sticky question. When you go into an office-supply superstore, you're confronted with spindles of blank discs boasting speeds all the way to 32X. 1X is the speed at which you can play an audio CD from start to finish, so you can burn an 8X disc in roughly one-sixth of an hour.

The problem is that, once again, we get into mutually assured destruction. Disc burners are dirt-cheap, and the only way a manufacturer can gain any advantage in the marketplace is to rush faster drives onto shelves. But with every speed increase comes a new set of physical specs for the discs, which means that a spindle of 32X discs may or may not work in an old drive that's only rated for 8X speed. *Most* media will work — it can handle being burned

at a slower speed — but when you buy discs at the top of the speed pile, tiny incompatibilities can trip you up. So don't buy the fastest discs expecting any sort of advantage.

Making things even more complicated, Apple's disc drivers are aware of these problems and try for maximum compatibility. So, if you try to use an 8X DVD-R with a Super-Drive that only works at slower speed, iDVD burns the disc just fine . . . but at 1X speed. So whatever the price difference was between the 1X and 8X discs, you might as well have given it to charity for all the good it did you.

Your best bet is to head on over to www.apple.com, click the Hardware tab, and look at the tech sheet for your specific model of Mac. If you look at the sheet for your 20" iMac, for example, it promises that 32X CDs work just fine with it. When in doubt, buy slower discs.

DVD STANDARDS: LET'S LOBBY FOR SOME TECH DÉTENTE!

Why are there so many different kinds of DVDs? Because all the different drive manufacturers were pretty desperate to start selling burnable DVDs to consumers. Normally, they don't start turning the things out until they've all gotten together and chosen one standard that everyone can support, but when one manufacturer bolted off to be first to the marketplace, everyone else took off behind him. Thus demonstrating that maybe the Cold War had actually been a pretty clever scheme. With *one* system of global annihilation, nobody had any motivation to get ahead of anybody else. Oh, if only tech companies could work with each other as well as the U.S. and the Soviet Union did during the 1960s and '70s!

Finally, if you mean "Which *brand* of disc should I buy?," most stores sell the generic discs shrink-wrapped into huge, 100-disc cylinders and sold so cheap that if you manage to find a rebate coupon online, you might actually make money buying one. Then there are the nice, name-brand discs that come in their own individual jewel cases.

There's no handy rule of thumb regarding which brand is the best or even if the generics are necessarily not as reliable as the name brands. You can pretty much trust that if a disc (a) burns successfully with no errors, and (b) you store it in an environment free from light, dust, and scratches, one is as good as the other. When you're burning audio CDs and video DVDs, intended to work in Any CD Player or Any DVD Player On The Planet, things get a little trickier. Some models of player are very finicky about their media. But it's impossible to predict in advance which media will or won't work with what player.

Still, I tend to keep both generics and name-brands in the office. The generics are for stuff I burn for fun and things I'm sending to friends. But when I'm archiving photos or backing up data, I use the name brands. Mechanically, they are a bit more rugged, and the fact that each one is stamped with the name of a big-time manufacturer means — naturally — that the company has to be worried about lawsuits. So, they're certainly going to do anything they can to ensure that they've been properly certified.

I forgot my login password.

Not a problem. If you're sharing this Mac with other people, find someone who (a) has an Administrator account, and (b) wasn't so foolish as to select "S00opER_!_!PHR333aKQUE928" as a login password. He or she has the power to change your password to something that's easier for you to remember and isn't a humiliating reference to a Rick James song.

If you're the lone wolf of the plains, reboot from your Tiger Install Disc (stick it in the drive and select Restart, and hold down the C on your keyboard). There's an item in the Tiger Installer's menu for resetting the system password.

Note

This is why you desperately need to keep this disc from falling into the wrong hands, assuming of course that you lead such a lifestyle of way-hey-hey excitement and thrills that someone might conceivably want to gain access to your Mac and take a look at your upcoming Rotisserie League hockey draft picks.

Can I send mail to people who don't have Macs?

Yup. Internet email is based upon a long-standing, well-documented, and free open standard, so you can read any email sent from any computer just fine on any other computer. Mail.app goes this one further: When you send a file attachment, it automatically uses more than one method to prepare it for its journey. So whether a Mac or a PC receives the file the recipient's mail program can decode it properly. For safety's sake, Mail also has a "Windows-friendly file attachment" option.

My PowerBook (or iBook or iPod) battery won't hold a full charge.

Stinks, doesn't it? Lilith 6, my current PowerBook, can only last about 45 minutes on battery, as opposed to nearly 3 hours when it was new. It's all due to the chemistry of modern batteries. They're going to wear out eventually, and the symptom of age is reduced capacity.

If you want to prolong the useful life of your battery, always give it a full charge after you use it. Doesn't matter if you only used it for 15 or 20 minutes. The most damaging thing you can do is run your PowerBook all the way down to its low-battery warning and then charge it back up again.

 Tip

One of the best investments you can make is a second power adapter. If you're constantly taking your PowerBook down to the living room to answer email while watching CourtTV, leave one plugged in next to the sofa and the daily routine won't have the slightest impact on your battery. A new PowerBook battery costs about $150. A new adapter costs about $60. No contest. Learn from my mistakes: When I fly from Boston to San Francisco, I have to spend those 6 hours *reading,* for God's sake.

It's just that I was talking with your mother the other day, and she kept saying how *nice* you would look with short hair.

Well, I just prefer to wear it long.

What's the difference between Automator and AppleScript?

It's a lot like the difference between baseball and cricket, or the difference between a nice, tight Pinot Noir and an ice-cold Yoo-Hoo. By which I mean it's nothing at all like either of those things. I'm just sort of fumbling for an answer here because that's a good, subtle question and the answer is best hashed out over dinner.

I suppose it's best to say that they're two departments in the same store. They're both in the same business: you

provide a list of steps for Tiger to perform (steps which might involve applications performing actions) and Tiger will perform them as commanded. The difference is that Automator's a better choice for linear sort of processes. Step One: get a list of images from iPhoto; Step Two: import them into a new document; Step Three: generate thumbnail images; Step Four: upload them to your website. AppleScript is what you pull out when the process you're describing sounds more like formal *software,* with lots of variables and decisions that have to be made along the way. Like, if you want your Mac to evaluate every image in an iPhoto library and then either email it to your gramma, upload it to your *Star Trek* costuming website, or throw it in the Trash depending on how it's been tagged. AppleScript is also the obvious choice when you're creating a solution with lots of user interaction.

The bumper-sticker version of this answer is, "Automator is obedient, while AppleScript is *smart.*" You can train a dog to run to a box, grab the ball that's inside it, and run back and drop the ball inside a basket. But you can't tell it "Run to the box. If there's a ball in there, pick it up and drop it in the basket. If it's a bone, drop it at my feet." That's a snap with AppleScript.

But to be sure, the line between AppleScript and Automator is a blurry one. Plus, remember: Automator is brand-new. It's certain to evolve as the years and decades march along.

My advice? Start off with Automator. It's easier to learn and you can get stellar results with little investment of time. And you can integrate an Automator workflow into an AppleScript. . . so if later on you need to do something that Automator can't handle, you can drop your work into AppleScript and continue from there. You can also incorporate an AppleScript into an Automator workflow, to give your worksflow a little dose of Smarts.

Why is my Mac so *slow* all of a sudden?

You probably just need to log out and then log back in again, or restart your Mac. When Tiger's performance drops down to the sort of speed that would cause a snail to cross over into oncoming traffic and blow past it while honking its horn and flipping it the bird, it's usually because over the past X days or weeks of nonstop operation the system's need for memory has just kept growing and growing.

Tiger, like all Unixes, relies on a system of virtual memory. Your Mac might have 512 MB of actual RAM, but if you open so many applications that the OS needs more, it treats disk space as though it were memory, shuttling information between drive and RAM as needed. Normally, this scheme works great. If some of the software you're running is slightly defective, it leads to torpor. (I learned that word in second grade and have used it about once a week ever since. Thank you, Mrs. Bellisamo!)

When a program no longer needs a hunk of memory, it's supposed to tell Tiger that it's okay to free that hunk up for other purposes. If it doesn't, the app just keeps calling for more and more hunks, which means that Tiger has to use more and more virtual memory, which ultimately means that your Mac can't figure out what 62 divided by 0 is without having to access the hard drive.

▼ Note

Web browsers are *particularly* notorious offenders. If I've had Safari up and running for several days, a dozen Safari windows often means having to wait an extra couple of seconds every time I click a link. I don't need to restart my Mac all that often, but I usually wind up restarting Safari at least once every couple of days.

Thus, you're probably going to want to restart your Mac once a week. Keeps things healthy. All of Tiger's memory is set back to zero, and you have a nice, fast, clean slate.

This sort of problem is more profoundly explained in Chapter 24. One way to minimize these problems is to make sure there's plenty of free space on your hard drive, so that Tiger can always "manufacture" big chunks of virtual memory whenever it needs to.

If these slowdowns are happening so often that you're imagining what the wall of your office would look like with a Macintosh-shaped hole in it, you *might* want to think about reinstalling Tiger (see Chapter 2). It's possible that a critical part of the OS has gotten thrashed sometime in the year or so you've been using it. Internally, a simple one-step process for getting a piece of system information becomes the extended director's cut of Abbott and Costello's "Who's on First?" routine as one bit of software goes through endlessly protracted and patient discussions with a defective part of the OS to make this happen.

▼ Note

This, incidentally, is true of every single OS I use. It's not just a Mac OS X problem. Over the years, I've become convinced that if there's just one simple tip for keeping computers healthy, it's to reinstall the OS from scratch once a year. It's like spring cleaning.

That said, I never seem to encounter these slowdowns on my Windows XP machines. It's one of the few things I prefer about Windows. The only other advantage is that you really don't feel sad or guilty after you wield your keyboard like a broadsword and beat the crap out of a Windows machine.

How about if you kept the long hair, but just cut it short up front?

Then I'd have a freakin' *mullet*. As a geek, doesn't society judge me harshly *enough* without my actively feeding the fire by getting a Billy Ray Cyrus haircut?!?

Thomas Jefferson had a ponytail. Paul Revere had a ponytail. Mozart wore a ponytail made out of real pony hair. Why can't you get behind me on this?

Is my Mac compatible with Windows?

Depends on what you're asking, but the answer's the same either way. Mac OS X Tiger uses most of the same standards as Windows, so you can drop it on a network and share files and resources with any Windows machine without any extra software. The drives are compatible, so you can pop a Windows-formatted CD into a Mac or plug a Windows-formatted keychain memory drive into a USB port and it'll be appear in the Finder just like any other drive. You won't be able to use a Mac-formatted hard drive, though.

Nearly all Windows files are Mac-compatible as well; in fact, the Windows and Macintosh editions of Microsoft Office write the exact same files. If a Windows person emails me a Word document, it'll open in my copy of Word with nothing more than a double-click.

Out of the box, Tiger won't actually *run* Windows software, of course. But if that's a hang up for you, send Microsoft a little money and buy a copy of VirtualPC. This piece of software emulates a full-featured Windows PC and will allow you to run Windows apps right alongside Mac apps.

I think this software Installer is stuck. It started off okay but the little progress thermometer hasn't budged an inch in a long time.

Hmm. That's a possibility. But whether you're installing a single application or the entire OS, there are procedures involved that can take a long, long time to complete. That progress indicator doesn't mark the amount of time the process takes; it moves forward as the Installer completes each task. So, if the Installer program has to do 30 things and the last one is Convert every document on this 30 GB hard drive to Mandarin Pig Latin and then back again, well, that extra one-thirtieth is going to take a while.

Here's what I do. If the progress indicator seems stuck, I move my mouse pointer so that its point is parked right at the thermometer's current position. That gives me a fixed, known landmark with which to compare the bar's movement. Then I go off and read monster comics or whatever for a while. If I come back and I see that the progress bar has advanced a few pixels, then I don't worry.

You don't want to interrupt an installation while it's in progress. There are easier ways to render your Mac inoperable, but it involves vodka and an open flame. If I have to, I'll leave a Mac running overnight rather than force a restart.

I keep trying to print, but nothing comes out! And I'm not getting any error messages!

That's because as far as your word processor and Tiger are concerned, the printing system is working just fine. There's no direct connection between an app and a printer. The app hands the job off to Tiger's print manager, which hangs on to the job until the printer's ready to handle it.

It's great from the perspective that you can print 170 pages of documents and then go off and watch a movie while the print manager acts as traffic cop. There's supposed to be enough communication between the entities that if something goes wrong, you'll learn about it, but the error-reporting system isn't perfect. So, while the manager is waiting patiently, the user is sometimes left wondering just what in the name of shampoo-and-conditioner-in-one is going on.

If you've been left wondering just what in the name of shampoo-and-conditioner-in-one is going on, go to the Dock. If it's working on a print job, the printer's icon should appear there; clicking it brings up a list detailing what it's working on.

If there's an error message in there instead, and it isn't a friendly message like "The Printer is out of paper" then 99 times out of 100 — I checked; hey, I'm a professional — you can get things moving again by deleting any pending print jobs (select them in the list, and then click the Delete button), and then walking over to your printer and turning the power off and then on again.

It's also possible that at some point you clicked the Stop Jobs button, which tells the print manager to accept print jobs but not to actually print them until someone starts the print queue again. But you said that there was no error message when you printed. Tiger is supposed to warn you about that before accepting the print job.

I'm *supposed* to be able to access my network from nearly a football field away through my wireless AirPort base station. I'm lucky to make it from the rec room to the bedroom!

Well, it's your own damned fault. Don't give me that look, either; you're the one who insisted on getting a brick and natural-stone treatment for the north wall of the living room. I told you that if you just painted the wall a reflective white, you'd save $6,000, and only half of that savings would cover the cost of a wall-sized projector that hooks right up to your Mac.

THE TRIALS AND TRIBULATIONS OF GETTING A GOOD WIRELESS SIGNAL

If you have a titanium PowerBook G4, just try to accept that this world is a vale of tears and that mankind is born to suffer. The G4 was one of the first Macs to have AirPort antennas built in, and, boy, did Apple make some poor choices. First, it located the antennas at the bottom half of the machine under your wrists, where they're almost certain to be covered up by something. Secondly, titanium isn't very transparent to radio waves, so the end result is that the PowerBook G4 is about as stealthy as an F117A fighter, which is to say, not very.

On later PowerBooks and iBooks, Apple moved the antennas to the top of the screen. I bought my new PowerBook for lots of reasons. Chiefly, there was no room for any more stickers on the old one, but the one feature I appreciated the most was the fact that for the first time in 2 years, I could actually access my home wireless network from the comfy chair.

Not only is that so-called grown-up wall treatment expensive, it also blocks radio signals. If you imagine the AirPort as a big light bulb that throws off radio signals, no computer in that wall's shadow can connect.

That's just one problem with getting a base station to work properly. Every wall between you and the base degrades the signal. Everything pumping out RF (like a TV or a cordless phone) can cause interference. Metal shelving can screw things up, too.

Two things to try. First, just try rotating the base station 90 degrees along various axes. It's a simple trick, but the difference between a base station that sits flat and one that hangs vertically on a wall can be dramatic. The same thing often works for your computers. Obviously, you can't use a PowerBook while hanging upside down, but you can rotate your chair so that you're facing the southern wall instead of the eastern one.

You can also try adding an external antenna to the base station. AirPort Extreme base stations have external antenna connectors built in; the standard base station requires a little warranty-voiding surgery. The chief benefit of buying and installing an external antenna is directionality. Normally, the base is like a bare light bulb, spreading its signal in all directions. An external antenna helps you focus its output where you need it.

But don't expect miracles. If none of the above succeeds in elevating the performance of your AirPort network from Utterly Wretched to Better Than Utterly Wretched, then your only alternative is to buy a second AirPort, Airport Extreme, or AirPort Express base station and then set it up to extend your existing Network, using the Airport Admin Utility or the Airport Setup Assistant. Instead of being a base station for a second, separate network, it'll simply receive the signals from the first base station and rebroadcast them. It's like a line of firemen passing buckets of water from hand to hand, only just try and sell a calendar of burly, oiled wireless base stations in interesting poses sometime and you'll fully understand the difference between the two species.

What if you get it cut, and if you don't like it, you just grow it back?

Give my best to Uncle Joad, Auntie. Talk to you next week, okay?

23

Drop the Book and Come Out Peacefully: Online Resources

The Mothership • News • Features and Product Reviews
Help/Community • Software • Shop

The temptation is for me to tell you that hey, there's a big wide world outside the pages of this book, and that now that I've shared as much Truth, Beauty, and Wisdom with you as my page count permits, you need to get hip to great resources on the Web. But this sort of betrays a problem with my worldview. Is my definition of exploration *really* "putting a book down on the coffee table and seeing what adventure I can find by staying on the sofa *but* working with a computer?"

Well, yes. I'm afraid so. Still, there's no reason for *you* to take this same insular attitude. Take a night course in flower arranging. Become active in community theater. Organize a neighborhood recycling program. But when you come back and you want to hook up with people, answers, and software, these websites will be waiting for you.

THE MOTHERSHIP

I'm just a bit amazed that every new Mac doesn't come with a simple sheet of paper, taped right to the top of the box, listing all of the online resources that Apple maintains for the benefit of its users. How much does paper cost? Exactly. And when you buy it in bulk-packs instead of in individual sheets, the price is even lower.

▼ Note

But when I say "I'm just a bit amazed," maybe you should keep in mind that I'm also pretty amazed that my rice cooker always knows *exactly* when the stuff is done. Light and fluffy, tender but not mushy, sticking together just enough to give the portion some heft but not enough to challenge the durable matzo ball for impenetrability. I've had some discussions with the cooker, asking if it wouldn't mind taking a look at my 401K, but it always changes the subject and starts talking about rice again.

Well, I suppose you have to admire an appliance for sticking to its strengths. So if that sheet of paper added three dollars to the cost of the hardware, it'd still be well worth it. It'd save users a huge amount of strife. I'm something of an expert on the Mac — I don't want to brag, but I've actually written entire books about the things; you should really check them out sometime — and yet I'm never more than a day or three away from the last time I plugged `www.apple.com` into a web browser to look for some info or troubleshoot a problem.

Apple Service & Support (www.apple.com/support/)

It's unlikely that you're the *first* person to experience a specific problem with your Mac, or to be confused by the right way to install memory or to customize the Dock. Whenever the dominant thought in your head can be summarized by the single, powerful syllable "Huh?" you'll want to consult Apple's vast collection of technical notes, procedures, and advisories. They're nicely sorted by product and software category, and can be searched.

And it's exhaustive. If you've recently acquired a Macintosh SE and an original ImageWriter printer and you want to learn how to get 'em working (i.e., you're either one of those saintly folk who refurbishes old computers and donates them to needy organizations, or else you lack the common sense to just keep on driving until you find a *better* Mac along the side of the road) it doesn't matter that Apple hasn't sold these things for more than a decade . . . full documentation and data is just one keyword-search away.

MY MASTER PLAN

I should state in my own defense that this whole "live life through a cozy filter of technology at all times" policy is part of a larger strategy. See, I didn't find out about girls until after college, which, as you all know, is the best time to hook a life-mate. Women's tolerance for nincompoop-like behavior is at their greatest during this critical period when they're not yet aware that they can do far, far better than you.

So my plan is to stay inside and off the map until the women my age have been through their second divorce or have buried their first husbands. When I hit my Forties, all my competition will have leathery, sun-damaged skin and be buckling under the emotional and financial burdens of alimony and child support. Whereas *I'll* be like a copy of Detective Comics #27 in Mint to Near-Mint condition, with white, unblemished pages. Unique, valuable, and highly desirable.

Provided that I don't blow it by continually coming up with comic-book references to everything. But hey, I still have almost ten years to work on that.

Even if you're serene in your mastery of Macintosh knowledge, you should check this page regularly. It's where Apple posts all of its software updates (your Mac's built-in Software Update app ought to download those things for you automagically, but the individual patches are online just as a backup). And while Apple is a blameless and holy creature, far beyond any mortal weaknesses, once in a blue moon they discover a problem with hardware that they've already shipped. Maybe it's a bunch of PowerBooks whose screens are a little dim, or some Macs whose power supplies acquire an annoying little hum after a few months. And so, visitors to support.apple.com will discover a little notice explaining that anyone who has an iMac with such-and-such a serial number is invited to drop by their nearest Apple Store for a free swap-out.

Apple Discussion Groups (discussions.info.apple.com/)

Apple's "official" town hall for chat about Macs, the OS, and (Heaven forfend) any problems. Heading to this spot and doing a keyword search is like eavesdropping on a thousand conversations that took place among tens of thousands of Mac users over hundreds of days.

And if you fill out a free registration, you can post messages and actually discuss your problems with the community. It's chockablock with solid, common-sense advice. Unlike other message boards, this community is well-moderated and so the signal-to-noise ratio is superb. You'll drop into practical, valuable discussions about why your PowerBook keeps going to sleep unexpectedly without having to sort through about three-dozen message threads about why Han Solo could, like, *totally* kick Captain Kirk's butt.

Apple User Groups (www.apple.com/usergroups/)

No matter how handy Apple's virtual help files and virtual discussion groups might be, there's often no substitute for getting out there and interacting with the Humans. Apple User Groups are independent organizations of ordinary users who meet (typically once a month) in nearly every major community across the country and throughout the globe.

Apple doesn't run these groups, but they maintain a database you can search to locate a group nearby.

Apple Mac OS X Downloads (www.apple.com/downloads/macosx/)

Apple has its own download area for Mac OS X shareware and freeware. The library isn't nearly as extensive as MacUpdate's or VersionTracker's (which shall be discussed, anon), but it has a more professional, catalogue-ish appearance that I find appealing. You won't find anything edgy in this collection, but it's all USDA Prime choice. No fillers, no extenders, and not a speck of cereal.

The Apple Store (www.apple.com/retail/)

The analog kind, not the kind you access through a web browser, I mean. A lot of folks (myself included) were a little skeptical when Apple announced that it would be opening a handful of company-run stores across America. But boy, this idea was a stroke of brilliance. They're much, much more than mere retail outlets. It's more like Apple was a small Baltic nation, and chose to open embassies in every nation to tend to the needs of its expatriate citizens.

Even if you resolutely insist on keeping your Mastercard in the wallet, the location of the nearest Store is solid info. This URL will lead you to Store Central, where you can see what's open in your region. Every store has a "Genius Bar" staffed by specially trained technicians, and if your Mac suddenly digs its heels in and refuses to start up, hauling its butt down to the mall and handing it over to a Genius for a spanking will usually set things right. And if it's something that can be fixed just by running a repair utility or working some diagnostic mojo from the keyboard, it'll be fixed free of charge.

You don't *need* to reserve a Genius in advance, but this site will take reservations anyway. Plus, each Apple Store has a regular roster of free classes and demonstrations, and checking the webpage of your local Store will often give you something to do on a Wednesday night. Apart from being disappointed and disgusted by animal-based reality TV shows on the Fox Network, of course.

Your online universe extends well beyond the divine margins of Apple Computer, o'course. Some more URLs that you need to bookmark, pronto:

NEWS

MacCentral (www.macworld.com/news/)

MacCentral is the online news presence of Macworld magazine. It's the CNN of the Mac world: it's furiously updated with ferocious and tenacious frequency and it has the broadest range of coverage. It's a great first-click-of-the-morning; in one collection of headlines you find news about products, partnerships, Apple as a company, future strategies, and links to outside news stories that aren't directly Mac-related but are likely to influence the Macintosh Experience in the weeks and months to come. MacNN.com is another nice Mac news site and is certainly worth a visit, but MacCentral is the place I go first thing in the morning.

MacObserver (www.macobserver.com/)

Like MacCentral, this is a news site, but if it covers breaking stories with less intensity, it makes up for it with a stable of columnists and commentators (including yours truly), and tips and techniques.

MacSurfer (www.macsurfer.com)

MacSurfer is a metasite; its real purpose is to link to news and articles on other websites. MacCentral, MacObserver, MacNN and the rest are good entities on their own, but MacSurfer will point to Mac-oriented articles that appeared in The Boston Globe, Forbes, Rolling Stone (just to mention three sites at the top of MacSurfer's headlines a moment ago), as well as The Usual Macintosh News Sites.

AppleInsider (www.appleinsider.com)

There are News sites and then there are Rumor sites. AppleInsider (somewhat uneasily) bridges both worlds. They'll cover the big stories, but they'll also report that a former Apple executive is suing for wrongful termination and that a new experimental build of Apple's next landmark OS has just shipped to software developers for testing. And if they come across a rumor that smells like lilacs, sure, they'll pass it along.

LIVING IN A STATE OF SYN

Incidentally, nearly all of the websites mentioned in this chapter have RSS syndication feeds. So by loading the webpage and clicking on Safari's "RSS" button, Safari can automatically locate and summarize newly-posted articles.

MacOS Rumors (www.macosrumors.com/)
Think Secret (www.thinksecret.com/)

Rumor sites are a lot of fun, so long as you make sure your eyes keep flickering to that URL — Mac Rumors. You can't safely consider their contents News. This is gossip and scuttlebutt about future Apple hardware and software releases and the anticipated moves of Mac-related companies. Oftentimes, the rumors on this site prove to be right on the money. Oftentimes, you wonder if the software used to post new items shouldn't be hooked up to a Breathalyzer or something to make sure such obvious rubbish isn't posted again. But this site is always an illuminating read, particularly when they simply note that Apple has just hired so-and-so, who is a known expert on such-and-such, which would imply that "such-and-such" will soon be part of an upcoming Apple product.

FEATURES AND PRODUCT REVIEWS

Macworld (www.macworld.com/)
MacAddict (www.macaddict.com)

The two most important magazines on the newsstand also have two of the most important Mac-related sites on the Web. Timely news isn't their forte; they produce material on monthly deadlines, not hourly ones, so if yours truly is ever arrested for breaking into an amusement park while wearing a firefighter's helmet and the bottom half of the Philly Phanatic costume, you won't read it there (not for a few weeks, anyway — and don't judge me; you just don't know what love is).

But they have the production resources of a full magazine staff, which means that they have extended product reviews, detailed how-to articles, and highly professional content

from top to bottom. In addition, these magazines often produce web-only content that's well worth checking out.

TidBITS (www.tidbits.com/)

TidBITS is that most unusual of beasts: an online-only publication that can punch in the same weight class as the print magazines. Its reviews are reliable, its analysis always insightful, and it has a unique editorial voice and point of view.

The Cult Of Mac (www.wired.com/news/mac/)

This is the Macintosh page of Wired Magazine's website, and I absolutely freakin' love it. The page is more oriented towards information and articles that the Mac community will find Interesting, as opposed to *useful*. The best way to explain is to describe today's headlines: a description of how to build your own re-creation of an Apple I personal computer; Los Angeles-area Apple Store employees dish dirt about their most and least favorite celebrity-shopping experiences; a story about how Microsoft managers are irritated because the vast majority of the employees in its main campus listen to iPods and not Windows Media Player devices; a guy can control his Mac from anywhere in the world using his PDA. New articles appear only a few times a week, but it's reliably good stuff.

HELP/COMMUNITY

MacInTouch (www.macintouch.com/)

MacInTouch was (along with TidBITS) one of the very first Mac-oriented electronic publications. In the past few years its focus has shifted slightly, taking it away from

457

breaking news and into community discussions of new software and developments. That is, while MacInTouch duly reports on the release of a new public beta of iChat, the real reason why you click on the link is to read the MacInTouch community's debate on its pros and cons. When you install a system update and you start to have problems, this is the place to read about other users' experiences. Because again, unless you've led an unusually evil and unchaste life, it's unlikely that you're the *only* iMac user whose machine started vomiting pea soup through its disc slot the moment you installed the latest update to QuickTime.

Slashdot (http://apple.slashdot.org/)

Slashdot is a lot of things (news site, message board, merchandise mart), but I think any smart definition of what it is begins and ends with the phrase, "Slashdot is so . . . itself." Its Apple subsection contains some of the most passionate and informed (and occasionally confusing above all) discussion about what's going on in the Mac world. Bonus: The Web site's software rates the karma (aka, trustworthiness, respectability, civility) of the person posting the message, so each post comes with an indication of how much credibility you can attach to it.

MacSlash (www.macslash.org/) brings much of Slashdot's vibe with less of its intimidation.

MacFixIt (www.macfixit.com/)

This site is a real lifesaver. It focuses on one concept: problem-solution. If items start disappearing from your Dock for no reason, there's probably a report up on MacFixIt that explains the cause of the problem and how to fix it. The only downside is that it's a pay site. New items are free, but searching through MacFixIt's handy archives is going to cost you.

SOFTWARE

VersionTracker (www.versiontracker.com/) MacUpdate (www.macupdate.com/)

Some of the best Mac software is available as downloadable shareware or freeware. I have a hard time choosing between these two as my favorite Macintosh download site. They both diligently assemble a wide range of apps. Both offer a simple, searchable database. On both sites, every file is backed up by user ratings and comments, so you can steer yourself straight to the best iPod utility of the 12 available for downloading. And both are nice enough to list all of the latest software right on the top page. It's always worthwhile to check in from time-to-time just to see what's new, and, better yet, to discover a great app that (a) You've never heard of and (b) would never have found on your own.

In the end, it's unimportant to rate one of them as the winner; between them you have the capability to totally choke your ISP's bandwidth with downloads.

MacDirectory (www.macdirectory.com/)

And then I suppose you're also going to be interested in commercial software, too. MacDirectory is chiefly an information resource that tries to list every piece of software available for the Mac, along with hardware and accessories. Lately they've had ambitions to become a more general-interest Mac zine, but it's still a good place to head for when you hope to find a Mac OS X app for managing a church bowling league.

SHOP

DealMac (www.dealmac.com/)

I'm not going to recommend any one store to you. Instead, I'll recommend DealMac, the site that always steers you toward the best bargains. It knows every one-day price drop, every coupon code, every rebate, and sometimes its news items are so compelling that you can't bear not to buy products. The online vendor keyed in the wrong price . . . plus there's a $30 rebate, plus there's a coupon code for 20 percent off any purchase and a free shipping promotion that ends on the 27th, for a total savings of 60 percent. See? I can tell that you're already getting out your Visa card, and you don't even know what the product is!

DealMac is especially handy when the item you're shopping for has volatile prices that change day-to-day. If you're in the market for a gigabyte of RAM, just stay tuned to Deal-Mac (or sign up for keyword-based email alerts). When the price is (quote) "The lowest we've ever seen on memory modules of this capacity," you know it's time to bite.

Finally, I ought to steer you towards

ANDY IHNATKO'S COLOSSAL WASTE OF BANDWIDTH (WWW.ANDYI.COM/)

A Web site and blog that truly live up to the name. Low expectations yield the most satisfying results, I find. But hey, do feel free to click on the link and send me some email.

Troubleshooting by the Seat of Your Pants

Macs are wonderfully stable and reliable, particularly when they run Tiger. But the only way to ensure that your Mac never experiences any slowdowns or random crashes or other signs of petulance is to perform the following steps, in this exact order: (1) carefully install Tiger on a compatible machine, following Apple's guidelines and instructions precisely, (2) Run the Software Update app to make sure that you've received all the most recent and most important updates and bug fixes to the OS; and then (3) shut down your Mac, unplug it, seal it in three layers of plastic sheeting, and with an indelible black marker, write, "Angry and vengeful monkey inside; DO NOT TOUCH." Apple doesn't tell you that in the ads. I've written and everything, to no avail.

Ideally, when your Mac starts acting funny, you would have a very experienced and knowledgeable friend or relative in your address book. You'd explain the problem and he or she'd walk you through some diagnostics and then tell you how to fix it.

 Tip

Incidentally, consider making a friend of a very experienced and knowledgeable Macintosh user. We're easy and affordable to maintain, sleep on any absorbent shredded bedding, and you can purchase our special food supplements in any establishment where you're allowed to speak into a fiberglass cartoon character from the comfort of your car.

Not everybody's quite so lucky, though. For your benefit, here's the standard ladder of things to try when your Mac acts up on you and you have no clue why.

This isn't a step-by-step list. It's just a batch of techniques that often tend to solve the problem, and they're arranged so that the procedures that are easiest to perform, require the least amount of your time, and carry the lowest amount of risk appear nearest the top. Numbers One through Three can be accompanied with a shrug of the shoulders and a cheerful muttering of "Why not? *The Simpsons* is a rerun tonight."

By the time you get to the bottom, you should wipe perspiration (real or imagined) from your brow, silently ask yourself if you have any right to play God, and then breathe deeply and move forward. You're building character, only *this* time you didn't have to spend three hours behind your dad's push-mower to acquire it.

DO NOTHING

And, yes, that is indeed a serious and solid piece of advice. When your Mac grinds to a halt and appears to lock up, or if the screen seems to update in odd ways, or if weird ghostly images of menus and windows cut in and out briefly, as if drawn by a contractor who's already been paid for this job and isn't interested in making things look good, it's possible that nothing's wrong that the Mac can't fix on its own once it gets the chance.

Your Mac has to do a lot of behind-the-scenes bookkeeping to keep the OS and all of its applications running smoothly. Sometimes these bookkeeping chores get a little backlogged, and it tries to do far too much all at once. This doesn't cause any *damage*, mind you, but it means that Tiger might temporarily act slow, ugly, and clumsy until it completes all the items on its to-do list.

So take this as an opportunity to go off and get a Coke. You have a couple of chicken fingers left over from last night's takeout. Heat 'em up and enjoy. Have you phoned your Mom recently? Well, *shouldn't* you?

Give your Mac some Alone Time. Let it have a good cry; maybe give it a copy of *Beaches* or *Steel Magnolias* to watch, just to let it get everything all out. By the time you sit back down at the keyboard, the torpor might be a thing of the past.

 Info

And sometimes, "Your Mac needs to let everything all out" is literally true. There are system-maintenance tasks that your Mac is supposed to automatically perform at daily, weekly, and monthly intervals. Usually these tasks are performed late at night, when few people use their Macs, but if you're up until the wee hours, you might discover that for a half-hour period, your Mac transforms from a sleek, swift Tiger, the Land Shark of Predators, to Gerald R. Tiger of Weymouth, Massachusetts. Oh, wait ... you've probably never met him. He used to work at this video store where I used to always get my movies. Ask him the most basic question and he'd stroll off into the back room, not emerging until lunchtime. I was *so glad* when Blockbuster moved into town and put him completely out of business.

This, incidentally, is one reason why it's a good idea to have Tiger display the current time within your menu bar (go to System Preferences, click Date & Time, click the Clock preference tab, and click Show the date and time). So long as 2:31 p.m. becomes 2:32 p.m. becomes 2:33 p.m., I'm willing to wait a problem out. However, when the clock is frozen, that's usually the sign of a more serious problem.

QUIT PEACEFULLY

If a complete lack of effort on your part accomplishes nothing, then quit the app that's acting up. It's possible that you can't access the menus, but press ⌘+Q anyway (the system software that drives the keyboard almost never slows down or crashes). And *then* walk away and get yourself another drink.

Admittedly, Quitting Peacefully isn't likely to work if Doing Nothing has already failed. But it's like when the police say, "Drop the weapon and lay facedown on the ground" to the man with the gun, the bags of charred

"DO NOTHING" WORKED FOR APOLLO 11

"When in doubt, first, do nothing" was one of the most important rules that NASA's mission controllers developed during the early days of the space program. The lunar module's landing radar kept freezing up and giving cryptic error codes during Apollo 11's descent to the lunar surface. The controllers didn't know exactly what the problem was, so instead of just guessing (or aborting the mission) they let the computer sort things out on its own. Result: perfect landing. Apollo 12 got hit by lightning *twice* during its launch, throwing entire systems offline. Astronaut Pete Conrad had his hand on an Abort handle that would blast the entire crew module safely away with just one twist, but he did nothing until the ship reached orbit, and discovered that the system could easily reset itself.

And as a taxpayer, the computers on board Apollo were the most expensive computers you've ever owned. So if it worked for *them* …

money, and the face full of dye that he got when he walked out past the bank's doorway. The next step is pretty inevitable, but it's also rather extreme and you'd like to be able to explain to people that you tried to do the peaceful and polite thing first.

▼ Note

But this tip actually *does* work well with Web browsers. These apps just have a fundamental nature to run more slowly the longer you've been using them. When Safari takes more time to do a Google search than it'd take me to visit a professor of literature at his home and ask him the title of the play-within-a-play in *Hamlet,* I quit and relaunch it. And suddenly, it is once again the snappy, sprightly browser I used to know.

FORCE QUIT

You want to try to Quit peacefully before force quitting because taking the latter action on a running app (even a troubled one, an app that never benefited from the many advantages that you or I took for granted growing up; in a

word, an app that was never held closely and told, "You are *loved*") can cause problems later on.

What problems? At minimum, you'll probably lose any unsaved changes in the app's open documents. At worst, an unseen but important file that Tiger or the frozen app uses for internal bookkeeping won't close properly — or it could become corrupted and unreadable — leading only to additional instability to the app and possibly even to the OS at some future date.

▼ Note

Reader: *You, too, are loved.* I'm sorry it's taken me more than 20 chapters to say that, but I usually keep my emotions pretty wrapped up. I guess I've just been a damned, prideful fool. Can you forgive me?

FREE UP SPACE ON YOUR HARD DRIVE

Mac OS X is based on Unix, and if Unix has a need for additional memory, it grabs some chunks of unused space

THE WISDOM OF IHNATKO

I don't know what idiot looked at the Ten Warning Signs of Alcoholism and snuck in the phrase, "Do you ever drink alone or when you're depressed?" I'm sure that this is something that alcoholics do, but this also describes what a system manager is doing and feeling when a computer is suddenly acting all petulant on him for no apparent reason.

So don't worry about it. Go down to the kitchen and get yourself another beer. So long as you're not driving, or singing "Radar Love" so loud that it disturbs the other tenants.

on your hard drive and treats it as virtual memory. Which makes it very, very important that you not fill your drive to capacity; if your drive is crammed to the gills, your Mac won't be able to "create" new memory when an app needs it. Apps may refuse to launch, and the ones that are running may run as slow as Slow Bob Slowley of Slowdon, last-place finisher of the World's Slowest Slow Person competition, who runs as if he is waist-deep in pancake batter.

▼ **Tip**

Yeah, I know. It's not your fault. Clutter is just plain attracted to your hard drive. The Omni Group (www.omnigroup.com) has a really nifty little utility that I use all the time. OmniDiskSweeper can scan your drive and highlight all its biggest space hogs. If you pay the $15 shareware fee, you can delete 'em with the click of a button. Don't worry; it warns you before you delete anything that the OS needs.

The first time I ran ODS, it instantly and painlessly freed up 3GB from my PowerBook's 40GB drive. Seems that months and months earlier, I'd tested a device that lets you tune in TV signals and record them on your Mac. Plumb forgot that I had 3 hours of TV shows on that drive.

As a general rule, I like to keep 10 percent of my hard drive free. I *prefer* to keep it at 20 percent. It keeps my Mac running nice 'n' regular, and it also means that I can install new software or slurp photos into iPhoto from my digital camera without having to go in and delete stuff to make room.

WEED OUT DUPLICATE FONTS

Yeah, I know. You're telling me that you've got aphids on your rose bushes and I'm telling you to go inside and turn down the temperature in your refrigerator. But seriously: launch the Font Book utility and select Resolve Duplicates from the Edit menu.

See, fonts are things that *every* app uses. If an app tries to build a Font menu and it finds two copies of the exact same font, befuddlement and bamboozlement can ensue. Did we learn nothing from Shakespeare's *The Comedy Of Errors,* in which Antipholus and Dromio, two sets of identical twins, engage in a madcap series of madcap misunderstandings in the 16th-century port city of Ephesus?

No?

How about that episode of *The Brady Bunch* where Peter Brady discovers that there's this other kid at school who looks exactly like him, except he wears glasses?

There you go. So duplicate fonts can cause all sorts of subtle problems. If that's the source of your pain, Font Utility should fix everything with minimal effort.

SPANKING INDIVIDUAL APPS

Oftentimes you're only having problems with one app, and not the whole Mac. An app keeps slowing down and stalling; an app keeps crashing and quitting itself; an app intimates that your latest manuscript is suspiciously derivative of a G.K. Chesterton story entitled "The Awful Reason Of The Vicar's Visit" and threatens to communicate this to your publisher.

Usually, the culprit is one of those little support files I mentioned earlier. You can't see 'em. They're usually buried inside your Library folder, but they're crucial to the app's stable operation. Quit the app, root around in your Library/Preferences folder and look for a prefs file or a folder that contains the app's name. Move the file or folder out onto the Desktop and relaunch. The app won't find the thing that you moved and will assume that you're a new user. Don't worry about it. If the app now behaves, then you know that one of the things you moved was the culprit. If it doesn't, copy the files back into their original location.

Be especially wary if the oddness starts immediately after you've updated the OS, or updated the software. Code that was compatible with your old environment might be incompatible with the new one, and (hopefully) a further update will be released in a few days that'll set everything right.

RUN PERIODIC MAINTENANCE

Earlier, I hinted that Mac OS X automatically runs a few maintenance routines at regular intervals, designed to keep your Mac healthy, wealthy, and wise. The problem with this scheme is that it's a holdover from Old School Unix, when computers were refrigerator-sized slabs of technology that stayed up and running 24 hours a day. Thing is, maybe you shut down your Mac every night instead of putting it to sleep. Or maybe you have a PowerBook, and it spends its evenings packed away in your briefcase.

In both situations, those periodic maintenance tasks — scheduled to be done early early early early *early* in the morning, when there's nothing on TV but infomercials — never get performed. Your Mac is never awake then.

But if you have an Administrator-level account, you can tell your Mac to perform all those periodic tasks at once, and immediately. Just open the Terminal app and enter the command **sudo periodic daily weekly monthly.**

Your Mac will percolate for a while, doing all sorts of housekeeping. When it's done, cross your fingers and hope that your Mac's happier now. It sure won't hurt anything.

 Tip

There's actually a handy free utility called MacJanitor (download it from either www.macdownload.com or www.versiontracker.com) that brings pushbutton simplicity to this function, and can reschedule these maintenance tasks for a time of day when your Mac is going to be alert enough to actually perform 'em.

SHUT DOWN AND RESTART

Shutting down your Mac is, of course, the super-atomic-wedgie version of quitting a running app and restarting it. All of the benefits of restarting an app now apply to every last component of the OS. It's like getting a good night's sleep, or just taking the license plate and the stereo from your car and abandoning the vehicle right there on the highway. You emerge refreshed. There's a sense of renewal and of getting a fresh start.

Proving that on this wretched hunk of rock upon which I've been stranded for lo these past six centuries, there is absolutely no good thing that doesn't have a bad side. The fact that Mac OS X is so much more stable than all

YET ANOTHER APOLLO REFERENCE

Ahhhh! Another opportunity to make an Apollo reference. NASA had a similar experience with the Apollo command module. When Apollo 13 had its in-flight explosion and it had to coast back to Earth without power, its trajectory kept drifting too low and needed to be corrected. It turns out that one of the components in the craft had a design flaw that caused it to leak gasses in flight. It affected every Apollo ever built, but this was the first time it had ever made its presence known. Normally, the thrust of its rocket engines nullified the effect of the bug, times about 1 million.

It's an interesting part of space history, and it also means that the slip-cased library edition of Apollo mission logs for which I paid $140 is now tax-deductible. And don't think I don't appreciate your reading this.

previous editions of the Mac OS means that while you can keep it running for weeks and months without a crash, you probably wouldn't want to.

Until OS X, developers never had an opportunity to test their apps to see how they held up after weeks or even just days of runtime. Somewhere by Day Two, the user would cause a system crash (clearly ignoring Apple Technical Library Document #29283: "Do Not Look At Menu Bar Funny (09/19/93v12)"), and would have to restart the Mac.

Under OS X, tiny bugs, hitherto undetectable, quietly build in strength over the course of days until eventually they cause huge problems. And sadly, some of these microbugs are in the OS itself. So it's just good policy to shut down and restart your Mac once a week or two, whether it needs it or not.

And I *do* mean Shut Down, not simply ticking Restart. A Shut Down does a more complete job of clearing out all of the old aches and irks and starting everything fresh.

 Tip

Simply logging out (using the Log Out command at the bottom of the Apple menu) and then logging back in again can also deliver the desired kick in the pants. And you'll save a little time, besides. But it isn't as effective as shutting down and restarting. Logging out and back in is useful if you're trying to actively diagnose the problem, but if you're just trying to get things going again, a shutdown is the way to go.

Incidentally, this is why I don't usually give out tips on how to quit and restart the Finder or the Dock, two items that can cause odd problems if they get bugged up. There are ways to do that, but my advice is to just do a Shut Down and Restart. Any problem that's caused the Finder to require a restart has probably corrupted other running apps and drivers, too. Best to shut them all down and let God (that is, the Boot Manager) sort it out.

RESTART AND ZAP THE PRAM

⌘+Option+P+R is so ingrained upon the consciousness of the Mac community that I'm surprised that the sequence of keys hasn't appeared on a line of bracelets and jewelry yet. COPR is the patron saint of, "I don't know why my Mac is acting up, and now I'll try some things at random and hope that the thing magically starts working again."

Pressing those keys during startup causes a tiny speck of battery-backed RAM to clear itself. Why does this sometimes solve mysterious problems? Because this is the Mac's Parameter RAM, and it stores a few very basic settings that must be maintained even if the machine is powered off and left off. Among this info is the name and location of the drive off of which this Mac is supposed to boot. If some sort of bizarre malfunction causes your Mac's PRAM to become jam-packed with aerosol cheese, it can cause a problem that will persist from restart to restart.

This technique is nondestructive, and the only reason why it's so far down on the list is because it's a big pain to close all of your apps and documents and perform a Restart. And it's not like it always (or even often) solves the problem; it's just that it doesn't take too long to perform and you know it won't make things any worse.

RESTART IN SAFE BOOT MODE

Still not working, eh? Hmm. Maybe the last time you installed a piece of software (or, better yet, the drivers for a new piece of hardware) the Installer program introduced a snippet of software that causes Tiger to spin its head like a top and start speaking in tongues.

Restart the Mac and hold down the Shift key. This restarts Tiger in Safe Mode; that is, during the startup process only Tiger's standard, barebones, must-have components are loaded. If your Mac suddenly becomes a happy and giggling little girl, you know that there's something inside your System Directory that's mucking things up.

Safe Boot also automatically runs a Unix disk utility called FSCK. So if the problem is a munged hard drive and it's an easy fix, you'll be sitting on velvet by the end of the (very, very long) boot process.

If it's a problem with Tiger, the situation probably has just gotten a little more serious. You might want to jump straight down to the section "Reinstall Panther." Or . . . (well, if I say, "Your ac-May ight-may be oken-bray," it'll magically cause it to happen, I won't say it in open text.).

▼ **Tip**

A similar trick: Log on as a different user. It's faster than Safe Boot because Tiger won't perform an FSCK, but it still gives you an answer to the question, "Is the problem with Tiger, or is it a problem with something in my account?"

For this reason, it's an excellent idea to create a separate user account named "Trouble" or some such. Don't use this account for *anything* other than troubleshooting; you want to keep this account's contents as plain vanilla and unblemished as possible.

SHUT DOWN, UNPLUG ALL CABLES, AND RESTART

Take a deep breath.

Take another.

Close the door and pull down the curtains.

Take a third deep breath.

Okay. Now, check the back of your Mac. It's possible — I'm not saying this is it, I'm merely tabling the possibility — that the reason your keyboard is dead is because its USB cable has somehow come unplugged. And not, as you so loudly theorized, because your Mac is "a worthless unreliable piece of trash that somehow can just plain *sense* when you've got a big project deadline coming up and can be counted on to cause a system failure at the *worst possible moment!!!!!!!!*"

This is one of the most common sources of utterly bizarre, unpredictable, and irreproducible problems. If a FireWire cable works itself *partly* loose, your hard drive may stop working. And it might even cause Tiger to kernel-panic; it keeps trying to read the FireWire port, but it's linked in just such a way that the wrong connector on the Mac's interface is grounded for just a millisecond, and then — boom.

Thus, this is a good time for you to unplug absolutely everything except for the keyboard, mouse, and monitor, and restart. If the problem goes away, you know you have a bad connection somewhere.

It's also a good opportunity to make sure your cables are undamaged and in good condition. I was having a nightmare of a problem getting my new USB scanner to work. Finally, I looked for the weakest, cheapest-looking cable in my whole setup and replaced it with a nice, thick one. Presto: heading out to OfficeMax and buying a new $10 cable cut through a problem that gave me fits for hours.

One more question: Did you install new memory just before Tiger started treating you like that bass player who's just started dating your 19-year-old daughter? It's possible that you have a bad memory module or that you zorched it with static electricity during installation. Try removing it and restarting. If you had the module installed professionally, take your Mac back to the shop that did the work.

FORTY POUNDS OF SMARTS, NINE OUNCES OF BRAINS

The most embarrassing (and thus most influential) story comes from a memorable week I spent shooting a DVD with three of the Mac community's top experts. The production office's AirPort base station stopped connecting to the Internet at absolutely the worst possible time. Sometimes we could find Web sites, sometimes the Internet disappeared entirely, and sometimes we could get a connection, but it was a horribly slow one. So, Expert A started working on the theory that the base station didn't receive a needed firmware update; Expert B thought that one of the Macs on the network might have been flooding the gateway with bad packets; Expert C thought that the office's ISP had noticed our heavy use of the Internet and was capping our access; whereas I started working out ways we could access the Internet without using the base station at all.

Only after an hour of fruitless four-man effort did these Incredible Mac Experts think to check the cable that was plugged into the base station. And, um, it turned out that the little plastic locking-tab thingy that keeps the cable firmly connected to the base station had broken off.

I jammed the toothpick from my Swiss army knife into the connector, and it locked it in place. Presto, everything worked fine (provoking the three other experts to simultaneously bark "Hey! I fixed it!" from all corners of the office). Since then, I never go hunting for a unicorn when the more likely suspect is a common brown horse with a cracked USB connector sticking out of its ear.

REBOOT OFF A CD AND RUN DISK UTILITY

Get your Tiger installation disc. It contains a bootable copy of the operating system. Stick it in your drive, restart, and press C while your Mac boots.

This causes a two-pronged effect. Your Mac will boot off the copy of Tiger on the disc, and you won't be using your hard drive's installed copy of Tiger at all. If your Mac magically runs happy, fast, and stable, you can at least be relieved to know that it's not a hardware problem and that your Mac can (likely) be easily fixed.

The second prong of this procedure is the fact that the installation disc also contains a copy of the Disk Utility application. Disk Utility (click Applications ➜ Utilities) can work two different kinds of mojo on a hard drive. Clicking the Repair Disk button scans your boot drive (or any other drive you specify), examines its data structures for abnormalities, and fixes them.

Disk Utility also has that Repair Permissions button. Clicking the button causes the utility to examine every single one of Tiger's system files and to make sure that its Unix permissions flags are properly set. A system file may just be 2K in size and contain seemingly unimportant profile info, but if the OS expects to be able to read and write this file, and it can't because Unix thinks this file is locked and unchangeable, all sorts of unpredictable trouble can ensue.

Performing both these functions can take an awfully long time. That's why this advice is low on the list. In truth, you actually want to run Disk Utility and Repair Permissions on a regular basis (once or twice a month; it builds strong bodies nine different ways), but your Mac may be tied up with this for an hour or more.

While we're on the subject of booting off a CD and running a disk utility, give some thought to buying a copy of

MY DINNER WITH DISK UTILITY

Disk Utility is also referred to with fond affection as Soup Plus Coffee and Dessert. Because it often takes a long time to run through all of its tests and thus, if you start this before you leave for lunch, you have a gold-plated excuse to stay out for 2 whole hours. This utility could only be more helpful to the put-upon office worker if it actually included QuickTime video that coaches you on the best way to explain to your manager why it's utterly impossible for you to get those Q3 reports done today.

It is, unfortunately, up to you to justify spending the afternoon in the office park's courtyard playing Ultimate Frisbee in your underwear.

Alsoft's DiskWarrior. Disk Utility will spank a problematic hard drive, but DiskWarrior will get downright Medieval on it. It's far more sophisticated, and can fix a far greater range of problems. If your Mac won't start up at all, you can boot right off the DiskWarrior CD and run the utility directly. And like Disk Utility, running DiskWarrior regularly will keep your drive healthy, wealthy, and wise.

At this writing, DiskWarrior version 3.0.2, is $80. Which is dirt-cheap, compared to the cost of setting broken bones in your hand and patching a hole in the wall if your drive goes south three hours before deadline.

SLAVE YOUR MAC

Dang. If you're still reading this, then things have gotten rather desperate. It's that sad part of the news story when the guy from the Coast Guard announces that at this point, the collision between the 14-foot sport sailboat and

REPAIRING PERMISSIONS: DON'T THINK, JUST THROW

Disk Permissions is another one of those frustrating concepts that fundamentally affects nearly everything your Mac does, and as such, it's a factor that can make your Mac act seriously wacky.

Example: I'd spent *two months* importing every last track on every one of my 700 CDs into iTunes. Disc after disc after disc went into my Mac and came out again, and the result was a library of some 12,000 songs. I was thrilled ... for about a month, until when I'd connect my iPod, iTunes would attempt to load it up with randomly-selected songs, and everything could come to a dead halt after copying only a few dozen tracks. "One or more tracks could not be copied," said iTunes.

Thanks. Great. Spiffy. Which *ones* of the 12,000 were bad? I got no help from the app. So I took a guess. If for unknowable and unimportant reasons some of those tracks had had their file permissions messed up — the OS thinks that it's not allowed to read the files — well, that'd cause iTunes to fail. So I selected my iTunes Music folder in the Finder, did a Get Info, made sure that as the Owner I had Read & Write access, and then I clicked the "Apply to all items" button. Tiger hit all 12,000 files and applied the change to each one. Result: my iPod always contains a fresh mix of hype mixes.

If we can broaden the definition of "hype mixes" to include Stan Frieberg comedy records, Tony Bennett albums, and Broadway cast recordings, of course. You shouldn't do this lightly, and you shouldn't do it to our whole Home directory. First, it takes a lot of time to change permissions on thousands of folders. Second, remember that this will affect all contents of a selected folder, so if you have a batch of files and folders that have been Permissioned to allow other users to access them, you're going to have to manually apply those permissions again.

the Queen Mary 2 has ceased to become a Rescue Mission and moved into the Recovery phase.

You're probably eager to make sure your files are all intact. If you have two Macs, move them together. If you only have the one, it's time to haul your machine to their house, or entice him or her to visit you. Promise to order in a pizza. If they're on Atkins, just wave a raw steak in front of the phone when you invite 'em over. Works wonders.

Shut down the power to the problem Mac. Get out a FireWire cable and connect the two Macs' FireWire ports together. It's not necessary to shut down the healthy Mac first, but make sure the healthy one is up and running before you proceed to the next step, which is to start up

the problem Mac while holding down the T key on its keyboard.

This will start your Mac up in Target Disk Mode: the healthy Mac will see it as nothing more than an external FireWire hard disk. Unless your Mac is totally and obscenely messed up, your drive will mount right on your pal's desktop and you ought to be able to copy your important files. You can even go into the healthy Mac's System Preferences, click on the Startup Disk icon, and tell the healthy Mac to restart itself from the sick Mac's System folder. That way, you'll be able to run the apps on the bad Mac without any difficulties. You *could* try double-clicking the app directly from the bad Mac's drive, but that may or may not work.

MUST READ:

A duck wearing a little yellow hardhat walks into a bar. He hops up onto a stool, flips his hardhat onto the bar, and orders a beer. The bartender's too amazed to do anything but pour a tall one and set it down. The duck downs the beer in no time flat and then flips his hat back on his head. "Thanks, Mac!" he quacks. "Hey, I just started working at that construction site across the street, and I like to get a beer after I get off my shift. So start me a tab, OK? See you tomorrow!" And then he waddles out.

The bartender blinks and regains his senses. He grabs the phone and calls his brother. "You'll never believe who — I mean *what* — just came in here. A talking duck! You *gotta* come here tomorrow and *see* this!"

The next day, the duck waddles into the bar at the exact same time. He flips his hardhat onto the bar, quacks "Let me have my usual, Mac!" and starts to drink his beer.

The bartender's brother is sitting just two stools away and can't get over what he's just seen. "You're the most incredible duck I've ever seen!" he blurts, just as the duck is about to take another swig. "Look, I own the biggest traveling circus in the world. I'll give you your own bus, a personal assistant, ten thousand bucks a month! I've just *gotta* hire you!"

The duck shifts in his seat. "You say you own a circus?" he asks.

The man nods, eagerly.

"That's one of those places that takes place in a huge tent, three rings, the floor's all sawdust and you pack up and move every week?" he asks.

Another nod.

"Well, *jeez*," the duck says. "What the heck would you need a *bricklayer* for?"

This joke does nothing to solve your Mac problem, but at this state in the proceedings you could probably use a laugh. It's all part of the service here. Please! No tipping!

CALL IN A GENIUS

Well, team, things are looking pretty freakin' bleak right now. You've eliminated nearly every possibility but two: something, somewhere, somehow inside Tiger has become corrupted, corroded, malcontented, malformed, sticky, shiftless, demotivated, devolved, demonized, hypnotized . . . somethin' ain't right. You've waved both the Mojo Tooth

and the John de Conkeroo at it, to uniformly disappointing results.

At this stage, it's time to toss your Mac into the backseat of the Dodge and haul on over to your local Apple Store. Every Store has a Genius Bar behind which a bona-fide Expert sits, lonely and waiting, for someone just like you to bring in a Mac just like that one and turn it from A

YOUR IPOD IS *TOO* A COMPUTER PERIPHERAL!

If you have an iPod, you can make this even simpler: plug it into your Mac (back when your Mac was working just fine. Remember back when your Mac was working just fine?), mount it as a hard drive on your desktop, and install a copy of Tiger on it. It'll only eat up about 4 gigs of space (which might be a mere pittance to you; I have a 40 gig iPod and my interests in music are so selective and arrogant that I have a hard time finding more than 10 gigs of music for it) and once it's done, your iPod can function as a lifeboat.

Naturally you'll have to go into iTunes, open your iPod's "iPod Options" window, and click the "Enable disk use" checkbox in order to use it as a hard drive.

So! If your Mac suddenly refuses to boot from its internal hard drive, you can just plug in your iPod and restart your Mac while holding down the Option, Command, Shift, and Delete keys. This forces your Mac to ignore the internal drive and boot off of an external volume . . . i.e., your iPod. If you had the forethought to install your critical apps (a word processor, a spreadsheet, a mail client) on your iPod as well, you'll probably be able to get a full night's work done. At minimum, at least you can copy your critical files onto the iPod and then carry it to another Mac for editing.

One caveat, though: the iPod's hard drive was designed for sporadic use (load in a song, then spin down and wait two minutes to load in the next tune) and if you make a habit out of booting and working off your iPod, it'll probably limit the device's lifespan a bit. All the same, I always keep an OS and a few apps on my iPod. Saved my backside more than once.

Cool Looking Doorstop back into a Powerful and Functional Computer.

Don't worry about the expense, either. Most problems can be fixed by running some special utilities, or by pawing through the low-level bits of your OS and looking for files and structures that have gone out of whack. Chances are that they can fix it for free. If they can't, then you were going to have to take it somewhere to be physically repaired, anyway. Might as well pay a guy with an Apple logo on his name badge.

REINSTALL THE OS

If you can't get to an Apple Store and you need to get this Mac back on its feet right flippin' *now*, it's time to drop the A-bomb: Shut down, reboot off of your Tiger install disc, run the Tiger Install program, and perform a clean, new installation of the operating system (selecting the Archive and Install option; see Chapter 2 for details.).

Time-consuming? *Whoah, Nelly*, yes. Say goodbye to possibly a whole evening's worth of working with Tony Hawk Pro Skater 4 and other productivity apps. Destructive? Mmmmaybe. You shouldn't lose any of the contents of your Home folder, but it's possible that you'll lose some of your old settings files and will have to tweak your System Preferences settings all over again.

I'm a bit conflicted as to how best to paint this option: a scorched-earth approach of destroying your entire existing Tiger system directory and sticking something else in its place? It sounds like something Dirty Harry would do in *Magnum Force*, or what Sylvester Stallone will do to his management team if he winds up in just one more direct-to-video release. It just isn't *orderly*.

And yet I sit here, fortifying myself with another sip from my bottle of Coke, and finally typing the following words:

RELY UPON THE GOOD BOOK

Yes, at times like these, when you're struggling with one of those little challenges that Life so often throws at you, you're glad to have a copy of the Bible there in your study. If you're a practicing Christian, you'll find words of strength and inspiration therein. Read the book of Job. The world is still a good place and God is still a kind and loving God.

If you're not a practicing Christian, a Bible is typically a solid twelve-point hardcover block of paper and you can *really* beat the hell out of a petulant computer with one. Actually, forget what I said in the previous paragraph. Let all of us — man and woman, regardless of geography, religion, cultural heritage, sexual orientation, or political party — unite in the cleansing and highly positive ritual of exorcising your rage and hostility upon an inanimate object. "You feel like connecting to the Internet *now?*" you may feel inspired to shriek. "How about that file that you say you can't open? Starting to see things my way? Are you? *Are you?!?*"

No *real* harm done, except of course to your Macintosh, which may very well now have problems that can't be solved by restarting and holding down one of its buttons. But now that it's in 90 to 300 convenient pieces, it'll be all that much easier to take it off of your desk and replace it with a shiny new Macintosh G5. If you can locate a recognizable bit of the old Mac on the floor or on one of the walls — a bit of plastic with an Apple logo on it, say — place it on a pike and display it on a corner of your desk, as a warning to *future* hardware that might decide to show you a spinning beach ball cursor for nine minutes instead of the webpage that you wanted the thing to load. File it under "Preventative Maintenance."

"Completely wiping out your old OS and replacing it with a brand-new copy once or twice a year is actually very, very good advice."

It's not the *big* bugs and tics that I fear. That's not why I replace my OS from time to time. My word processor starts crashing on me, I fix it, I move on. No, it's the little, undetectable, unfixable, *incremental* problems that I worry about. Modern operating systems are so complex these days that they can indeed suffer a condition akin to termite damage. One little, nearly anonymous system file gets corrupted. And then a code library that uses that file screws up and messes up another file. And *those* two files cause four *more* bits of code to mess up; on and on, heaping complication upon complication like the first-act finale of a Gilbert & Sullivan operetta, until there's barely a Tiger component that is working up to spec.

That's when weird things start going wrong with your Mac. It's not enough to render your Mac useless, but it's enough to become an enormous pain. And the root cause of the problem is so far in the past that you will *never, ever* root it out, not even with a Cadbury caramel egg for bait and the force of a federal court order.

 Note

Witness the problem I was having with my PowerBook just last week. All of a sudden, it couldn't run any Installers. I got this nifty-keen new utility for making screenshots, but I couldn't install it. And Software Update kept telling me that there was a new version of iTunes available. The download went fine, but I had as much hope of getting them installed as I did of getting 20 minutes alone in a coat-check room with Uma Thurman.

So I reminded myself that this life was but a vale of tears, I got out my Install disc, I reinstalled the OS … and everything worked fine from then on out." What was the specific problem? I haven't a clue. But I didn't *need* to know. I just wanted my Mac to work again!!!

Sometimes things go wrong with Tiger, and the simplest and most effective way to solve the problem is to just shrug your shoulders and start anew with a fresh copy of the OS. Mind you, an Archive And Install isn't a trivial exercise. If you have any major projects going, it's best to finish them before doing a reinstall. But I prefer to think of this procedure as a spring-cleaning and not as tenting and bug-bombing your whole house.

If none of the above techniques work, then you should probably just move on to The Slight Overreaction, viz:

CONVINCE YOURSELF THAT YOU NEEDED A NEW MAC ANYWAY

Well, maybe you don't want to be *that* morbid about it. But if nothing has fixed or alleviated your Mac's pain, you've reached the practical limits of what I can do for you, given that all I know about you and your Mac is that you seem to own one, and that you were nice enough to buy my book.

Still, if you've been eyeing one of those super-cool new iMacs, or the sleek, purple aura of seething power that surrounds the latest and fastest new tower Mac, don't be afraid to use this as a gold-plated excuse. Particularly if (a) your boss' job is riding on this latest project, and (b) you can establish a paper trail of having long ago informed the jerk that your current Mac was on its last legs and was certain to go 100% failure at precisely the worst moment imaginable.

EVEN THE EXPERTS LIKE TO GET OUT OF THE HOUSE ON OCCASION

To be honest, you might want to move this step to a higher position on the Priority List. My closest Apple Store is nearly an hour's drive away, but if one were closer, I really wouldn't be timid about dragging a non-functional Mac there, if it didn't respond to my immediate attempts at CPR. They really do know their stuff. The folks behind the Genius Bar aren't just "some kid who says he knows a lot about Macs." They're especially bred for this role on a small farm in the wine country of Santa Rosa, and it's unlikely that you're going to throw something at them that they either haven't been trained for or that haven't already seen a hundred times. OK. A yellow rubber kitchen glove painted with the face of silent-film comedian Harold Lloyd would probably be a new one. But otherwise, they've seen and experienced it all.

Even if you *do* stump 'em … there's The Red Phone. A phone that connects them directly to an even *more* studly form of Mac Geniuses back at Apple. How studly? Back on the breeding farm, the parts of their brains that would normally be filled with subroutines for social interaction and community living are filled with (you guessed it) additional information about Macs. The downside is that they can't be allowed into the general populace. But they're well cared-for at the other end of that phone line and to be honest, they wouldn't know what to do in The Real World even if they had the opportunity to experience it. I understand that they don't even lock the doors on their campus.

Earlier on, I made mention of the fact that I sometimes need to use more than one Mac at a time. I have plenty of 'em here in the office and in storage. And every time I feel like I want to gloat about how much more elevated Macs are, how much *more reliable* and *easy to maintain* any Mac is compared to any Windows PC — I really like it when people get so frustrated with me that they rip a fire extinguisher off a nearby wall and tap me in the base of the skull with it; makes me think that I'm tapping a nerve when they're tapping my brainstem — well, I sort of pull back. I think about all the times when the simplest, most uncomplicated act required me to go to three different machines before I found a unit that was in 100 percent operational spec.

We can be proud of our Macs and deliriously happy with Tiger. But you can't lose sight of the fact that while a Mac is a Mac, it's still a *computer*. And the reason why God inserted computers into our lives is because He can no longer cause frogs and snakes to rain down on our heads whenever He wishes to invite a plague upon Humanity and so instead, he delivered a technology that would automate the process.

The frogs-and-snakes thing is still well within His powers, of course, but the animal-rights activists cause enough trouble afterward that it's just not worth the effort anymore.

Wheels of the Mine

Begrudgingly Acknowledging Other Operating Systems • The Great Survival Mechanism
A New Era At Apple • Finding Your Own Inner Macintosh Blowhard

You've had a pretty productive time of it, I reckon. You've patiently plowed through more than two dozen chapters of this book, and for that, I thank you. It wasn't easy going, I know; a Macintosh is probably the easiest computer there is to use and maintain, but there are still fundamental things about any computing experience that make you wonder if there isn't some sort of alien race whose spaceships run on impatience and disorientation, and the Earth is nothing more than the Exxon of this sector of the galaxy. I mean, take a look through a Mac or a Windows machine's full font library. You're not telling me that all those symbols were designed for people with mere binocular vision.

I also admit that, at times, your reading experience must have been like taking a cab ride through any major Italian city — lots of adrenaline and lots of worried glances and lots of desperately clinging to the thought that the driver is, apparently, a professional, and he must know what he's doing. Otherwise, he'd have been dead long before his Bonfat SL hopped the curb by the airport and he started tossing your luggage into the trunk and onto the hood.

You're nearing the end of our journey of Macintosh knowledge, but you're not at the end. Not just yet. There is still one final lesson to complete: You must equal me in single combat. Pick that light saber up off the floor and don't ask questions because my attack commences in five seconds. I swear this to you, young Jedi, you shall return to your home village either in glory or in pieces. Only your actions over the next seven hours will tell the tale. Sorry. Got away from myself, there. I get so few opportunities for macho posturing that I rarely know when it's inappropriate. Forget it ever happened.

What I meant to say was that before I let you go, I need to stress to you the extreme importance of maintaining an air of impenetrable purple glowing arrogance at all times. It's a fundamental part of the Macintosh Experience. Author Tom Clancy used to adapt an old saying favored among fighter pilots: "Never ask a man what kind of computer he uses. If he has a Mac, he'll tell you. And if he doesn't . . . why embarrass him?"

Brilliant stuff. Really brings the point home. It's only the first of many anti-everything-else jokes you'll pick up during your first few months of Mac ownership. And if you're an old hand at this, repeating these old standards only keeps them fresh in your mind, like the Boy Scout Oath.

BEGRUDGINGLY ACKNOWLEDGING OTHER OPERATING SYSTEMS

At previous points in this book, I might have said conciliatory or even — in a moment of weakness — even *positive* things about Windows and Linux. Disregard them. I wrote those bits when one of the boys from Legal was wandering through my part of the office, trying to mooch a Hot Pocket off of someone. It's all junk. Why would anyone want to use a Windows machine? The GUI totally lacks elegance, subtlety, or nuance; and every time I launch a Windows app, I'm increasingly convinced that most authors of Windows software are more interested in meeting a Hobbit one day than one of these users that they keep reading about on the Web.

And don't get me going on the hardware. I am a geek of admirable ecumenicism: I embrace technologies of all faiths and followings. I have three Windows machines in my home office and as an internationally-beloved technology pundit, I receive all kinds of Windows hardware in the mail every week. A recent peripheral is a typical example. I opened the box and the hardware inside was so tightly

sealed in red and yellow warning tape that I wondered if the delivery guy didn't make some sort of mistake, and instead of a new network adapter, it was actually a Smallpox-N-Anthrax Party Pack from the Martha Stewart catalogue that Mrs. Pocatelli from next door ordered.

I knew what the warning text would say but I read it anyway. "STOP!" it ordered. "DO NOT CONNECT THIS DEVICE until AFTER you have installed the PROVIDED SOFTWARE!"

See, Windows is supposed to be plug and play. You plug in a device, Windows automatically knows what it is, and then it makes whatever additions or changes to itself that are required to make the new hardware work. The problem is that sometimes Windows gets it totally wrong and all it actually accomplishes is to make additions and changes to itself that ensure that this new hardware will never, ever work. So it's absolutely vital that you install the manufacturer's software before Windows can get its mitts on it.

Things like that just don't happen with Macs. I still remember the astonished looks I received from some of my Windows-only pals when I came into their office with my PowerBook recently. They wanted copies of a couple of my files and while they argued over where they could scare up a blank CD-R or a key drive to copy them onto, I simply woke my laptop from sleep, joined their wireless network, found their office's five file servers, and deposited the files into their shared folders. All with just a few mouse-clicks.

One of them looked like he was about to cry. "I bought a new notebook a month ago," he finally told me. "What you just did in 30 seconds cost me a week of phone calls to tech support."

Being a beacon of human kindness, I, of course, sympathized with him. "Most of the Mac OS' networking happens automagically." I explained. "I'm sure Microsoft will

THE BETTER PART OF VALOR

It's important to be arrogant, you see, but it's even more important to manage a Windows user's reactions carefully. You want to keep them angry enough that they eventually wind up buying a new computer, but *not* so angry that the reason why they need a new one is because they beat you in the head with the old one. Remember: A shattered jaw that's held shut with titanium wire can't spread the Gospel of Macintosh. And you can't be a vain blowhard with only *yourself* as an audience.

have this sort of thing in its next release of Windows." But even here, I was arrogant. Had I exhaled with just a little more force, he would have sensed that my unspoken suffix was ". . . in 2006, which is the latest slip date to the next big Windows update."

What about Linux? Good OS; some fantastic software. Comparing Linux to Mac OS is a lot like comparing a vintage muscle car to a brand-new, mid-priced SUV. There are potent arguments to be made that the former has more power and provides an attractive hands-on driving experience. But when I want to go to the store for some peanut M&M's, I hop in my car and go. Linux people have to pour some additive into their gas tank, replace the header they took off earlier in the day, crank the ignition while listening to make sure the number three cylinder is firing right, pop the clutch at *exactly* the right moment . . . I mean, there are times when you want to be a Power User, and then there are times when you just want to buy some candy and maybe see if the new *People* magazine is out yet.

But in the end, the only time I've ever envied a Windows user was when something went wrong with my Mac and it let me down at exactly the worst time and I was frustrated and angry and in need of release. If I had thrown my Macintosh through the wall, I would have probably felt really bad about it later.

Tip

Still, Mac users are cautioned about using arrogance against Linux users. Their usual (and quite effective) defense is for one of them to trap you in a headlock while the other one pummels you about the upper body with endless technical trivia about his or her system's superior performance, using names, specifications, and benchmark data on window-manager software, and networking standards, and all sorts of things that no Mac user ever could or would need to care about. You're *supposed* to embarrass yourself by attempting to respond to this battery of data directly. If you find yourself in this situation, however, your best bet is to wait for the speaker to finish, allow for a 2-second pause, and then say, "And *this* makes you happy, then?" This usually leaves the speaker stumped. At which point, you waggle your sack of M&M's in their faces tauntingly and then drive off, leaving them to do whatever it is they need to do to unlock their car. I think it involves executing a sudo command and then running a Perl script.

THE GREAT SURVIVAL MECHANISM

Privately (privately) I concede that the Macintosh operating system is the product of mortal and fallible human beings and that the Tiger Golden Master CD was not ejected fully formed from Zeus's forehead, like the formula for Classic Coke. On the day when I'm called up to testify in front of a Congressional subcommittee (have you been watching C-SPAN these days? One day it'll be your turn, too), I will tell the fair and honest truth: Users should take inventory of what they want and expect from computers and software, acquiring as much experience as they can. Then finally they should buy whatever hardware and software makes the most sense for them, be it a Mac, a Windows box, or a cantaloupe with a USB keyboard jammed into the pulp and the outline of a screen hastily marked on the skin.

But — and here's a big secret that you can only learn if you make it to the very end of a Mac book — arrogance always has been and always will be essential to the Mac's long-term survival.

Survival? The thing would never have even been created without the warm, womb-like embrace of serene arrogance! There were two wildly popular computers back in the early 1980s: the Apple II line and the IBM PC. Apple owned the rights to the Apple II. They could have evolved it in any direction they wanted, or incorporated any of their technologies into a new product.

They did not. Apple chose to enter the market with a computer that would have 0 percent market share. They would run 0 percent of the world's software, interact with 0 percent of its hardware. Including the photographer who plugged it in and turned it on for the publicity photos, the original Mac 128 had an active user base of about 129. Apple succeeded thanks to the arrogant and unshiftable belief that this was a computer and an OS that needed to exist and which couldn't possibly fail to catch on.

And, well, whaddya know? Apple was right on both counts.

Over the past 20 years, arrogance has gotten us through the lean times and the fat times. Apple, and the Mac's few but fierce early users, didn't care that its one word processor could only handle ten pages of text before running out of memory: I'm right, you're wrong, come back when you fully appreciate that fact and are willing to run a lap

around this office in your underwear as a sign of your penitence and I'll happily teach you how to use this machine. The Mac became a success and arrogance led Apple to new expressions of ego, and nigh-invulnerability to outside opinions: Apple created the Newton MessagePad, the world's first PDA. It would die a deathly death, but even in failure Apple gets credit for showing the industry that handheld pen-based handhelds were a Good Idea and had a bright future.

My belief in the viability of the company isn't based on arrogance. It's based on numbers. Others point to the Mac's slim market share, but I point to the company's consistent profits and the fact that folks who want to use Macs find that a Macintosh is exactly the sort of computer they want to use — and Apple is the only company making them.

Ironically, the only time the future of the company really was in danger was when humble, calm people, who made decisions based on *facts* instead of personal emotions, ran the company. These were the Dark Times, when the air was filled with the sound of the beating of leathery wings and Apple finally decided to cave into the conventional (read: idiotic) wisdom that the only way the company could continue was to license the operating system to work on third-party hardware, as Microsoft had done. Boy, did *that* backfire. The idea was that the licensees would make affordable, dirt-cheap Macs (an area that Apple never excelled at), and leave the high-performance workstation market to Apple. Instead, companies like PowerComputing rushed to place the hottest chips in the newest Macs and Apple was making most of its money off those high-margin workstations, so they wound up bleeding Apple dry.

The management had effectively taken the batteries out of Apple's once-mighty Infinite Arrogance Generator. Now, it put them back in, only backward, with the effect of sucking the Apple campus bone-dry of every last wisp of confidence that could be found.

A NEW ERA AT APPLE

And then, Steve Jobs reclaimed a leadership role. Apple came back twice as arrogant and insufferable as it ever was, thanks to his infusion of confident, sandalwood-scented ego and his immediate directives. Clones: All licensing agreements are now null and void. Newton: It's finally starting to gain traction in the marketplace, but we're a Mac company and it's not a Mac so it's gotta go. We're going to build a *new* Macintosh and its most apparent feature will be that it's molded out of the same translucent colored plastic as a Battleship board game. We think you users will get by just fine without a floppy drive, too. Why? Don't ask dumb questions. Look! It's *green! Isn't that cool?*

It was the iMac, and it set the whole industry on fire. Other PC manufacturers are lucky to have some sort of detectible influence upon their specific, limited sector of the technology industry. The iMac was so influential that even *George Foreman freaking grills* started coming out in iMac colors. Most importantly, this expression of arrogance, this renewal of the idea that this computer was so good that it couldn't possibly fail and who cares what the market research does or does not say. . . well, all of this renewed the public's grudging confidence in Apple. And rumors of a takeover or buyout, which was once accepted by the mainstream press as an inevitability, rang dumber and dumber as the months rolled on.

Which brings us full circle to Mac OS X. Just when the iMac got Apple back on its feet, it was announced that Apple was jettisoning the OS they'd been building and improving since 1984 and would be replacing it with something completely new: Unix. Possibly the most un-Mac-like operating system there is, unless you can come up with one that can only be operated using pen-like styluses jammed into your nostrils.

Did Apple waffle? No. It arrogantly insisted that this was the way it was going to be. Did users consider abandoning the Mac? Oh, *hell* no. They had their doubts about Unix, and demanded that X live up to their expectations; but they were arrogantly confident that *anything* had to be more pleasant to use than Windows, even an OS that required that you stick the stylus into another bodily opening entirely.

FINDING YOUR OWN INNER MACINTOSH BLOWHARD

Arrogance — for lack of a better word and to pinch a line from one of Charlie Sheen's best films and one of Martin Sheen's worst — is good. Why? Because when we speak of arrogance as Mac users, we're not talking about being closed to alternative ideas and being contemptuous of people who think differently. I mean, we actually put that last phrase on posters and tee shirts and billboards.

Our arrogance is what allows us to commit to new ideas, committing to them wholly and completely. Once a new idea has earned our respect, our arrogance allows us to see past the Now of Mac OS X 10.0, an OS with practically zero commercial apps that was barely functional enough to print a document. Our arrogance allowed us to see what 10.1 and 10.2 and 10.3 would be like — operating systems that find and connect to networks automatically, use next-generation graphics rendering to create a truly beautiful user experience, and pack enough horsepower to become the OS of one of the five most powerful supercomputers on the planet.

So our arrogance is a survival mechanism. Reflect upon the fine example and the plain-spoken common sense exhibited by contestants on TV's *Fear Factor*. They believe that they can drink a milkshake containing brains, eyeballs, spleens, bugs and something the show's producers spotted leaking out of a rusty drum by the side of a highway. Result: They *do*. Success is success, regardless of how many legs and thoraxes you spit into the sink afterward.

Don't restrict your arrogance to the privacy of your home, either. Go to the electronics megastore and try to help out the people trying out the latest Windows hardware. "You're here because you need to replace broken, incapacitated, or obsolete gear," you might say, provided the shopper is a lot smaller than you and that you know for a fact that you haven't wandered into a part of the country with a conceal-carry handgun law. "But I'm here because the speed and power of my iMac got me out of the office shortly after lunchtime!"

When the IT people who support the computers in your company insist that they can't add Macs to the network, or that a necessary feature, application, or service isn't compatible with Mac OS, refuse to believe them. "You're not telling me that it's impossible," you should say in an email,

LEADING WITH CHARACTER

What is in a name? Even here, we see the superiority of Apple over Microsoft. Both create consumer products by sticking a letter of the alphabet in front of a common word, but Apple chooses "i" as if to suggest *it's all about you, the user. We're always thinking about you first, even when it comes to typing the names of our music players.* Whereas when Microsoft thinks of consumers they think "X" as in "unknown" or "X" as in "deleted." Or possibly "X" as in "kiss." I've met with Microsoft executives; selectively, that would indeed be a positive enticement but you really don't want to leave that sort of thing to random chance.

cc'ing it to the head of the company. "You're telling me that either you don't know how, or you don't want to be bothered." And just to be extra helpful, head on over to Monster.com and headhunt for a couple of new IT people on behalf of your (overworked and underappreciated) Human Resources department.

There is one claim to Windows superiority that's hard to challenge. Most of the greatest games do indeed come out for the Macintosh later than the Windows editions, if at all. But when confronted by this, you should note that for less than half the cost of the custom high-performance video card that a Windows user needs to buy and install in order to play games at cinematic quality, you went out and bought an Xbox.

If you're a more peaceful sort of person who dislikes direct confrontation, you may opt to simply wait until the Windows bigot foolishly leaves his or her car unattended and then let nature and an easy-to-use plasma cutter (rentable at attractive daily rates from any contractor's depot) make your argument for you.

Finally, remember that just because you're as absolutely and arrogantly intractable regarding your beliefs as the Windows user is about his or hers, that doesn't make you a bigot. *Only people who are wrong and who disagree with you are bigots.*

History will prove us right. Arrogance was the right way to go with the original Mac, it was the right way to go with the iMac, and it's the right way to go with Mac OS X and beyond. We're the winners. We cannot fail. We shall prevail.

Now, granted, this also happens to be the last thing that the Big Brother guy said in Apple's 1984 commercial, just before he got taken out by the blond, lateral-thinking decathlete with the sledgehammer. But with a properly egotistical attitude, you can spin that positively. Remember: Big Brother was a PC guy.

Index

The Mac OS X Panther Book
Developed for the Apple Community
Andy Ihnatko and Jan Harrington
0-7645-6794-2

The iLife '04 Book
Developed for the Apple Community
Andy Ihnatko
0-7645-6796-9

There's only one Andy Ihnatko...

0-7645-6797-7

The iPhoto 4 Book
Developed for the Apple Community
Andy Ihnatko

0-7645-7322-5

The GarageBand Book
Developed for the Apple Community
Andy Ihnatko and Tony Bove

. . . but fortunately, there's more than one book!
Each loaded with valuable information, anecdotes, and tidbits—pure Ihnatko.

WILEY
Now you know.
wiley.com